Landscape
Construction of a Reality

This catalogue is published
on the occasion of the
exhibitions

Landscape in Motion
Cinematic Visions of an
Uncertain Tomorrow

Kunsthaus Graz
Universalmuseum Joanneum
13 March – 26 October 2015

Disputed Landscape
Camera Austria
13 March – 6 September 2015

HyperAmerica
Landscape – Image – Reality

Kunsthaus Graz
Universalmuseum Joanneum
10 April – 30 August 2015

**Landscape: Transformation
of an Idea**
Art from 1800 to the Present
Day from the Collection of
the Neue Galerie Graz

Neue Galerie Graz
Universalmuseum Joanneum
19 June – 6 September 2015

Political Landscape
Art – Resistance –
Salzkammergut

Art in Public Space Styria
Universalmuseum Joanneum
From 11 July 2015,
Ausseerland
11 July – 6 September 2015,
Kunsthaus Graz

Edited by
Peter Pakesch, Katrin Bucher
Trantow, Katia Huemer

Preface

Peter Pakesch

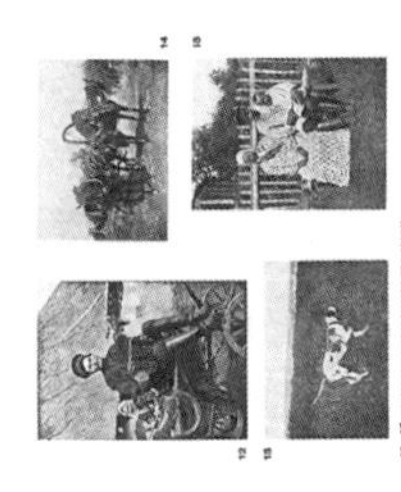

'The environment ("reality") which stimulates the Academician'

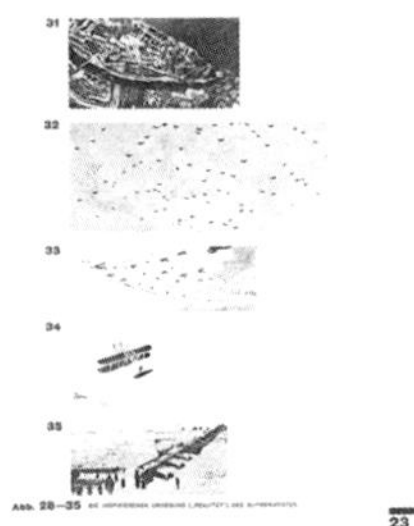

'The environment ("reality") which stimulates the Suprematist', pages from: *Suprematism. The World as Object-lessness* (1927) by Kazimir Malevich

In his groundbreaking text *Suprematism: The World as Objectlessness* of 1927, Kazimir Malevich considered various perspectives of looking at the world: he compared the academic view, for example, with that of the Impressionists, Futurists, Cubists and finally the Suprematists. In Suprematism Malevich saw an ideal way to interact with the world around us. He illustrated this comparison: the series of pictures begins with romantic academic views of people and landscapes, while at the end—having arrived at the world of Suprematism—we see landscapes depicting events on our earth and actions within it, viewed from far-off and above.

That art-theoretical reflections and polemics of this kind can have relevance, given the exhibitions we are holding on a specific theme in 2015, shows how much our dealings with the world as well as our view of the landscape are reflected in art, and how it accompanies develop-ments in it.

From the Early Modern Period up to Romanticism, people in our part of the world began to grapple with the notion of land beyond its practi-cal usage. From the late 18th and early 19th century, concurrent with Romanticism and the rise of such diverse fields as the natural sciences and tourism, landscape became the theme that we know today. Art is an instrument that helps us to comprehend this definitely new phenomenon, and as we shall see in the context of the present series of exhibitions, is also a driving force in view of the latest develop-ments not only in comprehending our notions of how to interact with our environment, but also surely in formulating new approaches to it. For this reason, prominent landscape researchers are also calling for comprehensive, integrative dealings with the phenomenon, with art and its development occupying a central role. What was still pure utopia in the world of Russian Constructivism has today become the real terrain of discourse—with images which in part are amazingly alike. These are the scenarios of present-day reflections on landscape

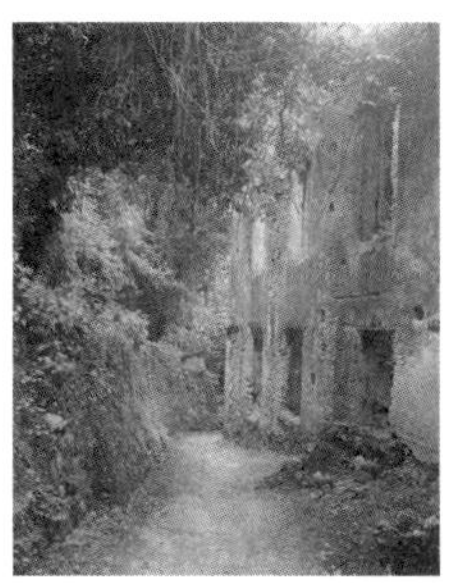

Darren Almond
Amalfi Sketchbook VI,
2014

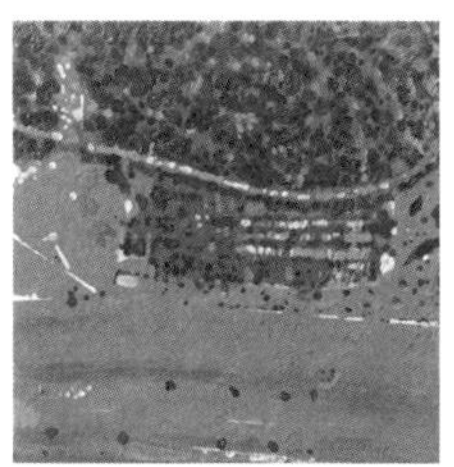

Wolfgang Temmel
Nordkoreanische Land-
schaft Nr. 6, 2012

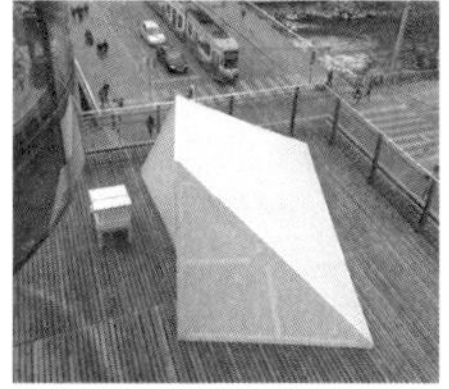

Sarah Bildstein
Der Bien, 2015

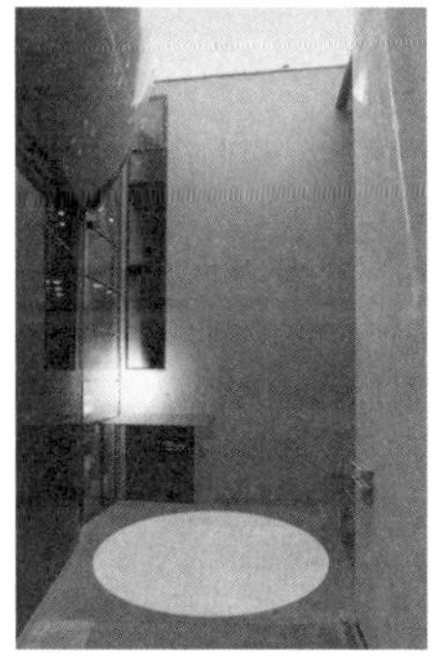

Bernhard Wolf
If you don't give the
mind something to do,
the mind will give you
something to do, 2015
(visualisation)

set against proclamations made of a new period in Earth's history, the Anthropocene, which is increasingly the subject of scientific and artistic discussions.

It is the paths leading to this that are the subject of this catalogue, which brings together an investigation into the concept of landscape in visual art. As a joint project between the Universalmuseum Joanneum and Camera Austria, the five exhibitions focus on examining the notion of landscape as a cultural dispositive and its construction as defined by the image. A three-part series of exhibitions, Camera Austria's *Disputed Landscapes* explores the contentious conceptuality of photographic images of landscape. In close cooperation, the Kunsthaus Graz presents the exhibition *Landscape in Motion* based on developments in cinematic vision. *HyperAmerica* (also at the Kunsthaus Graz) and *Landscape: Transformation of an Idea* (at the Neue Galerie Graz) open up perspectives on a historical evolution of the landscape picture and its notions ranging from the territorial through to the Romantic. At the Institute of Art in Public Space, *Political Landscape* takes the landscape back to its starting-point and reveals it as a sedimentary structure of history. Several artistic projects accompany the exhibition programme: as a visual revenant, Darren Almond's *Amalfi Sketchbook* is dedicated to the work of early Realist Karl Blechen in dialogue with the sketches of his contemporary Thomas Ender; while Wolfgang Temmel's *Nordkoreanische Landschaften* use Google Earth to make inaccessible regions visible. In a virtually exemplary fashion they create a connection between image construction with politics and history and reveal a multi-networked construct of an immense fragile landscape that determines us. Sarah Bildstein and Bernhard Wolf attended to the landscape around the Kunsthaus: Sarah Bildstein's installation *Der Bien* with its two beehives—located on the rooftop—is a metaphor for the adjustments to environmental changes, while Bernhard Wolf's work *If you don't give the mind something to do, the mind will give you something to do* directs vital sunlight into the courtyard of the Kunsthaus.

The exhibitions show a genesis of our view of landscape evolving over the last two centuries, and so offer perspectives on the future, the latter spanning from scientific domination of nature in theory and image to the domain of human intervention in political and ecological systems. The earth has become a different one—not only since we caught sight of it from outer space. Yet from this moment on, it has attained symbolic significance through the pictures taken of our finite planet as seen from the moon.

Landscape: Transformation of an Idea
Art from 1800 to the Present Day from the Collection of the Neue Galerie Graz

Gudrun Danzer, Günther Holler-Schuster

Landscape Depiction as a Construction of Reality

This exhibition does not aim to provide an overview of the history of landscape painting. Instead, it is an attempt to visualise a development that describes the influence of landscape painting on the way in which nature and reality are perceived and understood, using exhibits from the collection of the Neue Galerie Graz created between 1800 and today. The aim is to examine two seemingly unconnected epochs in relation to each other by juxtaposing time frames that are around 100 years apart, omitting the years between 1850 and 1950. This juxtaposition reveals not only differences but also surprising parallels.

It is important to consider not only artistic portrayals of the landscape but also all those images that have come into being due to the natural sciences or for practical purposes. After all, it was not only classical-ideal landscape art that was developing during this time period. The 17th century was also a time when the rationality of the objectifying natural sciences experienced important breakthroughs, a development that reached its climax in the 19th century. Ever since, experts such as geographers, instrument makers and fortress architects have been involved in creating different images of the landscape; knowledge and practical usage have been closely connected. The idea of landscape began to be transformed, becoming increasingly complex.[1] A dramatic expansion of horizons was prompted by images of nature that were entirely different to those of landscape art. Even today, images of the landscape develop from a diverse network of knowledge.
Parallel to landscape art for example, maps saw a further development in their role as an image of the world. However, the prominence of landscape painting prevented the artistic value of the map from being seen; it was not until the 20th century that terms such as 'mapping' or 'atlas' brought maps to a quasi-paradigmatic prominence. From the creation of maps to their refinement through satellite measurement (GPS), both the images of landscape and their function have changed. Both

[1]
See: Ulrike Gehring, Peter Weibel: *mapping spaces. Network of Knowledge in 17th Century Landscape Painting.* Munich 2015.

are/were primarily used to fulfil practical needs such as orientation, transportation, trade or war. With the development of additional ways to perceive reality, painting, which had always played a dominant role in describing and portraying the environment, began to be perceived in an increasingly narrow way. The tension between images motivated either by art or by other factors led to a discussion of representation and reality.

This fundamental tension can be seen both in art in general and in the portrayal of landscape specifically. It can be seen in the process of visualising reality and in the inclusion of true reality in art—from readymade to Land Art. The 19th century, which forms the starting-point of this exhibition, reveals an awareness of both aspects but nevertheless still defines the level of realism within the boundaries of representation, that is, the picture. During the 19th century, incredibly differentiated forms of landscape painting developed while, at the same time, people began to make intensive use of nature. Globalisation and economisation were driven by industrialisation. Realism did try to highlight also the dark side of people's living environment but, from today's perspective, it is clear that artists were not able to do justice to general developments in society. This realisation reveals that, in land-scape painting, the visual arts' connection to reality had in many cases become an antithesis of reality.

During the 19th century, there was an increase in the number of mechanisms and methods of visual representation. The development of technical visual media led to great scientific progress, which in turn had an effect on art. For example, before photography was developed around 1840, it was usual for artists to act as documentarians due to their formal skills. They worked in a field where science and art overlapped. Today, now that visual culture has taught us to understand visualisation in general and to perceive images as a whole, it is possible to see how advanced the results were. The function of these documentary pieces pushes beyond Realism as a style label and extends the aspect of rationality in art.

Images are shaped by ideas that are important for an individual's view of reality. This diverse world of ideas is part of a construction of reality that goes along with the interpretation of the way in which nature is perceived. For example, the politicising of the landscape began when visual clichés were established as an idealisation of national thought in all its different facets. Parallel to this, tourism began to act as a crea-tor of illusions, establishing image patterns in the eye of the viewer. These images continue to play an important role in the context of true perception of reality and in the way that it is increasingly shaped by the media.

The 20th century saw an increasingly unconditional call for reference to reality within the visual arts. Real objects became works of art; func-tions and real people's actions—also outside of an institutional con-text—became a means of expression in the art field. General criticism of social development communicated through art also became criticism of art itself. The avant-gardes of the 20th century no longer drew a dividing line between art and real events, unlike the art of the 19th century. Since the beginning of the 20th century, up until today, artists have consciously addressed the rationalistic basis of the objectifying natural sciences in order to make new statements in art. The patterns in the visual representation of nature developed previously were questioned, deconstructed and transformed into new formulations and content.

The term landscape thus not only refers to the portrayal of nature but rather to the transformation of nature by our emotions, imagination and perception. People take their external home—the landscape—for granted, only seeming to become consciously aware of it when a catastrophe occurs. The landscape is a real but also a profoundly emotional place.

The term landscape thus denotes the symbolic entity of nature and cultural patterns of appropriation. This includes the conquest of the landscape in the 19th century through travel as well as its emotional and sentimental interpretation within the medium of painting. Technical media—photography, film, video and computers—have supported the aspects of documentation and science and have mainly contributed to a transformation of reality.

Like landscape, nature has always been a construction of reality—maps do not simply present land but rather construct it. A map can be described as an image but also as an instrument for describing and constructing the world. Terms such as simulacrum and hyperreality are closely connected to the perception of nature and the way the landscape is seen. Furthermore, they play an important role in connection with the reception of art and provide additional differentiations for the perception of reality in general. This connection to reception, shaped by wide-ranging and ever multiplying theories, makes it possible to question whether reality can exist without medial construction. As a consequence, greater complexity has developed and it has become increasingly difficult to see which elements belong to the map and which belong to the land.

The transmutation of the world into images is clearly the result of a social and medial construction of reality. This construction of reality, society and public space is also highly political. Their deconstruction in the sense of relativising power relations is/should be a central topic in a democracy of educated observers.

Part 1 – Landscapes from the First Half of the 19th Century

In the earliest period discussed—the first half of the 19th century—the portrayal of landscape enfolds between different pairs of opposites. The most important pair of opposites seems to be that of the ideal and reality; other pairs include imagination and research, art and science, aesthetic standards and documentation, practical usage and ideological or ideal distortion, with individual images coming closer to one pole or another. Now that we are able to view the images from a temporal distance, it becomes clear that many images that we allocated to a

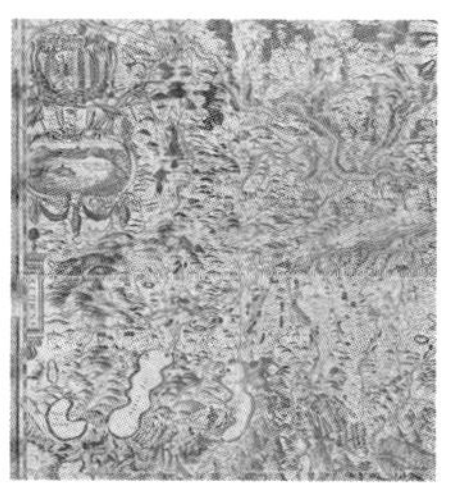

Georg Matthäus Vischer
Archiducatus Austriae Superioris Geographica Descriptio, 1667/69 (detail)

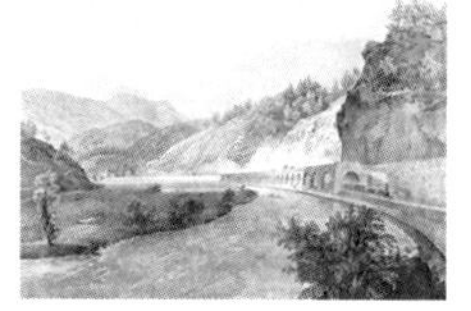

Joseph Kuwasseg
The Badelwand with Arches for Railway near Peggau in Styria, 1844

2
Jerry Brotton refers to the academic discussions as to whether 30,000-year-old rock carvings can be described as 'maps'. See: Jerry Brotton: *The History of the World in Twelve Maps*. London 2012.

3
Oskar Bätschmann: *Entfernung der Natur. Landschaftsmalerei 1750–1920*. Cologne 1989, p. 80.

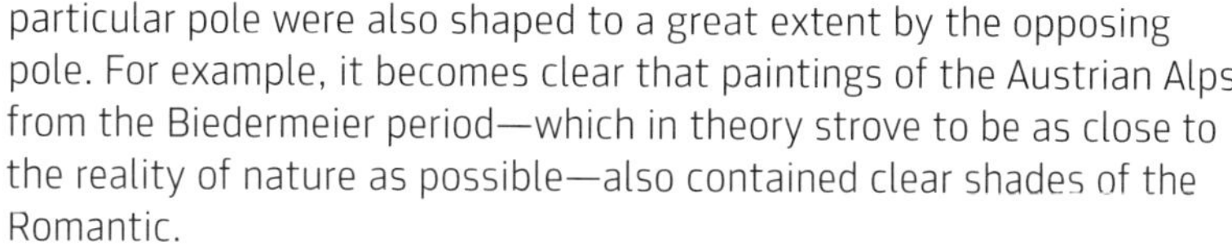

particular pole were also shaped to a great extent by the opposing pole. For example, it becomes clear that paintings of the Austrian Alps from the Biedermeier period—which in theory strove to be as close to the reality of nature as possible—also contained clear shades of the Romantic.

During this period of time, landscape painting freed itself from its inferior position in the artistic hierarchy, making its way right to the top. This process occurred parallel to a boom in the natural sciences, triggered by the enlightenment. As a result, the start of industrialisation and the increased use and exploitation of nature showed that it was possible for human behaviour and large-scale economic activity to transform both nature and landscape. The romanticisation and idealisation of the two can be interpreted as a reaction again this development.

Mapping the Landscape (Maps, Panoramas, Series of Views)

Specific resources are needed to understand and appropriate landscapes, and to be able to 'conquer' them for different purposes. Maps have long been used for this purpose. They have functioned as constructions that aim to combine practical experiences of landscape with ideas of the world as well as to locate people within their living environment.[2] With this in mind, we chose to include the map of Upper Austria, printed by Georg Matthäus Vischer in 1669, in the exhibition. This was the first map to be produced by the famous cartographer; it was drawn according to his own measurements and was used as a reference work for this geographical area for hundreds of years. Vischer combined schematic and naturalistic methods for representing geographical features to reproduce a hypothetical view of the landscape as seen from a great height. In the landscape painting of the 17th century, the horizon was placed in an increasingly high position, finally disappearing entirely in paintings such as Claude Monet's *Water-Lilies*. A similar dynamic can be seen in the relationship between landscape painting and maps.

While maps became ever more abstract, panoramas—which became increasingly fashionable at the end of the 18th century—tried to communicate a complete illusion of a landscape. As part of a new mass media, they were able to give the wider public an idea of what a few people had been able to experience since the first balloon flight was undertaken by the Montgolfier brothers in 1783: a panorama, an overview, the ability to visually appropriate a landscape. 'The view from above onto a panorama is the view of those who dominate and own. The illusion of the balloonists' freedom comes simply from the fact that they can fly over the heads of kings (...)'[3] It was the trains that truly opened up the landscape to a larger part of the population. The construction of the Südbahn, which went from Vienna via Semmering to Trieste (1842–1857), was also of great economic importance for both Graz and Styria as a whole. Joseph Kuwasseg created in the *Steirische Eisenbahn-Suite* [Styrian Railway Suite, ca. 1850] around 100 lithographic images of the landscape depicting the track layout of the train

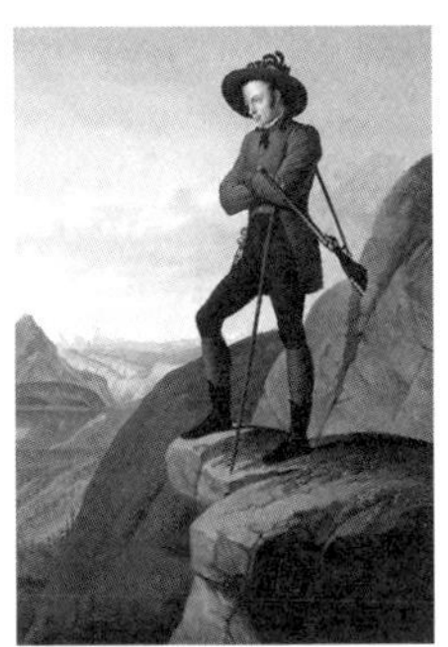

**Johann Huber after
Johann Peter Krafft**
*Archduke Johann on the
Hochschwab, 1817/1839*

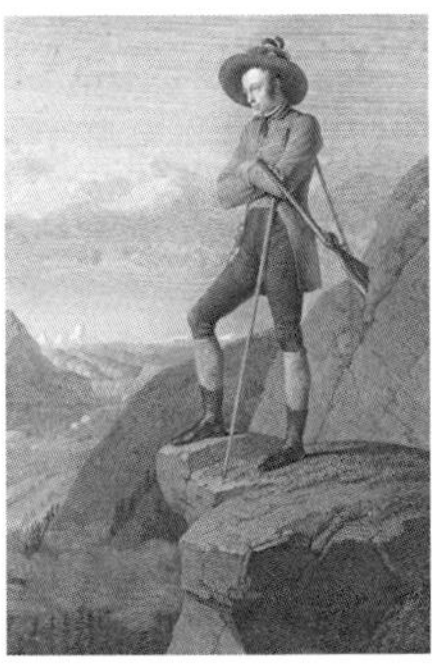

**Blasius Höfel after
Johann Peter Krafft**
*Johann Archduke of
Austria, 1817/1818*

4
The writer Xavier de
Maistre was put under
house arrest in 1790,
forcing him to stay at
home for 42 days. He
started an imaginary
journey through his
room. The result of
this journey was the
bestseller *Voyage
autour de ma chambre*.
He primarily described
the everyday objects
to be found in his
surroundings, conveying
the sense of a journey.

lines. This series of views gave people unable to undertake a train journey the opportunity to at least gain a visual impression, in a manner that reminds the viewer of the once famous room journeys.[4]

Ideologisation of Landscape

It is thanks to Archduke Johann von Habsburg-Lothringen (1782–1859) that the Südbahn was routed via Semmering through Styria and not through Hungary to avoid the mountains. Influenced by the ideas of the Enlightenment, the 'Styrian Prince' supported Styria and the Styrian population in many different ways in the first half of the 19th century, despite the fact that he did not actually have an important official or political function in the area. This involvement led to him being revered and adopted as one of their own by the people of Styria—feelings that are still evident today. Elements of this reverence can be found in the painting *Archduke Johann as Hunter of Chamois* (1817) by Johann Peter Krafft, which depicts a clear connection between the Archduke and the mountainous region of Styria. He is positioned on a rocky crag, allowing both him and the viewer to gaze down at the panorama from above. The Archduke is also literally raised up as the viewer sees him from below. This painting became almost iconic in its representation of a national hero. It constitutes an ideologically charged landscape that invites both identification and criticism, whose message has been spread in the form of numerous widespread copies, engravings, facsimiles and other reproductions. The image invokes the sense of a free, honest, simple and yet noble inhabitant of the Alps, inviting a contrast with the corrupt inhabitants of the city. It undoubtedly had a great deal of political power in the years following the Congress of Vienna, particularly bearing in mind the role that Archduke Johann played during the Napoleonic Wars. The first engraving of the image was created 1818 by Blasius Höfel, who consequently received a stern rebuke from the state police—the censorship authorities believed him to be spreading subversive ideas. A highly important aspect of the painting is the simple, traditional clothing of the Archduke, which he used in a conscious and symbolic manner and which the emperor banned from court. Like the mountainous landscape, traditional clothing was used to convey ideological aims, something that continued even after the time of Archduke Johann.[5]

Idealisation of the Alps

The majority of the large number of idealised Alpine images that emerged at the beginning of the 19th century were far less focused in their statements. Around the middle of the 18th century, the European mountain range was still perceived as inaccessible, forbidding and terrifying, and was therefore not seen as a suitable subject for painting. After this, the perception of mountains changed; they became a place that city-dwellers wished to visit in their search for edification and relaxation as well as for the opportunity to climb and conquer the

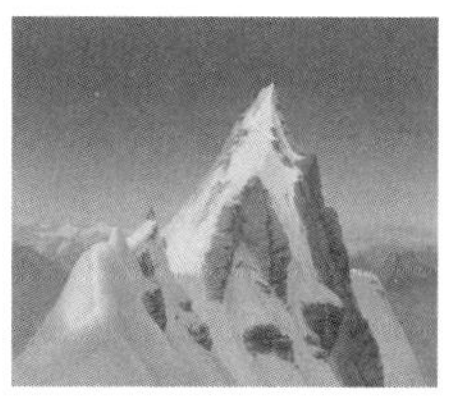

Markus Pernhart
Climbing the Groß-glockner, ca. 1850

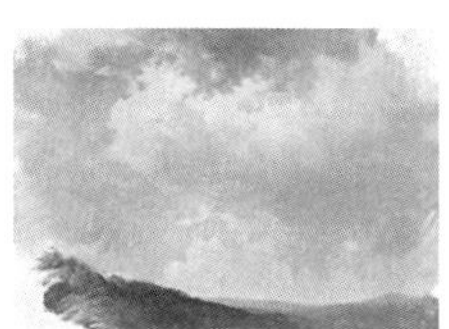

Friedrich Gauermann
Study of Clouds,
ca. 1830

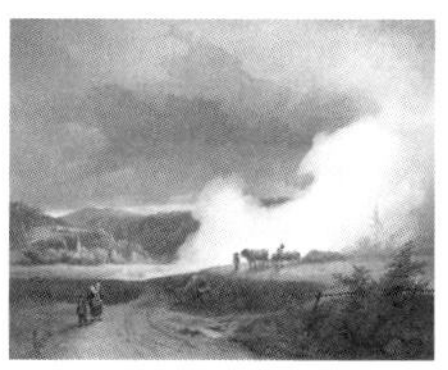

Ignaz Raffalt
Alpine Foothill Land-scape with Rising Mist, 1845

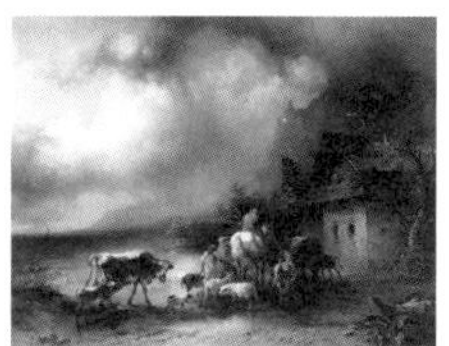

Friedrich Gauermann
Homecoming in the Thunderstorm on Attersee, 1856

5
Cf. Werner Telesko:
*Kulturraum Österreich.
Die Identität der
Regionen in der
bildenden Kunst des 19.
Jahrhunderts.* Vienna/
Cologne/Weimar 2008,
p. 371.

6
Cf. Johann Wolfgang
von Goethe: *Italienische
Reise.* Berlin 1976,
pp. 219–224.

highest peaks. Mountain-climbing in particular—with its dangers and the necessity of exercising self-discipline—led to stories of heroism and contributed to the Alps being viewed in an idealised manner. This idealised perspective was recorded, communicated and spread by the visual arts. The result was an interaction between the noble and pictur-esque 'painterly'—and thus also motifs and landscapes defined as such by painting—and the routes taken by tourists as well as the touristic development of the areas concerned. What is particularly noticeable from today's perspective is the obvious discrepancy between what was 'true to nature'—in other words, the realistic representations aspired to by the Austrian Biedermeier generation (whose paintings were often accompanied by the description 'created/drawn/painted according to nature') —and the obvious idealisation, idyllisation and exaggeration of their motifs. This use of motifs was clearly prompted by public taste: buyers liked some views so much that the painters created replicas of their own work. For example, there are currently three known versions of Steinfeld's *Hallstätter See*, which was painted around 1834, and two known versions of Ender's *Gastein*, which was painted around 1830.

Nature at Work

Many of the images created in the first half of the century, which reflect the development of Alpine tourism and the movement of travellers, ignore changes to the landscape itself triggered by the changing sea-sons and weather. However, as of around 1850, there was an increasing focus on the autonomous changes of nature. Changing cloud forma-tions were observed and sketched (Friedrich Gauermann) and artists experimented with their impact on the landscape's appearance. Ignaz Raffalt—also called 'Cloud Raffalt'—turned this development into an entire field of business. Artists liked to depict storms about to break, often including images of country people trying to bring the cattle or the harvest in safely in order to make the events more dramatic (Friedrich Gauermann, Joseph Heicke). From this point onwards, Alpine paintings developed into large pieces of powerful—and decorative— effect, with the more intimate atmospheric realism developing as a counter-movement.

Depictions of exceptional natural events and catastrophes, such as the two watercolours by Joseph Kuwasseg showing the flooding of the River Mur in Graz on the 8th June 1827 belong, however, more to the category of documentation and news coverage. Between 1631 and 1822, artists created copper engravings of the historic eruptions of Vesuvius, which were compiled in a book published by Nicolas Gervasi in 1823 in Naples, complimenting reports, vedutas, pieces of spectacu-lar effect and documentation of scientific research on the topic. Vesu-vius was very active during the second half of the 18th century, becom-ing a fixed point of call for those travelling through Italy. Many people such as Johann Wolfgang von Goethe, who visited the site in 1787, made use of their trip to combine their interest in both the natural sciences and history:[6] Observations of the eruptions of Vesuvius made

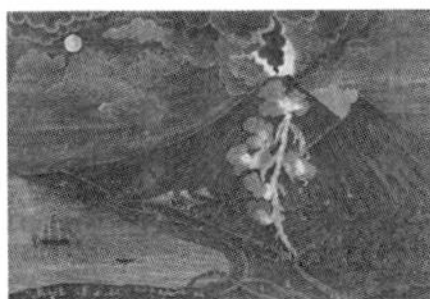

Nicolas Gervasi (ed.)
From: *Les incendies
du Mont Vesuve*,
Naples ca. 1823

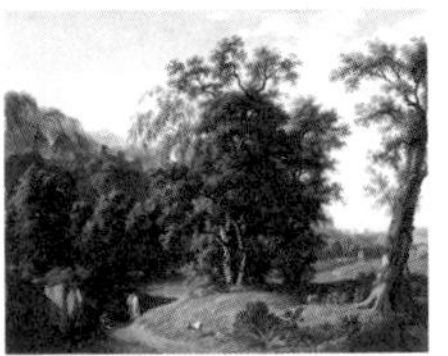

Johann Kniep
*Arcadian Mountain-
scape*, 1805

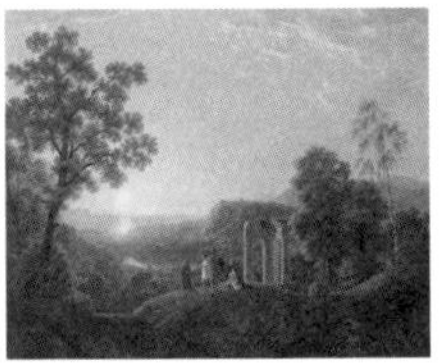

Johann Kniep
*Ideal Landscape
(with Sinking Sun)*,
1806

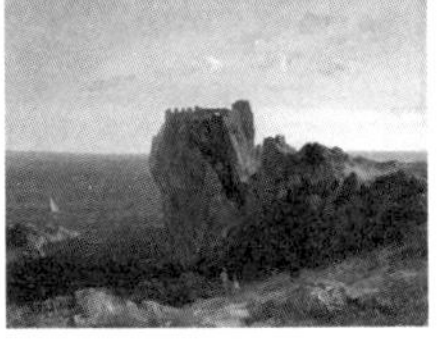

Thomas Ender
*The Cliff of Dante at
Duino*, ca. 1853

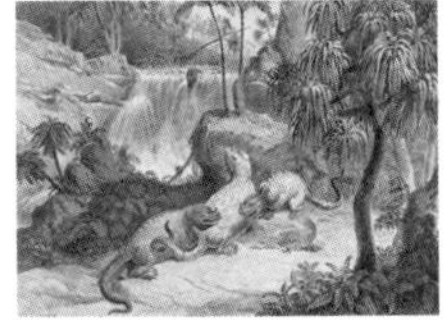

Joseph Kuwasseg
From: *The Primeval
World in Its Various
Stages of Formation*,
1846–49

an important contribution to the earth sciences, helping scientists to
make fundamental discoveries about the history of the Earth. At the
same time, archaeology experienced a boom with the excavations of
Herculaneum and Pompeii, greatly influencing the Neoclassicism of this
period. The two Roman cities were destroyed when Vesuvius erupted in
79 A.D. and were not rediscovered until the middle of the 18th century.[7]

Images of the Far-Off between Ideal and Reality and History of the Earth Research and Visual Representation

During the Classicism of around 1800, artists at the Academy of Fine
Arts Vienna also began to make use of old patterns of images from
idealist landscape painting. These images were influenced by classical
artists such as Claude Lorrain and his paintings of the Roman Cam-
pagna. Johann Kniep's two paintings from 1805 and 1806 thus consist
of combined individual elements, depicting an imagined hilly countryside, containing antique ruins and staffage figures. At this time Kniep
was also working as Archduke Johann's 'personal painter'. Pictures such
as his aimed to provide a perfect depiction of life in the ancient world:
ideal and harmonious and in keeping with nature. The numerous travellers who made their way to Italy are likely to have set off with these
very images in their minds.
One of these travellers was Thomas Ender, who accompanied the court
to Italy in 1819. He had already proven himself as a documentarian
during the Austrian expedition to Brazil in 1817/18. He tried to create
a relatively realistic record of events and sights in his sketches, but in
his work *Cliff of Dante at Duino*—though painted much later, in 1853—
the glorification of Italian culture still resonates in the manner that
remained typical for the ideal of humanistic education until well into
the 20th century.
During the 19th century there was a dramatic increase in the visualisation of research focussing on different times and places, which
followed a similar approach to that used in the depiction of journeys.
Patterns of images developed in the visual arts have an equally strong
impact on the visual result as the facts provided by the natural sciences or empirical research (in the case of expeditions). This means
that both aspects play an important role in the creation of the image.
Proof of this approach can be seen in the similarities between Joseph
Kuwasseg's watercolours depicting Ceylon and his *Primeval World*
series. The Ceylon pieces painted in 1855 were created by following
templates provided by his pupil Hermann von Königsbrun, which he
had brought back with him after travelling to the island. The 18-parts
Primeval World series was based on drawings created in close cooperation with palaeobotanist Dr Franz Unger, with the aim of depicting his
research. Unger worked at the Joanneum in Graz between 1835 and
1849 and his groundbreaking publication *The Primeval World in its
Various Stages of Formation* is seen as being one of the forerunners of
Darwin's theory of evolution.

Part 2 – The Depiction of Landscape since 1945

The first part of the exhibition spans a timeframe beginning around 1800 and ending in the middle of the 19th century. The second part continues on from 1945 and ends in the present. The works of art exhibited are not restricted by any formal stipulations—photography, drawings, paintings, sculpture, video and installations are placed next to each other as seems logical, in their medial singularity as well as in the conceptual connection between the works.
Separating artistic categories has long been obsolete and would, after all, not take the context of their creation properly into account. Surprisingly, it is still possible to see developments that stretch from the 19th century to today.
The exhibition shows how new ways of perceiving and visualising nature developed during the 19th century—not least due to the development of technical visual media. The natural sciences and rapid industrialisation also played an important role in drastically changing people's way of thinking and extending their scope of action. Our understanding of nature is no longer only shaped by different patterns of idealisation in landscape painting but by new perspectives provided by scientific research. The world has not increased in size but the areas that people can enter and begin to understand have become wider—and are continuing to expand today. It is surprising to see that the pictorial space found within landscape painting has also expanded, giving art new perspectives.
The language of art changed radically, at first only under the influence of new technology, then using it directly. Mechanically created images of science—generated by instruments used to measure and investigate the world and nature or, as was frequently the case, by photography— reflected the idea of nature recording itself. Illustrations of nature were not to be impaired by aesthetically motivated interventions or by choices or interpretation. In photography, people were prepared to accept technical limitations and the lack of colour in return for a piece that reflected the scientific ethos of non-intervention and contained no aesthetically motivated interventions. However, it is important to remember that all forms of presentation made available to art and science over the years, alter nature in their own way. Following the same train of thought, it can therefore also be said that nature can only speak for itself when you make it speak. Alteration is frequently connected with the choice of medium and it is this that makes up the construction of reality. For example, a photograph proves or shows in a different way to a drawing or a specimen. This laboratory situation was to continue to differentiate and specialise up to today. New technical media and new interactional contexts bring with them new ways of seeing things.
Living in a world where we are constantly being confronted with the fact that our existence and the way in which we treat the world could lead to its destruction, we are prompted to reach the same conclusion as Peter Finke: that 'we talk about landscape too much and do too

7
Compare in general: Joachim von der Thüsen: *Schönheit und Schrecken der Vulkane. Zur Kulturgeschichte des Vulkanismus.* Darmstadt 2008.

little for it'. He continues by saying that: 'The main problem that we have with landscape is neither a philosophical, historical nor psychological problem, nor is it a problem related to the theory of art or to literature. Instead it is a very real problem: its continuing destruction. Every time we focus on landscape today, we should do so in a way that works towards solving the problem.'[8] This militant approach, driven by a pragmatic desire to survive, is currently a ubiquitous aspect of contemporary art. Before a background shaped by awareness-raising and changing conditions, artists are not only performing direct interventions in nature, such as in the fields of Land Art and the later Environmental Art, but also making numerous attempts to depict nature.

This leads to a fundamental question within post-1945 art: Can art be relevant if it is not able to shape society and therefore does not influence key general problems that are of central importance in society? This may seem to be a rather inartistic demand, as it no longer reflects a traditional understanding of art. It could be said that there is no longer such a thing as a depoliticised landscape. Every debate regarding landscape has become a debate about nature, making it also a debate on the dominant living conditions and power relations. After all, images represent ideologies, worldviews and goals. During the 19th century, landscape depictions primarily focussed on the mapping, the opening up of the landscape. By the middle of the 20th century, there was an increasing objective to use artistic potential to actively participate in designing reality. This meant that landscape painting began to lose ground. After 1945, a new way of tackling landscape developed, which aimed to focus on real space and on the design of a real landscape. Artistic intervention made it possible to experience the landscape and the environment as a social construction.
The development of Fluxus, Happening, Performance Art and Concept Art increased the scope of art, therefore, together with technological progress, becoming important impulses within the artistic debate. Land Art made it possible to depict landscape as a subject in a sculptural way too. For example, a collection of stones presented in a gallery provides a material representation of a location in the landscape, which is deployed to an art space, thus becoming a non-place. Communication via photography and film can also be seen as a subtle form of representation. A conceptual approach to photography helps the substituting image of the place to become a representation. This medium of documentation also plays an ambivalent role in performative artistic expression. Photography takes the reality away from art works and equates image with reality. This aspect was seen as early as the 19th century, when reality was understood as being within the boundaries of representation.
The production of images from the beginning of the 20th century until today has become unmanageable; real spaces and problems resulting from ecology and industry have relativised the sublime as well as natural beauty. The depiction of places is not the only antipole to have developed opposite the classical representation of nature and

8
Peter Finke: 'Landschaftserfahrung und Landschaftserhaltung. Plädoyer für eine ökologische Landschaftsästhetik', in: Manfred Smuda (ed.): *Landschaft*. Frankfurt am Main 1986, p. 26.

landscape; there is now the additional element of actual changes to places. Analytical thinking and the deconstruction process have become important stimulations for art produced in the 20th century and later—and landscape depiction is no exception.

This has not stopped painting from existing but it has taken away its supremacy in the creation of visualisation. Demands for portrait, still life, genre or landscape have become obsolete. Remains of these divisions still exist but they have acquired a new meaning. Painting as a genre no longer truly exists. Now that we have entered a post-historical era, which presents itself as postmodernist synchrony, phenomena and developments are no longer received linearly but simultaneously. Reality has entered art, followed by the image as reality, something that is particularly evident in painting, where debates mostly take place in the context of medial discussions. The focus is no longer on finding an appropriate way of depicting nature in painting but on the defined patterns that developed over the course of the history of painting and are, in part, still operative today. This means that painting is limited in its depiction of reality; its way of interpreting nature is only acceptable in the light of tradition. Despite wide-ranging discoveries about nature, which also changed people's understanding of it, some significant 19th-century approaches still remain. Like art in general, painting continues to create antitheses to reality or use images to experience or create reality.

Travel as a Concept

Specialists from fields outside of art are involved and are developing this image. This also explains the significance of media, which took on a central role in portraying reality in the second half of the 20th century. The position previously held by the map, is now probably held by satellite photography ('Google Earth'). This development has since made it possible to call up a visual image of every place on earth at any time. The abstract map has been transformed into a realistic image—photography at its most advanced. At the same time, it is important to remember that disciplines such as drawing and painting have remained, either keeping themselves apart from technical visual media or including them in their artworks as a matter of course. In a post-media context, the mixing of disciplines and the resulting contextualisation in fields reflecting on the media are taken for granted. The formal aspect of the artwork is thereby transformed into an important part of the content; categories and media are constantly questioned and therefore also thematised.

While creating his monumental work on America, *K.C.C.P. in USA* (1992/93), Michael Schuster travelled through all 50 states of America. He photographed one place in each state that the respective local authorities said was the most visited by tourists and the most photographed. He was thus following the illusion machine of tourism, which is based on a constructed and standardised perception of reality. A Kodak Colour Control Patch was positioned in each image

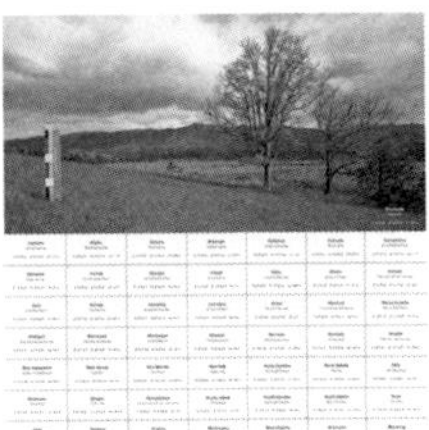

Michael Schuster
From: *K.C.C.P. in USA,*
1992/93

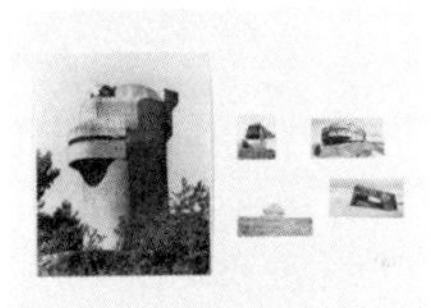

Paul Virilio
Bunker archéologie,
Karola, 1958-65/93

as a corrective, placed into the picture like an imaginary tourist, with the aim of prompting discussions about the objectivity of the photo. Schuster also made use of GPS to precisely document the location, do that the image was generally and fundamentally traceable, like a scientific experiment. In this artwork, Schuster deconstructed the construction of reality. The images did not show reality but rather the reality of the American consciousness. An ideological scene with any claims to reality was thus debunked. The context of the journey, a conceptualisation within the structure of an expedition, the way in which he recorded motifs and made them systematic, all this reminds the viewer of Land Art as well as of a form of documentarism, something that has always been thematised in different ways within photography. Contemporary tourism is about seeing everything fast, taking pictures and storing them in a tiny photo memory so that they can be used in different ways to prove that the journey took place. Ultimately, this ridiculousness is an expression of the idealisation of nature and landscape that began so long ago.

Paul Virilio counteracted this idealisation of reality in his project *Bunker archéologie* from 1958-65/93. He photographed the 'Atlantic Wall', concrete bunkers that the Nazis began to erect on the French coast in 1942. He describes this area, with its wartime constructions, as a landscape that shoots back. The shooters in the bunker cannot be seen, causing the landscape itself to be personified. The theoretical fragments that accompany the pictures provide no description. Instead, like the ruined fortifications, the information consists of fragments, which Virilio sees as being part of a poetic process. His project is based on the idea that the development of technology is also the development of accidents in the sense of *accidens*. The train may have initially been dedicated to the positive aim of opening up the landscape but it still also meant the development of the railway disaster. With the ship came shipwrecks, with the motorway came car crashes, with planes came another type of devastating crash. Virilio states that 'If we want to carry on using technology (and here I'm in no way thinking of going back to the Stone Age), I believe that we have to think about its essence *and* the respective accidens—here and now. For the essence is, at the same time, the object and its accidens, its accident.'[9] According to Virilio's logic, there must be an area that leads to collapse, although positive developments take place, due to the negative effects that develop in parallel. According to him, he claims that we remain silent about the negative sides of technology and speed, marginalising these aspects even today. Art can help to counterbalance this by raising awareness, something that is still a main impulse behind art.

9
'Technik und
Fragmentierung. Paul
Virilio im Gespräch
mit Sylvère Lotringer',
in: *Aisthesis.*
Wahrnehmung heute
oder Perspektiven
einer anderen Ästhetik.
Leipzig, 1991, p. 72.

The Impression of Land Art and
Landscape as Text

The context of travelling, of moving through the landscape, has had
different effects, two examples of which will be given here. Conceptu-
alisations are frequently responsible for transforming a non-art field
into an art field, prompted by a search for new ideas and statements.
In general, it is important to note that, since the end of the 1960s, the
topic of nature has been redefined in its position between Concept Art,
Minimal Art and Land Art. For example, Land Art became an aesthetic
visualisation of natural laws. Confronted with general developments, it
is necessary for art to provide a counterbalance; also in relation to the
construction of reality. Régis Debray says: 'Land use planning, the management of nature parks, representatives of the visual arts, landscape
protection, the ministries for environment and culture—all these institutions prove that landscape and art are no longer being experienced,
as was once the case—they are being constructed.'[10] Environmental Art
followed on from Land Art, taking up the task of finding new solutions
to climate and energy problems, well away from the art market. For
example, Peter Fend developed an alternative ecology based on the
protest movement of the late 1960s, creating a new type of cartog-
raphy of resources to encourage the creation of more effective energy
policies. In 1980, he founded the organisation 'Ocean Earth Construction and Development Corporation, OECD' together with other artists,
with the aim of monitoring and managing the planet to develop a more
stable food chain. Watersheds, reservoirs and bird migration patterns
were frequently used as parameters in reorientation and restructuring.
This example clearly shows that new art practices do not simply want
to depict places but to make actual changes, with art confronting economic, political, social and ecological conditions. This too can be seen
as a transformation process, moving from one construction to another.
It is, after all, a part of a general ecological movement.
Land art made use of cultic aspects that were transferred onto industrial wasteland and other inaccessible areas for the purpose of raising
awareness. The direct intervention in the natural context was strongly
shaped by form and, despite its closeness to reality, was still strongly
rooted in representation. The formulations of Concept Art that developed in parallel allowed a new language of forms to develop out of Land
Art. This language became the language of art, also using and quoting
elements from natural scientific research in different ways. Poetry, the
natural sciences and the cultic consciously entered into an alliance.
Wolfgang Buchner's work, for example, visualises physical processes
of change within nature. Since the late 1960s, the development of his
work has been influenced primarily by Land Art formulations. Specialist
knowledge of the natural sciences has been consolidated into artistic
design. A poetisation of the natural sciences has led to the development of a universal perspective that does not separate the humanities
and natural sciences. In his work series *Geopoesien*, made in 1975, the
artist presented layers of rock formations in display cabinets. In the

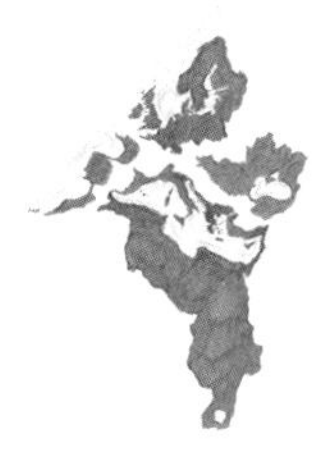

Peter Fend
*Wasserplanung für
Europa*, 1998

10
Régis Debray:
*Jenseits der Bilder.
Eine Geschichte der
Bildbetrachtung im
Abendland*. Berlin 2007,
p. 184.

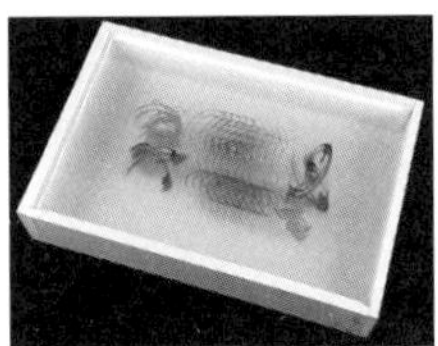

Wolfgang Buchner
Geopoesie III, 1975

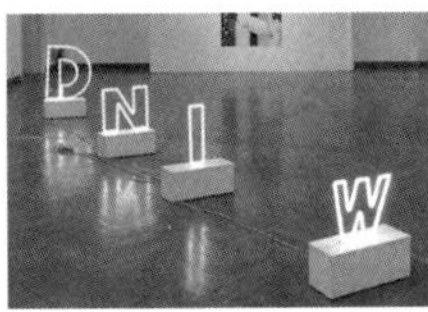

Peter Weibel
Wind, 1975

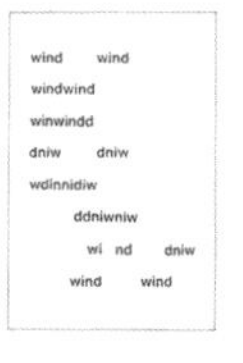

Heinz Gappmayr
Wind, 1961

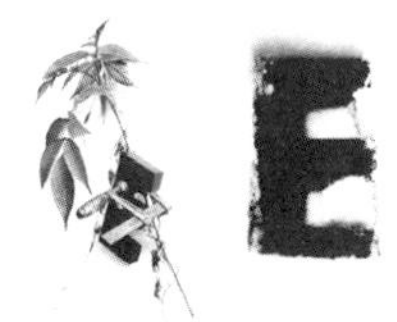

Josef Bauer
Sommer E – Winter E,
1976

11
Umberto Eco: *Ein-
führung in die Semiotik.*
Munich 1994, p. 38.

models consisting of glass layers, connections were made to geological methods and geodesy, with the models themselves seeming to
develop into free formations with a lyrical dimension. As is the case in
geometry, the space in which the artwork exists emerges as a space of
relationships consisting of dots, lines and curves; a limaçon of Pascal
as a poetic figure.

This conceptualising process can be followed through the exhibition
until a radical transformation of the landscape into text takes place.
Text as a model for creating order or explanation becomes important
when seen in the context of the post-historical condition, such as in
relation to postmodernism in general but also in art in particular. For
example, art from a specific nation can be thought of as a textual
structure, one that can be interpreted in a process of mutual exchange.
The intercultural similarities create a textual network that can be read
by all. However, for this to be possible, art cannot be seen as being
primarily an example of individual expression. Rather, it is connected to
a historical reference system. This desubjectivisation creates a degree
of objectification, the artwork is seen as a chain of signs, as a point in
a network of historical references, as part of a complete legible text.
According to Umberto Eco, all aspects of culture can be investigated as
communication phenomena. 'In culture any entity can become a semiotic phenomenon.' [11] The semiotics of culture sees culture as a symbolic
or textual context, within which individual cultural elements condense
to form a universe of texts. The semiotic approach pulls down the
barriers surrounding the classic definition of text. Not only linguistic
utterances but also landscapes, social acts, design or art in general can
be read as a text. Examples of work by Peter Weibel, Heinz Gappmayr,
Josef Bauer and Petra Maitz make this clear in the exhibition. All of
these pieces have in common the visual power of the text within a
tradition of linguistic criticism.

Landscape as Social Construction

The term landscape needs to be considered in relation to the existence
of the people who live and act within it. The effects of human behaviour
have never before been as evident as they are today. As a consequence,
the social construction of the landscape and reality is becoming an
additional central topos. The idea of nature being largely untouched
is in itself a construction. The way in which people live fundamentally
changes the appearance of the landscape.

In his extensive work of photography *Das Land*, Manfred Willmann
documented the southwest of Styria between 1981 and 1993, focussing on exactly this aspect. Following the tradition of the 'New Topographics' photographers of the 1970s, he recorded places that were
being shaped by interventions and actions on the part of people.[12] His
work focussed not on a landscape ideal but on viewing the living space
in a documentary manner, using photography to criticise civilisation.
Willmann shows country life in its existence between tradition, the
everyday and a thoroughly modern, rational economisation. He avoids

→ p. 242

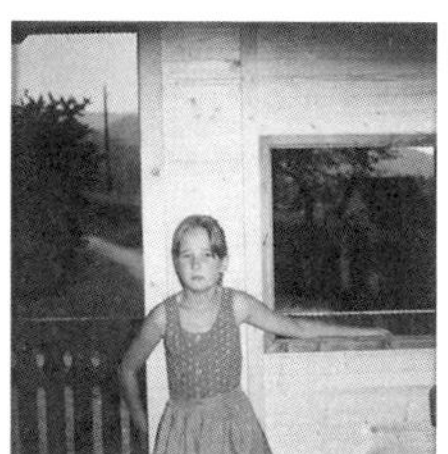

Manfred Willmann
From: *Das Land*,
1981-93/2013

12
The 'New Topographics'
movement developed
during the 1970s in the
USA. It was inspired by
a 1975 exhibition enti-
tled *New Topographics:
Photographs of a
Man-altered Landscape*,
which took place in
George Eastman House
in Rochester, New York.
The exhibition played
an important role in
photography becoming
a part of contemporary
art. Its international
influence on the next
generations of photo-
graphers cannot be
overestimated.

13
Arnulf Rohsmann:
'Abstraktion und
Abstrahieren in der
Österreichischen
Kunst', in: Peter Weibel,
Christa Steinle (eds.):
*Identität:Differenz.
Tribüne Trigon 1940–
1990. Eine Topografie
der Moderne.* Vienna/
Cologne/Weimar 1992,
p. 165.

picturesque modes of representation, placing himself in the same category as Dan Graham (*Homes for America*, 1966), Ed Ruscha (*Every Building on the Sunset Strip*, 1966) and Martha Rosler (*The Bowery in Two Inadequate Descriptive Systems*, 1974). Willmann not only creates a clear example of social criticism but also critically questions the medial level of photography focussing on documenting society. Walter Niedermayr can be seen as providing an antithesis, or an inten- sification of the same topic, in his photo documentation of touristic and functional landscapes, desolate abandoned sites and no-man's land. He creates an intense focus on darker places, which have been entirely used and used up by people. His photographs show these land- scapes irrefutably to be spaces of modern socialisation and places of modernity, revealing phenomena shaped by new determinative spatial planning and a new way of experiencing space.
In both cases, one is forced to come to the conclusion that there is no such thing as a non-ideological landscape. The positions of Willmann and Niedermayr are an example of a multiplicity of different formula- tions within a perception of landscape shaped by society, which have led to a condition of hyperreality caused by a many-layered process of transformation. Jean Baudrillard describes hyperreality as being an image of reality, which has been warped and deformed in such a way that reality can no longer be recognised in the image—only guessed at. We have set ourselves up in this simulacrum. This approach can be applied also beyond the positions mentioned—it has become the basis of a general understanding of reality. It becomes visible in different ways and is being deconstructed by artistic concepts.

Landscape Painting between Abstraction and Representation

The final focal point of the exhibition is again the art of painting, caught between abstraction and representation. Painting formed the basis of the fundamental impulses behind the depiction of landscape, as can clearly be seen in works from the 19th century. Even today, this medium still swings between the two poles of idealisation and documentation, although painting itself is now increasingly becoming the focus of discussions. The idea of a detail, where nature is seen as an entity in itself, is inherent both to the scientific image and the artistic image from the field of painting. However, there is now no one way in which people agree nature should be depicted within a paint- ing. Rather, different processes of abstraction attempt to find a new way of experiencing nature, which takes place at a conscious distance from approaches based in documentation or the natural sciences. Nature abstraction is used as a general term to describe the situation in Austria. It is often seen as being the opposing pole to abstraction, rather than as a part of it.[13] Positions such as those held by Max Weiler and Wolfgang Hollegha are received in this context. Forms found in the material world, in nature, in everyday life etc. are closely related to painterly conception, whether they provide the impetus and primary motif behind the design as is the case with Hollegha, or whether they

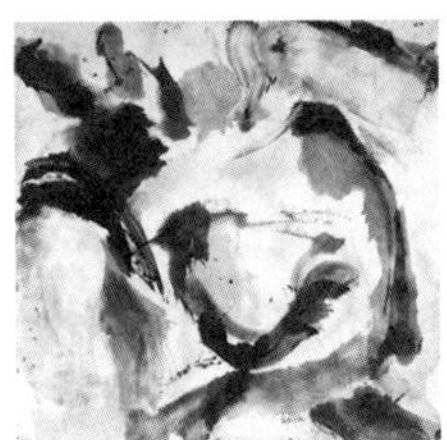

Wolfgang Hollegha
Holzstück III, 1966

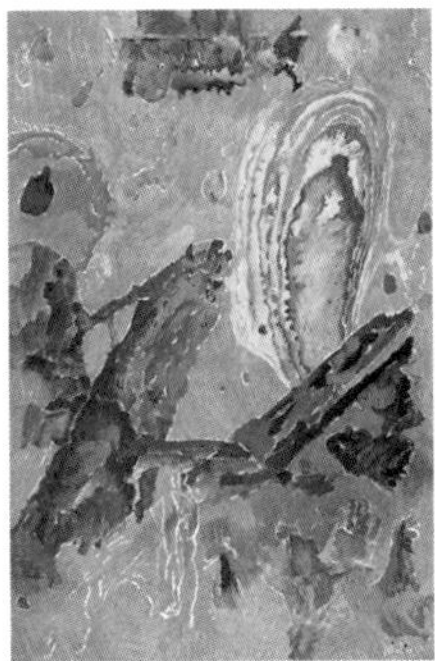

Max Weiler
Landschaft in Ocker,
1969

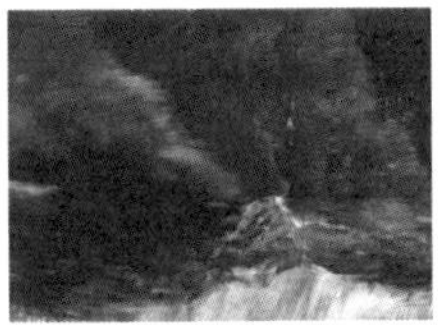

Herbert Brandl
ohne Titel, 2004
(detail)

14
Wolfgang Kos talking
to Herbert Brandl, in:
*Alpenblick. Die zeit-
genössische Kunst und
das Alpine*, Kunsthalle
Wien, Vienna 1997,
quoted from: Peter
Weibel, Günther Holler-
Schuster (eds.): *Herbert
Brandl*. Ostfildern-Ruit
2002, p. 255.

are used as inspiration for the shapes within the painting as is the case with Max Weiler. In this phase of painting, the understanding has been reached that nature consists of forces and energies, which are revealed through the power of nature. The focus lies not on the stability of things within nature, as is so often assumed. It is about taking a close look, which often means looking within. The artist's gaze falls below the line of the horizon, in the way of a map. However, the painters do not investigate the microscopic level of reality but rather unlock an emotional area motivated by inner images, which is both highly subjective and appears to be a variation of an unknown reality. Art does not reflect that which can be seen but rather makes visible.

In this exhibition, Herbert Brandl provides an example of a central position within the painting debate. Strongly influenced by the painting movement of the 1980s, he quickly established a form of painting that focussed on the medium itself, questioning it and demanding new styles. Far away from the discussion on abstraction or representation, the act of painting was turned into a new type of reality. The focus no longer lay on the connection to the reality of the subject but on the constants inherent to the medium of painting. Abstraction begins as soon as the painter begins to paint an object imported from reality—whether the end product is something that can be read or something abstract. In fact, even something abstract can be read as an object from certain perspectives. Brandl states: 'As soon as you start at the academies you learn: whatever is depicted, portrait formats always suggest trees or figures. And pictures using the landscape format will always be associated with landscape. (...) I always wanted to avoid the landscape but, before you can say Jack Robinson, the horizon appears again.'[14]

Brandl's paintings show how distinguishability between things disappears to make room for a continuum of paint splashes. The eye sees them as being just as thematic as that which they exist to represent. The subject therefore does not disappear in the field of painting. However, its representation is not the aim of the depiction but rather the reason for painting.

Overall, the exhibition reveals that nature and landscape operate in a different way in modern conditions than they did in the past. They are becoming more and more ambiguous; the location can be anywhere inside or outside of us. They are not limited to land or to the visible reality in front of our eyes. As has already been shown, images of modernism can be understood in the light of traditions. It no longer makes sense to differentiate between images that come specifically from the field of art and those that come from a non-art field such as the natural or social sciences. It is the generality in the visual entwined as it is in constant processes of transformation that determines our reality. The viewer is connected with this process as a matter of course, at the end discovering that they are a part of this increasingly dense construction of reality.

Themes and Artists of the Exhibition

Mapping the Landscape

Jakob Gauermann
b. 1773 in Öffingen/Württemberg (DE), † 1843 in Vienna (AT)

Josef Franz Kaiser
b. 1786 in Graz (AT), † 1859 in Graz (AT)

→ p. 141

Joseph Kuwasseg
b. 1799 in Trieste (IT), † 1859 in Graz (AT)
The Badelwand with Arches for Railway near Peggau in Styria, 1844
Lithograph on paper; 32 × 43.5 cm
Neue Galerie Graz, UMJ, Inv. no. II/11718

View of Graz from St. Peter (Panorama of Graz), ca. 1850
Sepia on paper; 46 × 72 cm
Neue Galerie Graz, UMJ, Inv. no. II/5419

Carl Reichert
b. 1836 in Vienna (AT), † 1918 in Graz (AT)

→ p. 140

Georg Matthäus Vischer
b. 1628 in Wenns/Tyrol (AT), † 1696 in Linz (AT)
Archiducatus Austriae Superioris Geographica Descriptio, 1667/69
Copper engraving of 12 plates on paper; 120.5 × 114 cm
Schloss Trautenfels, UMJ, Reg. no. TR 0012_12

Ideologisation of Landscape

→ p. 142

Blasius Höfel after Johann Peter Krafft
Blasius Höfel, b. 1792 in Vienna (AT), † 1863 in Aigen/Salzburg (AT);
Johann Peter Krafft, b. 1780 in Hanau/Hessia (DE), † 1856 in Vienna (AT)

Johann Archduke of Austria, 1817/1818
Copper engraving on paper; 61.5 × 39.4 cm
Neue Galerie Graz, UMJ, Inv. no. II/17804

→ p. 142

Johann Huber after Johann Peter Krafft
Johann Huber, active in Graz (AT) around 1840;
Johann Peter Krafft, b. 1780 in Hanau/Hessia (DE), † 1856 in Vienna (AT)

Archduke Johann on the Hochschwab, 1817/1839
Oil on canvas, 41.3 × 29.4 cm
Neue Galerie Graz, UMJ, Inv. no. I/2638

→ p. 142

Josef Kriehuber

b. 1800 in Vienna (AT), † 1876 in Vienna (AT)

Franz Josef I in Full-length as Hunter in Alpine Landscape, 1850s
Lithograph on paper; 77 × 57 cm
Neue Galerie Graz, UMJ, Inv. no. II/17670

→ p. 143

Melanie Stürgkh after Matthäus Loder

Melanie Stürgkh, b. 1898 in Graz (AT), † 1992 in Graz (AT);
Matthäus Loder, b. 1781 in Vienna (AT), † 1828 in Vordernberg/Styria (AT)

Curling on the Leopoldsteinersee, ca. 1822/ca. 1955
Watercolour on paper; 25 × 37.8 cm
Neue Galerie Graz, UMJ, Inv. no. II/10492

Boat Trip on the Grundlsee, 1822/1956
Watercolour on paper; 22.6 × 33.5 cm
Neue Galerie Graz, UMJ, Inv. no. II/10631

→ p. 142

Eduard Weixelgärtner and Josef Kriehuber after Johann Fischbach

Eduard Weixelgärtner, b. 1816 in Budapest (HU), † 1873 in Vienna (AT);
Josef Kriehuber, b. 1800 in Vienna (AT), † 1876 in Vienna (AT);
Johann Fischbach, b. 1797 in Grafenegg/Lower Austria (AT), † 1871 in Munich (DE)

The Old Huntsman with his Son, ca. 1850
Lithograph on paper; 83.5 × 64.5 cm
Neue Galerie Graz, UMJ, Inv. no. II/26479

Idealisation of the Alps

Thomas Ender

b. 1793 in Vienna (AT), † 1875 in Vienna (AT)

→ p. 144

Markus Pernhart

b. 1824 in Untermieger/Carinthia (AT), † 1871 in St. Ruprecht/Carinthia (AT)

Climbing the Großglockner, ca. 1850
Oil on canvas; 57.6 × 68.5 cm
Neue Galerie Graz, UMJ, Inv. no. I/777

Anton Schiffer

b. 1811 in Graz (AT), † 1876 in Vienna (AT)

→ p. 145

Franz Steinfeld

b. 1787 in Vienna (AT), † 1868 in Pisek (CZ)

Grundlsee, ca. 1845
Oil on canvas; 44.8 × 57.6 cm
Neue Galerie Graz, UMJ, Inv. no. I/434

Leopold Heinrich Voescher

b. 1830 in Vienna (AT), † 1877 in Vienna (AT)

Nature at Work

 Friedrich Gauermann
b. 1807 in Miesenbach/Lower Austria (AT), † 1862 in Vienna (AT)
Study of Clouds, ca. 1830
Oil on paper; 18 × 26 cm
Neue Galerie Graz, UMJ, Inv. no. II/2761

Homecoming in the Thunderstorm on Attersee, 1856
Oil on spruce wood; 62.6 × 82 cm
Neue Galerie Graz, UMJ, Inv. no. I/498

 Nicolas Gervasi (ed.)
Les incendies du Mont Vesuve, Naples ca. 1823
Book with 30 copper engravings; 36.7 × 48.2 × 1.3 cm
Neue Galerie Graz, UMJ, Inv. no. II/30432

Anton Hansch
b. 1813 in Vienna (AT), † 1876 in Salzburg (AT)

Joseph Heicke
b. 1811 in Vienna (AT), † 1861 in Vienna (AT)

Joseph Kuwasseg
b. 1799 in Trieste (IT), † 1859 in Graz (AT)

Christian Friedrich Mali
b. 1832 in Broekhuizen (NL), † 1906 in Munich (DE)

 Ignaz Raffalt
b. 1800 in Weißenkirchen/Styria (AT), † 1857 in Hainbach/Lower Austria (AT)
Alpine Foothill Landscape with Rising Mist, 1845
Oil on canvas; 42.2 × 52.8 cm
Neue Galerie Graz, UMJ, Inv. no. I/2576

Michael Wutky (attributed)
b. 1739 in Krems/Lower Austria (AT), † 1822 in Vienna (AT)

Images of the Far-Off between Ideal and Reality

 Thomas Ender
b. 1793 in Vienna (AT), † 1875 in Vienna (AT)
The Cliff of Dante at Duino, ca. 1853
Oil on paper on cardboard; 38.4 × 50 cm
Neue Galerie Graz, UMJ, Inv. no. I/1383

      Johann Kniep

b. 1779 in Vienna (AT), † 1809 in Vienna (AT)

Arcadian Mountainscape, 1805
Oil on canvas; 98 × 122 cm, golden frame
Neue Galerie Graz, UMJ, Inv. no. I/31

Ideal Landscape (with Sinking Sun), 1806
Oil on canvas; 95.5 × 121 cm
Neue Galerie Graz, UMJ, Inv. no. I/30

Vinzenz Kreuzer

b. 1809 in Graz (AT), † 1888 in Graz (AT)

Joseph Kuwasseg after Hermann von Königsbrun

Joseph Kuwasseg, b. 1799 in Trieste (IT), † 1859 in Graz (AT);
Hermann von Königsbrun, b. 1823 in Radkersburg/Styria (AT), † 1907 in Graz (AT)

Johann Nepomuk Passini after Thomas Ender

Johann Nepomuk Passini, b. 1798 in Vienna (AT), † 1874 in Graz (AT);
Thomas Ender, b. 1793 in Vienna (AT), † 1875 in Vienna (AT)

      Joseph Selleny

b. 1824 in Meidling near Vienna (AT), † 1875 in Inzersdorf/Lower Austria (AT)

Pine Grove in the Villa Doria-Pamphili in Rome, 1854
Oil on canvas; 78.8 × 51 cm
Neue Galerie Graz, UMJ, Inv. no. I/352

Alois Schönn

b. 1826 in Vienna (AT), † 1897 in Krumpendorf/Carinthia (AT)

History of the Earth Research and Visual Representation

      Joseph Kuwasseg

b. 1799 in Trieste (IT), † 1859 in Graz (AT)

The Primeval World in its Various Stages of Formation (after the Writings of Prof. Franz Unger), 1846–49
18 watercolours on paper; each 48 × 66.5 cm
Neue Galerie Graz, UMJ, Inv. no. II/38175-03 to 20

Joseph Selleny

b. 1824 in Meidling near Vienna (AT), † 1875 in Inzersdorf/Lower Austria (AT)

Travel as a Concept

Rosa Barba
b. 1972 in Agrigento/Sicily (IT), lives in Berlin (DE)

Gottfried Bechtold
b. 1947 in Bregenz (AT), lives in Hörbranz and Bregenz (AT)

Ger Dekkers
b. 1929 in Borne (NL), lives in Giethoorn (NL)

Hamish Fulton
b. 1946 in London (UK), lives in Canterbury (UK)

Richard Kriesche, Peter Gerwin Hoffmann, Seppo Gründler, Josef Klammer
Richard Kriesche, b. 1940 in Vienna (AT), lives in Graz (AT);
Peter Gerwin Hoffmann, b. 1945 in Gröbming/Styria (AT), lives in Graz (AT);
Seppo Gründler, b. 1956 in Graz (AT), lives in Graz (AT);
Josef Klammer, b. 1958 in Lienz/East Tyrol (AT), lives in Graz (AT)

→ p. 153 ### Michael Schuster
b. 1956 in Graz (AT), lives in Graz (AT)
K.C.C.P. in USA, 1992/93
Colour photograph on Diasec, 51 parts; each 60 × 120 cm
Neue Galerie Graz, UMJ, Inv. no. X/1728

Karl Stranzinger
b. 1953 in Graz (AT), † 2013 in Graz (AT)

Franco Vaccari
b. 1936 in Modena (IT), lives in Modena (IT)

→ p. 152 ### Paul Virilio
b. 1932 in Paris (FR), lives in Paris (FR)
Bunker archéologie, Karola, 1958–65/93
Photo collage on cardboard; 70 × 100 cm
Neue Galerie Graz, UMJ, Inv. no. X/1974

Bunker archéologie, Seeadler, 1958–65/93
Photo collage on cardboard; 70 × 100 cm
Neue Galerie Graz, UMJ, Inv. no. X/1873

The Impression of Land Art

→ p. 155

George Brecht
b. 1926 in New York, NY (US), † 2008 in Cologne (DE)
Landmass Translocation Project, 1969
Offset lithograph on paper; 21.8 × 29.7 cm
Neue Galerie Graz, UMJ, Inv. no. II/37761

Wolfgang Buchner
b. 1946 in Mürzzuschlag (AT), lives in Graz (AT)

Ernst Caramelle
b. 1952 in Hall in Tyrol (AT), lives in Karlsruhe (DE) and Frankfurt (DE)

→ p. 154

Christo
b. 1935 in Gabrowo (BG), † 2009 in New York, NY (US)
Wrapped Tree, 1970
Silkscreen on paper; 62 × 83 cm
Neue Galerie Graz, UMJ, Inv. no. II/3884

Braco Dimitrijevic
b. 1948 in Sarajevo (RS), lives in Paris (FR) und London (UK)

Peter Fend
b. 1950 in Ohio (US); lives in New York, NY (US)

Jochen Gerz
b. 1940 in Berlin (DE), lives in Kerry (IE)

Haus-Rucker-Co
1967 founded in Vienna by the architects Laurids Ortner, Günter Zamp Kelp and the painter Klaus Pinter

Hildegard Könighofer
b. 1954 in Rettenegg/Styria (AT), lives in Graz (AT)

Lukas Marxt
b. 1983 in Schladming (AT), lives in Cologne (DE), Leipzig (DE), Brussels (BE) and Graz (AT)

→ p. 155

Max Peintner
b. 1937 in Hall in Tyrol (AT), lives in Vienna (AT)
Verschiebbare Hügel und künstliche Wolken zur Belebung eintöniger Autobahnfahrten, 1969
Pencil on paper; 43.9 × 62 cm
Neue Galerie Graz, UMJ, Inv. no. II/37258

Ed Ruscha
b. 1937 in Omaha, NE (US), lives in Culver City, CA (US)

Josef Taucher
b. 1948 in Weiz (AT), lives near Graz (AT)

→ p. 154 ## Mario Terzic
b. 1945 in Feldkirch (AT), lives in Vienna (AT)
Humusbett, 1973
Pencil, watercolour on paper; 59.6 × 79.6 cm
Neue Galerie Graz, UMJ, Inv. no. II/14163

Luciano Trojanis
b. 1921 in Trieste (IT), † 2004 in Trieste (IT)

Landscape as Text

→ p. 157 ## Josef Bauer
b. 1934 in Gunskirchen/Upper Austria (AT), lives in Linz (AT)
Sommer E – Winter E, 1976
Diptych, b/w photographs; 49.3 × 38.2 cm
Neue Galerie Graz, UMJ, Inv. no. X/1153-1154

→ p. 157 ## Heinz Gappmayr
b. 1925 in Innsbruck (AT), † 2010 in Innsbruck (AT)
Wind, 1961
Indian ink on cardboard; 29.6 × 21 cm
Neue Galerie Graz, UMJ, Inv. no. II/35870

o. T. (21.3.-20.6./21.6.-22.9./23.9.-20.12./21.12.-20.3.), 1983
Letraset on cardboard
Neue Galerie Graz, UMJ, Inv. no. II/34982.

Frantisek Lesák
b. 1943 in Prague (CZ), lives in Vienna (AT)

Petra Maitz
b. 1962 in Vienna (AT), lives in Vienna (AT) and Hamburg (DE)

→ p. 156 ## Peter Weibel
b. 1944 in Odessa (RU), lives in Vienna (AT) and Karlsruhe (DE)
Wind, 1975
4 neon tubes, 4 metal bases, electronic; variable dimensions
Neue Galerie Graz, UMJ, Inv. no. III/539

Landscape as Social Construction

→ p. 158 **Peter Gerwin Hoffmann, Richard Kriesche**
Peter Gerwin Hoffmann, b. 1945 in Gröbming/Styria (AT), lives in Graz (AT);
Richard Kriesche, b. 1940 in Vienna (AT), lives in Graz (AT)

Humane Skulpturen, 1980
16 mm film on video, colour, sound; 20:03 min
Neue Galerie Graz, UMJ, Inv. no. IX/98

Alois Kiendlhofer
b. 1958 in Graz (AT), lives in Vienna (AT)

Branko Lenart
b. 1948 Ptuj (SI), lives in Graz (AT) and Piran (SI)

Walter Niedermayr
b. 1952 Bozen (IT), lives in Bozen (IT)

Hans Werner Poschauko
b. 1963 in Graz (AT), lives in Vienna (AT)

Liddy Scheffknecht
b. 1980 in Dornbirn (AT), lives in Vienna (AT)

Šempas-Family
1971 founded in Šempas (SI) by Marko Pogačnik, artists' collective that lasted until 1979

→ p. 159 **Manfred Willmann**
b. 1952 in Graz (AT), lives in Graz (AT)
Das Land, 1981–93/2013
C-prints, 125 parts; each 70 × 70 cm
Neue Galerie Graz, UMJ, Inv. no. X/1926

The Landscape Theme in Three Dimensions

Miroslav Šutej
b. 1936 in Duga Resa (HR), † 2005 Krapinska Toplice (HR)

Gustav Troger
b. 1951 in Kohlschwarz/Styria (AT), lives in Graz (AT)

Erwin Wurm
b. 1954 in Bruck/Mur (AT), lives in Vienna (AT)

Painting – Experience of Nature and Abstraction

Erwin Bohatsch
b. 1951 in Mürzzuschlag/Styria (AT), lives in Vienna (AT)

→ p. 163

Franz Grabmayr
b. 1927 in Pfaffenberg/Carinthia (AT), lives in Vienna (AT)
Wurzelstück in der Sandgrube, 1983
Oil on canvas; 97 × 137 cm
Neue Galerie Graz, UMJ, Inv. no. I/2355

→ p. 160

Wolfgang Hollegha
b. 1929 in Klagenfurt (AT), lives in Rechberg/Styria (AT)
Holzstück III, 1966
Oil on canvas; 194 × 199 cm
Neue Galerie Graz, UMJ, Inv. no. I/1357

→ p. 162

Elga Maly
b. 1921 in Munich (DE), † 1989 in Graz (AT)
Große arktische Landschaft, 1965
Oil on canvas; 116 × 140 cm
Neue Galerie Graz, UMJ, Inv. no. I/1539

Rudolf Pointner
b. 1907 in Zadar (HR), † 1991 in Graz (AT)

Hannes Priesch
b. 1954 in Volkersdorf/Styria (AT), lives in New York, NY (US)

→ p. 161

Max Weiler
b. 1910 in Absam/Tyrol (AT), † 2001 in Vienna (AT)
Landschaft in Ocker, 1969
Egg tempera on canvas; 200 × 135 cm
Neue Galerie Graz, UMJ, Inv. no. I/1514

Herbert Brandl – Between Representation and Abstraction

→ p. 164

Herbert Brandl
b. 1959 in Graz (AT), lives in Vienna (AT)
ohne Titel, 2004
Oil on canvas; 250 × 600 cm
Neue Galerie Graz, UMJ, Inv. Nr. I/2836

Painting – Experience of Nature and Representation

→ p. 167   Imre Bak
b. 1939 in Budapest (HU), lives in Budapest (HU)
Landschaftstransformation 2, 1974
Acrylic on canvas; 160 × 100 cm
Neue Galerie Graz, UMJ, Inv. no. I/1649

Mario Decleva
b. 1930 in Veli Losinj (HR), † 1979 in Vienna (AT)

→ p. 168   Alois Mosbacher
b. 1954 in Strallegg/Styria (AT), lives in Vienna (AT)
Die Schlucht, 1984
Oil on canvas; 150 × 130 cm
Neue Galerie Graz, UMJ, Inv. Nr. I/2343

→ p. 166   Franc Novinc
b. 1938 in Škofja Loka (SI), lives in Škofja Loka (SI)
Morgen, 1971
Acrylic on canvas; 100 × 139 cm
Neue Galerie Graz, UMJ, Inv. no. I/2249

Fritz Panzer
b. 1945 in Judenburg (AT), lives in Vienna (AT)

Drago J. Prelog
b. 1939 in Celje (SI), lives in Vienna (AT)

Alfons Pressnitz
b. 1982 in Wagna/Styria (AT), lives in Berlin (DE)

Peter Pongratz
b. 1940 in Eisenstadt (AT), lives in Vienna (AT)

→ p. 169   Hubert Schmalix
b. 1952 in Graz (AT), lives in Vienna (AT) and Los Angeles, CA (US)
Painted with My Own Hand (Landschaft), 2005
Oil on canvas; 200 × 150 cm
Neue Galerie Graz, UMJ, Inv. no. I/2753

Günter Waldorf
b. 1924 in Graz (AT), † 2012 in Graz (AT)

Wolfgang Wiedner
b. 1963 in Feldbach (AT), lives in Feldbach (AT)

HyperAmerica
Landscape – Image – Reality
Katia Huemer

The American landscape is shaped in many places by the 'American Dream'. While conceived in the country as free and independent, landscape as we understand it today has been formed by the human hand, and its depiction can no longer be seen separately from civilisation. Since the beginning of the 19th century, a special relationship with land has developed in America that is quite different from the equivalent in Europe: given a unique ideological slant as a result of the nation's *Manifest Destiny* to spread itself out over the continent and take possession of it, it is something that seems to have remained embedded in the collective consciousness of the USA to this day. And yet the great project of civilisation called America reveals a marked tension between a great desire for freedom and a simultaneous need for regulations, something one feels not least when roaming its land on its endless highways, observing the United States through the car window; a view that first became evident in 1957 with Jack Kerouac's novel *On the Road*, a literary homage to the highway as well as a foretaste of the modes of life on the margins of society to be realised in the following decade, then at the latest with the TV series *Route 66* at the beginning of the 1960s, influencing a whole generation of artists and the way they reflected on the country they lived in.

Especially in American painting of the post-war period, a development arose that had a deep impact on Western pictorial tradition. In Western tradition art was considered a depiction of a visual or a physical experience. This had been more or less the general consensus, and still applied to both Cubism and Abstract Expressionism. With a 'shift from nature to culture' (as Leo Steinberg put it, identifying a radical re-orientation) art now turned towards a radical symbolism, a principal reflected both in Pop Art and the painting of American Hyperrealism. Unlike Pop Art, Hyperrealism made no claims to social critique, but presented itself as noticeably apolitical. Supported by unbroken patriotism, an idealised image of America is conveyed, which superficially tells of glamour, wealth and power. Even during the period they were created in, the works of this genre seemed out of date; after all, the reality of the world in which the painters lived was completely different to that represented in the pictures. Often appearing unintentionally satirical, their subjects possess a bizarre distancing of the artist from their depictions. What interests the painter is not the motif, but rather the surfaces. An emotional attachment to the subject is expressly unwelcome, which is ultimately the main difficulty of this style: why paint something that means nothing, and even more so in a style that is so meticulous and so committed to (apparent) reality?

To pursue this question, we must look closely at the technique of these pictures. The painterly tool of Hyperrealism (Photorealism, as this style also is called) is the photographic model, and the unnatural, pointed view through the camera is the foundation of the painted picture. The photo motifs were meticulously copied, yet it was not a question of the painters imitating photography, but rather of questioning the claims to reality of this medium. Involvement with photography as an art form simply did not exist at this time, however (it was not until the 1970s that the importance of photography gradually began to grow). The photographic image, which many painters of Hyperrealism met with mistrust and contempt, was purely a means to the end of comprehending the exaggeration of a reality that could no longer get by without this medium in view of the triumphal march of popular culture. Richard Estes would be the most obvious name to mention in connection with this approach; his glowing, glossily reflecting cityscapes do not come from a single photographic model, but are created instead by superimposing several pictures from the same place, which the artist blurs into an ideal image. For Estes, the 'photo is just a convenience'.[1] The reality reproduced on it is unimportant for the picture. 'If I have to choose between authenticity and making a good painting, I'd rather have a good painting'.[2]

Hyperrealism achieved international recognition in Europe in 1972 at documenta 5, where curator Harald Szeemann carried out a *Survey of Reality*, in which all of its key figures took part. At the same time that the Hyperrealists were bringing concreteness back to art and dedicating themselves to the shining surfaces that expressed the American dream and associated values such as freedom, equality of opportunity and success, a handful of photographers turned their lens on the everyday and banal. 'The New Topographic Movement' was named after an exhibition in 1975 *(New Topographics: Photographs of a Man-altered Landscape)*, which took place in Rochester, New York, far removed from the art metropolises, and attracted extremely modest interest from the public; yet it was to turn out to be one of the key exhibitions of the 20th century. Curator William Jenkins gathered a selection of works by Robert Adams, Lewis Baltz, Bernd and Hilla Becher, Joe Deal, Frank Gohlke, Nicholas Nixon, John Schott, Stephen Shore and Henry Wessel Jr., and with these 168 photographs ushered in a paradigm shift in art history; moreover, the exhibition contributed essentially to the arrival of photography in the sacred halls of art. Likewise the influence wielded by the exhibited artists and their approach to the documentary

1
Louis Meisel, John Perreault (eds.): *Richard Estes. The Complete Paintings 1966–1985*. New York 1986, p. 19f.

2
Richard Estes, 1978, quoted from Jean-Claude Lebensztejn: 'Hyperrealismus. USA 1965–1975' (2003), in: Brigitte Franzen, Anna Sophia Schultz (eds.): *Closer than Fiction. Amerikanische Bildwelten um 1970*. Cologne 2011.

function of photography, was undeniably great. The noticeable characteristic inherent in all of the 'New Topographics' photographs, according to Jenkins, was the 'style-less style', which did not entirely depart from previous models, yet which had as its declared central goal the depiction of everyday motifs in the most neutral and non-judgemental way possible. In his foreword to the exhibition catalogue, Jenkins drew parallels to the early landscape photography of Timothy O'Sullivan, who had documented in photographic form the settlement of the American West, and this—of course largely due to the fact that the photography of that period had almost no past to draw on—without any stylistic and aesthetic claims. Yet even though the 'New Topographics' subjected their photographs to the most objective perspective possible, they shifted the landscape (and what they understood by it) to the centre of their attention, not only in terms of motif, but also above all as a mirror of the modern social order. The break with a notion of landscape restricted primarily to untouched nature came not least with the work of the human geographer, landscape scientist and founder of Cultural Landscape Studies, John Brinckerhoff Jackson. Prompted by his thoughts on the inseparability of natural and human landscape, which he had already formulated at the beginning of the 1950s in the magazine *Landscape* (whose editor was Jackson), the definition of landscape changed in that it was understood as a social and political concept, as a construct that was man-made, carrying with it the (American) lifestyle and the traditions associated with it. Equipped with the theories of 'Landscape Studies' and identifying with Jackson's fascination for the 'ugly development along the highways' and the reshaping of the landscape that accompanied it, photographers such as Stephen Shore, Robert Adams and Lewis Baltz set out on journeys across the USA in order to document a landscape that— mostly barren and uninhabited—seemed to be dominated by suburban settlements, street junctions, industrial zones and gas stations. This was accompanied by a de-mystification of the landscape of the American West, which, beginning with the progressive land grabs by the Anglo-American 'conquerors' in the second half of the 19th century and saturated with clichés of freedom and masculinity, had led to a glorification of the actual living conditions there.

Although the photography of 'New Topographics' and the painting of the Hyperrealists undeniably converged—the world-famous photograph of the Chevron gas station by Stephen Shore (*Stand*, 1975) can surely be compared in its aesthetic superficially with Ralph Goings' depictions of coolly parked pick-up trucks in front of various urban settings—the artistic philosophies of their creators nonetheless differed to the same extent. 'My paintings are about light, about the way things look in their environment and especially about how things look painted. Form, color and space are at the whim of reality, their discovery and organization is the assignment of the realist painter,' Ralph Goings said of the background to his works in 1978.

Shore's picture of the gas station—in colour! Where was abstraction, where the artistic demands?—was a symbol of pure civilisation. While

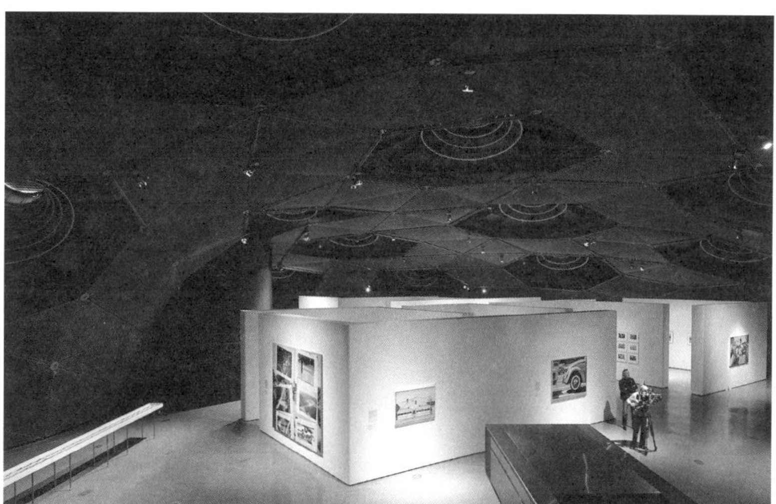

HyperAmerica,
exhibition view,
Kunsthaus Graz,
2015

not visible in the foreground, the human is undoubtedly illustrated, his traces ineradicable. In order to determine the differences and commonalities between these two art forms that developed side by side, the exhibition *HyperAmerica. Landscape – Image – Reality* places the painting of American Hyperrealists alongside photographs by 'New Topographics' and the positions associated with them. As a sort of reference to these chapters of art history and as a further link between painting and photography, the exhibition encompasses positions that accompanied these developments or which preceded them.

→ p. 172

Robert Adams

b. 1937 in Orange, NJ (US), lives in Astoria, OR (US)

The New West, 1968–71
Gelatin silver prints, 56 parts; each ca. 15.2 × 14.1 cm
Niedersächsische Sparkassenstiftung, Hanover

Federal 40. Mount Vernon Canyon. Jefferson County, Colorado, 1970
Pikes Peak, Colorado Springs, 1969

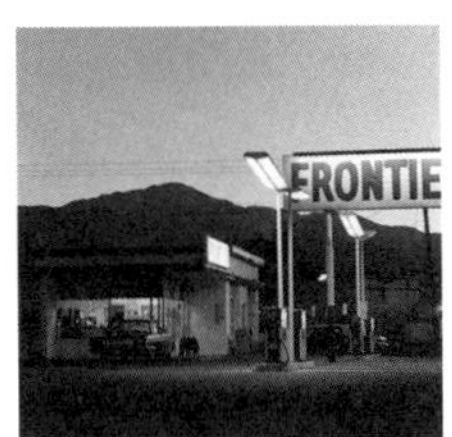

Robert Adams
*Pikes Peak, Colorado
Springs*, 1969
From the series: *The
New West*, 1968–71

After completing a PhD in English, Adams worked as a professor of English Literature for several years before devoting himself completely to photography in the mid-1970s. What followed is a career during which the almost self-taught Adams (the artist learned photographic technique from Myron Wood, a professional photographer in Colorado) showed in numerous exhibitions worldwide. In 1975 William Jenkins presented works by Robert Adams in the pioneering exhibition *New Topographics: Photographs of a Man-altered World* which marked the beginning of a new photographic view of the landscape.

Adams' work, always in series, shows regional moments of transition documented primarily in the Western and Midwestern United States, such as Denver's growing suburbanisation, for example, or the changing city of Los Angeles in the 1970s and 80s.

Adams' first, major photo series *The New West* was published as a book in 1974. 56 images in five sequences of pictures show the discrepancy between the romantic notion of the American West and the reality (at that time). The series reads like a photographic narrative, starting with a drive on a dirt road along endless farmland, only to focus a few moments later on a roadkill rabbit, its remains clinging to the asphalt. Everything about the landscape seems unfinished. Endless housing settlements, which show signs of decay despite being only half-finished, blend into the vastness of a country that only vaguely recalls the myriad images influenced by Wild West movies or the Hudson River School. And yet—as John Szarkowski, former head of the Department of Photography at the Museum of Modern Art in New York writes in his foreword for *The New West*—Adams manages to lend this boring collection of buildings a certain dignity. 'He has made them look not beautiful but important, as the relics of an ancient civilisation look important.'[1]

In a reserved, measured style and many shades of grey, Adams shows not only the serial houses, freeways and factory sites, but also the aspirations of the people who populated the landscape. As Robert Adams himself puts it, 'Paradoxically, however, we also need to see the whole geography, natural and man-made, to experience a peace; all land, no matter what has happened to it, has over it a grace, an absolutely persistent beauty.'[2] To end with Szarkowski's words, which also conclude his foreword: 'Though Robert Adams' book assumes no moral postures, it does have a moral. Its moral is that the landscape is, for us, the place we live. If we have used it badly, we cannot therefore scorn it, without scorning ourselves. If we have abused it, broken its health, and erected

1
John Szarkowski:
'Foreword', in: *Robert
Adams. The New West.
Landscapes Along the
Colorado Front Range.*
Boulder, Colorado 1974.

2
Robert Adams:
Introduction, in: *Robert
Adams. The New West.
Landscapes Along the
Colorado Front Range.*
Boulder, Colorado 1974.

upon it memorials to our ignorance, it is still our place, and before we can proceed we must learn to love it.' — *KH (AP)* –

→ p. 174

John Baeder

b. 1938 in South Bend, IN (US), lives in Nashville, TN (US)

Prout's Diner, 1974
Oil on canvas; 76 × 122 cm
Morris Museum of Art, Augusta, Georgia

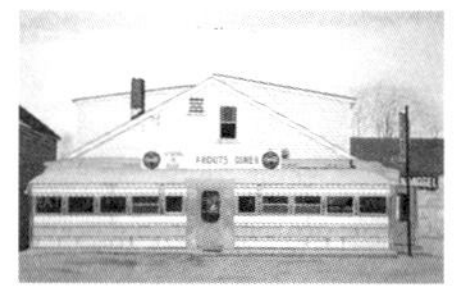

John Baeder
Prout's Diner, 1974

For over 40 years, John Baeder's work has explored his interest in diners, recording the distinctive American-style countertop restaurants with meticulous attention to detail and obvious sympathy for these locations. Often situated next to busy roads outside the city limits, these locales usually serve a purpose similar to rest stops along European highways. But for Americans living in the suburbs, they are also social meeting places. The painter's fascination for diners is tied not only to the architecture—diner interiors often nostalgically recall the economic boom-time of the 1950s—but also the specific experiences connected to them: the food, the stories, the people. Even when these elements are not visible in the image, the viewer clearly feels the basic conditions of this piece of American (sub)culture.

Like many artists of his generation, John Baeder was deeply influenced by cross-country road trips. Drives between his hometown of Atlanta, Georgia, and Alabama (and later out of a sheer desire to travel across the United States) became an important source of artistic inspiration. Like Robert Cottingham, Baeder also began his career as an art director in advertising, first in Atlanta and later, in the mid- to late-1960s, at Ted Bates in New York.

Never was the dialogue between advertising and the visual arts more intense than at that time, when Pop Art and Hyperrealism opposed Abstract Expressionism, and permeated everyday culture. Due to his experiences in advertising, many aspects of Baeder's works are still connected to the material world of America. Still, the time at Ted Bates was also important for other, very different reasons: The agency was located diagonally opposite the Museum of Modern Art, where Baeder frequently visited the photography department. Especially fascinated by works by FSA (Farm Security Administration) photographers such as Russell Lee, Ben Shahn and Walker Evans, he began to collect their work (among others) and was inspired to capture the rapidly-changing urban environment with his own camera.

However, it was not New York that delivered the impetus for Baeder's first paintings, but the images Baeder collected on several road trips— very often in the form of postcards showing 'roadside America', featuring diners, gas stations, motels and the like. Soon after, Ivan Karp invited John Baeder to join OK Harris Gallery, the same gallery that supported Photorealist artists Ralph Goings, Malcolm Morley, Robert Cottingham and Robert Bechtle, but also Pop artists Robert Rauschenberg, Roy

Lichtenstein, Andy Warhol, and Tom Wesselmann. Karp promoted these artists and played no small part in their success.

The documentary, historically-focused aspect of Baeder's paintings—the artist has painted hundreds of diners in recent decades, but the Silk City diner *Prout's Diner* in Sussex, NJ, is representative of his interests as a chronicler—is as indebted to role models in early photojournalism as it is to the FSA photography programme and the legacy of 19th- and 20th-century realist painters. Ultimately, we have Baeder to thank for creating a memorial to the iconic American diner—now more and more displaced by fast-food chains—and making space for the 'typical American's favourite restaurant' in visual art.   – *KH (AP)* –

→ p. 176

Lewis Baltz

b. 1945 in Newport Beach, CA (US), † 2014 in Paris (FR)

From the series: *Nevada*, 1977/78
Gelatin silver prints, 15 parts; each 16.2 × 24.2 cm
Niedersächsische Sparkassenstiftung, Hanover

Fluorescent Tube, 1977
Home Model, Shadow Mountain, 1977
Mustang Bridge Exit, Interstate 80, 1977

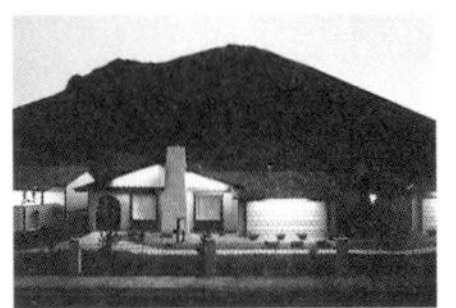

Lewis Baltz
Home Model,
Shadow Mountain,
1977, from the
series: *Nevada,*
1977/78

3
Lewis Baltz, quoted
in a documentary
video about the artist,
TateShots, 2012. www.
tate.org.uk/context-
comment/video/
tateshots-lewis-baltz.

4
Susanne Figner: 'Eine
obszöne Ästhetik. Von
der erhabenen Fassade
zum sublimen Dreck', in:
Susanne Figner, Walter
Moser (eds.): *Lewis
Baltz*. Cologne 2012,
p. 34.

Lewis Baltz was first exposed to photography at the age of eleven; by the time he was twelve, he knew he wanted to work artistically with photographic media. 'Photography as such is not necessarily interesting to me; it's interesting as an art medium where you can intersect with other aesthetic social questions.'[3]

Baltz's series do not show what is (conventionally) considered 'worthy of representation'; instead, he shows the ordinary and mundane by-products of the 'American High Sixties' outside of technological achievements and media spectacles like the moon landing: construction sites, industry, growing suburbia, wastelands. 'Baltz stages the social garbage and architectural decay of a dystopian world that stands not for progress, but for a step backwards,' Susanne Figner notes in a catalogue for one of the last retrospectives exhibited during Baltz's lifetime. 'It isn't blank horror that interests him, but the idea of connecting the beautiful with the terrible.'[4]

Like Robert Adams (whose *Tract Houses* photographs were shown with Lewis Baltz's images of half-finished residential and industrial areas in the 1975 exhibition *New Topographics: Photographs of a Man-altered Landscape*), Baltz captures the signs of decay already visible before or shortly after buildings are completed: cracks in the facades, construction debris or exposed pipes show the flipside of the 'American Sublime' with its promise of progress and hope. Baltz masked the inherent critique in his images with numerous quotations from Minimal Art, as well as Conceptual Art and Land Art. The precise aesthetic of Baltz's photo--graphs stems from his choice of very light-sensitive black-and-white films, long exposure times, eye-level perspective and (often) frontal views. Strong contrasts and shadowless image details make textured surfaces appear almost tangible, lending the objects an almost sculptural quality.

Despite the captivating formal language of the series, the artist's primary focus was its socially critical content. 'For me a work of art is something that's interesting to think about, more than something that's interesting to look at.'[5] In series like *New Industrial Parks near Irvine, California, Park City* or *The Prototype Works*, Lewis Baltz documented the 'fruits of American capitalism' and its conditions. Despite a palpable scepticism toward the supposed progress of urbanisation, the images are sober and conceptual in tone. Even the works' descriptive titles seem to withdraw any possible critical content *(Nevada)*, and yet they also contain allusions to the emerging real estate industry, for example, and the alluring views used in industry advertising *(Lemmon Valley, Looking North West, Toward Stead)*. The desert, a recurring motif (see *St. Quentin's Point* or *Near Reno*, for example), also appears in *Nevada*, symbolising the feeling of loneliness and emptiness evoked by Baltz's 'post-apocalyptic scenarios'.[6] The images are devoid of people (including the photographer himself). All that remains are their traces.   *– KH (AP) –*

→ p. 178

Robert Cottingham

b. 1935 in New York, NY (US), lives in Connecticut (US), New York, NY (US), Los Angeles, CA (US) and London (UK)

Carl's, 1975
Oil on canvas; 198 × 198 cm
museum moderner kunst stiftung ludwig wien
On loan from the Austrian Ludwig Foundation since 1981

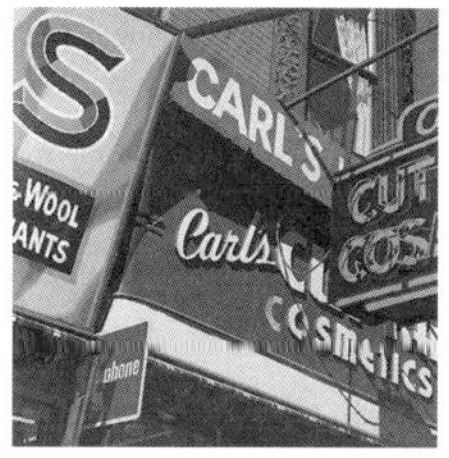

Robert Cottingham
Carl's, 1975

5
Lewis Baltz, quoted in TateShots, 2012.

6
See Walter Moser: 'Filmische Strategien im Werk von Lewis Baltz', in: Susanne Figner, Walter Moser (eds.): *Lewis Baltz*. Cologne 2012, pp. 128–144.

Robert Cottingham's artistic career began as an art director at a Los Angeles advertising company. It was a job the artist held for only a few years before devoting himself entirely to painting in the late 1960s, and yet it had a significant and conspicuous impact on the choice of motifs and visual vocabulary in his extensive oeuvre.

In the proliferation of urban signs it was usually the neon, commercial signs and architectural details of the American inner city locales that drew Cottingham's graphically-versed eye for advertising effect onto itself. He logically calls the focus of his paintings 'urban landscapes', and without explicitly depicting them, he speaks about the people, the way they handle their city, about *Americana* and the cultural creation of American society that is all too visible in the typical, colourful neon lights of large American cities.

Like most Hyperrealists, Cottingham also uses reference photographs to compose his paintings. These are not 1:1 copies on canvas, however, but staged, cropped images that do not prevent his paintings having the undeniable abstraction inherent to these motifs. The sensual aspect inherent to painting—which, in the artist's view, can only be achieved with freehand painting—is just as important as composition. So it is significant that Cottingham, who does not see himself as a Photorealist artist and has often stressed the abstract element in his work, names Piet Mondrian's works as an important source of inspiration for his art alongside Edward Hopper and Charles Demuth.

Cottingham plays with perspectives, crops signs and lettering so that their original visual message is lost and separates letters by tearing them out of their original context. In this way, Cottingham focuses on the advertising function of the signs and sends new messages, many of which contain wordplay. In the case of *Carl's* it is 'Wool Ants', woollen ants, a Cottinghamian species winding their way down the left side of the painting and into the viewer's line of sight.   *– KH (AP) –*

→ p. 180

Rackstraw Downes

b. 1939 in Pembury (UK), lives in New York, NY (US)

Dragon Cement Plant, Thomaston; View from the North End of the Clinker Barn, 1985
Oil on canvas; 54.4 × 196 cm
Ludwig Collection, Ludwig Forum for International Art, Aachen

Like many Hyperrealist painters, Rackstraw Downes started his artistic career with abstraction and only found his own, reality-indebted style after completing his studies at the Yale School of Art. 'When I changed over (…) one of the reasons was that I didn't want to be so damn conscious about my painting.(…) Should it be a symmetrical painting or an asymmetrical painting? And I found the question annoying! (…) What was the point in discussing this? Why not just look at something and paint it the way it is?'[7] Rackstraw Downes paints what and how he sees, without exaggerations. In his quest to depict reality, the artist (who does not see himself as a landscape painter), is interested in surroundings that reflect a 'man-shaped landscape' where Downes can see his own roots. 'I grew up in a landscape like that. England is very lived upon. All of Europe really is.'

In this way, Downes' spatial constructions shed new light on environments that most would describe as unattractive: landfills, construction sites, refineries, industrial plants and inhospitable places under large bridges; in the case of the work shown here, it is a concrete and cement factory belonging to the company Dragon, which Downes has painted using a complex sense of perspective.

Though photography is an important source of inspiration for the artist, it is not the photographs that this work is based on, but the actual places themselves. The artist works 'plein air' in such diverse locations as New York City, rural Maine or the Texas coast, creating paintings that invoke panoramic photography from the 19th century. These photographs, which were often assembled from several individual images or taken with special cameras that allowed a 180-degree view or more, were in many ways similar to Downes' paintings: not only did they show

7
Rackstraw Downes, quoted in a short documentary about the artist created by Betty Cuningham Gallery, 2012.

Eddy's use of reference photographs is not unlike the working method of Richard Estes, who also uses several photographs that he creates, develops and in some cases technically manipulates according to his needs. Even the reflections in Don Eddy's works from the 1970s recall the motivic interests of Richard Estes, and yet the two works are fundamentally different in both technical approach and subject matter. While his early works often drew on Pop Art and its affinity to mass culture, Eddy's paintings from the late 1960s and early 70s concentrate on detailed views of objects such as cars, aeroplanes or—later—storefront interiors. But the main interest in these motifs was less the objects themselves than a complex game with perception.

Untitled (Volkswagen), 1971, shows the unmistakeable detail of a VW Beetle, for a long time the leading export from Germany to the US. The picture illustrates what Don Eddy described as 'universal focus' and—conversely—as 'selective inattention': the viewer's gaze is directed through a gap between the bumpers of two parked cars, and confronted with a sudden blur. This effect, which Eddy borrows from photography on the one hand while alluding to natural visual perception on the other (since we tend to focus on one thing only, and not all of our field of vision is clear at the same time), is surprising in the medium of painting; the question as to why this blur is tolerable in photography when we are not aware of it in our everyday perception remains to be seen.

Eddy's game with focus is a reminder that every pictorial representation and viewing thereof depends on a single gaze that can never ever be objective, if only because it is unique. *– KH (AP) –*

→ p. 184

William Eggleston

b. 1939 in Memphis, TN (US), lives in Memphis, TN (US)
www.egglestontrust.com

From the series: *Los Alamos*, 1965–74
Dye transfer prints, 75 parts; each 30.5 × 45.1 cm or 45.1 × 30 cm
Museum Ludwig, Cologne

Memphis, 1971–74
Louisiana, 1971–74

William Eggleston is considered a pioneer of colour photography. His innovative use of colour and seemingly spontaneous visual compositions are enormously important to many photographers, artists and curators. This is evidenced by, among other things, the numerous exhibitions (including a major retrospective at the Whitney Museum of American Art, New York in 2008 and inclusion in the 2002 documenta 11 in Kassel) and many awards and grants (e.g. the Guggenheim Fellowship for Photography, 1974) Eggleston has received over the course of his long career.

At first glance, Eggleston's photographs seem like amateur snapshots, a stylistic feature that he very consciously employs in order to access a

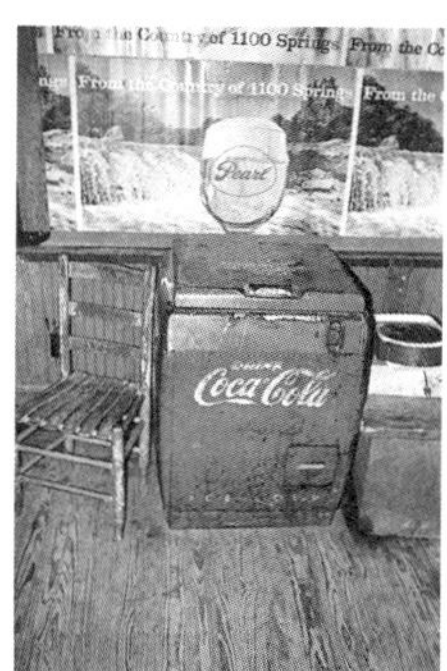

William Eggleston
Louisiana, 1971–74
From the series: *Los Alamos*, 1965–74

popular, easily accessible visual language. 'The result,' as Thomas Weski writes in his text for Eggleston's photo book *Los Alamos*, 'is paradoxical: Charged by the artist with a dimension hitherto unknown to us, the world presents itself as familiar and strange at the same time.' Apart from his choice of subject matter, Eggleston achieves this effect through the dye transfer process. Primarily used in advertising during the 1950s and 60s, the colour printing technique allowed Eggleston to add what would become the psychologising dimension typical of his work. The method enables the photographer to enhance and exaggerate specific colours by giving them an intense saturation. With this technique, the photographer gains control over colour and can act as a painter by selectively targeting specific colours and using them in a subjective way. Although Eggleston did not invent this process, he is considered the 'father of colour photography' and his artistic approach is credited with almost single-handedly paving the way for colour photography in the visual arts. Though almost incomprehensible from today's perspective, colour was far from an obvious choice for fine art photographers at that time, since it was equated with amateur photography. The connotation of the private snapshot might have had a positive effect on the reception of Eggleston's work, since his images also do without carefully staged motifs, and allow chance to play a decisive role in the composition. The more than forty-year-old photographs in the series *Los Alamos* have the look of a time capsule, showing us an American Southwest that no longer exists in that form. At the same time, the photographs are independent of place, have a timeless quality and are in no way nostalgic. Located in the state of New Mexico, Los Alamos County was the site of secret testing and development for the atomic bomb, a fact that gives the title more than just geographical significance (Eggleston's *Los Alamos* begins in his hometown of Memphis, and continues along a winding path westward from New Orleans to Las Vegas and southern California to the Santa Monica Pier). Instead, it implies an investigative attitude on the part of the photographer, who traces the abysses of his country under the deceptive calm of everyday life.

Originally, Eggleston planned a compendium of more than 2000 photographs for this project (incidentally, the first in colour) to be published in 20 volumes. He soon gave up this encyclopedic ambition, however, and only decades later condensed them into a portfolio of 75 photographs. William Eggleston's photographs show a world left to its own devices, one whose inhabitants—both objects and people—have taken on a strange life of their own, separated from their social contexts and freed of their practical functions. 'At the first glance, it seems associated with his environment, everyday life and its objects. Yet upon closer inspection, you notice that the photographs transcend the merely descriptive,'[8] notes Weski, who considers the journey for *Los Alamos* part of the artistic process. Together with colleagues and friends such as actor and director Dennis Hopper, Eggleston went on an aimless search for different ways of representing of everyday life in the American cultural landscape. 'I consider a photograph interesting whenever a photographer's view of reality does not double my knowledge of the world, but a

8
Thomas Weski: 'Draft of a Presentation,' in: *William Eggleston. Los Alamos*. New York 2003.

difference between our respective perception occurs,' Weski writes. It has, in other words, less to do with 'a precise representation of reality than the formulation of the representation of the world'. With this, Weski pinpoints what both captivates and perplexes us about Eggleston's photographs: an aesthetic of strangeness, coupled with the picture of everyday life, gives a sense of familiarity while simultaneously showing us that reality is uniquely, exclusively tied to our accustomed ways of seeing.

– KH (AP) –

→ p. 186

Richard Estes

b. 1932 in Kewanee, IL (US), lives in New York, NY (US) and Maine (US)

Rappaport Pharmacy, 1976
Oil on canvas; 92 × 122 cm
Peter and Irene Ludwig Foundation, Aachen
Permanent loan at the Ludwig Museum —Museum of Contemporary Art, Budapest

Downtown, 1978
Oil on canvas; 122 × 152 cm
museum moderner kunst stiftung ludwig wien
On loan from the Austrian Ludwig Foundation since 1991

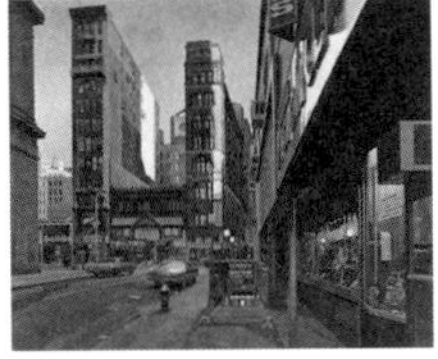

Richard Estes
Downtown, 1978

Richard Estes' detailed urban portraits look so much like photographs of New York that a viewer has to look twice to see the painting. Nevertheless, the artist's work is a true example of traditional painting sui generis. Highly suspicious of the photographic image, Estes views it purely as a means to an end—a way of grasping the intensification of a reality that, with the triumph of popular culture in the second half of the 20th century, could no longer manage without this medium. Estes' gleaming cityscapes and reflected urban surroundings are not based on a single photograph, but on several, superimposed pictures of the same place (75 in the case of *Downtown*), which the artist merges to form a single, ideal image. For Estes, 'the photo is just a convenience'.[9] The reality it presents is irrelevant for the painting. In a very traditional approach, the photo prints, which Estes himself takes in duplicate (one exposed for light, one for shadow) are also 'sketches' that serve as the basis for the actual artwork. The wide-angle perspective is another convenience of photography that the artist appropriates for his painting and transfers to the canvas, as though it corresponded to our usual way of seeing.
But it isn't just Estes' rejection of photography as an art form that seems anachronistic from today's perspective; the only 'true art' the artist acknowledges is realistic painting, applied to canvas using a brush. Thus, it seems only fitting that all of Estes' role models—both stylistically and in terms of subject matter—are exclusively in the realist tradition, such as the Ashcan School. Though Estes' work also shows some elements from 1930s social realists such as Edward Hopper, who responded to difficult living conditions during the Great Depression with a critical view

9
Louis Meisel, John Perreault (eds.): *Richard Estes. The Complete Paintings 1966–1985.* New York 1986, p. 19f.

of the 'American way of life', Estes expressly distances himself from emotional attachment to the subjects, something the psychological painters would not have done completely.

Certainly, Estes' virtuosity is presented in overlayering several pictorial planes of a big city typified by fast living and anonymity, but just as the storefront in *Rappaport Pharmacy* reflects the cold images of the big city, the artist's emotional world bounces off of the shining surfaces. *Downtown* also depicts a 'typical' New York street situation. Yet the stairs leading to the subway station—the same station that gives the painting its name—are almost inconspicuously placed at the bottom right edge of the image, overshadowed by the dominant vertical architecture in the centre of the canvas. The picture is a good example of Richard Estes' skill as a painter and his ability to manipulate space through a composition of light reflections, focal distance, perspectives or focal points, shifting these so that changes to the actual place are concealed from the viewer.

– KH (AP) –

→ p. 188

Walker Evans

b. 1903 in St. Louis, MI (US), † 1975 in New Haven, CT (US)

Roadside Store, Vicinity Greensboro, Alabama, 1936
Gelatin silver print, 19 × 23.8 cm
Neue Galerie Graz, Universalmuseum Joanneum

Negro Church, South Carolina, 1936/2002
Digital pigment print, 29.2 × 23.5 cm
Die Photographische Sammlung / SK Stiftung Kultur, Cologne

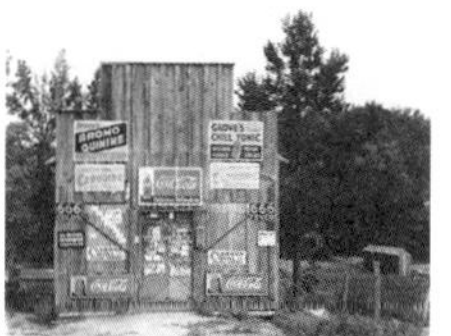

Walker Evans
*Roadside Store,
Vicinity Greensboro,
Alabama*, 1936

Initially rooted in the New York literary scene, Walker Evans began taking photographs in the late 1920s. From 1935 to 1938, at the height of the Great Depression, Evans worked for the Resettlement Administration (later the Farm Security Administration), a 'New Deal' government organisation created to assist the impoverished and especially hard-hit rural workers in the South. Walker's task was to photographically document the precarious living conditions of the poor, white population, to identify problems and observe any possible progress. 'In one way the Depression was good for artists, because those who didn't want to get sucked in to fulltime commercial work were unable to anyway; there wasn't any commercial work to do. I was very innocent about government, about Washington, but not if I could get a job there. I did it so carelessly, I just photographed everything that attracted me that time and rather unconsciously recorded that period (...).'

In 1936, Evans interrupted his work for the government for a collaborative project with writer James Agee, who was commissioned by Fortune magazine to write an article about impoverished sharecroppers in Alabama and Mississippi. Using portraits of three families from Akron in Hale County, Alabama, Evans and Agee reported on the life circumstances among the rural population, and the impact of the global

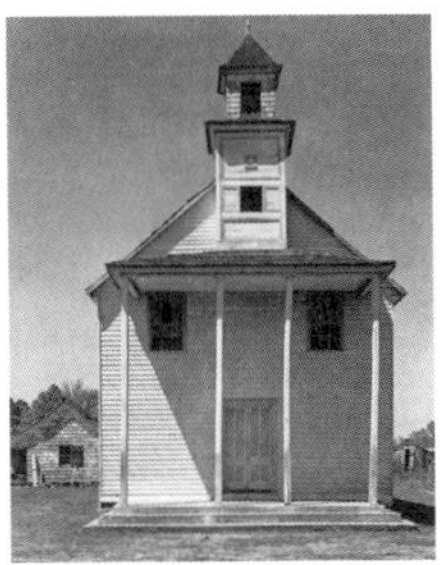

Walker Evans
*Negro Church, South
Carolina*, 1936/2002

economic crisis: 'The work produced in the Great Depression looks like
Social protest. It wasn't intended to be. It wasn't intended to be used as
propaganda for any cause. I suppose I was interested in calling attention
to something and even shocking people. But I don't think I had the purpose of improving the world. I like saying what's what.' When Fortune
Magazine decided not to publish the article, Agee and Walker compiled
the results of their research in the 1941 groundbreaking book *Let Us
Now Praise Famous Men*, which has long since attained the status of an
important historical document. Hardly noticed in a time of war, the significance of *Let Us Now Praise Famous Men* was only recognised in the
1960s, not least thanks to next-generation photographers like Lee
Friedlander, who constantly stressed Walker's influence on their own
work.
Walker Evans' pioneering work in the field of art photography is also
evident in his early solo exhibition at the Museum of Modern Art in New
York in 1938—the museum's first solo exhibition of a photographer.

– KH (AP) –

→ p. 190

Lee Friedlander

b. 1934 in Aberdeen, WA (US), lives in New York, NY (US)

From the series: *The New Cars: 1964*, 1963/2011
Gelatin silver prints, 33 parts; 21.6 × 32.7 cm or 32.7 × 21.6 cm

Detroit (Lincoln Continental)
32.7 × 21.6 cm
Niedersächsische Sparkassenstiftung, Hanover

'I'm not a premeditative photographer. I see a picture and I make it. If I
had a chance, I'd be out shooting all the time. You don't have to go looking for pictures. The material is generous. You go out and the pictures
are staring at you.'[10] Lee Friedlander's approach to photography, as we
see very clearly here, is direct and immediate; his main subject is the
characteristic 'American social landscape'. Using a 35 mm Leica camera
that Friedlander always operated by hand, the artist documented the
1960s zeitgeist as it was most impressively reflected on the streets of
New York. Yet despite all the signs of economic recovery, the pictures
also have palpably depressed overtones.
Friedlander's preoccupation with photography began in high school. He
later studied in Los Angeles at the Art Center School of Design, but left
to study painting under Edward Kaminski when his previous photography classes started to bore him. Kaminski, a painter and photographer,
recognised Friedlander's potential. In the years that followed, he became
Friedlander's most important mentor and enabler. In 1956 Friedlander
moved to New York, where he photographed portraits of jazz musicians
for album covers. It was in New York City that he also began his career as
a 'street photographer', a trajectory that would make him famous. John
Szarkowski gave the photographer a major career boost in 1967, when he

10
Lee Friedlander, quoted
in: *Documentary
Photography*. New York
1972, p. 178.

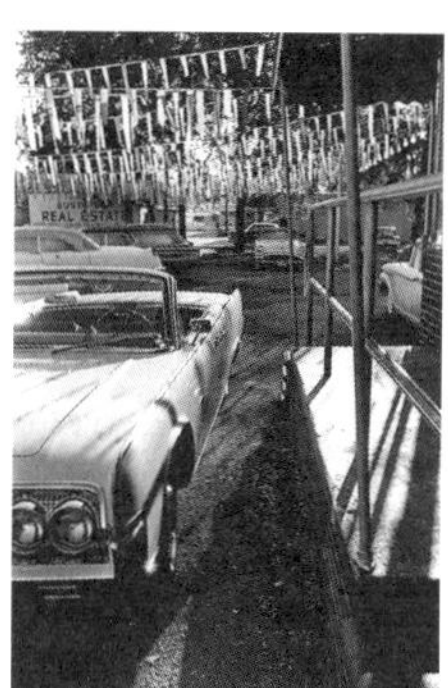

Lee Friedlander
Detroit (Lincoln Continental)
From the series: *The New Cars: 1964*,
1963/2011

exhibited Friedlander's works (along with those of Diane Arbus and Garry Winogrand) at the Museum of Modern Art in New York: the *New Documents* exhibition became a milestone for the development of art photography. In the press release for *New Documents*, Szarkowski wrote: 'In the past decade, this new generation of photographers has redirected the technique and aesthetic of documentary photography to more personal ends. Their aim has been not to reform life but to know it, not to persuade but to understand.'[11]

Unlike the 'New Topographics' photographers, who took a consciously distanced approach to the subject, Friedlander sometimes inserts himself in his pictures. Even when we see him only in hints of window reflections, shadows or mirror reflections, the photographer's presence is still visible and proof of his participation in society. Self-portraits of this type are also found in the series *The New Cars*, created in 1964 as a commissioned work for the fashion and lifestyle magazine Harper's Bazaar. The then 30-year-old, emerging Friedlander was hired to document the new, long-awaited 1964 models from manufacturers Chrysler, Lincoln, Buick and Cadillac. But Friedlander did not photograph the cars according to the advertising aesthetic Harper's Bazaar had been expecting; instead he showed them in their 'natural' environment: in parking lots, at the drive-in cinema, on the side of the road, etc. 'I just put the cars out in the world, instead of on a pedestal'. The photographs were not published for fear of losing the car companies as advertising clients in the magazine. It was only in 2010 that Friedlander rescued them from obscurity, turning them into a photo book that impressively shows the artistic intention of this series: it was not the cars that interested Friedlander. The series is part of his lifelong preoccupation with the distinctive visual landscape of the United States. The cars represent the economic boom of the post-war period, which Friedlander photographs with a wink. At once subversive, humorous and touching, Friedlander's *New Cars* are no less than an unmasking of the 'American Dream.'   *– KH (AP) –*

→ p. 192

Ralph Goings

b. 1928 in Corning, CA (US), lives in Charlotteville, NY (US), and Santa Cruz, CA (US)

Airstream, 1970
Oil on molino; 152 × 213.5 cm
museum moderner kunst stiftung ludwig wien
On loan from the Ludwig Collection, Aachen since 1978

'America's Vermeer', as Edward Lucie-Smith describes Ralph Goings,[12] devoted himself to the American scenery like almost no other painter since Hopper. After a classical painting education at the California College of the Arts in Oakland, California, his 'de Kooning' phase (as Goings calls his excursion into abstraction) behind him, Goings shocked his 1963 artistic milieu by meticulously copying photographs he projected on the wall. Goings' chosen subjects also appeared unworthy of art: parked pick-ups in suburban settings, diner interiors and finally,

11
Museum of Modern Art archives, press release, February 28, 1967. www.moma.org.

12
Edward Lucie-Smith: 'RALPH GOINGS. America's Vermeer', in: The Butler Institute of American Art (ed.): *Ralph Goings. Four Decades of Realism.* Youngstown 2004.

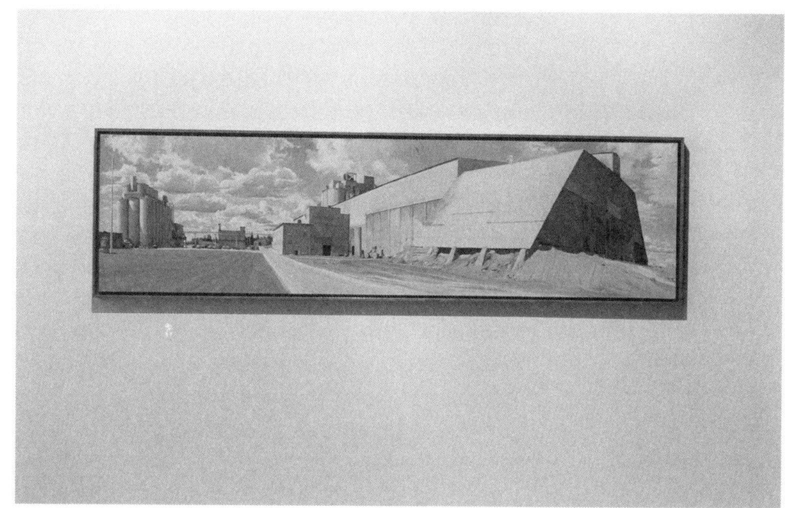

landscape from an extremely wide viewing angle (Downes' canvases are also usually extreme horizontal formats), they also captured a non-allegorical America far removed from the romantic tradition of the Hudson River School—an image fitting the reality of settlement and Westward expansion.

– KH (AP) –

→ p. 182

Don Eddy

b. 1944 in Long Beach, CA (US), lives in New York, NY (US)

Untitled (Volkswagen), 1971
Acrylic on canvas; 121.9 × 167.6 cm
museum moderner kunst stiftung ludwig wien
On loan from the Austrian Ludwig Foundation since 1991

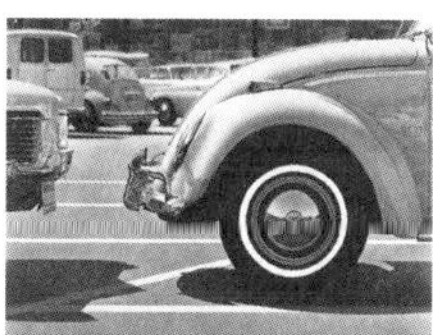

Don Eddy
*Untitled
(Volkswagen)*, 1971

As one of the key figures of American photorealism, Don Eddy stands for the modernist, abstract tendency in this art movement. Like Richard Artschwager, Chuck Close and Richard Morley, Eddy paints following a grid, a typical feature of both abstract and conceptual art from Mondrian to Sol LeWitt. With it came a fascination for the virtuosity of old masters such as Raphael and Jean-Auguste-Dominique Ingres, who evidently influenced Eddy's approach to painting.

Each little section of a Don Eddy painting is a small microcosm unto itself: tiny circles approximately 1.5 mm in diameter—invisible to the naked eye—form the basis for the painting, which appears to be a homogeneous surface when seen from a distance. Using an airbrush technique, Eddy applies the same green, ochre and violet paints in a three-step process. It is only on canvas, in the superposition of several layers of different paint, that the colours mix and become the 'underpainting' that forms the basis for his elaborately detailed 'overpainting', which in turn consists of up to 20 local layers of colour.

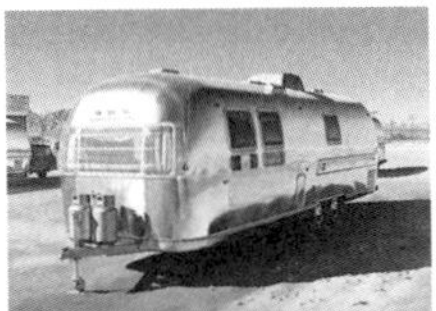

Ralph Goings
Airstream, 1970

somewhat later, still lifes showing ketchup bottles next to shiny napkin dispensers, ashtrays and salt and pepper shakers. At a time when photography was frowned upon as an art form and the general understanding was that mass media should stay far away from artistic practice, Goings stunned with a painterly style that suggested our knowledge of reality was essentially derived from photographic reproductions. To emphasise this, the painter transfers the blue tint of a photo to the canvas, thereby influencing the colour of the object depicted. Goings' stated goal was to depict ordinary things in an artistic way in order to make us more conscious of reality. The painter's real interest was not the object depicted in the image, but first and foremost light reflections, glare and the play of light and shadow: 'My paintings are about light, about the way things look in their environment and especially about how things look painted. Form, colour and space are at the whim of reality, their discovery and organisation is the assignment of the realist painter.'

Though certainly attracted to the trailer's shimmering surface, Goings was also drawn to the *Airstream* for the 'American way of life' these trailers symbolised at that time. First manufactured in the 1930s, it is no coincidence that the unpainted, spacious Airstream campers—lightweight and towable by any car—became emblematic of growing mobility on the American continent, and many Americans associated them with the dream of freedom. This painting, which Harald Szeemann chose for the 1972 exhibition documenta 5 (the same exhibition that catapulted the hyperrealists to their major breakthrough) is not only evidence of his technical precision—Goings showed every imperfection in the metal—it also shows the artist's flair for portraying American life, a defining characteristic of his work to this day. *– KH (AP) –*

→ p. 194

Richard McLean

b. 1934 in Hoquiam, WA (US), lives in Oakland, CA (US)

Rustler Charger, 1971
Oil on blended fabrics; 167 × 167 cm
museum moderner kunst stiftung ludwig wien
On loan from the Austrian Ludwig Foundation since 1981

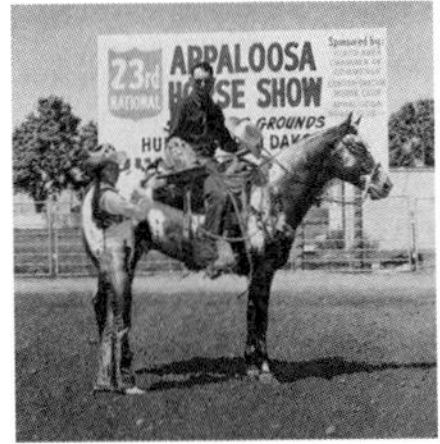

Richard McLean
Rustler Charger,
1971

Richard McLean is another Hyperrealist of the first hour, an artist whose creative path—fuelled by the triumph of Pop Art—veered away from Abstract Expressionism in favour of Realism. The change was not especially difficult for him, he says, especially since the latter seemed extremely abstract to him. McLean finds the abstruse subjects of his paintings in magazines aimed at horse breeders and athletes. Nevertheless, the artist dismisses the (admittedly natural) assumption that McLean's interest in these subjects stems from a love of horses or even a past as a rodeo rider. His focus is not the noble animals nor their proud owners, trainers and grooms, but the hyper-real artificiality that these initial images radiate, and their endless reservoir of profoundly American themes. McLean's affinity for horse subjects began in the 1960s, when he noticed that, despite horse's strong presence on canvases from the 18th and 19th century, 'serious' contemporary painters did not consider the subject at all. The ironic undertone of McLean's exclusive focus on this very sentimental subject is hard to miss. By eliminating any personal access and, like a still life, considering the animals purely as objects, McLean reverses the romance of historical horse portraits and their owners. Instead he infuses the image of the noble animal with the manmade background noise that 20th- (and 21st-) century equestrian sports—and everything else—entails: with filled garbage bags, plastic tubs, an inconspicuous rubber mat, a rusty horse trailer, etc. In the case of *Rustler Charger*, it is a huge sign that contextualises the depicted event as the 'Appaloosa Horse Show' while indicating the sponsors who made the event possible.

'Like other photorealist painters, I'm attracted to visual squalor, uninteresting stuff that can be made interesting by painting it. This is the kind of crap you find just beyond the suburbs—decay and neglect and all that stuff. When you put it in the pictorial context, it's important because it's right where it should be. Things fall together in seemingly haphazard ways. The mystery of painting to me is how right and appropriate they look once you paint them.'[13] The merciless sharpness and downright dream-factory-like colours exaggerate the already absurd reality of what is being represented, amplifying the painting's fantastic effect.

– KH (AP) –

→ p. 196 ## Ed Ruscha

b. 1937 in Omaha, NE (US), lives in Culver City, CA (US)

The Back of Hollywood, 1977
Oil on canvas; 56 × 203 cm
Musée d'art contemporain de Lyon

→ p. 242 *Every Building on the Sunset Strip*, 1966
Leporello photo book; 17.8 × 760.7 cm
Neue Galerie Graz, Universalmuseum Joanneum

Vacant Lots, 1970/2003
Gelatin silver prints; 54.6 × 54.6 cm
Sprüth Magers

The work of California artist Ed Ruscha defies easy categorisation. He is considered a trailblazer in the integration of language and mass culture symbols into visual art, and yet Ruscha has always resisted the Pop Art label and (despite the conceptual approaches of his photo books and monosyllabic language-pictures from the early 1960s) Ruscha's work cannot be subsumed under the term Conceptual Art, either. The ideas Ruscha has explored over the course of his long artistic career are too diverse for classification, and yet all follow an undeniable stringency

13
Richard McLean, quoted in Jesse Hamlin: 'Richard McLean Retrospective at St. Mary's College', in: *SFGATE*, 12.05.2012 www.sfgate.com/art/article/Richard-McLean-retrospective-at-St-Mary-s-College-3528649.php#photo-2890032.

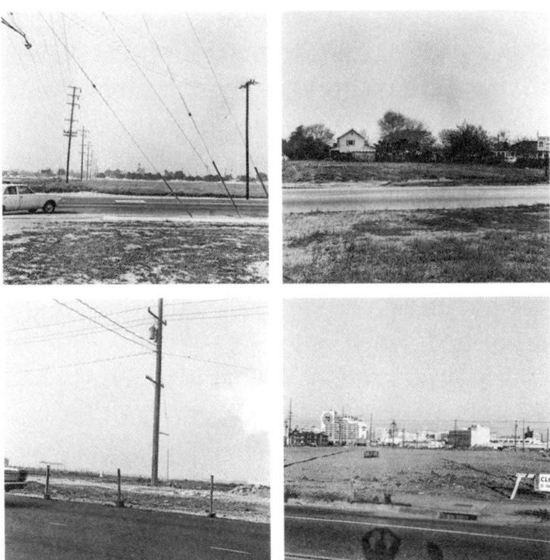

Ed Ruscha
Vacant Lots,
1970/2003

that made his work so important for subsequent generations of artists.
Though his primary media are photography and painting, the latter resonates with a suspicion that caused Ruscha to slow and eventually quit
painting after 1969. He would not paint again until the late 1970s. The
extreme horizontal formats Ruscha favoured at that time reflect the artist's life in Los Angeles, a city shaped by Hollywood and Disney. Allusions to film are evident not only in the cinemascope format, but also in
the narrative image content and graphic style of these paintings.

The question as to whether *Hollywood*—Ruscha's 1968 lithograph showing the most iconic, three-dimensional sign in the world—is to be read
ironically is an open one. (The artist himself has always refrained from
making statements about his work.) But almost ten years later, *The Back
of Hollywood,* 1977, contains a much more explicit, visual critique. Ruscha paints the sign in the warm light of sunset, palpably unmasking the
film industry that both creates myths and is sustained by them.

Like many others, as a prospective student Ruscha took a hope-filled
roadtrip across the United States to the West Coast, and the impressions he collected on this journey would influence his entire artistic body
of work. He was interested in the trip itself and the landscape as seen
from the road. Although both Ruscha's paintings and his photographs
showing highways, billboards, gas stations, slogans and words were and
are incredibly important to the way the American landscape is perceived,
there is a significant difference in the way Ruscha visualises his subject
matter in the two different media. While the prints and paintings—full of
double entendres and puns—ironically exaggerate what is depicted, the
artist takes a more distanced perspective in his photo series. His stated
artistic restraint in the field of photography, which sought to satisfy the
documentary requirements of photojournalism, became an important
reference for the 'New Topographics' artists, a group whose pictures
privileged ordinary subjects photographed in an objective way. But
despite the formal and thematic similarities, there is a big difference

14
Quoted in Gretchen
Garner: *Disappearing
Witness. Change in
Twentieth-Century
American Photography.*
Baltimore 2003, p. 164.

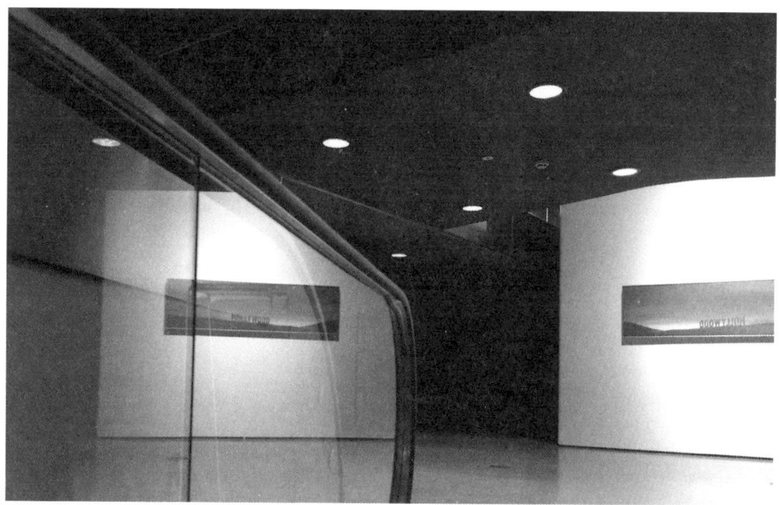

Ed Ruscha
The Back of Holly-wood, 1977,
exhibition view,
Kunsthaus Graz,
2015

between Ed Ruscha and the 'New Topographics' photographers in their understanding of what an image shows. As 'New Topographics' photographer John Schott succinctly put it, 'They [Ruscha's pictures] are not statements about the world through art, they are statements about art through the world.'[14]

Every Building on the Sunset Strip, which Ruscha conceived as a more than 7-metre-long foldout that already resembles a real estate agent's prospectus on account of its format, was printed in an edition of 1000 copies. It continues a series of typological photographs around the iconography of the American city. The shots are cool and documentary. The artist negates image structure and composition, denying the pictures any artistic ambition whatsoever. Ruscha's *Sunset Strip* shows all of the buildings on both sides of the street, each carefully numbered, but without comment. This lack of emotion is compounded by the fact Ruscha himself did not operate the camera. It was mounted to the back of his moving pick-up truck; the film in this 35-mm camera was advanced automatically, the subjective eye switched off in favour of mechanical objectivity.

– KH (AP) –

→ p. 198

John Salt

b. 1937 in Birmingham (UK), lives in Bucknell, Shropshire (UK)

Albuquerque Wreck Yard (Sandia Auto Electric), 1972
Oil on canvas; 121.9 × 182.9 cm
Courtesy of Louis K. Meisel Gallery, New York

Twentieth-century American folklore is defined by the highway and the automobile that drives it, two epitomes of the dream of endless space and unlimited mobility that so powerfully shaped the times. With such clear and prevalent cultural models, the equally enormous fascination

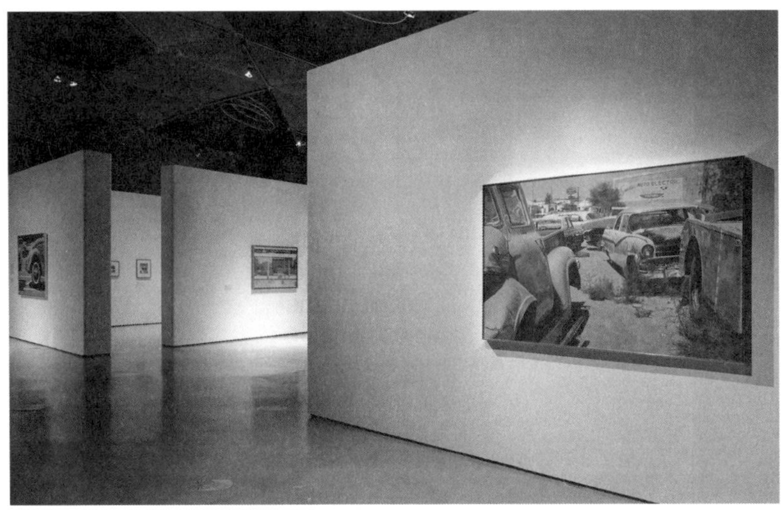

John Salt
Albuquerque Wreck Yard (Sandia Auto Electric), 1972, exhibition view, Kunsthaus Graz, 2015

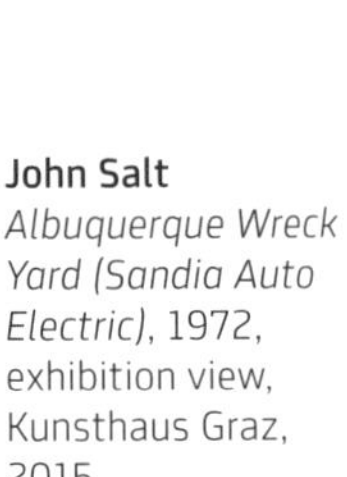

with the flip-side comes as no surprise: the sudden end of the ride, the shining miracle of technology, the promise of individual freedom—then an abrupt end: crash. But there is beauty in the crash as well, new geometries, new textures. On the one hand, the wreck as the end of the dream. On the other hand, everything has an expiration date. Every automobile is eventually bound for the junkyard. From this perspective, the highway is only the place where this certainty is suppressed.

John Salt's biography as the son of a garage owner might explain his fascination with wrecked automobiles—cars abandoned on the roadside or in junkyards by once-proud owners, given over to dust and sand. It is a motif that has characterised Salt's work since the late 1960s, and been inextricably linked with his name ever since. To Salt, these wrecks are of course a statement about American consumer culture, which, starting in the 1950s, began to spread inexorably across the world. Yet they also expand the traditional repertoire of images and increase viewers' understanding of the American landscape.

Suburban scenes from a semi-rural US are stages that Salt makes the subject and content of his paintings, even then as he returns to England after 20 years in Baltimore and New York. Virtually indistinguishable from the photographs on which they were based, his snapshot-like compositions are created using airbrush and stencil—a process that can take up to two years and almost completely restrains individual artistic expression.

Salt first discovered the documentary aspect of art during his graduate studies in Baltimore, when he happened upon the book *Contemporary Photographers Towards a Social Landscape*, with photographs by Lee Friedlander and Garry Winogrand. Fascinated by the possibility of escaping individual artistic style and making complete objectivity the guiding principle of the work, Salt turned away from Abstract Expressionism, a long-time influence, and towards photorealism. This stylistic and philosophical change in Salt's oeuvre finds expression in the painterly interpretation of a photograph by Garry Winogrand, showing a worn car seat. He does not give the work a title (*Untitled,* 1968).

Like many other works made since then, the car in *Albuquerque Wreck Yard (Sandia Auto Electric)* is no longer a symbol of the 'American way of life', but a monument and memorial to that same, abrupt end that is inevitable to every journey.
– KH (AP) –

→ p. 200

Ben Schonzeit

b. 1942 in Brooklyn, New York, NY (US), lives in New York, NY (US)

www.benschonzeit.com

Sugar, 1972
Acrylic on canvas; 244 × 305 cm
Collection Migros Museum für Gegenwartskunst

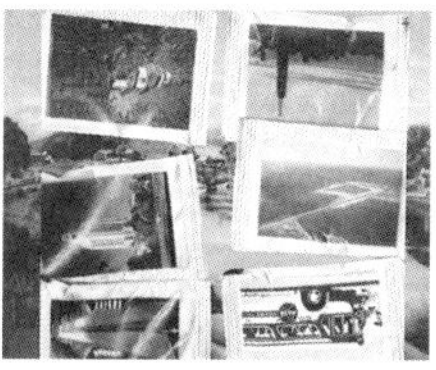

Ben Schonzeit
Sugar, 1972

'Why would someone paint a photograph? I don't paint a photograph; I paint a painting,' Ben Schonzeit explained to the audience at 'The Artist Speaks', a talk held in New York in November 2014. Considered one of the foremost photorealists since his participation in documenta 5 (although Schonzeit adamantly resists this kind of classification), the artist tries to express that, while almost identical on a formal level, the photograph upon which the painting is based can never have the aura of an original painting. Schonzeit, who lost an eye in a childhood accident, developed a 'different' kind of perception than that shared by most people, and is driven by a desire to communicate his experiences. At the same time, it is usually the 'worthless nothing' that brings captivating beauty to his large-scale canvases, with the aim of sensitising viewers to everyday objects. The artist paints, in other words, 'abstract spaces': 'I think that what I'm doing is a combination of painting a picture and creating a place that I'm in—almost a stage set—a smaller picture of a whole life.'[15]

While his almost classically composed still-lifes of recent years depict Technicolor-style fruit, flower vases or vegetables, Schonzeit's oeuvre from the late 1960s and early 70s reflects the uncertainty of the Vietnam War, drugs, but also a time shaped by the first images of outer space, which the artist handled metaphorically: objects floating in the picture appear pin-sharp in front of blurred backgrounds, while the relationship between these two image planes remains vague. Cupcakes against a lunar landscape, Warhol bananas over indistinct Ritz crackers or—as we see in the case of *Sugar,* 1972—sugar packets featuring American (landscape) icons that almost completely obscure a romantic-looking, idyllic lake landscape.

The focus is on the six packets, which appear carelessly tossed, upside down, cut off or rotated. Like other 'composites', as Schonzeit calls them, in Sugar the artist concentrates on the spatial relationship between colour and supporting surface. Schonzeit, whose missing eye prevents him from perceiving three dimensions in the way most would recognise as universal, plays with the relationship between fore- and background by

15
Cf. www.
nancyhoffmangallery.
com/artist/display/45/
Ben_Schonzeit.

superimposing three-dimensional objects (sugar packets) onto the two-dimensional (such as the photograph of a landscape). He then photographs this ensemble and ultimately translates it into a painting. The eye is deceptive—reality even more so. — *KH (AP)* —

→ p. 202

Stephen Shore

b. 1947 in New York, NY (US), lives in New York, NY (US)
www.stephenshore.net

From the series: *Uncommon Places*, 1973–83
C-prints; each 50.8 × 61 cm
Courtesy of Sprüth Magers Berlin London and 303 Gallery, New York

Chestnut & 4th St., Harrisburg, PA, July 4, 1973
4th and Main, Delphos, OH, July 6, 1973
Pittsburgh, Pennsylvania, US 30 Facing East, July 5, 1973
Abandoned Cabins, Gaylord, Michigan, July 8, 1973
Victoria Avenue & Albert Street, Regina, Saskatchewan,
August 17, 1974
Cherry Street, Fort Worth, TX, June 14, 1976

From the series: *The Roadtrip Journals*, 1973
Pigment print on rag paper; 45.7 × 67.3 cm (edition 1/5)
Courtesy of Sprüth Magers Berlin London and 303 Gallery, New York

July 6, 1973

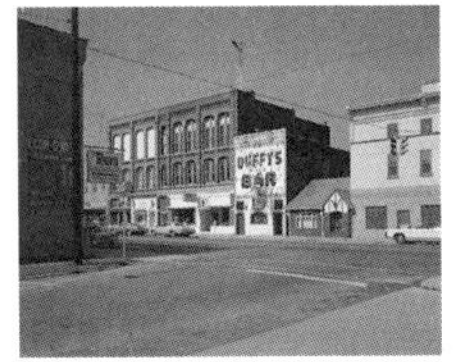

Stephen Shore
*4th and Main
Delphos, OH, July 6,
1973*
From the series:
*Uncommon Places,
1973-83*

16
Stephen Shore, 1982,
quoted in: *UNCOMMON
PLACES. An Interview
with Stephen Shore,
by Aaron Schuman.*
SeeSaw Productions,
2005.

Stephen Shore's works have been globally acclaimed for more than 40 years. A participant in the influential exhibition *New Topographics: Photographs of a Man-altered Landscape* in 1975, Shore was one of the young 'New Topographics' photographers who heralded a changed attitude towards landscape as a subject in photography. Shore is also considered one of the pioneers of colour photography, which left the realm of purely amateur photography at the start of the 1970s and slowly gained in importance and prestige in art as well.

Shore's artistic career began very early, when he stumbled upon a copy of Walker Evan's photo book *American Photographs* at the age of nine. What he saw piqued his interest in photography and its ability to represent cultural observations. At 17, Shore met Andy Warhol and moved into the 'Factory', where he observed and documented the lives of the artistic avant-garde through the lens of his camera *(The Velvet Years)*. And yet the turning-point of his career did not happen in New York City, but on a cross-country trip through the United States in 1972: 'Until I was twenty-three, I lived mostly in a few square miles in Manhattan. In 1972, I set out with a friend for Amarillo, Texas. I didn't drive, so my first view of America was framed by the passenger's window. It was a shock!'.[16] The cultural diversity he saw there became the focus of his subsequent work. While at first Shore almost manically photographed everything

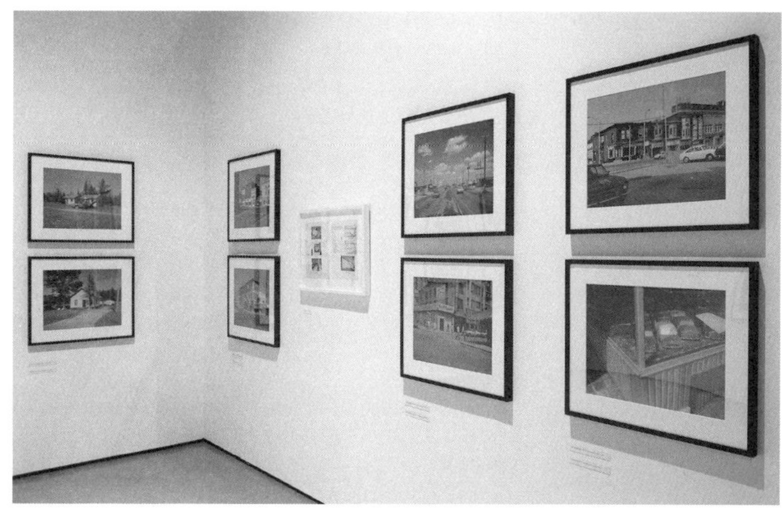

Stephen Shore
Uncommon Places,
1973-83 and *The*
Roadtrip Journals,
1973, exhibition
view, Kunsthaus
Graz, 2015

and everyone that crossed his lens in his travels through the country *(American Surfaces),* in 1973 he began to consider the medium of photography as an analytical process (with a large-format camera and tripod) and to ask structural questions. As a consequence of his formal investigations, the photographs began to show fewer portraits and still-lifes than buildings and streets. What did not change was his interest in seemingly mundane subject matter that challenges both the artist and his viewers more than dramatic motifs.

Published in 1982 from a selection of 40 photographs, the photo book *Uncommon Places* became a key influence for many artists in the generation that followed. In a new edition of *Uncommon Places* published in 2004, Shore expanded the series with several new photographs and another component a few years later: The *Road Trip Journals.* In the style of the 'New Topographics', who tried to avoid emotion and judgment, Shore documented the course of his trip down to the smallest detail. Using notes, archived receipts, collected brochures, postcards, newspaper clippings and photographs, the photographer recounts the minutiae of what he ate, where he slept, how many miles he drove and what he perceived in the meantime. The at first glance cool, distanced photographs in *Uncommon Places* are not least very personal images and shed light on an artist whose goal is to convey visual experience. What the camera captures are surfaces, and yet these surfaces hint at what lurks behind them, unseen. A closer look at Shore's photographs allows us to develop a sensitivity towards the peculiarities and special features of everyday life. *– KH (AP) –*

→ p. 204

Art Sinsabaugh

b. 1924 in Irvington, NJ (US), † 1983 in Chicago, IL (US)

Midwest Landscape #34, 1961
6.4 × 48.9 cm

Midwest Landscape #20, 1961
7.6 × 49.5 cm

Gelatin silver prints
Collection F. C. Gundlach

Art Sinsabaugh developed a documentary style for photographing land-scapes a full decade before the 'New Topographics' turned traditional Western landscape photography on its head. Sinsabaugh's work was long unrecognised, however, and did not influence the next generation of artists. Like painter Edward Hopper, it was typically the ordinary, inhabited areas that caught Sinsabaugh's poetic eye. Using a giant banquet camera that produced 12 × 20-inch negatives, he developed a unique methodology that cropped the upper and lower edges of the extra-large contact sheets to create very small, but cinematic formats. Sinsabaugh's work explored the Great Plains in the early 1960s—the broad expanse of flat land stretching nearly 1,600 km over Illinois from Chicago to the Rocky Mountains.

In Sinsabaugh's photographs, the huge farms for which the region is known become artificial horizons strewn with buildings, grain silos like small towns. Like Adams, Shore or Baltz ten years later, Sinsabaugh maintained a straightforward, detached attitude toward the photo-graphed landscape. For him, it was not about documenting rural life or agricultural labour. The perspective he assumes is that of a car driver; the highway remains an ever-palpable presence.

In the mid-1960s, Sinsabaugh returned to Chicago, where he taught photography at the Institute of Design from 1949 to 1959 and at the University of Illinois from 1959 until his sudden death in 1983.

As part of an ambitious urban development programme that would expand the city with a new system of expressways and an airport, the Chicago Department of Planning and Development commissioned Sinsabaugh to photograph the development work, giving the artist unrestricted access to the construction sites. 'Neighborhoods were just sliced open and laid bare for my inspection,' Sinsabaugh noted. Yet despite the official documentary nature of the commission, the titles that the photographer chose for this and other series was as vaguely formulated as possible: *Chicago #162*, for example, or even more obscure: *Midwest Landscape #20*. The photographs show a city trying to shake off its dusty image and transform itself into a modern, urban, mobile system. Details of this modernisation—parking garages, highway loops and skyscrapers towering higher and higher in the sky—come to focus as well as the overall picture of a changing city. The automobile reigns supreme, making pedestrians an insignificant part of urban life. Though

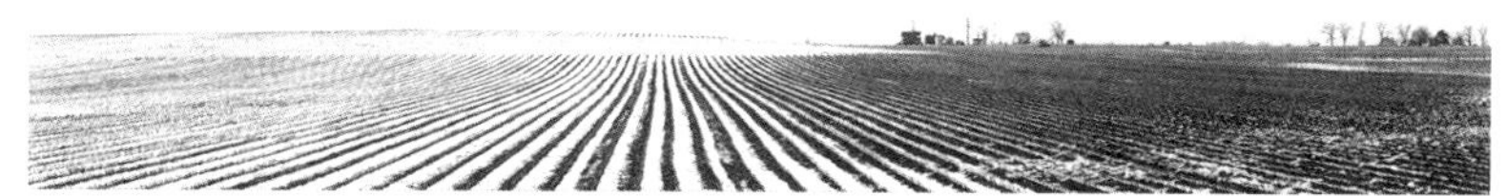

it is difficult to judge how relevant and important Sinsabaugh's photographs were to the City Hall commissioners, if one considers that his work was used as a basis for urban planning decisions, Sinsabaugh succeeded like no other in transforming art photography into geography.

– KH (AP) –

→ p. 206

Joel Sternfeld

b. 1944 in New York, NY (US), lives in New York, NY (US)

From the series: *American Prospects*, 1978–87
C-prints
Sammlung Fotomuseum Winterthur, gift of George Reinhart

McLean, Virginia, December 1978
38 × 47.8 cm
After a Flash Flood, Rancho Mirage, California, July 1979
40.5 × 50.6 cm
Wet'n Wild Aquatic Theme Park, Orlando, Florida, September 1980
40.3 × 51 cm
Pendleton, Oregon, June 1980
40.3 × 51 cm

'To discover America is to discover oneself,'[17] writes Andy Grundberg in his introduction to Joel Sternfeld's photography book *American Prospects*. The statement evokes both literary 'wanderers' such as Huckleberry Finn or Sal Paradise in Jack Kerouac's novel *On the Road*, and photographers (and adventurers) William Henry Jackson and Timothy O'Sullivan, who documented the American West in the years after the Civil War. Commissioned by the US government, the latters' landscape photographs presented a very different picture than the romanticised one seen in paintings by the Hudson River School or the literature of that era: that of rugged nature—inhospitable, merciless and forbidding.

Joel Sternfeld's work can also be seen in this tradition, which Walker Evans had continued in the 1930s. Taken in the 1970s and 80s during his sometimes months-long travels in a VW bus, the photographs in Sternfeld's *American Prospects* series are characterised by a strange mix of tragedy, black humour and boredom. Prospects, glimpses into the American lifeworld—the ambiguousness of the title is as multilayered as Sternfeld's own work capturing the consequences of US expansion across the continent. He leads us into a rich country full of technological achievements that is lost in the midst of progress; the desolation we see stands in stark contrast to the promise of salvation and the values of a

17
Andy Grundberg: 'The Itinerant Vision', in: *American Prospects. Photographs by Joel Sternfeld*. New York 1987.

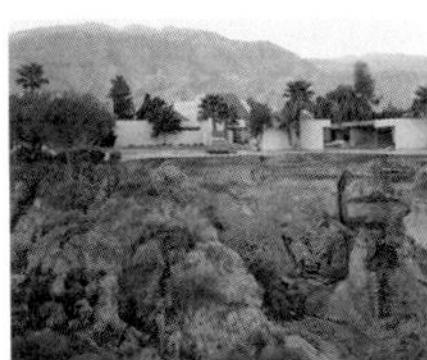

Joel Sternfeld
*After a Flash Flood,
Rancho Mirage, Cali-
fornia, July 1979*
From the series:
*American Prospects,
1978–87*

society with freedom and justice enshrined in its Constitution. The scenes that Sternfeld captures with his large-format camera are neither urban nor rural; instead it is the in-between and the middle-class suburbs that most impressively reflect American reality. Sternfeld's photographs show 'man as the earth's caretaker,'[18] however without being visible in every shot. *American Prospects* documents man's intervention in the landscape, be it agriculture, industry, residential areas or leisure activities. Other photographs show events that put man in his place, through floods *(After a Flash Flood, Rancho Mirage, California, July 1979)* or other acts of nature.

The position the photographer took was distanced, in the strictest sense of the word (Sternfeld almost always positions his camera about 20 metres from the subject, at a slight elevation), creating an almost voyeuristic remove between subject and observer. Like the 'New Topographics', he takes an objective view of his subjects, though there is nothing detached about Sternfeld's pictures. Although the images are very narrative, some background knowledge is useful for understanding the photographs: *Manville Corporation World Headquarters, Littleton, Colorado,* for example, shows the (then) brand new headquarters of a bankrupt New York asbestos factory, the shine of which can be seen many kilometres away from the original, troubled company.

Sternfeld's photographs almost always show the 'white noise' of everyday life—a warship on the beach, a firefighter buying a pumpkin from a farmer as his house burns in the background, a runaway elephant lies exhausted on a country road, surrounded by police. Sternfeld does not stage these incidents, but knows how to frame the scenario through the conscious use of light, colour and perspective. The optical appeal of his photographs is what draws us in, pulling us closer to what we might otherwise overlook. *– KH (AP) –*

18
Anne W. Tucher:
'American Beauty in
Atypical Places', in:
*American Prospects.
Photographs by Joel
Sternfeld*. New York
1987.

Landscape in Motion
Cinematic Visions of an Uncertain Tomorrow

Katrin Bucher Trantow, Monika Holzer-Kernbichler

Max Frisch authored *Man in the Holocene* as early as the late 1970s. The story of an approaching storm is an ominous parable about the position of man and the earthly destiny of decay and mortality. Like so many generations since the Industrial Revolution and subsequent rapid growth of cities, Frisch's protagonist Herr Geiser has retreated into an unspoilt landscape, and it is there that he tries to collate the accumulated knowledge of the world and importance of humanity into a kind of 'super-encyclopedia of Modernity'.

Today's scholars speak of the *Anthropocene*, an era in which human activity is a fundamental factor for developments on Earth. The term contributes to a changing picture of humankind's ability to shape the world; it gives us back our responsibility, but also the potential power of determinability.

Untouched nature has become a rare phenomenon. For millennia now, humankind has had an influence on their environment through their way of life, by changing the ground and the air above areas of land and so contributing to global warming.[1] Industrialisation, however, has led to an acceleration in human interventions, and their scale is also growing exponentially. As a result, Nobel Prize winner Paul J. Crutzen [2] proposed in 2000 that we stop using the term 'Holocene' in the geological timescale and instead speak of the 'Anthropocene' (ancient Greek: *ánthropos*, man). He had recognised that chemicals were attacking the protective ozone layer around the Earth and argued spontaneously and fairly heatedly at a conference[3] that it was clear that the Age of Man had dawned. The debate continues as to whether this term for the latest geological age should be officially adopted.[4] It must first be demonstrated that man has already had such a significant impact on the Earth and its structure that we have fundamentally altered its characteristics and its climate. Irrespective of this, the discussion has triggered deeper reflections[5] about humankind's treatment of the world, about its resources, climate change and potential global perspectives for the future. Very few areas survive where human traces are

[1] For approximately 8,000 years now, man has continued to act in ways that alter the global climate—through large-scale slash and burn techniques to make land arable, for example, or through the rice cultivation that became popular in Asia some 1,000 years ago. Both examples are proven significant contributors to global warming. However, the most serious increase in greenhouse gases in the atmosphere came only with the onset of the Industrial Revolution. Cf. also, for example, studies conducted by climate researchers at the ETH Lausanne: Jed Oliver Kaplan, Kristen Krumhardt, E. C. Ellis, W. F. Ruddiman, C. Lemmen, K. K. Goldewijk [etc]: 'Holocene Carbon Emissions as a Result of Anthropogenic Land Cover Change', in: *The Holocene*, vol. 21. no. 5, 2011, pp. 775-791.

not already inscribed: cities, arable and pasture lands, industrial zones, landfill sites, forestry plantations, roads, mining operations and vast reservoirs demonstrate at a global level the power of humankind to exploit the Earth's resources exhaustively. Areas that are not scattered with the traces of mankind's activities or signs of its consequences have become a rarity.[6]

Landscape happens. It needs perspective, and is defined through the gaze. As a human environment, it is structured by our culturally, socially and politically shaped perception and largely depends on the mind's eye. *Landscape in Motion* is a plea for a complex view of landscape and its visual representation. The starting-point is a study of cinematic developments and interpretations of landscape. The exhibition begins with a selection of works at a time when our view of the human environment has changed fundamentally since the moon landing in 1969: on the one hand, we very clearly see the Earth's limits, while technological advances and territorial expansion in (outer) space dramatically expand our sense of sight at the same time. New imaging techniques shed light on landscape as a usable surface defined by extension, shift and transformation. Taking a cue from Foucault and his pioneering essay *Of Other Spaces* (1967), the exhibition broadly considers a space shaped by different events and points of view. An open road system configuration, it leads to an understanding of landscape as a moving space for social interaction. Loosely structured, it comprises topics related to a *material formed by technology*, a *political and economic territory*, *landscape as narrative* and *landscape as a resource for the future*.

Landscape is often seen as a characteristic expression of the nature of a particular area of land. When we think about landscape, then often the images that come to mind are of distant horizons and memorable light and weather conditions, but also those of urban landscapes, roofscapes or seascapes. We talk about untouched natural landscapes, of cultivated landscapes, of intact landscapes, protected landscapes, but less readily about spoiled or even destroyed landscapes. The notion of landscape seems to hold largely positive connotations. 'Why is landscape beautiful?' Lucius Burckhardt—the founder of strollology—asked in 1979, so demonstrating that landscape is chiefly a construct.[7] It is not to be found primarily in the phenomena of the environment, but rather in the minds of the viewers. The more our expectations are met by what we see, the greater our satisfaction. The capacity to filter our gaze and blank out any irritations is also an advantage in this process.

From Technology-Shaped Material to Political and Economic Territory ...

Ever since the moon landing and even a year before, when the first pictures of the Blue Planet—still the most published image in the world— came out in 1968, we radically saw the limitedness of landscapes as

2
In 1995, meteorologist Paul J. Crutzen (b. 1933) received the Nobel Prize for Chemistry because of his groundbreaking work on atmospheric chemistry. He is considered one of the pioneers in the study of the ozone hole. For more on his research on the Anthropocene, see Paul J. Crutzen: 'Geology of Mankind', in: *Nature*, 415, 2002, p. 23. www.nature.com.

3
At a conference for the Intergovernmental Panel on Climate Change (IPCC) in 2000, Crutzen intervened when many of the participants were still referring to the Holocene. The term Holocene refers to the moderate warm period that has enabled human development for the past 11,700 years. Crutzen was the first to dispute the term, the validity of which had gone unquestioned since 1885.

4
Even today, the concept of the Anthropocene is not yet officially confirmed. 'A proposal to formalise the "Anthropocene" is being developed by the "Anthropocene" Working Group for consideration by the International Commission on Stratigraphy, with a current target date of 2016.' In: WORKING GROUP ON THE 'ANTHROPOCENE', http://quaternary.stratigraphy.org/workinggroups/anthropocene (14.03.2015).

useable areas with our own eyes. It was the era of science fiction, the search for life on other planets, and yet was also a war-weary time of struggle against control and widespread student revolt. Signs of an incipient ecological movement could be seen as early as 1962, with *Silent Spring* by Rachel Carson and *Whole Earth Catalog* somewhat later, and thus also a view of landscape as a finite resource.[8] Rapid technical and media developments went hand-in-hand with changes to artistic approaches as well, and the landscape became a connected, Earth-bound surface to be used and shaped. Film became a medium for the visual arts, and art ventured out of the gallery and into the realm of cities and landscapes. Building on developments in Hard-edge painting and Happenings, for example, artists from the OHO group in Slovenia to Richard Long in England and Robert Smithson in the United States shifted away from the 'white cube' and restrictive norms of the art establishment and into the space of the real, working directly on the Earth's surface. At the same time, Land Art developed in the Western world as an expansion of the concept of painting and sculpture, from a feeling of connectedness with the cosmic and the knowledge of (one's own) finiteness in global interconnectedness. Robert Smithson's colossal basalt sculpture *Spiral Jetty* (1970) in the Great Salt Lake in Utah shows a visionary combination of technological and industrial sculpture in a world of natural entropy. As a cinematic narrative about an almost mystical landscape monument in flux, the work shows an impressive artistic intervention created with the help of industrial machinery. The powerful event becomes a sculptural process. *Spiral Jetty* was a seminal work that fascinated subsequent generations of artists including James Benning and Tacita Dean, for example, who explicitly reference the piece in works of their own. But aside from its conceptual power, the work's significance stems from its recognition of the ambivalent beauty and power of the technological: Seen from a helicopter and with the necessary spatial distance, the bulldozer reveals its own nature as a workhorse that, along with the human beings controlling it, becomes part of a natural system of growth and decay. *Spiral Jetty* shows a complete picture of a cycle in which landscape, human and technological development are inextricably connected.

Ed Ruscha's *Every Building on the Sunset Strip* (1966) and Michael Snow's 360-degree film *La Région Centrale* (1971) also show a heightened perception of time and space in technology-enabled 'moving' vision. When Ruscha attaches a camera to his moving car for his photographic surveys, he references the enormous importance of the car as machine for seeing and creation—a machine that turns the modern roaded landscape into an absurd merry-go-round in Walter Niedermayr's *Seiersberg I* (1997).

To the eyes of 20th-century passengers, landscape unfurls as a moving experience and—as we see in Shi Guorui's long-time exposures—as a cinematic 'seeing in time'. Evidence of this can be found in the ever-growing number of road movies and narratives, from Jack Kerouac's *On*

5
See, for example, the comprehensive programme of events for 'Basic Cultural Research using the Means of Art and Science', held 2013/2014 at the House of World Cultures in Berlin. Cf: www.hkw.de/de/programm/projekte/2014/anthropozaen/anthropozaen_2013_2014.php.

6
Cf. for example Christian Schwägerl: *Menschenzeit. Zerstören oder gestalten? Die entscheidende Epoche unseres Planeten.* Munich 2010.

7
Lucius Burckhardt: *Warum ist Landschaft schön? Die Spaziergangswissenschaft.* Kassel 2008.

8
The Whole Earth Catalog, founded in 1968 by Stewart Brand. The publication put the Blue Planet on its cover one year before the moon landing, making knowledge from NASA generally accessible for the first time. It drew connections between such significant social issues as ecology and nature romanticism, cybernetics and new technologies, psychodelia and the cult of computers.

9
In 1856, French photographer Felix Nadar created the first aerial photographs using wet collodion plates and a darkroom in the basket of a hot-air balloon.

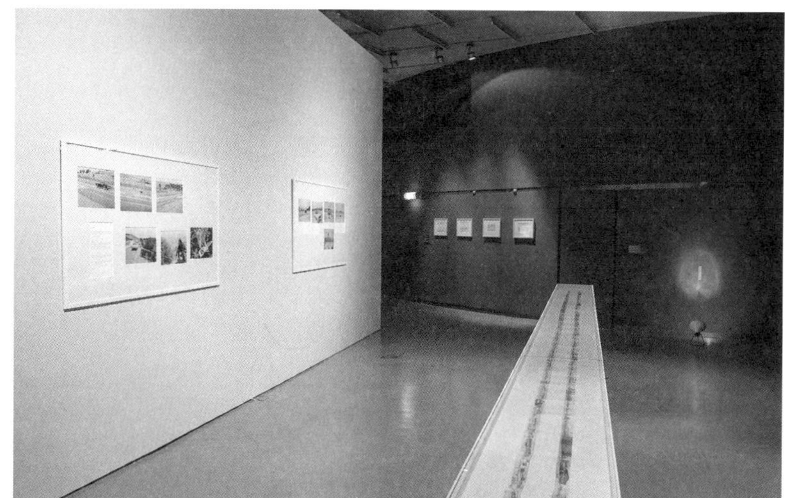

Landscape in Motion, exhibition view, Kunsthaus Graz, 2015

the Road (1957) to Cormac McCarthy's *The Road* (2006). And yet it is precisely the view from above that shaped the representation of landscape as a network of paths between centres of power production, as we see particularly in the work of James Benning, the Center for Land Use Interpretation (CLUI) and Darren Almond.

Flying, and the techniques of photography and also film have altered our view of the landscape. In the mid-19th century, hot air balloon photographs pioneered by Frenchman Felix Nadar[9] provided the first glimpses of Paris from a bird's eye view. The 1860s also saw the first aerial photographs in America, showing Boston from above.[10] Seeing the landscape from above, through the lens of a camera, overthrew central perspective for the first time since the Renaissance. 'La terre se déroule en un immense tapis sans bords, sans commencement, ni fin,'[11] writes Nadar, whose photographs changed not only how landscape is seen, but also had a profound impact on painting. The new perspective inspired the Impressionists; abandoning Euclidean space in the representation of subjects eventually became the testing ground for the Cubists as well.

Viewing the landscape from above is also politically motivated, particularly when it comes to flight.[12] Military interests have constantly advanced and expanded the technologies and scope of landscape photography. Nowadays, unmanned drones are already taking over this work. Thus the camera has broken away not only from the ground but also from the eye of the filmmaker.

The growing speed of flight and increase in the distance from the Earth's surface broadened the overview: we could see further, see more, and see faster and faster. The overcoming of gravity and the development of space travel made a view of the entire globe possible from the perspective of motion. A number of built structures and geographical

10
See: Thierry Gervais: 'Expérimentations photographiques. La vision en plongée, de Nadar (1858) á Gaston Tissandier (1885)', in: *Vues d'en haut,* Exh. cat. Centre Pompidou-Metz 2013, pp. 51-61.

11
Felix Nadar, *Quand j'etais photographe.* Paris 1900, reprint Paris 1979, p. 22.

12
As early as 1859, the Italian Ministry of War invited Nadar to exploit balloon photography for 'reconnaissance purposes' in the campaign against Austria. But Solferino's photographs fell short of what was needed. The American Civil War saw the first usable shots from the balloon, so the work of the photographer and aeronaut Lowe finally led to military successes. Cf. Edouard Dolezal, Vienna: *Verein zur Verbreitung naturwissenschaftlicher Kenntnisse 1910,* p. 22.

13
The first pictures of Earth as seen from space were taken in 1947, and it was military interests that made those possible as well. Wernher von Braun was an engineer and a member of the Nazi Party and the SS. Working with Nazi Germany, he developed the V-2 rocket for the bombing of enemy cities. He also became the father of the US space programme having surrendered to the US army a few days before the war ended. The V-2 was developed on US soil. During test flights in 1947, researchers were able to load the rocket with instruments. On board was a camera that took a picture every 1.5 seconds. These were the first shots taken outside the Earth's atmosphere at an altitude of 160 km, and clearly showed the curvature of the Earth against black outer space. Cf. Stefan Schmitt: 'Raumfahrt-Geschichte: Die ersten Erd-Fotos aus dem All', in: *Spiegel Online*, December 18, 2006, accessed April 14, 2015. www.spiegel.de/wissenschaft/weltall/raumfahrt-geschichte-die-ersten-erd-fotos-aus-dem-all-a-454903.html.

14
Cf. Fred Truniger: 'Filmische Landvermessung: Landschaftsverständnis und visuelle Kultur', PhD diss. Zurich 2008, p. 9.

changes caused by humankind have reached such proportions that they are visible from space. The *Whole Earth Catalog*, started by Stewart Brand in 1968, not only put the Blue Planet on its cover a year before the moon landing,[13] it also discussed significant social issues such as the incipient ecological movement.

In the meantime, we have become used to the bird's eye view. Any one of us can use Google Maps at home to view the whole world from above, to zoom in and fly about in the virtual world. Actual flight has become a standard for global mobility, leaving profound traces on the Earth's climate.

To the same degree that technical changes have impacted image production and thus the perception of the Earth and its landscapes, the Industrial Revolution accelerated transformation in the scenery itself.

Both CLUI's flight over the endless Texas oil fields and Benning's views of industry-marked California bear witness to this accelerated Industrial Revolution and, like Lukas Marxt's *Captive Horizon* (2014), are investigations of a universal, aesthetic pattern of growth. Marxt's survey of the landscape with a drone becomes an intelligence-seeking journey between microscopic and macroscopic structures, and allows time—hence the intrinsic relationship to Land Art—to become an undetermined mass whose permanency is reflected in entropic change.

... On Landscape as a Narrative and the Prospect of a Landscape as a Resource for the Future ...

In the 1950s, John Brinckerhoff Jackson founded the newspaper *Landscape*. In it, he denounced the still dominant idealisation of landscape and instead focused on his immediate surroundings. He noted that the landscape has long been heavily impacted by humans and described it as a space of social interaction that assumes communicative functions within society and in doing so, can become a space of projection for subjective moods, social utopias or atmospheric qualities.[14]

EDEN'S EDGE (2014) by Leo Calice and Gerhard Treml investigates this space of projection in material and method, and a cinematic landscape model is blended with personal stories that open space for a narrative construction of landscape. Mathias Kessler and Rosa Barba also describe the landscape as a contested narrative. Their visual and language-based critical approach focuses on deconstructing landscape and sculptural concepts, and reveal them to be inadequate and system-dependant norms. Qiu Anxiong's animation, on the other hand, shows the landscape to be politically and culturally determined, as an endless series of interconnected sediments that are traces of human expansionistic policy in the spirit of Martin Warnke or Martin Pollack.

It seems clear that 'man' can no longer be thought of as separate from 'nature', and that he is indisputably connected to the Earth system. French sociologist Bruno Latour has for some time now been trying to

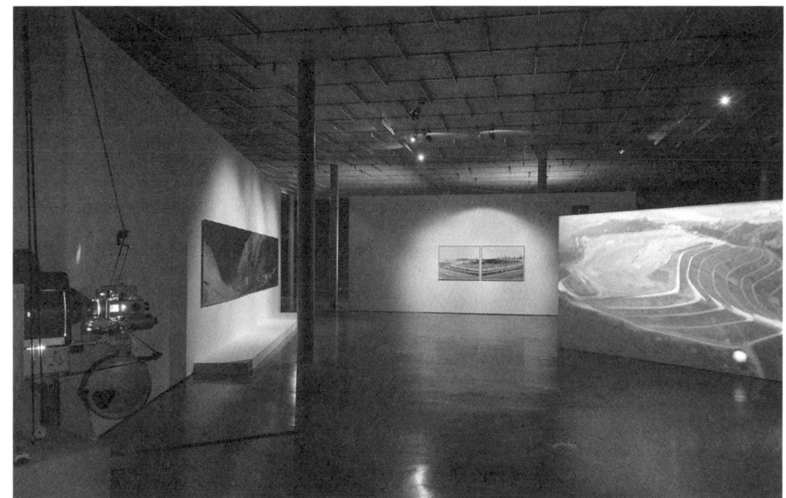

challenge the thinking behind this, and to call attention to a Parliament of Things:[15] humankind is only part of a greater system, just as animals or other things are. We should be reworking our notion of the natural sciences as supposedly objective sciences, and exposing the political powers that exploit them. As a relatively young science, political ecology has the task of investigating the effects of ecological changes on human communities, but should also question the extent to which terms such as 'nature' and 'environment' are constructions. The opposing interests and aims of politics, the economy or science inevitably lead to problems in this—we should be finding strategies for resolving these together. According to Latour, we need a new culture that mediates between different modes of existence.[16]
The growing exploitation of nature for human requirements that began with industrialisation is also reflected in the relevance of the theme within art. Art takes a look at different landscapes and the range in their qualities.

The works of Markus Jeschaunig, David Nez, Klaus Schafler and Ursula Biemann analyse landscape with an eye to man's responsibility for the environment he exploits. Markus Jeschaunig's hour glass of petroleum, Ursula Biemann's film showing the eerie global connections between oil production and rising sea levels, Klaus Schafler's studies on excessive sand consumption and finally David Nez' visionary metaphor for the threat of global warming—all reference mankind in the Anthropocene, a humanity that is beginning to see the effect of geological changes, and how connections cross all boundaries between disciplines and areas of knowledge. Guido van der Werve sees humanity as a species walking on thin ice, behind it the threatening technology he has called a ghost of his creation. Armin Linke sees the hurricane rising before before us and Marine Hugonnier looks to the world of tomorrow as the world of yesterday.

15
Bruno Latour: *We Have Never Been Modern.* Cambridge, MA 1993.

16
Bruno Latour: *An Inquiry into Modes of Existence. An Anthropology of the Moderns.* Cambridge, MA 2013.

These artistic calls to action have to be taken seriously—an exhortation that, for the past 40 years, has urged human beings to claim responsibility in an era of finite resources, human-driven exploitation and profound structural change on the planet, and to view landscape as a subjective counterpart. Let us not forget that the landscape is shaped multidimensionally by its various political, personal, cultural, and economic uses; landscape is above all a moving construct that not only includes human beings and their needs, but also defines them.

For Frisch, the modernist desire for order yields to the equanimity of postmodernism; a gust of wind enters Herr Geiser's refuge, miserably wrecking his experiment. The limits of the encyclopedic are exposed, but so are those of an information society.
'What does Holocene mean! Nature does not need names. This much Herr Geiser knows. The stones do not need his memory.'[17] Herr Geiser comes to the conclusion: 'Man is forever a layperson.' He is resigned to the unconscious in Nature: 'Only man knows catastrophes, to the extent that he survives them; nature knows no disasters.'

15
Bruno Latour: *We Have Never Been Modern.* Cambridge, MA 1993.

16
Bruno Latour: *An Inquiry into Modes of Existence. An Anthropology of the Moderns.* Cambridge, MA 2013.

17
Max Frisch: *Man in the Holocene. A Story.* New York 1980.

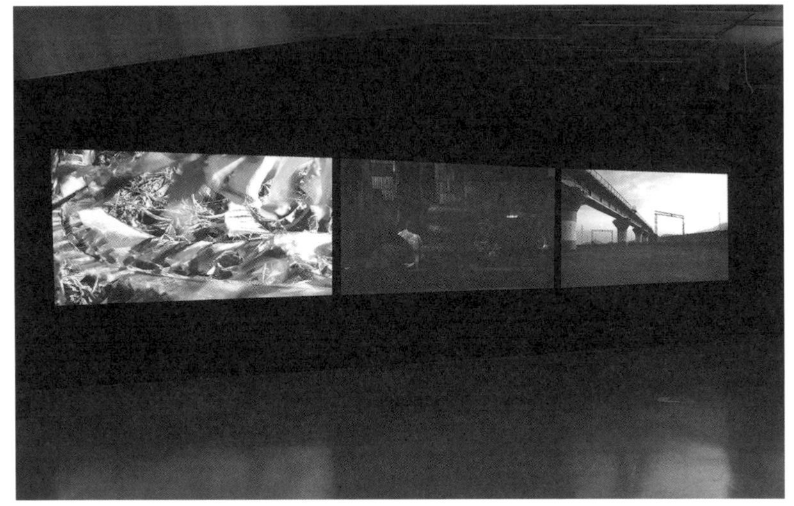

Darren Almond
In the Between,
2006, exhibition
view, Kunsthaus
Graz, 2015

→ p. 210

Darren Almond
b. 1971 in Wigan (UK), lives in London (UK)

In the Between, 2006
3 channel HD video, colour, sound; 14 min
Courtesy of the artist

Darren Almond achieved prominence in 1997 with his oversized digital clock in the exhibition *Sensation* in London (1997), with his video installations on loss and mourning that are visible from far-off—such as the personal portrait of his grandmother in *If I Had You* (2003)—and his spectacular full-moon photographs using extended exposure. His unsentimental, objective, documentary-style works deal with time, location and history: with collective memory as much as with personal experience and endurance. His (partially mechanical and time-measuring) sculptures, his films, photographs and paper works are all based on journeys that lead him from full moon photographs and re-interpretations of Carl Blechen's romantic oil studies of the Amalfi coast to the labour camps of Siberia or the sulphur mines of Java, Indonesia.
His video *In the Between* is devoted to the symbolic explosive force of the most elevated railway line in the world—at over 4000 metres above sea level—between Quinghai in China and Lhasa in Tibet. It is the third part of an intensive involvement with this form of transportation and is part of a railway trilogy that began with *Schwebebahn* (1995), in which he portrayed the first suspended railway in the world in Wuppertal, Germany, and continued with *Geisterbahn* (1999) from the Prater in Vienna. In it he recognises the railway as a multi-layered tool for conquering the countryside. *In the Between* refers to the title of the sutras known today as *The Book of the Dead (Bardo Thödröl)* which function as a spiritual guide for the transition from life to death. At the same time Almond refers to the situation of moving from one culture to another, as well as

from one part of the train trilogy to the other in intermediary fashion, the one symbolising emerging life, the other gloomy death.

During the 14-minute video, Buddhist monks from this monastery—Lhasa's oldest—can be seen most of the time in the central image of the video, which is set up as a triptych. Filmed with a static camera shot, the monks eat, sing and meditate, while on the projection surfaces on both sides the thundering train rushes through the sand-coloured, arid landscape and seems on one occasion to be roaring straight towards them. Sometimes the camera is also positioned in the train, sometimes it looks straight out into the passing landscape, into the luminously blue sky and up to the Himalayas looming in the distance. The train whizzes through empty railway stations—the only humans present being the soldiers on guard—through uninhabited landscape, while it observes the deployment of troops on the border and brings goods and commercial travellers as well as tourists—in the first year there were over 1.5 million passengers—to the spiritual centre of the Tibetans and Buddhists. The visible contrast between the technological, industrial and spiritual world turns the train into a penetrating aggressor. The triptych thus becomes a precisely composed epic on the territorial and social claim to power made by China, which is manifested in the construction of the routes completed for the 2006 Olympic Games, and thus refers both metaphorically and actually to the Chinese invasion of 1950–51. The video becomes a political exploration of time, image and space, accompanied by the supporting soundtrack of prayer songs and cymbals. – *KBT (AH)* –

→ p. 212 **Rosa Barba**

b. 1972 in Agrigento/Sicily (IT), lives in Berlin (DE)
www.rosabarba.com

Definition Landfill, 2014
35 mm film, colour, sound; 5 min
Courtesy of the artist, Meyer Riegger, Berlin
and Gio Marconi, Milan

Like many past works of the Berlin-based Italian artist Rosa Barba, *Definition Landfill* deals with hidden perceptive and narrative characteristics of filmic narrative. The physical and conceptual components of filmic presentation are thus taken apart, made abstract and then reconstituted. Since her spectacular work *Coro Spezzato,* which she showed in 2009 as part of the Venice Biennale and which won her the Nam June Paik Award in 2010, she has become known to a wider public. The multipart projection work, which was based on the practice of Venetian polyphony that arose in the Renaissance, had five 16 mm projectors project words onto the exhibition room walls at pre-set, alternating periods, to generate in this way a kind of 'audio trompe l'œil' effect.

Definition Landfill was created as an analogue film in 2014 during a residency in San Antonio. The installation-like film work is the portrait of a monumental landfill overgrown with grass not far from Los Angeles. In

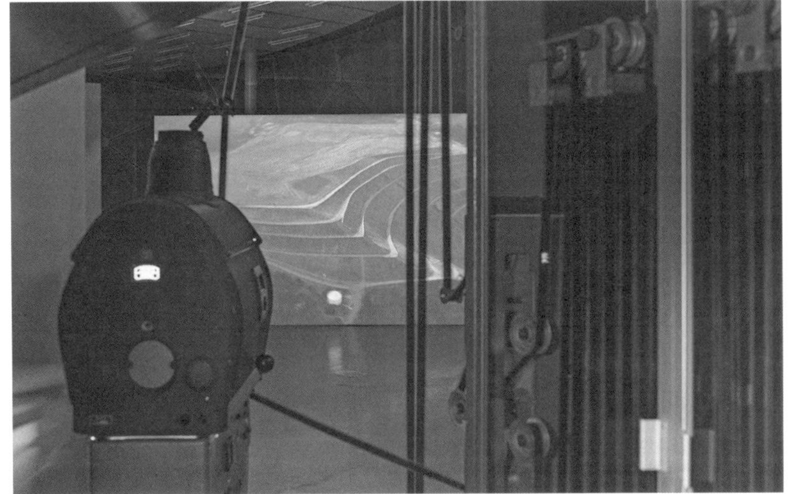

Rosa Barba
Definition Landfill,
2014, exhibition
view, Kunsthaus
Graz, 2015

the space, the man-sized 35 mm projector documents the physical, even sculptural presence of the film event. Stretched over nearly endless rolls and loop lashings, the narrative and pictorially powerful story of the unreal landscape monument is projected onto a massive, freestanding projection wall.

Within the film, Barba observes from the perspective of the circling helicopter an artificial elevation within a hilly landscape, scans it by means of the film material and then analyses it through the medium, image and language. It is a topographical perspective that offers the marvelling eye of the viewer images of a fantastic aesthetic and creates warm pictures in chrome with the dancing, kinematic light on the wall. An uncanny, almost nostalgic environment is created, reminiscent of the Expanded Cinema of the 1970s—such as Anthony McCall's pioneering work *Line describing a cone* (1973) —and which can be walked through and in a certain sense accessed by the public.

In the linguistic analysis of the filmic narrative, Barba exaggerates in turn the logic of Conceptual Art by having a robotic computer voice read out her self-created definition of the term 'landfill'. The monotonous voice, a typical voice recognition programme that is as artificial as the landscape it describes, speaks of the possibility of seeing the landfill as an arranged accumulation of found objects—in a certain sense as Ready-mades—so that they in turn reveal an independent work. It is a sardonic text that settles accounts with civilisation, which Barba has read out by a voice devoid of emotion. Barba's scepticism in using the language of art targets a range of subjects, from the archaeological use of the term 'landfill' as an accumulation of artefacts, terms such as 'earthworks' which are borrowed from Land Art, through to American land appropriation, global over-utilisation, excessive exploitation and wastage. In the analogous recreation, the spatial-temporal dimension residing within the landscape can be experienced both physically and intellectually. Barba's engagement with landscape is analytical and visionary at the same time. It is marked by an ambivalent attitude towards the intoxicating beauty and power of the unsettling to be found in a culture rendered technological, systematic, and obsessively objectified.   *– KBT (AH) –*

→ p. 214

James Benning

b. 1942 in Milwaukee, WI (US), lives in Valencia, CA (US)

From: *California Trilogy*, 1999–2001
16 mm film, colour, sound; each 90 min

El Valley Centro, 1999
Los, 2000
Sogobi, 2001

casting a glance, 2007
16 mm film, transferred to digital media, colour, sound; 77 min

Courtesy of the artist

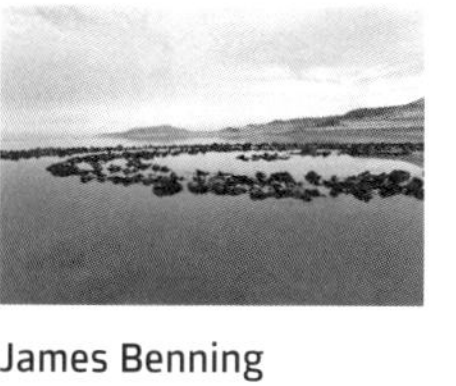

James Benning
casting a glance,
2007, film still

1
The 'California
Aqueduct', officially
the 'Governor Edmund
G. Brown California
Aqueduct', is a system
of canals, tunnels, and
pipelines that conveys
water collected from
the Sierra Nevada
Mountains and valleys
of Northern and Central
California to Southern
California. http://
en.wikipedia.org/wiki/
California_Aqueduct.

The avant-garde film-maker and trained mathematician James Benning is known for his strictly composed filmic engagements with landscape. *California Trilogy* concerns a three-part topographical study of the 'Golden State'. The first part, *El Valley Centro* (1999), shows photographs of the extended Californian valley, which is shaped above all by agricultural mass production. The second part, *Los* (2000), is devoted to the greater Los Angeles area, while the last part, *Sogobi* (2001), is a portrait of the Californian wilderness. All three films are marked by the precise design of the picture and Benning's unspoken 'social commentary': they each last 90 minutes and consist of 35 shots of exactly two-and-a-half minutes' length. The precisely chosen view frame emphasises the three-dimensionality of what is shown, the panoramic or the sublime nature of a landscape. This kind of recording alludes to early cinema, emphasising the space outside of the field of view: a form of staging that breaks the ostensibly documentary character of the shots. Undoubtedly it is the author's subjective view that we are dealing with here. At the end of all the films of the trilogy, a political reading, which is contained in all the images only implicitly, is finally given concrete form: the credits list the film locations and turn the ownership relations into a theme. The landscape is thus presented not only as the result of a pictorial tradition of the romantic and the sublime, but is pervaded with work and ownership relationships, with industry and the circulation of goods, the most precious of which is water. The 'California Aqueduct'[1] also links all three films as an overarching theme.

California Trilogy shows not only Benning's mastery of interlacing aesthetics and politics, but also his sensitive handling of his own status as a film-maker who, as the member of a privileged class, directs his focus on the asymmetrical power and ownership relations that reach deep into the history of the USA and its appropriation of land. In the titles he uses

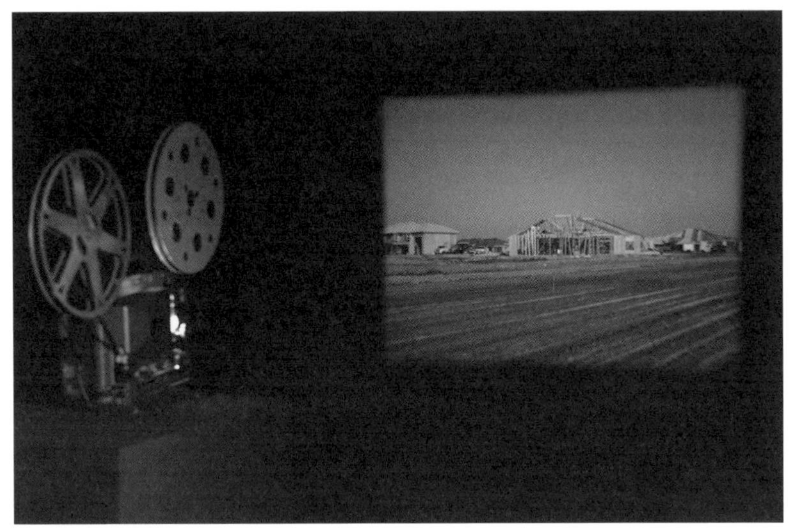

a mixture of Spanish and English for the extended Californian valley *(El Valley Centro)*, the Spanish abbreviation for Los Angeles *(Los)* and the Shoshonean word for earth *(Sogobi)*.[2]

The protagonist in Benning's complex time study *casting a glance* (2007) is Robert Smithson's famous Land Art work *Spiral Jetty* (1970). Benning undertook a total of 16 journeys within two years and projected this period of filming onto the whole history to date of the *Spiral Jetty* since 1970. Beginning with 'April 30, 1970' and ending with 'May 15, 2007'—according to the inserts—*casting a glance* recapitulates the work's degree of visibility (between 1984 and 1988 the jetty was completely submerged under water). The water level concerned was mathematically reconstructed by Benning and reproduced by a corresponding photograph. The highly composed feel of the film only emerges by means of this extra information, which shows perfectly how time can be stretched artificially, without using force on the latter. Audio recordings with hidden homages made in situ form the soundtrack: one tranquil evening—the jetty is peacefully resting in the water just then—a version of the Country song 'Love Hurts' sounds from far away; it was recorded by Emmylou Harris and Gram Parsons in the year that Smithson died in a plane crash (1973). Such homages in no way undermine the view of the essential, however: the temporal, also the seasonal dimension, indeed the shifting, historical disappearance and then re-emergence of the mythically formed headland. 'The film is my personal homage to this important artwork and how difficult it is to be recognised by people', to quote James Benning.[3]   *– CS, CH (AH) –*

2
Revised extract from the text by Claudia Slanar for the booklet accompanying the DVD edition filmmuseum 78. *James Benning. California Trilogy.*

3
Revised extract from the text by Christian Höller for the booklet accompanying the DVD edition filmmuseum 78. 76. *James Benning. casting a glance/RR.*

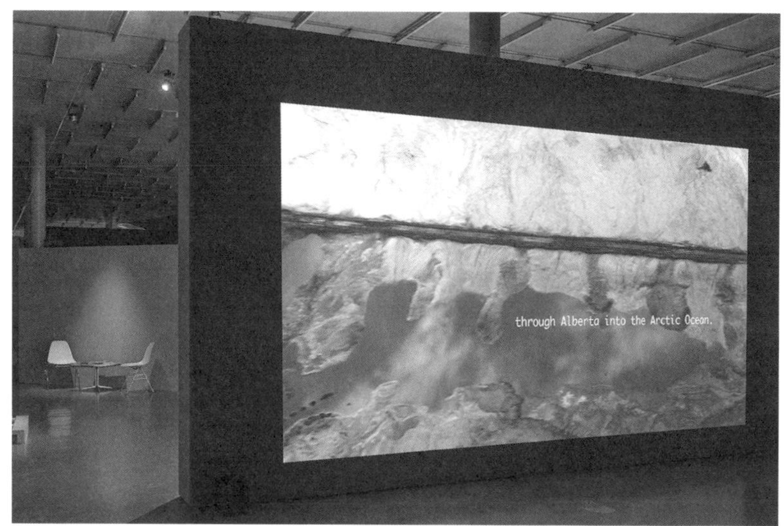

Ursula Biemann
Deep Weather, 2013,
exhibition view,
Kunsthaus Graz,
2015

→ p. 216

Ursula Biemann

b. 1955 in Zurich (CH), lives in Zurich (CH)
www.geobodies.org

Deep Weather, 2013
HD video, colour, sound; 9 min
Courtesy of the artist

Artist, curator and networker Ursula Biemann examines the (seemingly objective and distanced) real circumstances, global contexts, political topics and information that circulate in online and print media every day. For Ursula Biemann, art is a medium for learning how to understand the world. Her video essays organise complex global relationships, combining on-site video recordings, expert interviews, archival material, virtual information sources and theoretical texts in a way that goes against the objective documentation of reality.

Biemann works with the traditional tools of documentation—she conducts interviews, researches scholarly literature, films and photographs but rather than assume the sober, objective nature of reportage, the work encourages viewers to join the discussion. Her non-linear narratives about climate change, immigration- and gender politics or the economy emphasise an intensive dialogue with the local people who are directly affected.

The video *Deep Weather* is the result of a research trip to two locations: Alberta, the wealthiest province in Canada, and Bangladesh, one of the poorest countries in the world. Visually stunning and informative, the work approaches the topics of ecology, oil and water in a global context. The first part of *Deep Weather* shows the dark, battered landscape in Alberta in northern Canada, a city dominated by government-sponsored oil sands mining. Its global consequences—including rising greenhouse gas emissions and the associated global warming—are felt in other places, such as Bangladesh, for example. For the second part of her work, Biemann travelled to the other side of the world where the Delta inhabitants of Bangladesh build powerful earthen walls by hand, as protection against impending floods from the melting Himalayan glaciers.

– ES (AP) –

→ p. 218

Lucius Burckhardt

b. 1925 in Davos (CH), † 2003 in Basel (CH)
www.lucius-burckhardt.org

Kriegerische Landschaft, n. d.
17 × 24.1 cm

Friedliche Landschaft, n. d.
17 × 24.1 cm

Das unsichtbare Matterhorn, n. d.
12,5 × 18 cm

Ohne Titel [Atomkraftwerk auf Staffelei], n. d.
23 × 31.1 cm

Watercolour on paper
Courtesy of the Public Library of the University of Basel and Estate of Lucius and Annemarie Burckhardt-Wackernagel

→ p. 335

Walking stick with metal leaf *Hier ist es schön* [Here it is beautiful] by Andreas Gram for Lucius Burckhardt, Kassel 1993
Wood; 93 × 13.5 × 3.2 cm, multiple, ex. 43/50
Courtesy of the Public Library of the University of Basel and Estate Lucius and Annemarie Burckhardt-Wackernagel, Donation of Andreas Gram and Galerie Martin Schmitz

Why Is Landscape Beautiful? This is the title of a publication on Lucius Burckhardt's thinking as a cultural studies scholar, philosopher and sociologist. This question was the starting-point for the founder of strollology—the 'science of walking'—at the beginning of the 1980s to investigate the aesthetics of landscape. Besides his theoretical texts, he also left behind numerous watercolours, in which his thoughts on the perception of landscape are revealed.

With the words, 'one sees what one has learned', Burckhardt trenchantly sums up his deliberations: if the watercolours show us a cypress tree with a small temple, we think of countless pictures of idealised landscapes in Italy. Likewise with the case of the Matterhorn, its striking form having inscribed itself on our collective memory. Both motives are used by Burckhardt time and again like props in his watercolours so as to illustrate the process of perceiving landscape: 'The perception of landscape is an achievement of integration, a completely synthetic and

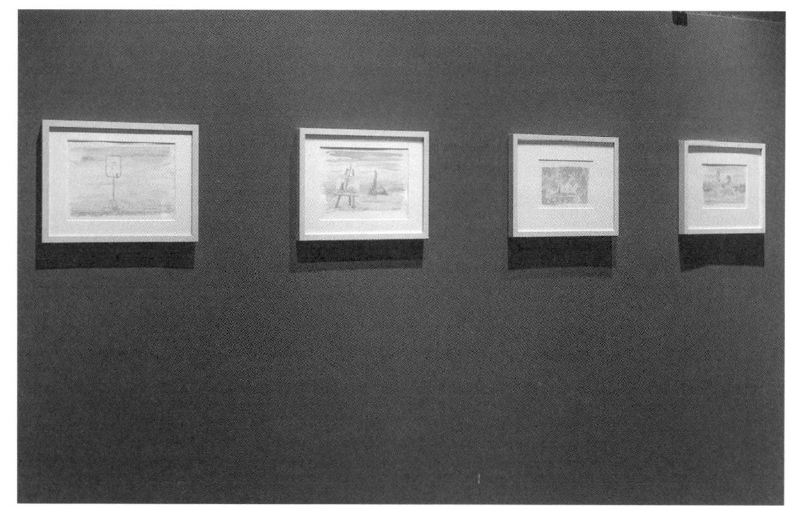

Lucius Burckhardt
Exhibition view,
Kunsthaus Graz,
2015

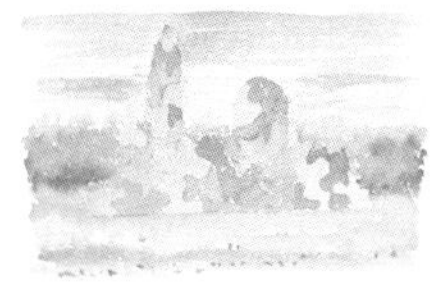

Lucius Burckhardt
*Friedliche
Landschaft*, n. d.

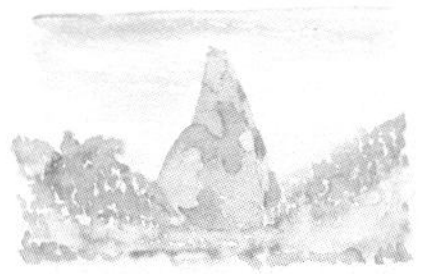

Lucius Burckhardt
*Das unsichtbare
Matterhorn*, n. d.

artistic construction which has little in common with the actual realities of nature.'

His watercolours *Friedliche Landschaft* [Peaceful Landscape] and *Das unsichtbare Matterhorn* [The Invisible Matterhorn] provide evidence of his theory of camouflage: to perceive something means at the same moment to not perceive something else—the perception of space which happens in time is always linear and does not enable us to perceive all that is real in the same moment.

Besides the consciously employed technique of the watercolour, which played an important role primarily in the 19th century in 'open-air' painting, Burckhardt undertook walks with his students in Kassel, such as 'Crossing the Zebra', in which the exhibited walking-stick with the universal pin 'It's beautiful here' was also employed. Lucius Burckhardt walked through Kassel with his students without obeying the existing zebra crossings and traffic lights, using instead a portable zebra rug, which allowed them to cross streets at places they chose themselves. It was a subversive act of appropriating public space. With this method of walking, Burckhardt attempted to rediscover the act of viewing, and for Burckhardt 'viewing' means 'opening up new perspectives, trying out ways of seeing, perceiving the unusual, revealing disruptive elements, making mistakes and noticing them in oneself.'

Lucius Burckhardt taught at the Hochschule für Gestaltung in Ulm, at ETH Zurich as well as the Universität Münster in Dortmund, and was the founding Deacon of the Faculty of Design at the Bauhaus-Universität Weimar. As the Professor for Urban Construction at the Gesamthochschule Kassel, Burckhardt initiated a planning event from 1980 to 1982 parallel to the *documenta urbana*, a model estate in the tradition of building exhibitions; the event was realised as part of documenta 7 based on an idea of the documenta founder Arnold Bode. 15 of the so-called problem locations in the city of Kassel were identified and sent to artists, architects and educational institutions, so as to enable the population to become involved in the creative planning process and share responsibility. In 2014 Burckhardt was represented at the Architecture Biennale in the Swiss Pavilion.   *– ES (AH) –*

→ p. 220   **Leo Calice, Gerhard Treml**

Leo Calice, b. 1980 in St. Gotthard (AT), lives in Vienna (AT);
Gerhard Treml, b. 1963 in Salzburg (AT), lives in Vienna (AT)

EDEN'S EDGE, 2014
Research team: Lissy Marko, Edith Schwarzl, Christina Linortner
Video and sound installation: 3 projections on sand:
Water & Worms, Time Square, Turtle Island

HD videos, colour, sound; 5:35 min, 6:03 min, 7:09 min
Courtesy of the artists

The artists Gerhard Treml and Leo Calice work in a wide range of media. In *EDEN'S EDGE* (2014) we look down on a sandy, dry landscape, the ground of the 'Wild West', on a stereotypical road movie set in the horizontal cinematic format. EDEN's EDGE is the nine-part episodic film of the 'Office for Narrative Landscape Design' on the one hand, and a multipart floor projection—far removed from cinema—on the other. In collaboration with the University of Applied Arts and the Institute for Landscape Design in Vienna, the goal was to realise a research project on narrative landscape design. Using various industrial techniques, such as filming with a hot-air balloon or as a final solution in the Greenscreen, and scientific methods, such as Mikhail Bakhtin's script writing, the intention is to make landscape accessible to perception as a narrative. The main roles in the film sequences are played by various people who have ventured into the Californian desert in order to live away from civilisation. Their stories are miniatures that negotiate the border between fiction and reality in Wonder Valley. This is to be found not far from Hollywood, where the American dream of the land of endless opportunities is dreamed time and again. In the reconstructed Wonder Valley, the gaze is focused on the story of the individuals. The landscape, which was reconstructed as a model for the film, becomes pure fiction, driving the narrative. Like God's eye, the gaze is from above looking down, unobserved, and undisturbed, one warms oneself up for the stories as if standing at a fire, and—no less important—for the voices that accompany them. American slang, nowadays as familiar to all and sundry as one's own image, pulls us into the orchestrated simplicity of the set. This simplicity is based on a common, strictly adhered-to, clearly visible basic pattern: from a height of around 15 metres, we see minimalist stages on grey to yellow desert sand, arranged into a harmonious image with few props, but with the automobile typically always present.
Small and somewhat lost, the protagonists move within them; they are hermits, outsiders and freaks in the best sense. They have all gone to the desert in order to redesign their lives on the margins of society (that

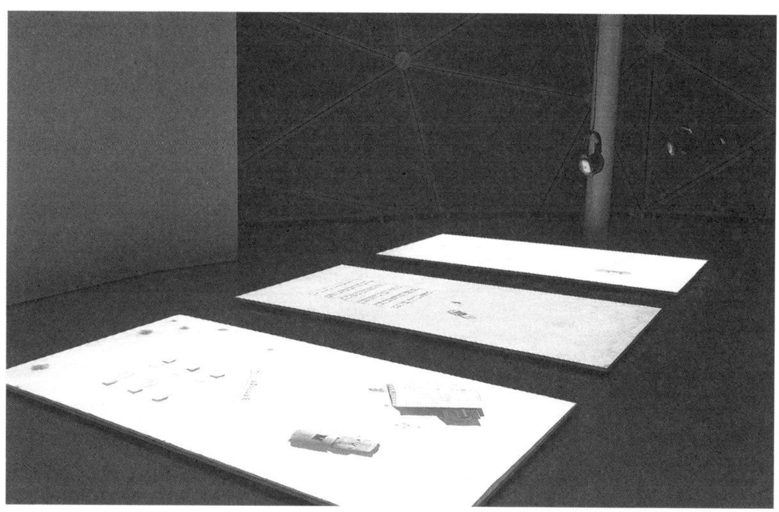

has become unbearable for them): the schizophrenic, who is actually a shaman and who leaves his car behind in the car park in order to re-establish contact with his roots; the barmaid, who falls in love with the wise drinker and builds him a carousel in the desert; or the laundress, who takes care of an artistic project. While they all drag themselves ponderously through the sun-drenched set, they can be heard recounting their fate, while in the background sounds the lonely cry of a desert bird. All in all, an intense essay on a landscape for unconventional modes of existence. 'Rarely,' according to Christian Höller, 'are the boundaries of the paradisiacal so concisely fathomed, rarely are the spaces for withdrawal that remain to non-conformists so precisely outlined'.

– KBT (AH) –

→ p. 222 **Center for Land Use Interpretation**

1994 founded in Los Angeles, CA (US)
www.clui.org

Houston Petrochemical Corridor, Texas, 2000
HD video, colour, sound; 14:12 min

Great Salt Lake Evaporation Ponds, Utah, 2013
HD video, colour, sound; 19:13 min

The Grapevine, California, 2010
HD video, colour, sound; 7 min

Courtesy of the Center for Land Use Interpretation

The Center for Land Use Interpretation (CLUI) describes itself as a research and educational organisation with the goal of recording, archiving and cataloguing landscapes in the United States as well as illustrating the functional and aesthetic use of the American landscape. This centre's interest lies with human interaction with landscape, the differing perspectives on landscape, the production of space and its perception. Since its founding in 1994, CLUI—as a subversive mixture of an environmental organisation, scientific research institute and open artists' collective—has already produced dozens of exhibitions and books on themes related to land usage.

CLUI has a highly official, almost state-like presence, suggesting that the very lack of a clear definition of this group is employed as an artistic strategy so as to think and work in a way that is not steered, though networked. Thus they succeed in accessing various usage and funding groups as well as an interdisciplinary and broadly distributed bank of knowledge. The organisation carries out educational work on an individual level, e. g. guided tours through landscapes; it administers a comprehensive online archive on projects and programmes to date and is the leading organisation of the American Land Museum: a federal-wide network of exhibition locations that represents various functional, cultural, economic and historical regions of the United States and that communally sets out to create a dynamic and contemporary image of the USA—a museum that exists both in and of the American landscape.

The three exhibited films are so-called *Landscans*, a series of exclusively American landscape images from above. *Houston Petrochemical Corridor, Texas* (2008) shows images of a giant field of crude oil processing and production. A helicopter flies, taking a route that the viewer cannot trace, the flight sounds of which set the backdrop for the images of steel constructions, parking lots, streets, silo and pond complexes, workers' housing settlements, freight trains and ships: the inconceivably large industrial region in Texas. Just as powerful in terms of image and colour are the pictures of the Great Salt Lake in Utah. The Great Salt Lake and its salt extraction ponds are the protagonists of *Great Salt Lake Evaporation Ponds, Utah* (2013). Initially creating the impression of depicting nature as untouched by human hand, pictures immediately row up composed of fine lines made of pink, turquoise and white-coloured squares and rectangles. *The Grapevine, California* (2010) is a perfect example of the intensive engagement of CLUI with the history of each location concerned and of the conscientious research that precedes each film. The Landscan shows images of the receding, over-settled landscape of Los Angeles up to the point where the flat, agricultural, extended valley of California begins. The eponymous *Grapevine* is California's 'richest' road, a mountainous passage separating the population of Southern California from the rest of the state and whose course is followed by water, gas and electricity infrastructures. The three roads that follow upon one another in the film represent three periods of modern transport: the *Ridge Route* (1915), the *Alternate Ridge Route* or *Highway 99* (early 1930s) and today's *Interstate 5*, which, as the most important transport axis along the whole of the west coast, leads from the Mexican to the Canadian border.

The films show apparently objective topological data and leave the viewers free to interpret the images as they choose—in formal or socially critical terms. These are pictures lined up in a non-hierarchical fashion: art next to science, the trivial beside the sublime, the official next to the forbidden. Together they produce something diffuse, which becomes their exciting and elucidating approach, with which they link up with Robert Smithson's ability to lead perception to other places, in order—as they formulate it themselves—'to read the cultural inscription in the landscape formed by the human hand, in order to better understand who we are and what we are doing.'

– ES (AH) –

→ p. 224

Tacita Dean

b. 1965 in Canterbury (UK), lives in Berlin (DE)
www.tacitadean.net

Trying to Find the Spiral Jetty, 1997
Audio CD; 27 min
Courtesy of the artist, Marian Goodman Gallery, New York and Frith Street Gallery, London

→ p. 250

Time, landscape, change, Surrealism, re-positioning, history and language play a significant role in Tacita Dean's films, photographs, paintings and drawings. Her often multimedia works frequently focus on people or buildings, through which the artist examines the relationship between the past and present. With *Trying to Find the Spiral Jetty*, Dean goes in search of one of the oldest and best-known examples of Land Art, the *Spiral Jetty* by Robert Smithson, a spiral heaped with sand, stones and rocks at the edge of the Great Salt Lake in the Utah desert. Dean's audio work was made 27 years after Smithson's *Spiral Jetty*—when time and natural forces had all but obliterated the artist's interventions, and not just physically. Tacita Dean received detailed directions to the *Spiral Jetty* from the Utah Arts Council, and she and a colleague set off to find it.
Her audio installation consists of recordings from this journey. The two talk continually about the directions they were given; though they are detailed, changes in the landscape have left much open for interpretation. Again and again they stop, ask for street names, walk for a bit and take pictures of the landscape that has captivated them both: 'Maybe it is about getting people to come here, because it is a beautiful place.' It was one of the last sentences said before they turned around and left, without having seen the *Spiral Jetty*. With their dialogue, they take the audience on a road trip that (as is so often the case when travelling) becomes a search for one's own artistic role and position in a landscape of forebears. The experience of the futile search for the *Spiral Jetty* became the point of departure for Dean's latest 35-mm film *JG*, 2013.
Once the work *Trying to Find the Spiral Jetty* became public, an intensive exchange developed between the artist and British essayist and New Wave story author J. G. Ballard (1930–2009), after whom the film is named. In 1960, Ballard wrote the science fiction short story *The Voices of Time*, which ends with a mandala being drawn in a landscape. Demonstrably, Robert Smithson owned a copy of this publication. It was above all the

intersections in Ballard's and Smithson's work—the study of time, change and landscape—that awakened Dean's interest in complex concatenations in history.

– ES (AP) –

→ p. 226

Marine Hugonnier

b. 1969 in Paris (FR), lives in London (UK)
www.marinehugonnier.com

From the series: *Towards Tomorrow*, 2001–03
C-prints on aluminium; each 180 × 300 cm
Courtesy of 49 Nord 6 Est – Frac Lorraine Collection

Towards Tomorrow (International Date Line, Alaska) #1
Sunset over the Bering Strait in Alaska
Towards Tomorrow (International Date Line, Alaska) #2
End of the sunset over the Bering Strait in Alaska

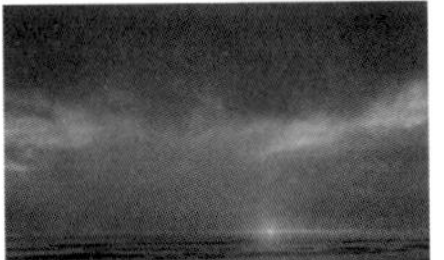

Marine Hugonnier
*Towards Tomorrow
(International Date
Line, Alaska) #1,*
from the series
Towards Tomorrow,
2001-03

Marine Hugonnier's conceptual works often blur the line between documentary and fiction. The artist exposes invisible processes behind obvious or supposed realities, thereby undermining clear definitions. Influenced by her background in philosophy and anthropology, Hugonnier examines the historical, social and cultural legacies of images through the paradigm of representative landscapes.

The two photographs show a romantic, dramatic sunset with a deep, almost endless horizon—a sunset reminiscent of Romantic landscape paintings, where nature is sublimated and removed from reality. Looking at them sets our thoughts in motion, carrying us to far-off horizons. Hugonnier investigates these recurring images as they appear in everyday life, and how they affect us. Her films, photographs, books and installations explore and deconstruct cultural constructions and representational modes.

The series *Towards Tomorrow* was created during Marine Hugonnier's travels to the Bering Strait in Alaska, a strait between the easternmost point of Asia (Siberia) and the westernmost point of mainland America (Alaska). Right there, at the 180th meridian, is the generally accepted International Date Line. Whoever moves from Alaska to Siberia at this location enters a zone with a different calendar date, because according to an international agreement, Siberia is 24 hours ahead of Alaska. The view in the photographs crosses the International Date Line and literally captures a look into the future. This fictional and yet reality-based moment—the ability to see into tomorrow, and capture it photographically—is characteristic of many of Marine Hugonnier's works. *– ES (AP) –*

→ p. 228

Markus Jeschaunig

b. 1982 in Graz (AT), lives in Unterpremstätten near Graz (AT)
www.agencyinbiosphere.com

Barrel You!, 2012
Installation: crude oil, glass, brass, wood, stone; 45 × 45 × 220 cm
Courtesy of the artist (Agency in Biosphere)

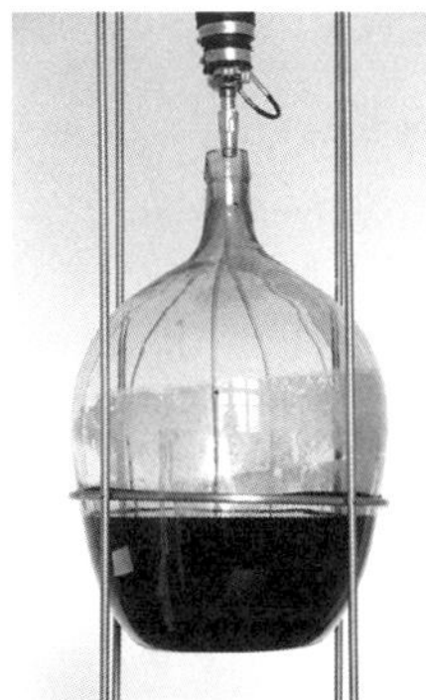
Markus Jeschaunig
Barrel You!, 2012,
exhibition view,
Ogms gallery, Sofia/
Bulgaria, 2014
(detail)

Markus Jeschaunig's artistic material is energy and how it is used. As an artistic visionary he weds in his 'poor' and highly poetic works the conditions of the economy with the logic of ecology. His works deal with geographical and landscape-related themes and are attempts at capturing and measuring spaces, landscapes and resources. The artist describes the work in the following words:
Barrel You! is an installation in the form of a large hourglass that is filled with a resource we never see in its pure form, but which strongly dominates our daily lives: petroleum. Fuel, oil, plastics, medicine, and cosmetics are all fossil products based on petroleum and have become indispensable for our daily lives. For more than 150 years this toxic material has been extracted from the depths of the Earth and has ever since formed the basis for technological progress and for countless products and materials. Today all sectors of the economy, industry and transport depend on petroleum. About 81 % of global energy needs are met by fossil fuels. Yet fossil energy sources are finite. By the end of the 21st century most global petroleum resources may well be exhausted. In the foreseeable future we will have to source our everyday energy needs entirely from renewable energy sources. The installation *Barrel You!* reveals crude oil in its pure form, making it vulnerable and visible in the shape of an hourglass, hinting with every drip at the future and the finite demise of the material. The liquid volume of the upper glass bottle contains two-tenths of a Barrel (1 bbl. = 158.987294928 litres), the international trading unit of mineral oil. The drip interval is matched to the period of the exhibition, allowing around 32 litres of the precious raw material to drip down continuously.' *– KBT (AH) –*

→ p. 230

Mathias Kessler

b. 1968 in Kampten (DE), Austrian citizen, lives in New York, NY (US)
www.mathiaskessler.com

*Jarrells Cemetery, N37°53.96' W81°34.71', Eunice Mountain,
West Virginia*, 2012
From: *Graveyard*
Inkjet print on site-specific wallpaper installation; size variable
Courtesy of the artist and Galerie Heike Strelow

The works of the New York-based Austrian Mathias Kessler are investigations into the historical and current effects of an enduring western, eurocentric fantasy of a natural world: They reveal an understanding of

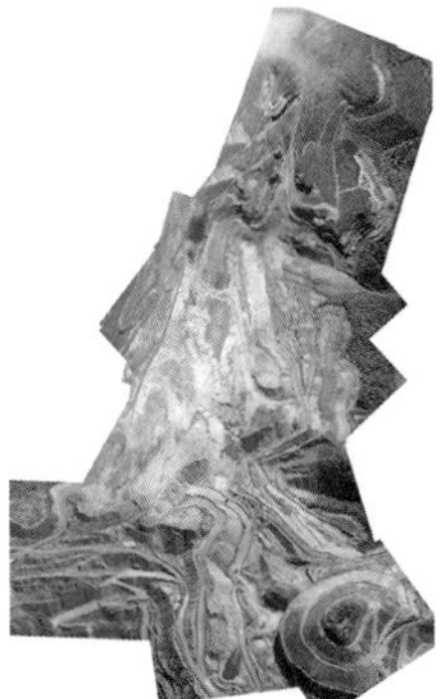

Mathias Kessler
*Jarrells Cemetery,
N37°53.96'
W81°34.71', Eunice
Mountain, West
Virginia*, 2012

nature that derives from this as both a terrifying unknown and a usable resource. In *Jarrells Cemetery, N37°53.96' W81°34.71'. Eunice Mountain. West Virginia* (2012) Kessler focuses on a landscape marked by the ravages of the industrial exploitation of a thriving coal mine in Western Virginia. In the midst of this arises the only evidence of humans, a cemetery—lifeless and utterly abandoned—which forms a tragicomic image of an era of mankind in decline. The artist documented a place that can no longer be found on official maps by using assembled topographical photographs, bringing them back to interior space as wallpaper. *Jarrells Cemetery* thus shows itself as a political focal point and as a metaphor, in which private interest clashes with public interest, and in which the worlds of local, economic and political interests battle with one another. Documented by Kessler in photographs and sound, the story of *Jarrells Cemetery* reveals an emotional—albeit in a sense ironic—loss of a landscape that once existed here and which seems directly connected to the people. Kessler's approach to the concept of landscape deciphers the complex relationship between man and nature in relation to *natura naturans* (self-creating nature) on the one hand and *natura naturata* (created nature) on the other, without him adopting a purely environmentalist approach in the process. Through photography, installation and social sculpture Kessler instead examines the contemporary notion of nature and landscape employing a pictorial language that is borrowed from the genre of romantic landscape as well as that of expedition photography. In his artistic, far-reaching explorations he uses the 'sublime' and 'empirical reason' as opposite poles. He thus sets out to determine the complicated political and economic powers that have so drastically altered the social and natural landscape. Kessler's visually captivating images and their participatory context confront the observer with contemporary fears. They reflect the environment and globalisation, digitalisation and artificial realities, post-industrial decay and natural disasters.   *– KBT (AH) –*

→ p. 232

Armin Linke
b. 1966 in Milan (IT), lives in Milan (IT) and Berlin (DE)
www.arminlinke.com

Whirlwind, Pantelleria, Italy, 2007
C-print on aluminium; 150 × 200 cm
Courtesy of the artist and Galleria Vistamare, Pescara

Armin Linke became known for his multimedia installation *Alpi* about the contemporary Alpine landscape, for which he was distinguished in 2004 at the 9th International Architecture Exhibition in Venice and in 2006 at the 7th Media and Architecture Biennale in Graz. He is currently a professor of photography at the Hochschule für Gestaltung in Karlsruhe.
Armin Linke travels the world as a photographer and film-maker, working on an ever-expanding archive that he describes as a 'photographic atlas of a globalised world'. It is a collection of images showing human life and

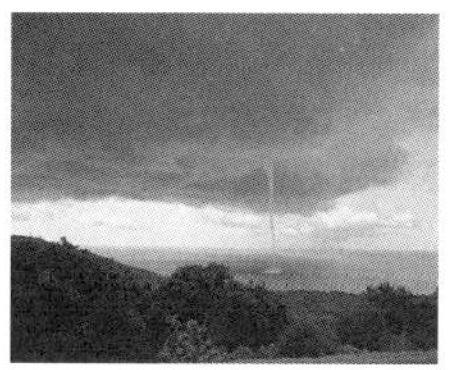

Armin Linke
Whirlwind,
Pantelleria, Italy,
2007

a vast variety of natural and man-made landscapes. The artist gravitates to scenes where the boundaries between fact and fiction blur or become invisible: a flower market at Amsterdam airport, a ski and toboggan slope with alpine scenery in a giant cold store in Dubai, a Bollywood film set in Switzerland or, as we see in *Whirlwind, Pantelleria, Italy*, a cyclone in the Mediterranean off the Sicilian island of Pantelleria.

Linke's artistic method of archiving and of collective, interdisciplinary collaboration makes it possible for him to use the image archive as a kind of set piece, as currently seen in the context of the project #4 *The Dark Abyss of Time: Fourth Episode of the Anthropocene Observatory* at the House of World Cultures in Berlin. In previous exhibitions—such as the 2007 exhibition *Phenotypes / Limited Forms* at Stift Admont—Linke has allowed visitors access to his photographic collection (or part of it) so that they can create a personalised photo travel prospectus. The artist's easily accessible, humorous approach is a testament to his interest in the developing and shaping of landscapes, from 'reality' to a reality in which fiction and absurdity become inherent parameters.   – ES (AP) –

→ p. 234

Lukas Marxt

b. 1983 in Schladming (AT), lives in Cologne (DE), Leipzig (DE), Brussels (BE) and Graz (AT)
www.lukasmarxt.com

Captive Horizon, 2014
Video installation: HD video, colour, sound; 14:12 min
Frottages on aluminium; dimensions variable
Courtesy of the artist

Landscape is the medium and the material with which the Styria-born Lukas Marxt effects his filmic investigation into the perception of time. Time and again, isolated, eternal-seeming landscapes function in his work as filmic measurers of space and time. As commentaries on a perception shaped by images, they superimpose themselves over inner pictures of the landscape like transparent film, living from a surreal chargedness of minimalistic emptiness. *Captive Horizon* shows views of Lanzarote from a bird's-eye view. Human traces are largely blanked out, the landscape becoming the protagonist of an entropic course of the world. Marxt works with fascination for a mysterious, autonomous nature, in which humankind has shifted into the role of the examining observer. With award-winning films such as *Reign of Silence* (2013) and *Nella Fantasia* (2012), the camera's eye in search of insight focuses on water as the carrier of information and poses questions about the reality and aura of panoramic cinema images.

In the installation *Captive Horizon*, as in the trailer for the Diagonale 2015 which was created parallel to it, he devotes himself for the third time—after the film *It seems to be loneliness, but it is not* (2013) and the artist's book of the same name—to the inhospitable lunar landscape of Lanzarote. From the bird's-eye perspective a camera moves over surface structures which cannot always be matched with particular

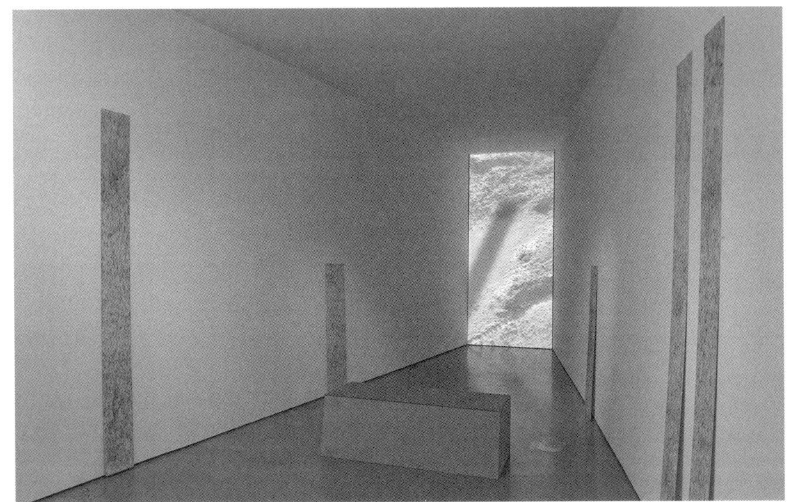

micro- or macro-structures. As with Robert Smithson, the sound of a helicopter can be heard occasionally, which merges into the roar of the water, opening thereby a narrative of landscape that evokes technologically shaped, apocalyptic visions and revealing an indecipherable, inner connection between human technology and natural evolution. Marxt films the surreal landscape with a drone, measuring it and squeezing the resulting six-part film into a spatial corset, which adds another layer of alienation to the chargedness of the puzzling structures. In the elongated high format, the constantly shifting surface images are pushed as dazzling views into the tapering, clinically white exhibition space, evoking associations of scientific, enlarged picture-worlds, which alternate with the structures of a psycho-diagnostic Rorschach test or of sci-fi visions such as Andrei Tarkovsky's *Solaris*, for example. When entering the cramping and at the same time glittering room, a strange unsettled feeling dominates one's own sense of spatialisation. The suction effect of the room and the developing film superimposes itself on this feeling, however, and together with the frottages of Lanzarote's ground, the public is then—quite literally—located and grounded.   *– KBT (AH) –*

→ p. 236

David Nez

b. 1949 in Massachusetts (US), lives in Portland, OR (US)

*Project – a heater warms the thermometer on the wall,
Novi Sad*, 1969
Installation: Heater, thermometer; dimensions variable
Courtesy of the artist and the Marinko Sudac Collection

David Nez was born in Massachusetts (USA) in 1949 and is of Croatian origin. He had already spent time in Yugoslavia as a teenager when his father was involved in reconstruction work as an engineer after the great

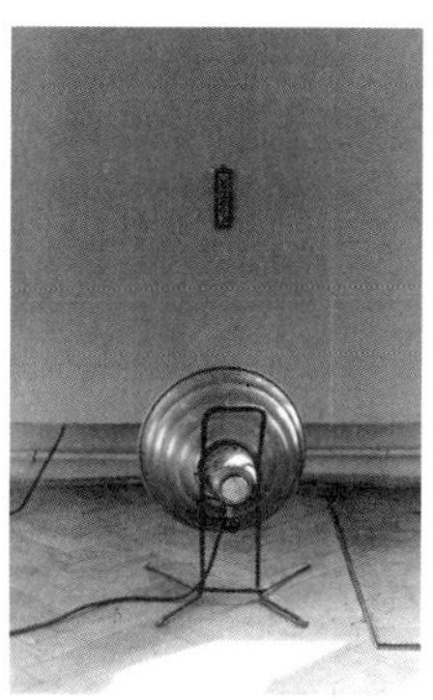

David Nez
*Project – a heater
warms the
thermometer on the
wall, Novi Sad,* 1969,
exhibition view,
Moderna galerija
Ljubljana, 1969

earthquake in Macedonia (1963). As a student he was interested in the state's political conditions and returned to Ljubljana. There he studied at the Academy of Fine Arts, becoming a member of the Actionist group *OHO* in 1968. Committed to the ideas of the Fluxus movement and Arte Povera, he took part in joint exhibitions, organised Happenings, photo and film projects, along with constant actions in public space. At first he designed pictorial objects bound to Hard Edge painting, then increasingly made installations that extended the pictorial space and which, especially since the 'Summer Projects' of the OHO group in 1969—parallel to the development of Land Art in America—penetrated into landscape space.

For example, David Nez produced—inspired by Smithson's *Mirror Displacements* from 1969—in the same year a work of mirror installations in the landscape. In them, landscape became an accessible environment for expanding one's consciousness as well as a fractal structure in photography, which identifies the three-dimensional in continuous movement between the positive and negative form. Later on, Nez worked primarily with process-driven works, in which time and place—as well as their mutual conditionality and dependence—were pushed to the foreground of the engagement.

Also stemming from this period is *Project – a heater warms the thermometer on the wall, Novi Sad*, which he showed in an exhibition of the OHO group in the Moderna galerija in Ljubljana in 1969. The work, which has been reconstructed for the first time for the exhibition *Landscape in Motion*, turns man's environment into a metaphorical body, which we change with technological developments. The world, moved here into a self-constructed fever, shows Nez as a visionary artist, who recognises the environment in the sense of an emerging ecological awareness and a connection that is implanted in all things. Using the vocabulary of Concept Art he transfers the extended concept of sculpture on to the materiality of the institutional, political as well as organic structure. Nez, from 1970 onwards a member of the *Šempas Family*, an artists' commune that arose from the OHO group, thus turned his life into his artistic and sculptural work. Works that established a link between technical, industrial material and the natural, and then in turn formed a special, also spiritually charged cosmology of an art that is in a certain sense conciliatory, became pioneering for the group. After graduating in 1972 Nez left Yugoslavia and the group and returned to America where, beyond his sculptural and performative works, he has been reworking an interest in esoteric spirituality—also as a writer—that he has fostered since the times of OHO. In 2015 he will publish a self-illustrated book on the historical roots of western esotericism.   *– KBT (AH) –*

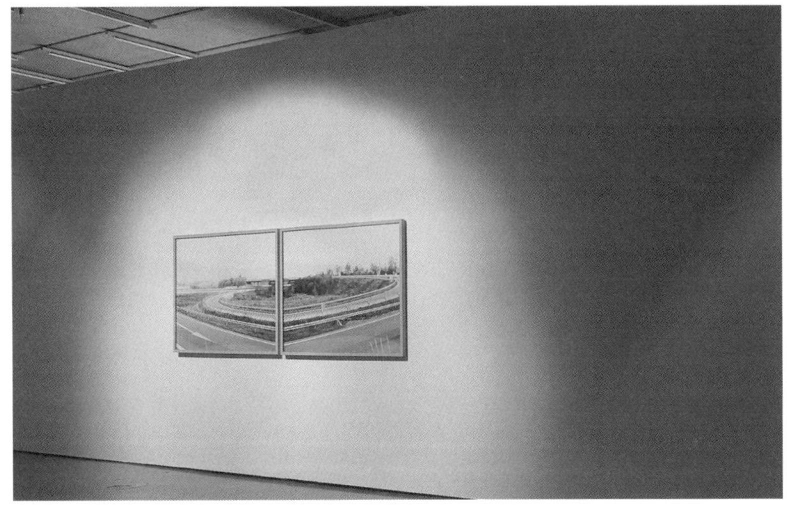

Walter Niedermayr
Seiersberg I, 1997,
exhibition view,
Kunsthaus Graz,
2015

→ p. 238

Walter Niedermayr
b. 1952 in Bolzano (IT), lives in Bolzano (IT)

From the series: *Artefakte*
C-prints, 2 parts; each 103 × 129.5 cm
Courtesy of the Grazer Kunstverein Collection

Seiersberg I, 1997

'I'm interested in places where humankind appears in the landscape,' says photographer Walter Niedermayr, in an interview discussing his photographs of alpine landscapes, architecture and infrastructure—a series for which he has been well-known in the German-speaking world since the 1990s.
Seiersberg I (1997) shows the Seiersberg exit from the Pyhrn highway A9 from two different perspectives. Since 2002, Seiersberg—a suburb of the Styrian provincial capital approximately two kilometres south of Graz—has been home to the third-largest shopping mall in Austria. The diptych belongs to the series *Artefakte* [Artifacts], which Niedermayr began in 1992: urban landscapes, overpasses, highway bridges, intersections and junctions are evidence of human activity in landscapes, yet the interventions also take on a life of their own, independent of human beings.
Through repetition in diptychs and the simultaneous shift in perspective, he successfully challenges the power of the unique image and perspective. The levelling of the depicted spaces is made more pronounced by the lightness that is typical of his work: what looks like overexposure is actually an underexposure of the negative. The effect is a flattening and unification of the picture surface. Though Niedermayr's images resonate with a certain critique of mediated reality, he sees himself as someone who captures spaces, landscapes and facts as they appear in motion:

'It's only by moving, moving through the space that a possible implementation occurs to me. I once read a quote about how movement creates a spatialisation, an extension of the space. This experience also comes from working with landscape; you have to move in it and then find the right spot for yourself. At the same time, you subconsciously work out other things, which can be used again in another context of movement.'[4]

– ES (AP) –

→ p. 240

Qiu Anxiong

b. 1972 in Sichuan (CN), lives in Shanghai (CN)

Minguo Landscape, 2007
Video animation, b/w, sound; 14:33 min
Courtesy of the artist

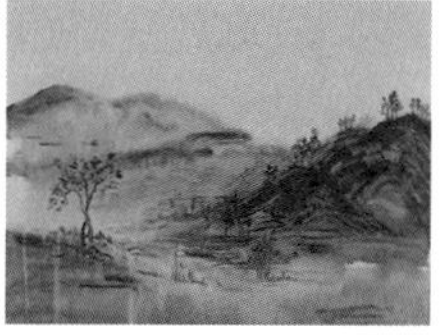

Qiu Anxiong
Minguo Landscape,
2007, video still

Qiu Anxiong, who lives in Shanghai, speaks in his melancholy animation *Minguo Landscape* of a long-since vanished era of deep-reaching changes in China over the past century. *Minguo* describes the eventful, often forgotten past or equally frequently idealised period of the Republic of China from 1912 to 1949, which concluded with the end of the Civil War and the assumption of power by Mao Zedong. The Japanese invasion, the Civil War and the beginning of Communism are taken up in a melancholy series of pictures and sounds, which absorb the style of traditional Chinese ink drawings and which are connected with what is surely the most popular musical piece from the Minguo period—the song *The Age of Bloom (Hua Yang De Nianhua)* by the singer and actress Zhou Xuan—in the most unsettling way. The combination turns into a strangely alienating, vortex-seeming portrait of a dystopian, constantly changing landscape of forbearance. With almost dreamy lyricism and subtly expressed criticism, Qiu describes the social advances made in China—which according to the official Chinese history narrative has liberated 600 million people from poverty—as a destructive and far-reaching change in the environment and society.

Educated at the Sichuan Academy of Fine Arts in Chongqing and the University of Art in Kassel, the painter Qiu Anxiong is known for his filmic and installation-like animations. Since his return in 2004 to Shanghai—where he also holds the position of Professor at the Normal University—he has designed them as a link between Chinese and western traditions and as a reflexion embedded within them on the different modernities. An example would be his stop motion films, which distantly recall William Kentridge: not small-format ink drawings, rather a sequence of numerous large-format canvas paintings in oil. So the images of his films fill half a studio, with every frame an independent work and a physically worked object. His portrayed figures are equally autonomous, sometimes growing from the screen and film into elaborate sound or synthetic-resin sculptures. They thus quote productions of popular animated film culture on the one hand, and are also manifestations of his concept of evolution on the other, a concept shaped by a blend of fictive

4
Walter Niedermayr
in an interview with
Andrea Domesle, *Eikon*
Sonderdruck #7, 2001.

archaeology, visionary science fiction, and elements both Buddhist-Confucian and poetic-literary. His works, which revolve around the thematic group of history, remembrance and memory, chart the course of the world as a recurring epoch, in which the Chinese tanks of the Cultural Revolution turn into dinosaurs, for instance, or peasants repeatedly climb hills with their burdens, Sisyphus-like. It is an image of the world bound to a Buddhist conception of reincarnation and a striving for the next stage of development, and in which criticism of our thoughtlessness in how we treat the Earth plays a vital role, committed to his own suppressed or forgotten culture.

– KBT (AH) –

→ p. 242

Ed Ruscha

b. 1937 in Omaha, NE (US), lives n Culver City, CA (US)

Every Building on the Sunset Strip, 1966
Leporello photo book; 17.8 × 760.7 cm
Courtesy of SAMMLUNG VERBUND, Vienna

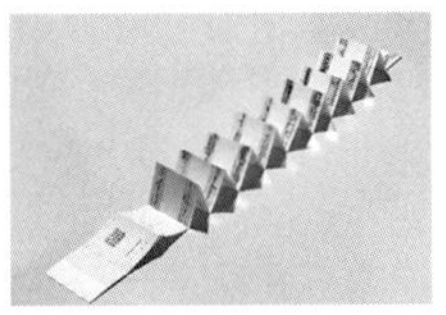

Ed Ruscha
*Every Building on
the Sunset Strip,*
1966

Every Building on the Sunset Strip, which Ed Ruscha conceived as a more than 7-metre-long foldout that already resembles a real estate agent's prospectus on account of its format, was printed in an edition of 1000 copies. It continues a series of typological photographs around the iconography of the American city. The shots are cool and documentary. The artist negates image structure and composition, denying the pictures any artistic ambition whatsoever. Ruscha's *Sunset Strip* shows all of the buildings on both sides of the street, each carefully numbered, but without comment. This lack of emotion is compounded by the fact Ruscha himself did not operate the camera. It was mounted to the back of his moving pick-up truck; the film in this 35-mm camera was advanced automatically, the subjective eye switched off in favour of mechanical objectivity.[5]

– KH (AP) –

→ p. 244

Klaus Schafler

b. 1966 in Graz (AT), lives in Vienna (AT)
www.schafler.net

Sandbank, 2015
Installation: Wood, Alu-Dibond, concrete, sand sacks; dimensions variable
Courtesy of the artist

The interdisciplinary works of Styrian-born Klaus Schafler have a situational character. For many years his performative, socially cultural and critical interventions have revolved around the usage, exploitation and abuse of the planet in the sense of public property. Climatic changes and threats are the central field of the investigation in his artistic formulations, which find expression in illustrative, pseudo-laboratory situations.

[5]
Excerpt; the complete
text on Ed Ruscha is to
be found on p. 49.

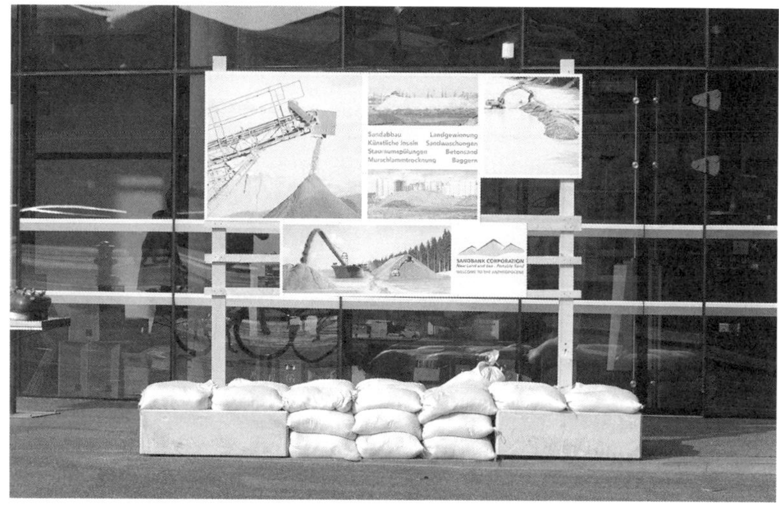

Klaus Schafler
Sandbank, 2015,
exhibition view,
Kunsthaus Graz,
2015

Ecological, political or technical decisions are carefully formulated for this as film, installation or performance right to their conclusion or up to their visible effect: erroneous forecasts and social realities and codes are unmasked in this way as well as confirmed occasionally in their simple logic.

In its dialogue with various researchers his long-term research project *2050*—named after the year forecast as the point of fundamental climate change—is devoted to the debate concerning worldwide weather and climate manipulation as well as the various aspects of this debate about a market-dependent living environment in the radically different Anthropocene era.

With the installation *Sandbank*, Schafler created an intervention for the Kunsthaus Graz that consists of an information sign and a found footage film without any commentary. The work parks itself in front of the entrance to the Kunsthaus in the form of an ironic 'welcome to the Anthropocene'. As a semi-fictitious advertising sign for the 'Sandbank Corporation', the installation advertises a company of global sand consumption. In the city and in front of the technological-looking Kunsthaus architecture, this interactive work is a call—ironically meant, too—for awareness of a little known resource, which is however only available in limited amounts and fought over, and of enormous importance globally: sand. Weathered rock, which is present all over the earth's surface, a small, mobile, geological carrier of information, driven forward by water, rivers, wind, erosion and increasingly by human and technological interventions too, modified, excavated and then piled up again at another place in the service of reclaiming and expanding the land appropriated for geo-political claims to power, such as the infamous 'Spratly Islands' in the South China Sea. Sand is disappearing in the controversial process of fracking, in which it is pumped together with chemicals into deep layers of rock and used to extract oil, or in the course of sand change, too, whereby in the case of hydropower plants it is removed to improve the flow-speed of water, so that hardly any river transports sand—immensely important for ecological balance—to the sea without obstacles. Sand is also used for the production of glass and microchips, but mainly of cement and concrete—annually an estimated two tons of sand per global inhabitant are processed, which when projected adds up to 15 billion tons.

The *Sandbank* project takes these perceptions and connections as its theme with the help of the fictitious 'Sandbank Corporation', a company that moves sand globally, which points out the conditions and problems of the current geological era of the Anthropocene through performative shows by the artist in situ also, and thus represents a call to become a responsible part of the system as well as—subversively—to return sand to the rivers and to the gearing mechanisms of sand logic.

SANDBANK CORPORATION
New Land and Sea – Portable Sand
WELCOME TO THE ANTHROPOCENE   *– KBT (AH) –*

→ p. 246

Allan Sekula

b. 1951 in Erie, PA, (US), † 2013 in Los Angeles, CA (US)

From: *California Stories*, 1973–77
Gelatin silver prints, printed paper on tableau; each 91.4 × 180 cm
Courtesy of Ludwig Museum – Museum of Contemporary Art, Budapest

Cliffhanger, San Pedro, July 1975, 1975/2011
Vietnam Village, San Pedro, July 1975, 1975/2011

In *Vietnam Village, San Pedro, July 1975* and *Cliffhanger, San Pedro, July 1975*, the theme of immigration plays a central role: one element common to all the photographs is the fence, which delineates a landscape in which a refugee camp for Vietnamese immigrants is to be found, with those in the camp going through a six-month programme of naturalisation. Reality that is constructed over conventions; decisions made over and above landscape and people; the process of making pictures: all these are measured and rendered visible in Sekula's photographs. Both works can be understood as conceptual road trip photographs: like an artistic storyboard, they are films cut up into single pictures, loosely arranged on a tableau and partially expanded with text. The photographs were created in California in the 1970s already, almost at the same time as Sekula's early and now well-known photographs of the working class (*Untitled Slide Sequence*, 1972). Both photo series—the *California Stories* has only been on show in exhibitions since 2011—draw one's attention to the relationship between pictorial and textual language, conveying his thinking: landscape as space that has been inhabited and altered by man and which is per se 'social topography which is unavoidably a place of class struggle, of land appropriation, of oppression and power'. With these words Allan Sekula adopts an alternative position towards

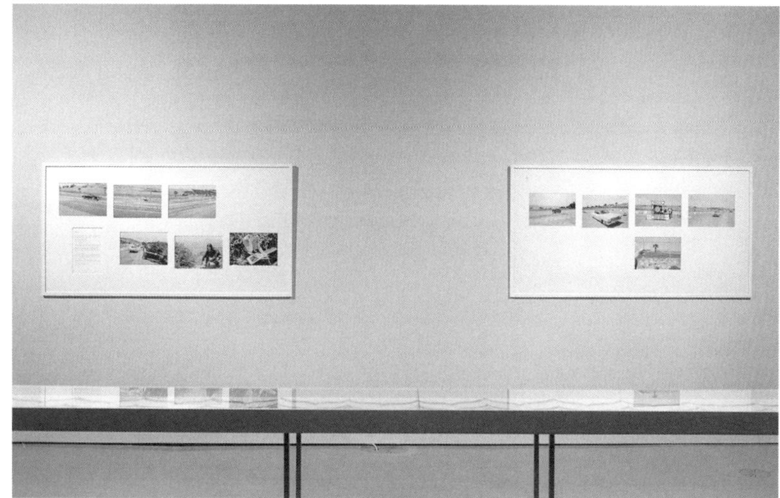

the 'New Topographics'—a photographic movement in the 1970s in the United States who attempted a neutral reproduction of man-made structures within larger contexts such as landscapes.

In his conceptual works as a photographer, writer and film maker, Allan Sekula reflects on the strategies of representation, speaking and writing. Adopting a purist aesthetic, he questions the function of documentary photography as well as generally the political status of pictures in the media, art and society. His early works are particularly concerned with socially manifested roles—especially in the workers' milieu from which he himself comes—and with the consequences of material systems and economic changes as a result of globalisation. Despite his early death he left behind artistic and theoretical work that has achieved worldwide recognition. For nearly 30 years Sekula taught photography and media art at the California Institute of the Arts in Los Angeles.   *– ES (AH) –*

→ p. 248

Shi Guorui
b. 1964 in Shanxi (CN), lives in Beijing (CN)

Himalayas: The Mount Everest 8843.43, 20 January 2006, 2006
Gelatin silver on Alu-Dibond, 2 parts; in total 129 × 790 cm
Courtesy of the M+ Sigg Collection, Hong Kong (gift)

This monumental, almost 8-metre-long photograph was taken in the Himalayas as a long-exposure photograph on photosensitive paper. Mount Everest, the highest mountain in the world, inscribes itself directly into the material, so that it can be approached on foot and (almost) physically experienced. For this project, Shi Guorui built a camera obscura at an altitude of 5,200 metres on a mountain near Mount Everest: a completely darkened room into which the sunlight could penetrate only through a small hole. Light through the 1.6 mm opening

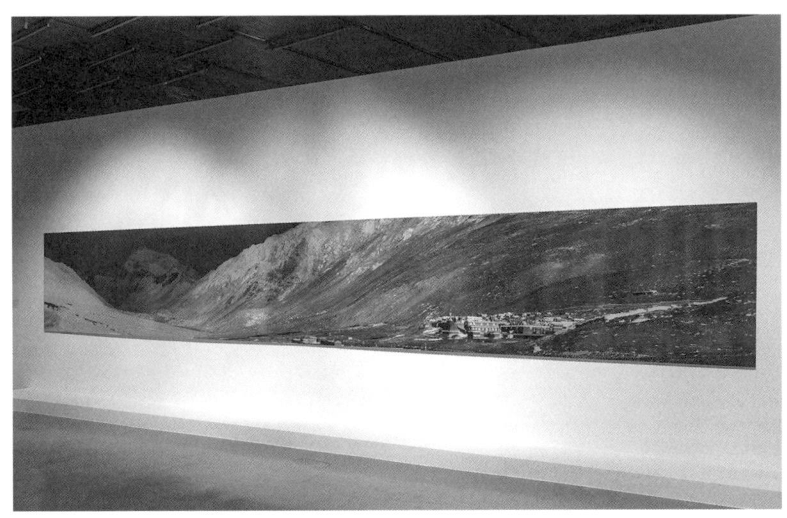

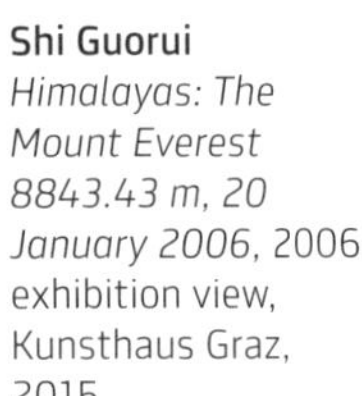

created a laterally reversed, upside-down projection on the opposite wall, which the photographer captured on silver gelatin. Shi Guorui persisted for hours during numerous expeditions into the mountains and under extreme weather conditions (the average exposure time was around eight hours) to capture the ideal image of the mountain.

Shi Guorui has been experimenting with the camera obscura since 2000: all of the places he has captured so far are iconic and reflect analyses of Chinese history, including the Great Wall of China and views of the Shanghai cityscape, which show a contrast between old colonial (The Bund or Waitan) and new China (Pudong). Mount Everest has an almost magical status both within China and around the world; for many climbers, its remoteness stands for the ultimate challenge. Shi Guorui's photograph conveys a surreal impression of this fabled mountain: any motion or activity becomes invisible, the subject is stripped to the essentials. The landscape is a place unto itself, shown in enormous detail and impressive depth. For Shi Guorui, the process of creation is as important as the final photograph; the long exposure time means that rapidly moving objects become invisible, making this a spiritual and meditative act. The waiting and watching is also something Shi Guorui asks of his viewers: 'In China, we believe that only a thorough examination of this world can ever lead to a deeper understanding of the image. Those who do not do this only ever see the surface.'   *– ES (AP) –*

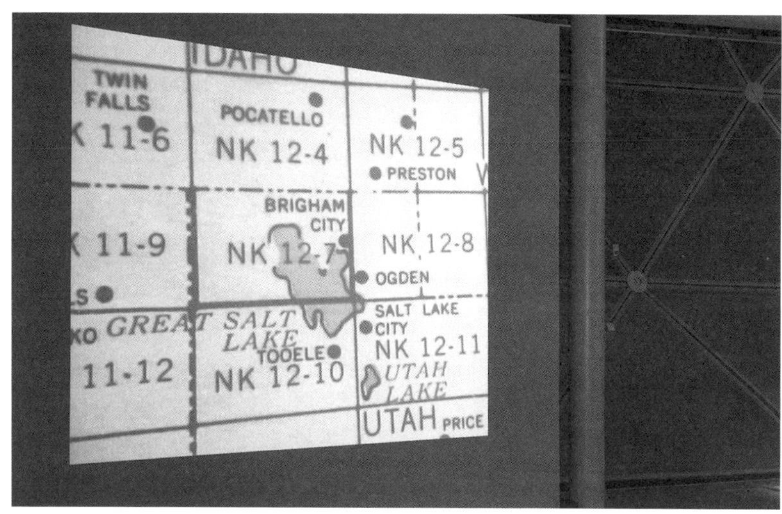

Robert Smithson
Spiral Jetty, 1970,
exhibition view,
Kunsthaus Graz,
2015

→ p. 250

Robert Smithson

b. 1938 in Passaic, NJ (US), † 1973 in Amarillo, TX (US)

Spiral Jetty, 1970
Camera: Robert Fiore, Nancy Holt, Robert Logan, Robert Smithson
16 mm film, transferred to digital medium, colour, sound; 35 min
Courtesy of Robert Smithson Foundation, James Cohan Gallery,
New York / Shanghai and Electronic Arts Intermix (EAI), New York

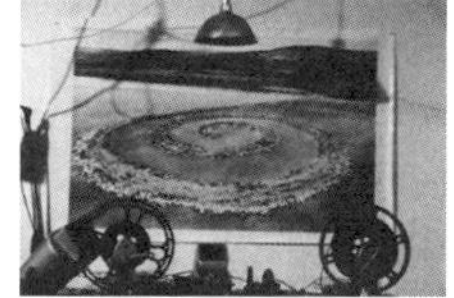

Robert Smithson
Spiral Jetty, 1970,
film still

Robert Smithson is considered a visionary among artists of the late 1960s, his works with and in landscape seminal for the development of Land Art. Crucial to this were the perspective from above, flying over areas and the accompanying apocalyptic visions. *Spiral Jetty*, 1970, in the Great Salt Lake of Utah is seen as one of his main works. 6000 tons of basalt rock boulders lay out a spiral-shaped jetty that is 460 metres long and five metres wide, an aesthetic pattern in the salt lake.

Following extensive logistical preparations, the giant volcanic rocks were placed in the lake over a period of three months consuming 625 man hours, and captured by Robert Fiore, the film-maker who transferred Smithson and Nancy Holt's works into the medium of film.

Fiore, who entered film history with the documentary *Pumping Iron* (1977, with the young Arnold Schwarzenegger), chose shots from the air which observed the artist walking joyously along the finished jetty, thus demonstrating the scale of a human compared to the sculpture placed in the landscape. Smithson's voice in the film accompanies the event in which monstrous excavators shove the basalt boulders weighing tons into the lake as prehistoric rocks and into the form of the spiral. And time and again it is the permanent rise and fall of the water that shapes the experimental film. Smithson chose a place in the desert with which the oil industry was already finished, yet its traces had been left behind in the form of rubble and industrial waste. His interest in this work lay in the dichotomy between nature and culture, which were balanced out in the entropy. The influence of industry and technology on the landscape played a key role in his finding a form, as did nature, too: salt crystals grow in a spiral-shaped net.

Robert Smithson, who died in a plane crash in 1973, created works which take as their theme temporal changes in landscapes, drawing on their own transience. The created work needs to be experienced in the landscape and in time itself: it requires movement through the landscape, the changed water levels and prevailing weather conditions. Land Art thereby completed a liberating step (especially in the USA) away from the exhibition spaces with their prescribed conditions and out into the multi-dimensionality of the landscape.

In the case of Smithson, documentary film and programmatic essays such as *The Monuments of Passaic* (1967)[6] are part of his sculptural work. They enable the survival and reception of the work in the context of art, far away from the giant jetty in the salt lake, whose visibility depends on the natural conditions concerned. On the other hand they point to the dependence of all seeing on the written word. '"Nature" is simply another 18th- and 19th-century fiction,' said Robert Smithson, thus emphasising his reservations concerning a positive ideology of progress and its irreversible changes.

For him the *Spiral Jetty* is a return to our origins in the midst of the industrial ruins of a modern-prehistorical world, and a vision of the endlessly repeating entropic structure of all becoming. Through Smithson's work the abandoned place was lent a new attractiveness, drawing tourists and other curious onlookers, inspiring artists such as James Benning or Tacita Dean, and is regarded by an entire generation of followers as an icon of a fundamentally altered view of the landscape, in which everything is included—industrial ruins, too. *– KBT, MHK (AH) –*

→ p. 252

Michael Snow
b. 1929 in Toronto (CA), lives in Toronto (CA)

La Région Centrale, 1971
16 mm film transferred to digital media, colour, sound; 180 min
Courtesy of the artist and Jack Shainman Gallery, New York

Known above all for his avant-garde films, the Canadian painter, sculptor and experimental film-maker Michael Snow made his most spectacular and at the same time most ambitious composed and constructed film in 1971, which was to lead the way for directors such as Stanley Kubrick. His three-hour epic, set to a bizarre soundtrack consisting of repetitive electro-acoustical signals, shows a revolving continuum of a landscape, a sky and geological formations that resembles photos of the moon and show the earth permanently rotating.

For *La Région Centrale* (1971) Michael Snow mounted a camera firmly anchored in the midst of the isolated mountain peak of Quebec. He had the camera rotate in all directions over a period of five days, with only

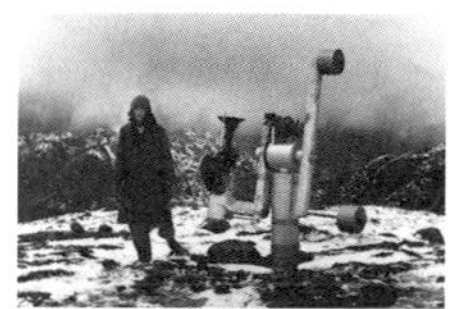

Michael Snow
La Région Centrale,
1971, production
study

the speed of the camera movements preset and accelerating over time. *La Région Centrale* shows the landscape at a real place, whereby the (picture) view frame concerned seems to wander randomly with the eye of the camera. While the film is removed from being documentary on account of the unusual picture movement, it nonetheless reflects in a fully authentic way the rugged mountainous world in its cosmic abandonment through the isolation of its location.

Given the background of the 1969 moon landing and the view of the rotating earth from outer space, this film must also be read as a commentary on our own finiteness. Yet at the same time it reflects the social climate of a hope, ignited by technological developments, of another life beyond our planet. Snow speaks of how he planned a filmic manifesto with *La Région Centrale*, which tells of a changing planet as a legacy and a message to alien life. His structural landscape portrait is arranged and organised using highly developed technology, and thus defined in terms of media technology. With *La Région Centrale Snow* succeeded in producing moving images that no human eye could have imagined until then, and through the multitude of shifting axes and accelerations, in enabling us to experience the sheer infinity of a perspective that encompasses 360°.

– KBT (AH) –

→ p. 254

Guido van der Werve

b. 1977 in Papendrecht (NL), lives in Hassi (FI), Berlin (DE) and Amsterdam (NL)
www.roofvogel.org

Nummer acht, everything is going to be alright,
Golf of Bothnia FI, 2007
16 mm film transferred to digital media, colour, sound; 10:10 min
Courtesy of the artist and Monitor Gallery Rome, Gallery Juliette Jongma Amsterdam, Marc Foxx Los Angeles, Luhring Augustine, New York

Film recordings made in the Gulf of Bothnia in Finland show the artist as he seems to walk just a few steps away from an icebreaker—it was actually just 10-12 metres away—as it pushes its way through the gulf. The ship is fast on his heels as he approaches the position of the camera or the viewer. The heroic icebreaker's approach is reinforced by the increasingly loud sounds of breaking ice. The film *Nummer acht* can be considered an interpretation of the painting *Das Eismeer* [The Sea of Ice], 1823/24 by Caspar David Friedrich, a leading proponent of 19th-century Romantic landscape painting. As is characteristic for Van der Werve, he sarcastically undermines Romantic landscape painting in that, unlike Caspar David Friedrich (in whose paintings the ship is sinking), the force of nature is not destroying man. Instead it is the human being—embodied by the artist—who shows the boat the way, leaving a path of destruction in the frozen landscape. There are two moments in this observation: first, the human being is marching ahead of the ship with the conviction that everything will be all right, as it says in the title of the work. On the

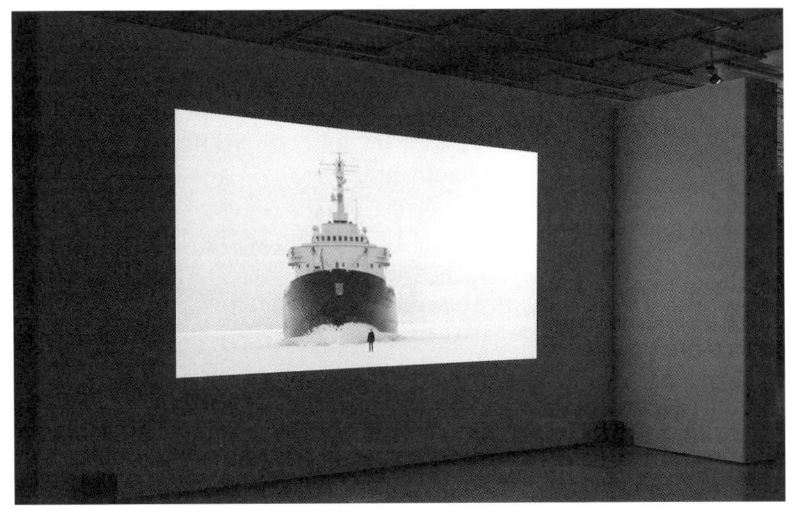

Guido van der Werve
Nummer acht,
everything is going
to be alright, Golf of
Bothnia FI, 2007
exhibition view,
Kunsthaus Graz,
2015

other hand, the ship—a technical achievement of humankind—becomes an immediate threat to both man and nature.
The Dutch artist works with the media of film, photography and performance, also composing music, which generally plays a large role in his work. Van der Werve appreciates music's directness and ability to immediately communicate emotions that reach every recipient—an effect he also employs as a visual artist. Since 2003, the artist has created 11 short films and has prefixed each title with a number similar to the way in which musical compositions are numbered, without forming a contiguous series. The film *Nummer acht* brings together a number of recurring themes in Guido van der Werve's oeuvre: physical endurance, man's struggle with nature, interfaces between history and geography, melancholy and loneliness.   *– ES (AP) –*

Disputed Landscape
Estelle Blaschke, Reinhard Braun

The Visual Paradigm
Conception of Landscape

Photographs of landscapes appear, in the history of the medium, as a highly fragmentary genre that eludes clear definition. Talbot's idea of *The Pencil of Nature*,[1] of photography as a utensil for 'writing nature' and the quasi-automatic origination of an image through exposure to light, signifies the immanent relationship between photography and the representation of space and landscape, in terms of both aesthetics and geography. Accordingly, numerous picturesque views of landscapes, inspired by painting, can be found in Talbot's work and in that of his French contemporaries, such as Gustave Le Gray, Henri Le Secq and Hippolyte Bayard, originating around 1850.

The interest of photographers was soon trained on other subjects. As an invention of the industrial age, photography was always particularly concerned with representing the opposite of nature. It proved to be the perfect medium for visual chroniclers and flâneurs, who in the photographic image preserved the urban activity and the continual changes playing out in transitioning cities from the mid-19th century onwards. According to Susan Sontag, the photographer is 'an armed version of the solitary walker reconnoitering, stalking, cruising the urban inferno, the voyeuristic stroller who discovers the city as a landscape of voluptuous extremes'.[2] If one of the essential features of photography is its inherent link to and fixation of time, then photographs of nature and landscape appear to entirely elude this noêma. Hiroshi Sugimoto's spherical landscape allegories called *Seascapes* (as of 1980) illustrate this in an exemplary way. The rendered view existed before it was photographed, and it will continue to exist long after. Rather than quality being drawn from the ephemeral moment, potential constellations, or 'voluptuous extremes', a sustained tranquillity is contained within depictions of nature and landscapes. They suggest timelessness.

1
William Henry Fox Talbot: *The Pencil of Nature*, 1844–46. www.gutenberg.org/files/33447/33447-pdf (18.02.2015).

2
Susan Sontag: *On Photography*. London 2002, p. 55.

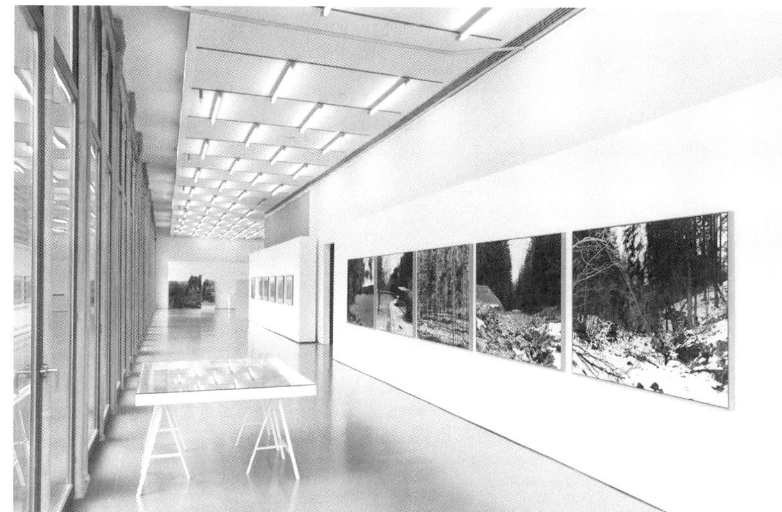

The history of landscape photography is a fragmentary history because it is particularly localisable in those areas long excluded from the museum context: tourist imagery, commercially available stereographs, and landscape photographs taken on research trips to attain measurable or scientifically utilisable data. In the 1980s, Rosalind Krauss specifically criticised the decontextualisation of Timothy O'Sullivan's photographs, which had been taken within the scope of state-funded geological expeditions into the American West during the 1860s and 1870s, due to the related musealisation of his work. In the eyes of Krauss, the intention and function of these pictures—a visual surveying that served the ends of territorial annexation and exercise of control—were invalidated by this museum-based presentation and positioning within aesthetic discourse, and the meaning of the images was distorted.[3]

This criticism is echoed in the work *Through Historic Hole in the Rock Mormons Blasted a Path to Their Promised Land* (2011) by Christian Mayer, inspired by the enlarged black-and-white photograph from a *National Geographic* article published in 1949 about the blasting of the Hole-In-The-Rock gorge along the Colorado River, undertaken by Mormon settlers on their way to Utah. These photographic images, now printed in large format and captioned with the original titles, show the penetration of the gorge and also a few cowboys who are once again conquering the land, this time in a motorised way.[4] Mayer printed the enlargements of the magazine pages on honeycomb panels made of medium-density fibreboard, forming a free-standing, pop-up-like mountain range in the exhibition space. With this panel and three others, the artist moves beyond a mere thematisation of the topos of the 'great American landscape' and the canon of early American landscape photographs like those of Timothy O'Sullivan and William Henry Jackson and their formal aesthetics, which recur in this re-enactment

3
Rosalind Krauss:
'Photography's
Discursive Spaces:
Landscape/View', in:
Art Journal, 42, no. 4
(Winter 1982), pp. 313ff.

4
Jack Breed: 'First Motor
Sortie into Escalante
Land', in: *National
Geographic Magazine*,
96, no. 3 (September
1949), pp. 369–404.

of the photo reportage. Mayer's installation likewise references the history of technology and the exhibition strategies employed in presenting the medium of photography. Indeed, at the time, this *National Geographic* series basically equated to blatant advertising for Kodachrome colour film, which started being commercialised for the masses in the late 1940s. The image spread was printed in full colour and the accompanying caption heralded the landscape as a paradise for any photographer: 'The few natives,' said the photographer of the series, 'called this area Thorny Pasture. But we renamed it Kodachrome Flat, because of the astonishing variety of contrasting colors in the formations.'[5] Moreover, Mayer's installation—situated between the magazine form and a state of objectness—is reminiscent of the display strategies of American propaganda exhibitions, especially Edward Steichen's MoMA show *Road to Victory* mounted in 1942. To cite Krauss's line of argumentation, (landscape) photography all too frequently masks the intention of its makers, having been (and still being) an instrument for appropriation and for exercising power. There is hardly another genre where the illusion of space engendered by the apparatus and the material planarity of the photograph collide as strongly as in landscape photography.

Such shifting between spaces of illusion and surfaces is taken further in Ricarda Roggan's series *natura nova, Sedimente* (2008/10). The artist contrasts the far-reaching view of landscape, which is an important element in many painted or photographed landscape portrayals, with a wall made of stone and gravel. The constellation of sediments and porous layers makes it almost impossible to determine the positioning of the beholder and the actual vantage point: there is no up, no down, no beginning, and no end. Through continual observation, selection of detail view, and intervention into the given state, Roggan succeeds in photographing the sedimentary deposits in such a way that they advance from an incidental state to a dramatic-seeming system of forms and monochromatic colour nuances. One appears to be taken forward or backward in time to a place where nature leads an independent existence irrespective of human life. With *natura nova, Sedimente*, Roggan appears to be clearly contradicting the idea that nature is shaped and dominated by humans, and also the concept of an Anthropocene period, as present in photography since the groundbreaking exhibition *New Topographics: Photographs of a Man-altered Landscape* in 1975. Accordingly, one interpretative approach to Roggan's work implies that not only the conventions of representing the genre are challenged, but also the existing perspectives of nature that were first made possible by the photographic apparatus.

It also becomes evident how little the documentary character of landscape photography is fundamentally questioned, despite it having always provided only dubious or imprecise data, when examining the work of the artist Stephanie Kiwitt and the artist duo Nicole Six & Paul Petritsch. Kiwitt's close-up shots of an industrial area and wasteland

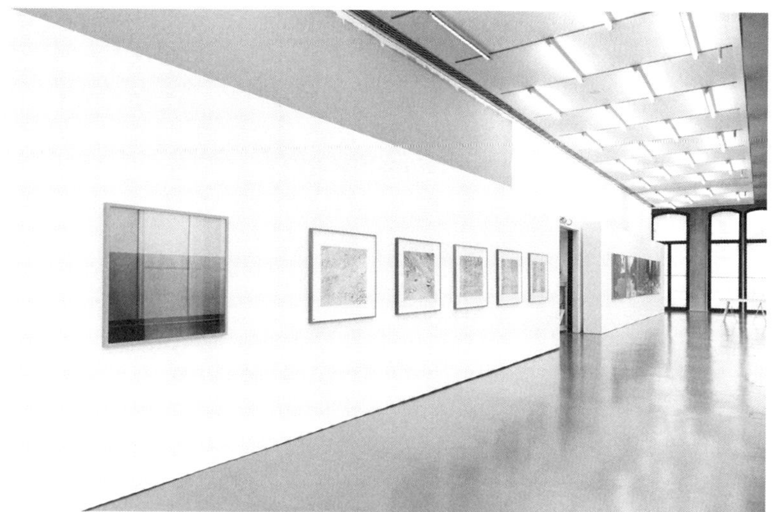

(*Wondelgemse Meersen*, 2012) near the Belgian city of Ghent document the repercussions of the utilisation and destruction of nature by humans. Taking an approach similar to that of an archaeologist, Kiwitt exposes the traces, scars, and erosion of vegetation and earth, before subsequently arranging them according to the digital document name as a kind of collection of evidence. The pictorial series *Die Innere Grenze / Notranja meja* (2008) by Nicole Six & Paul Petritsch, in turn, deals with an invisible boundary in a region that in the past was claimed by the Kingdom of Serbs, Croatians and Slovenes and also by Austria. Here, the delineation of borders from a geopolitical perspective seems just as vague as it is fictitious in the unspectacular pictures of woodlands, lake scenery, and mountain landscapes. In Kiwitt's series, which is clearly critical of society, the visual traces and supposed evidence disintegrate into abstract, aesthetic entities of inherently autonomous nature through the artist's act of photographic reproduction. In Six & Petritsch's *Die Innere Grenze*, the history of the border and its political implications remain opaque despite a 'neutral' method of representation. The photographs refuse, or so it seems, to be instrumentalised as data, documents, or evidence. The works exhibited here by Kiwitt and Six & Petritsch record hybrid intermediate states that no longer lend themselves to clear deciphering as either/or—as landscape photography or not.

The tendency of landscape photographs to seemingly elude, again and again, a more complex reading is also contingent on—as Robin Kelsey has argued in allusion to Krauss and W. J. T. Mitchell[6]—their exhibition history and that of the institutions showing them. According to these authors, the notion that a landscape photograph is a veracious, pure, and ultimately passive rendering has been decisively shaped by the context of the White Cube, which has in turn influenced our conception of landscape and also later artistic works. It must therefore be the

6
Robin E. Kelsey:
'Viewing the Archive.
Timothy O'Sullivan's
Photographs for the
Wheeler Survey, 1871–
74', in: *The Art Bulletin*,
85, no. 4 (December
2003), pp. 702–723
and W. J. T. Mitchell:
'Imperial Landscape',
in: W. J. T. Mitchell (ed.):
Landscape and Power.
Chicago 2002,
pp. 14–15.

objective of a contemporary artistic and curatorial exploration of the genre of landscape photography to allow the inherent contradictions evoked here to implode. *– EB (DD) –*

Uncovering History

Since Alain Resnais's *Night and Fog* (*Nuit et brouillard*, 1955) we have known that there is nothing to see, that catastrophe and crime do not always leave traces in the visible realm. Resnais drew on a wide variety of pictorial material—from different sites and various sources—for the history that his film seeks to reconstruct, rather than trusting in the gaze focused on what can be seen. In a remarkable way, but also quite oppressively, this film oscillates between authenticity and the impossibility of any vestige of authenticity. We are tempted to follow the lead of Claude Lanzmann in speaking of an utterly fundamental and ineluctable unrepresentability[7]—but only when dealing with a kind of reclamation, with an act of making-visible-again, with an attempt to show something that did happen but is now gone. Yet how can this succeed? Are not all 'images in spite of all'[8] necessary in order to highlight those places that have become inscribed into collective memory, which is in turn also full of images? Do not the images, despite everything and although arriving too late, again inscribe this history into those pathological places (and landscapes) that have become the showplaces of the inconceivable? And do not these images surface precisely at the vanishing point of this inconceivability?

The second segment of the *Disputed Landscape* exhibition project, *Uncovering History,* examines such questions dealing with pictorial voids or gaps that the pictures fill or where they arise, especially those that history leaves behind—when merely banal traces of the events themselves remain. In the series *As Terras do Fim do Mundo* (*The Lands of the End of the World*, 2010), Jo Ractliffe documents her journey to the south of Angola seeking vestiges of the Namibian War of Independence. She travelled with former soldiers who were revisiting, for the first time since achieving independence in 1990, the places where they had fought, in the hope of learning more about the events and correlating the places, images and events. Yet even the soldiers themselves almost failed to recognise these sites. The remnants of the war still visible—wreckage, ruins, near-derelict bomb shelters—make it barely possible to identify former battlefields. Sometimes it seems as if the war had just finished, sometimes as if the land had been utterly desolate and untouched for ages. 'Sometimes I'm not even sure what it is I'm looking at. I am here without language. It is hard to read the signs,' says Jo Ractliffe. Here, too, the images come too late, raising the question as to whether they always arrive too late and fall short of their desire to picture something. What difference would it make to have been 'present' at the time? Does the visibly rendered actually even provide us with information about what happened?

7
See Jacques Rancière: *The Future of the Image*. London/New York 2007, pp. 127ff.

8
Georges Didi-Huberman: *Images in Spite of All. Four Photographs from Auschwitz* (trans. Shane B. Lillis). Chicago 2008.

Philippe Dubois speaks of a tear in the body of the image itself, of a schism that can hardly be concealed: on the one hand 'the identity object, the representation, the form, the motif, the referentially designated (recognised as the same)—and on the other hand, precisely its other, its lack of form, which generates a spot or a symptom, its flawed symbol that wounds us and leaves us speechless and that proliferates in images as soon as we begin to look for it.'[9] For Georges Didi-Huberman, too, the photographic image is riven: 'The dual system of the image will therefore occupy every moment of this experience: between a *certain* knowledge of what is represented and an *uncertain* recognition of what is seen; between the uncertainty of *having seen* and the certainty of having *experienced*.'[10]

Ractliffe's images navigate this uncertainty of having seen and the certainty of having experienced. They show the silence and the vacuity of the landscape where there is so little to see. Yet it is precisely this silence and vacuity of the images, their sometimes spectral quietude, that gives history the room to appear, even if in absence. Is it not first possible to lend visuality to something when the tear remains open to this end? When it does not want to succumb to disappearance under the weight of a description, a representational identity?

In her series *100 Years* (2007), Efrat Shvili likewise shows something different to what is visible. The boscage of the forest not only literally hinders the view of whatever is situated behind or amidst this thicket; it also camouflages the history of this forest, or more aptly put: it redoubles the act of making-invisible that is targeted by the history of this forest. Planted more than a hundred years ago by the Jewish National Fund as part of a reforestation programme in Palestine, the forest is indicative of an inscription onto the land, but also of the superimposition of a different history. The beauty and texture of the photographs suggest an authenticity that contrasts with the artificiality and the political 'nature' of this forest. With the images focusing on what cannot be seen, Shvili also shifts the pictures of her identity relationship into the realm of uncertainty and thus into another visual realm. And once again, within this shift, the 'space' where history itself does not appear but can assume *presence* is granted in the image. Although the exhibition title speaks of uncovering history, this does not actually imply that it suddenly becomes visible or could be presented. But perhaps it does mean that history can begin to proliferate in the pictorial voids, as a *symptom* of the images, as per Dubois.[11]

When Tatiana Lecomte combines completely different archives in *Die El Alamein-Stellung. Eine Montage* [Positions at El Alamein. A Montage] in order to construct a simultaneously fictional and documentary history of the scene of a battle during the Second World War—the beach of El Alamein—she also opens up a terrain between the images and within the narrative, where something can 'take place' that transpires only between the pictures. The nude photos of a woman, taken decades

9
Translated from Philippe Dubois: 'Plastizität und Film. Die Frage des Figuralen als Störzeichen', in: Oliver Fahle (ed.): *Störzeichen. Das Bild angesichts des Realen.* Weimar 2003, pp. 113–136, esp. p. 126.

10
Georges Didi-Huberman: op. cit., p. 86.

11
Philippe Dubois, op. cit., p. 128.

after the war, collide with wartime pictures. Although it is hardly possible to differentiate between the different sources, and although the artist herself presents to us the pictures within pictures (and thus basically authenticates and verifies them), it at least becomes evident that private obsessions meet with a collective traumatic event here, that a private space is erected within the narration of history.

Anthony Haughey's series *Disputed Territory* (since 2006), created in part at the border separating Northern Ireland and the Republic of Ireland, also sometimes shows strange environments with hard-to-identify traces and obscure utilisations, places that have long been perceived and defined by the conflicting parties in totally different ways. The environs and landscapes, which are first made visible thanks to the artist, the interventions and traces that he hereby shows in the photos, are connected to complex power relations, changing history, and conflicting memories. Many of the markings, objects and interventions remain indecipherable and require a meticulous and complex interpretative approach (be it planting, excavation, or what appears to be rubbish but is actually spent munitions). It is the attempt to win back and decipher these meanings that first politicises such landscapes and re-inscribes them into the history of the conflict, but at the same time into the contested history of an uncertain recognition of what is seen. *– RB (DD) –*

Enacting Landscape

'Vision is as important as language in mediating social relations, and it is not reducible to language, to the "sign", or to discourse.'[12] Landscape is not only the designation for the 'world outside' but always also for something that is defined through social use—a social use in which vision plays a dominant role. Landscape is thus not only a social covenant, a convention, but also a visual phenomenon, an aesthetic construction.[13] From this perspective we might assert that landscape 'as such' does not exist, that it is continually yielded through cultural production, however not solely—or by no means primarily—through agriculture, urbanism and economics, but instead as a social formation, as a visual topography that follows social distribution. And if it is true that visual culture is 'the visual construction of the social, not just the social construction of vision',[14] then aesthetics and imagery, aesthetics and bodies, culture and imagery are directly interwoven. Or, even more radically, 'the object is inconceivable beyond the forms of its visual presence'.[15] So landscape would then be something that arises, or is at least designed, through a kind of performativity of the visual. 'Enacting Landscape', the idea of restaging landscape, ties into this conception of landscape that is not always already there, but that is carried out, becoming permanently generated, actualised, and ultimately picturised, something that does not exist outside or in front of the image but that is first elicited through the images themselves. With this elicitation the boundaries between the documentation and staging of landscape

12
W. J. T. Mitchell: *What Do Pictures Want? The Lives and Loves of Images*. Chicago 2005, p. 47.

13
See Rainer Guldin: *Politische Landschaften: Zum Verhältnis von Raum und nationaler Identität*. Bielefeld 2014, p. 26.

14
W. J. T. Mitchell: 'Showing seeing. A critique of visual culture', in: *Journal of Visual Culture*, 1/2 August 2002, pp. 165–181, esp. p. 170.

15
Translated from Philippe Dubois: 'Plastizität und Film: Die Frage des Figuralen als Störzeichen', in: Oliver Fahle (ed.): *Störzeichen. Das Bid angesichts des Realen*. Weimar 2003, pp. 113–136, esp. p. 118.

become blurred; that is, between their representation and their engenderment through and with the aid of (photographic) action—landscape as something that is not merely visible, but as something that first becomes perceptible and imaginable through a kind of 'use', through a process of visualisation, and that arrives at this 'staging' through different practices of visualising it.

The quest for traces that Sharon Ya'ari pursues in Israel can be interpreted as just such a staging. He has rephotographed many sites over the course of up to several years, thus documenting the processes of change that have passed through these places: archaeological excavations, a street corner, a picnic area, a ficus tree standing at the corner of a house. It is not historically significant events that fascinate Ya'ari, but instead the overlooked changes: a felled tree, a neglected plant, or flooded farmland. The idea here is to keep 'in memory' the changes impacting a country whose further development remains conflict-ridden and disputed. The diptychs and series that arise in the process allow a concept of landscape to unfold that is directly associated with this practice of chronicling and representing, with traces that usually elude our perception. When one is confronted with Ya'ari's photographs, the immediate impression is that these landscapes and detailed landscape views would be inconceivable outside of their visual presence. However, in this form the sights and vistas are not common or familiar—on the contrary: 'the more documentary, authentic, unfiltered, and unmanipulated an image is, the higher the cultural and psychological abstraction of what it "shows".'[16] Indeed, in the work of Sharon Ya'ari, the landscape surrounding us is not taken for granted; rather, it is something that must first be made visible, that emerges in these complex technocultural processes of visualisation.

In the work of Michael Höpfner, the concept of performativity seems to be most self-evident, with his photographs created during hiking expeditions lasting several weeks to remote geographical regions, like the highlands of Tibet. One might initially think that the reinvention of something would be most successful where the burden of one's own culture feels the lightest: in distant places, far away, in a different culture, on a different continent, beyond the reaches of civilisation, where one might finally find something like unadulterated nature. But this utopian vision is radically refuted by Höpfner's projects: in places where we would expect to find nature, there is instead a landscape evincing traces of industrialisation. What is more, a yearning for 'the other', 'the natural', for 'the East' as a place of longing similar to Karl May's 'wild Kurdistan' will be disappointed: this is an invention, a projection, a discourse. Höpfner's method thus lies not in showing panoramic images of this landscape in a state of destruction (as an accusation or expression of sorrow), but rather in showing the discrepancy between expectation and the found material as visually engaging with this landscape. *Lie Down, Get Up, Walk On* (2015) initially describes the practice itself: pausing, taking a picture, standing up, walking a few

16
Translated from Tom Holert: 'Die Erscheinung des Dokumentarischen', in: Karin Gludovatz (ed.): *Auf den Spuren des Realen. Kunst und Dokumentarismus.* Vienna 2003, pp. 43–64, esp. p. 55.

steps, taking another picture, then walking on. In an enlarged contact print we see a few such images, while the rest remains black, as if only marginal insight could be given about this landscape through which the artist frequently meanders for weeks on end, as if almost everything remained concealed to him. Landscape in Höpfner's work arises from a performance, from walking, halting, taking pictures, walking on. In this sense the artist is showing us a very personal creation, one that rests on collective conceptions—from which he cannot escape—about how to contradict. So in Höpfner's photographic work landscape is literally staged and re-enacted.

Landscapes or motifs associable with landscape are repeatedly found in Philipp Gaißer's work. Sometimes as multiply exposed silhouettes of a desert landscape with cacti, as in *Tour d'Horizon* (2013), then again as a conceptual model in *Untitled (Ocean, Biosphere II)* (2013), as a kind of road-movie still in *One Is Passing While I Am Watching the Scene I* (2013), or at the boundary between staging and documentation in *Made by Cactus Tactical Supply* (2013). 'That is a characteristic of Philip Gaißer's photography: for all their documentary-like objectivity, his pictures retain something puzzling; there is always a tipping moment or a directed ambivalence. That remains a constant, even when themes and subjects vary: besides landscape and architectural photographs and precisely illuminated arrangements in the style of studio photography, we also just find the atmospherically flitting snapshot or the open, stage-like setting.'[17]

As is the case in Ricarda Roggan's work (see 'The Visual Paradigm'), when viewing Gaißer's photographs the question of staging inevitably arises, even though the artist does not use interventions in front of the camera to direct his pictorial creation. Considering what is seen in his pictures, the beholder is often immersed in a feeling of improbability and artificiality. So in both cases, the artists allow the act of presentation as such to evolve. According to Jacques Rancière, the 'newly visible' has very special qualities: 'It does not make visible; it imposes presence.'[18] But these works may also show that, outside of the forms of its visual presence and performance, reality—and thus also landscape—eludes definition.
– RB (DD) –

17
See Jens Asthoff's contribution to this catalogue, p. 108.

18
Jacques Rancière: *The Future of the Image.* London/New York 2007, p. 121.

→ p. 258

Philip Gaißer

b. 1980 in Hamburg (DE), lives in Hamburg (DE) and Leipzig (DE)
www.philipgaisser.de

From: *The Ground is Mine the Sky is Yours*
Made by Cactus Tactical Supply, 2013
156 × 127 cm

From: *The Outside Looks more Fetching than the Inside*
Untitled (Ocean, Biosphere II), 2013
39 × 48 cm

C-prints
Courtesy of Galerie Conradi, Hamburg

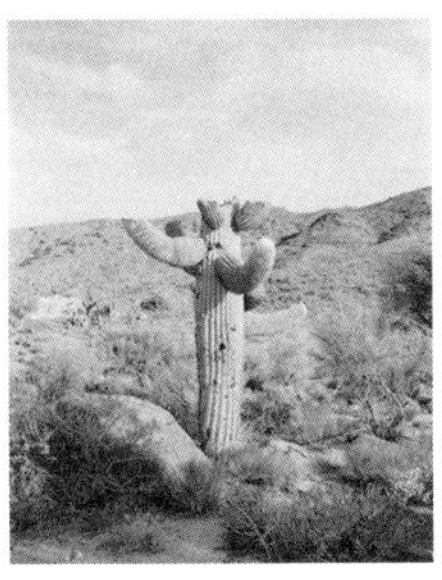

Philip Gaißer
Made by Cactus Tactical Supply, 2013
From: *The Ground is Mine the Sky is Yours*

Philip Gaißer's works are conceived as complex visual arrangements. They arise from mutually interrelated thematic complexes and present landscapes, plants, artificial and also sculptural forms. They blend the documentary register with iconic staging and construction—things become allegories of themselves. Embedding the individual images in installational contexts, Gaißer creates formal analogies between them. Some of these are comprehensible on the level of content, while others are owed to free association, producing arrangements of motifs that lend themselves to multiple readings—such as fragile inner fibre networks of a cactus plant converging with the geodetical cupola in the deserts of Arizona. Thus the artist's production of images also always includes a conceptual component, a reference back to the image's own qualities as a medium and the material reality of the means of representation. His current publication *Alma* was published by Spector Books in 2014.

The Saguaro cactus stands there like a memorial, soaring heavenwards between two lumps of rock in a stony, weed-covered area of desert landscape. Behind it rise karst hills, sketching a jagged horizon before light clouds. A typical setting, somewhere in Arizona or Mexico—also very recognisable for Europeans, the scenery of films set in the Wild West. And yet a certain irritation encroaches on this almost clichéd familiar: this specimen of a *Carnegiea gigantea* has been amputated at what looks like mid-height, cut across its trunk and side-arms. As the interfaces here coincide exactly with the transition between ground and sky, we automatically think of a montage or imagine the action has been carried out by the photographer's own hand. A picture like an open question—but whatever might have happened here: the amazing congruence of figure and background integrating a moment of the artificial into the picture Gaißer nature, narrating the landscape as a construction.

This is a characteristic of Philip Gaißer's photography: for all their documentary-like objectivity, his pictures retain something puzzling; there is always a tipping moment or a directed ambivalence. This remains a constant, even when themes and subjects vary: besides landscape and architectural photographs and precisely illuminated arrangements in the style of studio photography, we also simply find the atmospherically flitting snapshot or the open, stage-like setting. The photo with the objective yet puzzling title of *Made by Cactus Tactical Supply* (2013) stages an intervention found in the landscape. The photograph was created on the practice grounds of the US company 'Cactus Tactical Supply Enterprise' near Phoenix, Arizona: a weapons supplier that rents a total of twelve such desert areas for shooting practice. During the shooting, this mutilated *Carnegiea* became a target. As if in a mercifully revelatory act of harmonisation, Gaißer takes his photo from exactly the perspective that lines up the fragmented plant torso with the line of the horizon. His method of depiction matches the subject and surroundings more intensely; moreover, Gaißer used infrared-sensitive film here, which reproduces the relatively dark green of the Saguaro somewhat more brightly. These and similar staged gestures are the means by which Gaißer infiltrates irritation into the immediateness of the photographic given—thereby opening and forming the gaze onto landscape.

– JA (AH) –

→ p. 260

Anthony Haughey

b. 1963 in Armagh, Northern Ireland (GB), lives in Dublin (IE)
www.anthonyhaughey.com

From the series: *Disputed Territory*, 2006
C-prints; 100 × 100 cm and 50 × 100 cm
Courtesy of the artist

Red Coffins, Glogjani, Kosovo, 2006
Men Digging, Pristina, 2006
British Army Fortifications, Orange Order Protest, 2006

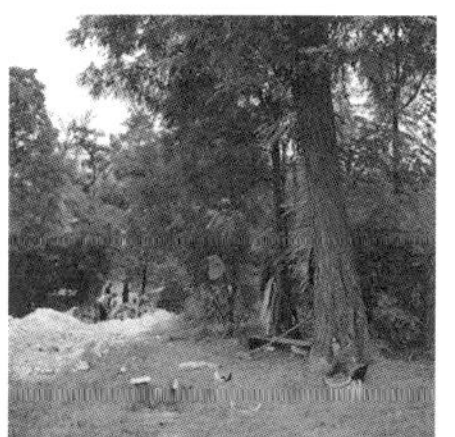

Anthony Haughey
*Men Digging,
Pristina, 2006*
From the series:
Disputed Territory,
2006

Besides his artistic work, Haughey also works as a lecturer. He supervises practice-based doctoral theses at the Dublin Institute of Technology. Previously he was a Research Fellow at the Interface Centre for Research in Art, Technologies and Design at the University of Ulster Belfast, where he completed his doctorate in 2009. His art practice is based on the premise of a basic situatedness of art in space and community and its connection through dialogical exchange. He has cooperated on a broad basis with various social groups and individuals and thereby blurred the borders between subject and viewer. Between 2008 and 2012 he produced a series of video installations and art interventions with *The Global Migration Research Network*.

His work has been widely exhibited and collected at an international level. Among his exhibitions in 2014 are *Soundings* (dlr Lexicon, Dublin), *Motivational Deficit* (Crawford Gallery, Cork), *Making History* and *Homelands* (Colombo Art Biennale). In 2013 he was represented in the exhibitions *Northern Ireland: 30 years of photography* (MAC and Belfast Exposed), *New Irish Landscapes* (Three Shadows Gallery, Beijing), *Homelands* (exhibition of the British Council, which toured through South-east Asia), *Citizen* (Highlanes Gallery, Drogheda and MCAC, Portadown), as well as *Strike!* and *Labour and Lockout* (Limerick City Gallery). In addition, he produced a commissioned work for the *Aftermath* project, which toured through Ireland in 2013. His monographs include *The Edge of Europe* (1996), *Disputed Territory* (2006) and the artists' book *State* (2011). He has also written numerous articles for catalogues and magazines. His works can be found in international public and private collections; moreover, he is editorial consultant to the Routledge magazine *Photographies*. Recently he was awarded the *Create Intercultural Art Bursary*.

Anthony Haughey's projects mostly revolve around economic, social or political disruptions in present-day Europe. Linked to this are both historical and current conflicts based around territories and the drawing of borders. *Disputed Territory* (since 2006) is a long-term project that investigates European territorial and identity-related tensions based on the effects of the conflicts in Ireland, Bosnia and Kosovo, showing the landscape as controversial and fought-over borderland. The artist lived near the border between Northern Ireland and the Republic of Ireland for several years. At the climax of the 'Northern Ireland Conflict' during the 1970s and 1980s, it was one of the most heavily guarded and militarised zones outside of the then Eastern Bloc—yet this demarcation line remained virtually invisible and would have been almost impossible to identify without the use of relevant maps.

Haughey's pictures of this border between Northern Ireland and the Republic of Ireland in part show strange surroundings with barely identifiable traces and unclear usage, which were long perceived and defined in completely different ways by the two conflicting parties. The surroundings and landscapes that he makes visible in the first place, together with the interventions and traces that he thereby shows, are connected with complex power relations, with shifting history and contradictory memories. Many of the markings, objects and interventions remain incomprehensible and demand a precise and complex method of interpretation (whether planting, excavations or apparent rubbish that turns out to be spent ammunition). The landscape only becomes political when the attempt is made to win back these meanings, to decode them. The acts of suppressing, forgetting or remembering of this encoding are neither neutral nor innocent acts, however; rather, they are part of the politics and power that the landscapes have also inscribed on themselves. In this sense Haughey's pictures bring up to date the unease caused by memory and history, revealing them to us once again. It is not just an attempt to counteract the disappearance of this memory and history, but also a concern with investigating ideological and political narratives through these pictures, which have left their imprint on this conflict-ridden history as 'contested territory'.   *– RB (AH) –*

→ p. 262

Michael Höpfner

b. 1972 in Krems/Donau (AT), lives in Berlin (DE) and Vienna (AT)

Lie Down, Get Up, Walk On, day 11, 25-9-2012, 2015
Lie Down, Get Up, Walk On, day 6, 4-9-2014, 2015
Contact sheets, numbered and signed
Courtesy of Galerie Hubert Winter, Vienna

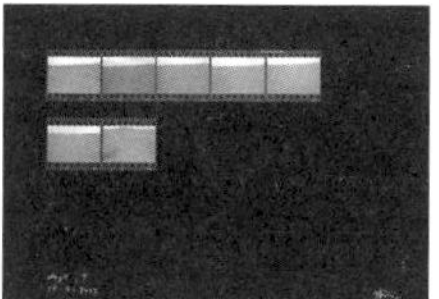

Michael Höpfner
*Lie Down, Get Up,
Walk On, day 11,
25-9-2012*, 2015

Michael Höpfner studied at the Academy of Fine Arts Vienna and at the Glasgow School of Art. His work is based on travel and walking, which since 1995 has taken him mostly to remote and uninhabited regions in the Ukraine, Tajikistan, Kazakhstan, Northern India, Nepal, Western China, South Korea, Senegal, Libya, Iceland and Scotland, for example. His current work *Lie Down, Get Up, Walk On* (2015) was produced in connection with his stay on the high plateau of Chang Tang in western Tibet. It focuses on hiking, the rhythm of movement as a physical appropriation of the landscape and the relationship between one's own place and a virtually delocated landscape. Höpfner takes a picture, goes a few steps further, takes another picture, and repeats this four to five times. A sequence emerges that does not attempt primarily to document the landscape, but instead depicts a specific form of access to the space of the landscape, to its surface, to that which is simultaneously present and uncertain about its presence. From these sequences there arises a kind of (re-)staging of landscape, its reconstruction, which is based on the 'performance' of walking, stopping, settling and then moving on.
Yet there is a conflict and a contradiction at the heart of this performative representation: that which is located between the completely different concepts of time and space of the Tibetan Highland cultures, and the post-postmodern consumerist society. The high plains of Tibet seem like natural space, yet are marked throughout with traces of industrialisation. The fantasy of untouched nature collides with the inexorable spread of its exploitation and destruction. Similarly, the belief in nature and spirits of the nomadic culture of the Tibetans collides with the destructive political and social powers of globalisation. The wide expanse of the East symbolises a place of—no longer attainable—promise and authenticity, yet also a space of—similarly vanished—secrets and barbarism, of the threat of the uncontrollable. The landscapes through which Höpfner hikes seem to be expanses of nature, yet are a space that is also created discursively—by the West—which, while it can be localised, is at the same time omnipresent as a threat. To this extent Höpfner's projects are highly personal approaches to his own, yet also collective yearnings and perceptions of an environment, to strata of history, and to the rapid change in a landscape and its social structures.

– RB (AH) –

→ p. 264

Stephanie Kiwitt

b. 1972 in Bonn (DE), lives in Brussels (BE)

From: *Wondelgemse Meersen. Archiv*, 2012/15
Courtesy of the artist

Schwarz, 15 inkjet prints; each 15 × 10 cm
#3, inkjet print; 121.9 × 81.3 cm

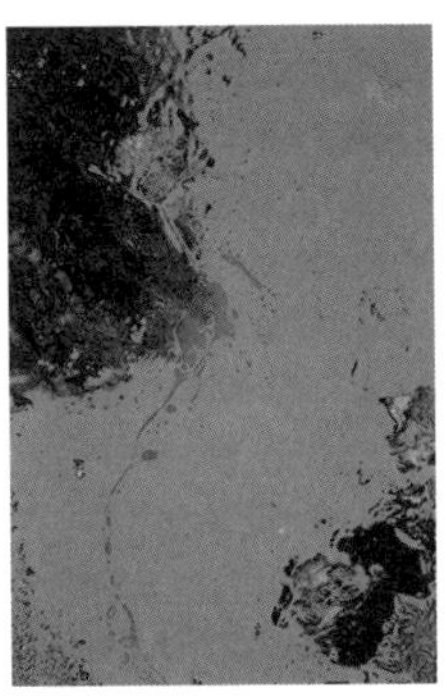

Stephanie Kiwitt
#3, 2012/15
From: *Wondelgemse
Meersen. Archiv,*
2012/15

Stephanie Kiwitt studied photography at the Academy of Visual Arts Leipzig (HGB). Serving as point of departure for her work is the photographic observation of places that represent a steady commercialisation of public space and everyday spheres of life. She works with series and ensembles of pictures, each assuming a specific form in a book or an exhibition space. She has received numerous awards: in 2009 she was artist-in-residence at WIELS in Brussels, and in 2010 she was awarded the Stiftungspreis für Fotokunst der Stiftung Alison und Peter Klein. From 2010–12 Kiwitt participated in the photography research project 'De fotograaf in de stad' at the Royal Academy of Fine Arts (KASK) in Ghent. It was in this context that her publication *Wondelgemse Meersen*, published by Kodoji Press, was created.

In *Wondelgemse Meersen* (2012) Kiwitt photographed wasteland in the north of the Belgian city of Ghent. The area, some 100 hectares in size, was originally marshland and is today surrounded by transport routes, industrial and residential zones and empty factory buildings. Meticulously, and in countless pictures—printed in the book of the same name largely in grid form, only occasionally punctuated by full-page pictures—Stephanie Kiwitt documents this semi-urban area, showing numerous details without ever offering an overview of the landscape itself. Our gaze is mostly directed towards the ground, to traces, rubbish, puddles, mud, strewn objects, tyre marks. If we look up, then it is only so far as to notice ruins, tree stumps and burned-out wrecks of cars; only very rarely can the horizon be seen, a pylon for example, rising up behind a tree trunk, a car in the adjoining car park on the other side of a fence. It seems like a visual scanning, sounding-out, exploring—Kiwitt orders these pictures in groups, almost as though she were working on a typology or an inventory of the objects found at the site. Within this typology, culture and nature collide; different (former) usages are hinted at, though in fragmented form and lacking a context. It makes us suspect that informal accommodation existed here, that this area is both enclosed and out of bounds, a space that fences one in and excludes one, beyond order and normality, a territory of refuge and fear. The trash and destruction in the pictures could be a metaphor for the dystopias of our age, a swansong to consumerist culture and gentrification. Landscape, like society, is divided up into separate parts and would have to be laboriously reconstructed, rediscovered. All these assumed, ascribed elements are based, however, on a documentary as a non-documentary, which evokes a terrain and a landscape that perhaps does not exist at all in this form—that in any case remains inaccessible and unknown. No concept is created of the terrain, of its location, topography, of its dimensions, its boundaries, and above all no conception of what could await us beyond this terrain.

– RB (AH) –

→ p. 266

Tatiana Lecomte

b. 1971 in Bordeaux (FR), lives in Vienna (AT)

Die El Alamein-Stellung. Eine Montage, 2012
Projection of 81 slides; dimension variable
Courtesy of the artist

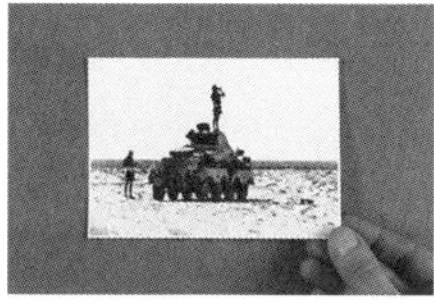
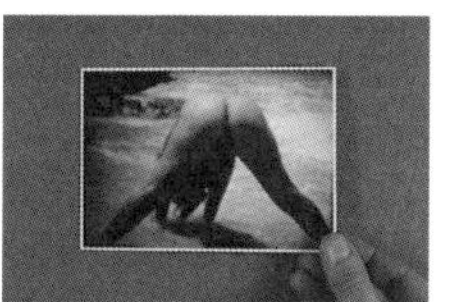

Tatiana Lecomte
From: *Die El Alamein-Stellung. Eine Montage*, 2012

In recent years Tatiana Lecomte has worked exclusively with found picture material that she reproduces and changes in the repeated process of development and enlargement, picking out details, producing new sequences from them or revealing the materiality of the original through powerful enlargements.

For *Die El Alamein Stellung. Eine Montage* [Positions at El Alamein. A Montage] (2012) she also draws on a private archive of slides that she found in the waste in front of her house. In this archive—obviously spread over several decades—the same woman can be seen time and again, mostly in erotic poses and at numerous 'locations' all over the world. Some of these slides show this woman on the beach of the Egyptian town of El Alamein, which in 1942 was the scene of a battle in which the Allies forced the German-Italian troops to retreat from Africa in two decisive clashes. She combines these photographs with military archive pictures, which were likewise created at this place, or at least could have been—soldiers and burning vehicles in a desert-like landscape, maps, aeroplanes, troop movements. It mostly concerns single scenes that leave the overall context unclear. Between these war pictures a woman crops up time and again, posing lasciviously; she could equally come from a private picture collection of one of the fighting soldiers. Each photograph is shown to us by the artist's hand before a green background, as if someone was presenting a photo album to us, as if reporting on her or his participation in this historically important event. This gesture of authenticating what is being shown conflicts, however, with the uncertainty over the sources from which these pictures actually derive. The 81 slides unfold an artificially constructed history of violence and sexuality, of war and private obsessions, of the violence of power, and the force that pictures exert over bodies and history. In this ambivalence concerning what is shown and narrated, Lecomte in the end localises the ambivalence of photographic representation, too, which is linked to a lack of knowledge and context, and which ultimately throws doubt on the meaning of the pictures.

In 2011, Tatiana Lecomte's work was shown in a solo exhibition (with Šejla Kamerić) at Camera Austria, and in the same year her publication *Dissolution* was published by Edition Camera Austria.

– RB (AH) –

→ p. 268

Christian Mayer

b. 1976 in Sigmaringen (DE), lives in Vienna (AT)

From Boynton's Lookout the Author Photographs the Grandeur of Escalante Canyon, 2011
197 × 183 × 97 cm

Through Historic Hole in the Rock Mormons Blasted a Path to Their Promised Land, 2011
130 × 181 × 4 cm

Escalante Expedition Named This Glowing Valley "Kodachrome Flat", 2011
172 × 215 × 80 cm

In Earth's Age-old Battle with the Elements, Giant Chimney Stands Undefeated, 2011
183 × 130 × 4 cm

UV direct prints on lightweight panels with paper honeycomb core
Courtesy of the artist and Galerie Nagel Draxler, Berlin

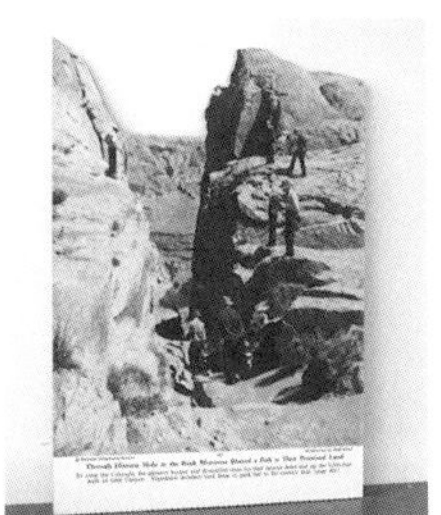

Christian Mayer
Through Historic Hole in the Rock Mormons Blasted a Path to Their Promised Land, 2011

Christian Mayer's exhibitions and projects address memory, preservation and rediscovery. His interest lies in testing the methods with which these subjects can be handled in an aesthetically unusual way: techniques of reversal, compression and expansion of time, of the simultaneous observation of things from two sides. He creates situations in which there is beauty to be found in the way one thing leads to another. His works have recently been shown at a number of international exhibitions including mumok, Belvedere, Zamek Poznan, at Kunststiftung Baden-Württemberg, Galerie Nagel Draxler, Galerie Mezzanin and others. He is also co-editor of a magazine that appears under a different name each time, depending on the font it uses (www.ztscrpt.net).

In his contribution to the exhibition Mayer uses the story of an expedition of the National Geographic Society in Basin State Park, Utah undertaken in 1949. The report published in the *National Geographic Magazine* of the same year covering this undertaking enthusiastically describes the photogenic quality of the undeveloped area and mentions the renaming of the landscape by the expeditioners from 'Thorny Pasture', as it was called by the indigenous inhabitants, to 'Kodachrome Flat'. Since this symbolic act the landscape has been linked with the brand name of the first commercially successful colour film with which the National Geographic photographers first recorded it. Even the final shutting-down of Kodachrome Films production in 2009 has not changed this name in any way.

For the installation Lion the original picture-text pages of the *National Geographic Magazine* article undergo a multiple translation: enlarged many times, printed on MDF honeycomb panels and cut along the horizon line, they are transformed into stage-like elements that spatialise the reproduced landscape again. Mayer has in large part removed the colour so significant for Kodachrome and only left in colour the expeditioners, who are clothed in red, so recalling a stylistic approach of the National Geographic photographers that later was to be given the name 'Red Shirt School of Photography': in order to make the picture printed in colour more prominent, and to differentiate the subjects from the landscape, people were placed in the picture who wore conspicuously red colours. With this group of works Christian Mayer illustrates how the perception of landscape is closely connected with the cultural techniques of their recording, representation, dissemination and archiving. By 'reloading' a picture technology no longer available today, he emphasises those aspects and processes that determine the visualising and archiving of reality, in particular of landscape. That the history of perception is not only linked to materials and aesthetics, but always with a policy, too, is shown here perfectly with the situation of a renamed landscape which confirms and legitimises its appropriation, thus extinguishing and over-writing a previously existing history. *– RB (AH) –*

→ p. 270

Jo Ractliffe

b. 1961 in Cape Town (ZA), lives in Johannesburg (ZA)

From: *As Terras do Fim do Mundo (The Lands of the End of the World)*, 2009/10
Hand-printed silver gelatin prints; 45 × 56 cm
Courtesy of Stevenson, Cape Town / Johannesburg

Unmarked mass grave on the outskirts of Cuito Cuanavale, 2009
Unidentified memorial in the desert, south of Namibe, 2009

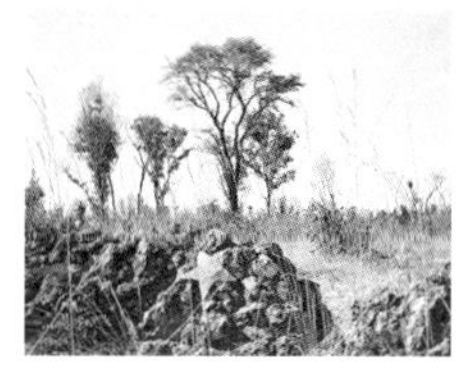

Jo Ractliffe
Unmarked mass grave on the outskirts of Cuito Cuanavale, 2009
From: *As Terras do Fim do Mundo (The Lands of the End of the World), 2009/10*

Jo Ractliffe's photographs reflect three decades of her involvement with the landscape of South Africa, and show clearly how differently this is depicted in the imagination of the country—above all, with regard to the violent legacy of apartheid. Since 2007, she has been closely concerned with the consequences of the war in Angola, in which South Africa was involved in a complex way. After *Terreno Ocupado*, 2008, and *As Terras do Fim do Mundo (The Lands of the End of the World)*, 2009/10 her latest work *The Borderlands*, 2013, deals with locations in South Africa that were affected by the mobilisation and aftermath of this war. 'Sometimes I'm not even sure what it is I'm looking at. I am here without language. It is hard to read the signs.' Between 2007 and 2010 Jo Ractliffe travelled to southern Angola several times on the trail of the Namibian War of Liberation. She travelled with former soldiers, who visited combat locations for the first time since independence was declared in 1990, places where they had fought and yet which they barely recognised, although in many places relics such as burned-out military vehicles could be seen—as if the landscape were a kind of open-air depot for the remnants of the fighting that had taken place here. Millions of people fled to the cities; hardly any animals were left, most having been slaughtered either by the troops or the starving population. But it is above all the mines that make resettlement almost impossible. Among other places Ractliffe also visited Cassinga, where the South African army attacked a SWAPO base in 1978, leading to the deaths of many civilians. The warring parties describe this attack either as fighting or as a massacre—controversial history that continues to the present day, both past and yet eerily present. Ractliffe's pictures bear witness to this history, to the quiet and emptiness of the landscape that conceals relics seemingly alien to it, yet which are important to define its present-day appearance. Her pictures, in part ghostly, revolve around the idea of a 'landscape as pathology' in the sense in which past violence—lasting and fleeting, visible and invisible at the same time—inscribes itself on the present, both in a forensic and symbolic way. This pathology, through which violent history pursues the present, forces us to become involved in these places that are still barely understood even today, for which we lack both the language and the images.

Jo Ractliffe teaches at the University of the Witwatersrand in Johannes-burg, where she works with Rory Bester on *PhotoFocus*—a pedagogical platform for photography training that spans disciplines, histories, loca-tions and experiences. She also teaches in the Market Photo Workshop and is a member of the advisory council there. In addition, she holds talks, workshops as well as courses at universities in South Africa and has initiated numerous independent public educational projects. In 2010 she received a writing scholarship at the Wits Institute for Social and Economic Research (WISER), and in 2011 and 2012 she was invited to teach at the Salzburg Summer Academy; in 2014 she was research asso-ciate at the Centre for Curating the Archive at the University of Cape Town.   *– RB (AH) –*

→ p. 272   **Ricarda Roggan**
b. 1972 in Dresden (DE), lives in Leipzig (DE)

From the series: *natura nova, Sedimente,* 2008–10
Bromide gelatin silver print; 66 × 75 cm
Courtesy of Galerie EIGEN + ART, Leipzig / Berlin

natura nova, Sedimente 6, 2010

Ricarda Roggan is one of the most important German photographers of her generation. She studied photography under Timm Rautert at the Academy of Visual Arts Leipzig (HGB) and continued at the Royal College of Art in London. Her artistic involvement with found places and spaces occurs through photography. Before realising her vision photographi-cally, she carries out methodical preparations by shielding the spaces from external factors such as indicators of the dimensions of time, mem-ory, narrative and imagination. She opposes the authenticity of the found situation with artificial modifications. The spaces are cleansed and enhanced through the artist's intervention in situ and by the

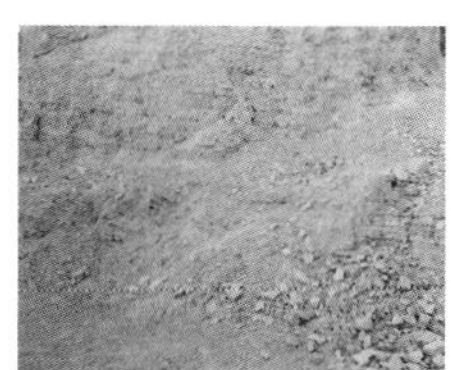

Ricarda Roggan
natura nova, Sedimente 6, 2010
From the series:
natura nova, Sedimente, 2008–10

elimination of external influences. Roggan's works are on show both in national and international solo and group exhibitions, and also in various public collections including the Art Collection Deutsche Börse, the Federal Collection of Contemporary Art in Bonn, the Art Collection of the German Federal Parliament, the Museum of Fine Arts Leipzig, the Olbricht Collection and the Pinakothek der Moderne, Munich.

Ricarda Roggan's work is characterised by a basic control over the photographic image. She greatly influences what we see and in what way we can see it. Her working method, however, is more accurately described by the term intervention rather than staging—its aim is not to produce something artificial or unlikely, but on the contrary to reveal or to bring to light that which at first seems obvious or even familiar. She also pursues this methodology in her works about nature, although nature—apparently—seems to contradict cultural production and basically evades any control.

In the series entitled *Baumstücke* (2007/08), belonging to the group of works *natura nova*, she crops foliage and branches of the groups of trees depicted so that they correspond to her visual concept. Primarily dramatic or attention-arousing details are thus removed; subsequently, the plasticity of the motif is reworked by means of post-exposure and retouching in the printing process, among other things. Landscape details emerge which blend with the surface and above all with the presence of the photographic image: structures of impenetrable verdancy, both borrowed from nature and a result of the materiality of the photography itself, simultaneously exemplary and puzzling and dislocated—found, and yet also created only through the picture itself. In the series *Sedimente* (2008–10), which was shot in quarries on Cyprus, we see stone formations heaped up in front of us like a wall, monumental and replete with the history of nature, an intersection through the ages. Yet for these pictures too, the artist moved debris and rock and thus added an extra form of 'preparation' to the artificial geological excavation. Through these interventions, which seem never to exceed the boundaries of probability and thus still appear to lay claim to something akin to authenticity, Roggan moves along the border between documentary and construction, reality and model, chance and typology, thus emphasising exactly at this border the definitional power of the visual for the perception of and reflection upon realities—and thus also for notions of landscape.

– RB (AH) –

→ p. 274

Ahlam Shibli

b. 1970 in Palestine
www.ahlamshibli.com

From the series: *The Valley, Arab al-Shibli, Palestine, 2007/08*
28 C-prints; 38 × 57.7 cm or 57.7 × 38 cm
Courtesy of the artist

Untitled (The Valley no. 5), Arab al-Shibli, Palestine, 2007/08
Untitled (The Valley no. 9), Arab al-Shibli, Palestine, 2007/08

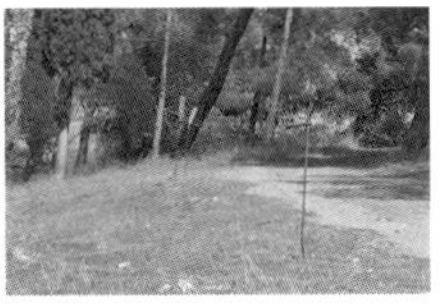

Ahlam Shibli
*Untitled (The Valley
no. 5), Arab al-Shibli,
Palestine, 2007/08*
From the series: *The
Valley, Arab al-
Shibli, Palestine,
2007/08*

In her photographic work, Ahlam Shibli uses a documentary aesthetic to focus on the contradictory implications of the notion of homeland. She deals with the loss of homeland and the struggle against it, but also with the restrictions and borders that are imposed due to the concept of homeland on individuals and communities subject to repressive identity policy.

The images of *The Valley* were taken in 2007 in the village of Arab al-Shibli and its lands in the Lower Galilee of Palestine/Israel. In this work Ahlam Shibli reads the landscape and the marks it bears against the backdrop of the village's history.

Half the inhabitants of the village of Arab al-Sbaih survived the war of 1948 by hiding in the caves of Mount Tabor, the mountain on whose flanks the village had been built. The other half of the people opposed the Jewish fighters in order to protect their lands, and as a consequence had to seek refuge in Jordan. In the camps where their descendants have been living to this day, the refugees kept the memory of their original home by using the old names and reproducing the previous social structure. The refugees' living conditions are the subject of Shibli's work *Arab al-Sbaih*.

When the people who had been hiding at the mountain returned to their property after the war they were forced to change the name of their village in order to avoid revenge from the victors. They renamed the village Arab al-Shibli after the name of one large family.

'In 1950, two years after the war and the establishment of the State of Israel, the people of the village were asked to exchange lands for one year: the good lands that were officially owned by the people who had stayed in the village, for the fallow lands of the people who had fled the village and which had been appropriated by the State of Israel. In 1952, things became worse. People from the village were arrested and others not allowed to leave the village. In 1954, the state official in charge of "absentee property" came to the village and claimed the lands that had belonged to the refugees and were given to the village people in the agreement of 1950. In 1957, when the village people asked for permission to build houses in their village, their request was rejected with the argument that their village didn't exist on the state map.' (Ahlam Shibli)

The Valley shows the way the people from Arab al-Shibli are presently forced to scar the mountain that had protected them during the war. In order to be able to build a house they had to give up the name of their village and the respect for the land. While they were deprived of their sense of home, the refugees in the camps in Jordan kept theirs but are without proper houses.

The images of *The Valley* are political through Shibli's practice 'to look at what is there, to read it and its conditions and to make an image of that reading'.

– RB (AH) –

→ p. 276

Efrat Shvili

b. 1955 in Jerusalem (IL), lives in Jerusalem (IL)

From the series: *100 Years*, 2007
11 black-and-white prints; 40 × 40 cm and 65 × 88 cm
Courtesy of Sommer Contemporary Art, Tel Aviv

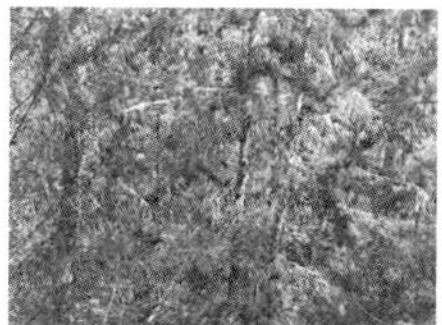

Efrat Shvili
From the series: *100 Years*, 2007

Efrat Shvili's photographs and videos give expression to socio-political processes and phenomena in a wide range of genres from landscape photography to portraiture. Her subject is Israeli society and identity, as well as the Israeli-Palestinian conflict. Her work combines formalistic perception with a conceptual approach, encompassing both socio-political and personal narratives. In its dialectical outlook, her oeuvre confronts the viewer with a complex position: point counterpoint, one reality vis-à-vis another, individual versus community.

Shvili became well-known for her two early series, *New Homes in Israel and the Occupied Territories* (1992–1998) and *Palestinian Cabinet Ministers 2000*. While the first series questioned the relationship between Israelis and the land through photographs of austere landscapes and construction sites, the second series gave visibility to a new image of the Palestinian as statesman rather than terrorist. In her later works, Shvili examined myths and rituals that have to do with the formation of the Israeli identity and collective memory.

During her career, Shvili has exhibited in a number of leading international venues including the 50th Venice Biennale, the NY Photography Triennial, the KW Center for Contemporary Art in Berlin, the Center for Contemporary Art Witte de With in Rotterdam, and the 8th International Istanbul Biennial.

In her series *100 Years* (2007), Efrat Shvili shows close-up photographs of trees and thickets, without any horizon or possible points of orientation. The almost graphical surface of the photographs shields us from these delocated woods, which seem to be reserved for nature alone: entangled, enchanted woods, which grow over everything in time and so bury and hide it. They may remind us of Sleeping Beauty's concealed castle, cut off from the world and slumbering away, as if fallen out of time. Yet like many of Shvili's earlier works, this series also revolves around the specific political situation in Israel, whereby precisely the vision of something dormant or buried under the mass of time, as in a fairy tale, plays a role.

100 Years shows a wood in the west of Jerusalem, which was created more than 100 years ago by the Jewish National Fund as part of a

Palestinian forestation programme. What today appears to be nature and like an ancient forest, was planted on former Palestinian territory to drive out the population from there and to appropriate the land—as has been the case up to the present day. The beauty and texture of the pictures thus suggests a naturalness that contradicts the artificiality and political 'nature' of this wood. Thus the pictures are also metaphors for a strategy of supplanting one landscape with another, of the oppression and rendering-invisible of history, which is always the history of others, of *the others*—a history that, like Sleeping Beauty in the fairy tale, was locked away and almost forgotten and requires an extraordinary act to bring it back to the present.

Thus the pictures of the series *100 Years* turn into a political metaphor, which not only deals with the space of the landscape, but also with the era of utopia: 'And what worries me is that the good life here (…) produc[es] a terrible delusion. After all, it's clear that things cannot go on like this for another hundred years – I am not sure they can go on for another 10 years.[1]

– *RB (AH)* –

→ p. 278

Nicole Six & Paul Petritsch

Nicole Six, b. 1971 in Vöcklabruck (AT), lives in Vienna (AT);
Paul Petritsch, b. 1968 in Friesach (AT), lives in Vienna (AT)

From the series: *Die Innere Grenze / Notranja meja*, 2008
74 C-prints; each 120 × 155 cm
On loan from Museum Moderner Kunst Kärnten, Klagenfurt

Die Innere Grenze / Notranja meja, Abb. 02 + 03 / Slika 02 + 03, 2008

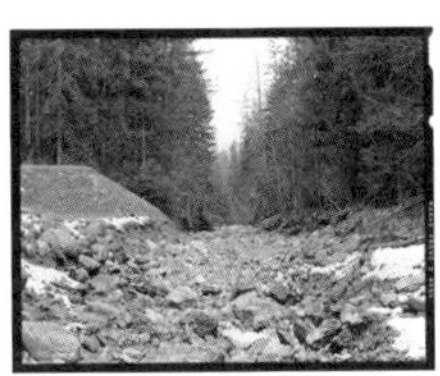

Nicole Six & Paul Petritsch
*Die Innere Grenze /
Notranja meja, Abb.
03 / Slika 03*, 2008

Since 1997, Nicole Six & Paul Petritsch have been realising joint performative, filmic, photographic and sculptural projects and regularly produce displays and projects in public space. In many series they work on the modern/modernistic paradigm of a discovery and measuring of the world, translating the spatial aspects of these conquests into representational systems that are acutely marked by abstract and statistical processes, and thus are in a relationship of mutual tension to the (photographic) image. In their project *Atlas* (2009/10) they documented the circumnavigation of the earth with two mopeds on a former race track in Spain by 24-hour exposures of pinhole cameras set up at twelve positions on the route. These pictures capture the whole time span of the 'journey' without those making the journey being visible.

In the series *Die Innere Grenze / Notranja meja* (2008), using historical maps and documents, they followed the former border between Austria and the 'SHS State' (the Kingdom of the Serbs, Croatians and Slovenes) that laid claim after the First World War to parts of present-day Carinthia. In 1920 the state affiliation of these areas was decided by plebiscite: nearly 60 % of the population living there voted to remain in Austria. In this case too, they subdivided the historical course of the border into sectors and every two kilometres took a picture in the direction of

1
Ze'ev Sternhell in an interview with Ari Shavit, Haaretz, March 2008.

the continuing border line, at 74 locations in total. In a certain way, here too almost the whole border is documented, yet not visible in the pictures. The landscape itself is turned into a visual context that surrounds emptiness. Although documentary in the full sense of the term, the landscape pictures remain full of empty spaces, uncertain meaning and a lack of knowledge within contexts merely hinted at through a brief description of the facts—and thus move along a border of documentary strategies: the continuation of a pictorial concept at places that oppose and evade this pictorial concept. In this way Six & Petritsch link up questions of the possibility of visual reconstruction and documentation with questions of the conditions of the landscape's political significance.

– RB (AH) –

→ p. 280

Sharon Ya'ari

b. 1966 in Holon (IL), lives in Tel Aviv (IL)
www.sharonyaari.com

Tel Yavne Archaeological Mound, Summer, 2012
124 × 156 cm

Tel Yavne Archaeological Mound, Summer, 2012
122 × 154 cm

Safe Room, Beersheba Zoo, Spring, 2013
42 × 52 cm

C-prints
Courtesy of Sommer Contemporary Art, Tel Aviv

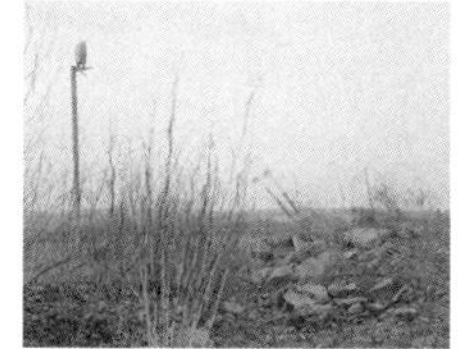

Sharon Ya'ari
Tel Yavne Archaeological Mound, Summer, 2012

Sharon Ya'ari studied photography at the Bezalel Academy of Art and Design, Jerusalem. His works focus on ordinary objects and routine life in his home country, at the same time drawing a range of complex socio-political sensitive insights. They depict the remainders of some past private actions and motivations, questions about local identity, and about the way trivial things become charged with meaning by being present over an extended period of time; simply lying there, piling up, accumulating, taking form. Ya'ari's images have a story—usually one related to existence and near-extinction.

He does not photograph combat zones, firing ranges, memorials or locations immediately identifiable as being in Israel. His interest lies far more in the mundane, in places passed time and again, a picnic spot, zoo, park, street corner, the unfinished ground floor of a building, the overgrown front gardens close to his own house, the shortcut through a green space; in between the desert, time and again, a landscape in which any change, any intervention receives special attention. Yet it is not the banality of the everyday that interests Sharon Ya'ari but rather time, history, which also changes these—apparently inconspicuous—places, inscribing itself on them and thus manifesting itself at these locations.

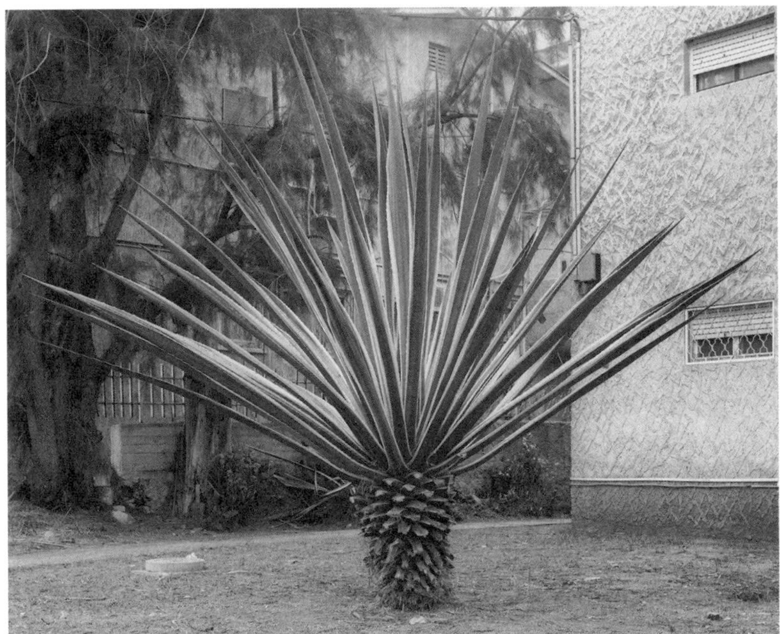

Sharon Ya'ari
Agave, Hadera, 2012

In Israel this history has primarily to do also with the appropriation of land too, with its reclamation, with utopias of landscape and society which brought the many immigrants to the country and who attempted their realisation—flying in the face of reason. Perhaps this is why much in Ya'ari's works seems strangely dislocated, as if artificially arranged, in any case unclear in its meaning. Ya'ari visits some of the places and landscapes at intervals of several years, such as a picnic spot or an archaeological memorial, in order to document the—in part almost eerie—mixture of standstill and collapse, of custody and neglect, nature and culture, memory and oblivion, an instable and precarious situation. Ya'ari is interested here less in documenting these changes per se, and more in a possible analogy with regard to future changes, in order also, as he himself says, to be able to predict the next catastrophe. These pictures thus appear less to be documenting, and more to be question-ing these places and landscapes in transition, in their uncertain signifi-cance for the production of identity and affiliation—not just for the present but also for the imminent, uncertain future. In them the moment of—always threatened, ephemeral, fragile and fleeting—being created and impermanence of rural settings becomes tangible.   *– RB (AH) –*

Political Landscape
Art – Resistance – Salzkammergut
Dirck Möllmann

'To change "landscape" from a noun to a verb.'
W. J. T. Mitchell

'landscaping' in Political Landscape

In Austria and, indeed, the entire Alpine region, the beauty of nature as a landscape promotes well-being and relaxation. This is one of the reasons why not only urban holidaymakers favour the destination, but also why creative people, writers, poets, musicians and painters flock to the countryside to work there. The Salzkammergut has become famous as a classic summer holiday region. Here, in the Styrian Ausseerland region, the *Political Landscape* art project is due to open in July 2015.

The landscape around Lake Aussee and the Totes Gebirge also bears a collective political history that has shaped this part of the countryside and its people. From 1943 to 1945, a great many actions both for and against Hitler's fascist rule were concentrated here in the Austrian Salzkammergut, a triangle that stretches between the high mountains of the present-day regions of Salzburg, Upper Austria and Styria. Sections of the proto-partisan-like Resistance used the impassable areas of the high mountains as a place of retreat. After the collapse of the Nazi regime, National Socialists also hid in the mountains or lived anonymously in the region. Like a burning lens, a great number of events had their focus here up until May 1945, such as art theft, betrayal, active and passive resistance, escape and murder. These complex and ambiguous times continue to have normative effects on our political system today, although fewer and fewer people are aware of it. 2015 marks 70 years since Europe's liberation from National Socialist totalitarianism, by which point few living witnesses will remain.

Political Landscape specifically addresses the landscape of the Salzkammergut and its political history, tackling the issue of individual and collective memory in several steps. This project was inspired by the artist Eva Grubinger. An international workshop of artists, theoreticians and regional experts in August 2014 connected aspects of the geology,

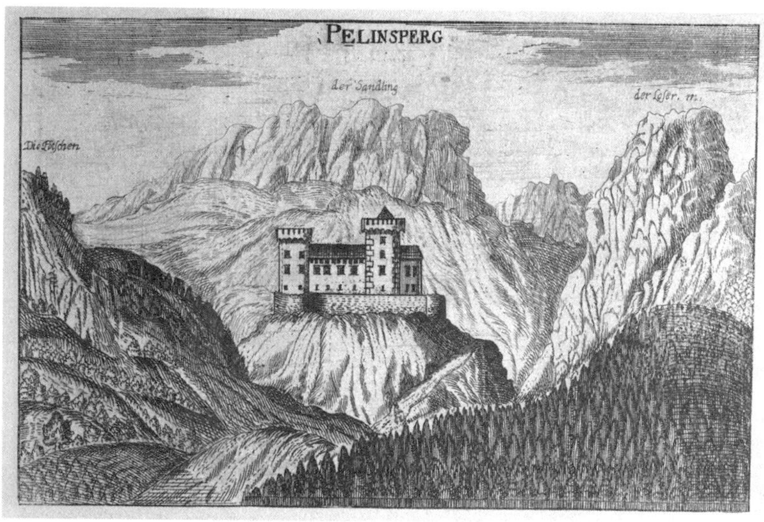

A classic image of the political landscape is the castle on a hill. Here we see fort Pflindsberg between Sandling and Loser nearby Altaussee, built in the 13th century, depicted by Georg Matthäus Vischer for *Topographia Ducatus Stiriae*, ca. 1681.

history and sociology of the Salzkammergut, including the current spatial planning of the region, in order to combine historical and contemporary information. Some of the project's outcome will be located in the valley, and another part in the high mountains, while a third part will be presented at Kunsthaus Graz. The artworks develop new perspectives on the landscape, enhancing broad regional debate and social awareness of the political nature of landscape and everyday culture from a contemporary artistic perspective.

Political Resistance in the Salzkammergut 1943–1945

During the 19th century, the Salzkammergut was a popular holiday destination. Today it is one of the most highly developed cultural and tourist regions in Austria. Its name is attributed to the salt mining carried out here under imperial rule; an eventful history has left its traces across the Salzkammergut's picture-book scenery. This is a history intertwined with the forestry, mining and tourism industries, with the literature and fine arts of the Romantic era, as well as the political events of the war years from 1939 to 1945. Salt mines were used as shelter during air raids, and misused by the Nazis as bunkers for their looted art. It was only thanks to insubordination and heroic efforts during the final days of the war that these cultural riches were salvaged from destruction by the Nazis. Legends are spun of Nazi treasures buried deep at the bottom of a lake. Yet these mountains also provided refuge and escape routes for members of the Austrian Resistance opposing the dictatorship of the Third Reich—their history is far less well known. In acts of non-violent local resistance, for instance, men and women helped escapees from concentration camps or army defectors hiding out in the mountains. Directly following the war, many activists involved in the events of this period were employed either in municipal or city councils. Later, with the onset of the Cold War and its

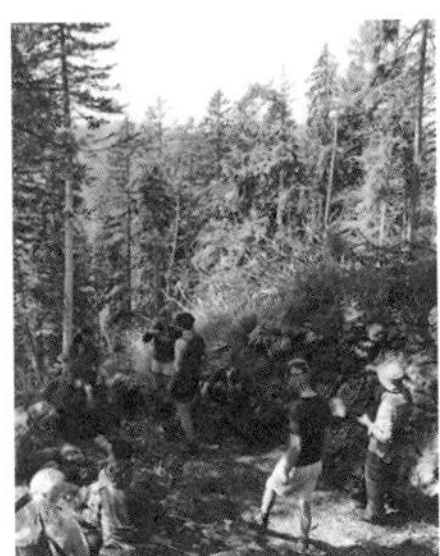

The hiking group at
the former 'Igel'
[Hedgehog]

ideological infighting, they found themselves once again on the defensive and, ultimately, sunk into oblivion. The scenes of these noteworthy events remain hidden from both locals and tourists to the region, with only a very few exceptions. The Ebensee Society for Contemporary History (Verein Zeitgeschichte Ebensee), for example, has marked the site of the Willy-Fred group's hiding place—'Igel' [Hedgehog] —with a commemorative plaque, albeit difficult to find. Individual works within the art project will lead to some of these historic sites.

However, the political aspect of landscape not only lies in dealing with complex social history or indicating a lack of will to do so in the past. Amongst other things, the title of the project also refers to Martin Warnke's investigation of the same name: 'Political Landscape' (1992). His opulent political iconography of art-historical images and real landmarks in the landscape (castles, monuments, memorials, parks and gardens) encreases one's awareness of how people exploited natural forms of landscape for purposes of military rule, feudal representation, conquest in the name of freedom, or, seen in totalitarian imagery, of legitimising power. His research shows that the instrumentalisation of nature went hand-in-hand with the acknowledgement of being 'an independent power in its own right', whose potential of 'action-guiding motives and experiences', however, is now exhausted owing to the pollution of civilisation[1].

Although relieved that nature can no longer be exploited to legitimise human interests, we share Warnke's pessimism in the light of the future development of global ecology and economy. In his conclusion, however, a further idea emerges to which he alludes without going into detail. This is because the above-mentioned power of nature surpasses the antagonistic relationship between the object nature and the human subject that enables modern day functional instrumentalisation and action-guiding acknowledgement of tamed nature in the first place. Going a little further, we arrive at an approach that transforms 'landscape' from a noun into a verb, thus fundamentally changing the perspective: 'Landscape, we suggest, doesn't merely signify or symbolize power relations; it is an instrument of cultural power, perhaps even an agent of power that is (or frequently represents itself as) independent of human intentions.'[2]

Apart from its natural appearance, this project views the mountain landscape as an agent, in constant interdependency with human acting, thinking and feeling. It is subject to historic and natural changes. In this perspective, landscape changes from a noun to a verb that we can read as 'landscaping'. Seen as an agent with its own power and in its own right, landscape thus describes a relationship of transfer as change that intervenes in human activities and transforms them. Because of this, it was crucial for all participants in this art project to experience both social history and landscape. For artefacts such as artworks are also able to change our perception or actions through the language of materials and forms. The *Political Landscape* project carefully places artworks in the landscape as a publicly accessible space. Artworks like these are by no means normative: they are intended

1
Martin Warnke:
*Politische Landschaft.
Zur Kunstgeschichte
der Natur.* Munich 1992,
pp. 171-173. Cf. Martin
Warnke: *Political Landscape. The Art History
of Nature.* Cambridge,
MA 1995.

2
W. J. T. Mitchell (ed.):
Landscape and Power.
Chicago 1994, 2nd
edition 2002, p. 1f.

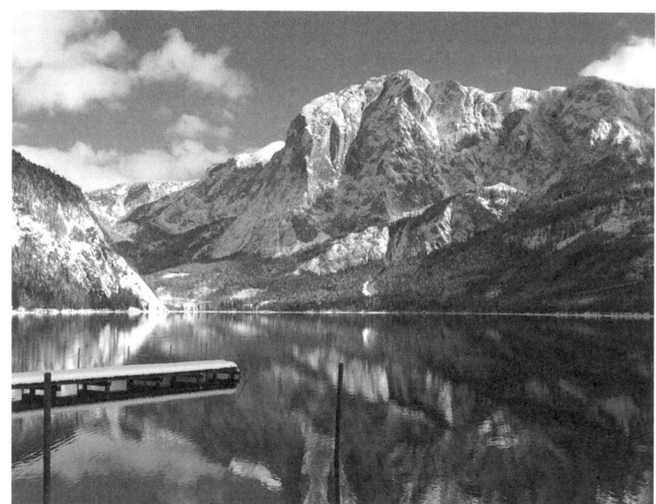

Lake Altaussee

neither as imperative nor as representative monuments, nor do they symbolise an image of legitimised nature or naturalise manmade relationships in the cultural medium. They rather provide an opportunity to reflect within a transformative relationship whose 'political or ethical dimension is actually [derived] from the fact that this articulation cannot be attributed solely to the power of human beings.'[3]

Prospect

Although public space was previously considered the terrain of the inner city, nowadays—due to growing urbanisation, tourism, transport infrastructure and new technology—it extends into the outlying countryside. The concept of public space can be applied to the mountain ranges outside the city, now freely accessible to everyone and even supported by Styrian law, based on the 'right to roam' (§ 5 Steiermärkisches Wegefreiheitsgesetz 1922). The art projects detailed on the following pages originate from a workshop that focused on researching the Salzkammergut and Ausseerland regions. The workshop was held from 14–24 August 2014 in Bad Mitterndorf, Bad Aussee, Altaussee, and Totes Gebirge. The artists are introduced here with reference to a selection of their individual works. Their respective proposals for Aussee are only briefly mentioned since, once realised, the project will enter a second phase. Certain sites, aspects and technical details may change within the individual designs over the course of the project.

[3] Kathrin Busch: *The Language of Things and the Magic of Language. On Walter Benjamin's Concept of Latent Potency*. http://eipcp.net/transversal/0107/busch/en (08.02.2015).

Clegg & Guttmann

Michael Clegg, b. 1957 in Dublin (IE), lives in Berlin (DE), Vienna (AT) and New York, NY (US);
Martin Guttmann, b. 1957 in Jerusalem (IL), lives in Berlin (DE), Vienna (AT) and New York, NY (US)

Library of Collective Memory 1945, 2015
Bookshelf filled with books on the subject, microphone (Shure SM58)
and stand, 2 PC computers (transmission and reception units), ampli-
fier, weather-resistant speaker, cable, software Max MSP
Courtesy of the artists

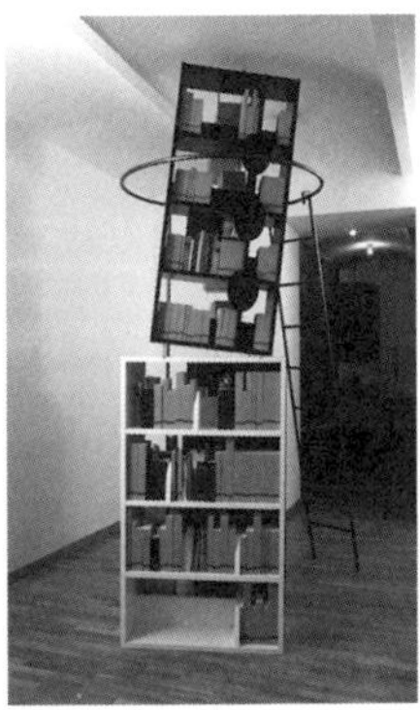

Clegg & Guttmann
Sha'at'nez or The Displacement Annex,
2004, Sigmund-Freud-Museum, Vienna

Clegg & Guttmann moved to New York in 1978 to study at the School of Visual Arts under Joseph Kosuth and formed a lasting artist duo in 1980. Their artwork is highly regarded internationally and was shown early on at documenta VIII (1988) and the 46th Venice Biennale (1995). Both frequently work in and with public space.

Through the mediums of photography, installation art, and object art, Clegg & Guttmann analyse the structures of societal power and its representation. This may lead to works of monumental scale thematising public commemoration and the problematic question of national identity, as with the *Monument of Monuments for Unity & Freedom* (2010), a proposal for a public competition in Berlin. But this is also achieved in a masterly way through the classic genre of portraiture, for the aesthetics of the stately portrait have remained closely associated with politics and sovereign power since the Renaissance and Baroque periods.

Assembled in a portrait, as in a landscape, are not only the individual features of a person or group of people, but also their claim to power and signs of their position within society. In Clegg & Guttmann's work, models that predominantly originate from their circle of acquaintances are arranged subtly and obviously in equal measure. They each assume a certain role, for instance in portraits of families, companies or artists. They become semiotic vehicles against an artificially imposed backdrop, which coalesces fragments from other pictorial traditions. The portraits become multilayered analyses of self-representation in the context of the social world—immersed in the artist duo's conceptual slant on art, which gives rise to a further realm for reflecting on medium, image, and subject of depiction.

Clegg & Guttmann establish connections between pictorial surfaces, three-dimensional objects, and their spatial order, thus directly addressing social communities. For example, their installed and freely accessible glass-encased bookshelves called *The Open Public Library*[1] were developed, starting in 1991, for public use and various locations. Each and every participant is allowed to remove books from the shelves and is invited most especially to place his or her own books inside. An almost consistent principle in the artistic work of Clegg & Guttmann is activating involvement on the part of the beholder. Together with those engaging with the social sculptures and installations in public space, these works sketch a vague collective picture of a group, a site, or a city district. In the town of Altaussee, Clegg & Guttmann plan to place literature on the topic of *Political Landscape* in the shop 'Buch & Boot' [Book & Boat]

1
The Open Public Library was situated in Graz in 1991, in Hamburg in 1993, at the Hofgarten in Augsburg in 2001, and has been at the Jewish Cemetery in Krems since 2004. Achim Könneke (ed.): *Clegg & Guttmann. die Offene Bibliothek / The Open Public Library*. Ostfildern 1994.

so that Aussee residents and visiting travellers can read select passages aloud. The readings will be broadcast into the mountains via microphone. Near the Blaa-Alm there is a receiving station designed to transmit the signal to a loudspeaker in the forest. People who just happen to be strolling past are then able to listen to the reading.   *– DM (SC, MN) –*

→ p. 286

Eva Grubinger

b. 1970 in Salzburg (AT), lives in Berlin (DE)
www.evagrubinger.com

Hedgehog, 2015
Glazed wood; 46,6 cm (h), ø 44 cm
Courtesy of the artist

Eva Grubinger's works appropriate form and site, establish new dimensional scales, and imbue them with new meaning. In Grubinger's artwork, content assumes artistic form through material, colour, proportion, corporeality, and ultimately also through the lightness of reduction and its playful elegance. Extensive thematic research flows into space-encompassing exhibition situations which appeal to the visitors in ways that are both candidly sensuous and aesthetically reflective. Here, Grubinger's works repeatedly hark back to the elementary questions of form posed during modernity, related to the function, utilisation, and autonomy of art. But her themes are political, with the artist subjecting the traces of modernity to interpretation from a present-day perspective. Smoking for example. Exhaled smoke communicates with the world. It expresses open enjoyment from the inside to the outside. Today, smoking has been 'excommunicated'. In the near-to-nature park at Bad Bentheim Clinic, a health centre in Lower Saxony near the Dutch border, Grubinger put up a black steel pavilion for the 2011 sculpture project *kunstwegen*. *Smoking Shelter* is a cubic sculpture in a beautiful setting underneath chestnut trees on the banks of a pond, almost literally breathing the form-follows-function idea of Modernism. Openly accessible to everyone, it invites users to smoke. The wide band of steel at head level provides anonymity, at the same time bursting with wit, for this perfectly designed shelter turns into a stage that both exposes and shields its actors. An ambivalent flash of irony in broad daylight.
In Altaussee, shelter is again referred to but in a completely different way. Grubinger will apply her project proposal to the fabled 'Igel' [Hedgehog] retreat in the Totes Gebirge region. This was used from 1943 to 1945 by Austrian oppositionists hiding from the National Socialists. The artist has designed a useable sculpture that provides visitors with a seat providing a view of the landscape. The round, bristly form of the wooden sculpture is enlarged from a similarly designed object of the same name once owned by Oscar Bondy. His collection was 'Aryanised' by the National Socialists in the 1930s. The most remarkable works in Bondy's collection were among the looted art stored in the Altaussee salt mine. Grubinger's sculpture is to be placed both at the 'Igel' retreat in the

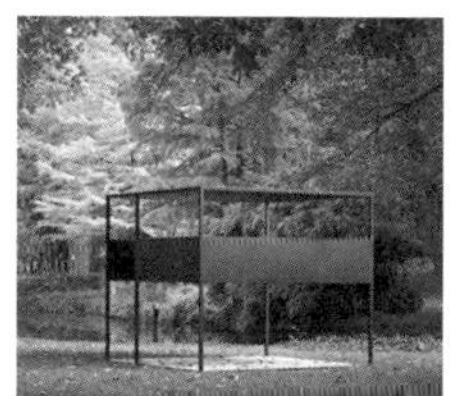

Eva Grubinger
Smoking Shelter,
2011, *kunstwegen,*
Bad Bentheim

mountains and in the communal park of Altaussee. Correlating two historical places, their setting reminds us of the terrible period of Aryanisation in the middle of this typical summer holiday resort. Here too, the art object becomes a stage—a stage for remembrance that is not immediately evident, but which nevertheless has a lasting impact as soon as it comes to light.

Eva Grubinger has exhibited internationally at important venues such as the Kiasma Museum of Contemporary Art, Helsinki (2001), Baltic Centre for Contemporary Art, Gateshead (2003), Berlinische Galerie, Berlin (2004), Schirn Kunsthalle, Frankfurt am Main (2007), Museum der Moderne, Salzburg (2009), and Museum Schloss Belvedere, Vienna (2012). She has participated in group exhibitions at Deichtorhallen Hamburg (2002), Taipei Fine Art Museum (2008), Krannert Art Museum, Illinois (2009), Marrakech Biennale (2012), Galeria Vermelho, São Paulo (2013), and Witte de With Centre for Contemporary Art, Rotterdam (2014). *– DM (SC, MN) –*

→ p. 288

Florian Hüttner

b. 1964 in Bad Tölz (DE), lives in Bad Tölz (DE) and Hamburg (DE)
www.florianhuettner.de

HIDEOUT (Turtle), 2015
Paint compatible with nature; dimensions variable
Courtesy of the artist

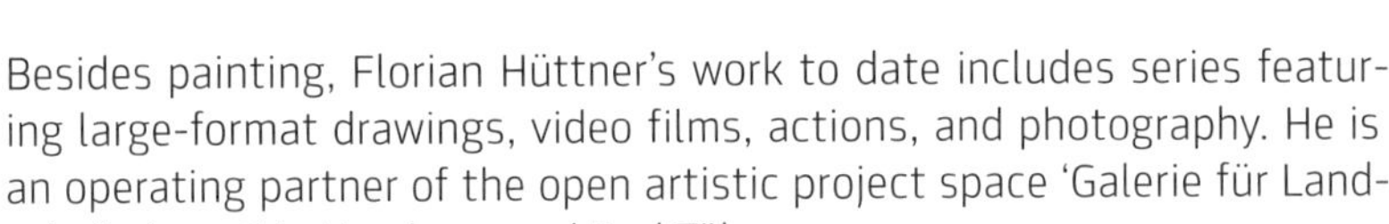

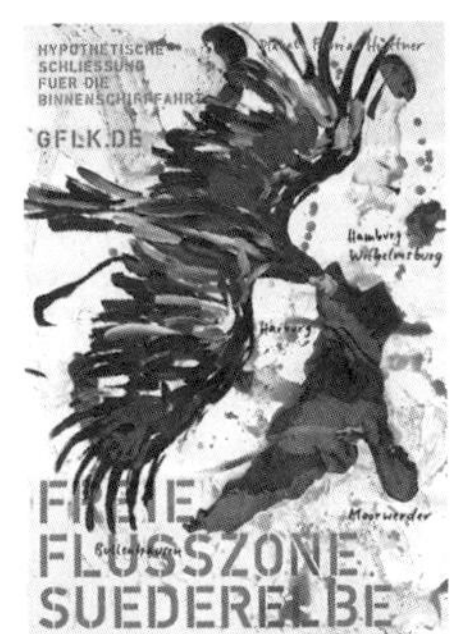

Florian Hüttner
*Freie Flusszone
Süderelbe*, 2012,
poster

Besides painting, Florian Hüttner's work to date includes series featuring large-format drawings, video films, actions, and photography. He is an operating partner of the open artistic project space 'Galerie für Landschaftskunst' in Hamburg und Bad Tölz.

Hüttner combines painting with drawing. From painting he borrows the large format, the expressive gestures, and the armamentarium—and with the spontaneity and levity of drawing he visually conflates his thinking. The large-format sheets eschew colour for the most part. The artist's line is often coarsely applied by the brush, yet some detailed ink strokes remain visible nonetheless. Traces of kinetic energy cover the pictorial surface like borderlines—contouring, encircling, or opening. Delineated in the work is a certain corporeality.

Hüttner overcomes any fixation on the surface in ways deviating from those used in modern painting, such as colour contrasting, to instead lend a literally space-consuming quality to his graphic works. Dimension, proportion and installation are the spatial parameters of his art. Many sheets first begin to unfold before the lingering eye. An initial impression is quickly imparted, but the delicate haziness of the motifs and themes requires more thorough reflection. It is indicative of spontaneous thrust reversal, hesitation and revision, roughness and delicacy. From the classic draft sketch to the ink drawing, and even including photography and video, Hüttner uses methods of production to both draw and record. His stance is contemporary. He expands his artistic methods to integrate mass media such as posters, videos, and radio broadcasting. In the Totes Gebirge region, Hüttner will be working on creating a kind of cave painting—in a seam, for example, or in a partial cavern or recess that is somewhat protected and remote. Caves can be perfect 'time capsules'. His rock painting is sculptural, working on and with the uneven ground. It is applied using biodegradable paints or pigments and is not meant to last for all eternity, exposed as it is to natural processes of change. Hüttner is inspired by the spatial situation of the 'Igel' [Hedgehog] hideaway, which he equates with a cave in terms of its protective function, and establishes a retreat comparable to the 'Igel' in a different place. The artist thematises the fact, still important today, that the Igel has given rise to narratives and legends, still anchored in local history like a myth. His mural sets out to express the vague, uncertain and also harsh and painful facets of the historical situation. At the entrance to the salt mine in Altaussee, information about the site in the mountains will be presented. *– DM (SC, MN) –*

→ p. 290

Angelika Loderer

b. 1984 in Feldbach (AT), lives in Vienna (AT)
www.angelikaloderer.at

Larches and Stones, 2015
Tree saplings (larch), wire, concrete, stones; dimensions variable
Courtesy of the artist

Styrian artist Angelika Loderer studied sculpture at the University of Applied Arts in Vienna and received several awards for her work, such as the Promotion Prize of the Province of Styria in 2013.
Loderer makes techniques, materials and forms of sculptural design the theme of her art. Draining, pouring, casting, ladling, layering, and pressing—as practised in skilled crafts and trades—are translated by the artist into free forms ranging from abstract to non-representational.
Assuming that we were encased in history today like a frozen flash of lightening, caught in a moment in time, then we would repeatedly encounter supra-historical phenomena and events that could liberate us from the burden of such human constraint. Research and art are two such methods that attempt a practical approach to staying clear of history's pitfalls. Certain artists tend to experiment with well-known techniques, discovering new paths in the process and venturing risks with montage or recontextualisation.
Angelika Loderer counts among these curious individuals—well trained in the canon of manual dexterity—who uncover moments of playful experimentation that eschew any given function yet without succumbing to the empty beauty of autotelic form. She takes the quartz sand used in bronze casting and presses it to create material collages in combination with found items from everyday life (*Untitled*, 2013) or with fragments from other works of art (*Untitled [With Dejan Dukic]*, 2014). She makes moulds of fragile mole burrows (*Casted Holes*, 2012) or rough

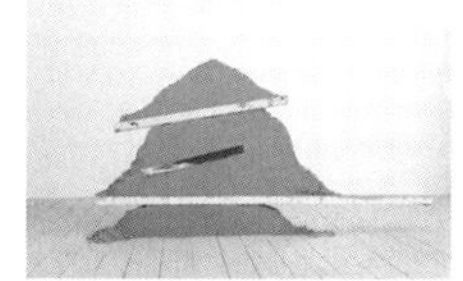

Angelika Loderer
Untitled [With Dejan Dukic], 2014

woodpecker cavities (*Untitled, [Buntspecht I-III]*, 2013) and casts them in bronze, displaying a breathtaking complexity of detail. Or she fashions *Death Masks* from grass, which slowly rot from the inside out, furnished with a layer of plaster *(Untitled [Totenmasken]*, 2014).

The landscape and social history of the Ausseerland region have inspired Loderer to work with pressure and gravity—with material pressure that can cause larch trees to exhibit strange deformations starting at about 900 metres above sea level and extending up to the treeline. Such deviant growth can be traced, among other factors, to the burden caused by heavy snow, the extended snowmelt, and the overlapping growth period in high-elevation mountain areas. Young trees are forced into whimsical forms. In her installation, Loderer uses, for instance, the weight of stones to coerce young tree saplings into unnatural shapes. Her natural sculptures allude to civil and political development in the region and also to the inhumane repercussions of the persecution practices pursued by a totalitarian regime, which left behind clear (though not immediately discernible) traces both in the valley and the highlands.   *– DM (SC, MN) –*

→ p. 292

Susan Philipsz

b. 1965 in Glasgow (GB), lives in Berlin (DE)

Slow Fresh Fount, 2015
Audio file, speakers, cable; dimensions variable
Courtesy of the artist

Slow, slow fresh fount. A musical setting by Edgar L Bainton of words by Ben Johnson. Copyright 1920 Joseph Williams.
Courtesy of Stainer & Bell Ltd

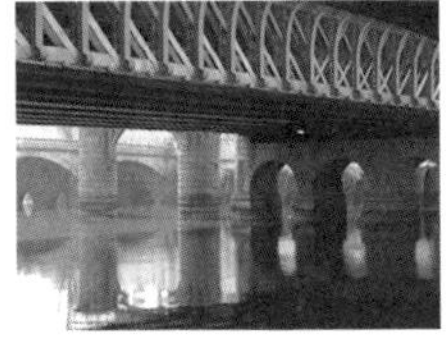

Susan Philipsz
Lowlands, 2010,
Glasgow International Festival of Visual Arts, Glasgow, 2010

Voice, sound, singing, tones and related environments comprise the sculptural material of Susan Philipsz, who works to define spaces through sound. Her installations establish connections to the setting in which they are audible, and they provide a new context for songs or sounds that are frequently of historical nature. Philipsz uses multitrack technology to transform comprehensive research on musical, literary and historical models into new sound pieces. On the one hand, the artist invokes her own untrained singing voice, such as in Münster with a song based on E. T. A. Hoffmann, *The Lost Reflection*, 2007, or in Glasgow (her hometown), where she tonally activated the hollow space under three bridges along the River Clyde with vocal scores in 2010.

In 2012 in Kassel, on the other hand, she disaggregated the *Study for String Orchestra* by Pavel Haas into sequences of sound. Haas's composition was originally composed in 1943 at the Theresienstadt concentration camp; the original score was lost and later reconstructed. At documenta 13 Philipsz distributed the different audio tracks featuring the individual instruments to the seven loudspeakers situated towards the end of the railway platforms at Kassel's central train station. This site had been the departure point for many deportation trains travelling to the extermination camp. The new sounds were just fragments of the score and blended with the everyday sounds populating the environment. The sounds thus activated both the individual power of imagination and collective memory, eliciting a heightened mindfulness of the site. The art of Susan Philipsz 'sits at a point where music becomes a kind of intangible sculptural material—or a material that points, often melancholically but not dogmatically, to absent bodies, absent objects.'[2] In the Altaussee salt mines—an ancient historical mining site that briefly served as one of several storage facilities for art looted by the National Socialists—Susan Philipsz will allow a two-voiced elegy from the year 1601 to resonate throughout the space. Its sound correlates with an installation playing at a nearby lake in the Ausseerland region.

Susan Philipsz studied in Dundee and Belfast. The sculptor is the 2010 recipient of the Turner Prize. She has presented solo exhibitions at Hamburger Bahnhof, Berlin (2014), K21, Düsseldorf (2013), Museum of Contemporary Art, Chicago (2010), among other venues, and has participated in group exhibitions at documenta 13 (2012), Biennale of Sydney (2008), and skulptur projekte münster (2007). Philipsz works in collaboration with the artist Eoghan McTigue. She has been awarded the Order of the British Empire.

– DM (SC, MN) –

→ p. 294

Bojan Šarčević

b. 1974 in Belgrade (RS), lives in Basel (CH) and Paris (FR)
www.bojansarcevic.net

The Partisan, 2015
Giant clam *Tridacna gigas*; 40 × 28 × 20 cm and 40 × 25 × 20 cm, ca. 17 kg
Courtesy of the artist

A giant clam from the South Pacific appears in the Totes Gebirge—for Bojan Šarčević, materials and things attain new meaning as artwork through reduction of form and dislocation to a new site. His sculptural works use this artistic method to appropriate clearly structured spaces so as to facilitate new aesthetic experiences.

For example, when the corner of a building earmarked for demolition in the Netherlands was removed for the work *World Corner* (1999) and subsequently placed in a gallery space in Germany, this process of transfer and displacement generated a plenitude of meaning. The item is still functioning as a corner but simultaneously implies more than a corner, for it connects the particles of its history with the information available about the new site. In a figurative sense, the work can be interpreted as a portrait of an existential shift in location, thus making the visual experience of those from other corners of the world accessible.

Here, the three dimensions explored by Šarčević as a sculptor also factor in time—not in a measurable dimension as with a clock, but in the unique time of *my* memory, *my* perception of present circumstances, and *my* expectations of future developments. In the artist's works, history

2
Martin Herbert: 'String Theories. On Susan Philipsz', in: Idem, *The Uncertainty Principle.* Berlin 2014.

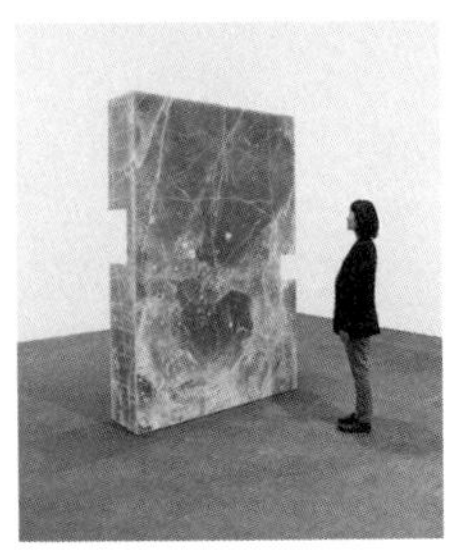

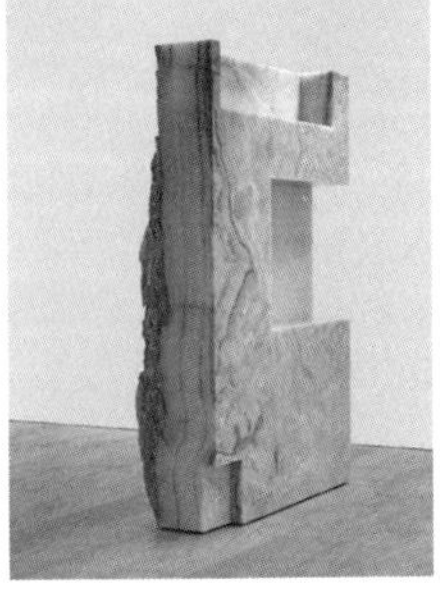

Bojan Šarčević
He, 2010
She, 2010

becomes an aesthetic moment of subjective perception, even when he alludes to prehistoric time.

A fold mountain range, the Alps were created millions of years ago due to continental drift. The limestone formations of the Totes Gebirge mountains even contain traces of primeval fossils. Šarčević is now setting out to generate a strange parenthetical state. In Bad Aussee he will be installing a giant clam *(Tridacna gigas)*, but each half in a different place: at a site that usually goes unnoticed, on the one hand, and near a hiking path in the Totes Gebirge on the other. The monumental sea creature originates from the South Pacific and is environmentally protected. Local use is only allowed if a permit is issued by the Austrian customs office. Decoratively placed atop concrete in the valley and artificially implanted in the highlands, the clam bridges gaps between time and space in a disconcerting way. While the open shell may appear vulnerably exposed to its surroundings, at the same time it is a fixed element within the mountainscape, similar to the 'Igel' [Hedgehog] hideaway.

Bojan Šarčević studied at the École des Beaux-Arts in Paris and at the Rijksakademie in Amsterdam. He took part in Manifesta 1998 and was invited to participate both in the 50th Venice Biennale in 2003 and, one year later, in the 3rd Berlin Biennale. In 2012, the Kunstmuseum Liechtenstein dedicated a large retrospective to Šarčević's work.

– DM (SC, MN) –

Abbildungen
Illustrations

Landschaft: Transformation einer Idee
Kunst von 1800 bis heute aus der Sammlung der Neuen Galerie Graz
Landscape: Transformation of an Idea
Art from 1800 to the Present Day from the Collection of the Neue Galerie Graz

Neue Galerie Graz

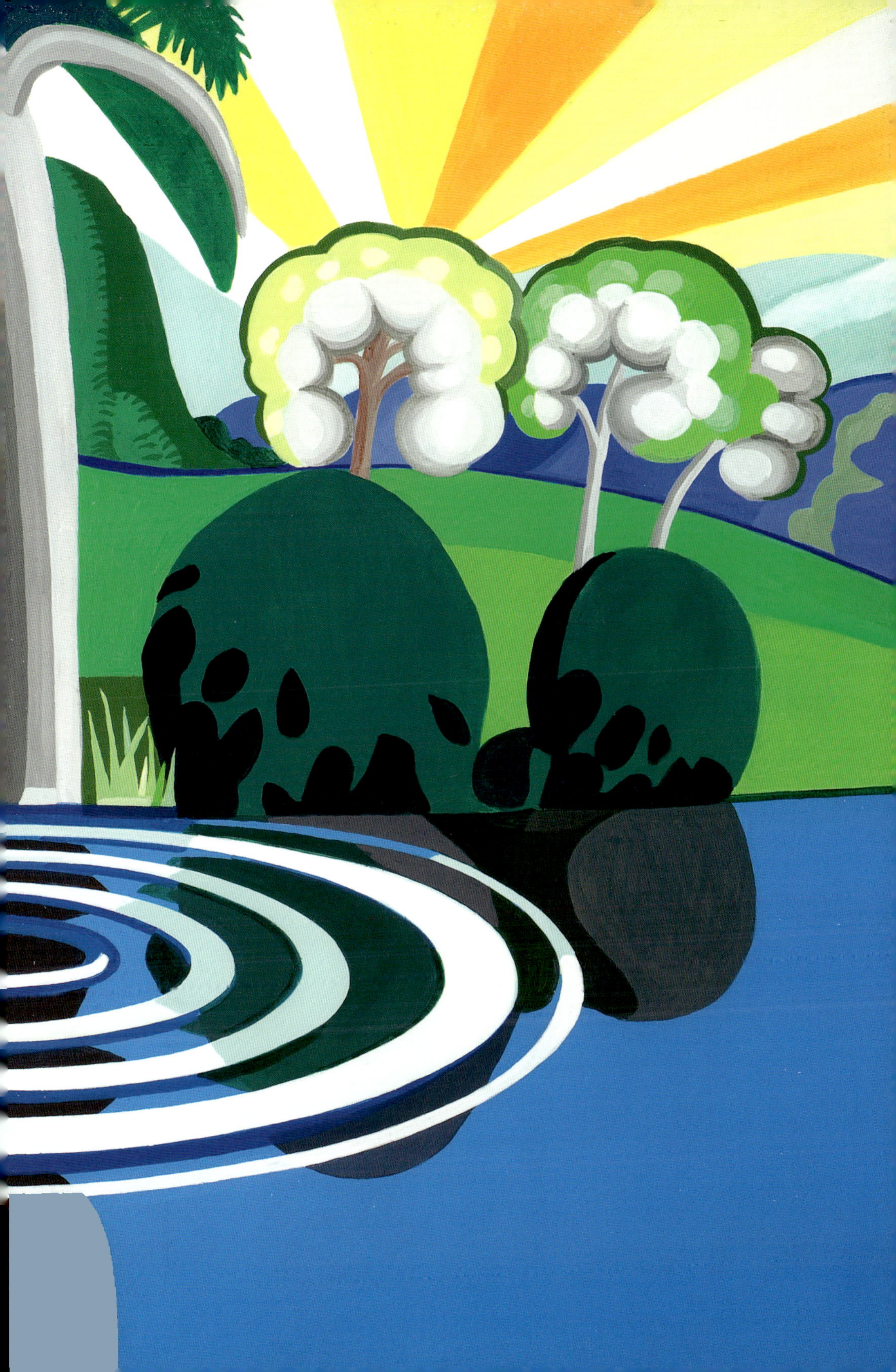

Erschließung der Landschaft / Mapping the Landscape

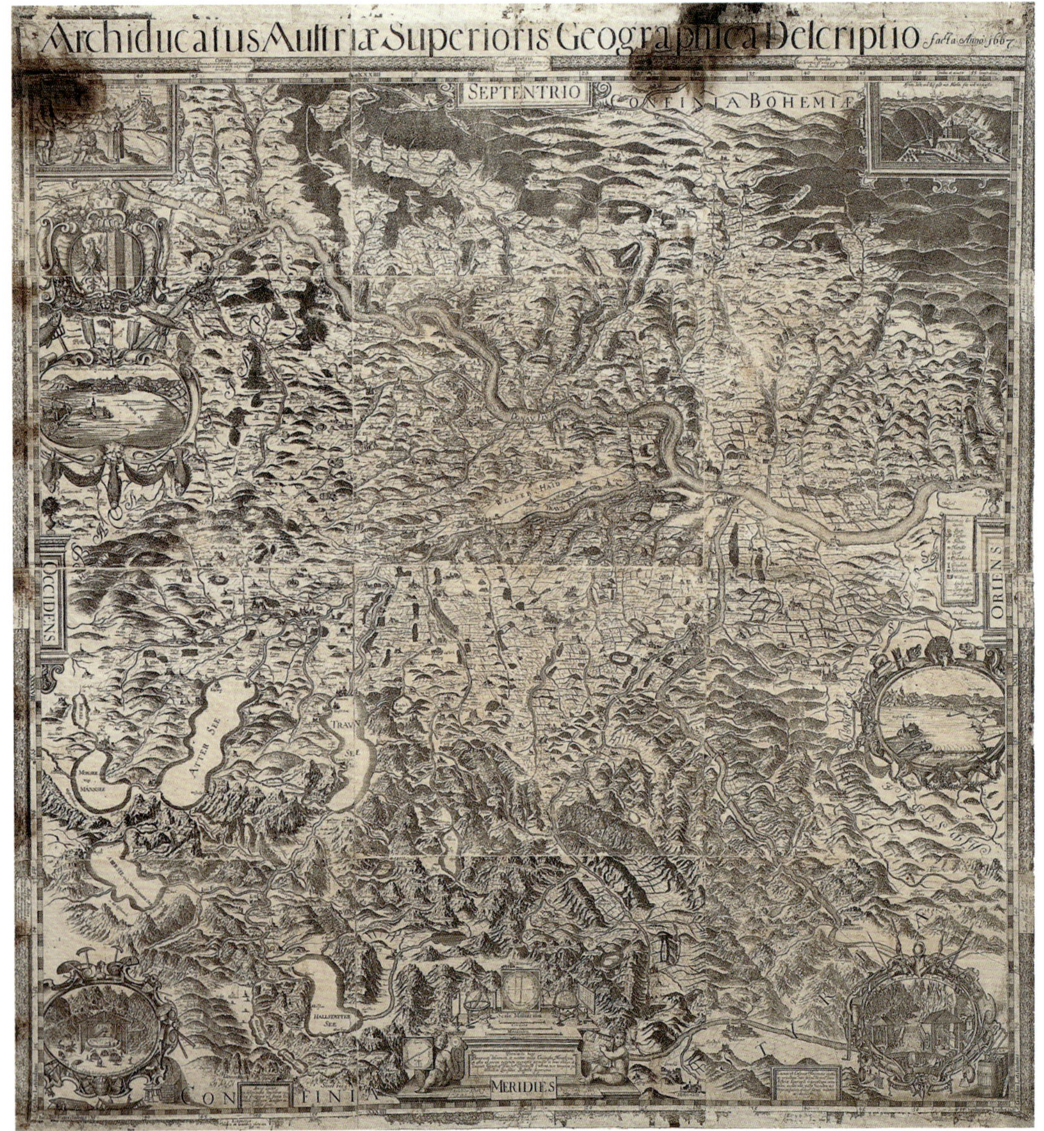

Georg Matthäus Vischer
Archiducatus Austriae Superioris Geographica Descriptio, 1667/69

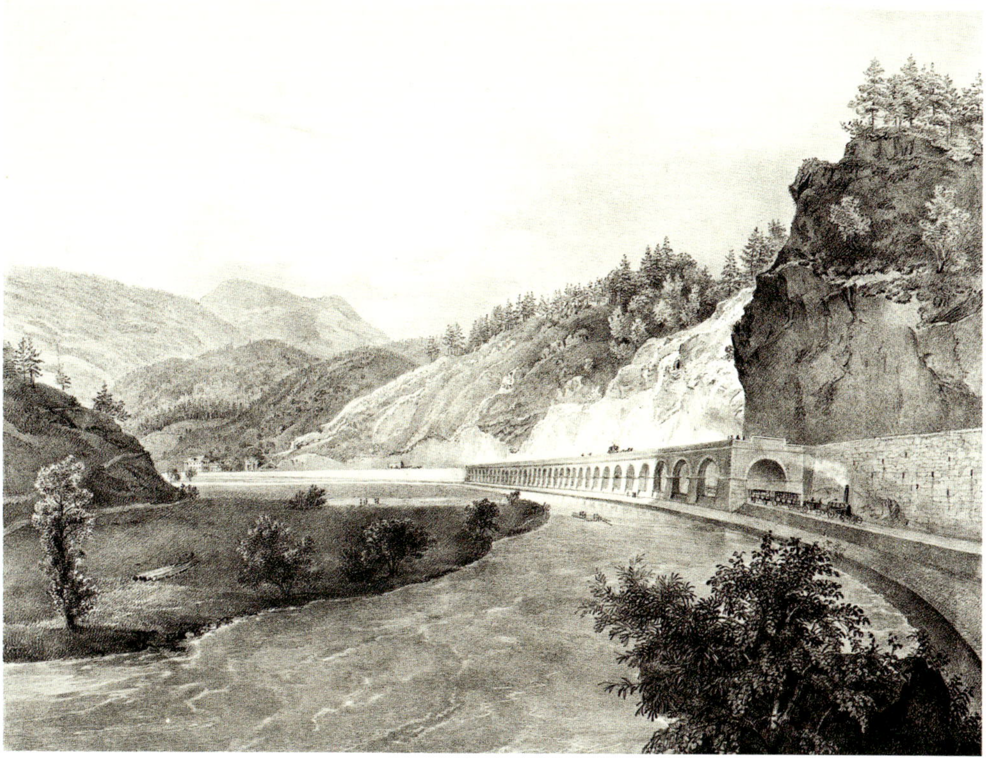

Joseph Kuwasseg
Die Badelwand mit den Gallerien zur Eisenbahn bei Peggau in Steiermark / The Badelwand with Arches for Railway near Peggau in Styria, 1844

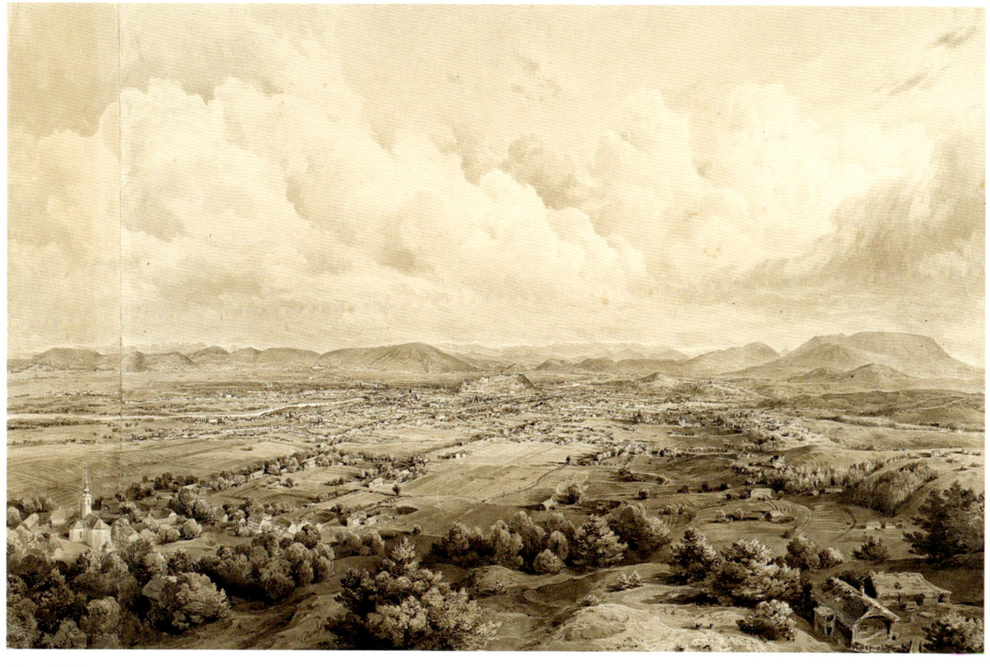

Joseph Kuwasseg
Blick auf Graz von St. Peter (Panorama von Graz) / View of Graz from St. Peter (Panorama of Graz), ca. 1850

Ideologisierung der Landschaft / Ideologisation of Landscape

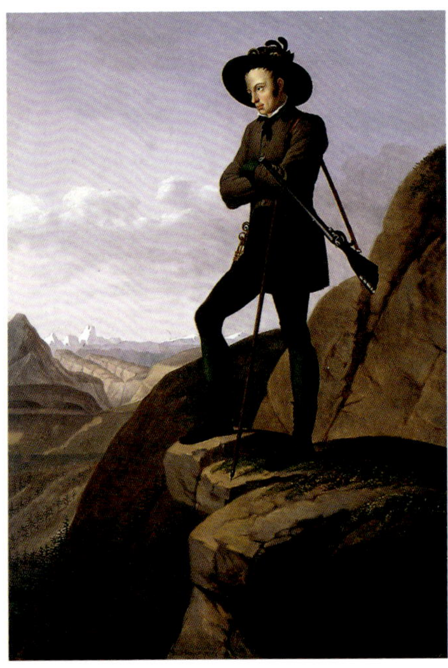

Johann Huber nach / after Johann Peter Krafft
Erzherzog Johann am Hochschwab / Archduke Johann on the Hochschwab, 1817/1839

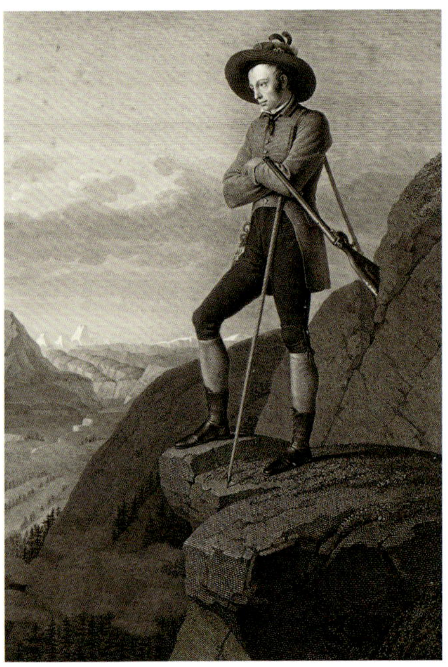

Blasius Höfel nach / after Johann Peter Krafft
Johann Erzherzog von Österreich / Johann Archduke of Austria, 1817/1818

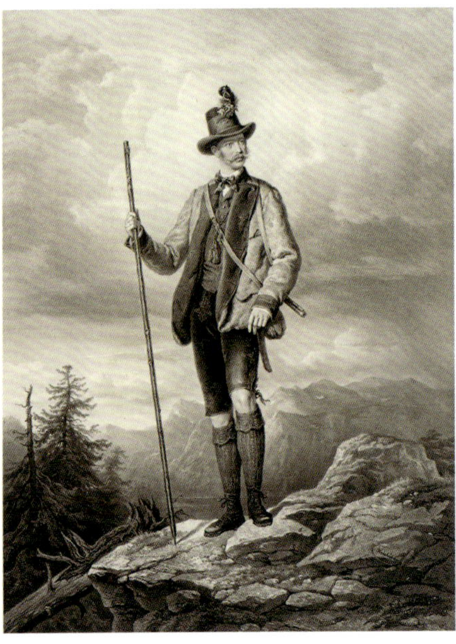

Josef Kriehuber
Franz Josef I. in ganzer Figur als Jäger in Alpenlandschaft / Franz Josef I in Full-length as Hunter in Alpine Landscape, 1850er-Jahre / 1850s

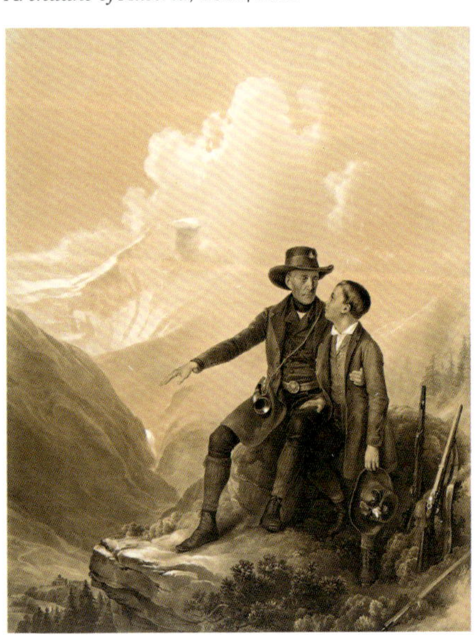

Eduard Weixelgärtner und / and Josef Kriehuber nach / after Johann Fischbach
Der alte Schütz mit seinem Sohn / The Old Huntsman with his Son, ca. 1850

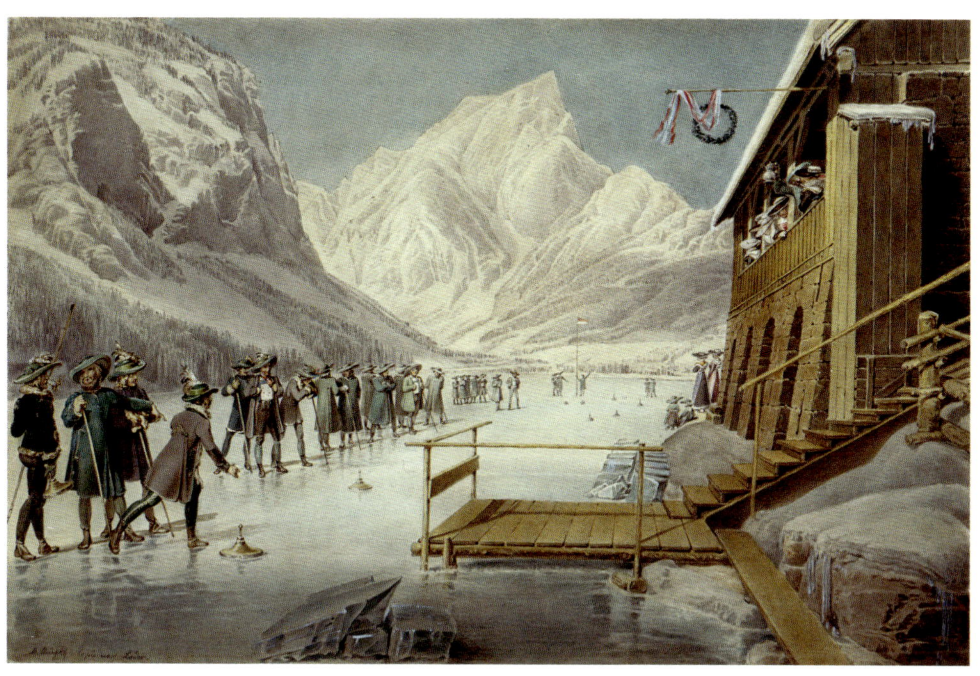

Melanie Stürgkh nach / after Matthäus Loder
Eisschießen auf dem Leopoldsteinersee / Curling on the Leopoldsteinersee, ca. 1822 / ca. 1955

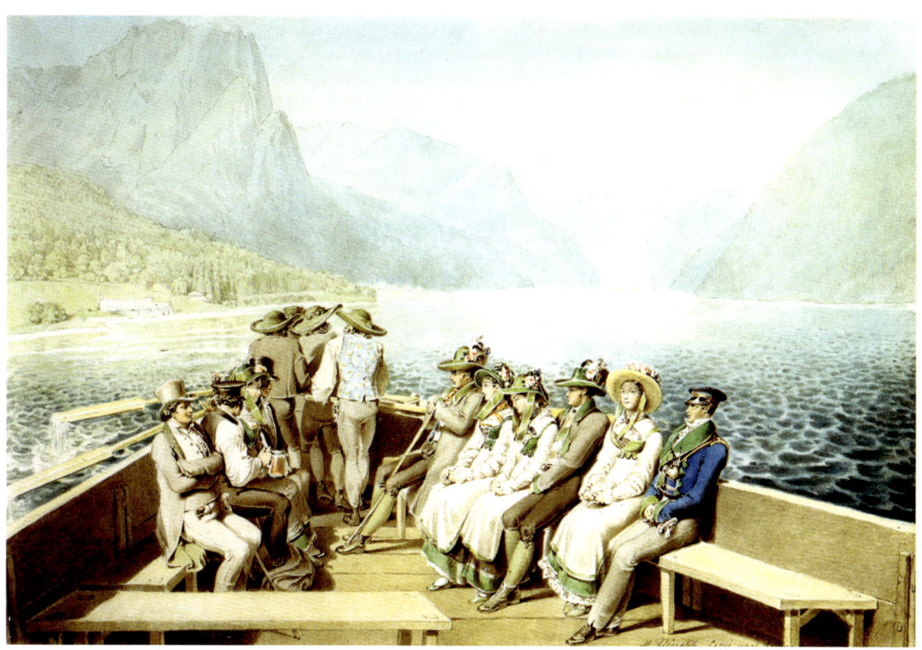

Melanie Stürgkh nach / after Matthäus Loder
Kahnfahrt auf dem Grundlsee / Boat Trip on the Grundlsee, 1822 / 1956

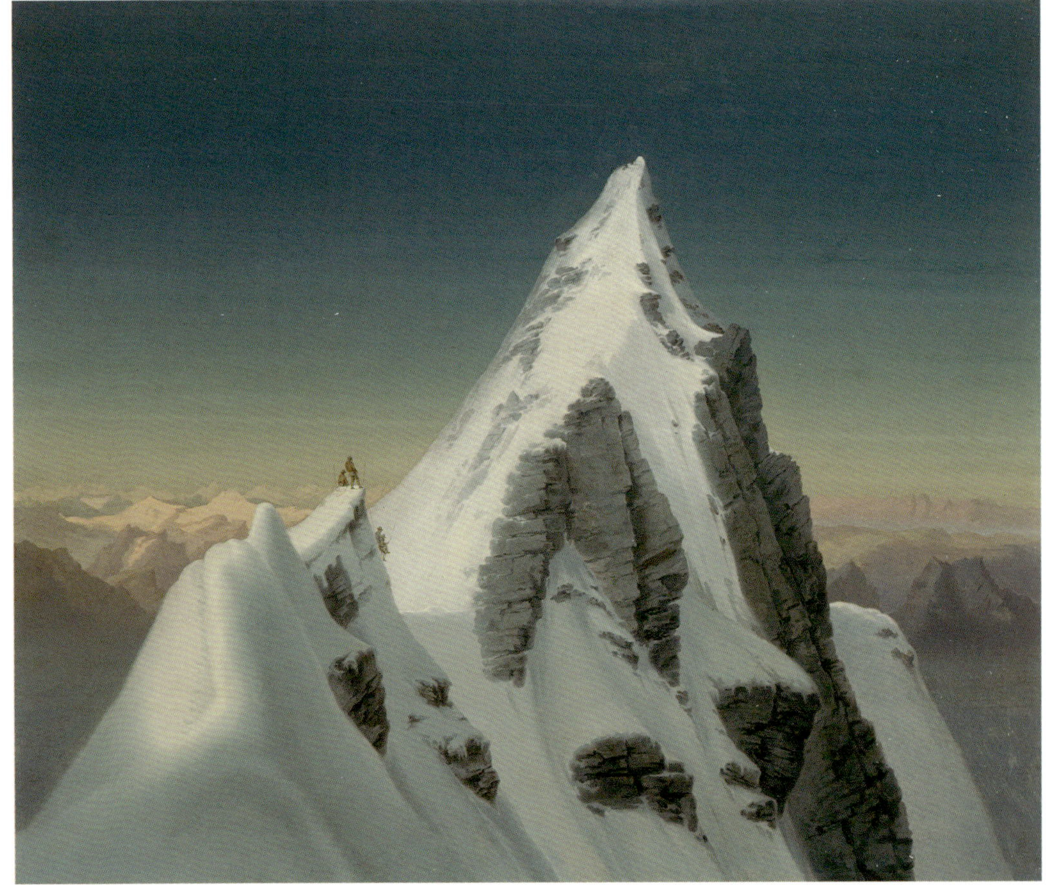

Markus Pernhart
Besteigung des Großglockners / Climbing the Großglockner, ca. 1850

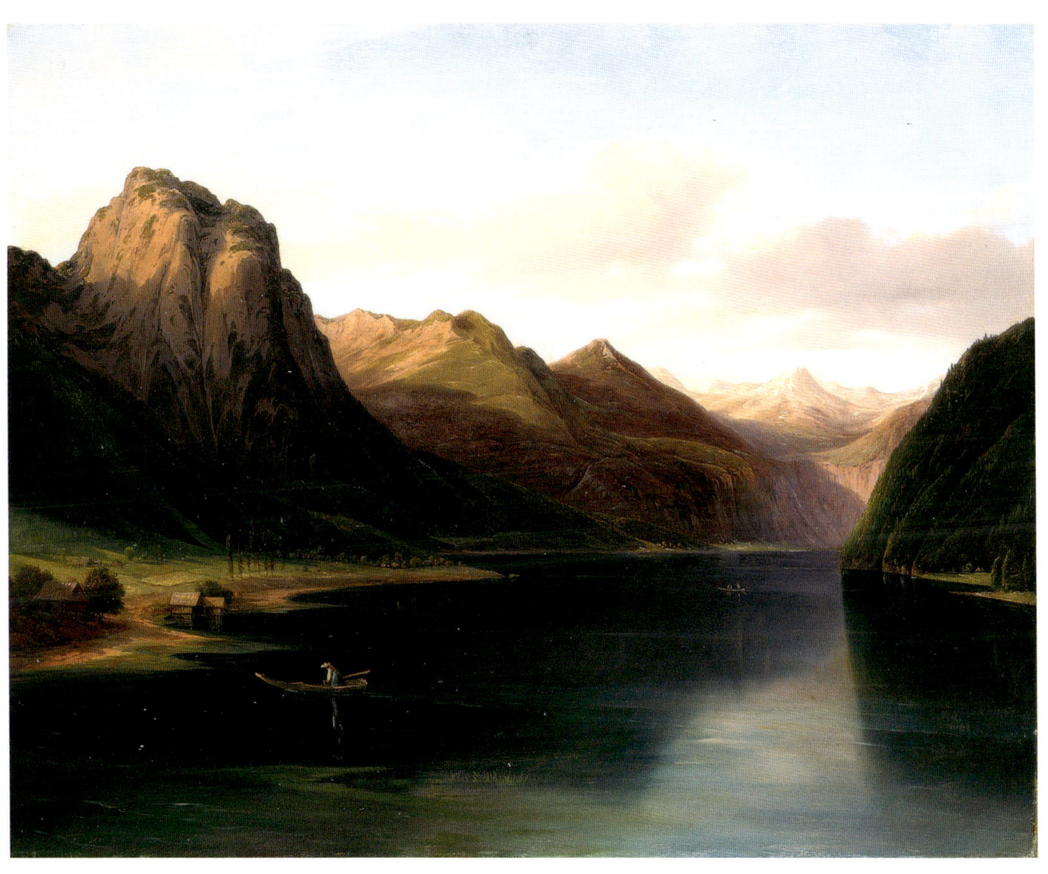

Franz Steinfeld
Grundlsee, ca. 1845

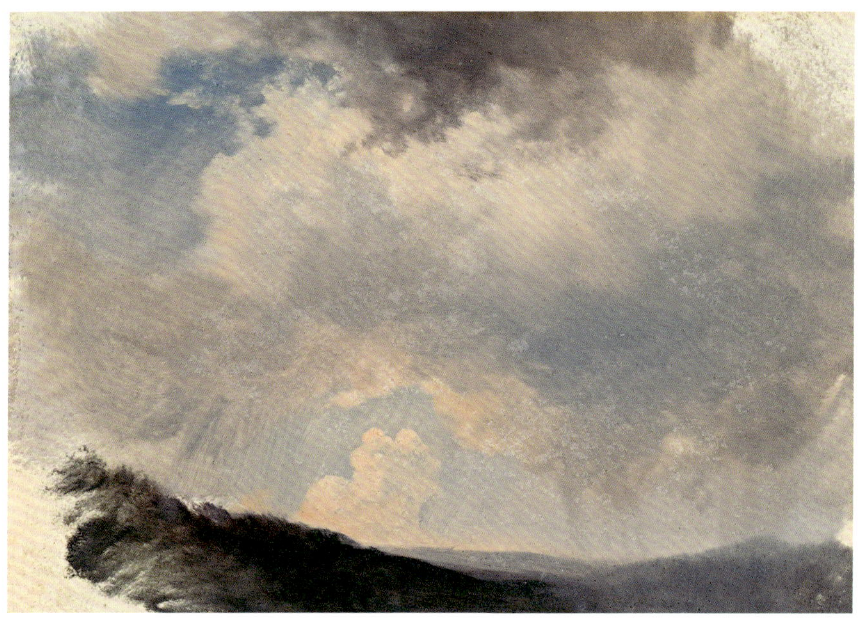

Friedrich Gauermann
Wolken-Studie / Study of Clouds, ca. 1830

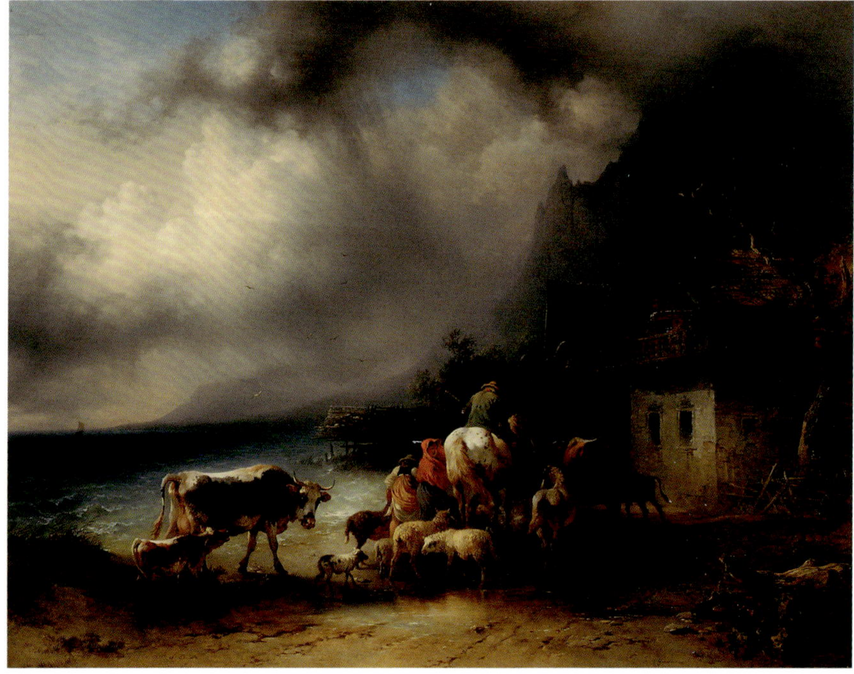

Friedrich Gauermann
Heimkehr im Gewitter am Attersee / Homecoming in the Thunderstorm on Attersee, 1856

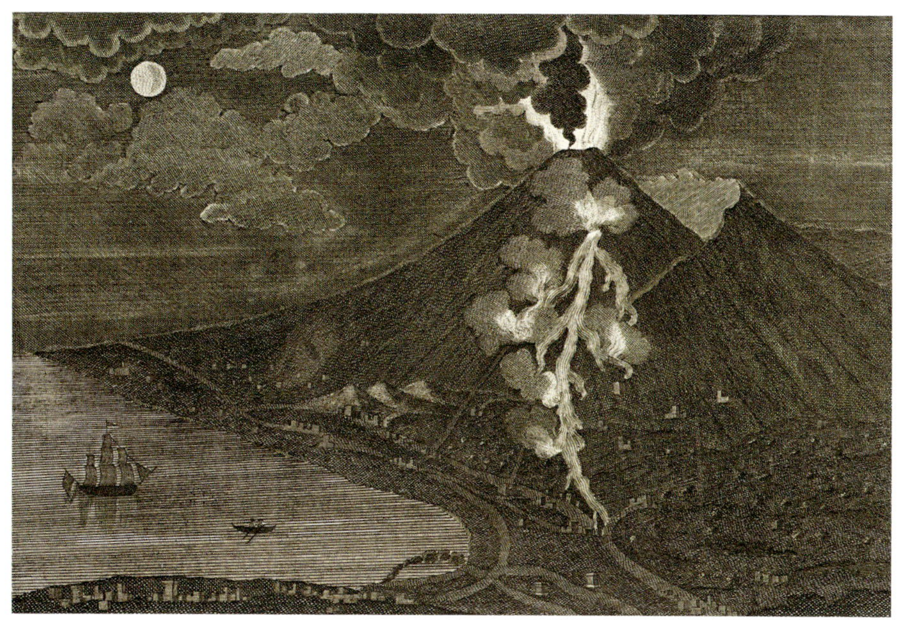

Nicolas Gervasi (Hg. / ed.)
Seite aus dem Buch / page from the book: *Les incendies du Mont Vesuve*, Neapel / Naples
ca. 1823

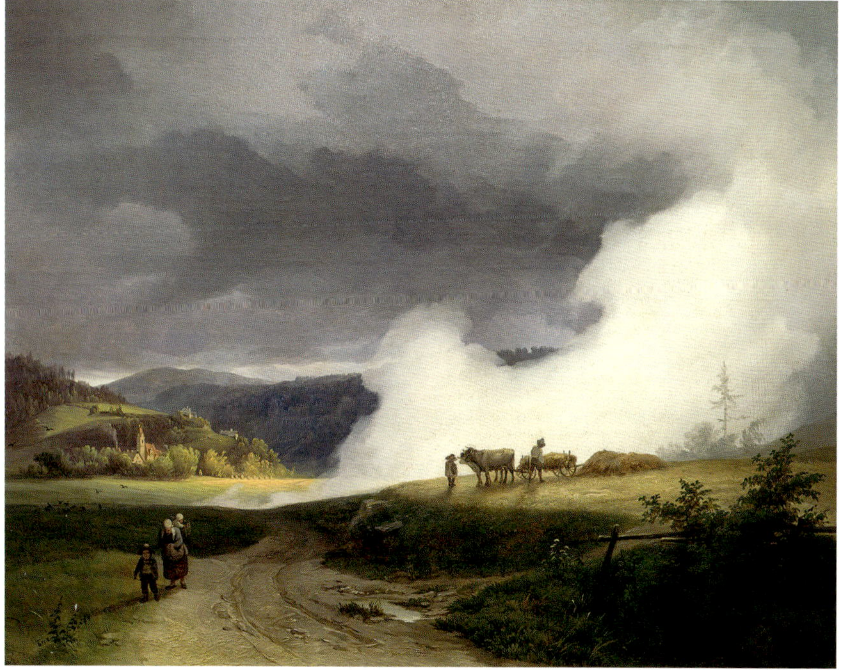

Ignaz Raffalt
Voralpenlandschaft mit aufsteigendem Nebel / Alpine Foothill Landscape with Rising Mist, 1845

Das Bild der Ferne zwischen Ideal und Wirklichkeit
Images of the Far-Off between Ideal and Reality

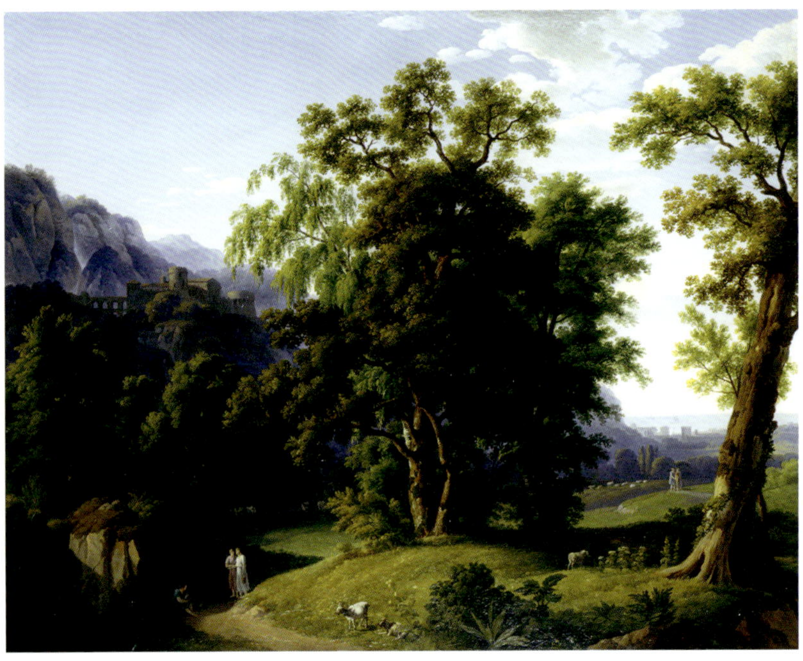

Johann Kniep
Arkadische Gebirgslandschaft / Arcadian Mountainscape, 1805

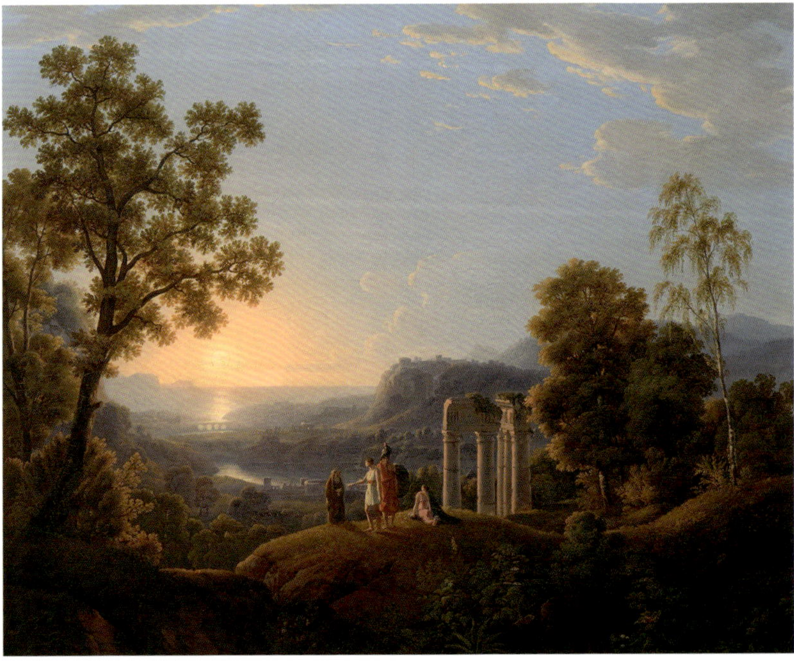

Johann Kniep
Ideale Landschaft (mit untergehender Sonne) / Ideal Landscape (with Sinking Sun), 1806

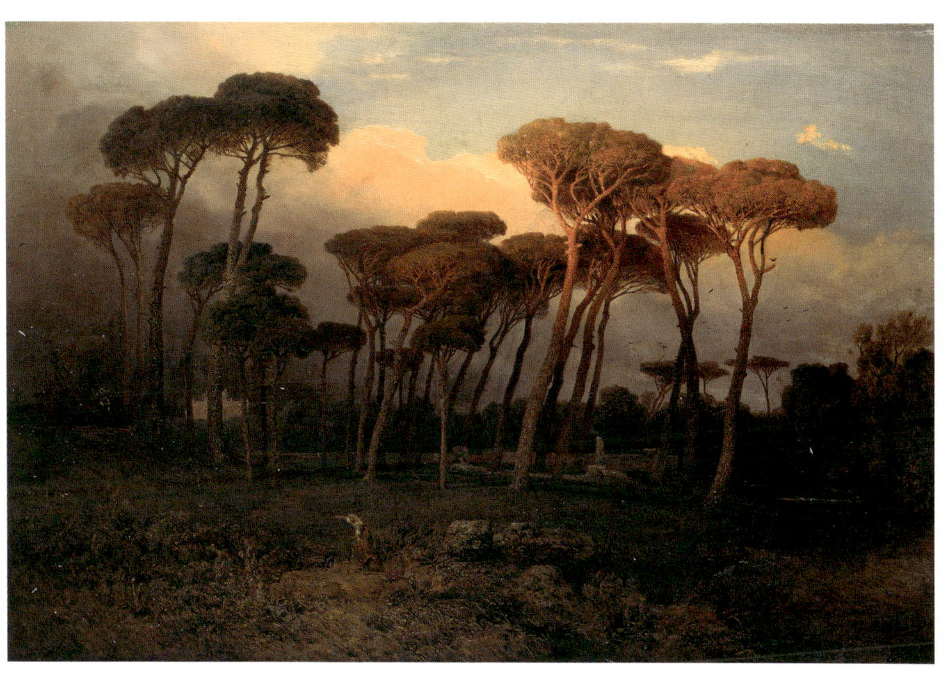

Joseph Selleny
Pinienhain in der Villa Doria-Pamphili in Rom / *Pine Grove in the Villa Doria-Pamphili in Rome*, 1854

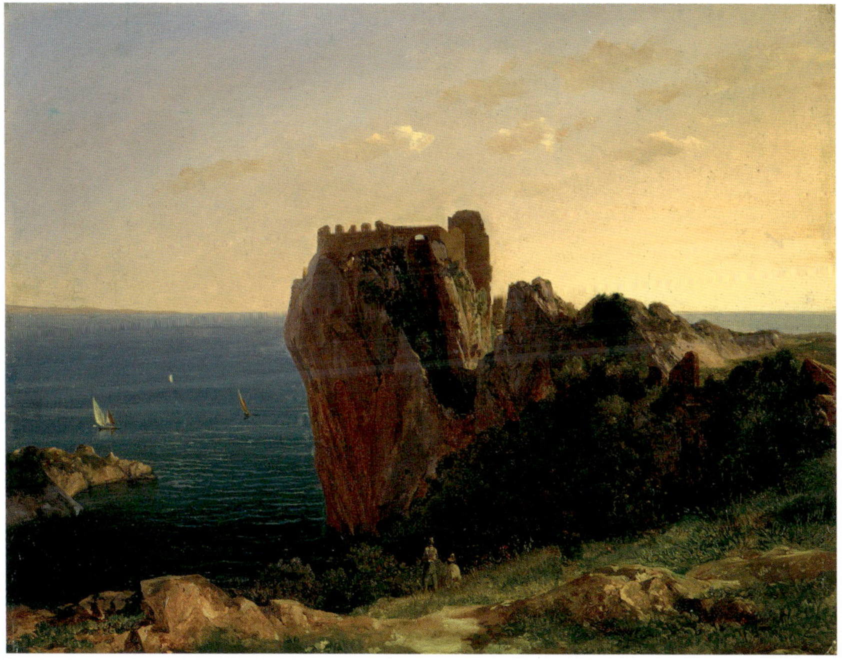

Thomas Ender
Der Dante-Felsen bei Duino / *The Cliff of Dante at Duino*, ca. 1853

Erdgeschichtsforschung und visuelle Darstellung
History of the Earth Research and Visual Represention

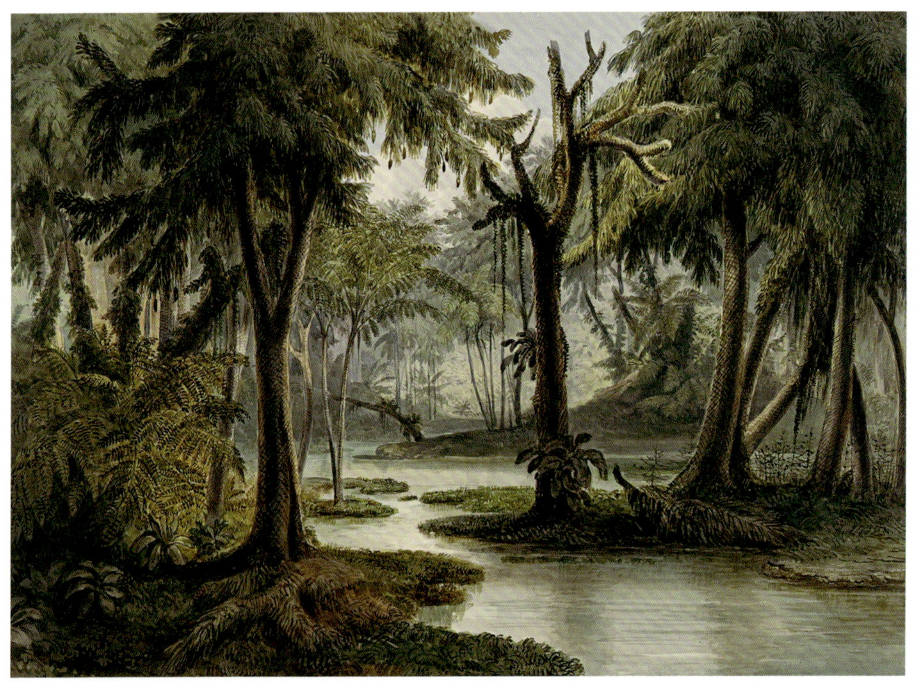

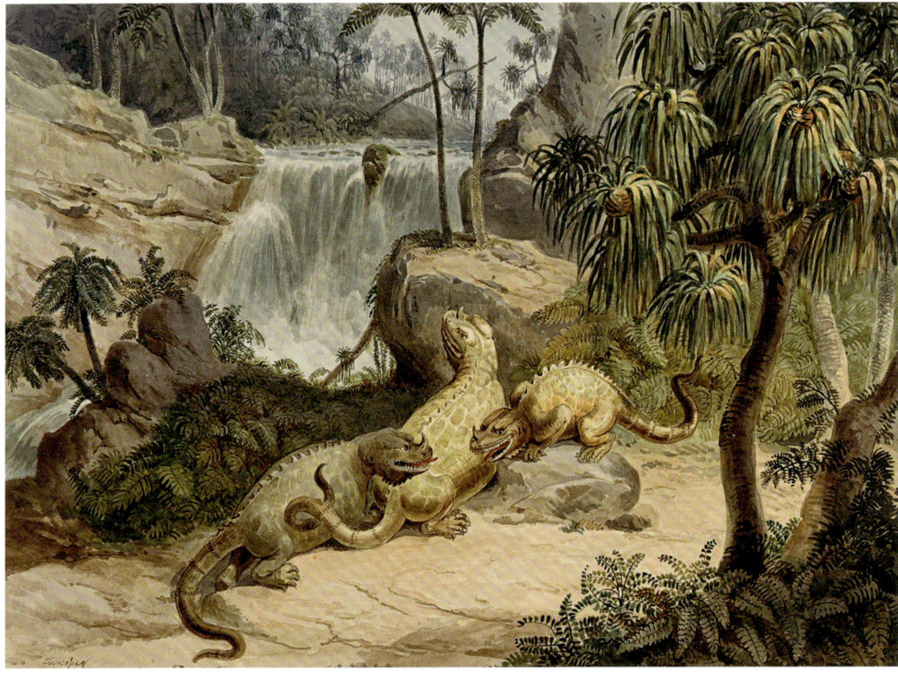

Joseph Kuwasseg
Aus | from: *Die Urwelt in ihren verschiedenen Bildungsperioden (nach der Schrift von Prof. Franz Unger)* /
The Primeval World in its Various Stages of Formation (after the Writings of Prof. Franz Unger), 1846–49

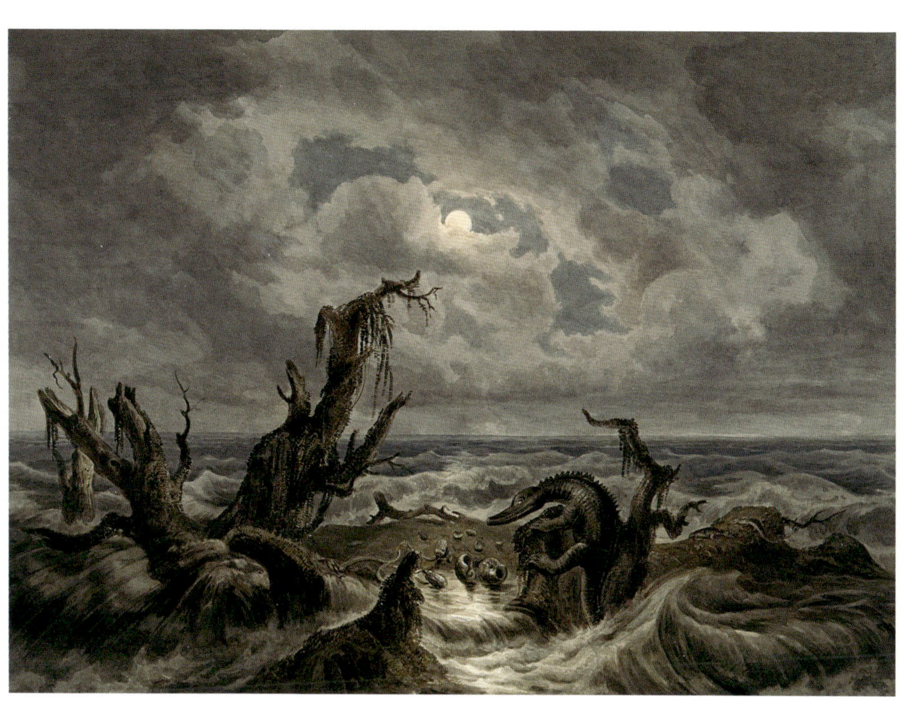

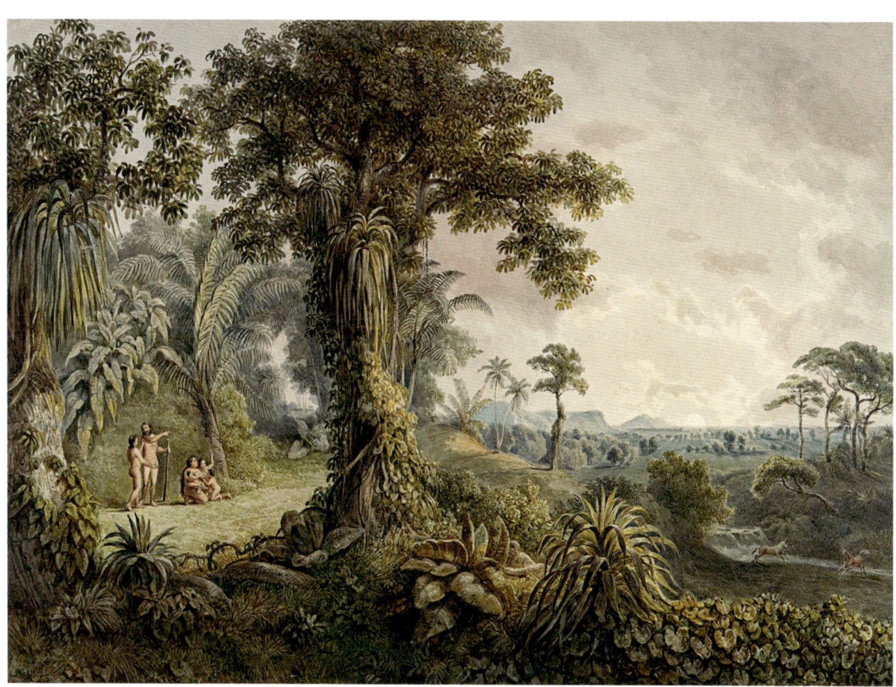

Reisen als Konzept / Travel as a Concept

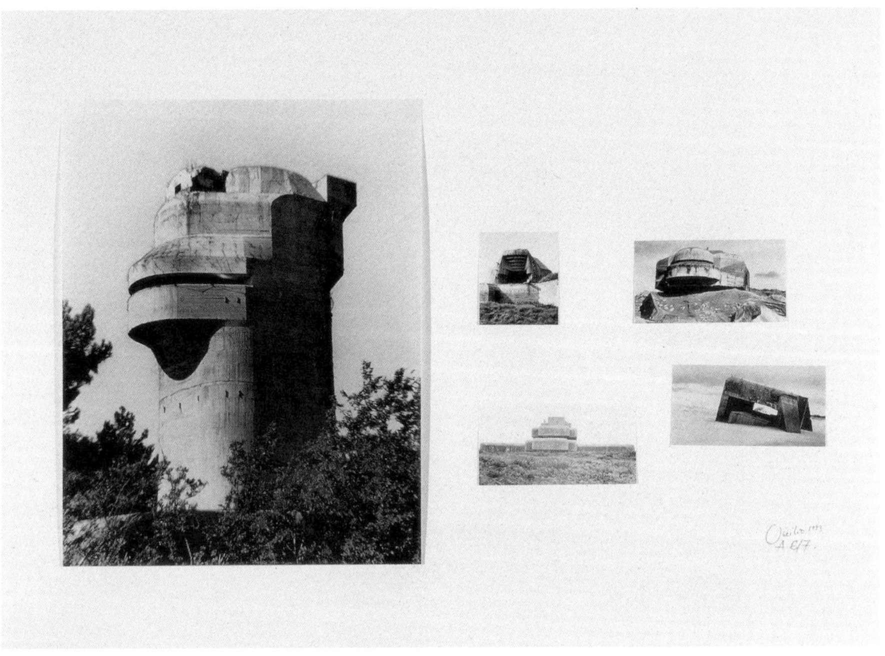

Paul Virilio
Bunker archéologie, Karola, 1958–65/93

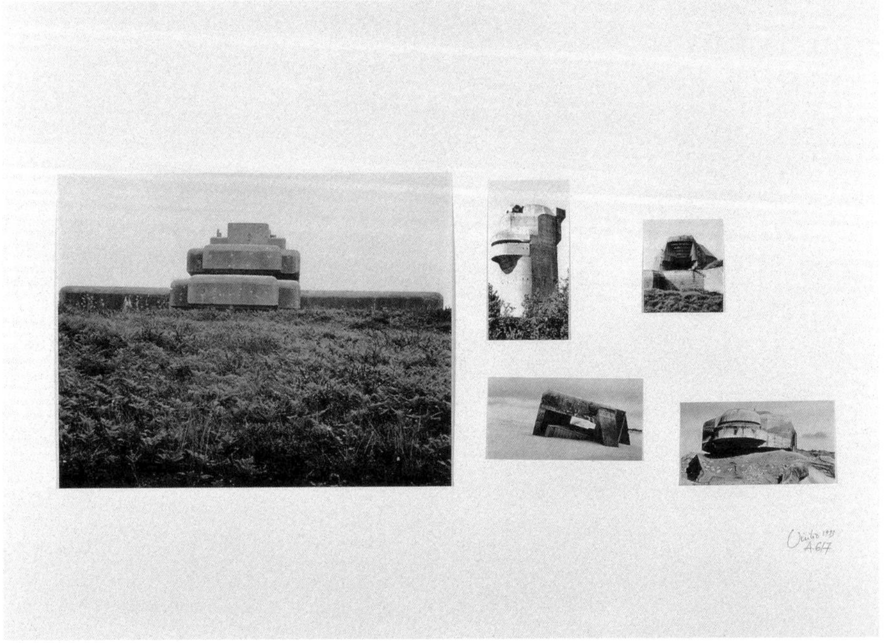

Paul Virilio
Bunker archéologie, Seeadler, 1958–65/93

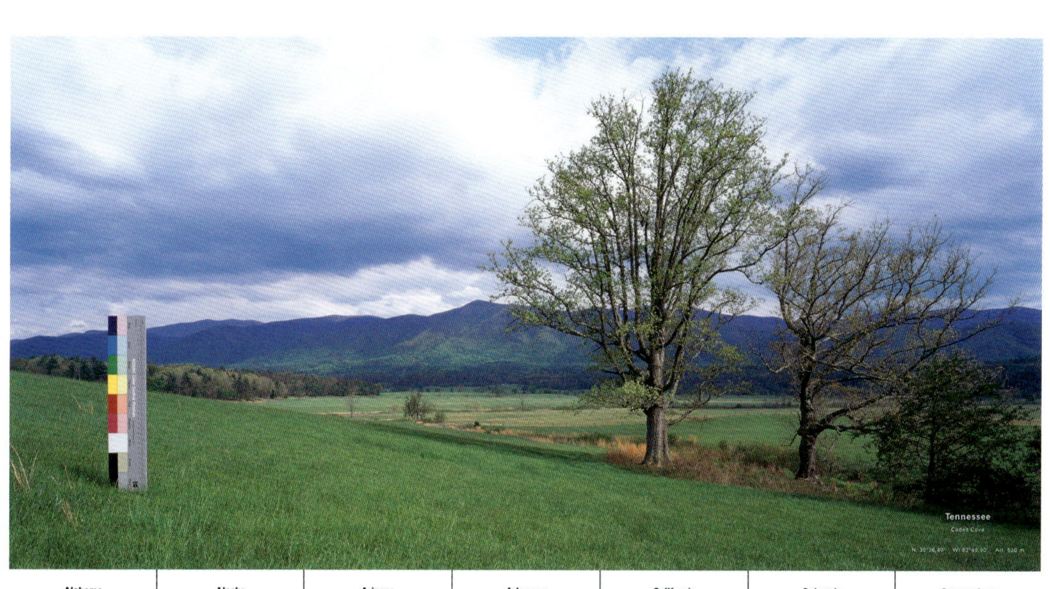

State	Location	Coordinates
Alabama	Lake Guntersville	N: 34°24,55' W: 86°10,77' Alt. 171 m
Alaska	Mendenhall Glacier	N: 58°25,30' W: 134°32,67' Alt. 17 m
Arizona	Grand Canyon	N: 36°02,73' W: 111°49,51' Alt. 2259 m
Arkansas	Old State House	N: 34°45,03' W: 92°16,26' Alt. 173 m
California	Golden Gate Bridge	N: 37°49,75' W: 122°29,36' Alt. 2 m
Colorado	Maroon Bells	N: 39°06,19' W: 106°56,26' Alt. 3016 m
Connecticut	Henry Whitfield House	N: 41°16,79' W: 72°40,44' Alt. 11 m
Delaware	Hagley Museum	N: 39°46,94' W: 75°34,12' Alt. 41 m
Florida	Kennedy Space Center	N: 28°37,55' W: 80°36,87' Alt. 13 m
Georgia	Stone Mountain Park	N: 33°48,71' W: 84°08,52' Alt. 316 m
Hawaii	Diamond Head	N: 21°16,65' W: 157°49,74' Alt. 2 m
Idaho	Sawtooth Mountains	N: 44°09,92' W: 114°54,18' Alt. 1988 m
Illinois	Skyline of Chicago	N: 41°52,59' W: 87°37,03' Alt. 142 m
Indiana	Indianapolis 500 Mile Raceway	N: 39°47,60' W: 86°14,29' Alt. 98 m
Iowa	Iowa State Capitol	N: 41°35,60' W: 93°36,02' Alt. 287 m
Kansas	The Flint Hills	N: 39°17,70' W: 96°36,54' Alt. 392 m
Kentucky	Bluegrass Horse Park	N: 38°09,11' W: 84°31,13' Alt. 271 m
Louisiana	St. Louis Cathedral	N: 29°57,52' W: 90°03,68' Alt. 4 m
Maine	Portland Head Light	N: 43°37,42' W: 70°12,37' Alt. 4 m
Maryland	The Paca House and Gardens	N: 38°58,90' W: 76°29,11' Alt. 47 m
Massachusetts	Boston, Acorn Street	N: 42°21,44' W: 71°03,98' Alt. 74 m
Michigan	Mackinac Island Grand Hotel	N: 45°51,11' W: 84°37,40' Alt. 151 m
Minnesota	Mississippi Headwaters	N: 47°14,52' W: 95°12,33' Alt. 450 m
Mississippi	Illinois Memorial	N: 32°21,63' W: 90°50,31' Alt. 119 m
Missouri	The Gateway Arch	N: 38°37,40' W: 90°10,55' Alt. 134 m
Montana	Glacier National Park	N: 48°41,88' W: 113°42,95' Alt. 2040 m
Nebraska	Chimney Rock	N: 41°42,22' W: 103°20,82' Alt. 1231 m
Nevada	Great Basin National Park	N: 39°01,24' W: 114°13,35' Alt. 2150 m
New Hampshire	Old Man of the Mountain	N: 44°10,08' W: 71°40,54' Alt. 526 m
New Jersey	Cape May	N: 38°56,03' W: 74°57,70' Alt. 2 m
New Mexiko	Taos Pueblo	N: 36°26,42' W: 105°32,56' Alt. 2257 m
New York	Niagara Falls	N: 43°05,28' W: 79°04,80' Alt. 168 m
North Carolina	Blue Ridge Parkway	N: 36°09,14' W: 81°41,40' Alt. 1021 m
North Dakota	Badlands	N: 47°36,15' W: 103°20,24' Alt. 623 m
Ohio	Ohio Statehouse	N: 39°57,85' W: 82°59,87' Alt. 316 m
Oklahoma	Turner Falls	N: 34°25,65' W: 97°08,71' Alt. 433 m
Oregon	Crater Lake	N: 42°56,82' W: 122°10,07' Alt. 2378 m
Pennsylvania	Independence National Historic Park	N: 39°56,97' W: 75°08,89' Alt. 6 m
Rhode Island	The Breakers	N: 41°28,24' W: 71°17,72' Alt. 7 m
South Carolina	Boone Hall Plantation	N: 32°51,52' W: 79°49,31' Alt. 10 m
South Dakota	Mount Rushmore	N: 43°52,72' W: 103°27,24' Alt. 1623 m
Texas	The Alamo	N: 29°25,64' W: 98°29,09' Alt. 249 m
Utah	Monument Valley	N: 37°02,06' W: 110°05,94' Alt. 1735 m
Vermont	Wells River	N: 44°06,00' W: 72°02,93' Alt. 362 m
Virginia	Mount Vernon	N: 38°42,58' W: 77°05,02' Alt. 19 m
Washington	Mount Rainier	N: 46°54,86' W: 121°38,37' Alt. 1901 m
West Virginia	Gristmill	N: 37°58,25' W: 80°56,46' Alt. 862 m
Wisconsin	Wyalusing State Park	N: 42°59,73' W: 91°07,23' Alt. 319 m
Wyoming	Yellowstone National Park	N: 44°43,76' W: 110°42,09' Alt. 2279 m

Michael Schuster
Aus | from: *K.C.C.P. in USA*, 1992/93

Im Eindruck der Land Art / The Impression of Land Art

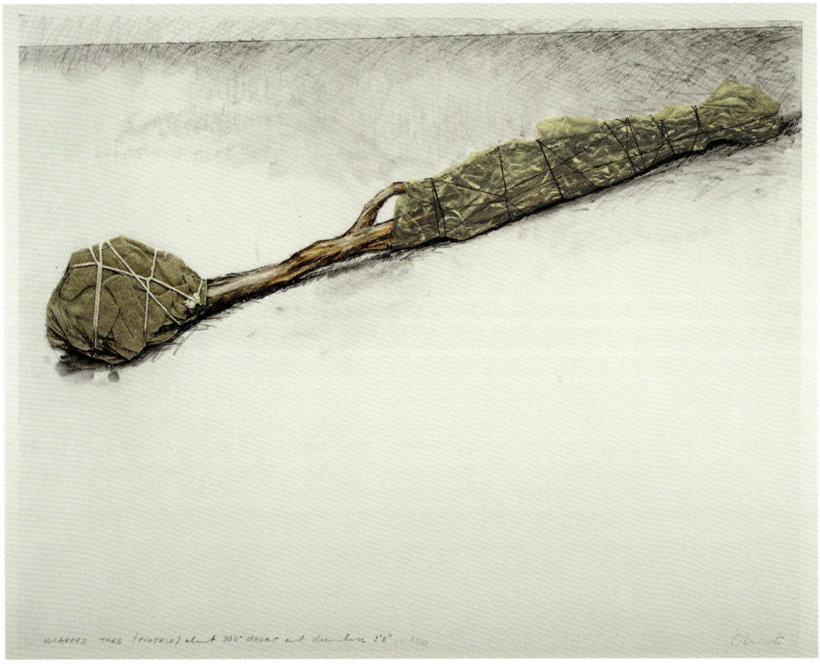

Christo
Wrapped Tree, 1970

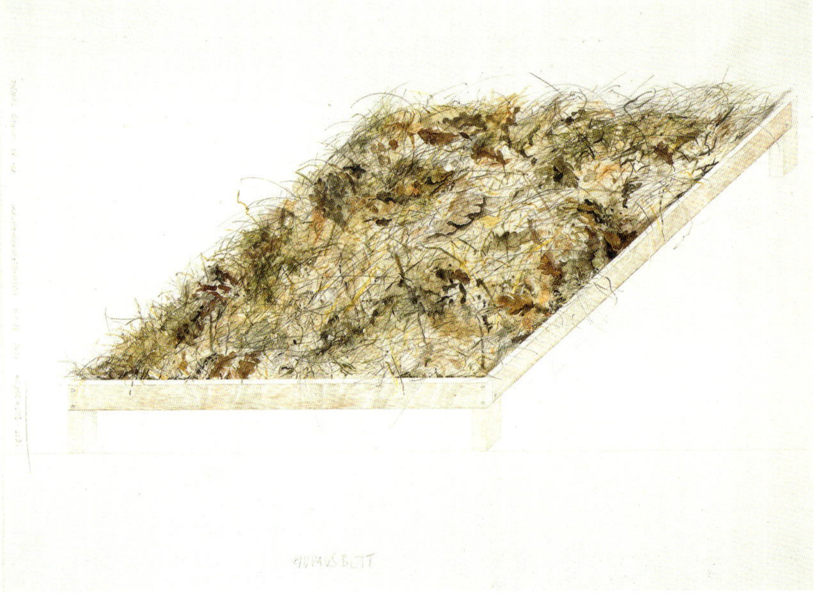

Mario Terzic
Humusbett, 1973

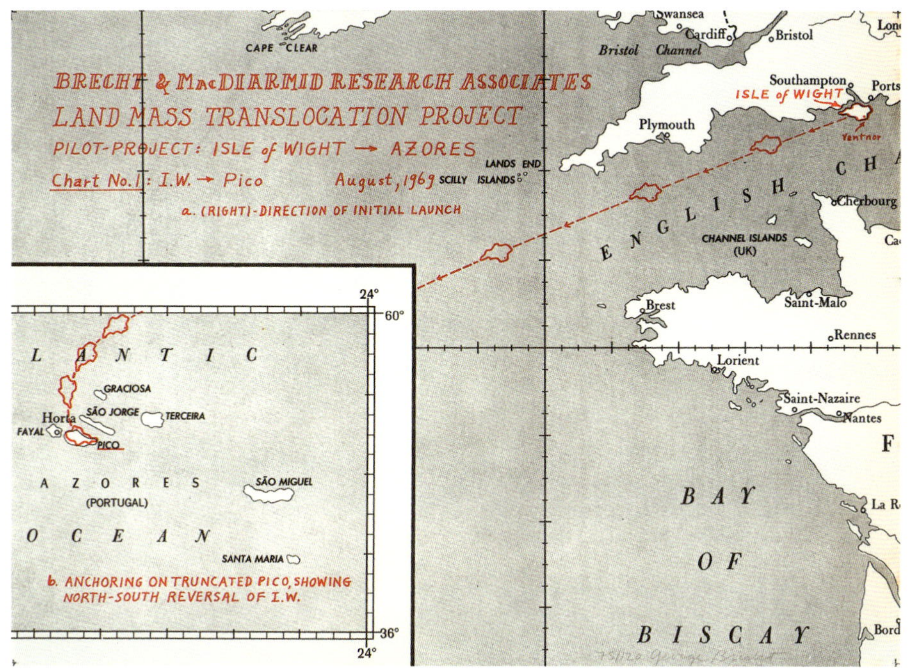

George Brecht
Landmass Translocation Project, 1969

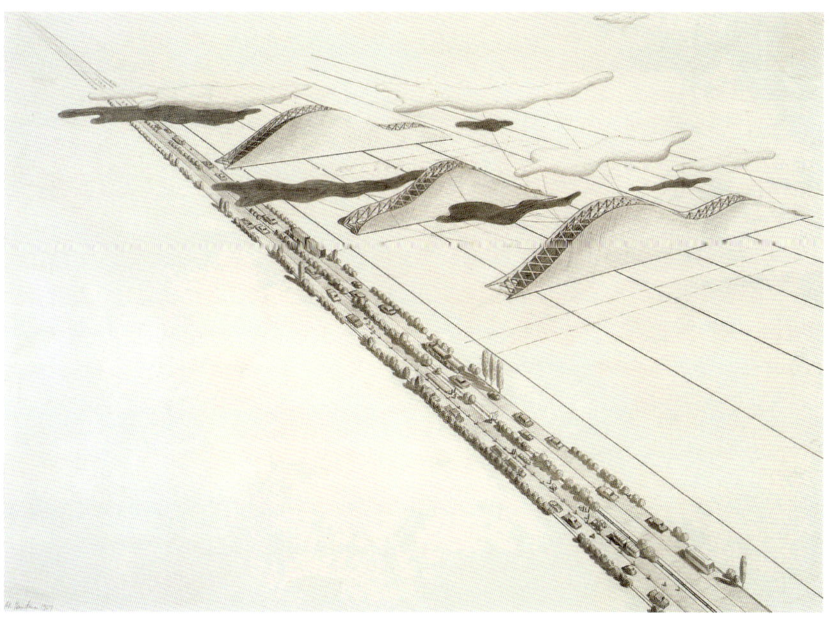

Max Peintner
Verschiebbare Hügel und künstliche Wolken zur Belebung eintöniger Autobahnfahrten, 1969

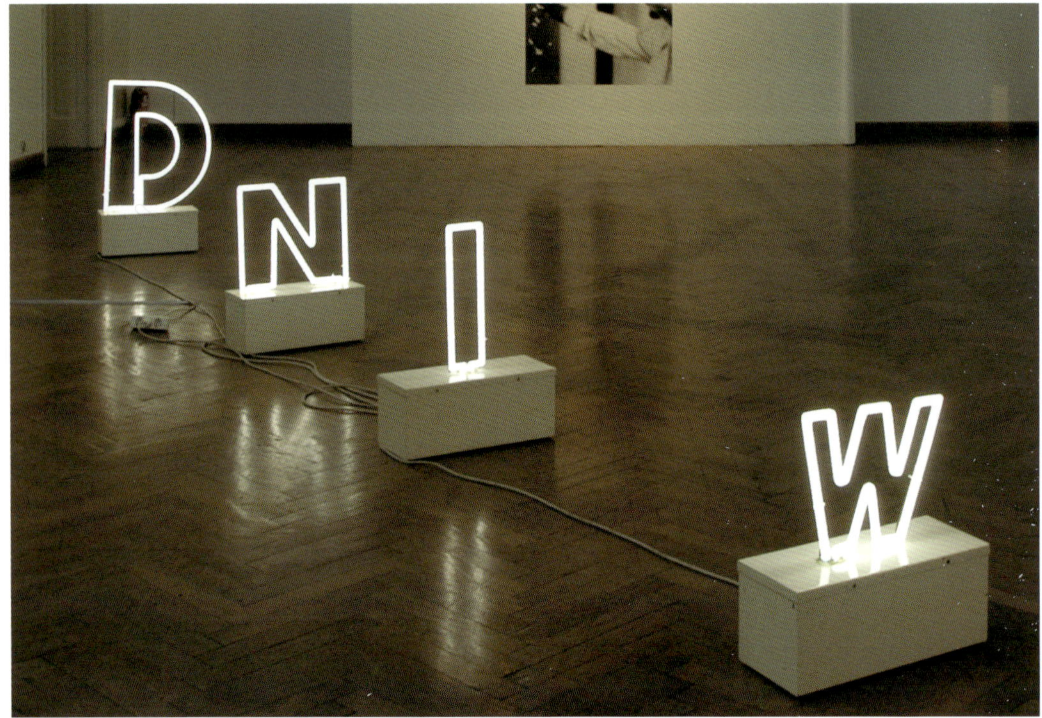

Peter Weibel
Wind, 1975, Ausstellungsansicht / exhibition view, Moderna galerija Ljublana, 2004

wind   wind

windwind

winwindd

dniw   dniw

wdinnidiw

   ddniwniw

    wi nd   dniw

   wind   wind

21. 3. - 20. 6.
21. 6. - 22. 9.
23. 9. - 20.12.
21.12. - 20. 3.

Heinz Gappmayr
Wind, 1961

Heinz Gappmayr
*o. T. (21.3.-20.6./21.6.-22.9./23.9.-
20.12./21.12.-20.3.)*, 1983

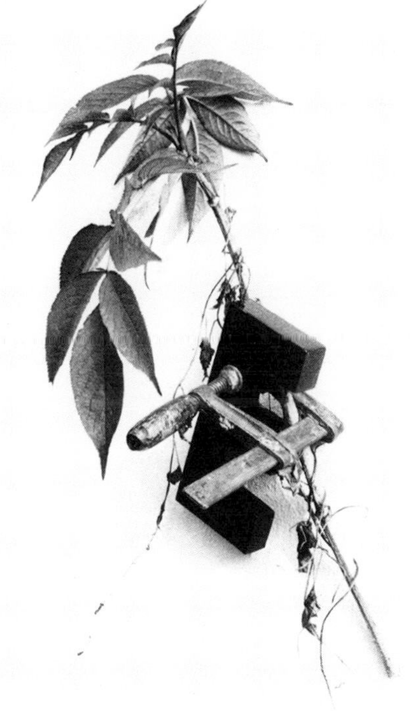

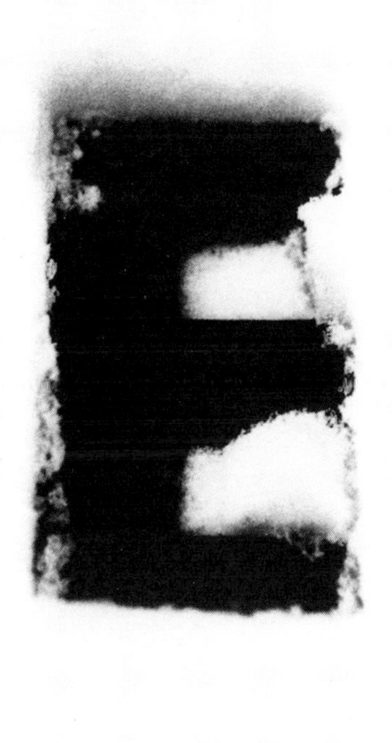

Josef Bauer
Sommer E – Winter E, 1976

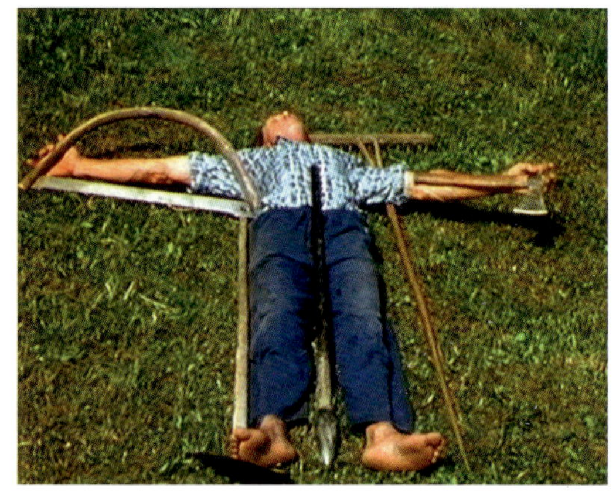

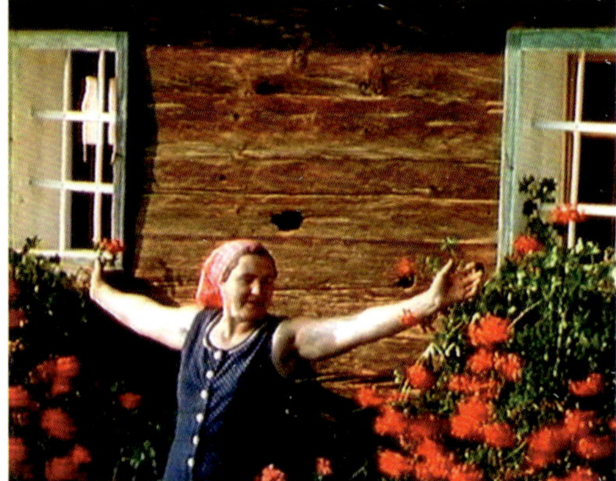

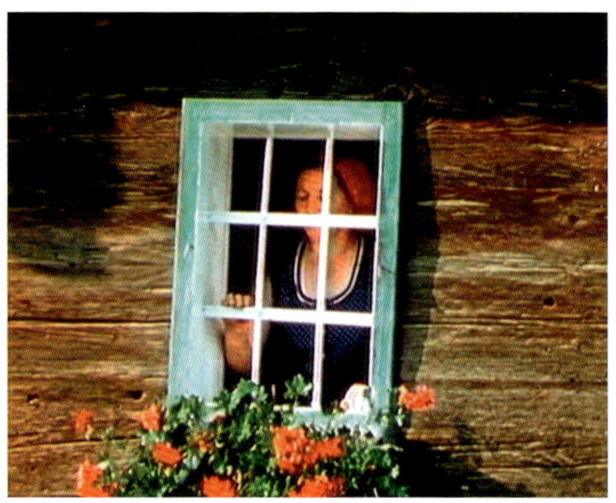

Peter Gerwin Hoffmann, Richard Kriesche
Aus / from: *Humane Skulpturen*, 1980
(Videostills / video stills)

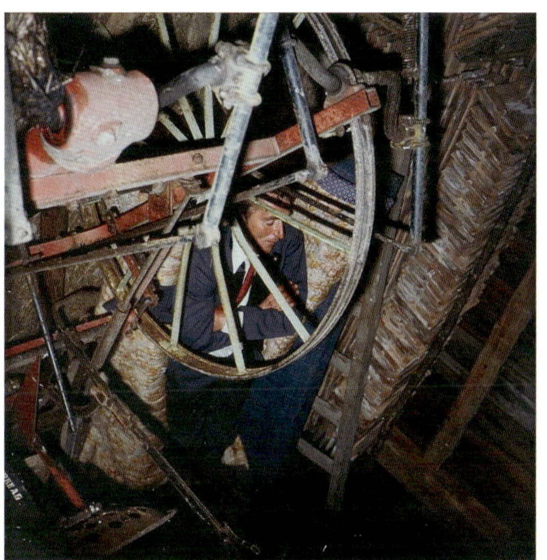
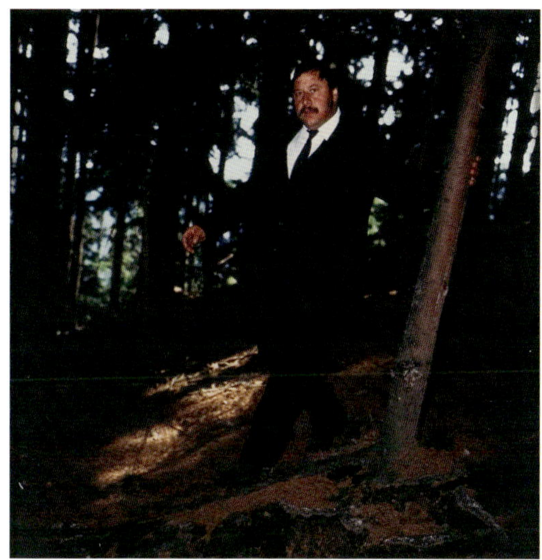
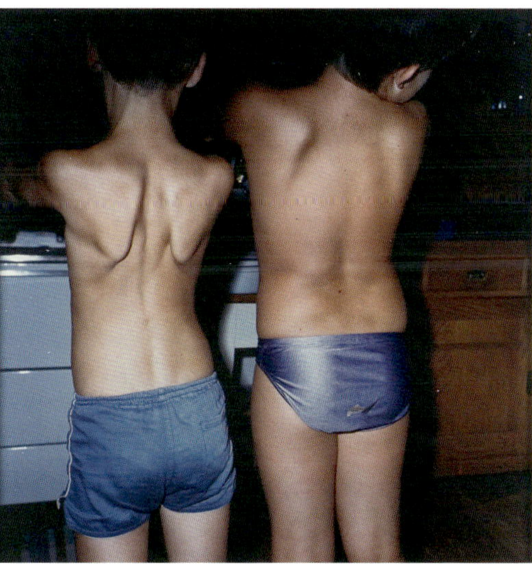
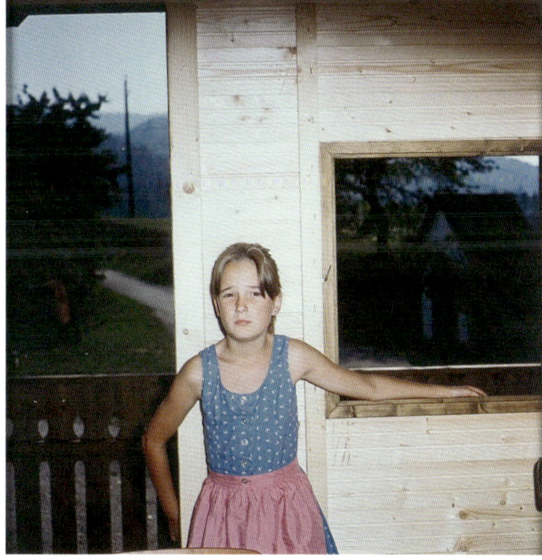

Manfred Willmann
Aus / from: *Das Land*, 1981–93/2013

Malerei – Naturerfahrung und Abstraktion I
Painting – Experience of Nature and Abstraction I

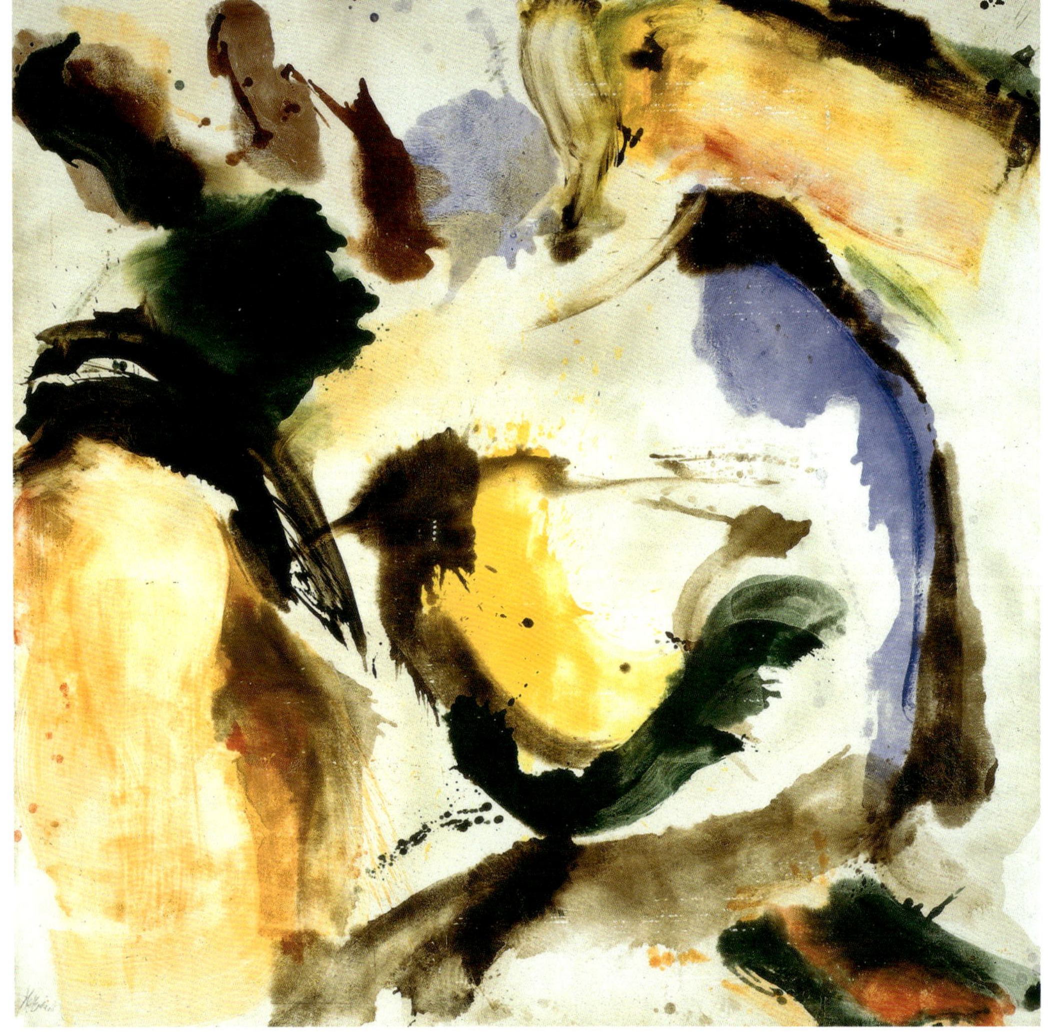

Wolfgang Hollegha
Holzstück III, 1966

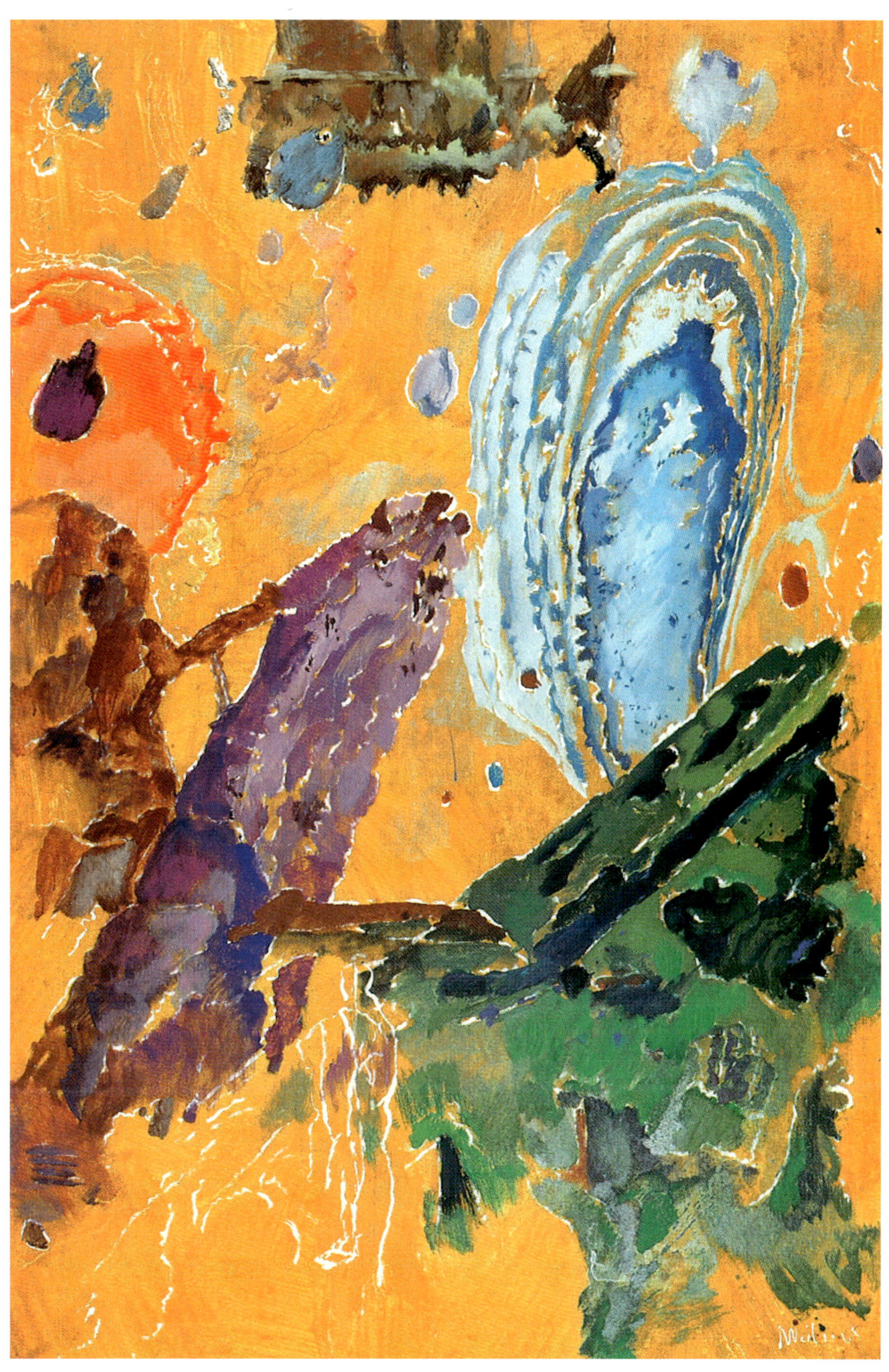

Max Weiler
Landschaft in Ocker, 1969

Malerei – Naturerfahrung und Abstraktion II
Painting – Experience of Nature and Abstraction II

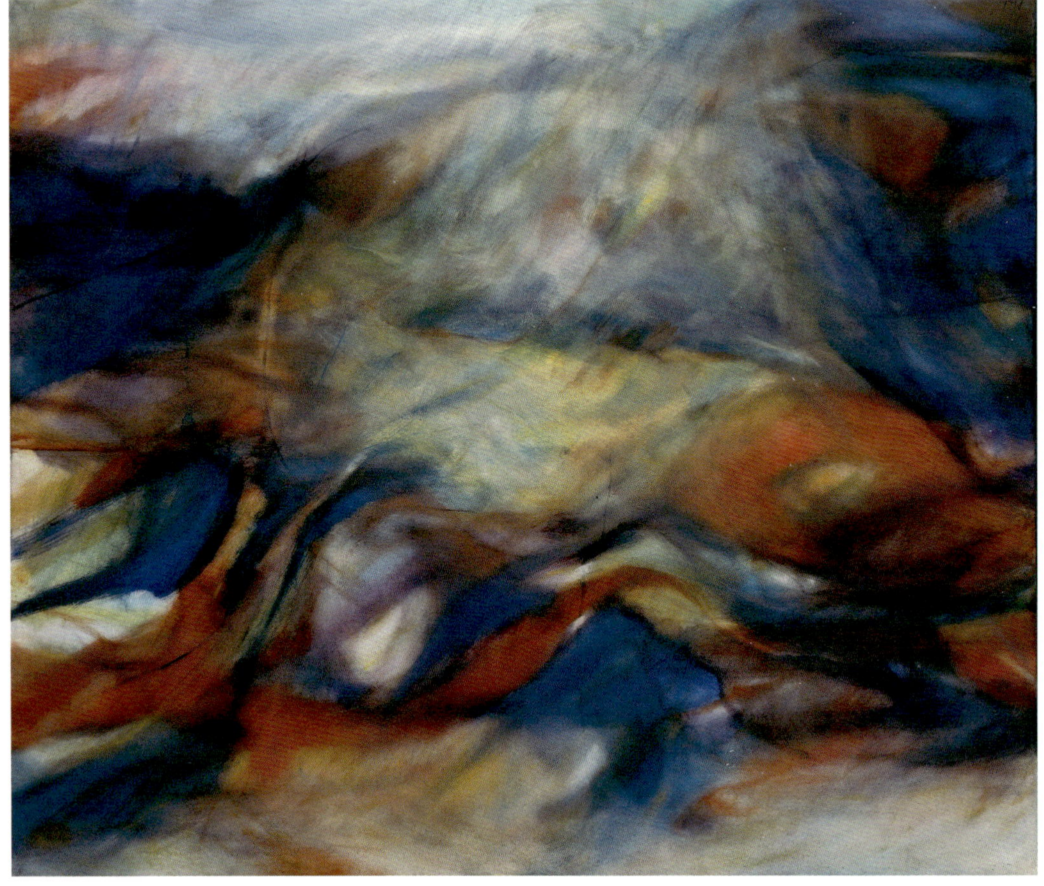

Elga Maly
Große arktische Landschaft, 1965

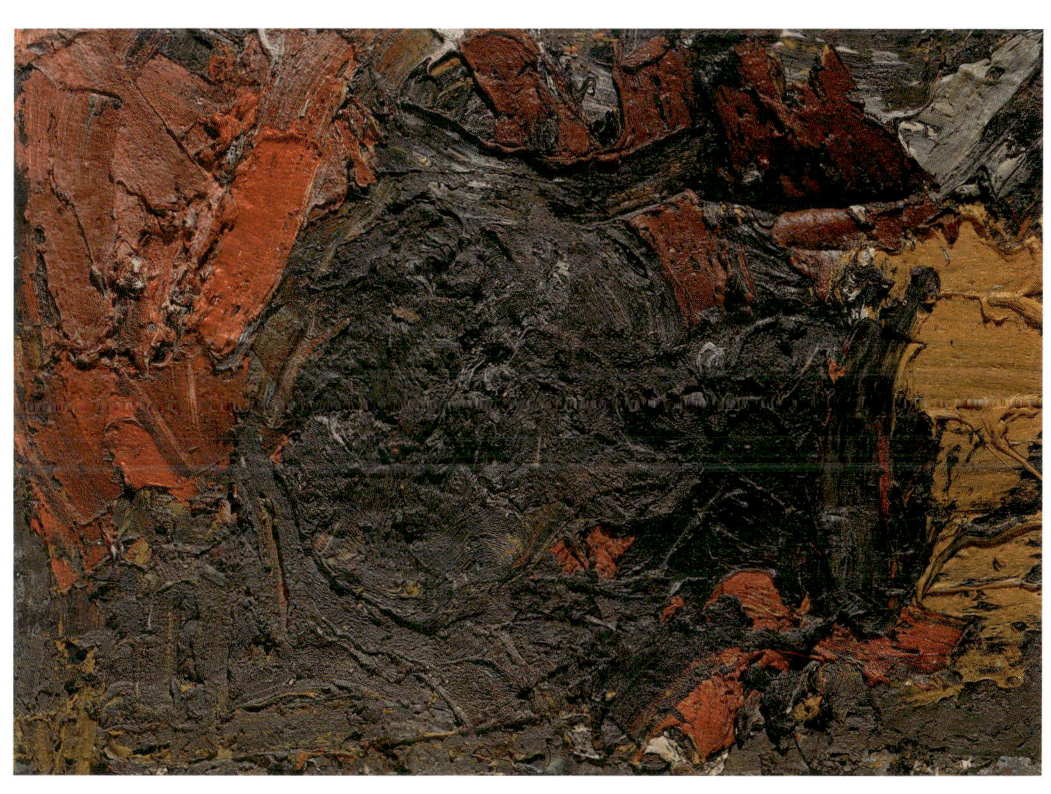

Franz Grabmayr
Wurzelstück in der Sandgrube, 1983

Herbert Brandl - Zwischen Gegenständlichkeit und Abstraktion
Herbert Brandl – Between Representation and Abstraction

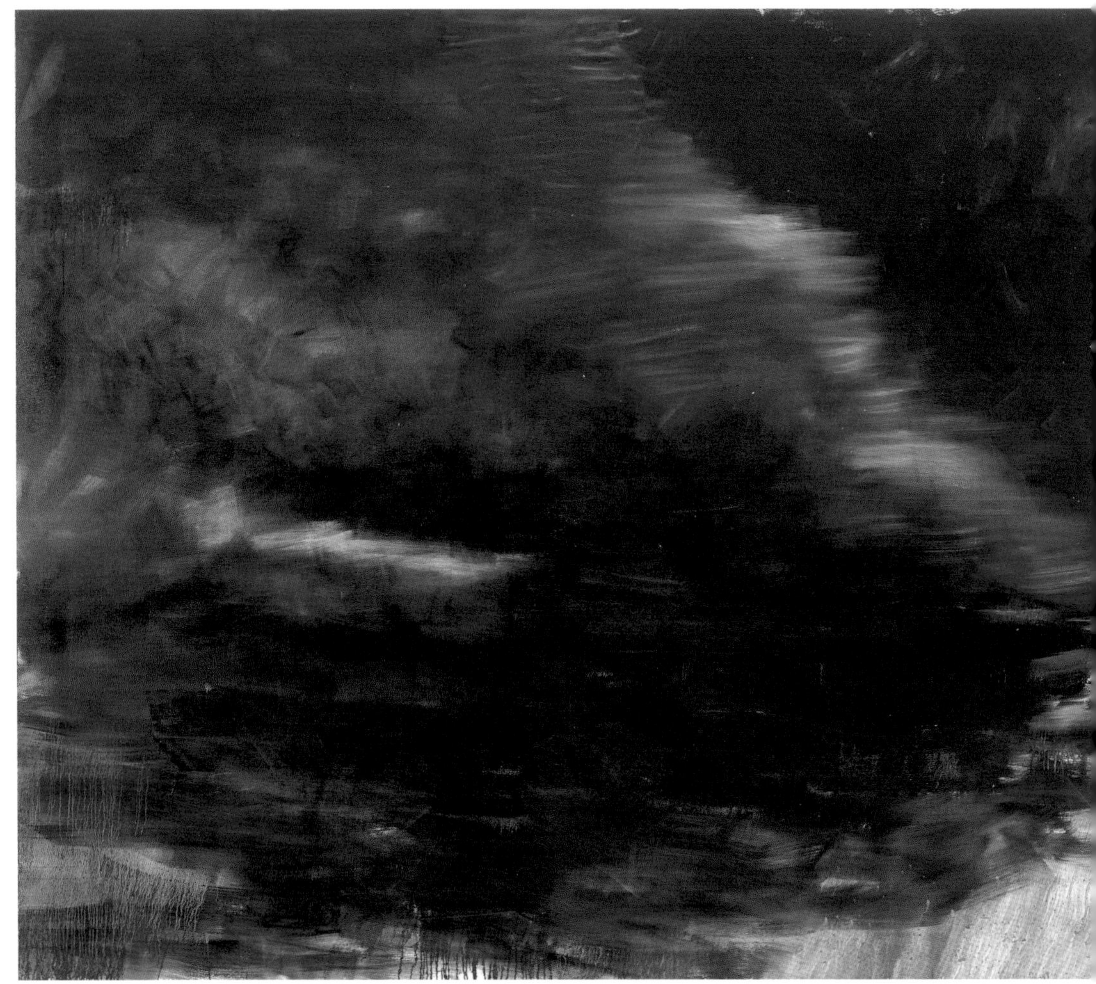

Herbert Brandl
ohne Titel, 2004

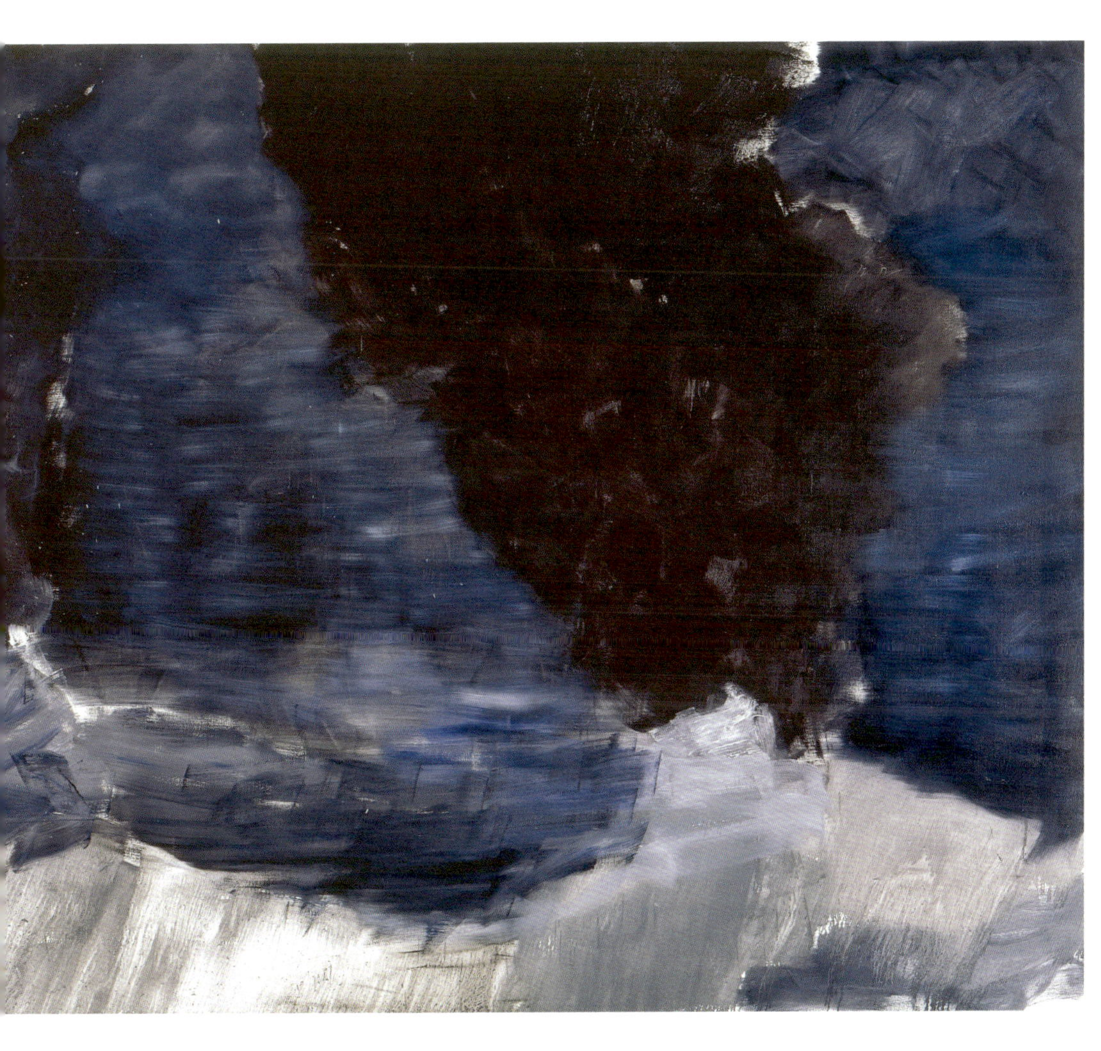

Malerei – Naturerfahrung und Gegenständlichkeit I
Painting – Experience of Nature and Representation I

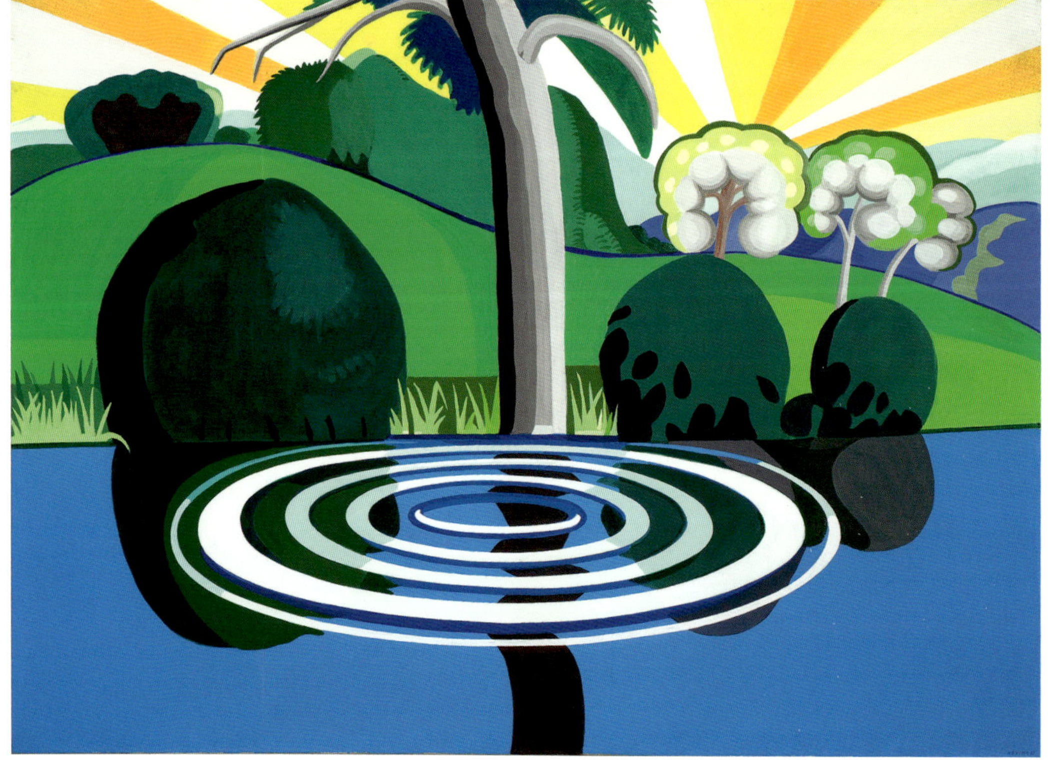

Franc Novinc
Morgen, 1971

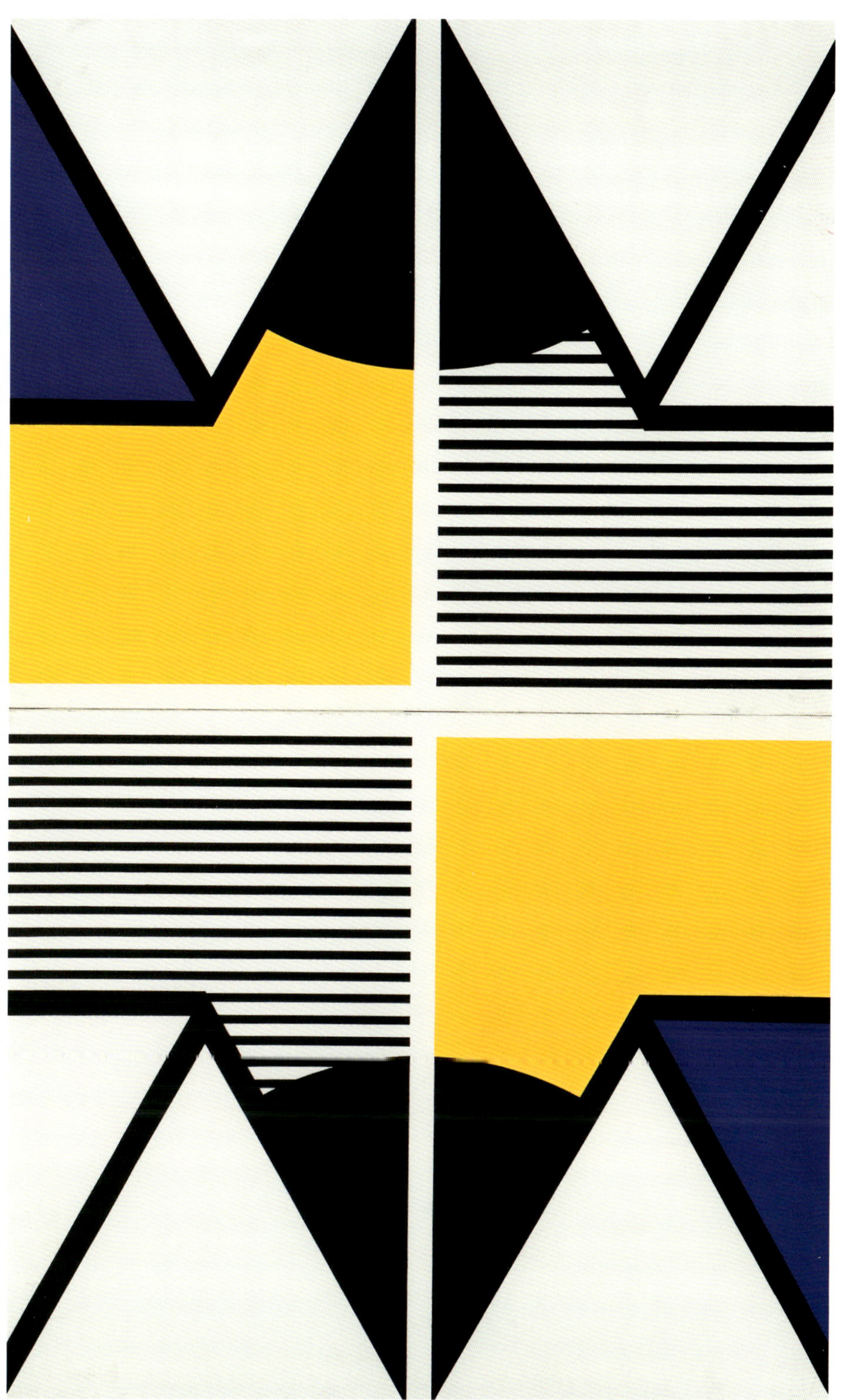

Imre Bak
Landschaftstransformation 2, 1974

Malerei – Naturerfahrung und Gegenständlichkeit II
Painting – Experience of Nature and Representation II

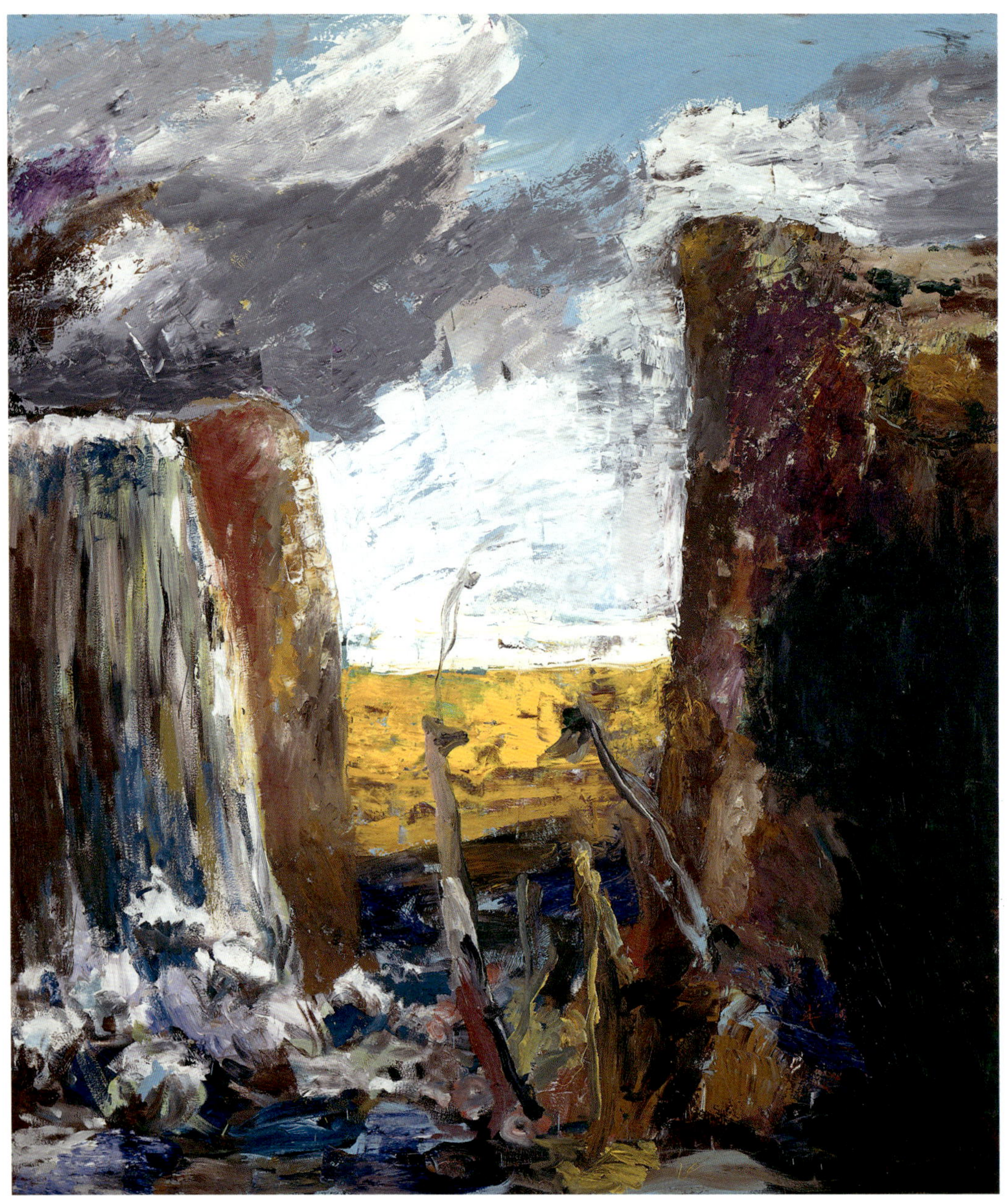

Alois Mosbacher
Die Schlucht, 1984

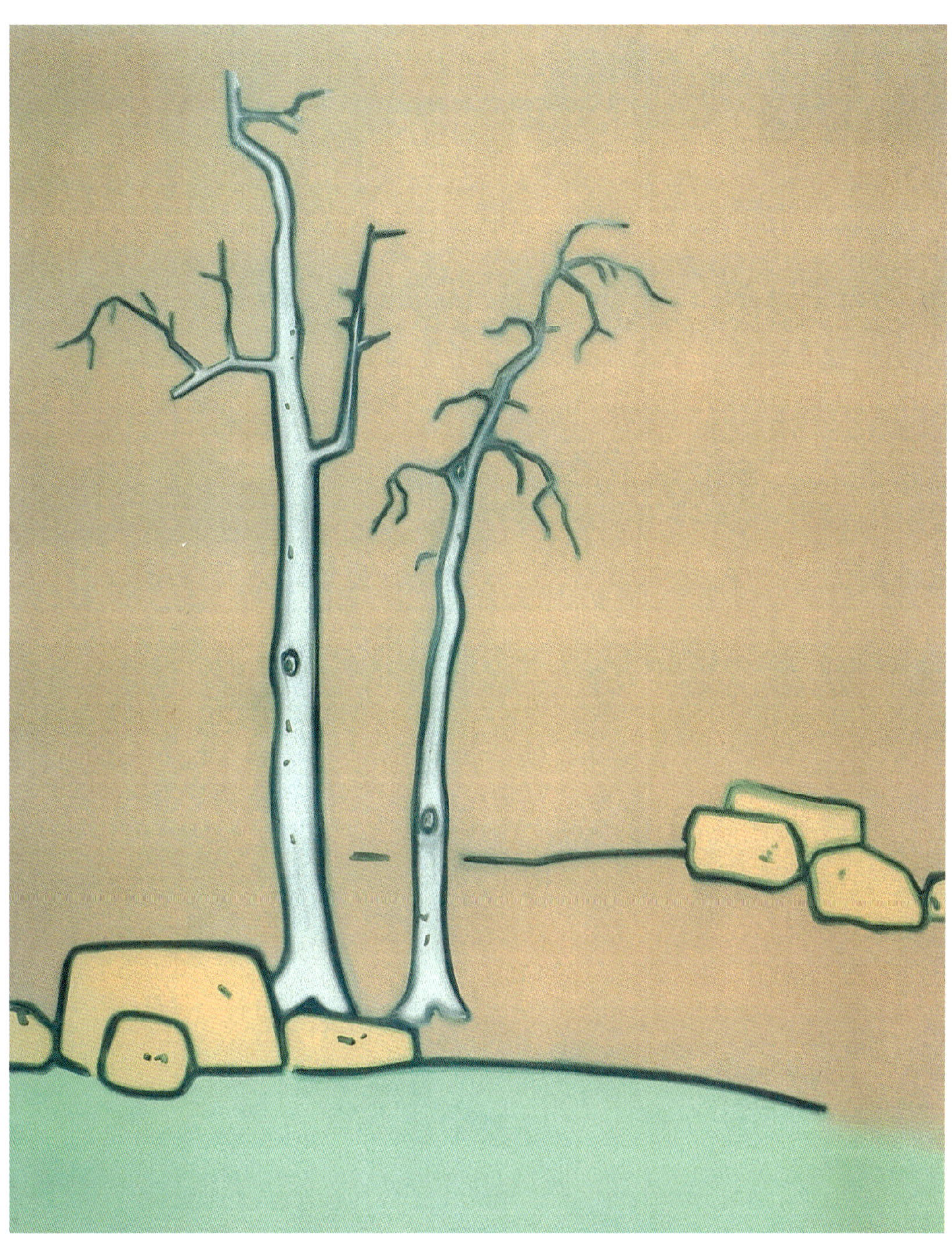

Hubert Schmalix
Painted with My Own Hand (Landschaft), 2005

HyperAmerika
Landschaft – Bild – Wirklichkeit
HyperAmerica
Landscape – Image – Reality

Kunsthaus Graz

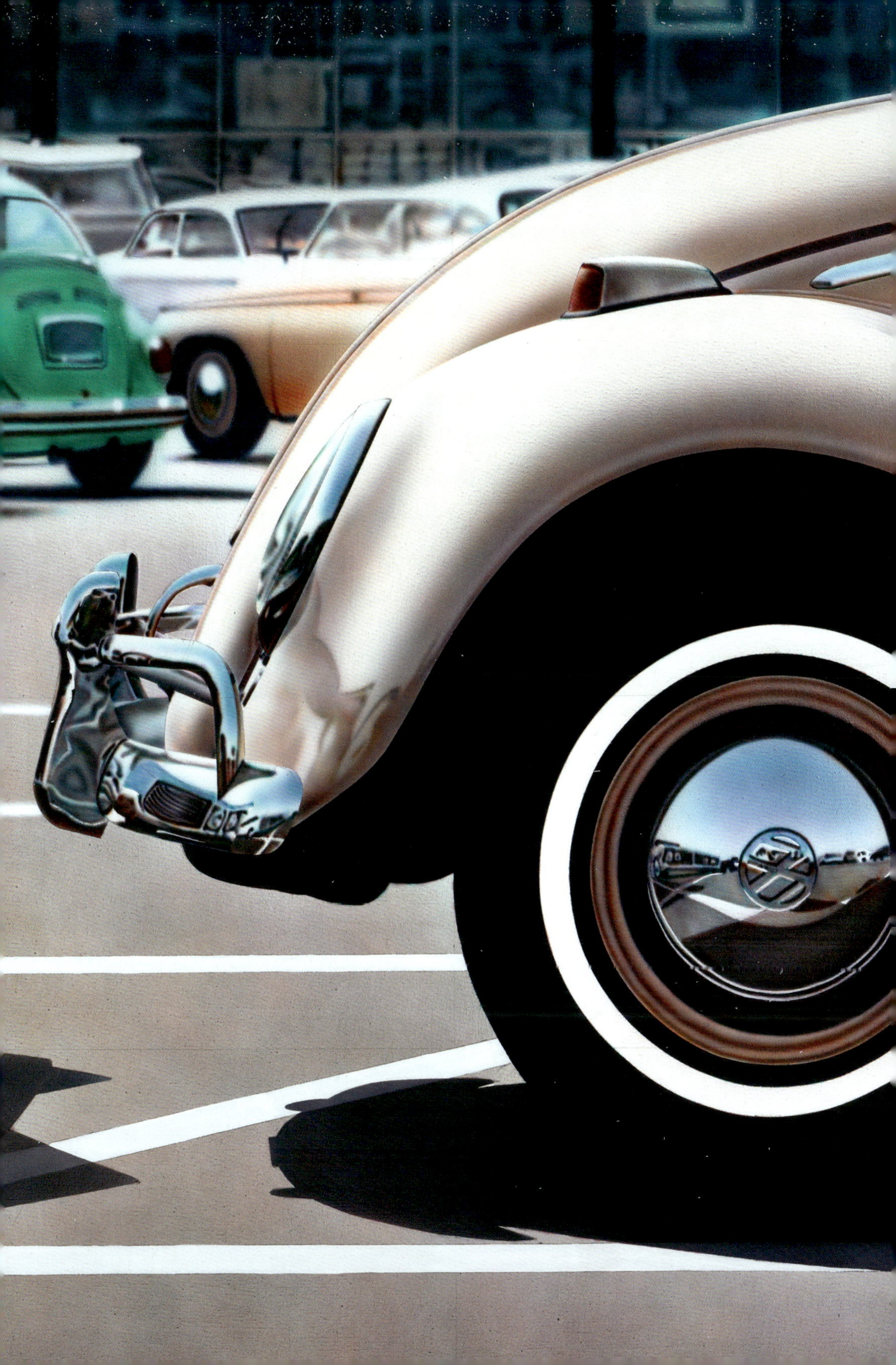

Robert Adams
Aus der Serie/from the series:
The New West, 1968–71

*Federal 40. Mount Vernon
Canyon. Jefferson County,
Colorado*, 1970

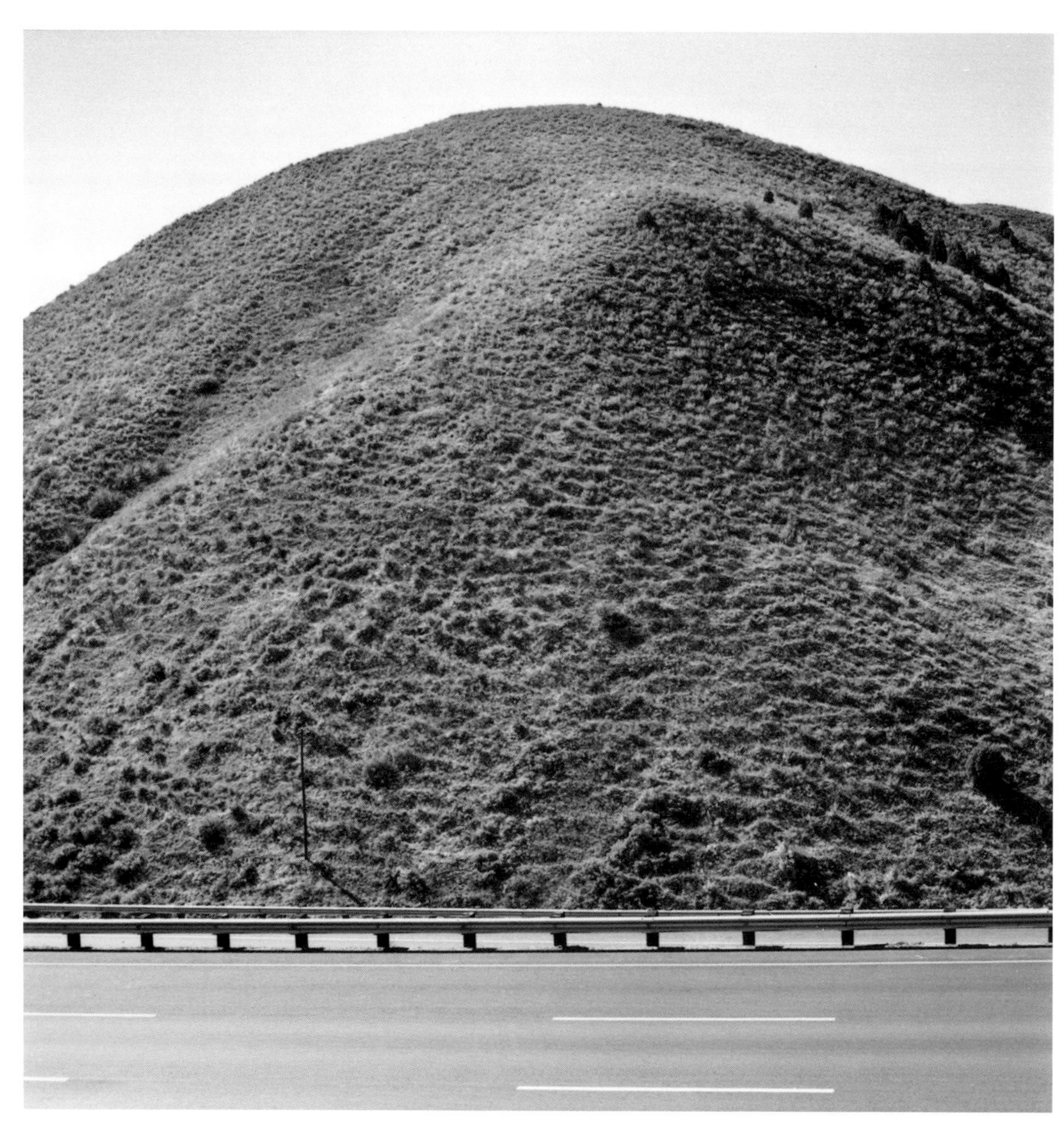

Robert Adams
Aus der Serie/from the series:
The New West, 1968–71

Pikes Peak, Colorado Springs, 1969

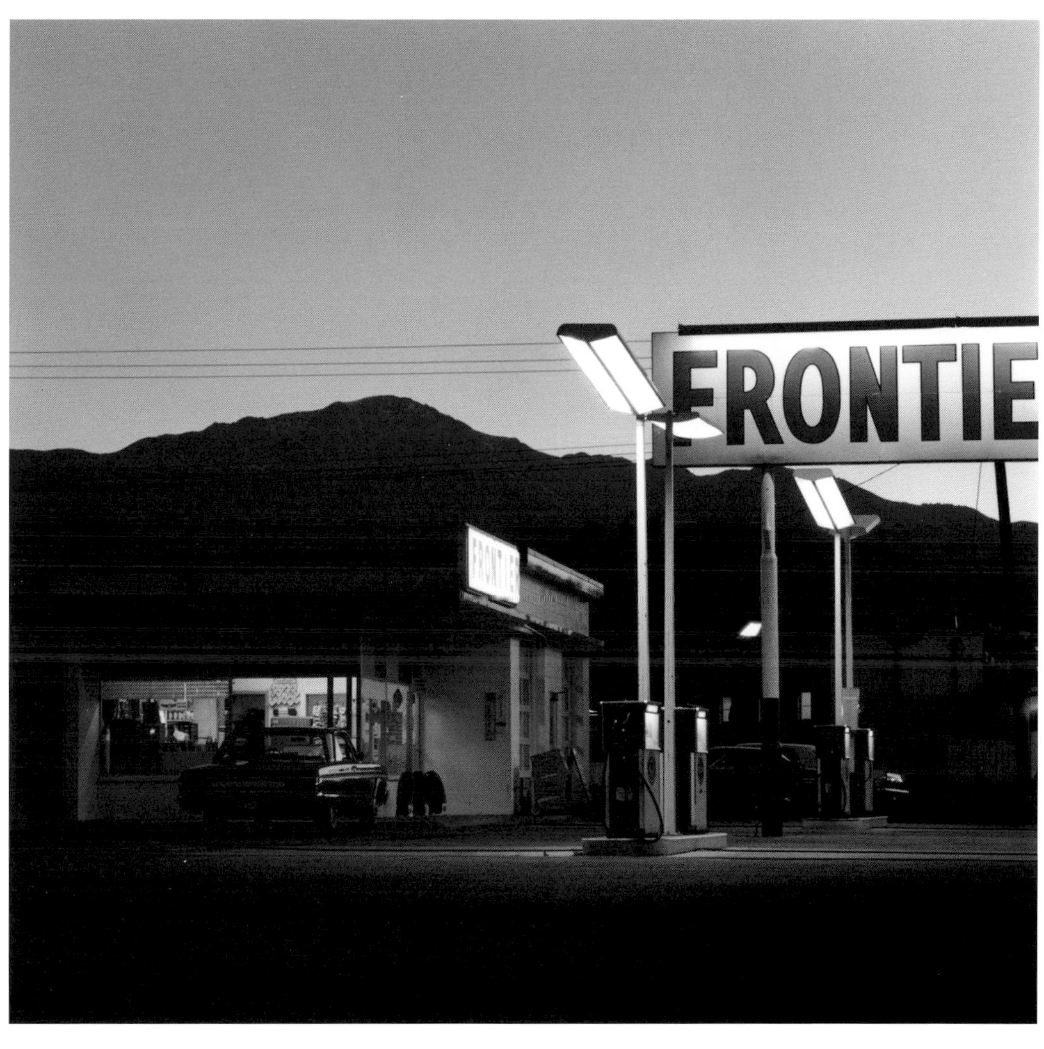

John Baeder
Prout's Diner, 1974

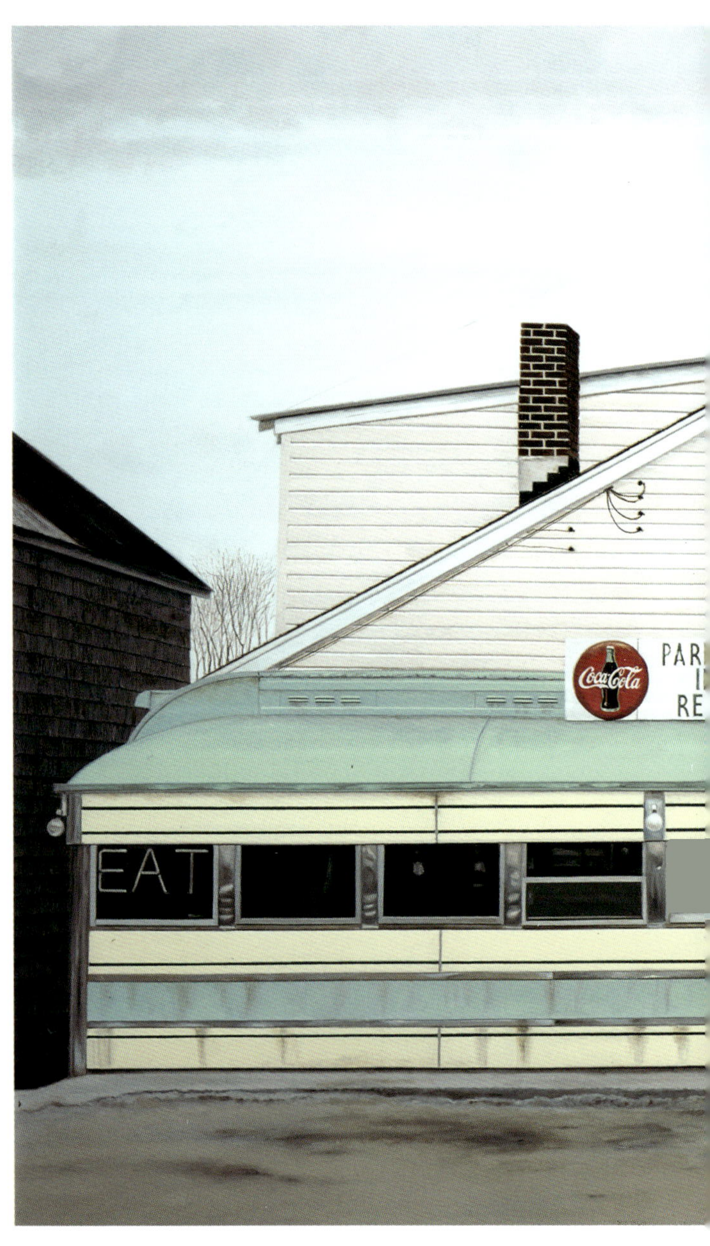

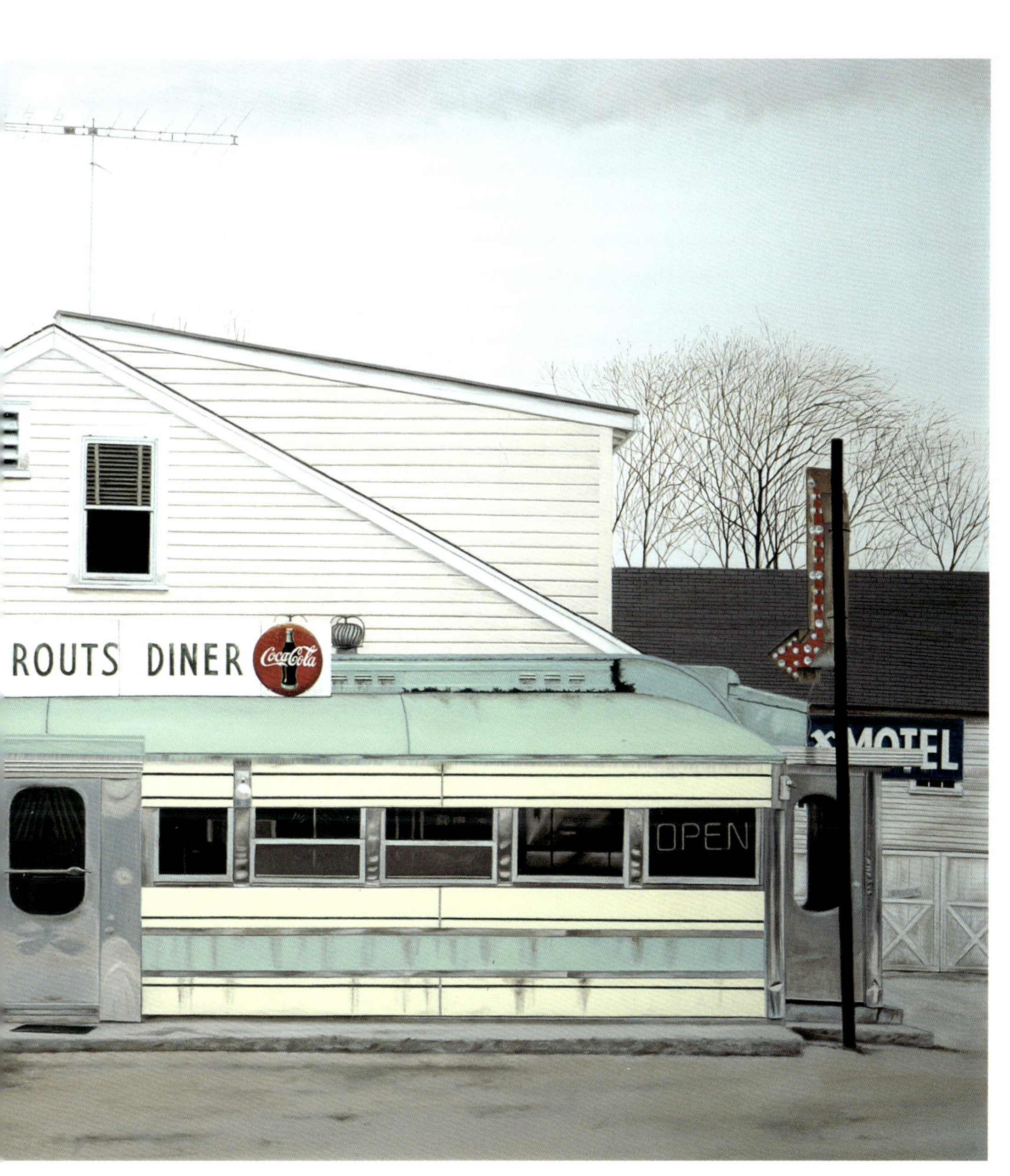

ROUTS DINER
Coca-Cola
OPEN
MOTEL

176—177

Lewis Baltz
Aus der Serie / from the series:
Nevada, 1977/78

Fluorescent Tube, 1977

*Home Model, Shadow
Mountain, 1977*

*Mustang Bridge Exit,
Interstate 80, 1977*

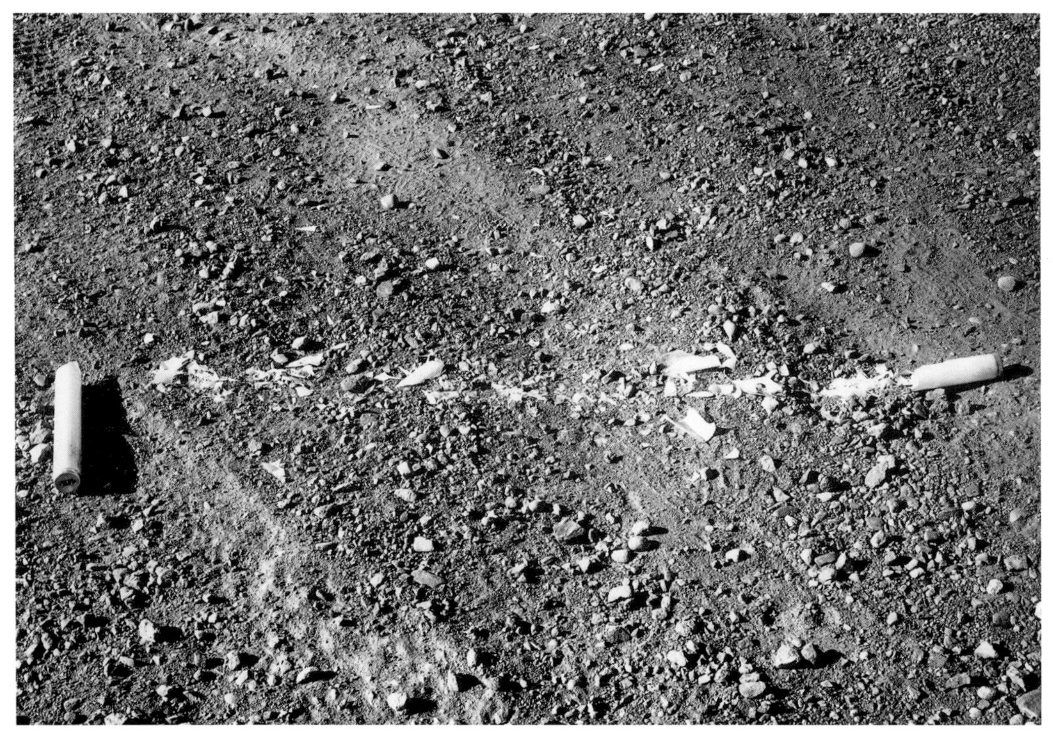

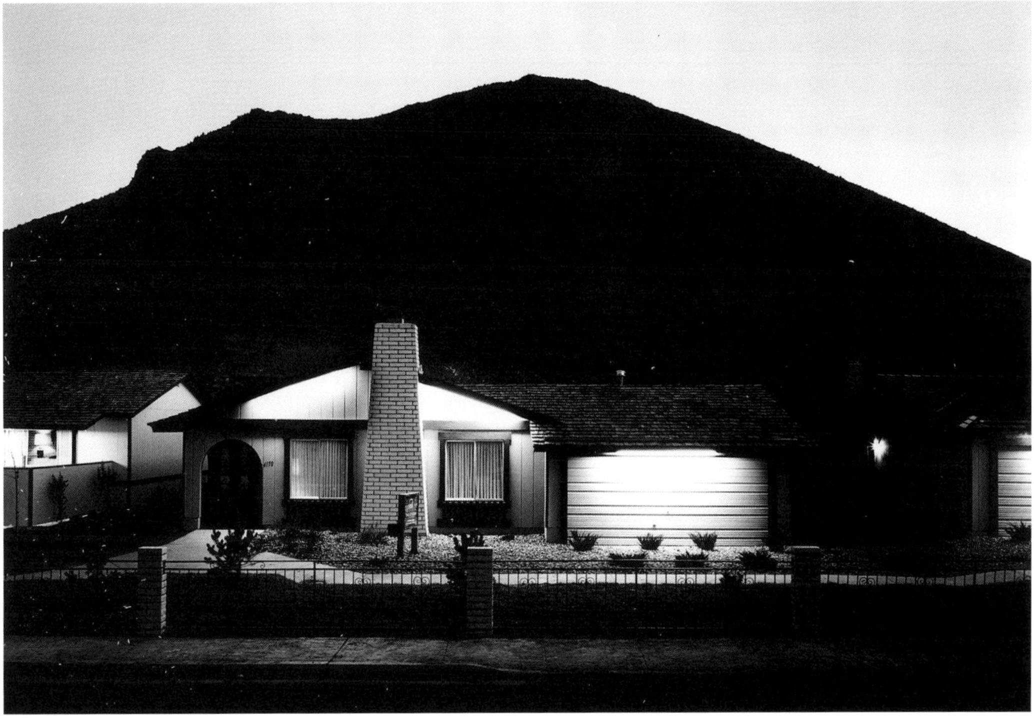

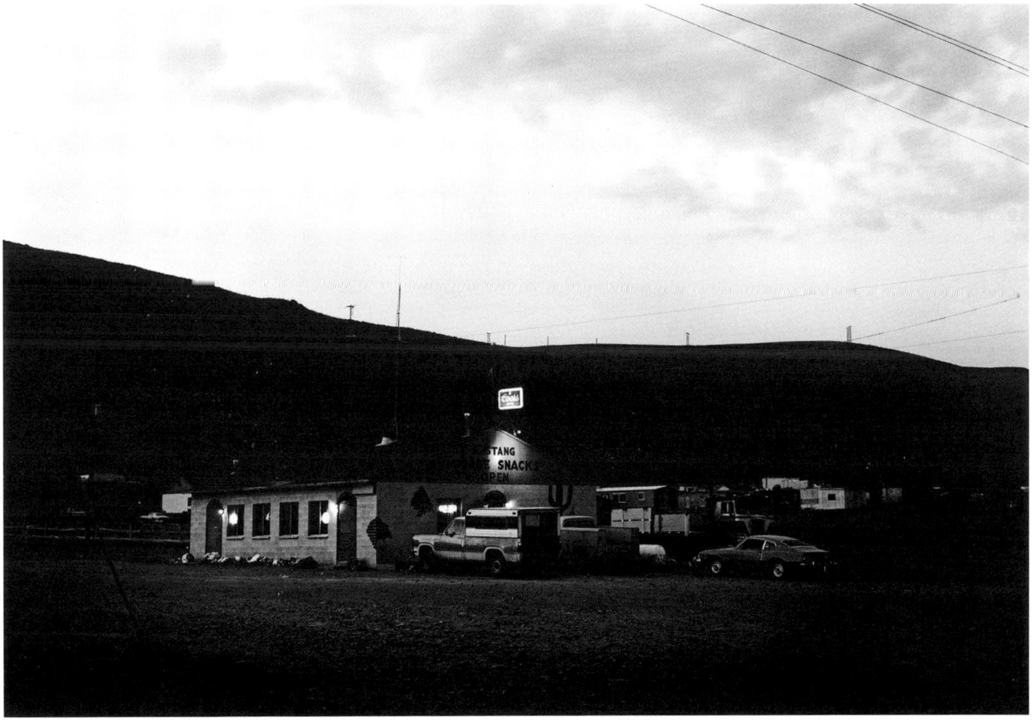

Robert Cottingham
Carl's, 1975

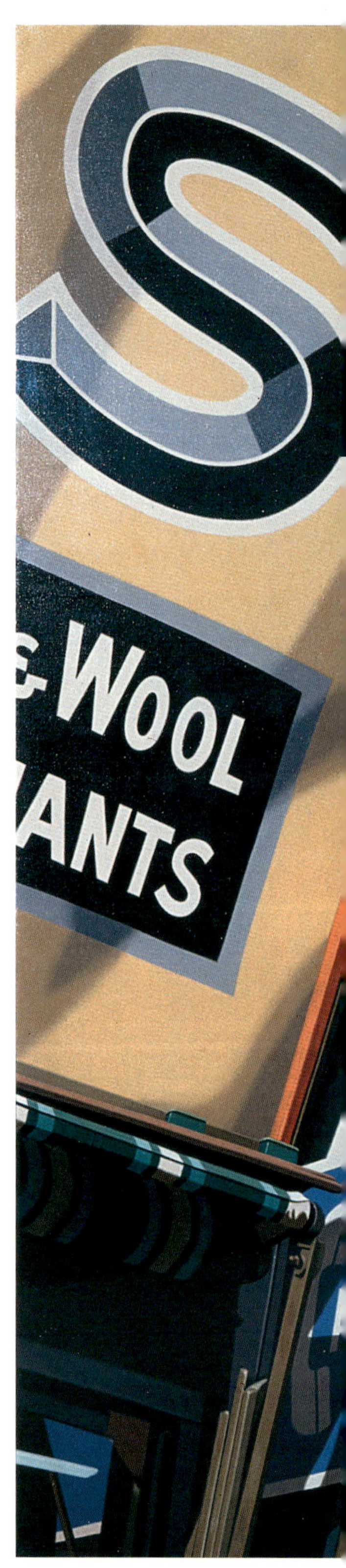

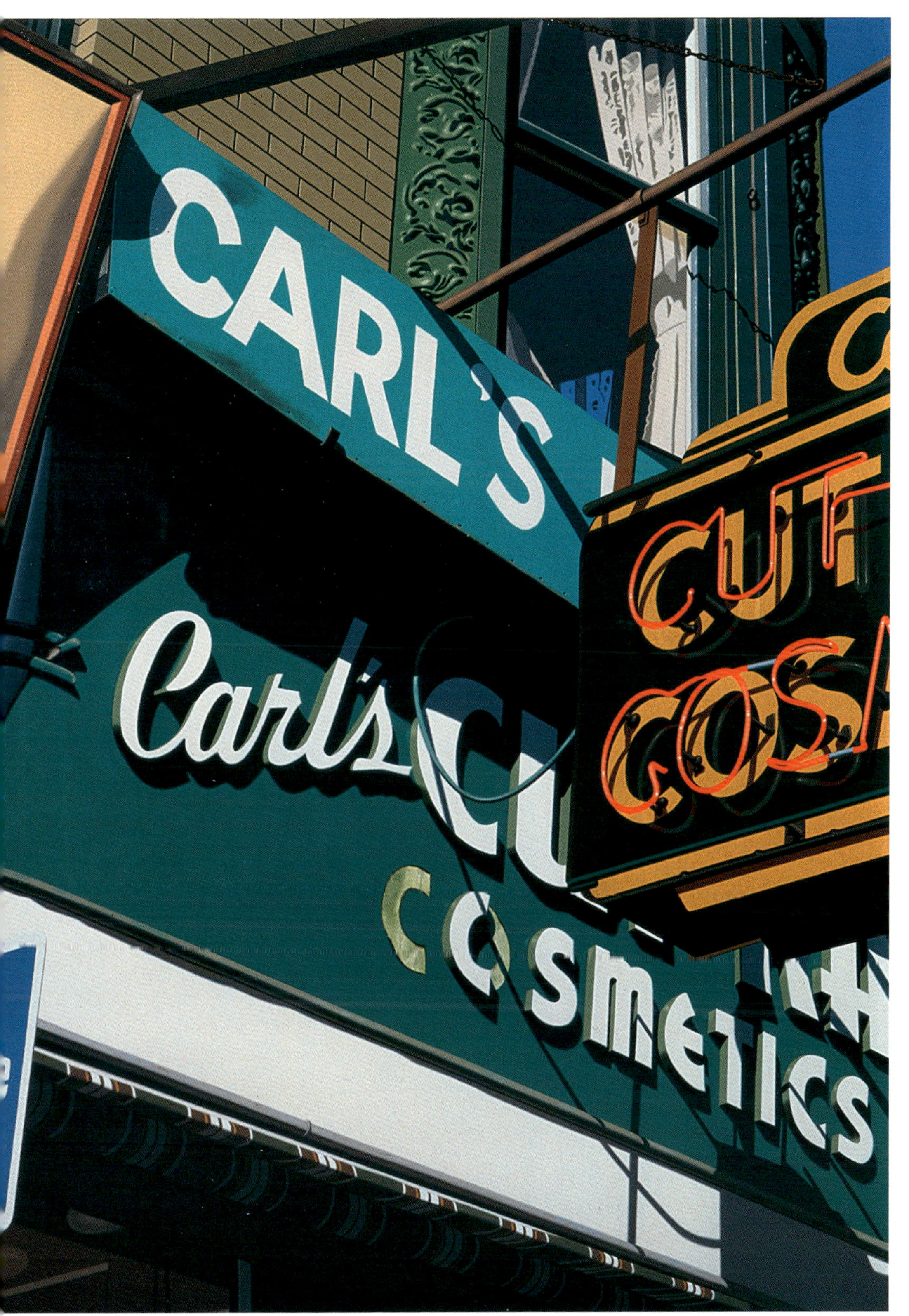
CARL'S
Carl's
COSMETICS
CUT
COS

Rackstraw Downes
Dragon Cement Plant, Thomaston;
View from the North End of the
Clinker Barn, 1985

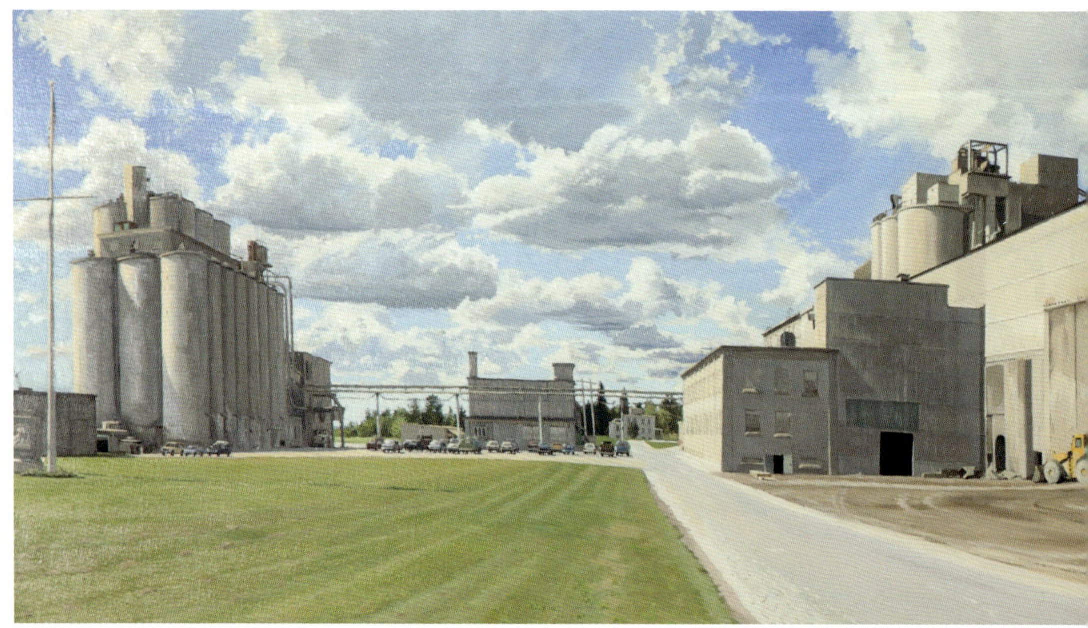

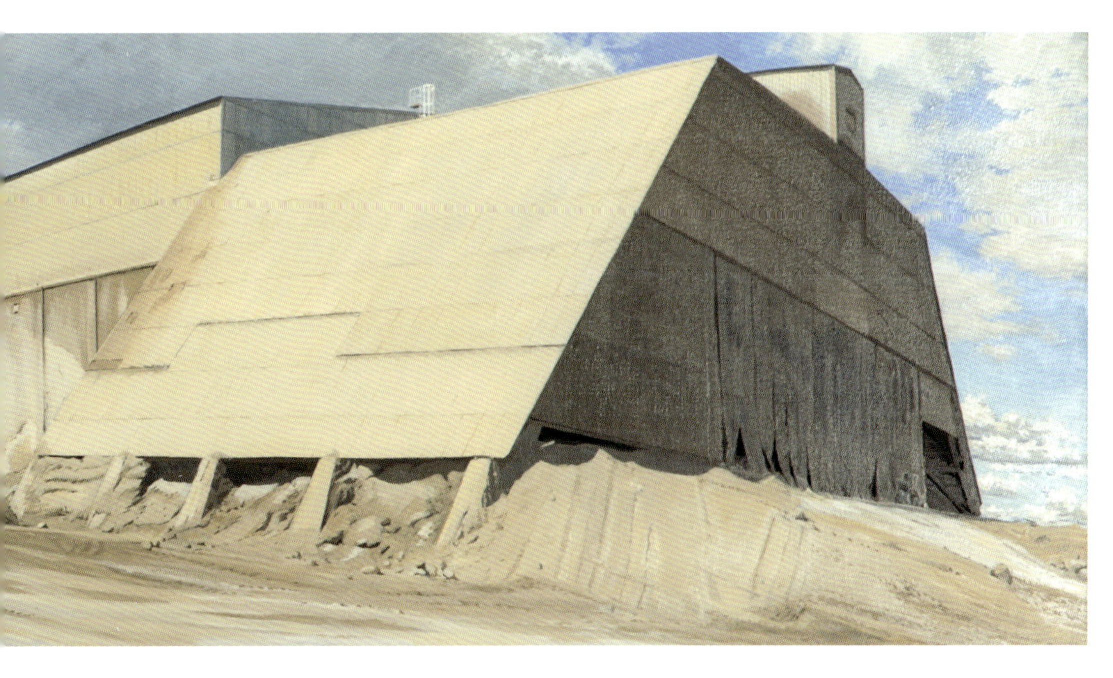

Don Eddy
*Untitled
(Volkswagen),*
1971

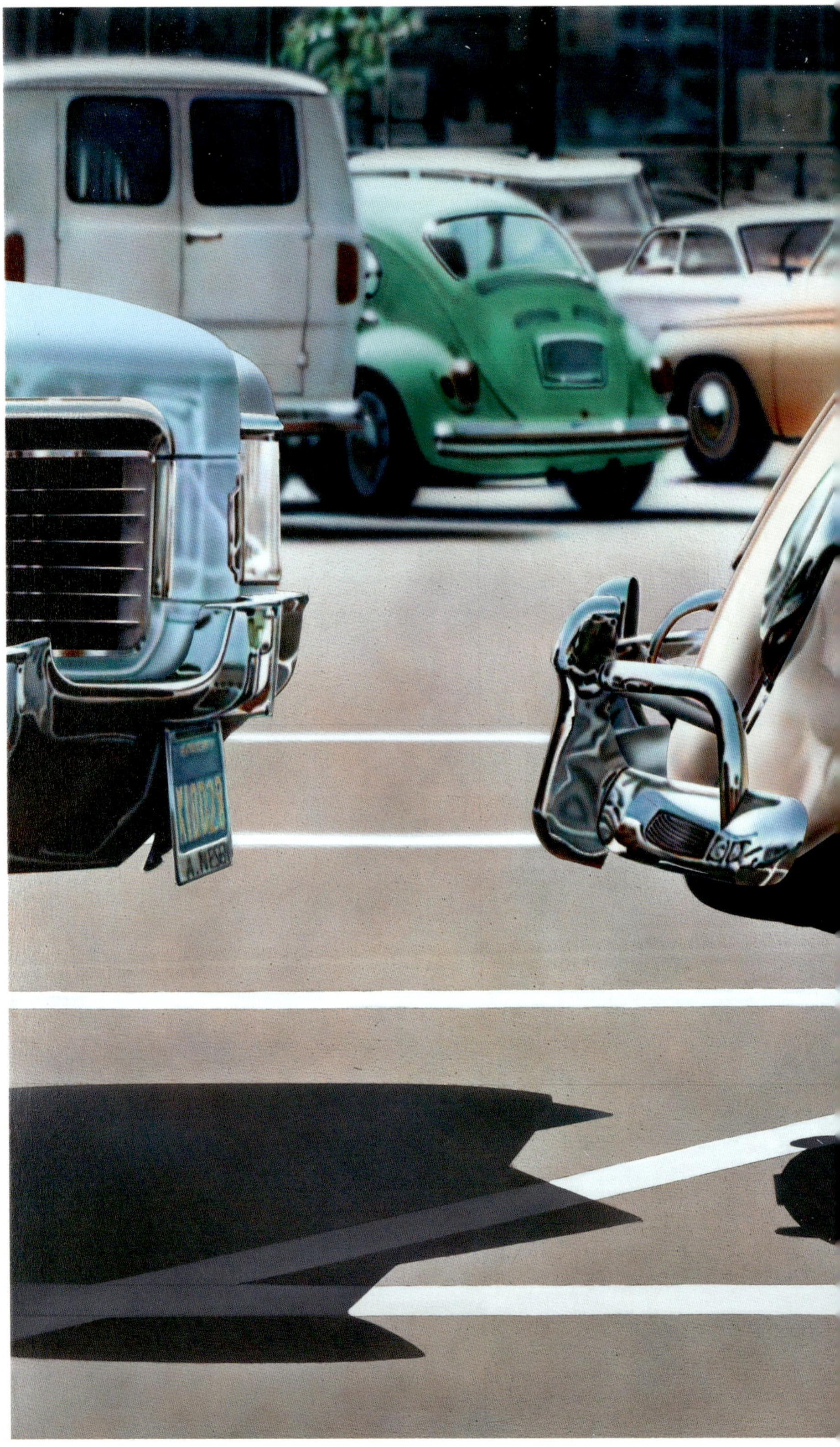

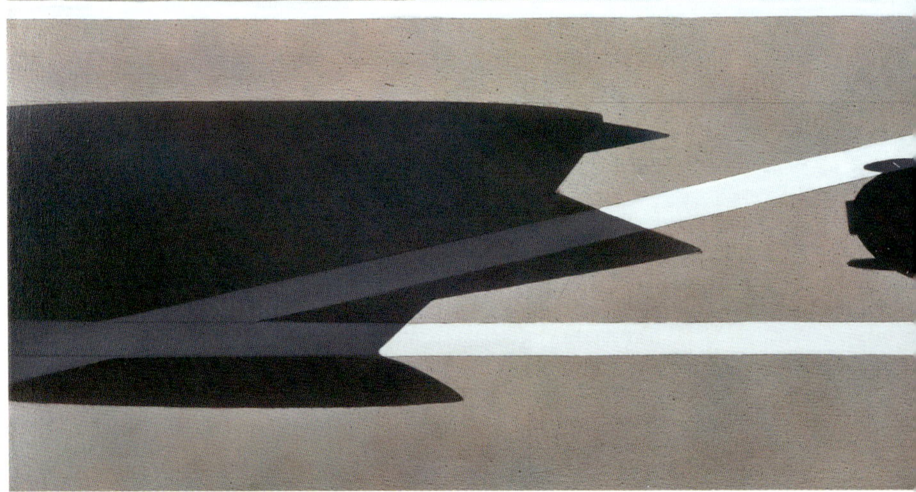

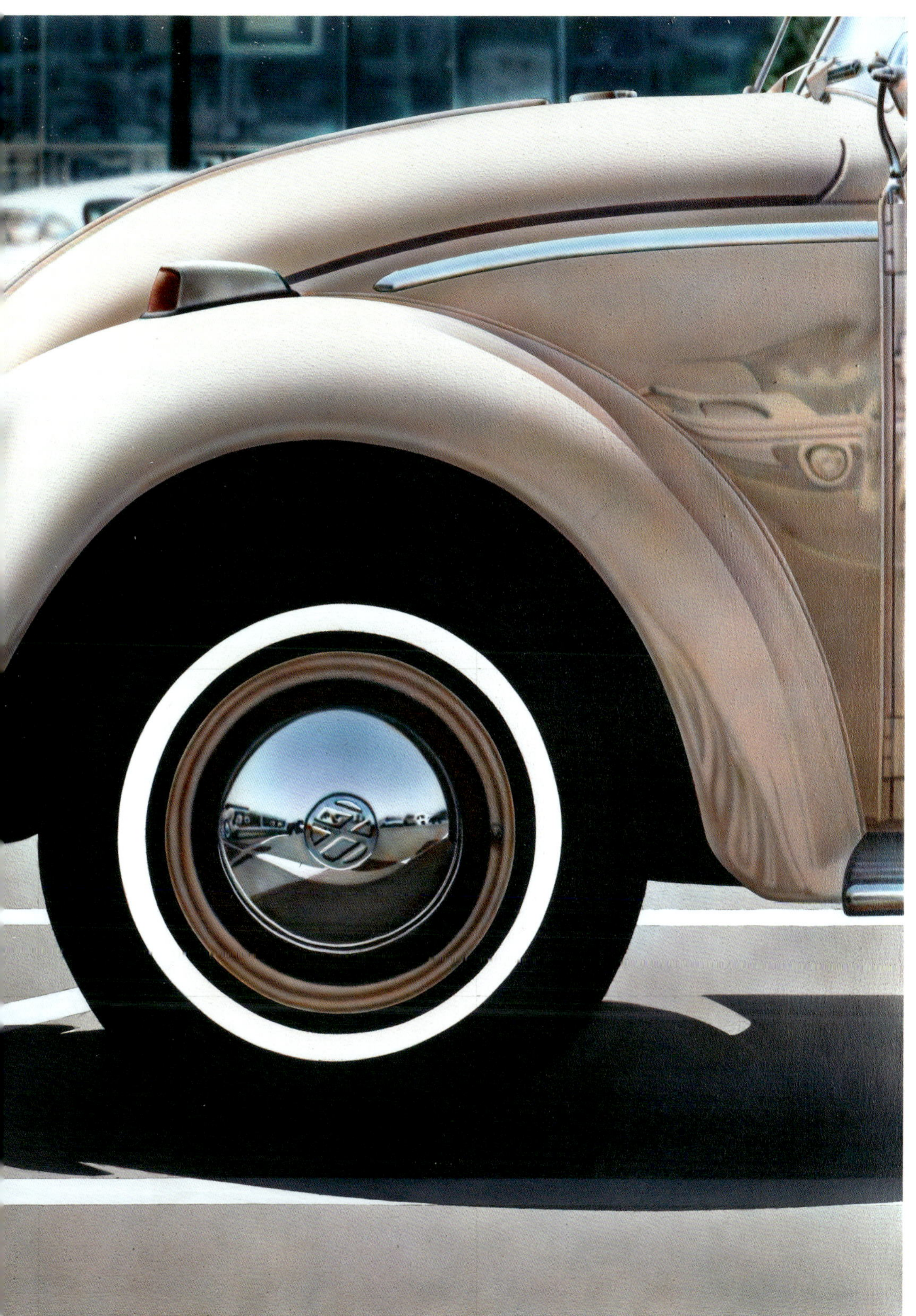

William Eggleston
Aus der Serie / from the series:
Los Alamos, 1966–74

Memphis, 1971-74

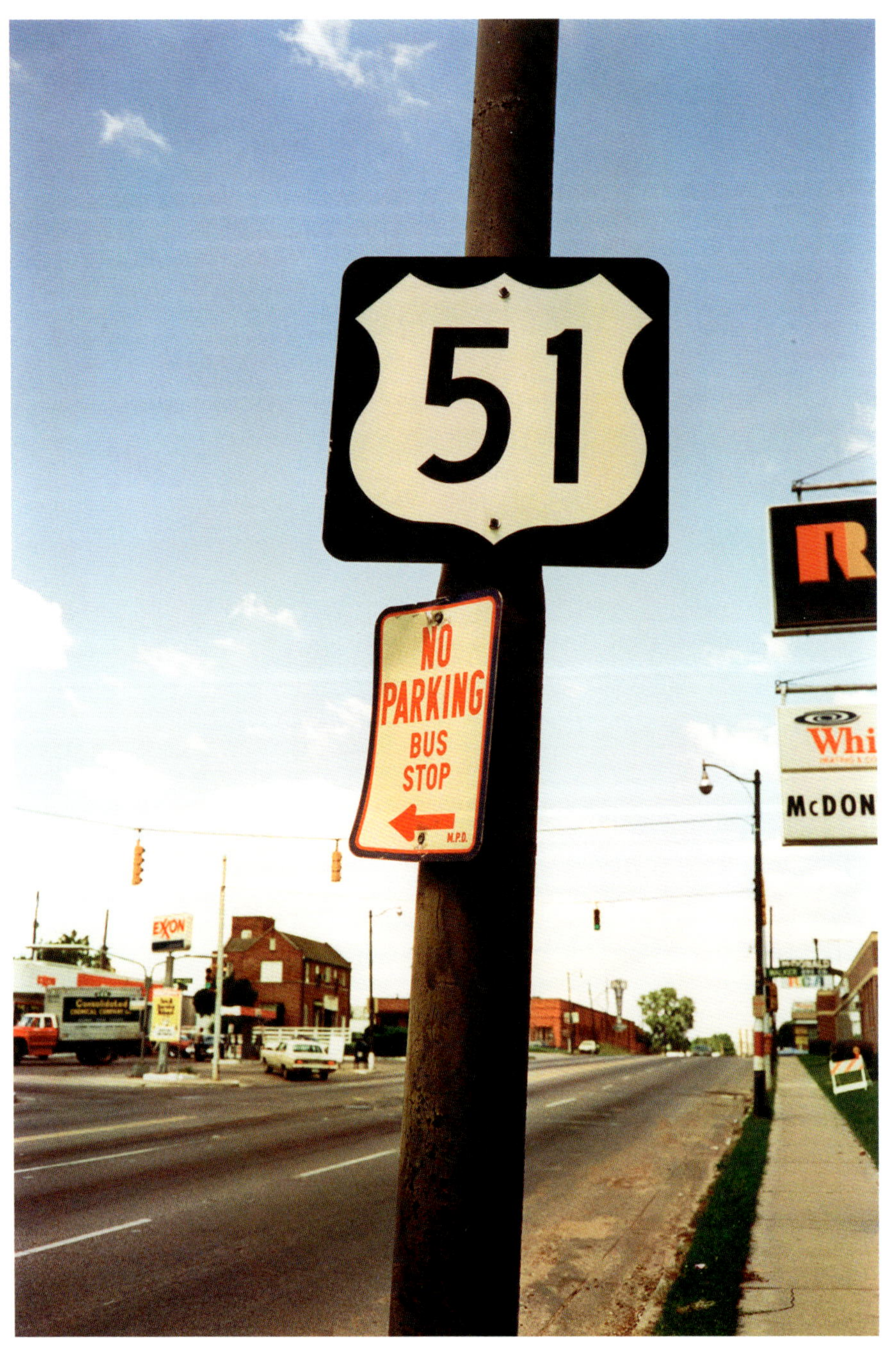

William Eggleston
Aus der Serie / from the series:
Los Alamos, 1966–74

Louisiana, 1971–74

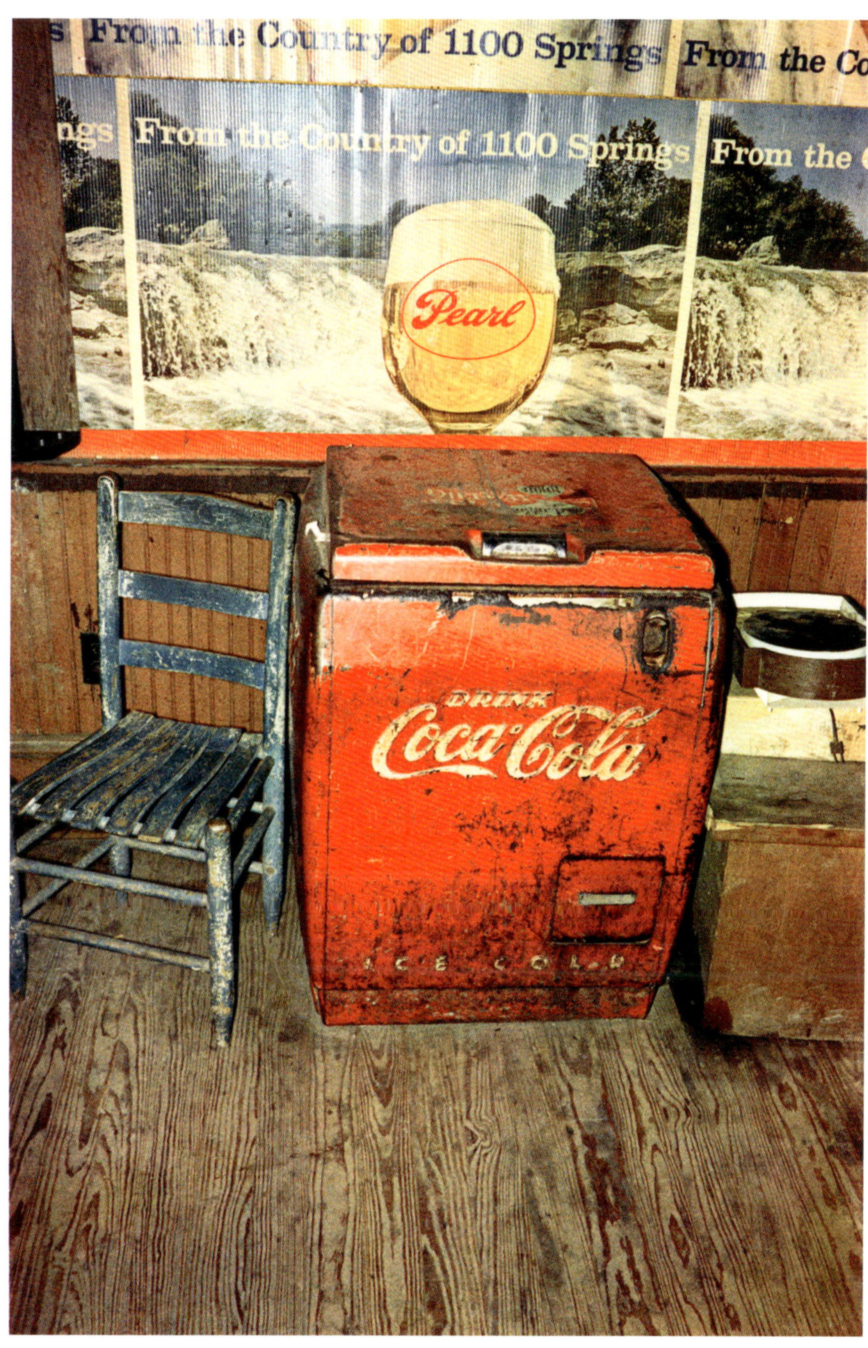

From the Country of 1100 Springs From the Co
From the Country of 1100 Springs From the
Pearl
DRINK
Coca-Cola
ICE COLD

Richard Estes
Rappaport Pharmacy, 1976

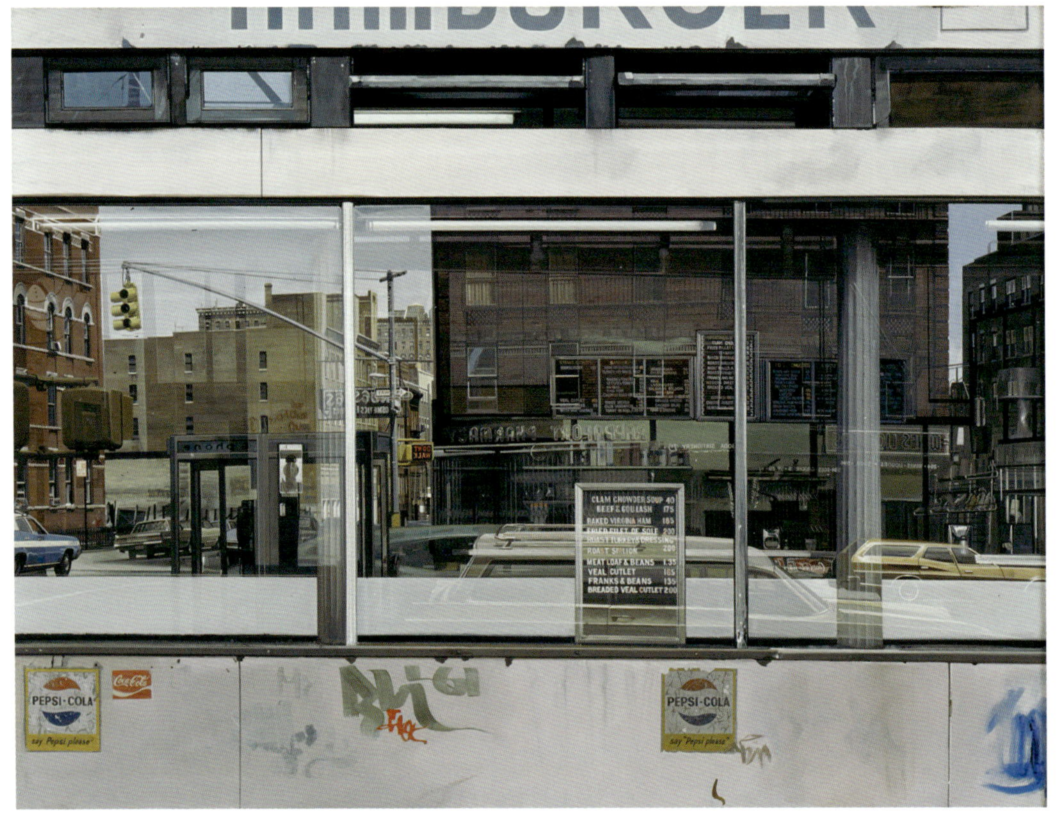

Richard Estes
Downtown, 1978

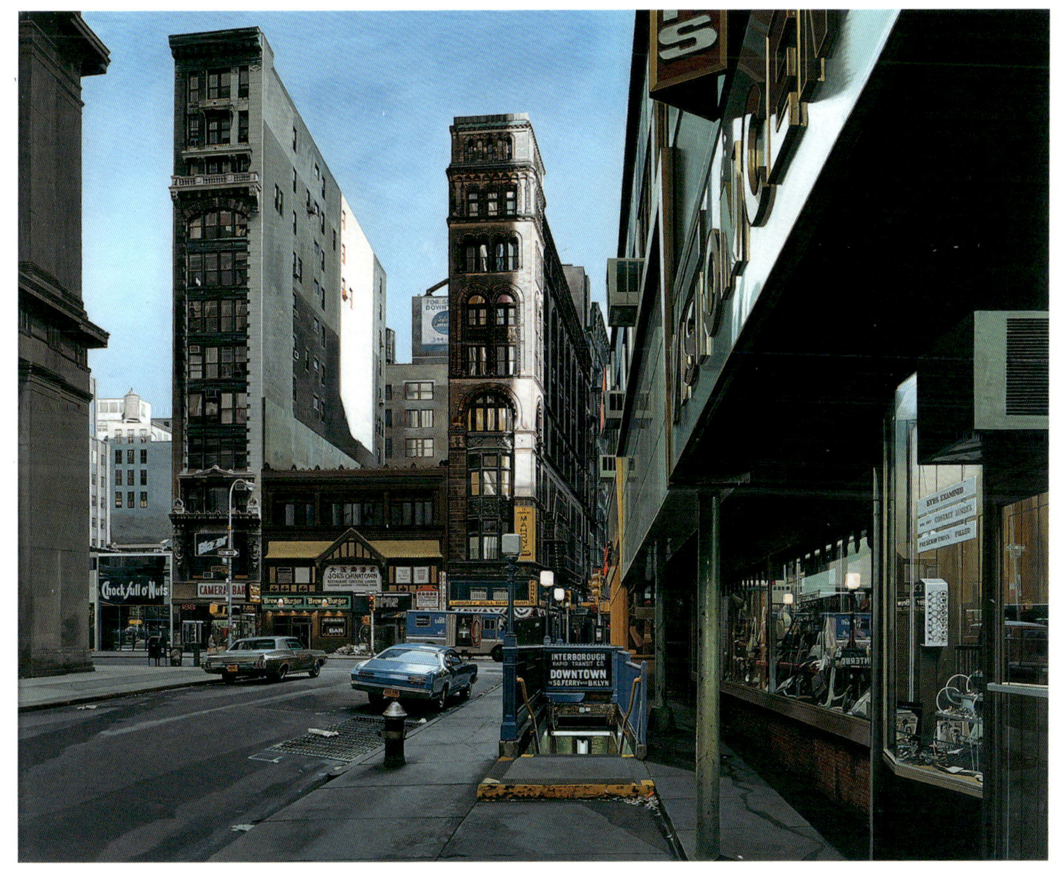

Walker Evans
Roadside Store, Vicinity
Greensboro, Alabama, 1936

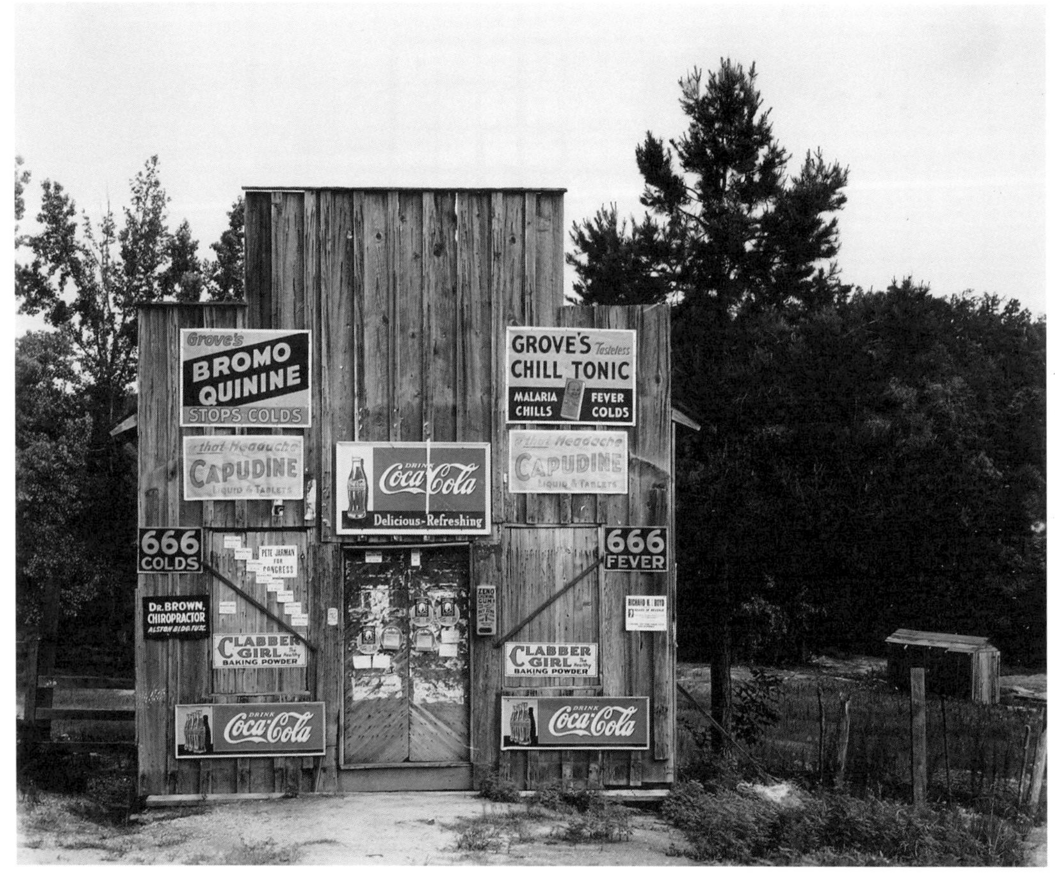

Walker Evans
Negro Church, South Carolina,
1936/2002

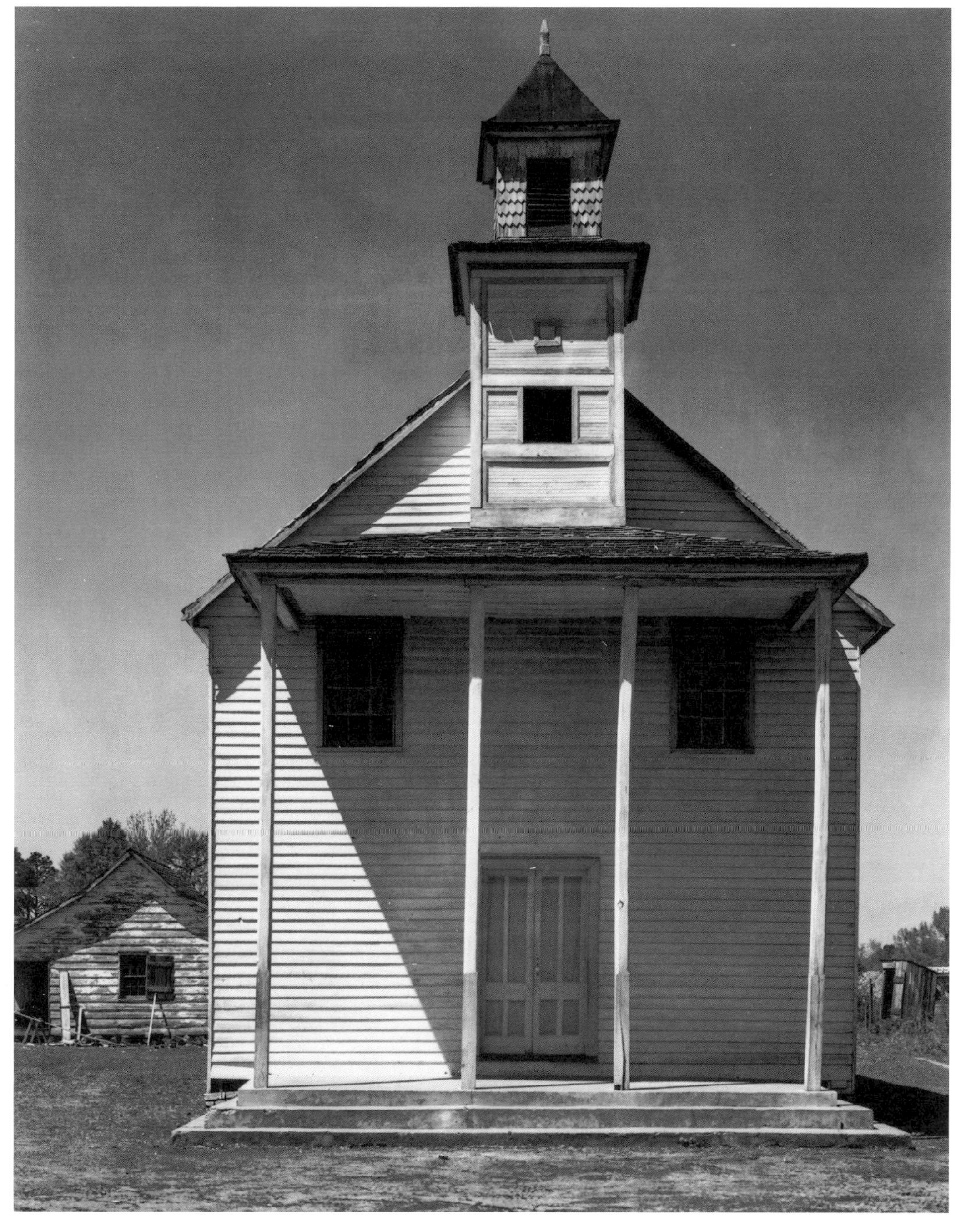

Lee Friedlander
Aus der Serie / from the series:
The New Cars: 1964, 1963/2011

Detroit (Lincoln Continental)

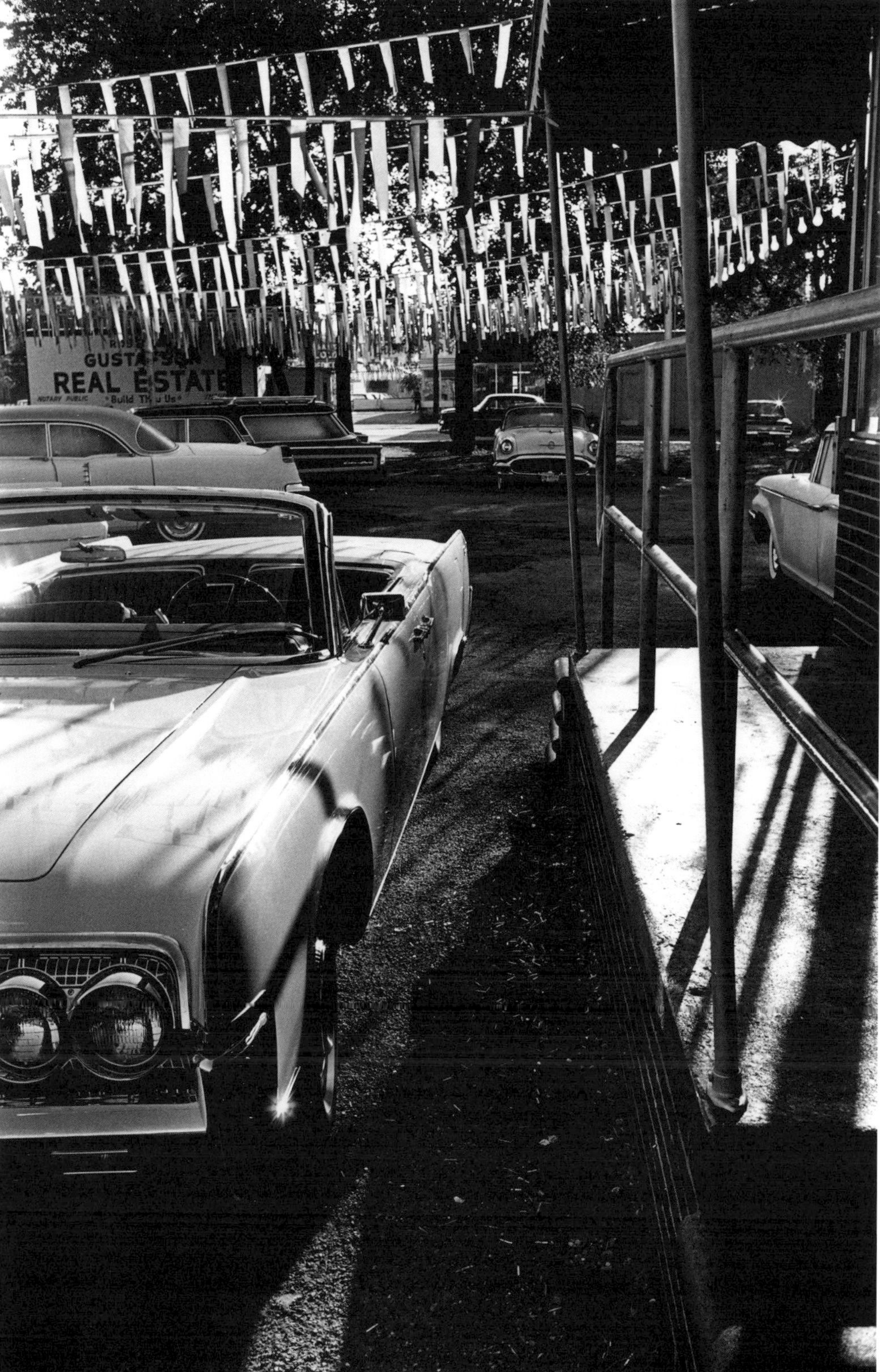
GUSTAFSON
REAL ESTATE
NOTARY PUBLIC   "Build Thru Us"

Ralph Goings
Airstream, 1970

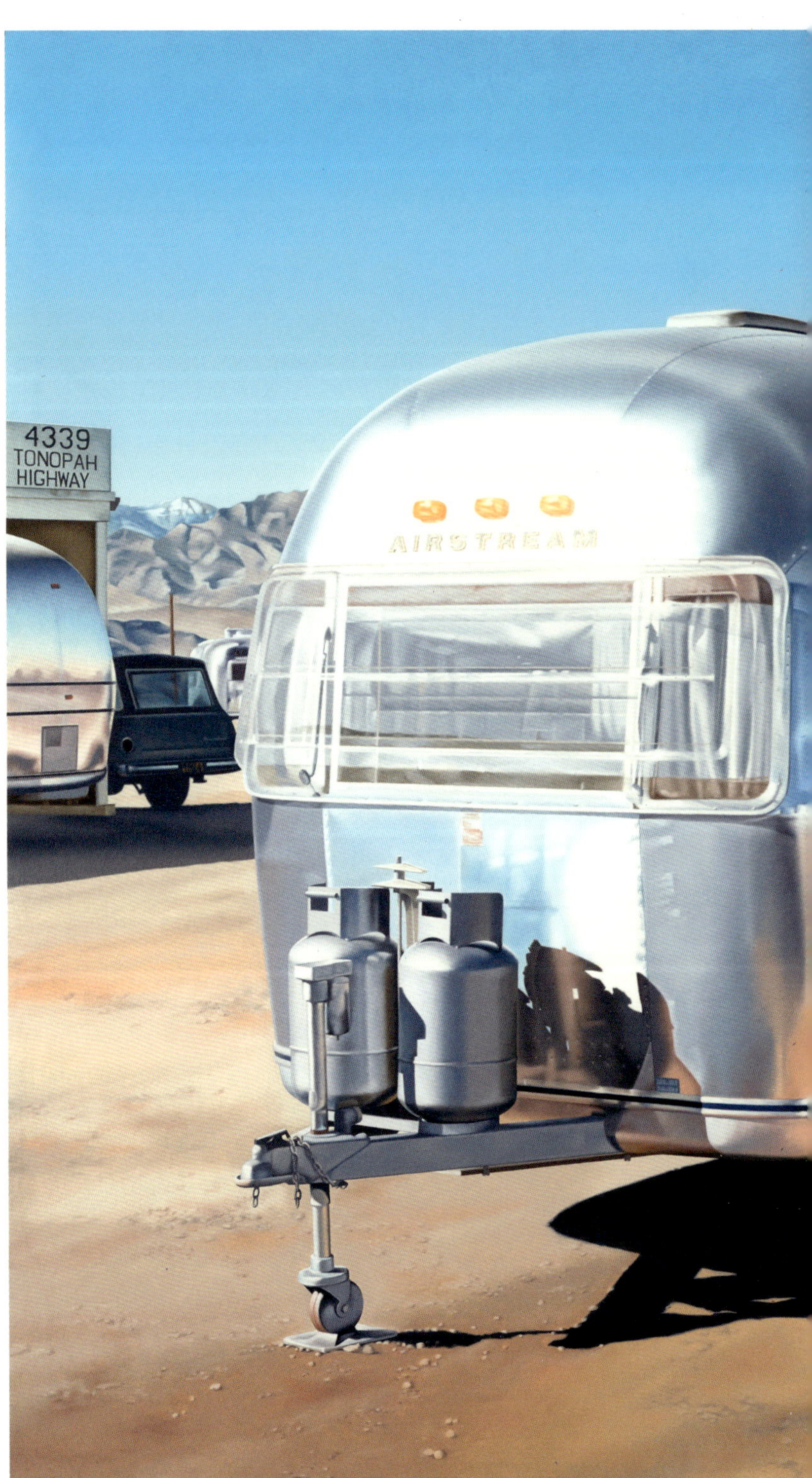

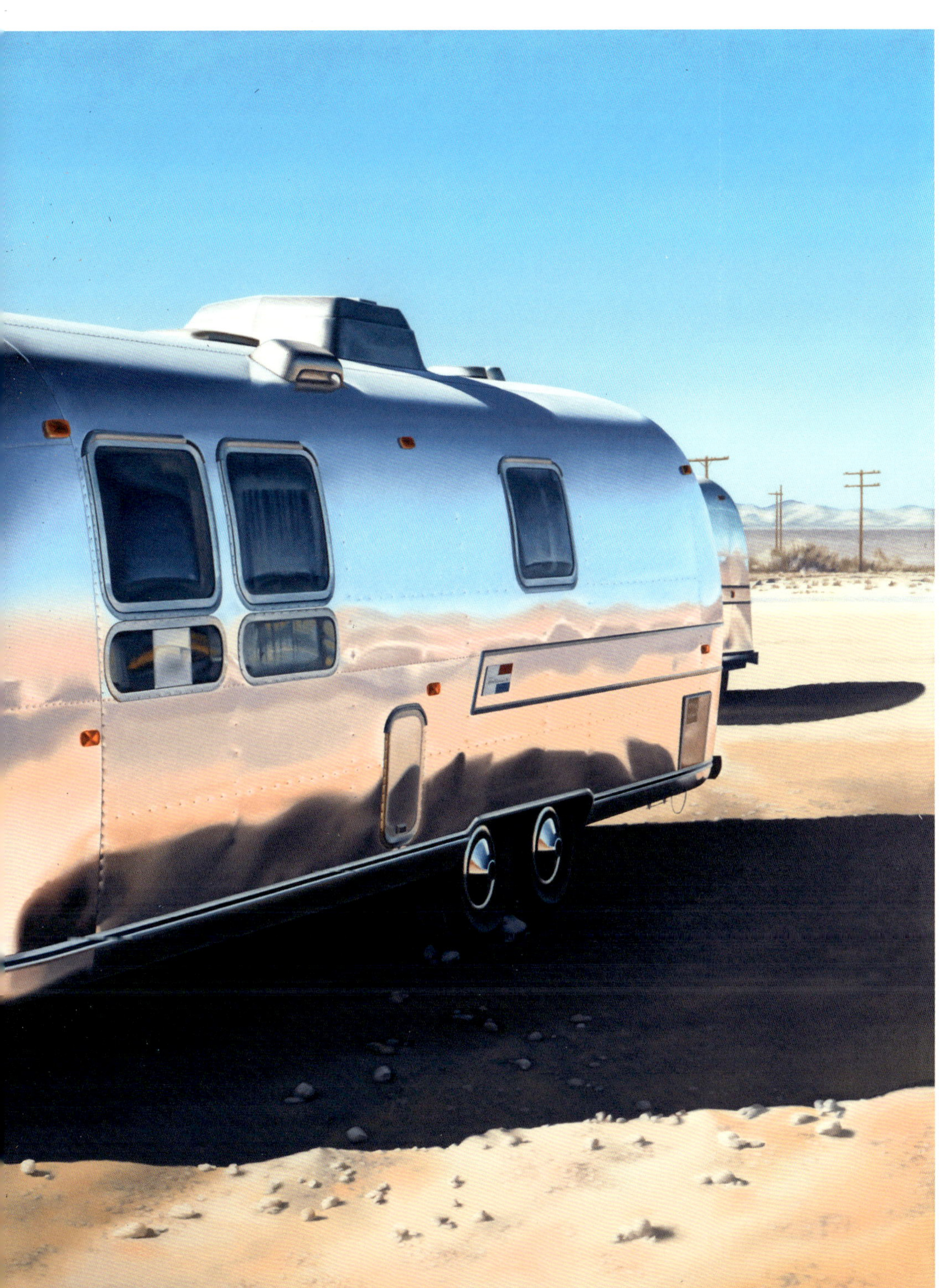

Richard McLean
Rustler Charger, 1971

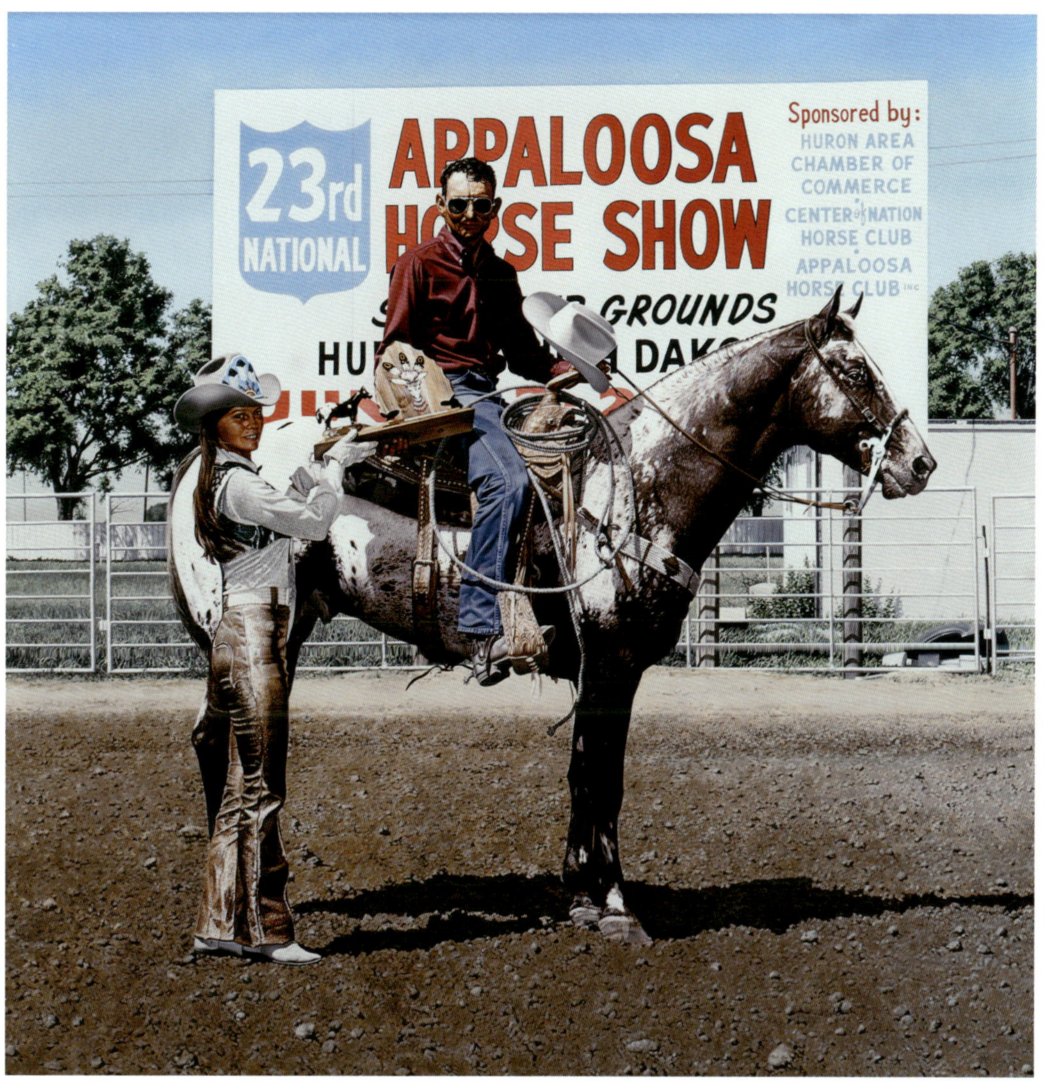
23rd
NATIONAL
APPALOOSA
HORSE SHOW
GROUNDS
HU DAKO
Sponsored by:
HURON AREA
CHAMBER OF
COMMERCE
CENTER of NATION
HORSE CLUB
APPALOOSA
HORSE CLUB INC

Ed Ruscha
The Back of Hollywood, 1977

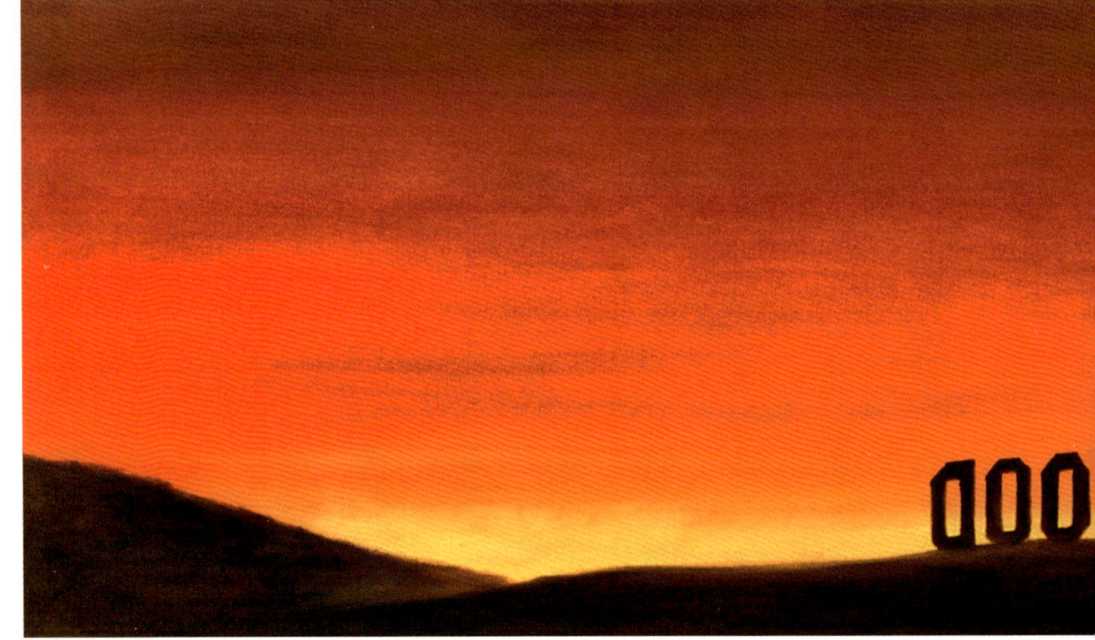

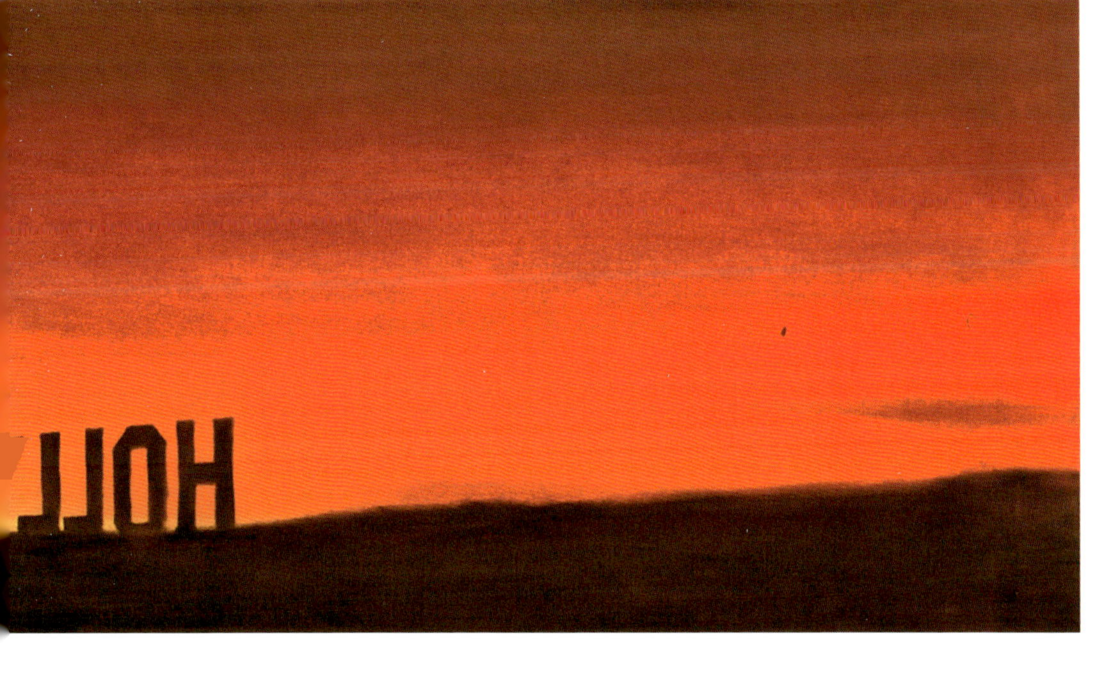
HOLT

John Salt
*Albuquerque Wreck Yard
(Sandia Auto Electric), 1972*

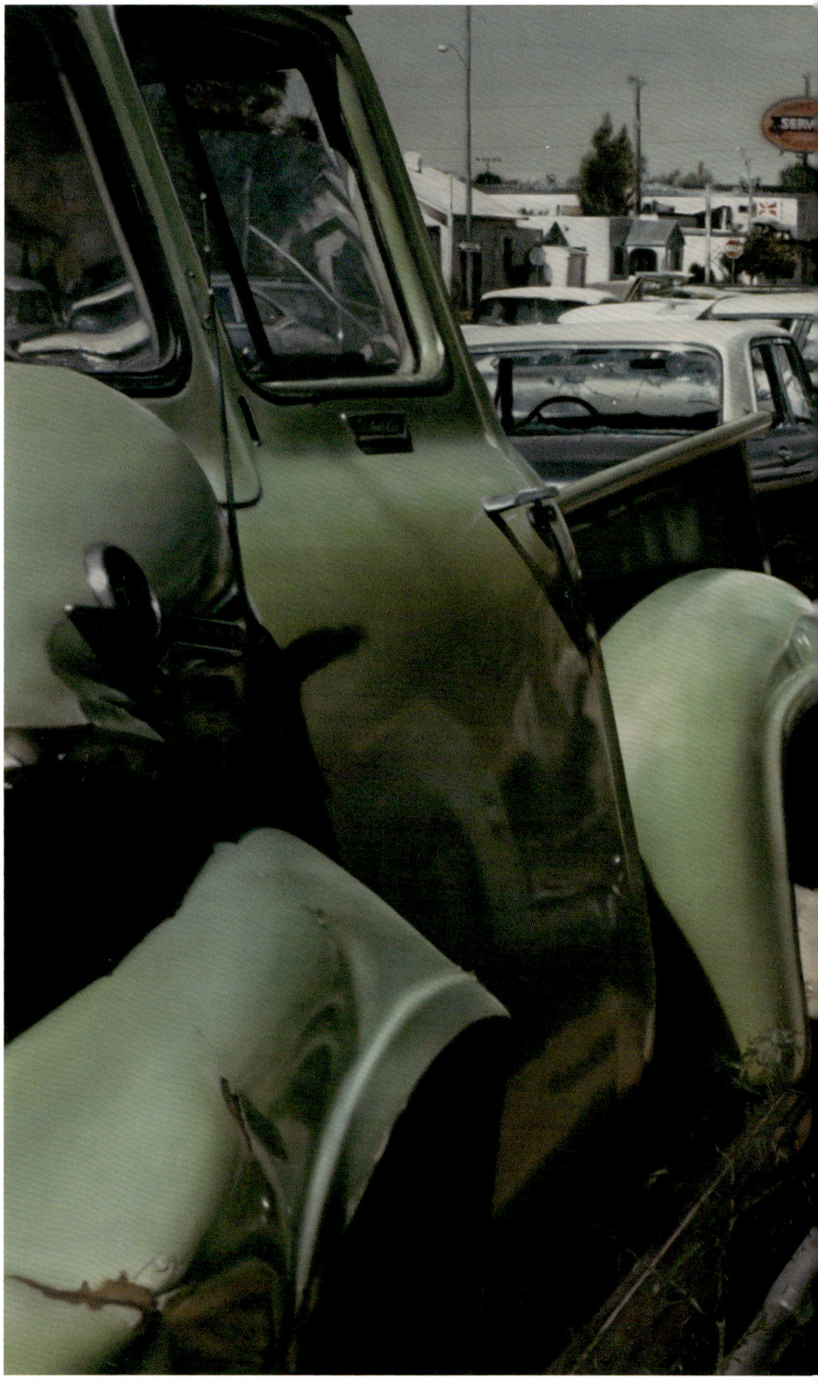

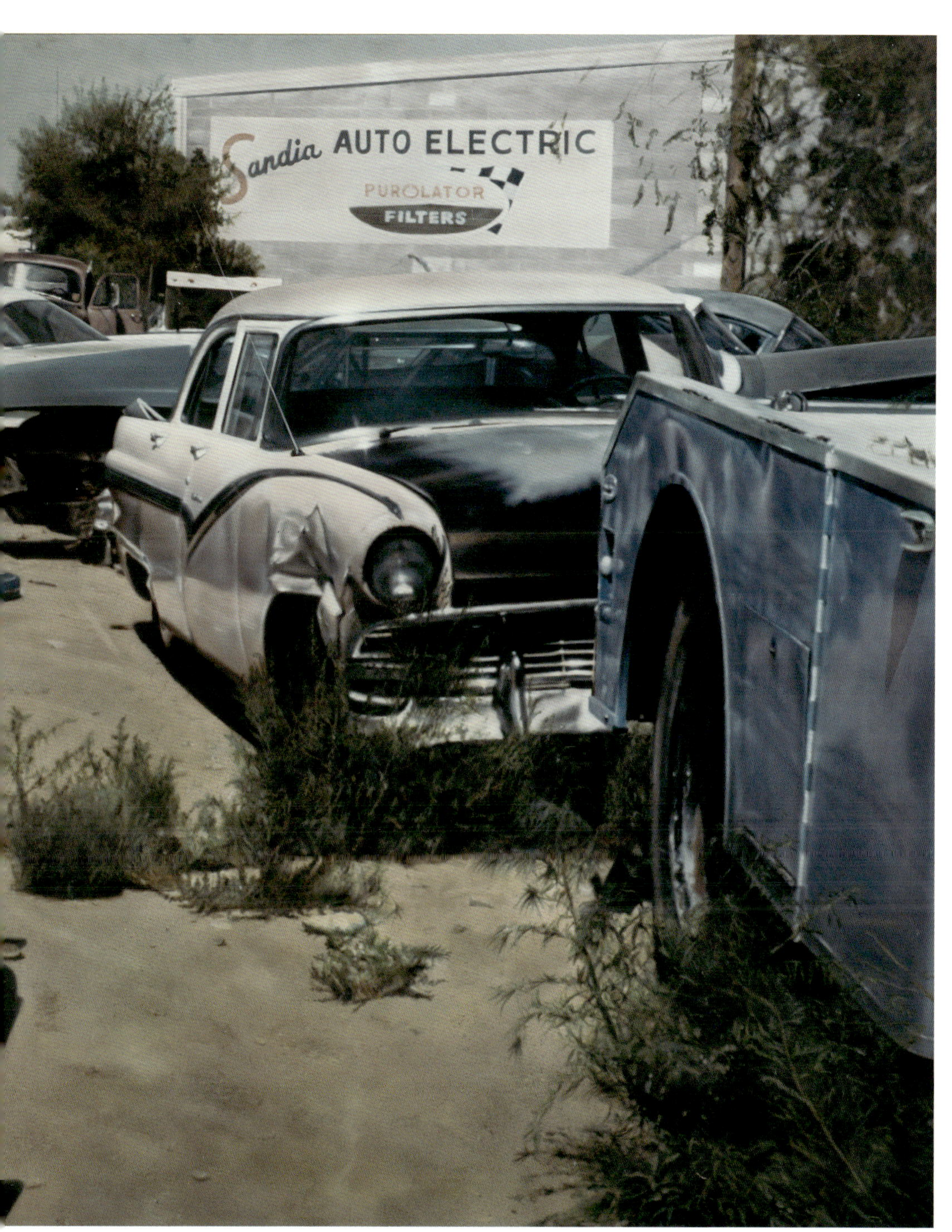

Sandia AUTO ELECTRIC
PUROLATOR
FILTERS

Ben Schonzeit
Sugar, 1972

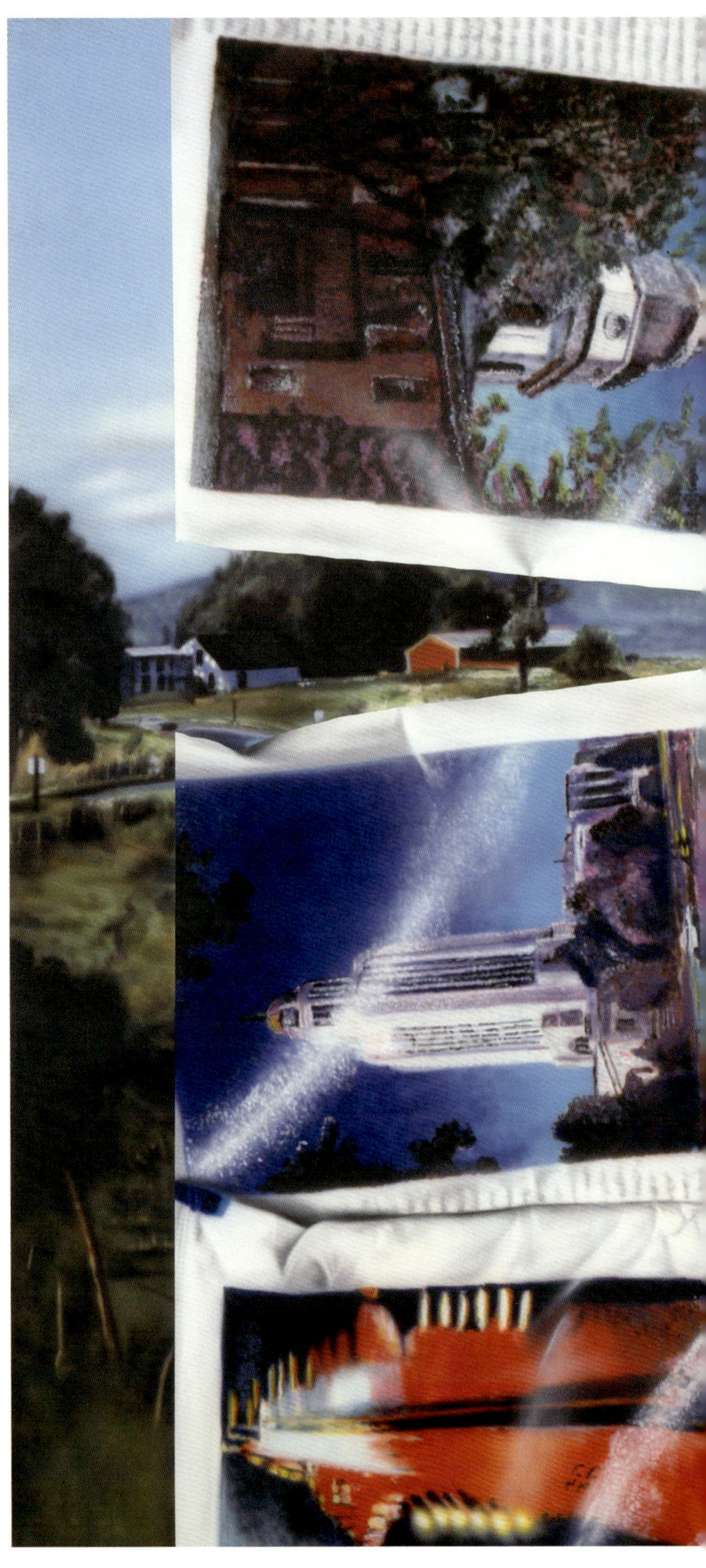

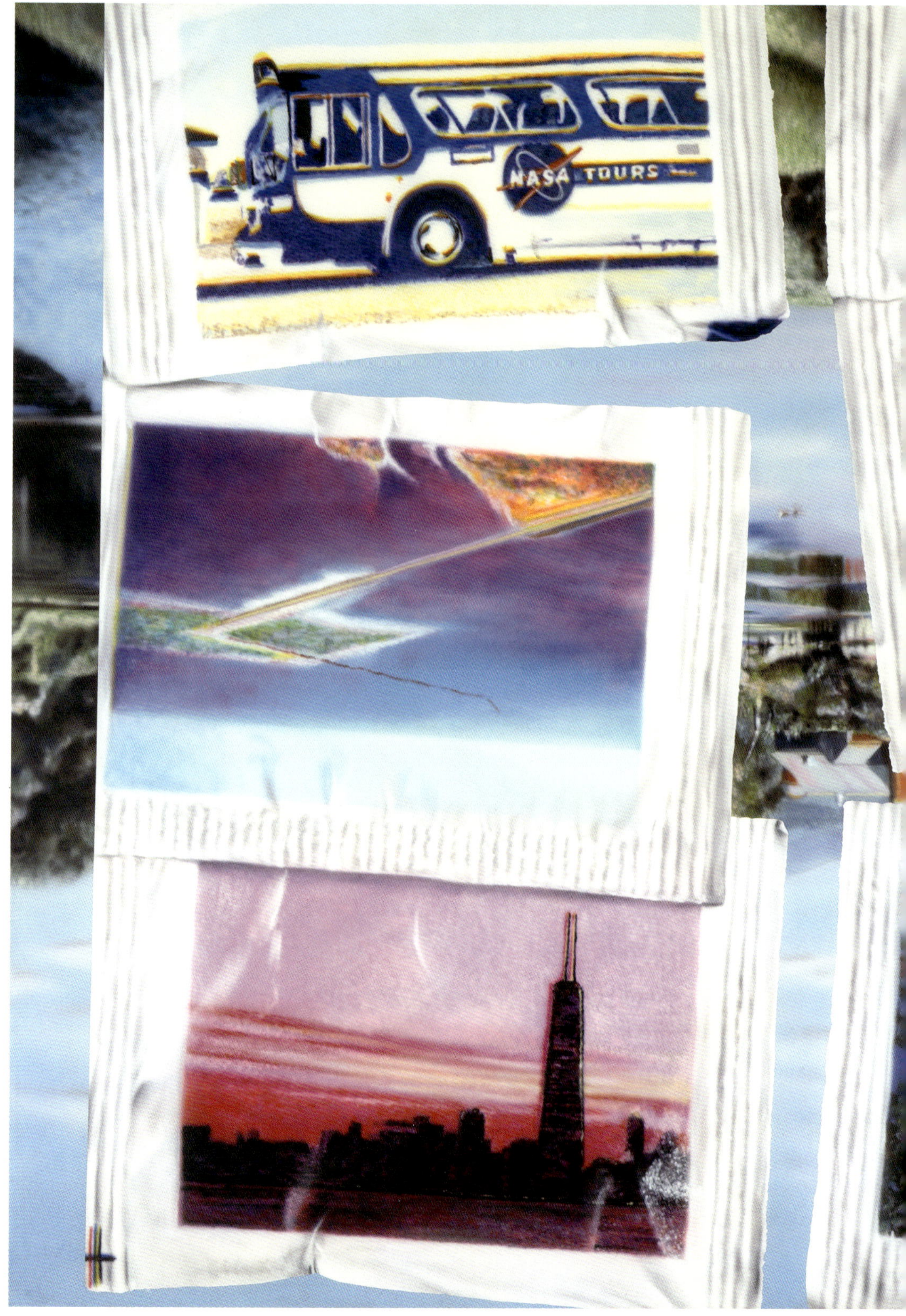
NASA TOURS

Stephen Shore
Aus der Serie / from the series: *Uncommon Places*, 1973–83

Chestnut & 4th St., Harrisburg, PA, July 4, 1973

4th and Main, Delphos, OH, July 6, 1973

Pittsburgh, Pennsylvania, US 30 Facing East, July 5, 1973

Stephen Shore
Aus der Serie / from the series: *Uncommon Places, 1973–83*

Abandoned Cabins, Gaylord, Michigan, July 8, 1973

Victoria Avenue & Albert Street, Regina, Saskatchewan, August 17, 1974

Cherry Street, Fort Worth, TX, June 14, 1976

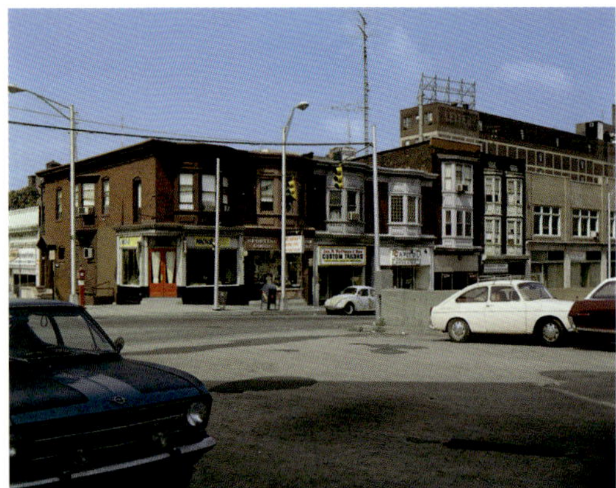

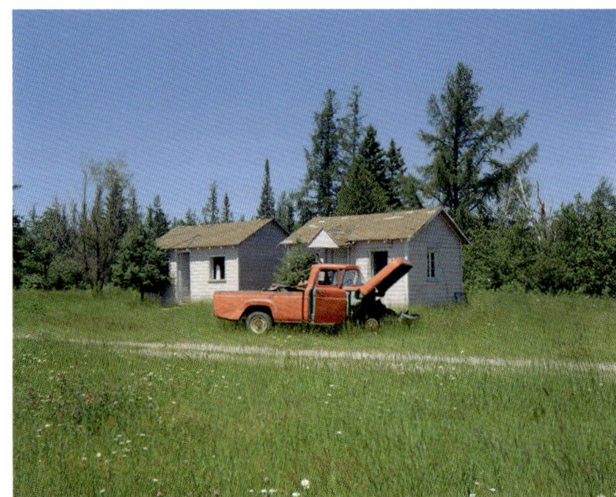

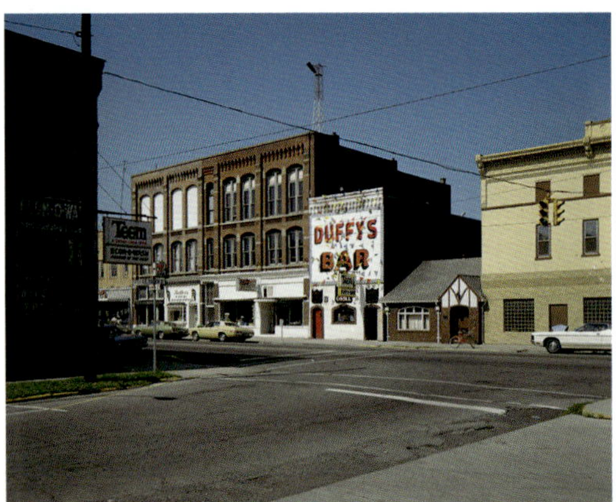

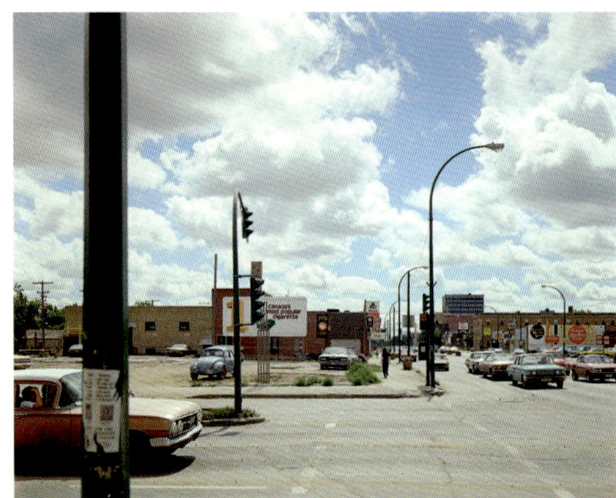

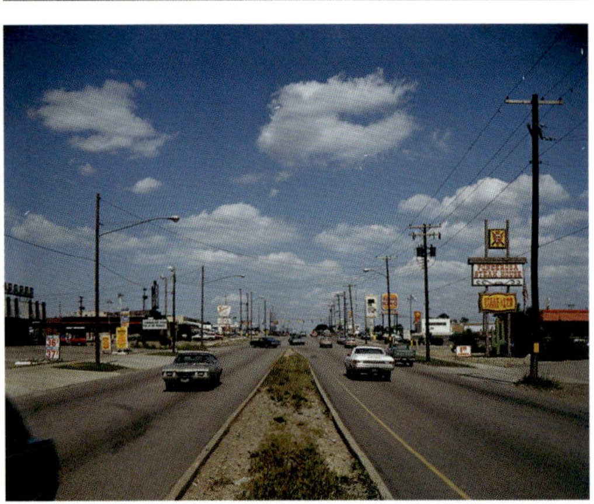

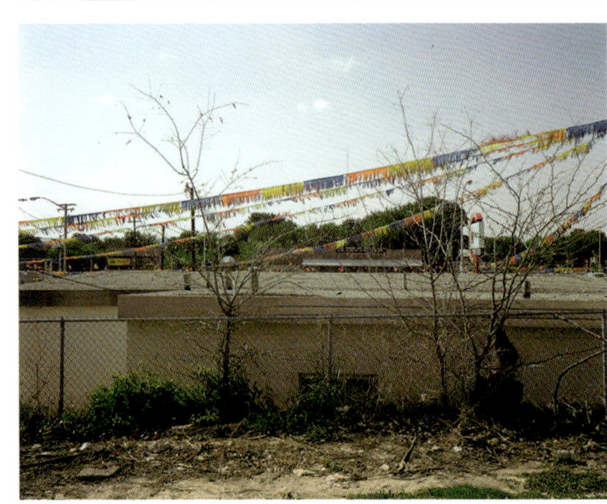

Stephen Shore
Aus der Serie / from the series:
The Roadtrip Journals, 1973

July 6, 1973

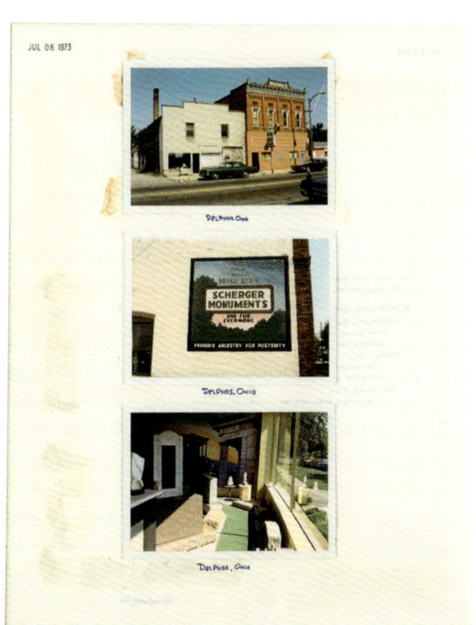

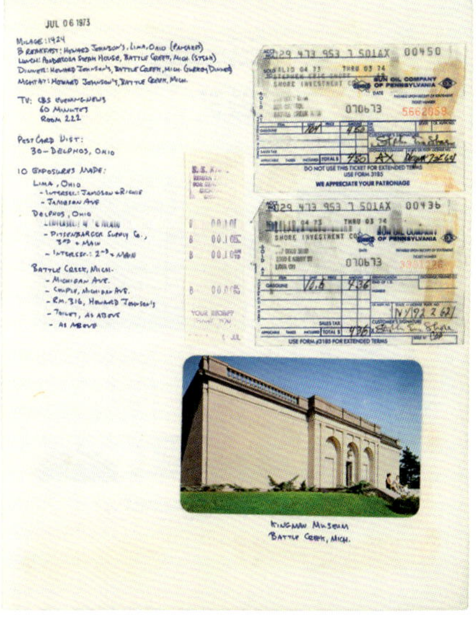

Art Sinsabaugh
Midwest Landscape #20, 1961

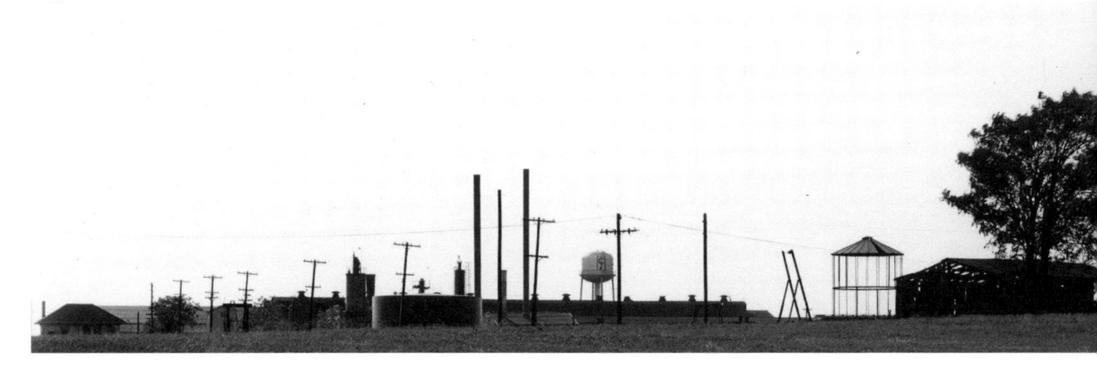

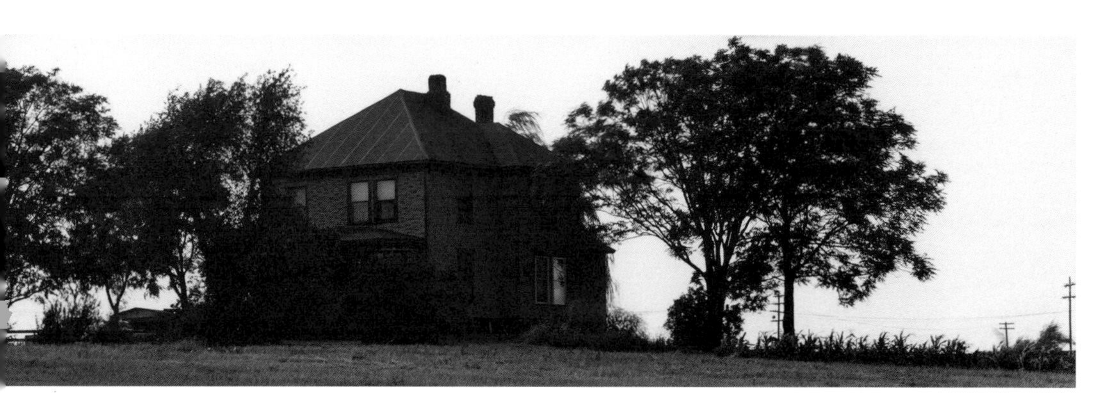

Joel Sternfeld
Aus der Serie / from the
series: *American Prospects,*
1978–87

McLean, Virginia,
December 1978

After a Flash Flood, Rancho
Mirage, California,
July 1979

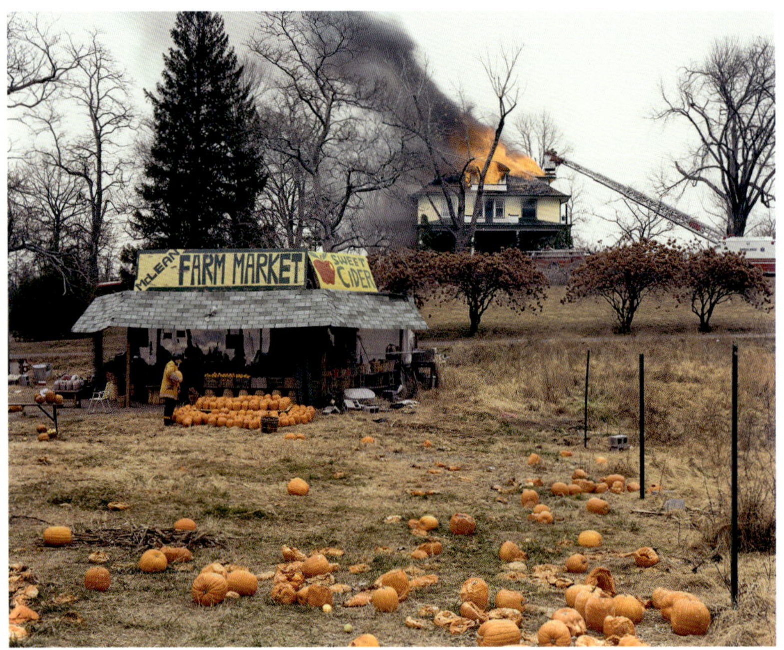

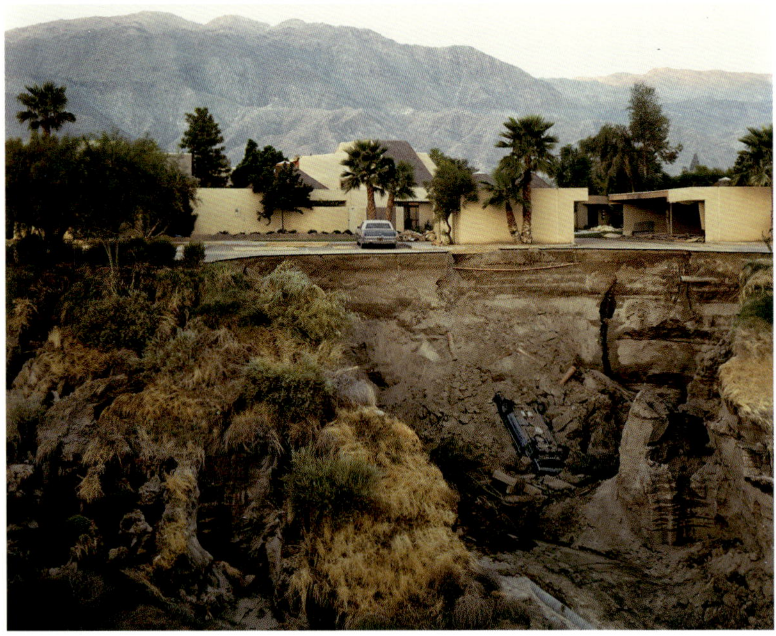

Joel Sternfeld
Aus der Serie / from the
series: *American Prospects*,
1978–87

*Wet'n Wild Aquatic Theme
Park, Orlando, Florida,
September 1980*

*Pendleton, Oregon,
June 1980*

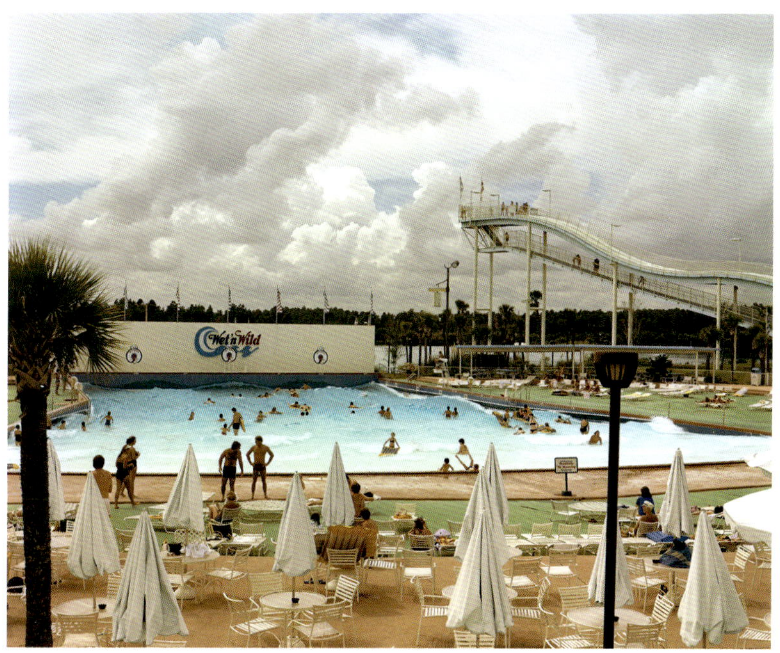

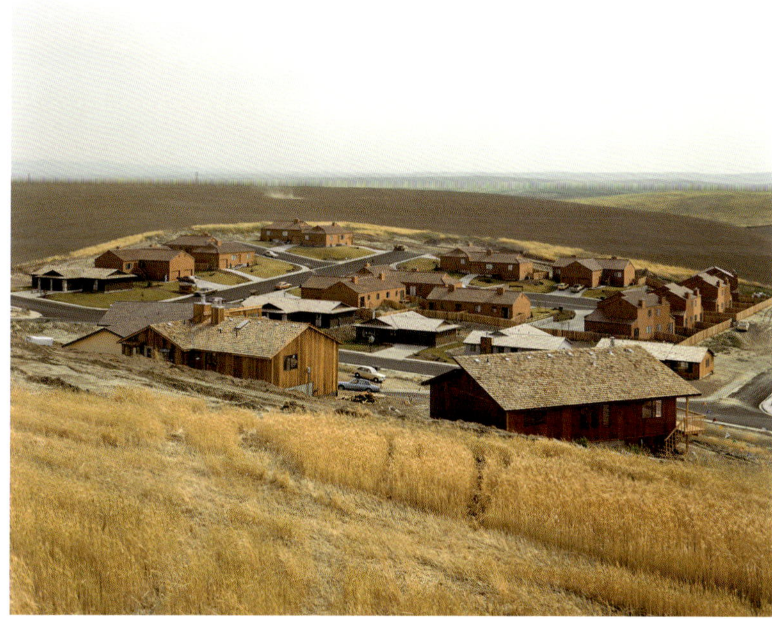

Landschaft in Bewegung
Filmische Ausblicke auf ein unbestimmtes Morgen
Landscape in Motion
Cinematic Visions of an Uncertain Tomorrow

Kunsthaus Graz

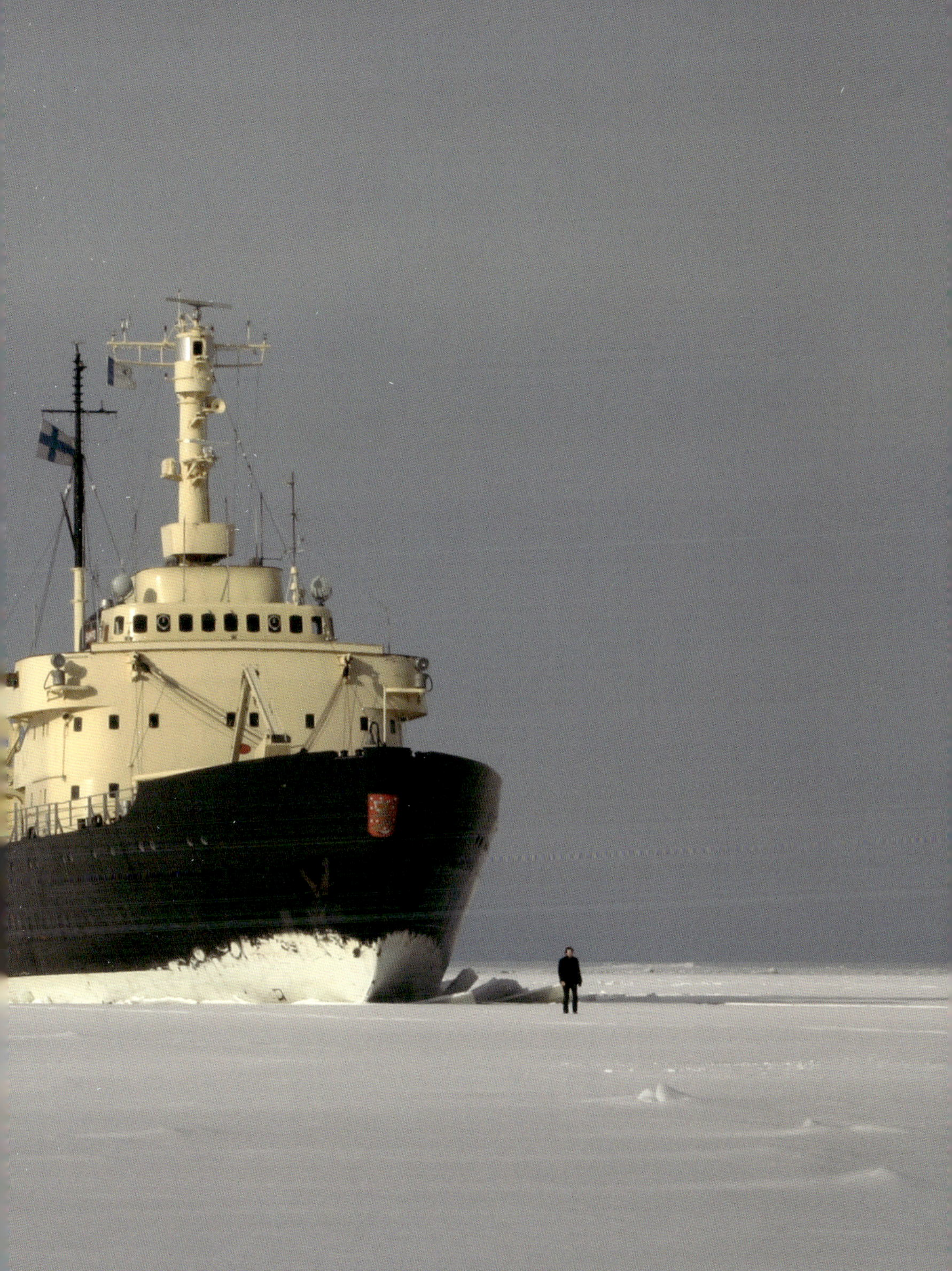

Darren Almond
In the Between, 2006
(Videostills / video stills)

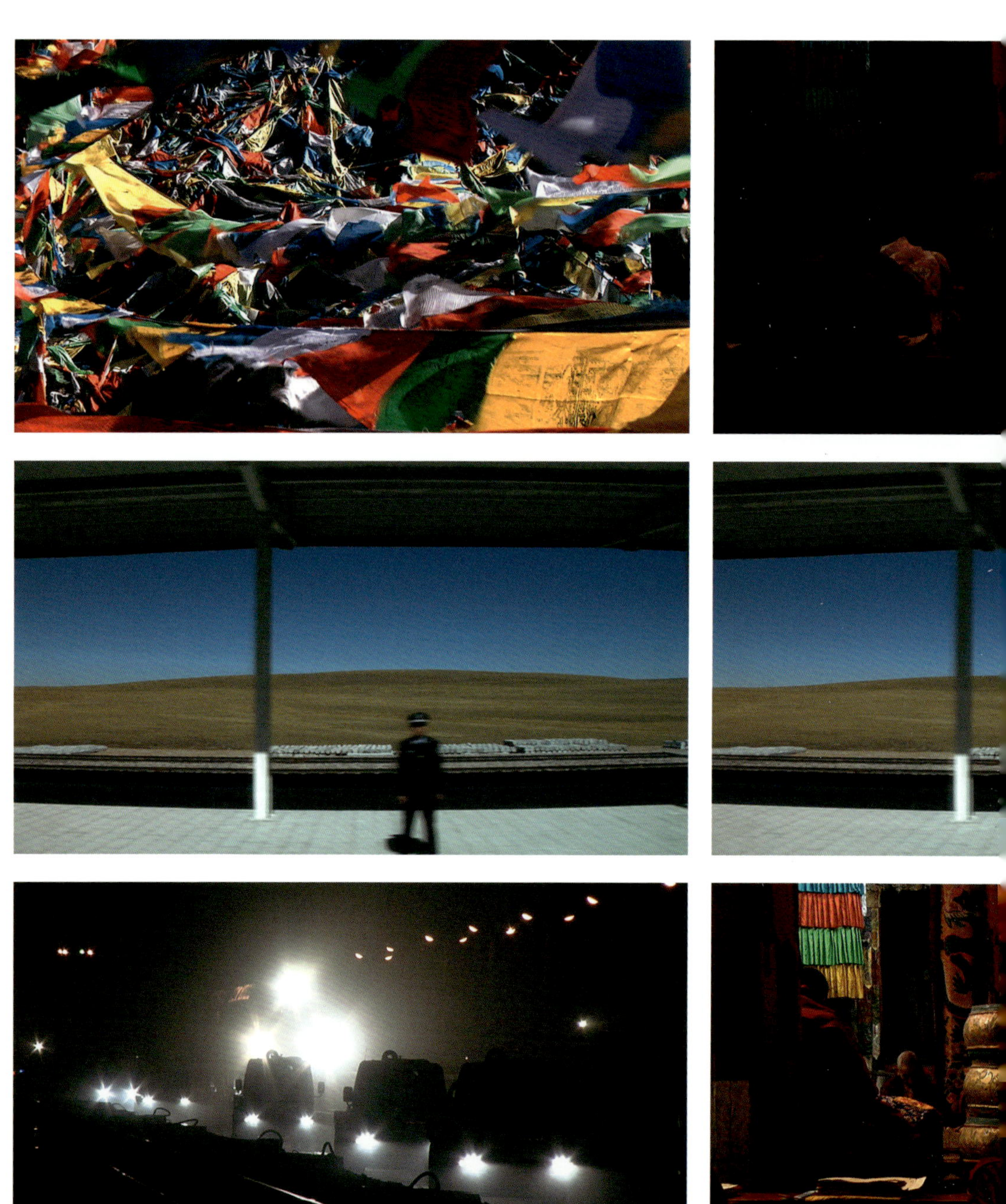

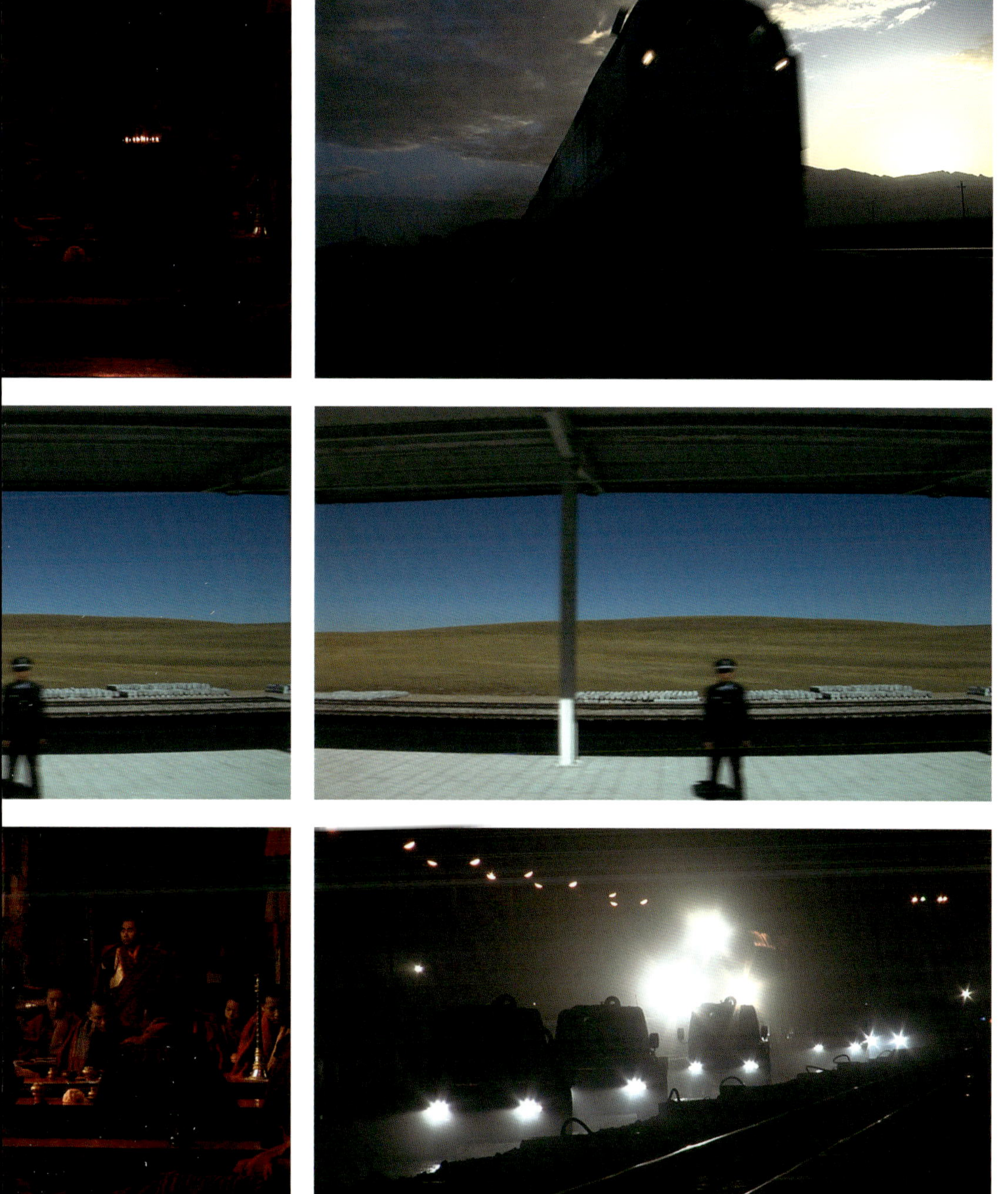

Rosa Barba
Definition Landfill, 2014
Ausstellungsansicht / **exhibition view**,
Artpace San Antonio, Texas

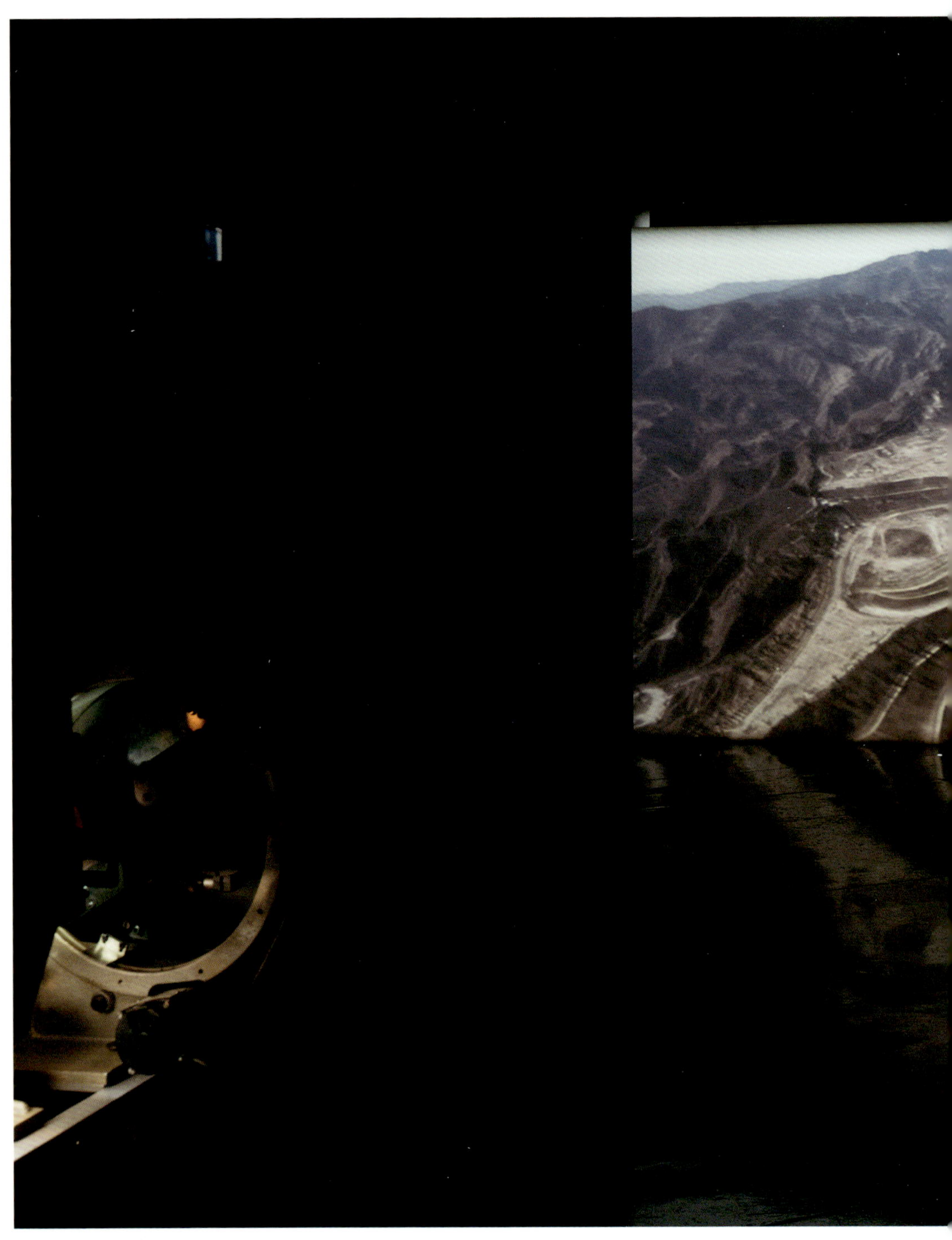

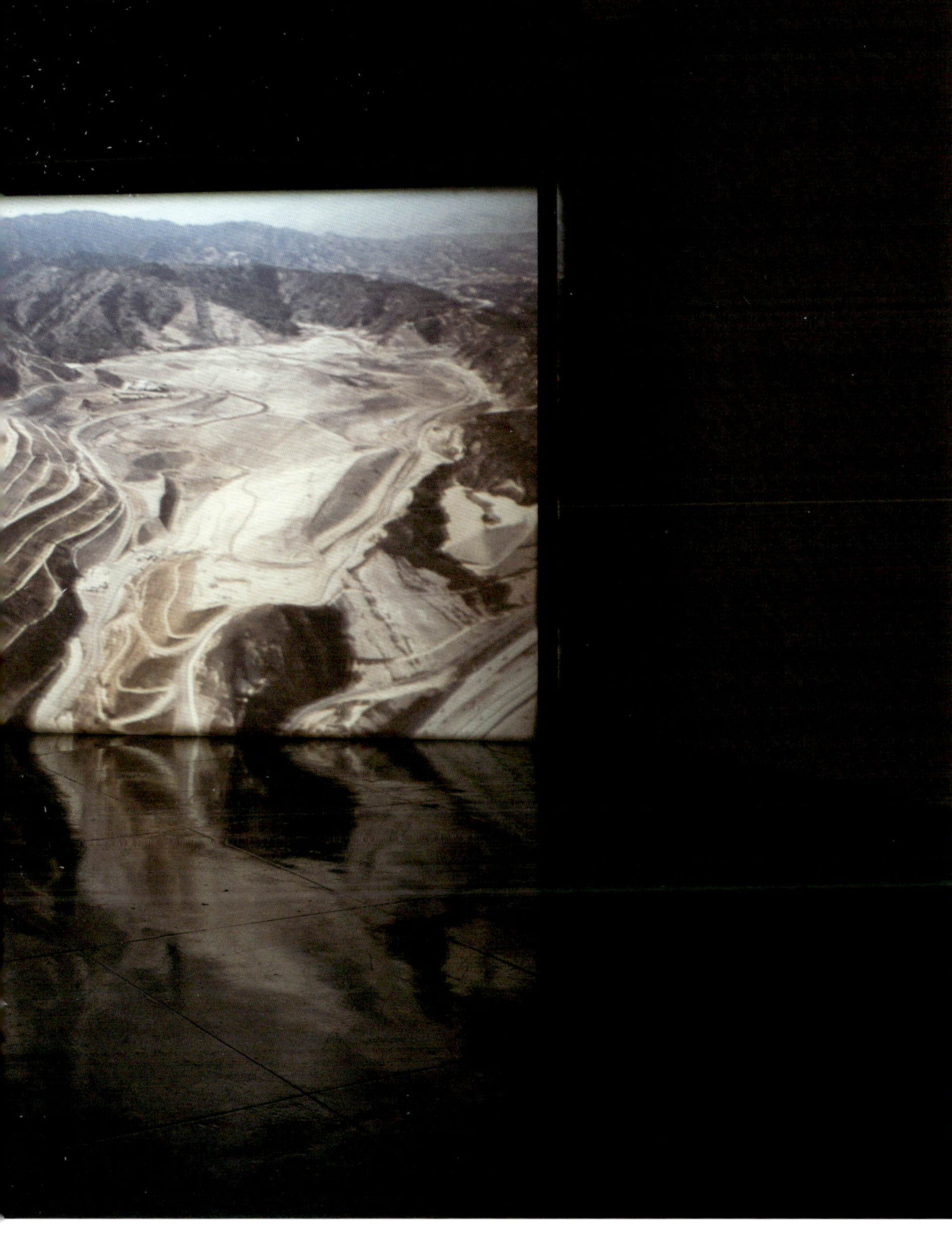

214 — 215

James Benning
Aus / from: *California Trilogy*,
1999–2001
(Filmstills / **film stills**)

El Valley Centro, 1999

Los, 2000

Sogobi, 2001

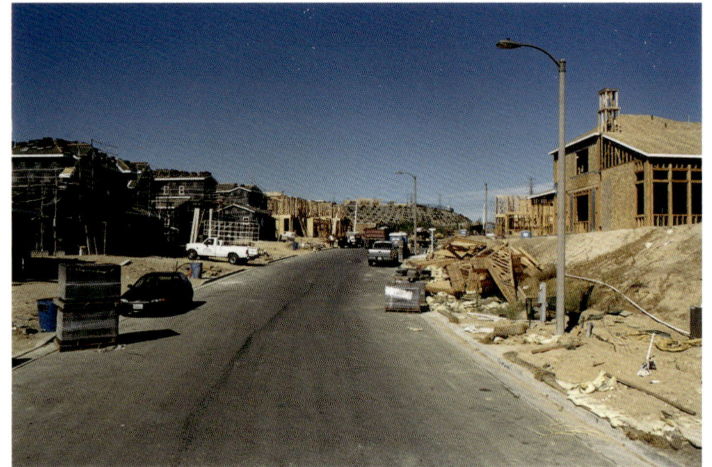

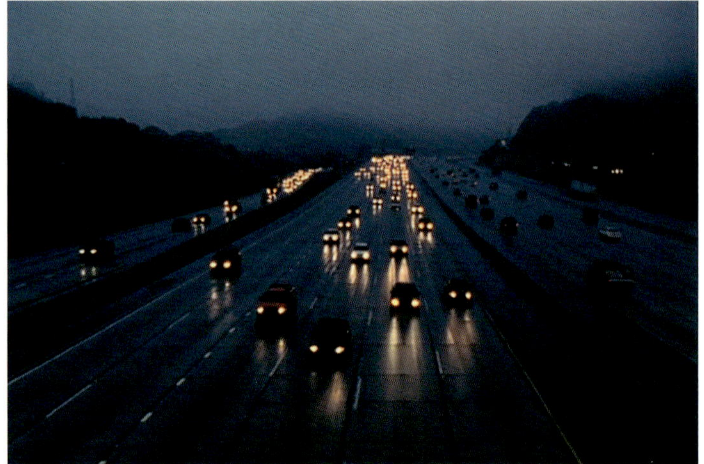

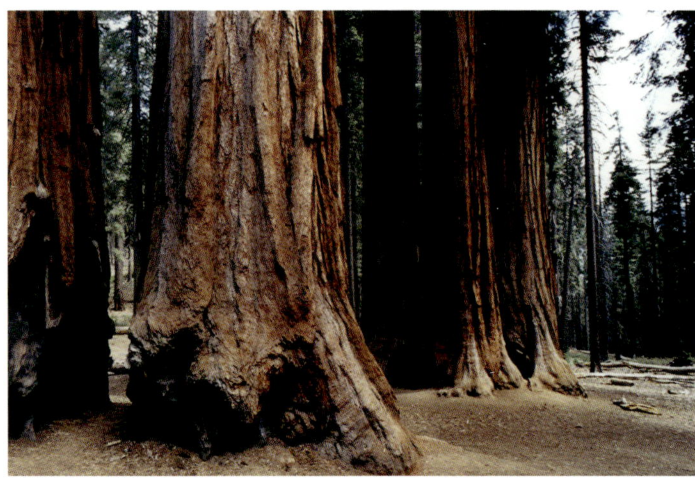

James Benning
casting a glance, 2007
(Filmstills / film stills)

James Benning
casting a glance, 2007
(Filmstills / film stills)

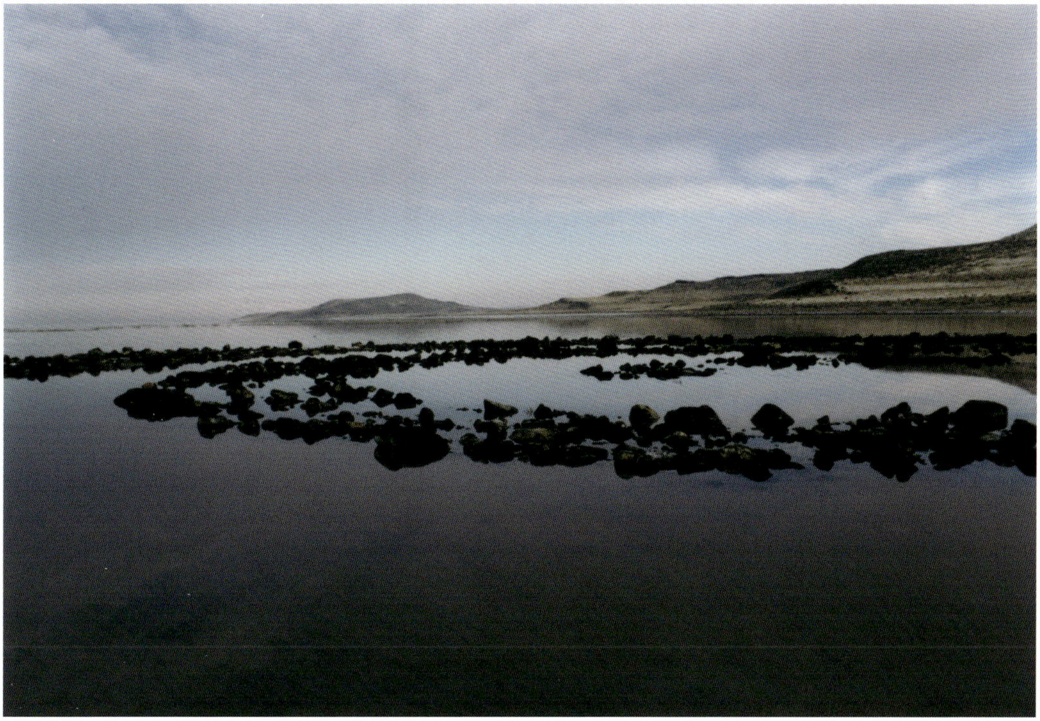

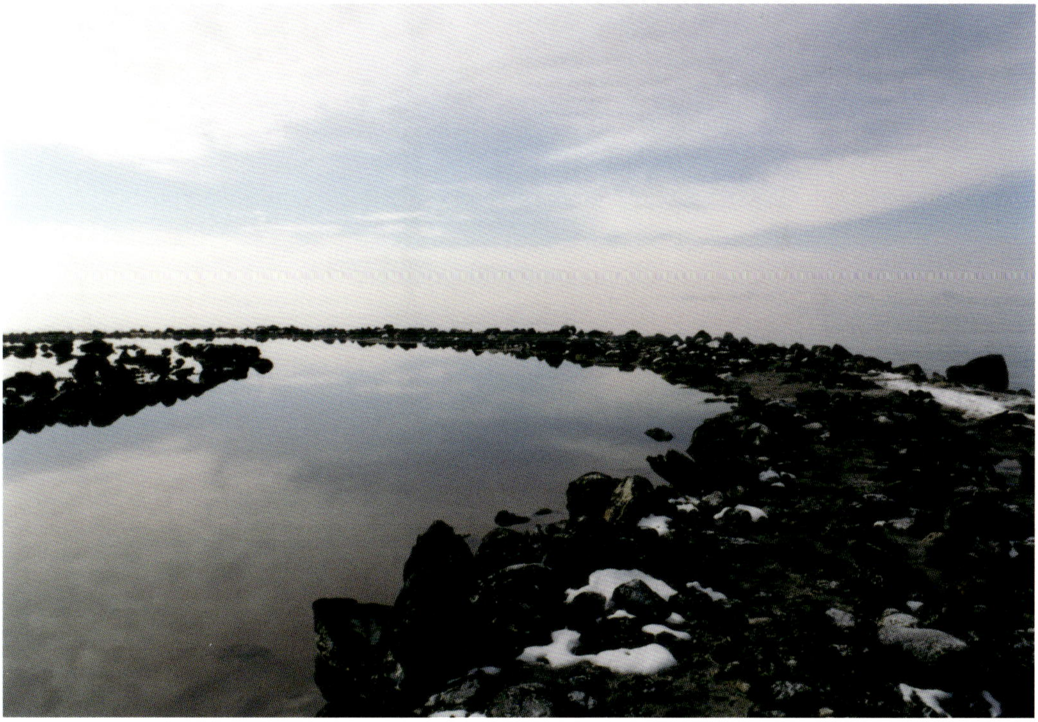

Ursula Biemann
Deep Weather, 2013
(Videostills / video stills)

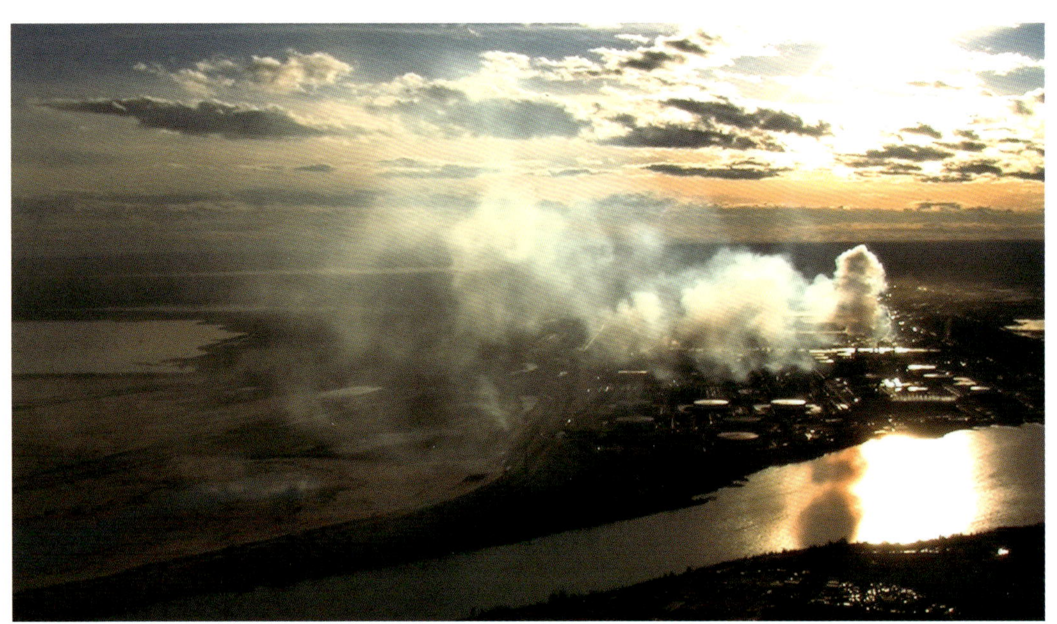

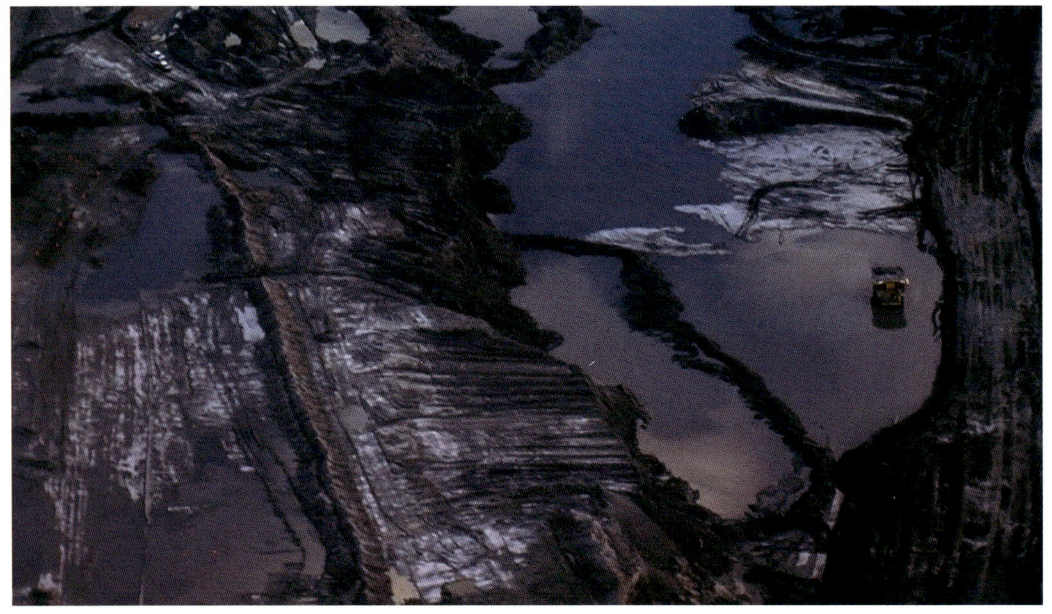

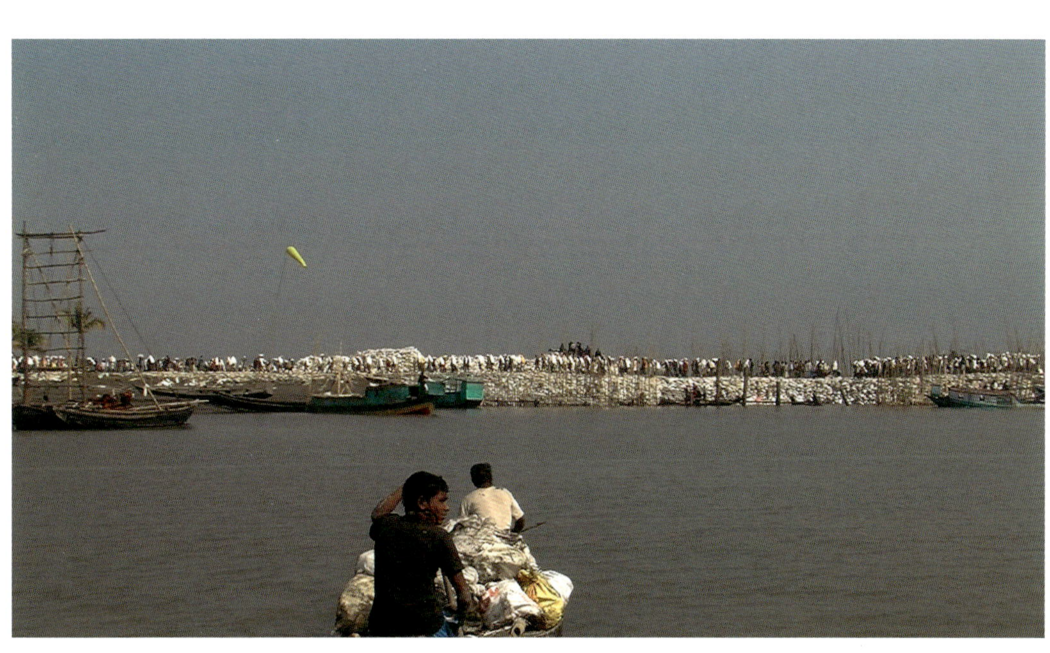

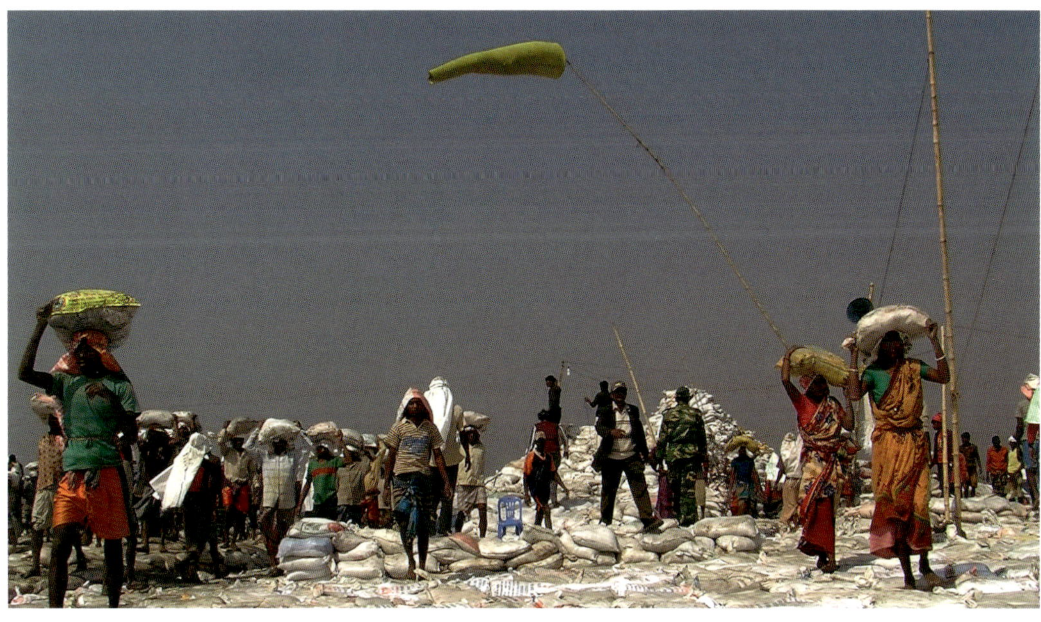

Lucius Burckhardt
Kriegerische Landschaft,
o. J. / *n. d.*

Friedliche Landschaft,
o. J. / *n. d.*

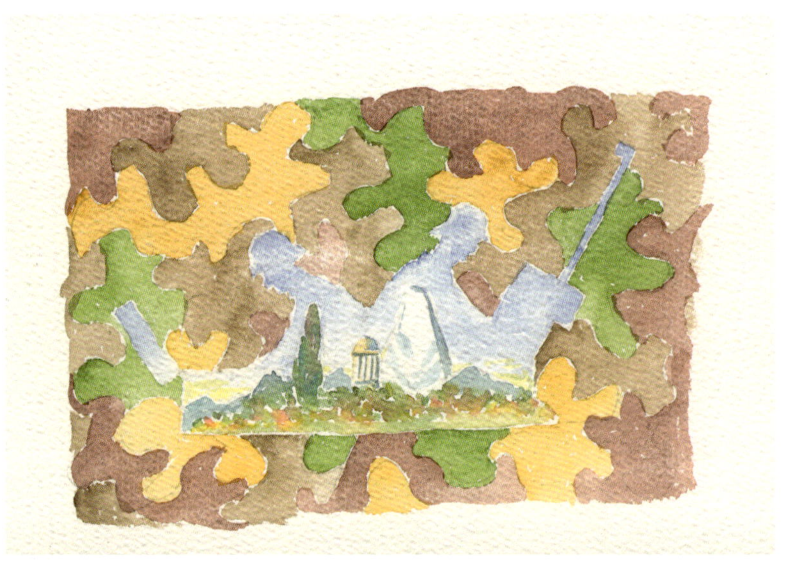

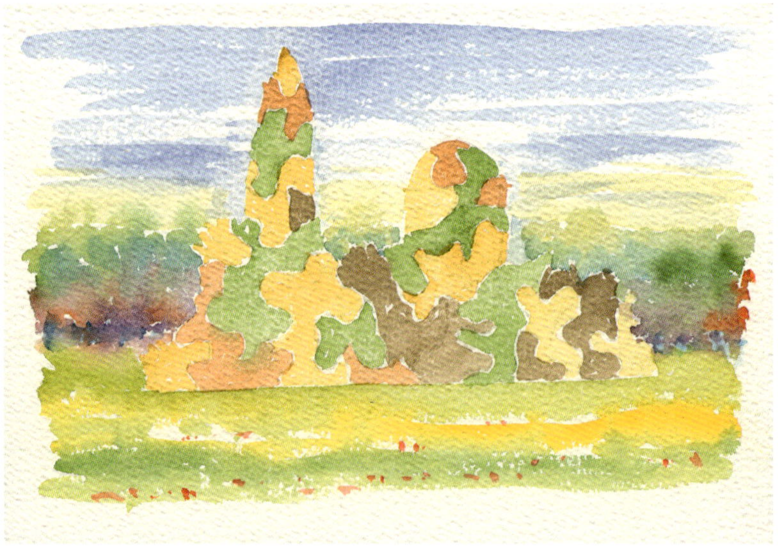

Lucius Burckhardt
Das unsichtbare Matterhorn,
o. J. / n. d.

Ohne Titel [Atomkraftwerk auf
Staffelei], o. J. / n. d.

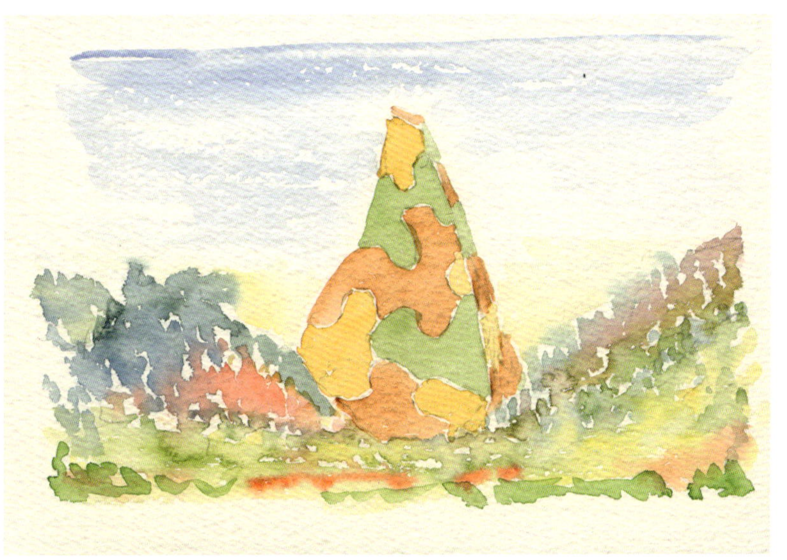

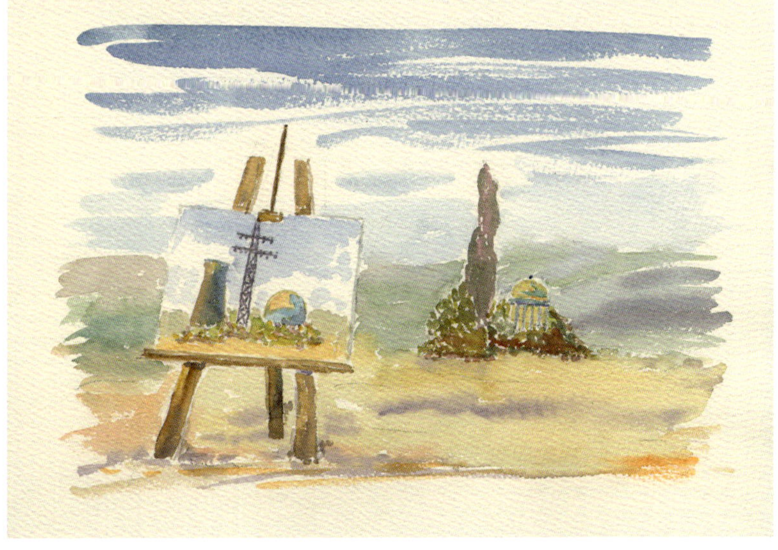

Leo Calice, Gerhard Treml
EDEN'S EDGE, 2014
(Videostills / video stills)

Time Square, 2014

Exile Park, 2014

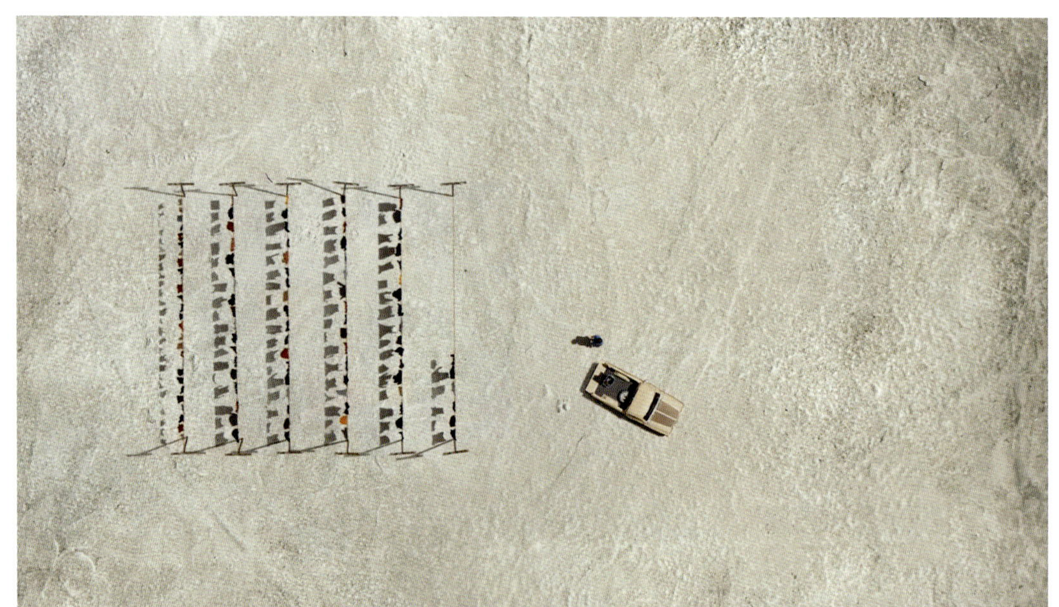

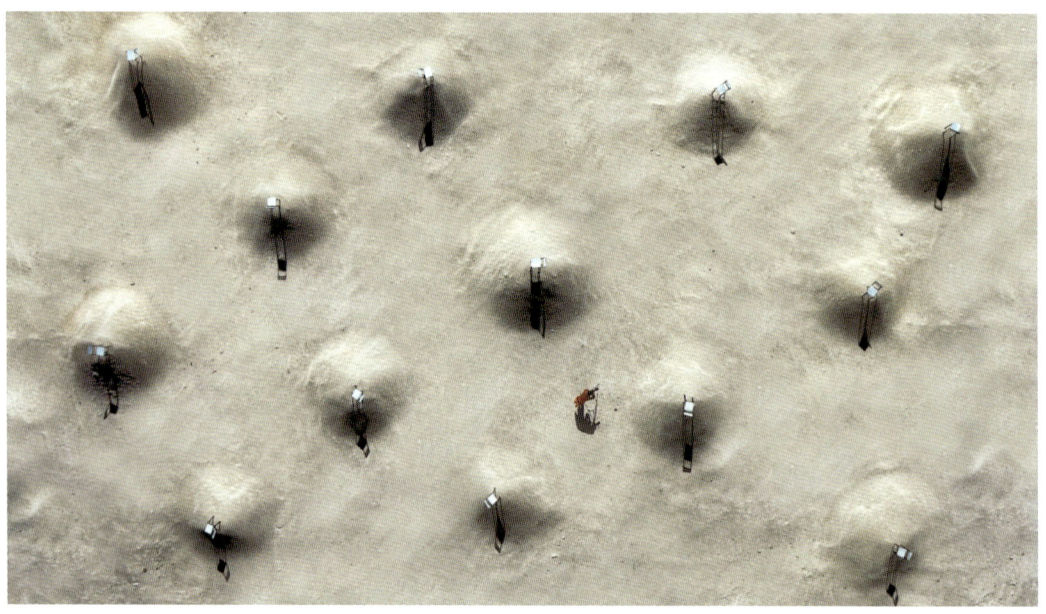

Leo Calice, Gerhard Treml
EDEN'S EDGE, 2014
(Videostills / video stills)

Turtle Island, 2014

Water and Worms, 2014

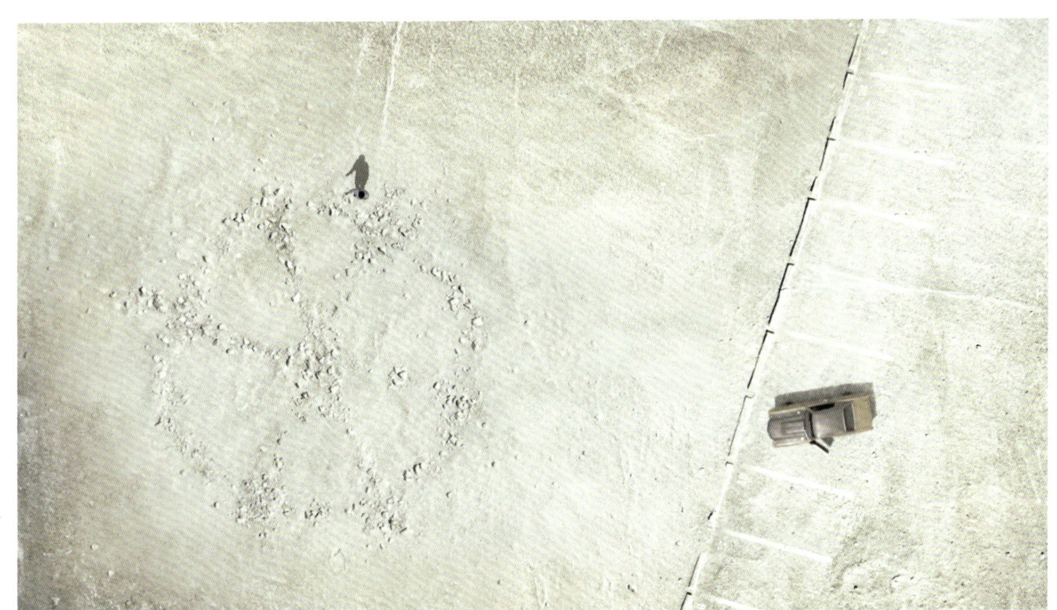

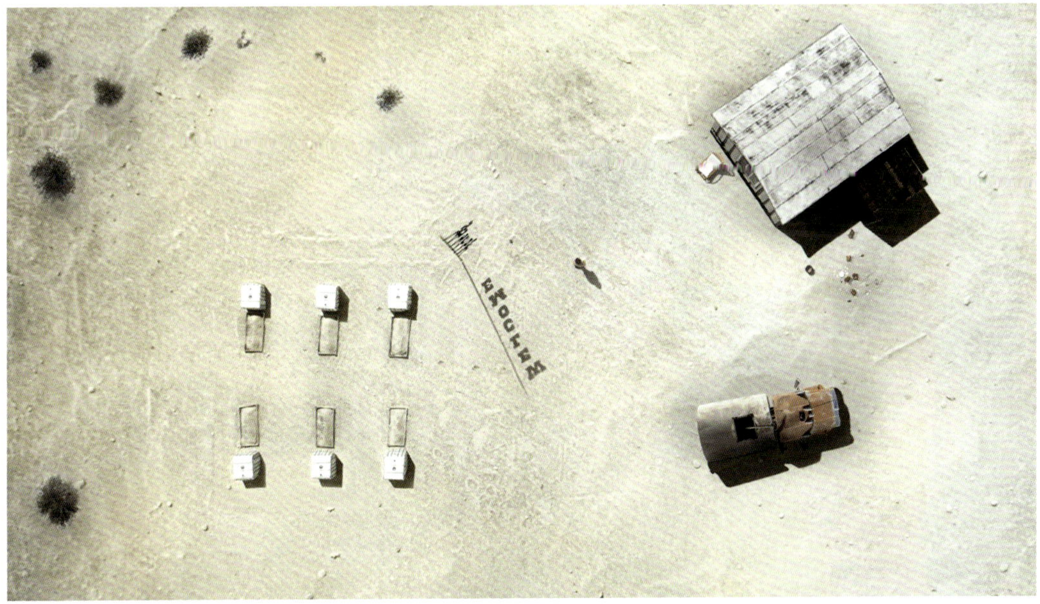

**Center for Land Use
Interpretation**
*Houston Petrochemical Corridor,
Texas, 2008*

*Great Salt Lake Evaporation
Ponds, Utah, 2013*

The Grapevine, California, 2010

(Videostills / **video stills**)

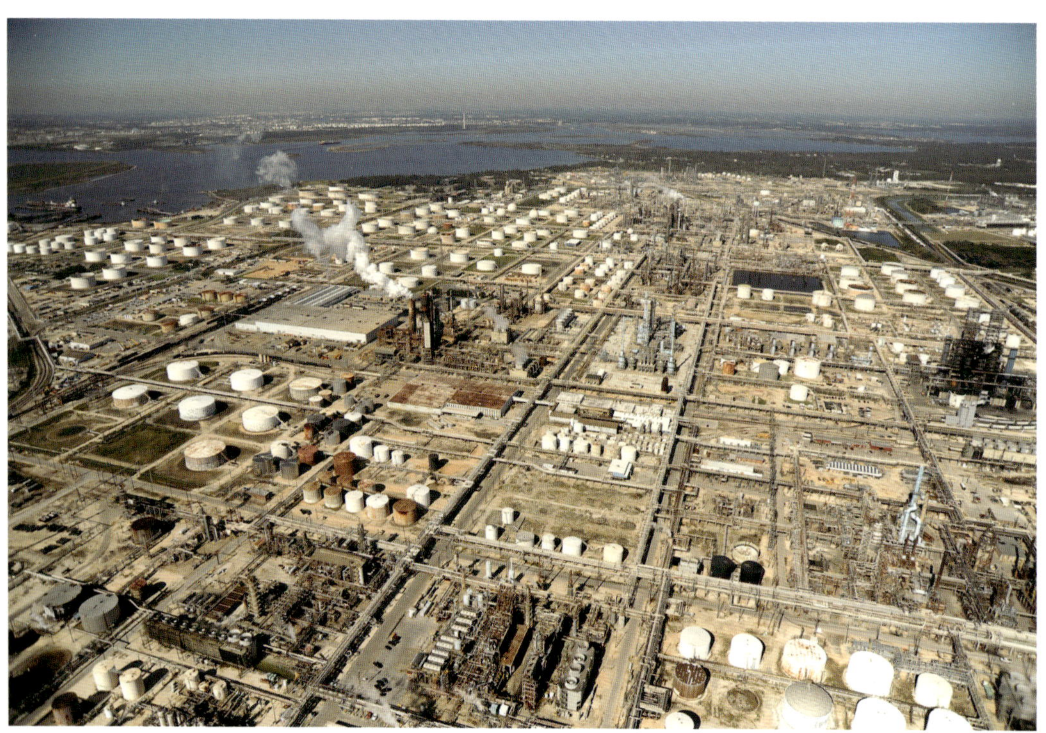

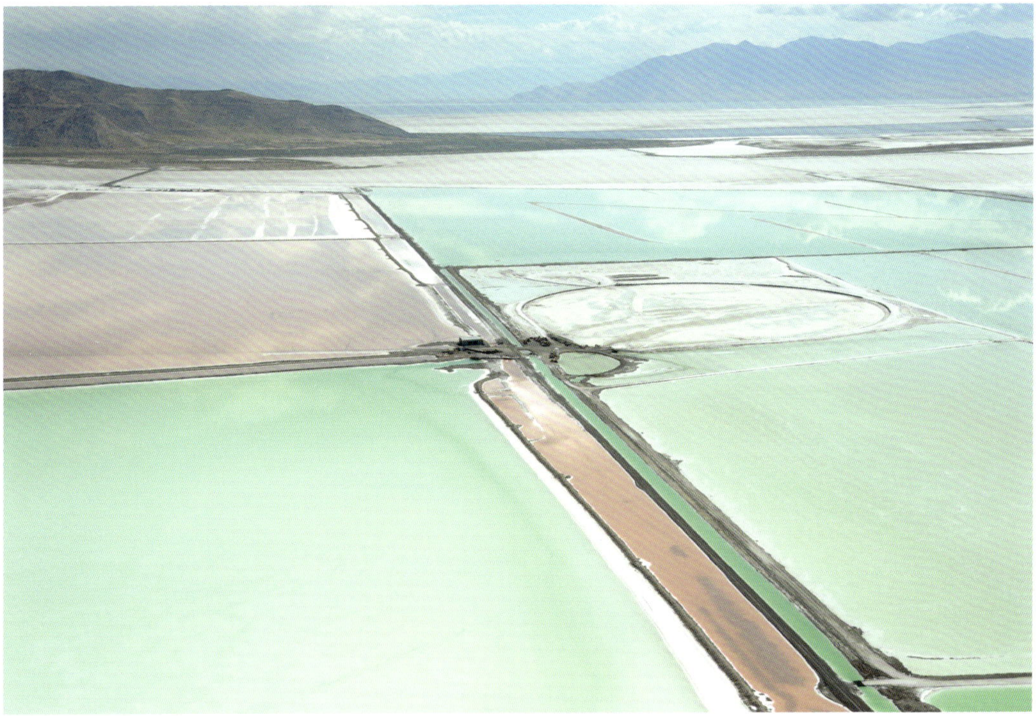

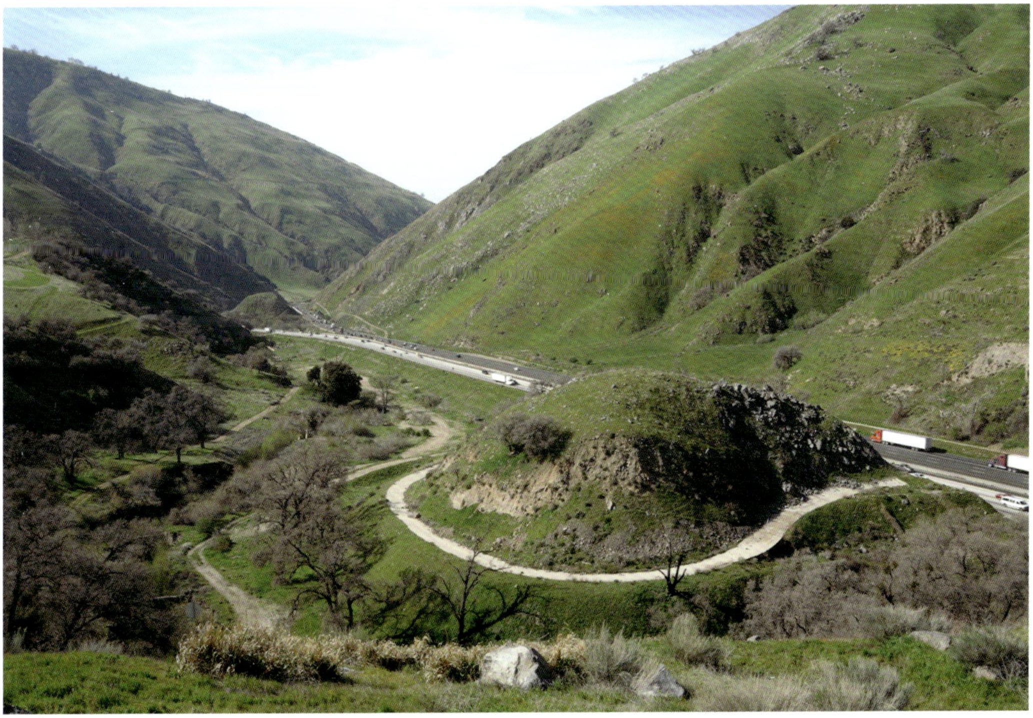

Tacita Dean
Trying to Find the Spiral Jetty, 1997
Gefaxte Wegbeschreibung für die
Suche nach Robert Smithsons *Spiral
Jetty* (1970) / faxed instructions for
finding Robert Smithson's *Spiral
Jetty* (1970)

06/23/97   09:29   FAX 801 533 6196   UTAH ARTS CNCL.   002/004

SPIRAL JETTY

Detailed directions:

1. Go to the Golden Spike National Historic Site (GSNHS), 30 miles west of Brigham City, Utah. The Spiral Jetty is 15.5 dirt-road miles southwest of the GSNHS.

To get there (from Salt Lake City) take I-80 north approximately 65 miles to the Corinne exit, just west of Brigham City, Utah. Exit and proceed 2.5 miles west, on State Highway 83, to Corinne. Proceed through Corinne, and drive another 17.7 miles west, still on highway 83, to Lampo Junction. Turn west off highway 83 at Lampo, and drive 7.7 miles up the east side of Promontory Pass to the GSNHS.

2. From the Visitor Center at the GSNHS, drive 5.6 miles west on the main dirt road running west from the Center. Remember to take the county dirt road...not the railroad grade.

3. Five point six miles will bring you to an intersection. From this vantage you can see the lake. And looking southwest, you can see the low foot hills that make up Rozel Point, 9.9 miles distant.

4. At this intersection the road forks: One road continues west and the other goes south. Take the south fork. Both forks are Box Elder County Class D (maintained) roads.

5. Immediately you cross a cattle guard. Call this cattle guard #1. Including this one, you will cross four cattle guards before you reach Rozel Point and the Spiral Jetty.

6. Drive 1.3 miles south. Here you will see a corral on the west side of the road. Here too, the road again forks. One fork continues south along the Promontory Mountains. This road leads to a locked gate. The other fork goes southwest toward the bottom of the valley and Rozel Point. Turn onto the southwest fork, just north of the corral. This is also a Box Elder County Class D road.

7. After you turn southwest, you will go 1.7 miles to cattle guard #2. Here, besides the cattle guard, you will find a fence but no gate.

8. Continue southeast 1.2 miles to cattle guard #3, a fence, a gate, and a sign on the gate which reads, "Promontory Ranch."

9. Another .50 miles will bring you to a fence but no cattle guard and no gate.

10. Continue 2.3 miles south/southwest to a combination

fence, cattle guard #4, iron-pipe gate...and a sign declaring
the property behind the fence to be that of the Rafter S
Ranch. Here too, is a "No Trespassing" sign.

11. If you choose to continue south for another 2.3 miles,
and around the east side of Rozel Point, you will see the
Lake and a jetty (not the Spiral Jetty) left by oil drilling
exploration in the 1950's. As you approach the Lake, you will
see an abandoned, pink and white trailer (mostly white), an
old army amphibious landing craft, an old Dodge truck...and
other assorted trash.

The trailer is the key to finding the road to the Spiral
Jetty. As you drive slowly past the trailer, turn immediately
to the west, passing on the south side of the Dodge, and onto
a two-track trail that contours above the oil-drilling debris
below. This is not much of a road! In fact, at first glance
it might not look to be a road at all. Go slow! The road is
narrow; brush might scratch your vehicle, and the rocks, if
not properly negotiated, could high center your vehicle.

12. Drive .6 miles west/northwest around Rozel Point and look
toward the Lake. The Spiral Jetty should be in sight.

Maps of the area:
     BLM 1:100,000 Surface Management maps - Available at the
     BLM's State Office Public Room, 324 South State Street,
     Salt Lake City, Utah 84111 phone: (801) 539-4001
          (1) Tremonton
          (2) Promontory

     U.S. Geological Survey, 7.5 minute series - Available at
     the U.S.G.S., Federal Building, 125 South State Street,
     Salt Lake City, Utah 84111 phone: (801) 524-5652
          (1) Golden Spike Monument Quadrangle
          (2) Rozel Quadrangle
          (3) Rozel Point Quadrangle

For Additional Information:

Bureau Of Land Management
Salt Lake District
2370 South 2300 West
Salt Lake City, Utah 84119
phone: (801) 977-4300

Golden Spike National Historic Site
P. O. Box 897
Brigham City, Utah 84302
phone: (801) 471-2209

Marine Hugonnier
Aus der Serie / from the series:
Towards Tomorrow, 2001-03

*Towards Tomorrow
(International Date Line,
Alaska) #1, 2001-03*
Sonnenuntergang über der
Beringstraße in Alaska /
Sunset across the Bering Strait
in Alaska

Marine Hugonnier
Aus der Serie / from the series:
Towards Tomorrow, 2001–03

*Towards Tomorrow
(International Date Line,
Alaska) #2*, 2001–03
Ende des Sonnenuntergangs
über der Beringstraße in Alaska /
End of sunset across the Bering
Strait in Alaska

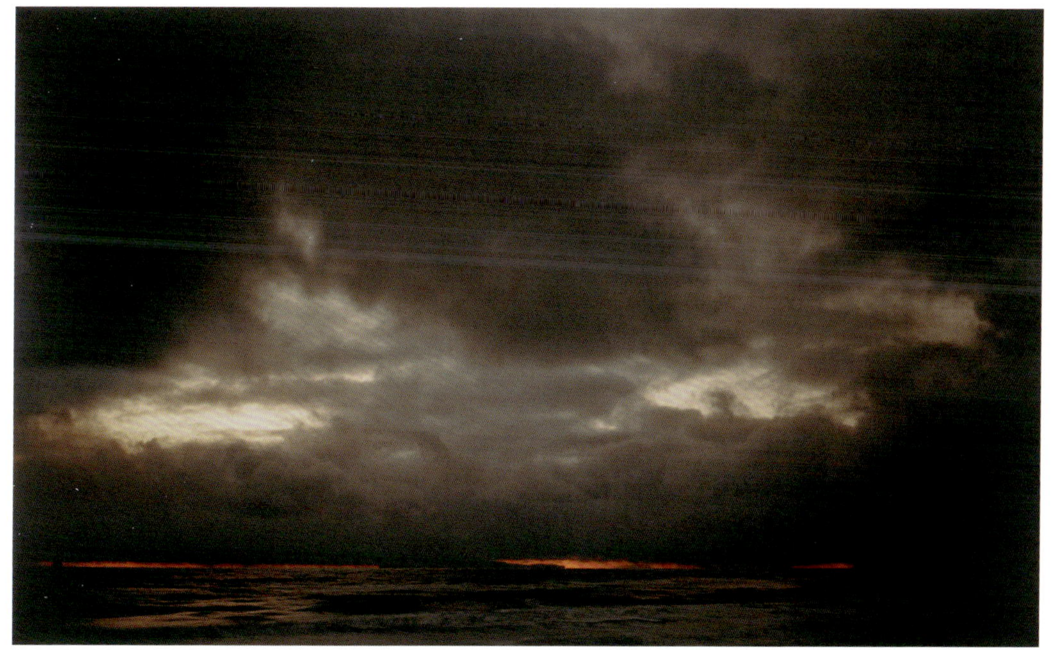

Markus Jeschaunig
Barrel You!, 2012
Ausstellungsansicht /
exhibition view, Kunsthaus
Graz, 2015

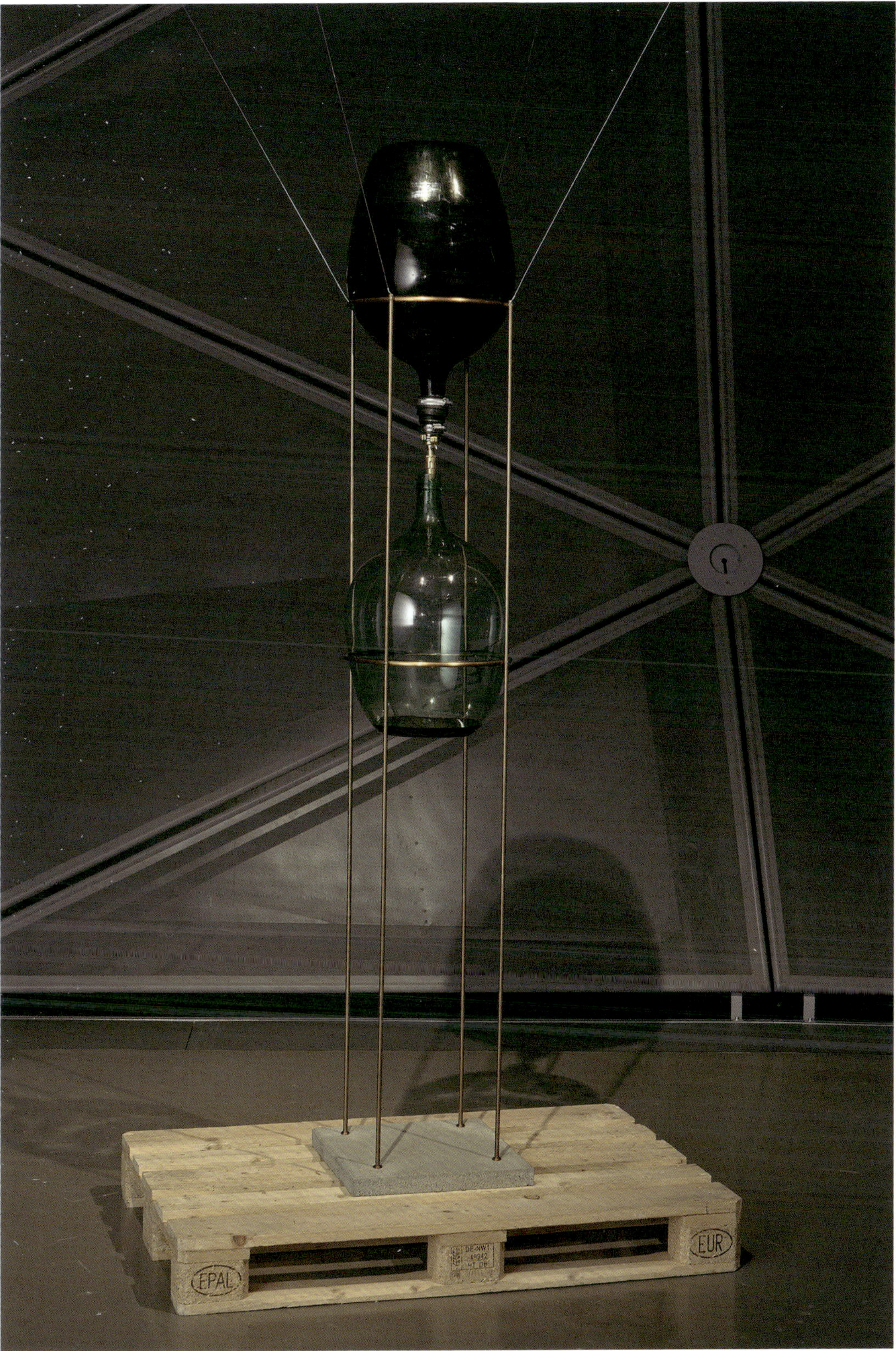
EPAL
EUR

Mathias Kessler
Jarrells Cemetery, N37°53.96'
W81°34.71', Eunice Mountain,
West Virginia, 2012
Ausstellungsansicht /
exhibition view, Kunsthaus
Graz, 2015

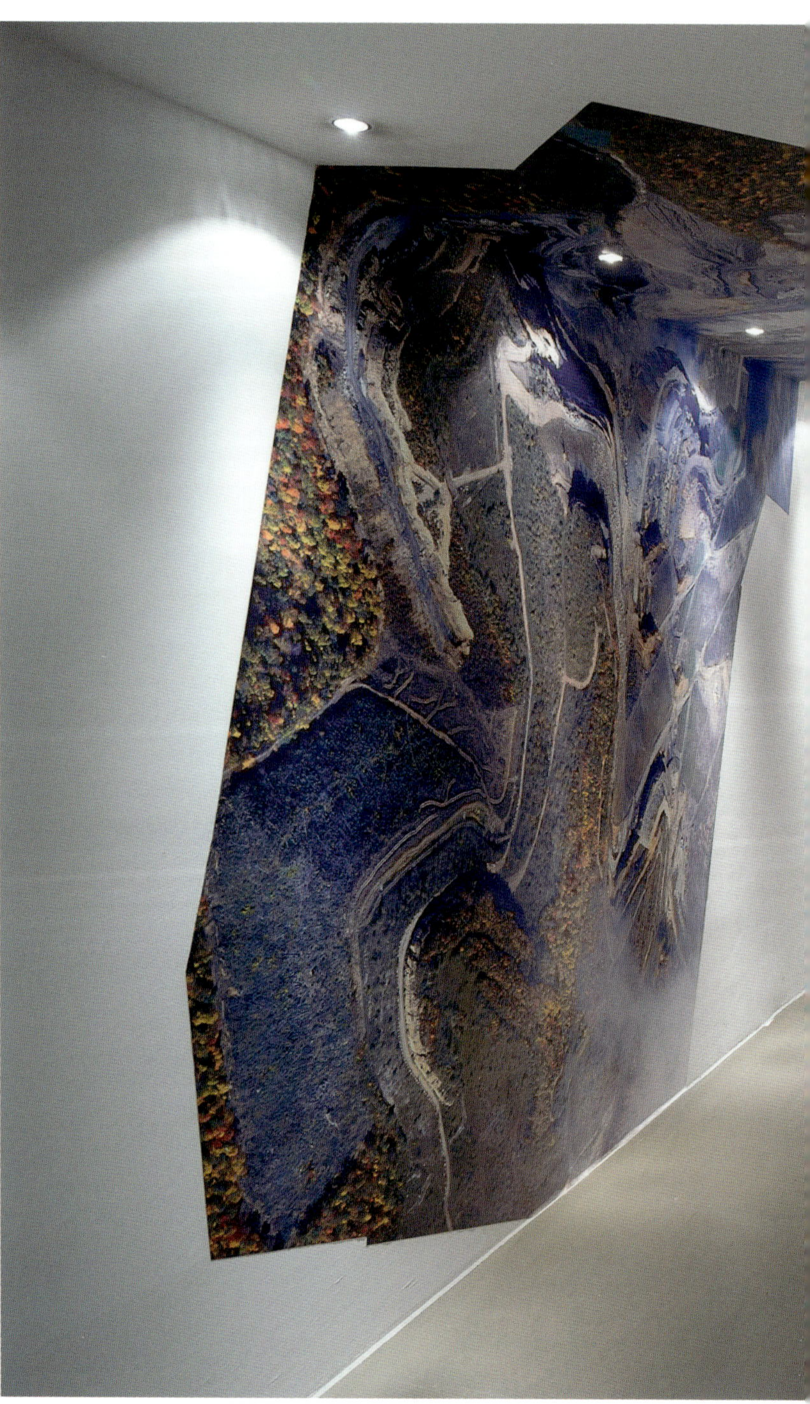

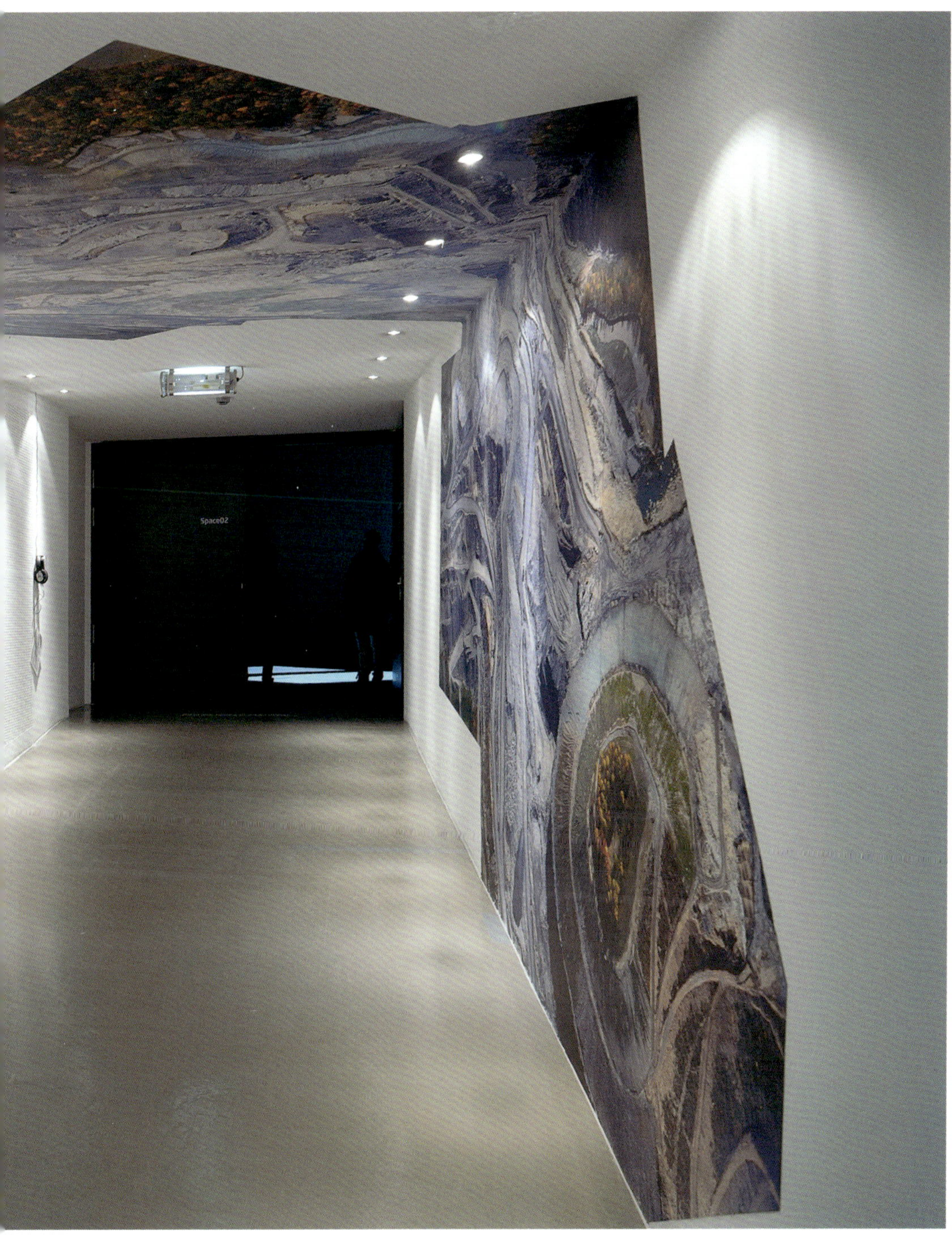
Space02

Armin Linke
*Whirlwind, Pantelleria,
Italy, 2007*

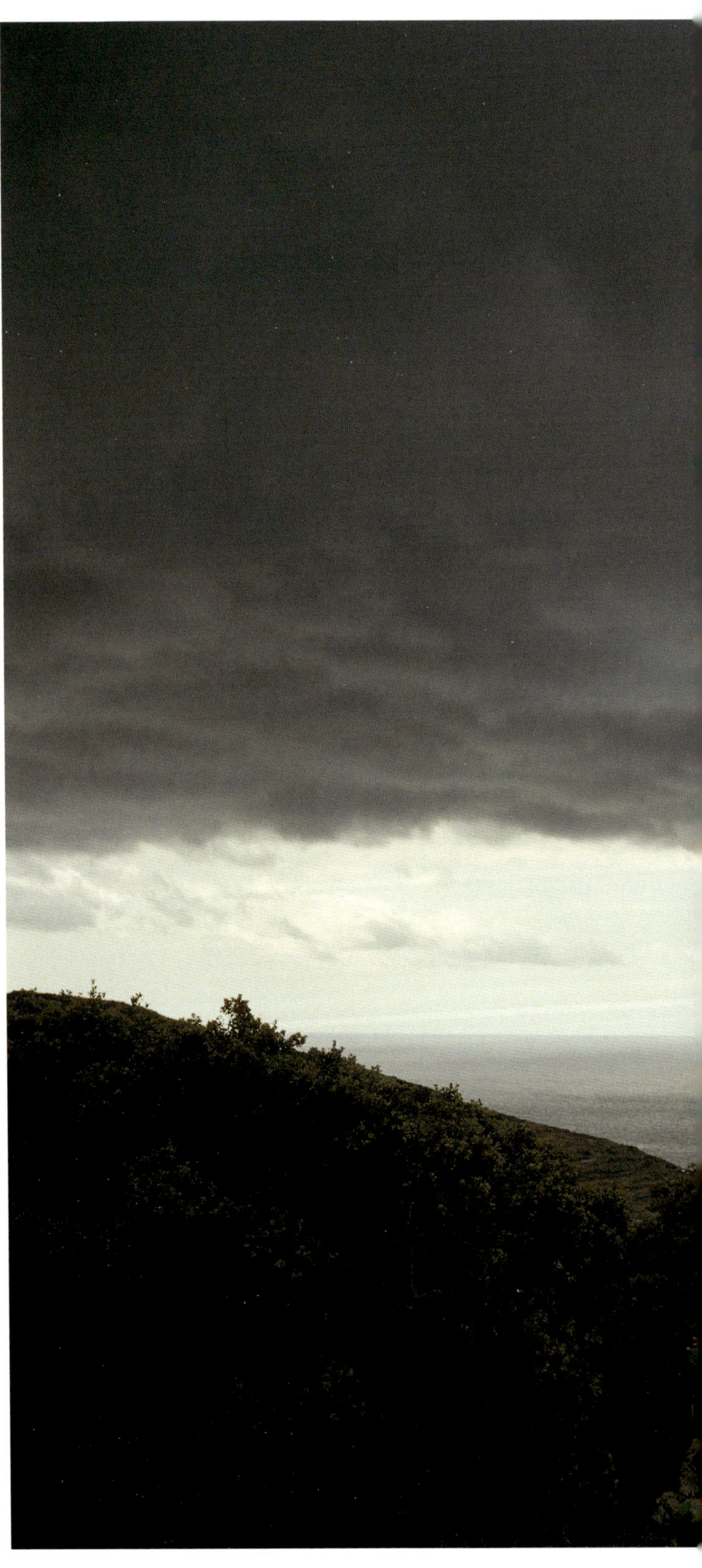

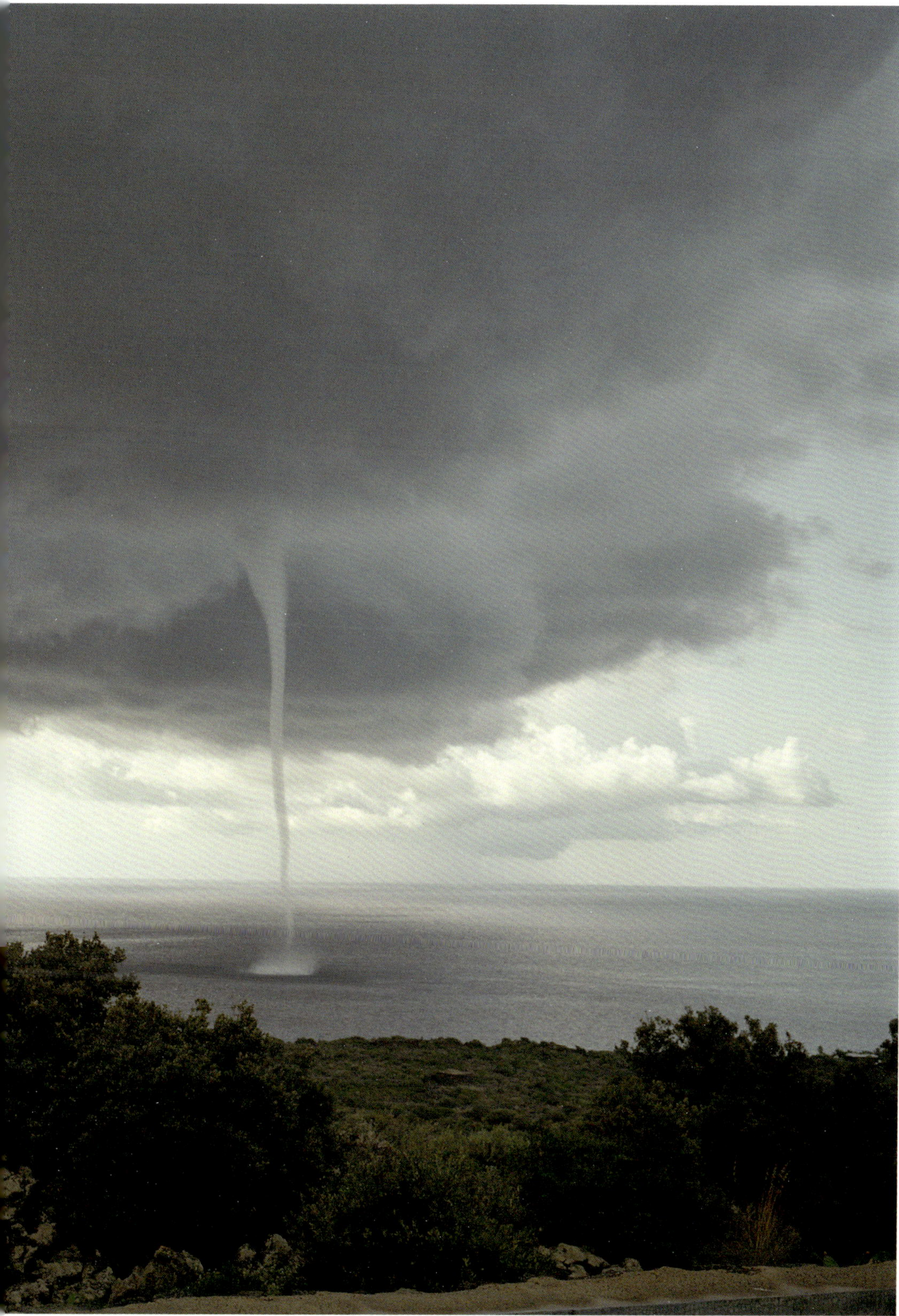

Lukas Marxt
Captive Horizon, 2014
(Videostills / video stills)

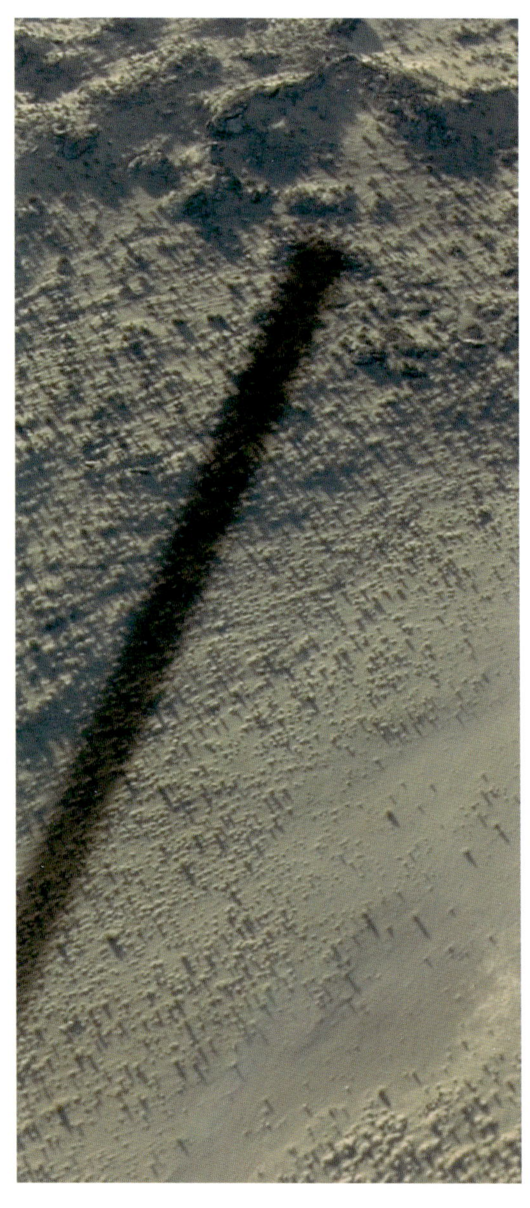

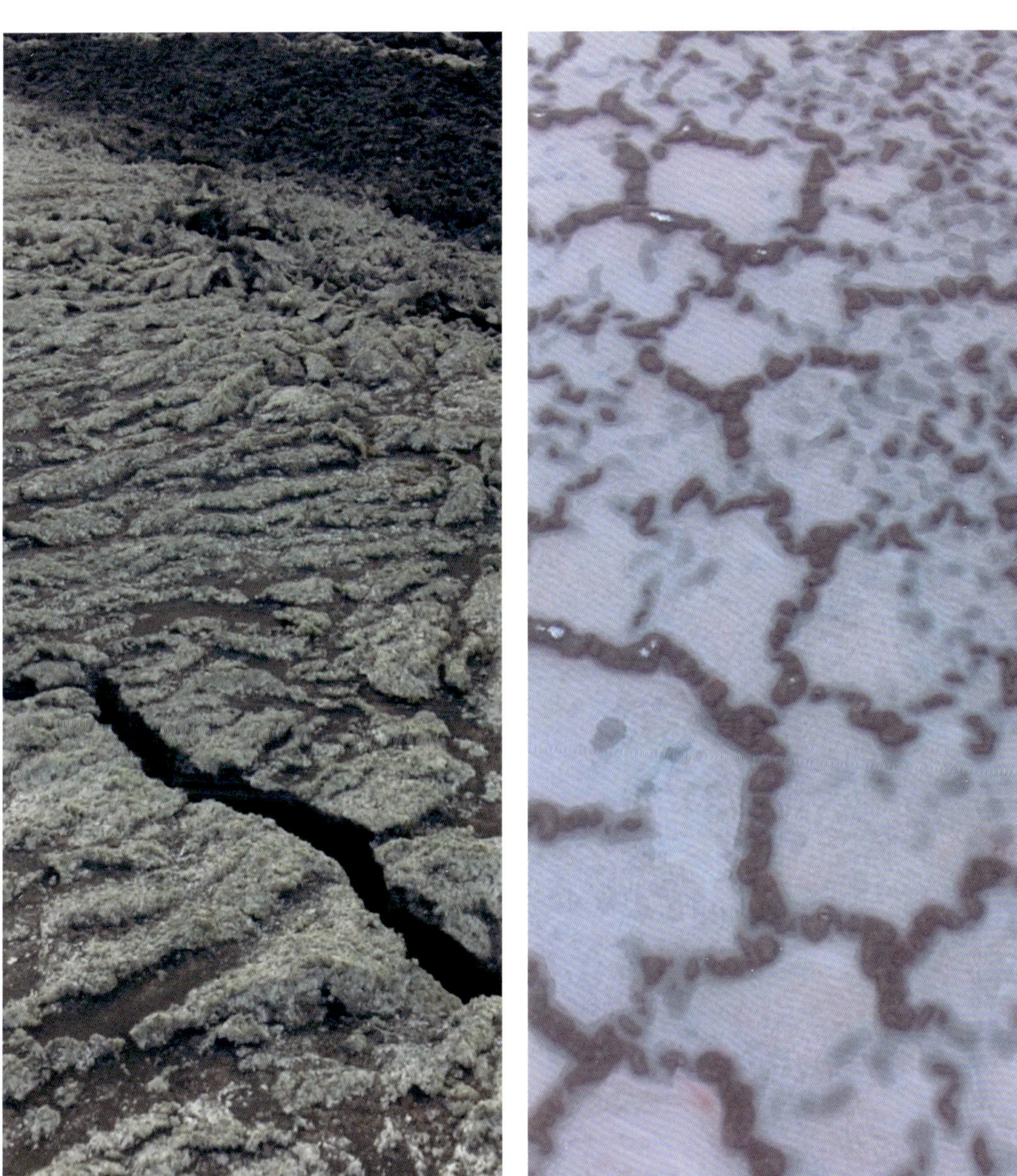

David Nez
Projekt – ein Heizgerät wärmt das Thermometer an der Wand, Novi Sad / Project – a heater warms the thermometer on the wall, Novi Sad, 1969
Ausstellungsansicht / exhibition view, Kunsthaus Graz, 2015

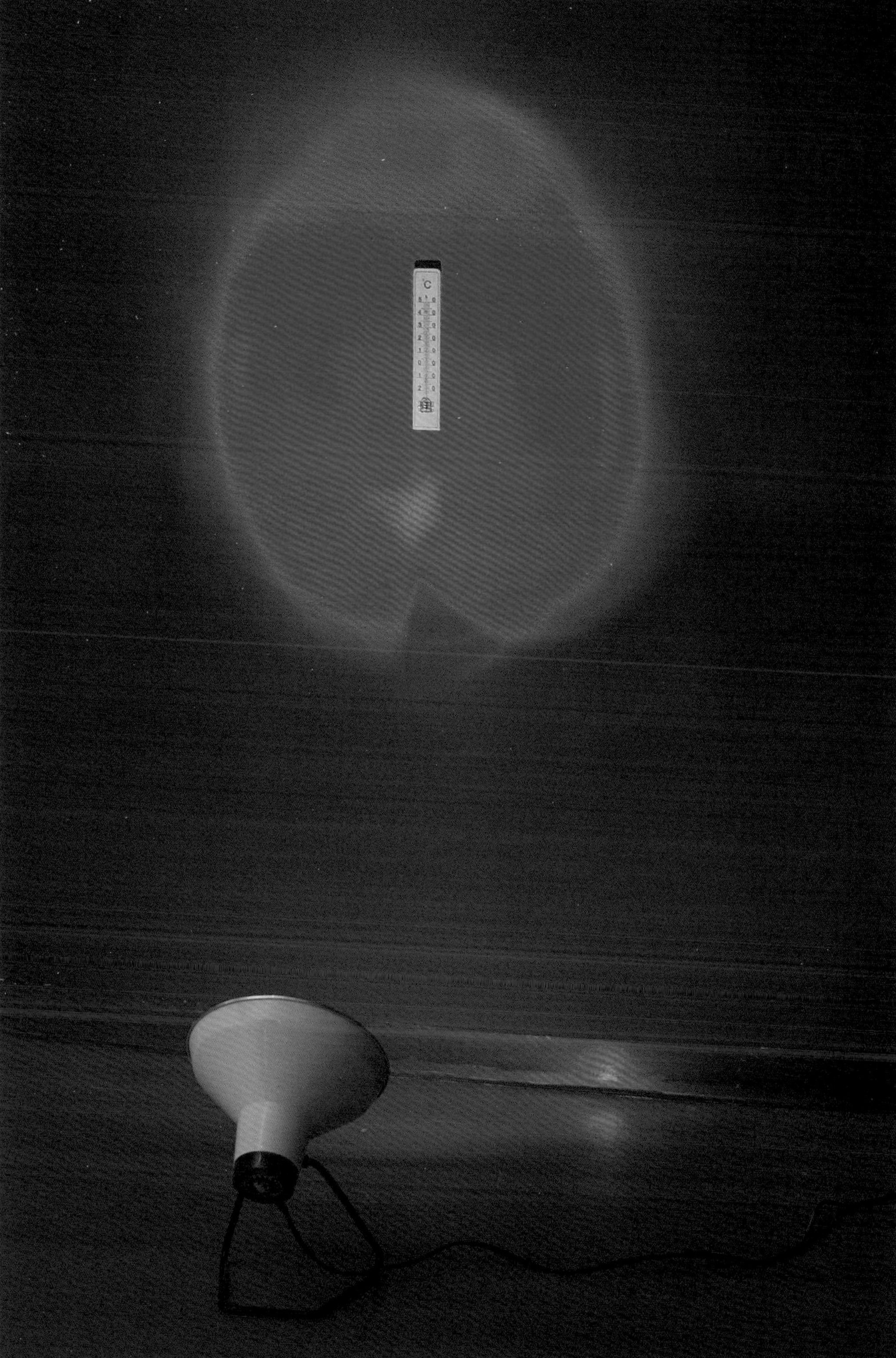
°C
5 0
4 0
3 0
2 0
1 0
0
2 0

Walter Niedermayr
Aus der Serie / from the series:
Artefakte, seit / since 1992

Seiersberg I, 1997

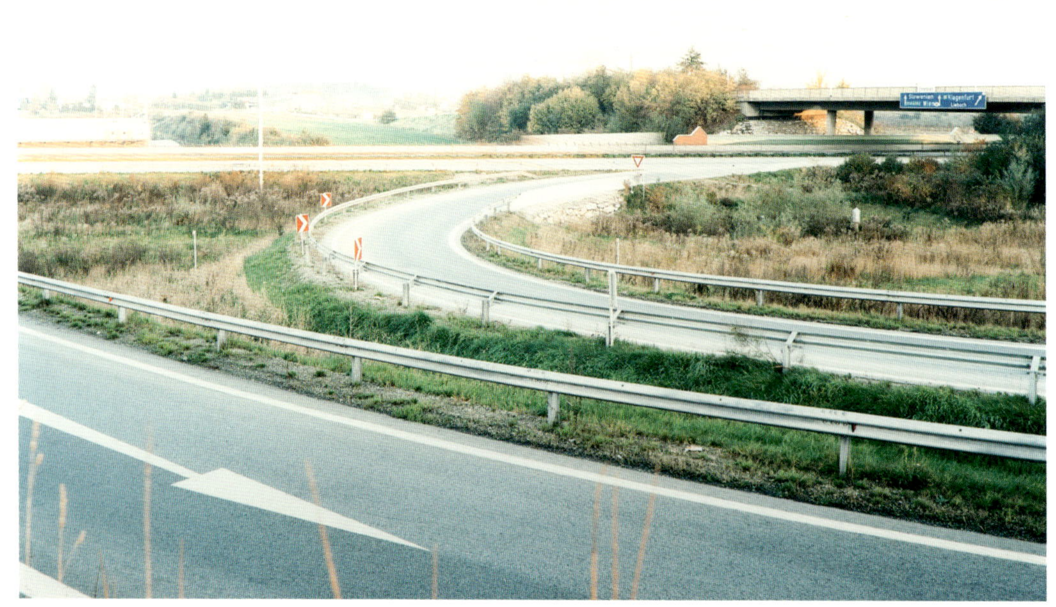

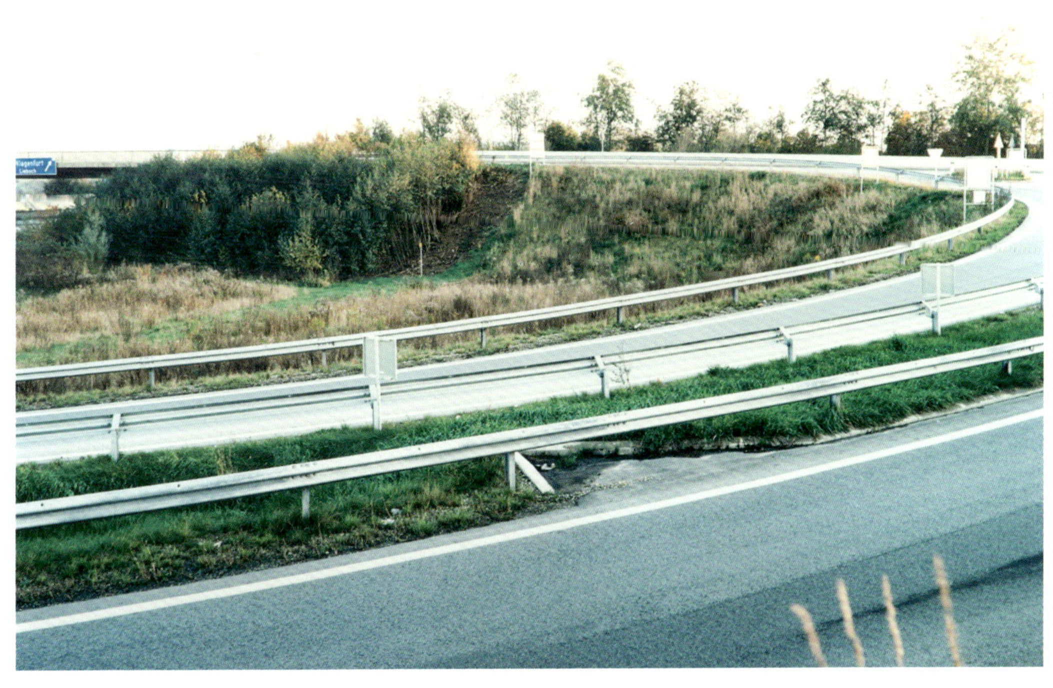

Qiu Anxiong
Minguo Landscape, 2007
(Videostills / video stills)

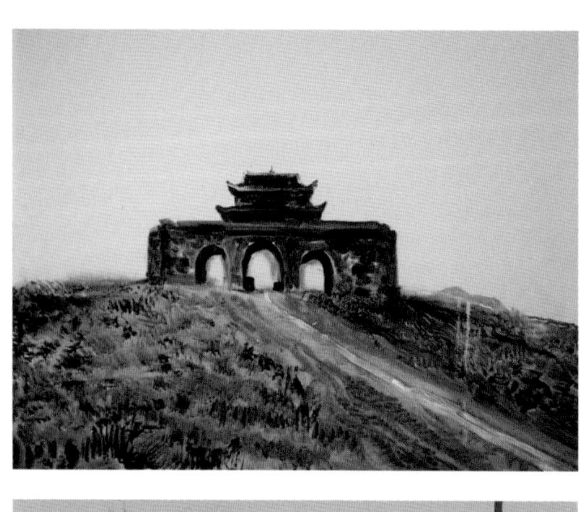

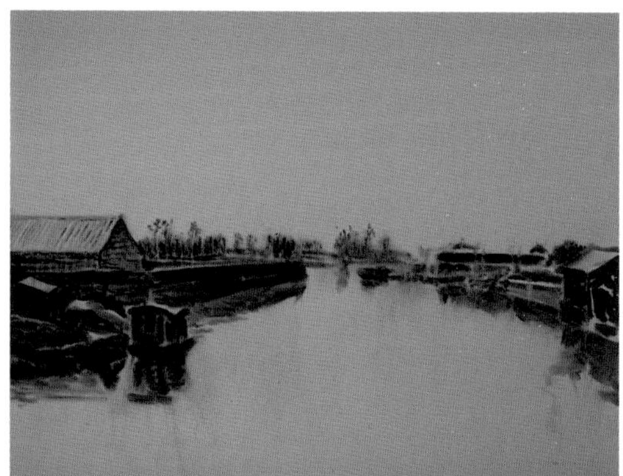

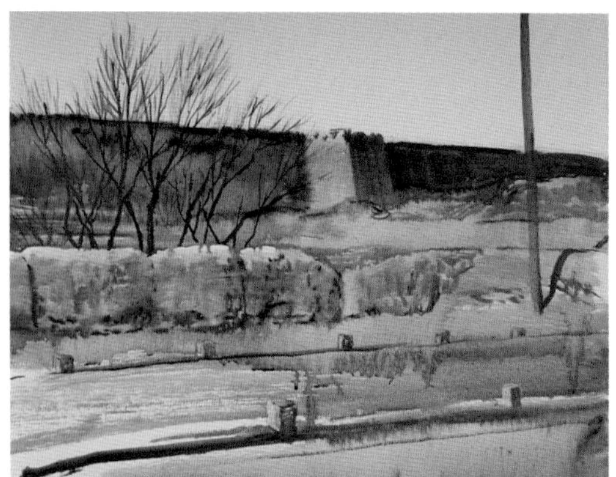

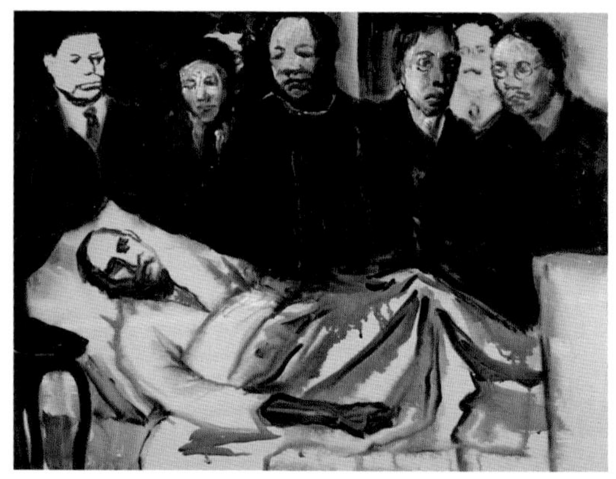

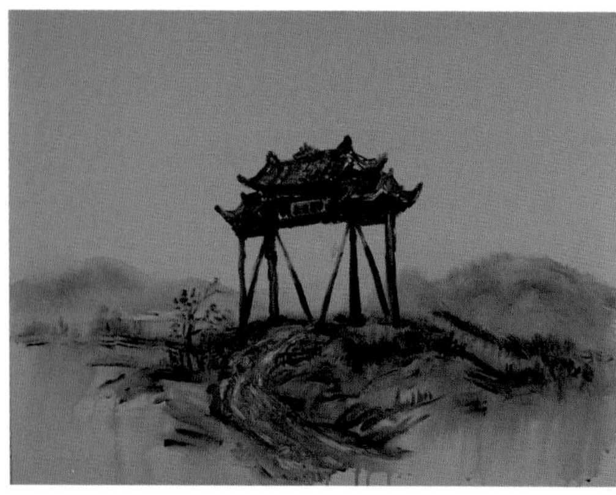

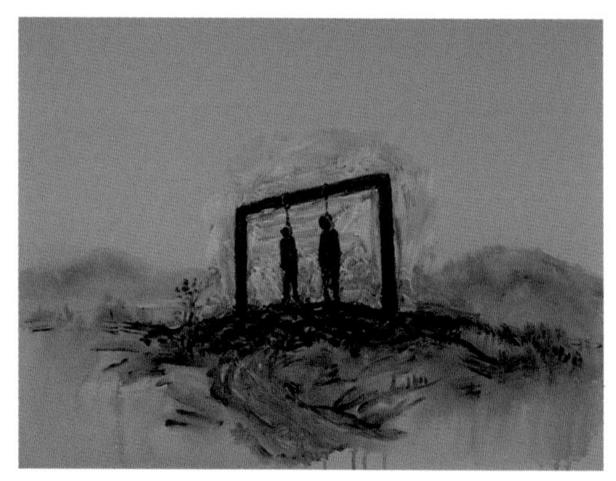

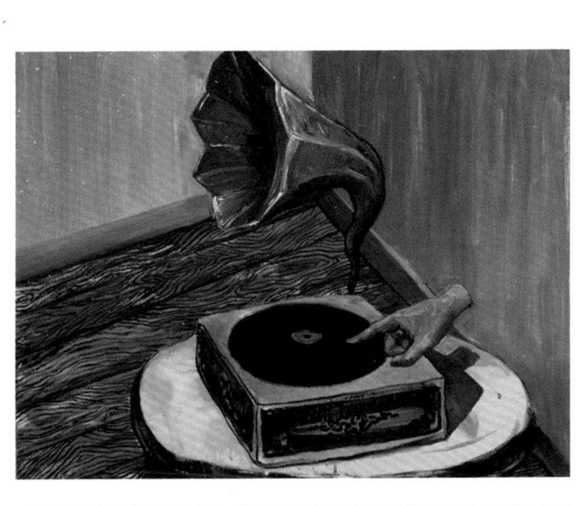

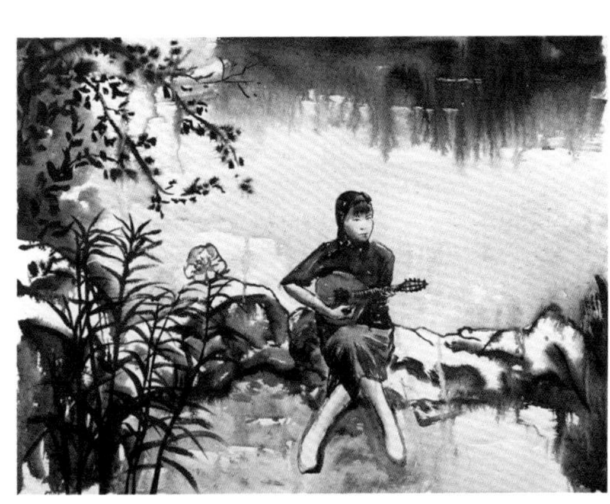

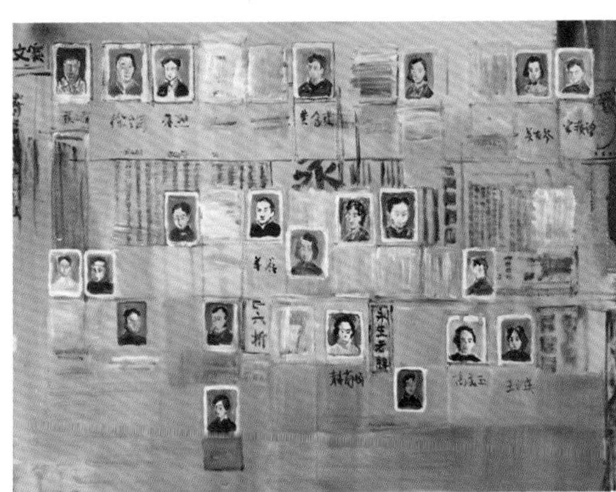

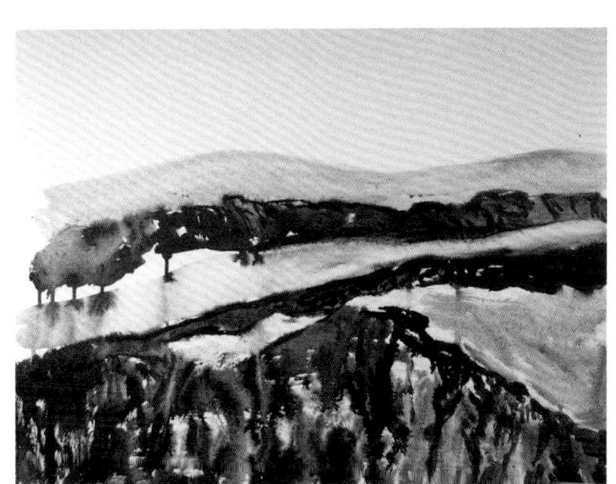

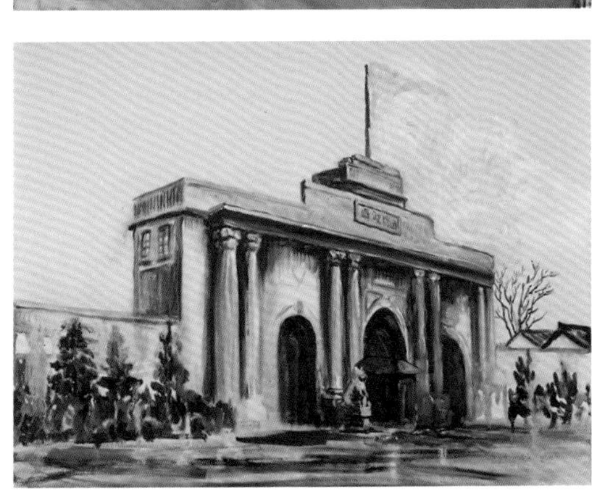

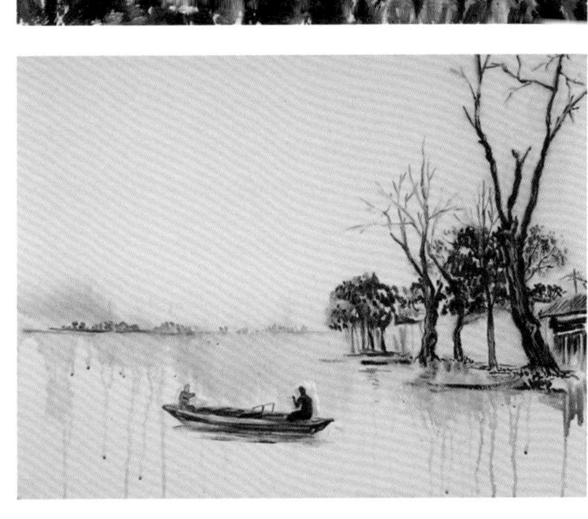

Ed Ruscha
Every Building on the
Sunset Strip, 1966
(Fotomontage / photomontage)

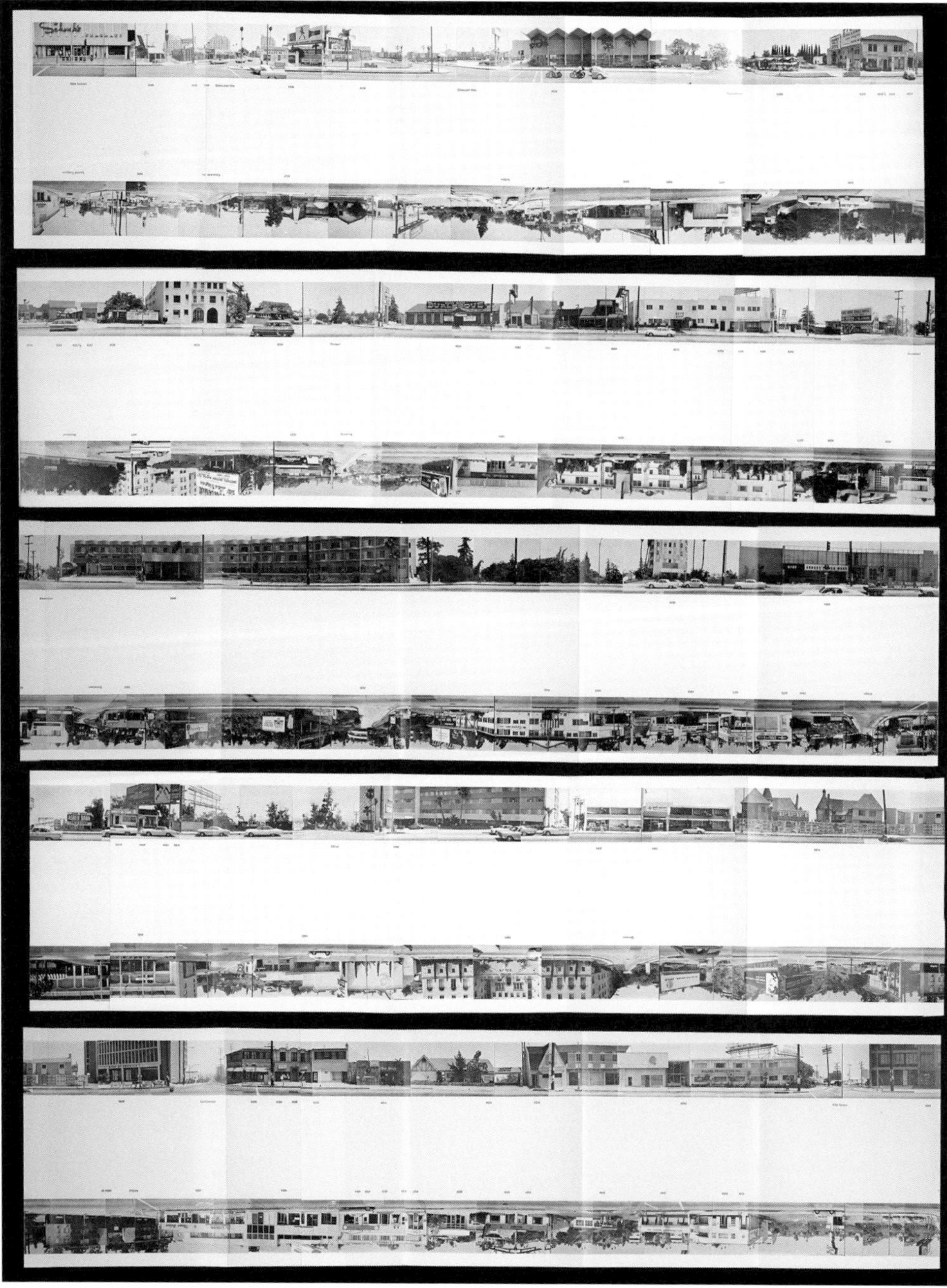

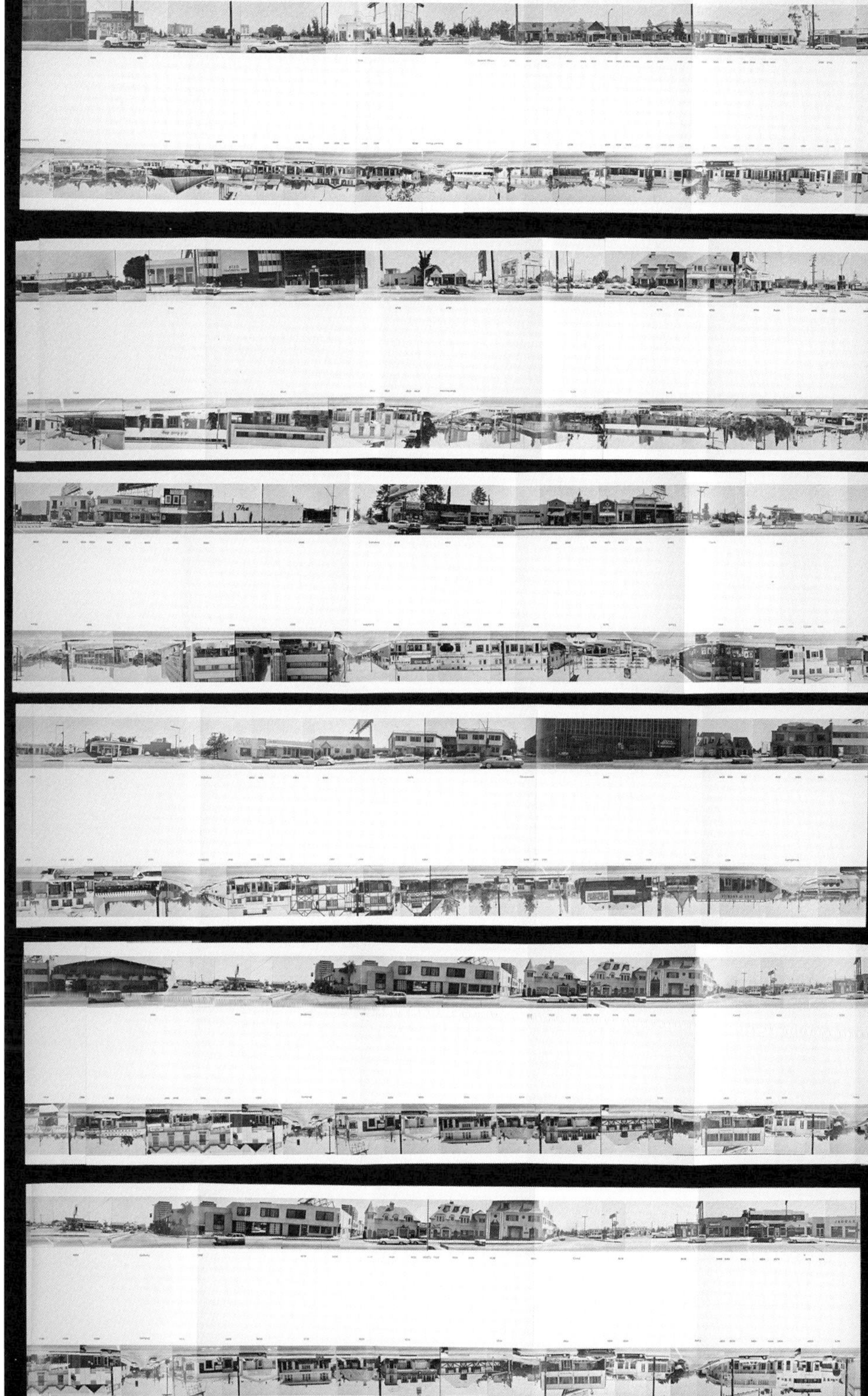

Klaus Schafler
Sandbank, 2015
Ausstellungsansicht /
exhibition view, Kunsthaus
Graz, 2015

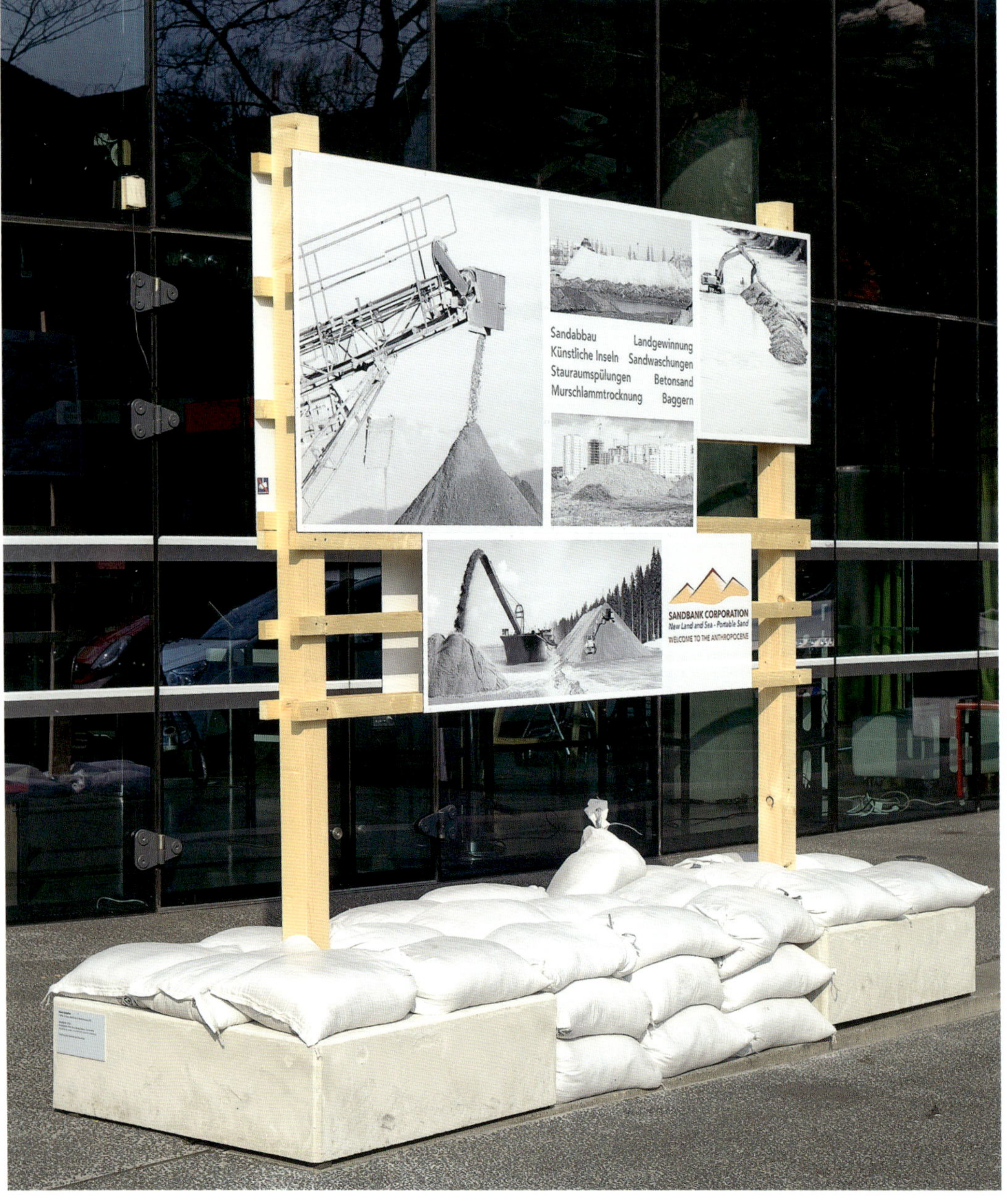

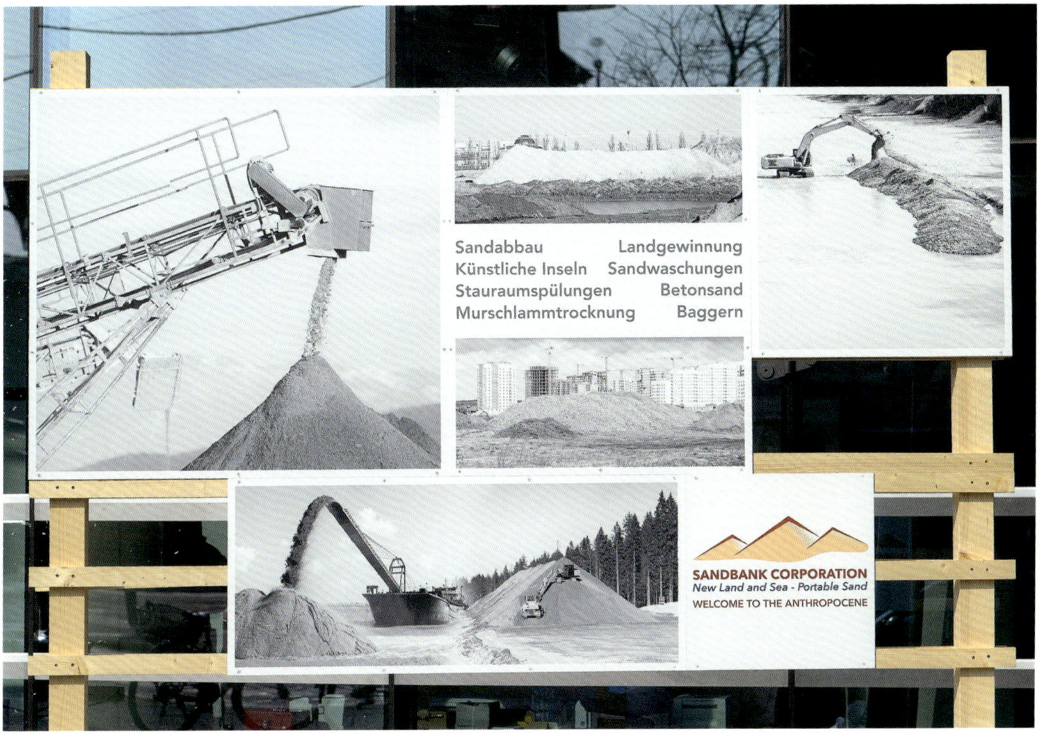

Sandabbau   Landgewinnung
Künstliche Inseln   Sandwaschungen
Stauraumspülungen   Betonsand
Murschlammtrocknung   Baggern
SANDBANK CORPORATION
New Land and Sea - Portable Sand
WELCOME TO THE ANTHROPOCENE

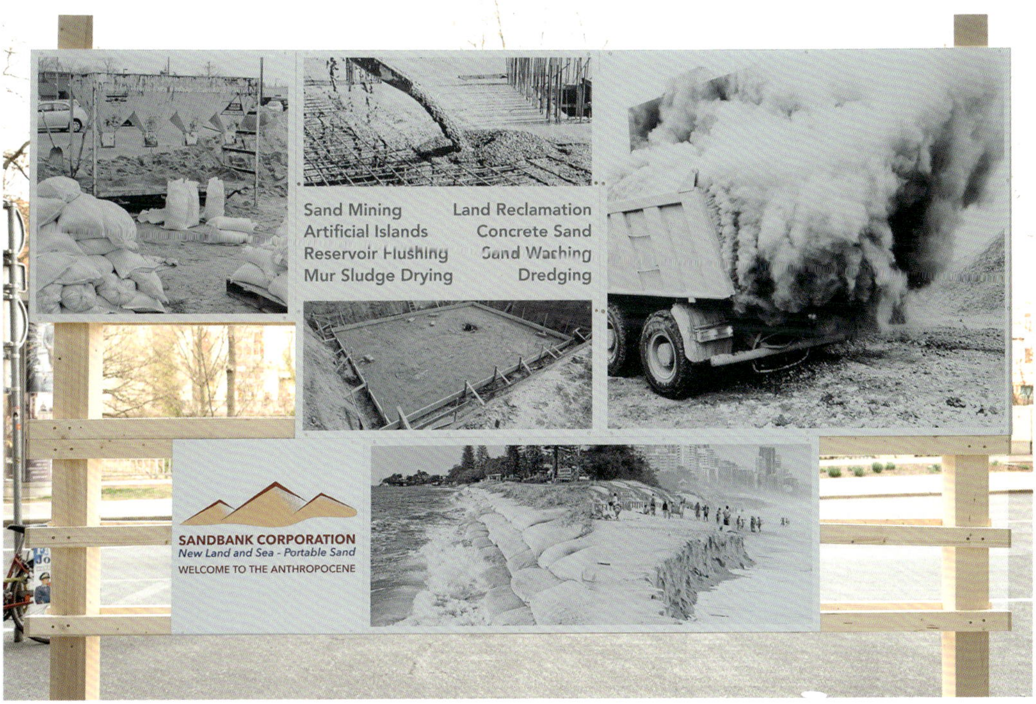

Sand Mining   Land Reclamation
Artificial Islands   Concrete Sand
Reservoir Flushing   Sand Washing
Mur Sludge Drying   Dredging
SANDBANK CORPORATION
New Land and Sea - Portable Sand
WELCOME TO THE ANTHROPOCENE

Allan Sekula
Aus | from: *California Stories,*
1973–77

Cliffhanger, San Pedro,
July, 1975, 1975/2011

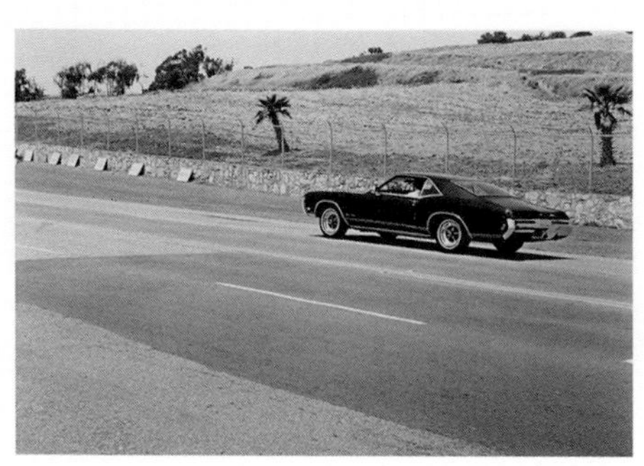

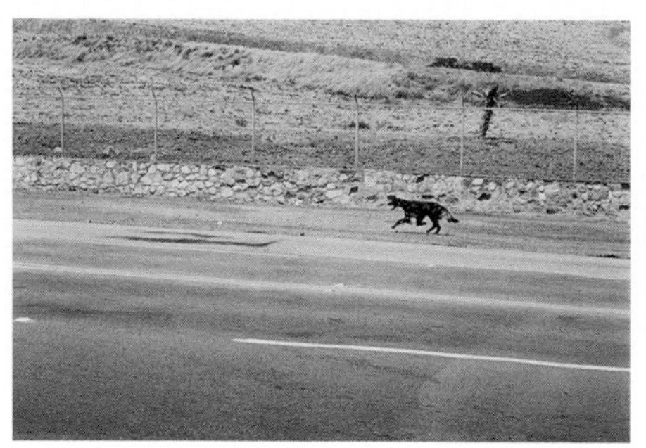

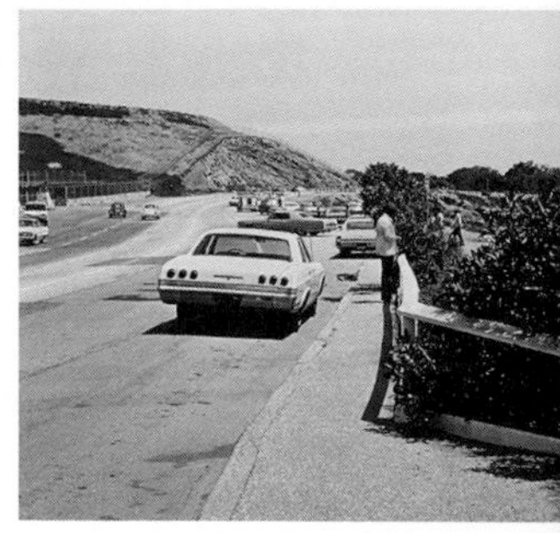

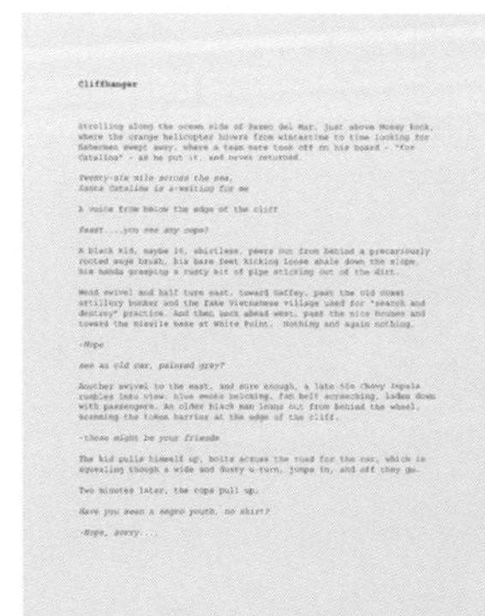

Cliffhanger

Strolling along the ocean side of Paseo del Mar, just above Mossy Rock, where the orange helicopter hovers from wintertime to time looking for fishermen swept away, where a team mate took off on his board – "for Catalina" – as he put it, and never returned.

Twenty-six mile across the sea,
Santa Catalina is a-waiting for me

A voice from below the edge of the cliff

Psst....you see any cops?

A black kid, maybe 16, shirtless, peers out from behind a precariously rooted sage brush, his bare feet kicking loose shale down the slope, his hands grasping a rusty bit of pipe sticking out of the dirt.

Head swivel and half turn east, toward Gaffey, past the old coast artillery bunker and the fake Vietnamese village used for "search and destroy" practice. And then back ahead west, past the nice houses and toward the missile base at White Point. Nothing and again nothing.

-Nope

see an old car, painted grey?

Another swivel to the east, and sure enough, a late 50s Chevy Impala rumbles into view, blue smoke belching, fan belt screeching, laden down with passengers. An older black man leans out from behind the wheel, scanning the fence barrier at the edge of the cliff.

-those might be your friends

The kid pulls himself up, bolts across the road for the car, which is squealing though a wide and dusty u-turn, jumps in, and off they go.

Two minutes later, the cops pull up.

Have you seen a negro youth, no shirt?

-Nope, sorry....

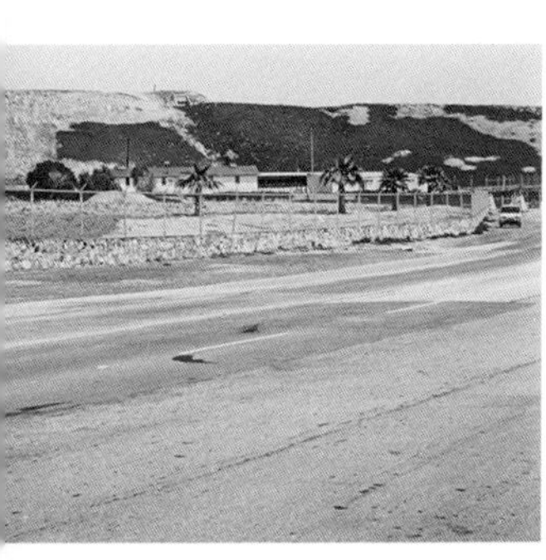

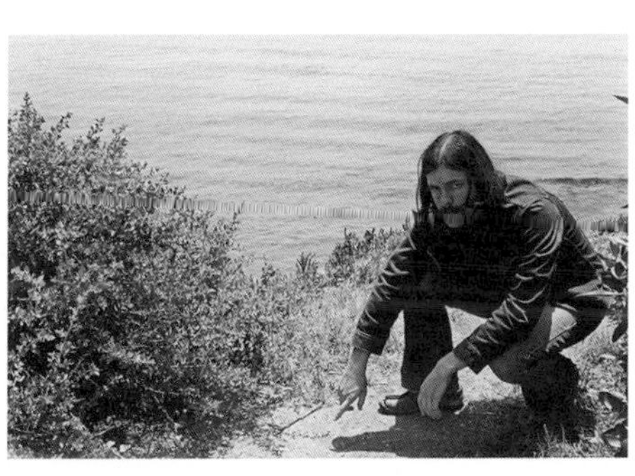

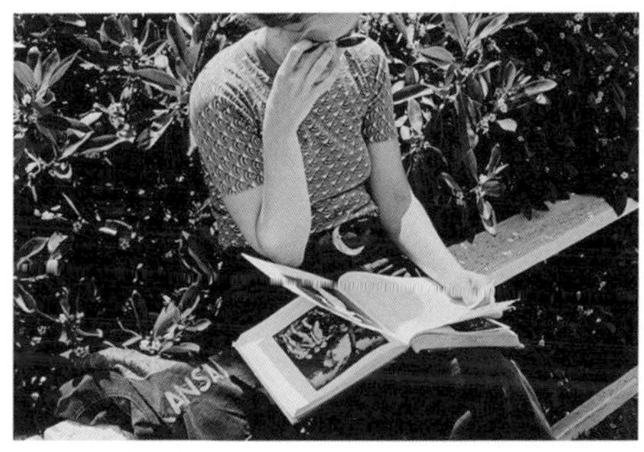

Shi Guorui
*Himalayas: The Mount Everest
8843.43 m, 20 January 2006,*
2006

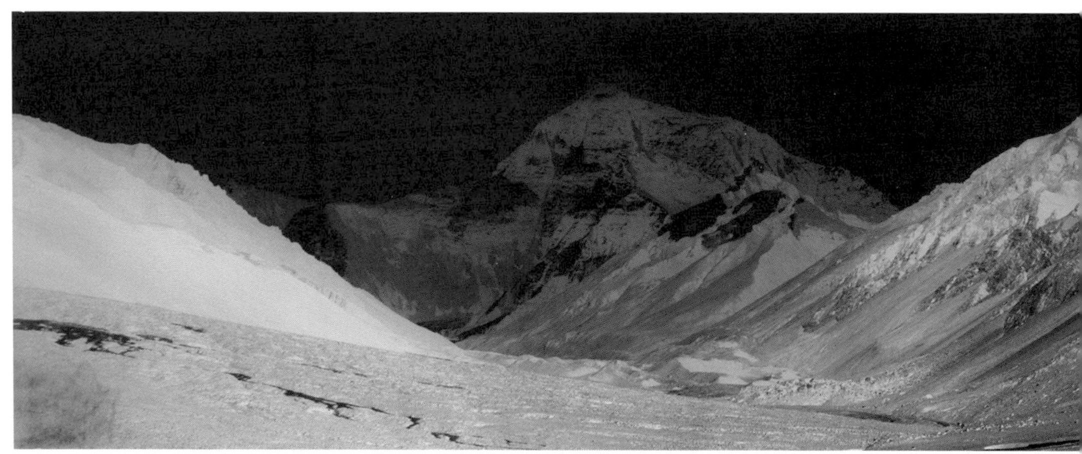

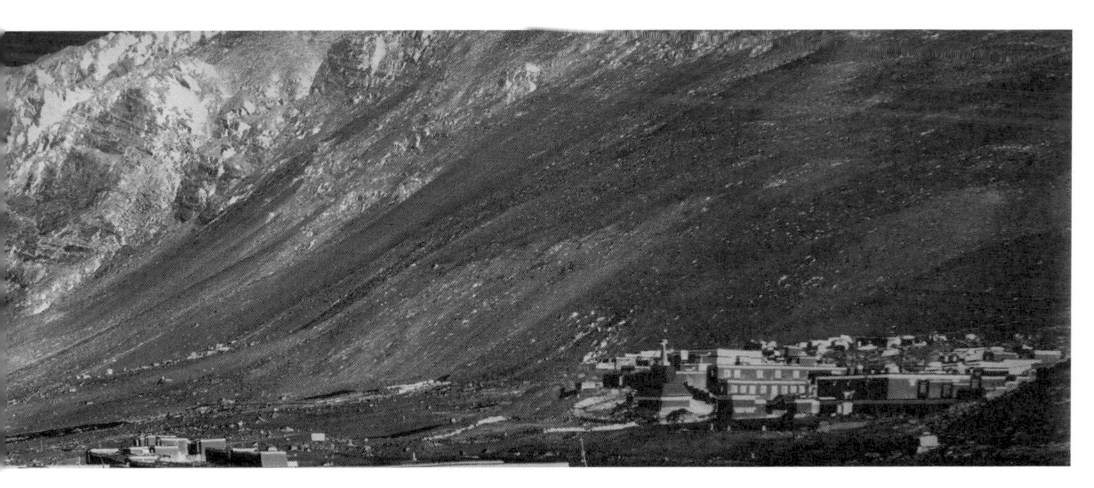

Robert Smithson
Spiral Jetty, 1970
(Filmstills / film stills)

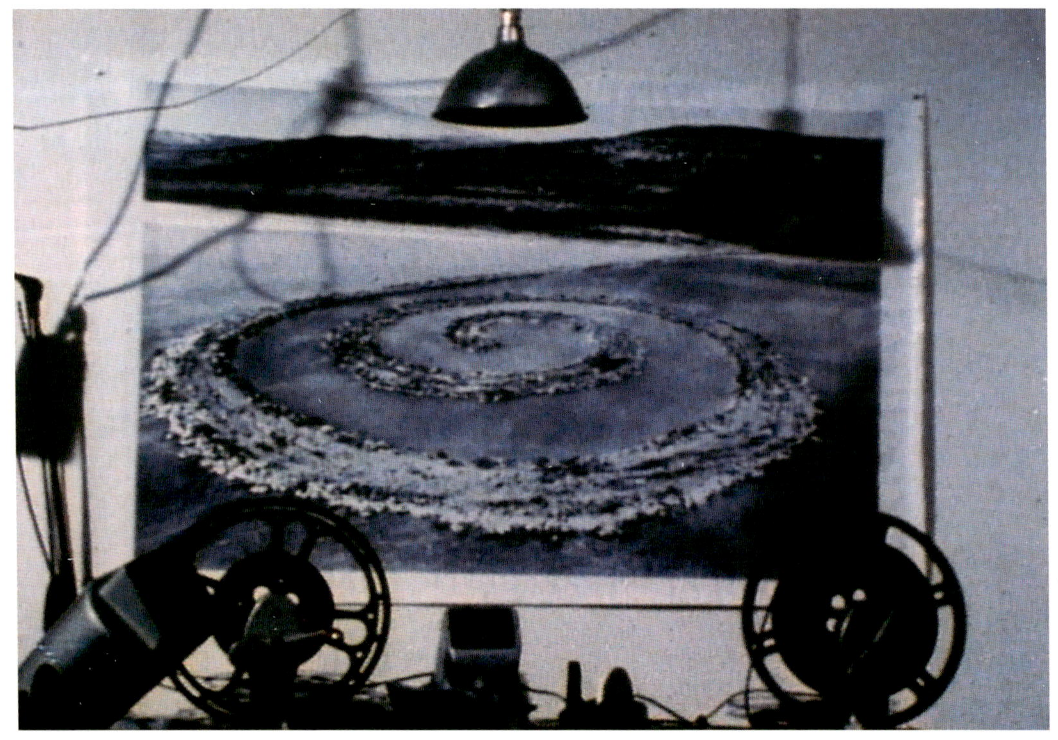

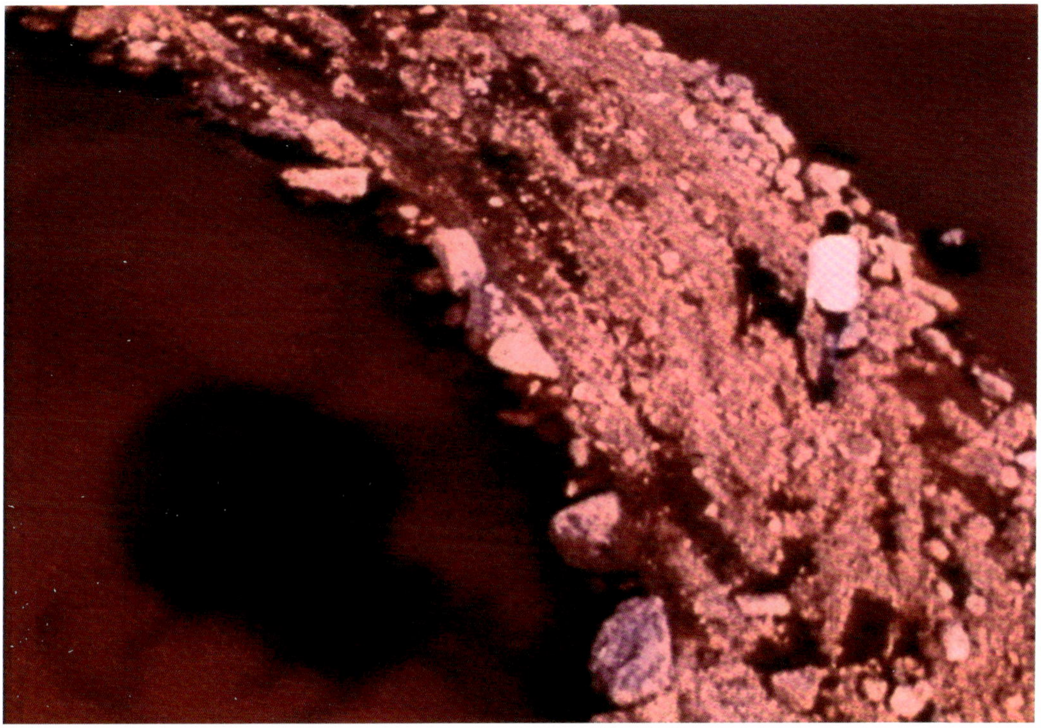

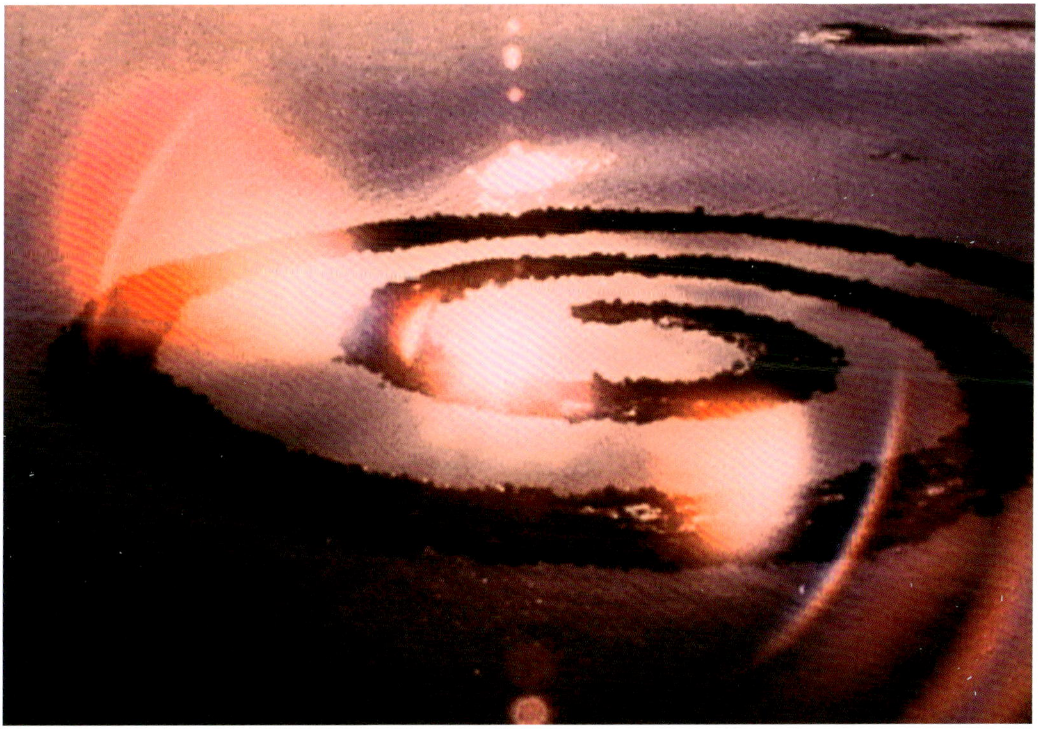

Michael Snow
La Région Centrale, 1971
(Produktionsstudie / production study)

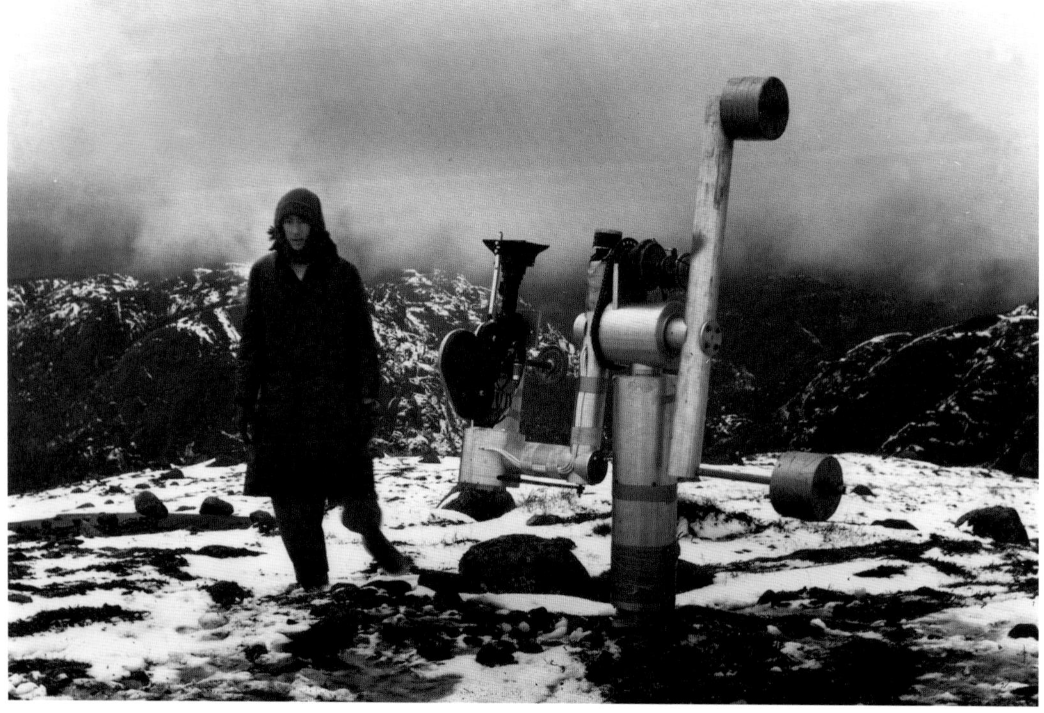

Michael Snow
La Région Centrale, 1971
(Filmstill / film still)

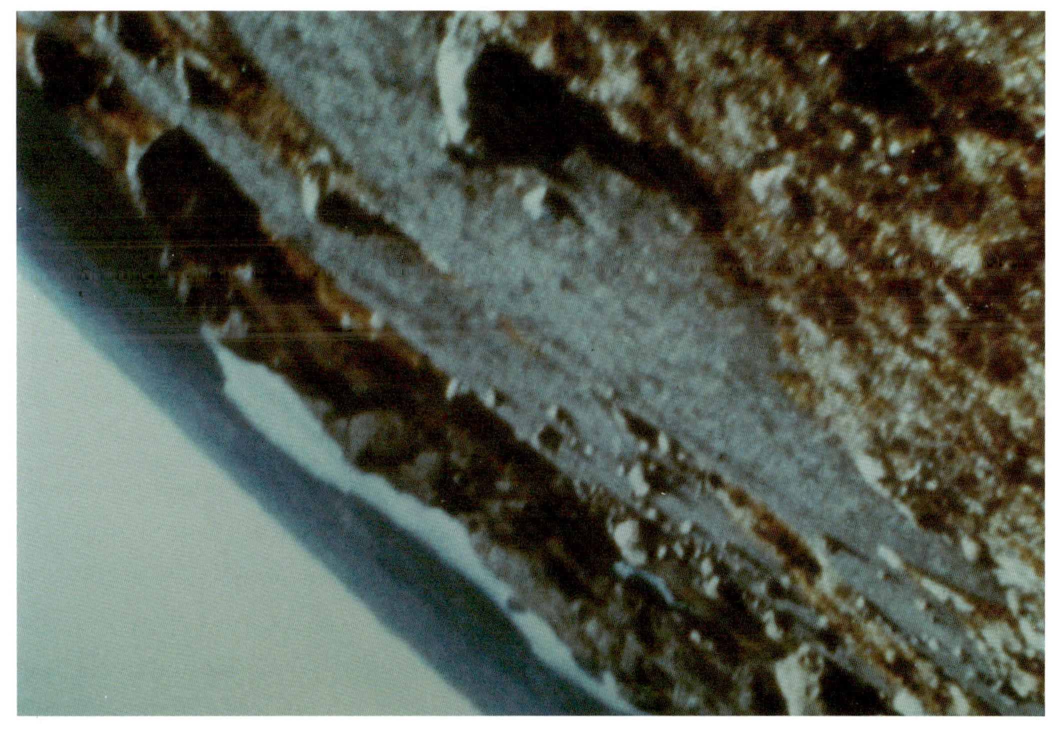

Guido van der Werve
Nummer acht, everything is going to be alright, Golf of Bothnia FI, 2007
(Filmstills / film stills)

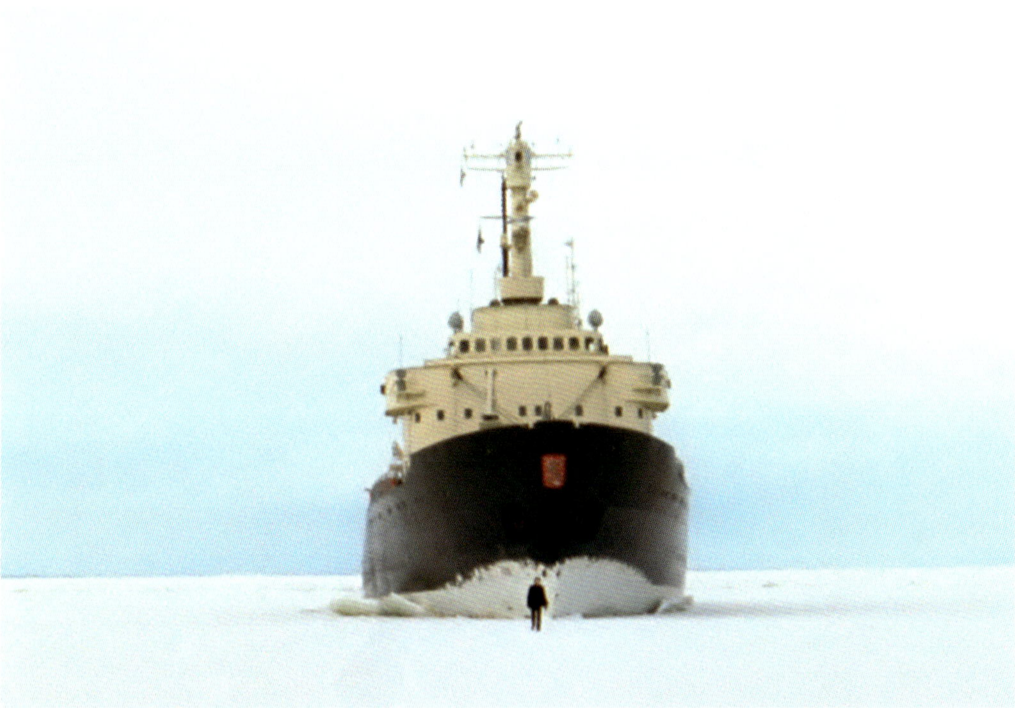

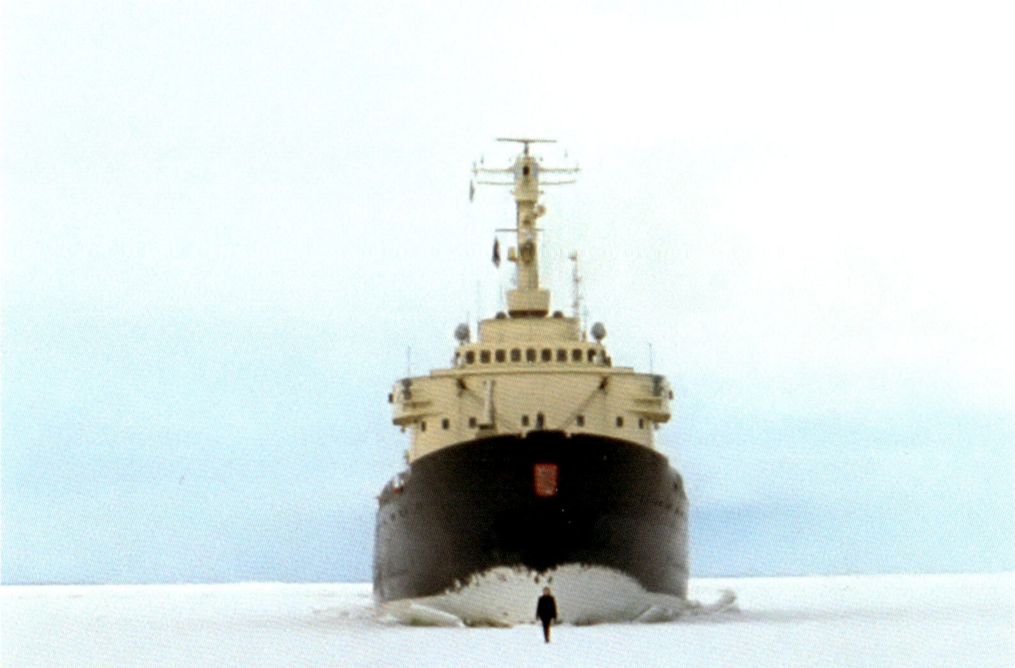

Disputed Landscape
The Visual Paradigm
Uncovering History
Enacting Landscape

Camera Austria

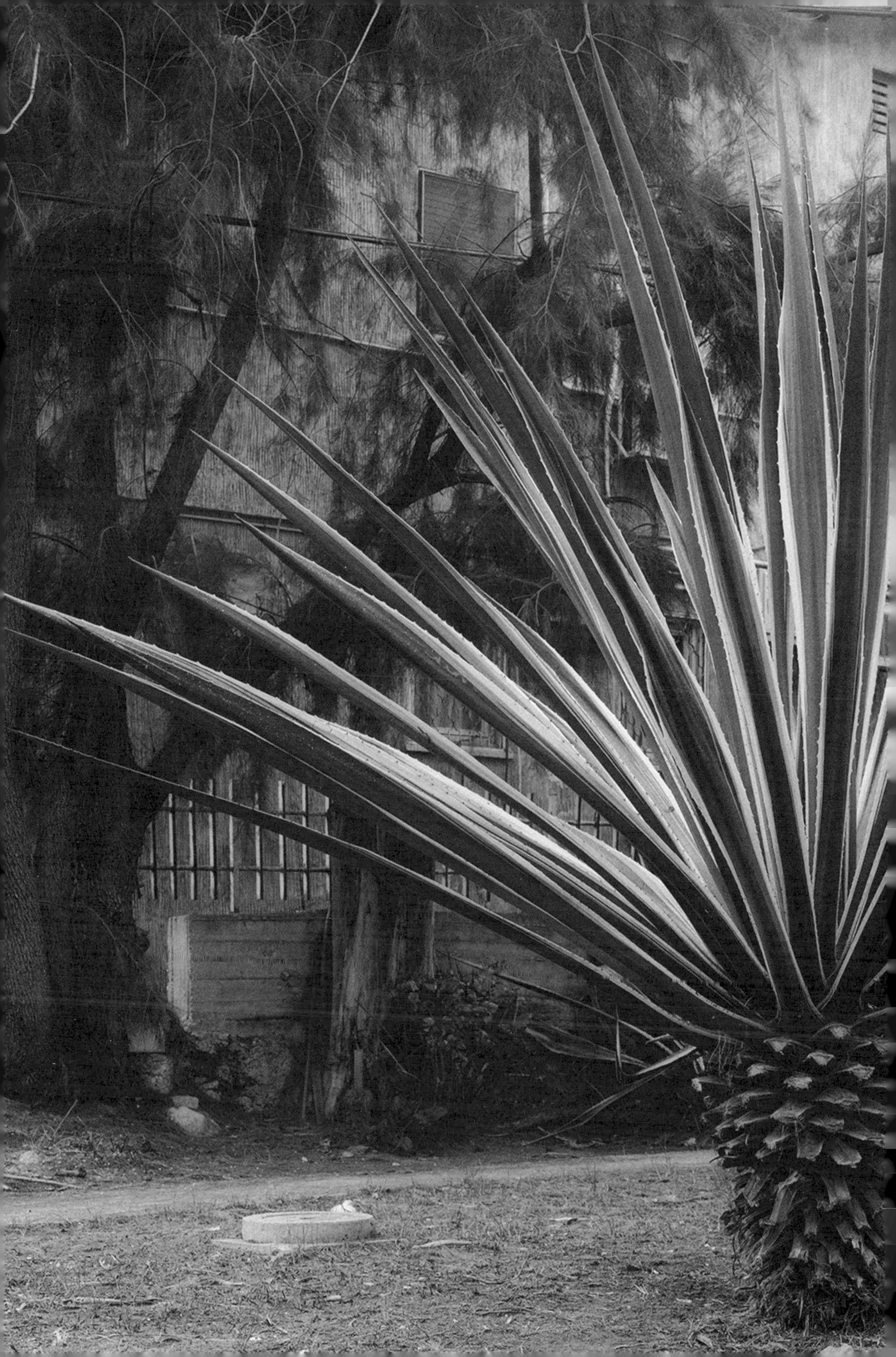

Philip Gaißer
Aus | from: *The Ground is Mine
the Sky is Yours*

*Made by Cactus Tactical
Supply, 2013*

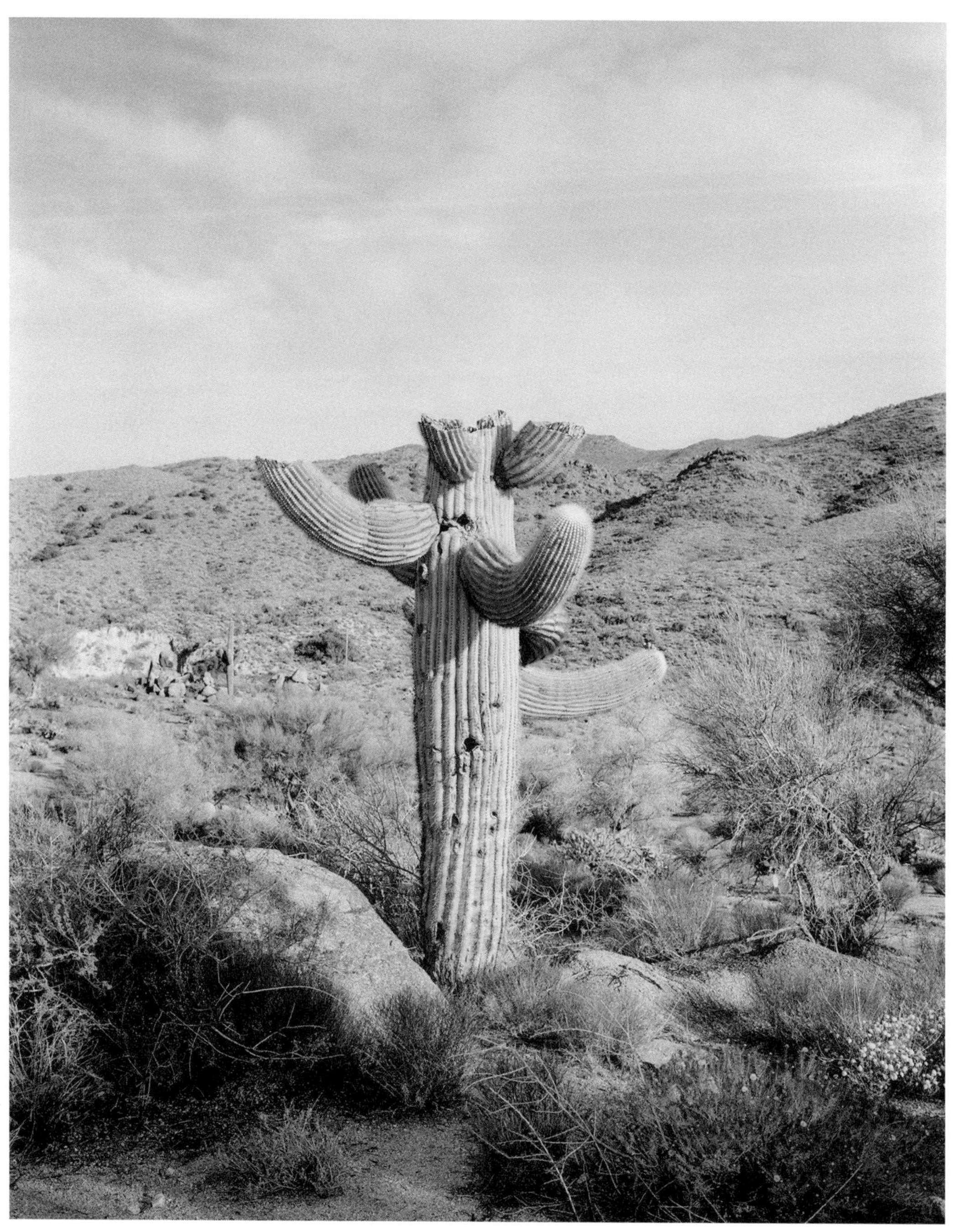

Philip Gaißer
Aus | from: *The Outside Looks
more Fetching than the Inside*

Untitled (Ocean, Biosphere II),
2013

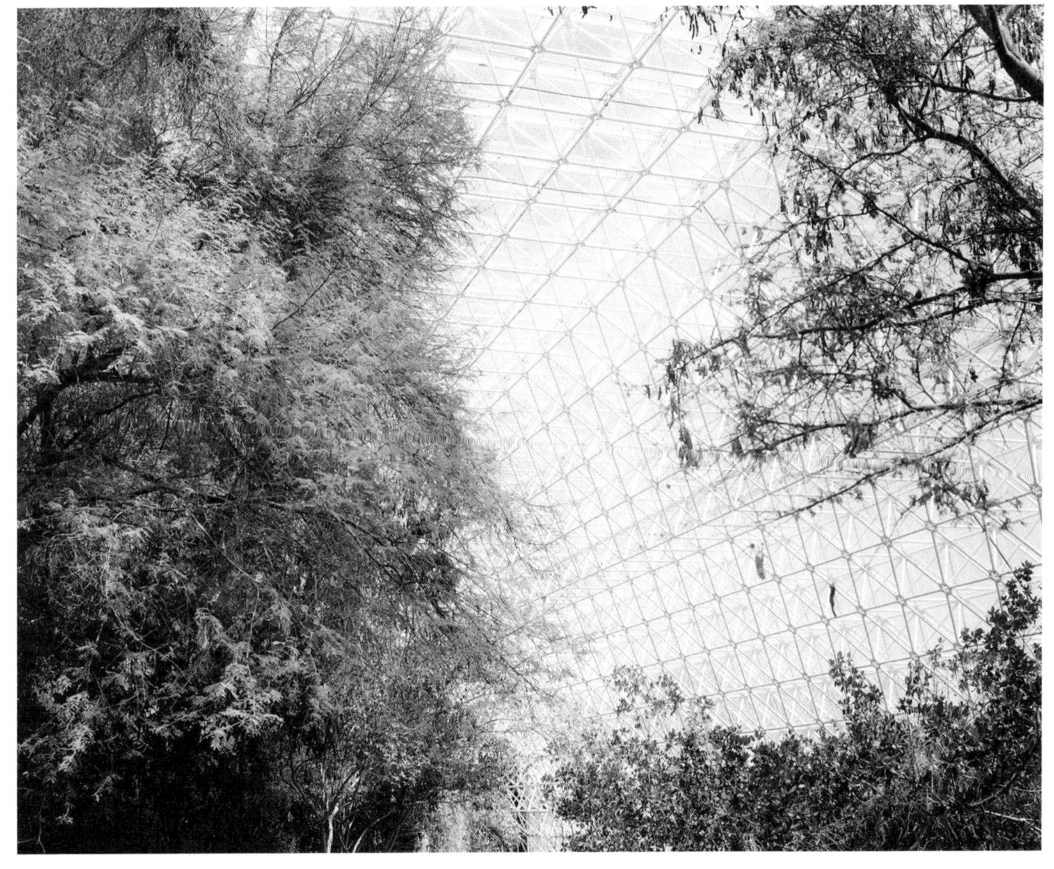

Anthony Haughey
Aus der Serie / from the series:
Disputed Territory, 2006

Red Coffins, Glogjani, Kosovo,
2006

Men Digging, Pristina, 2006

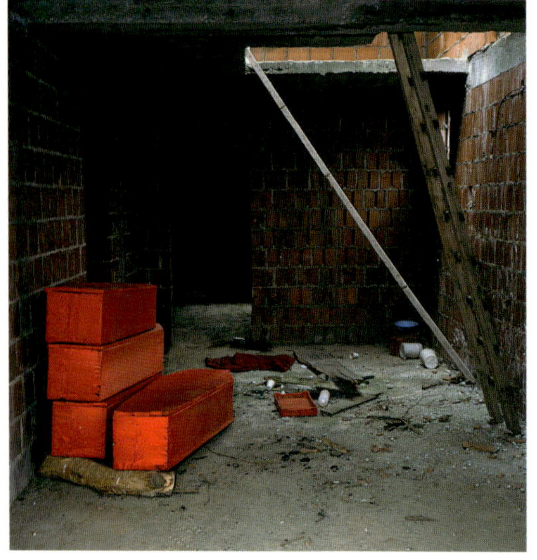

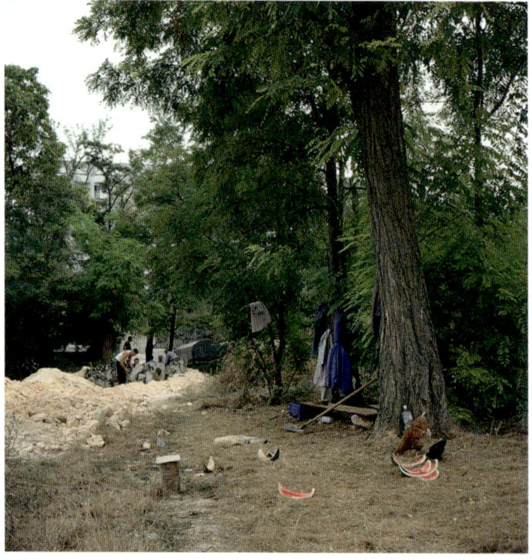

Anthony Haughey
Aus der Serie / from the series:
Disputed Territory, 2006

*British Army Fortifications,
Orange Order Protest, 2006*

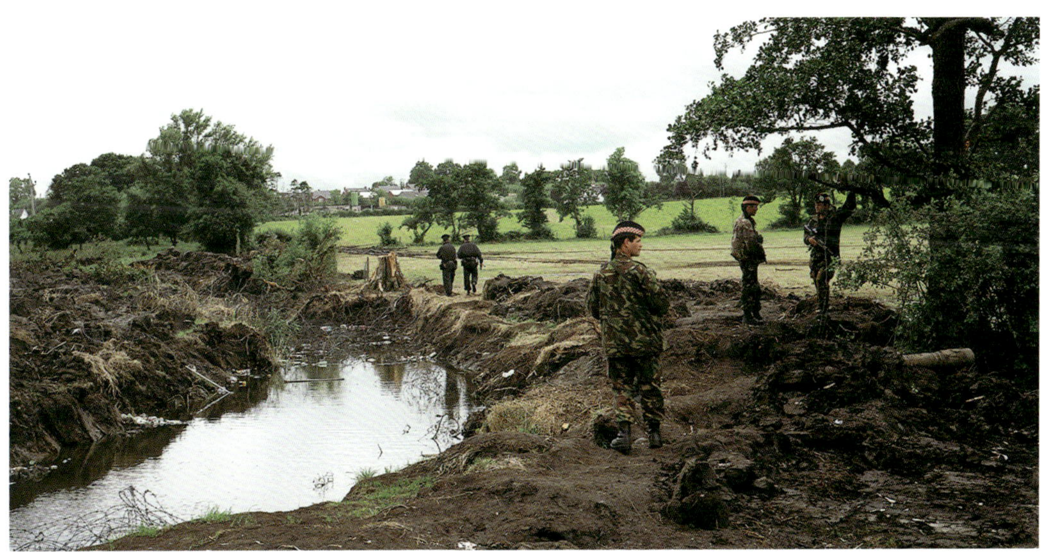

Michael Höpfner
Lie Down, Get Up, Walk On,
day 11, 25-9-2012, 2015

Michael Höpfner
Lie Down, Get Up, Walk On,
day 6, 4-9-2014, 2015

Stephanie Kiwitt
Aus / from: *Wondelgemse
Meersen. Archiv, 2012/15*

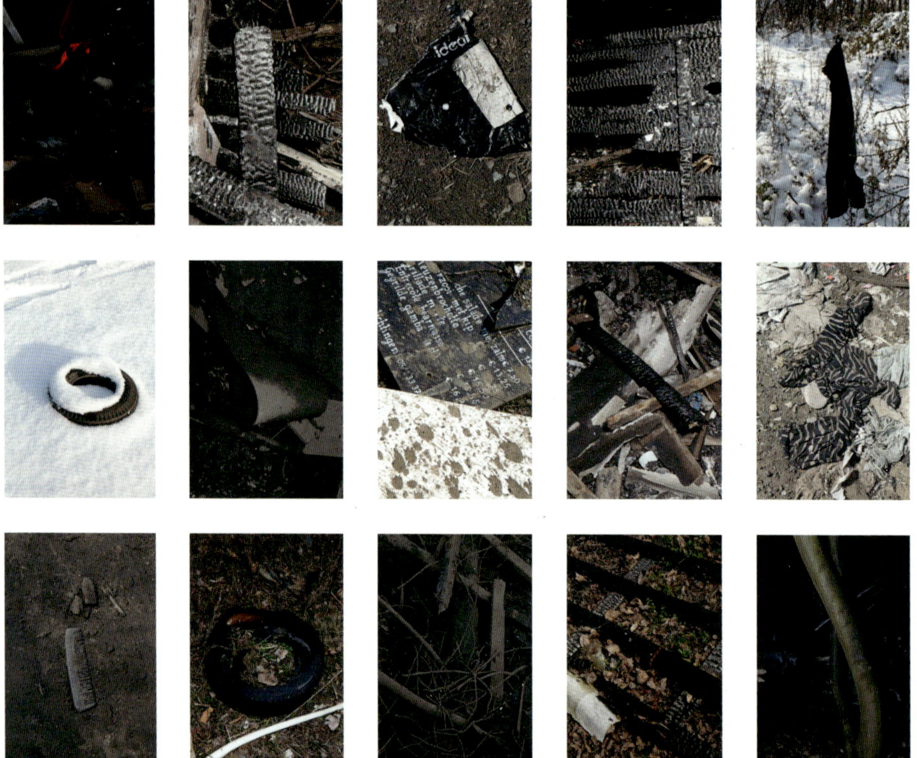

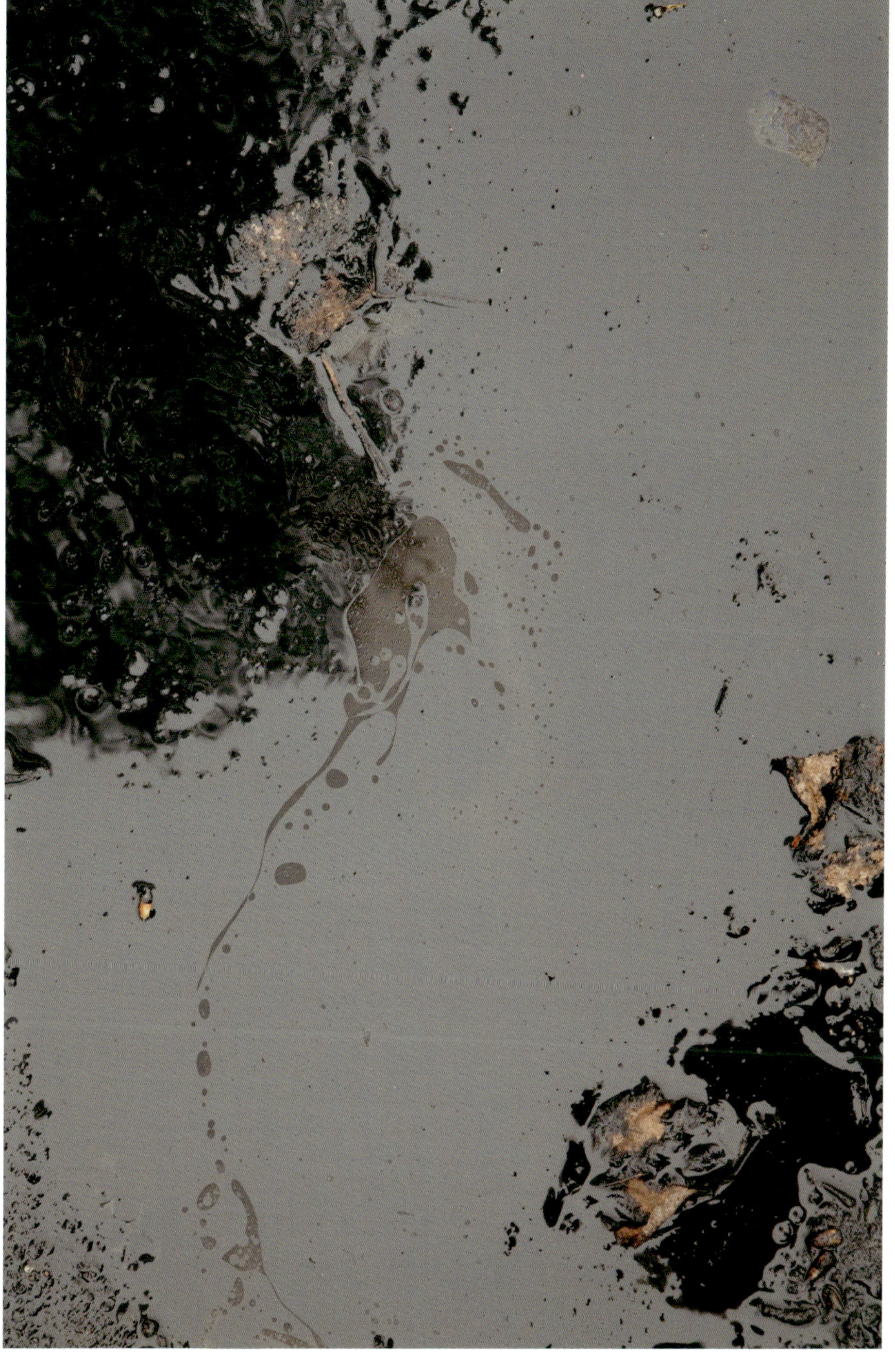

Tatiana Lecomte
Aus | from: *Die El Alamein-Stellung. Eine Montage*, 2012

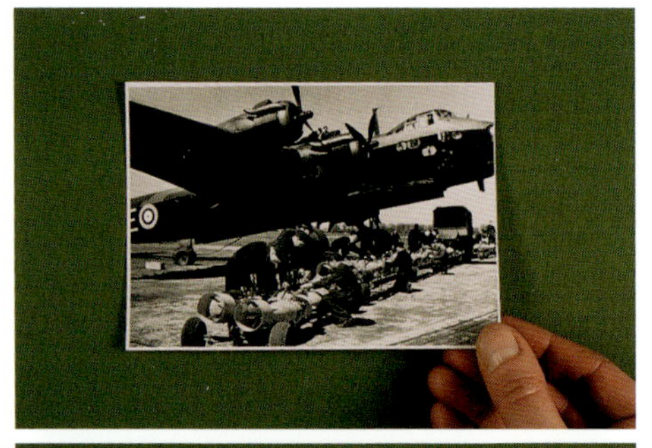

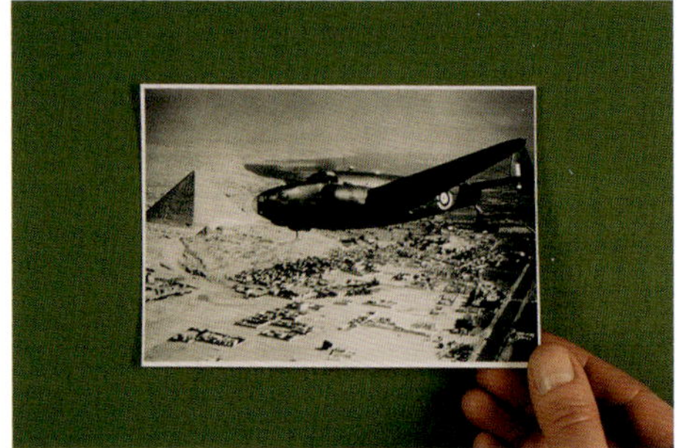

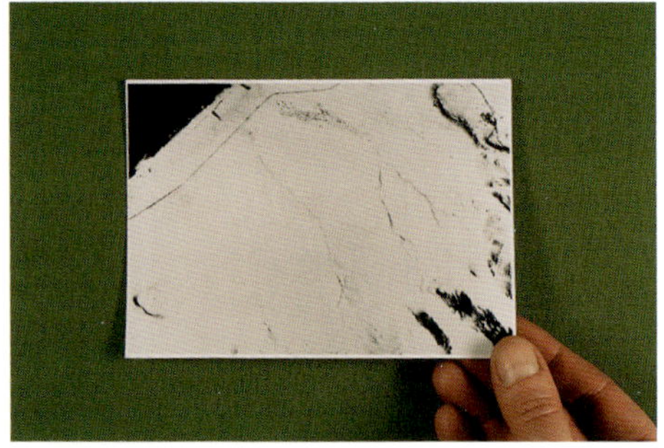

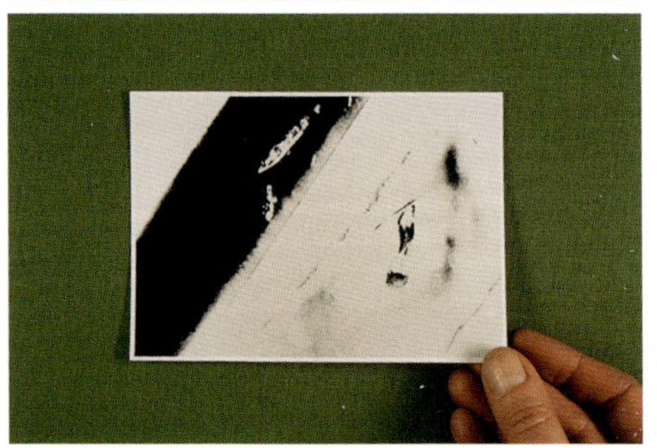

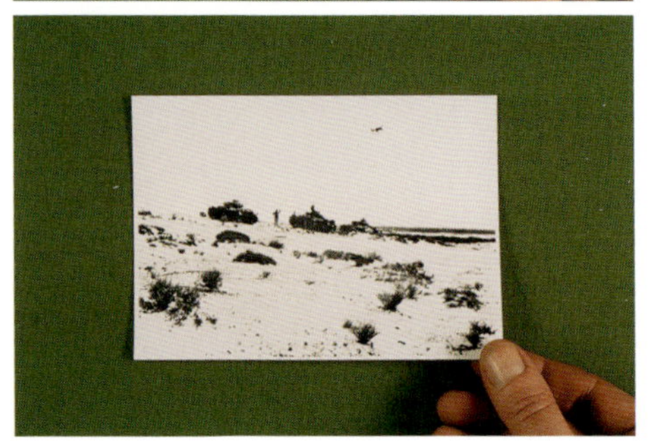

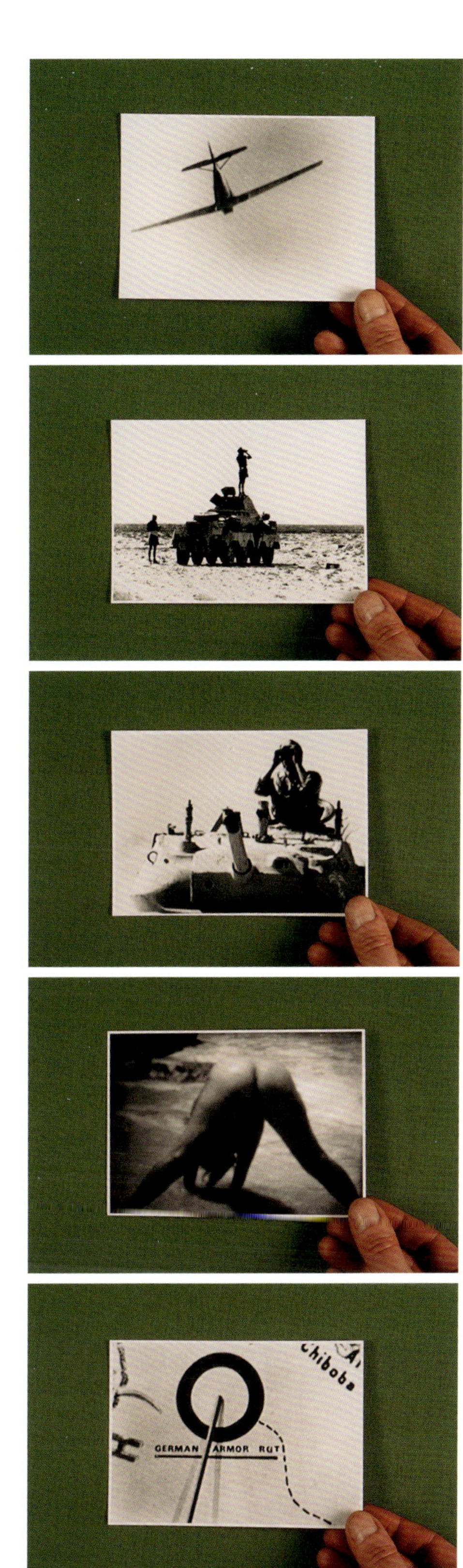
Chiboba
GERMAN ARMOR RUT

Christian Mayer
From Boynton's Lookout the
Author Photographs the
Grandeur of Escalante Canyon,
2011 (Detail)

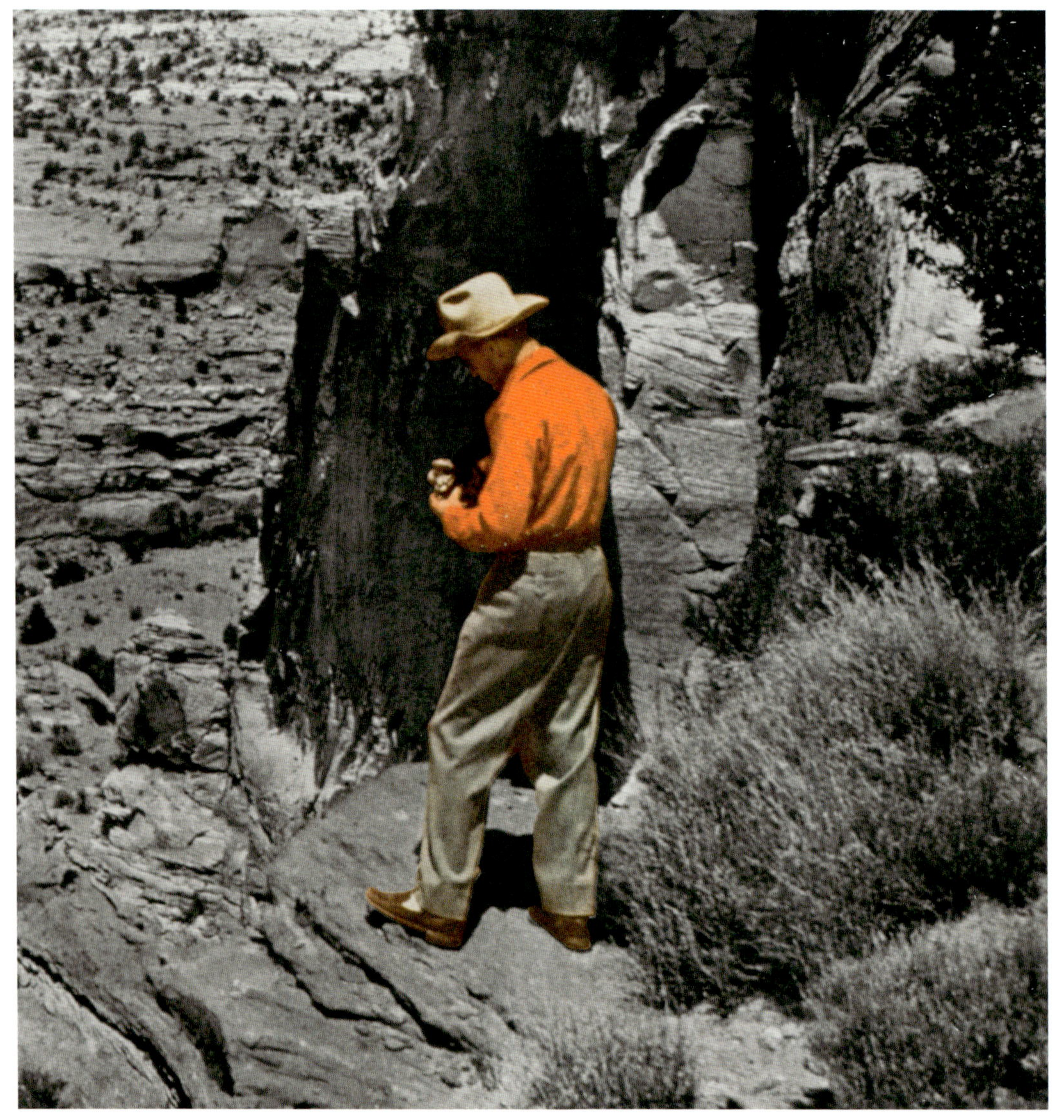

Christian Mayer
From Boynton's Lookout the Author Photographs the Grandeur of Escalante Canyon, 2011
Im Hintergrund / in the background: *Through Historic Hole in the Rock Mormons Blasted a Path to Their Promised Land,* 2011
Ausstellungsansicht / exhibition view, Camera Austria, Graz, 2015

Christian Mayer
Escalante Expedition Named This Glowing Valley "Kodachrome Flat", 2011
Im Hintergrund / in the background: *In Earth's Age-old Battle with the Elements, Giant Chimney Stands Undefeated,* 2011
Ausstellungsansicht / exhibition view, Camera Austria, Graz, 2015

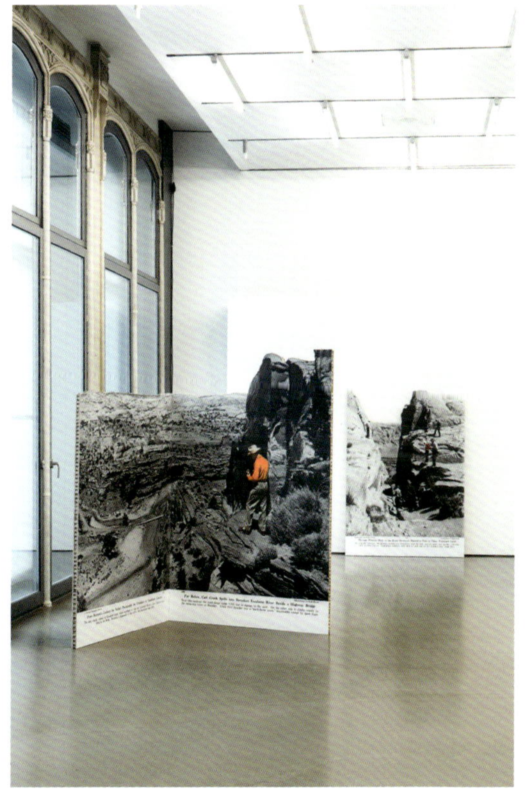

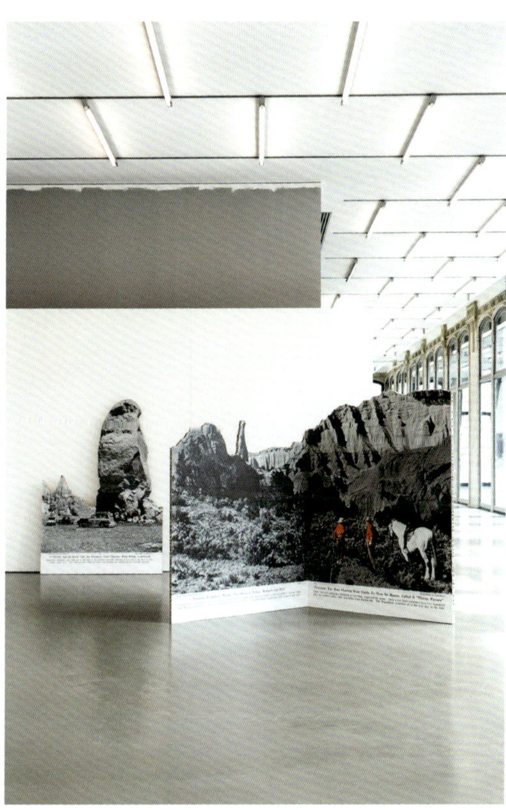

Jo Ractliffe
Aus | from: *As Terras do Fim do Mundo (The Lands of the End of the World)*, 2009/10

Unmarked mass grave on the outskirts of Cuito Cuanavale, 2009

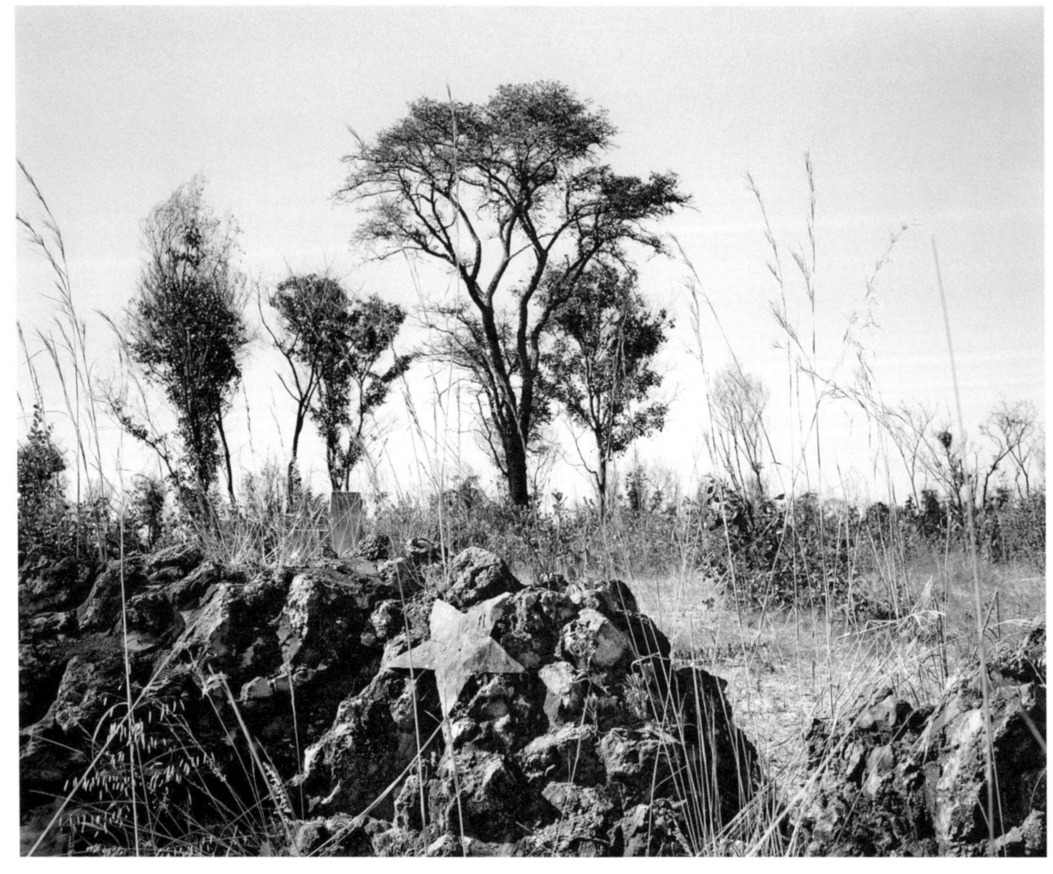

Jo Ractliffe
Aus | from: *As Terras do Fim
do Mundo (The Lands of the
End of the World)*, 2009/10

*Unidentified memorial in the
desert, south of Namibe, 2009*

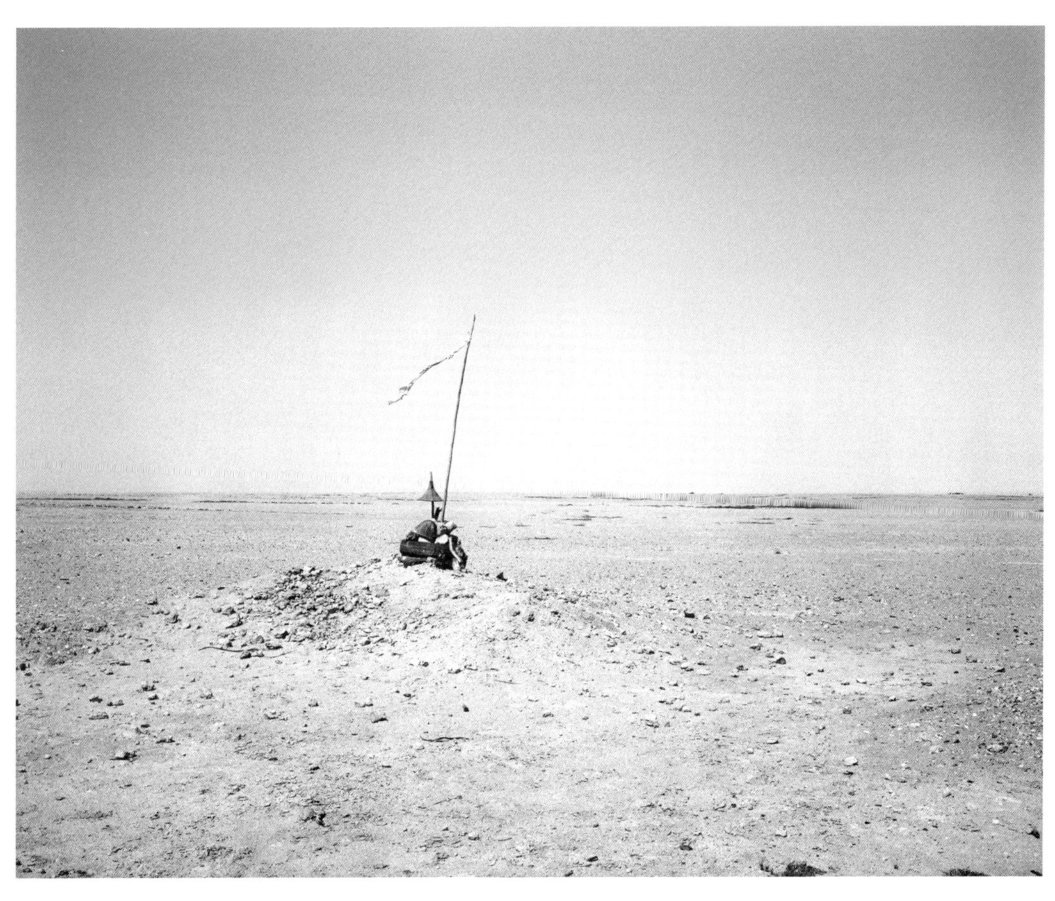

Ricarda Roggan
natura nova, Sedimente 6,
2010

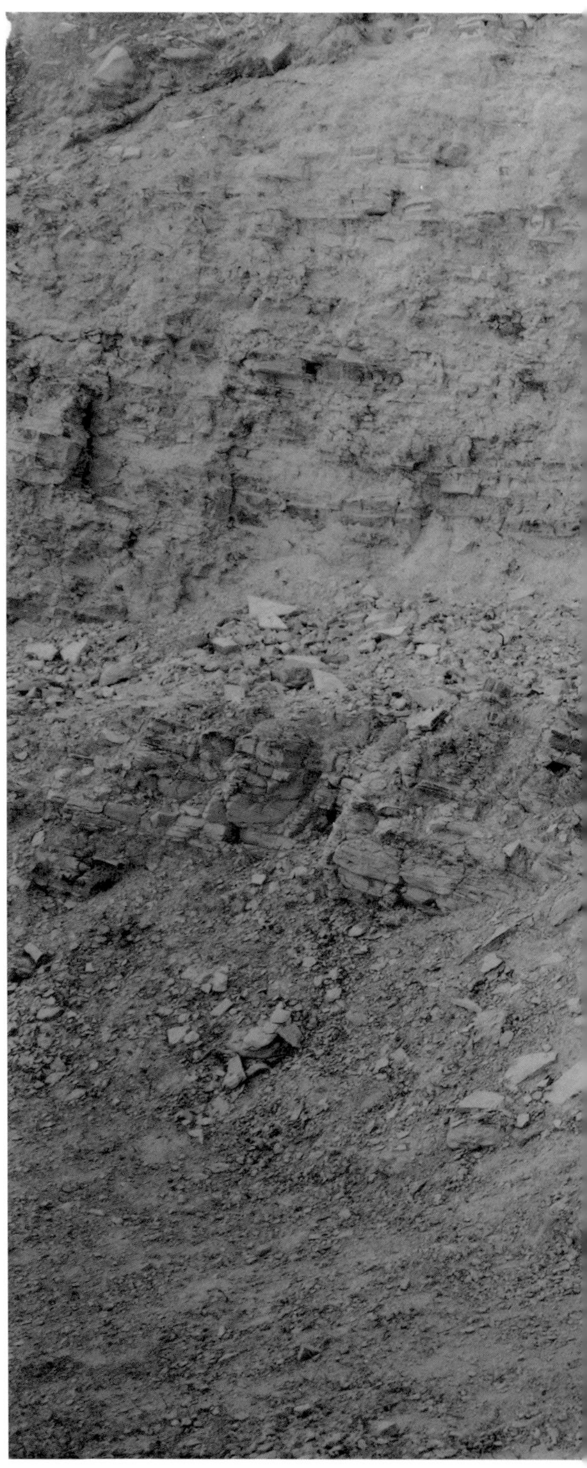

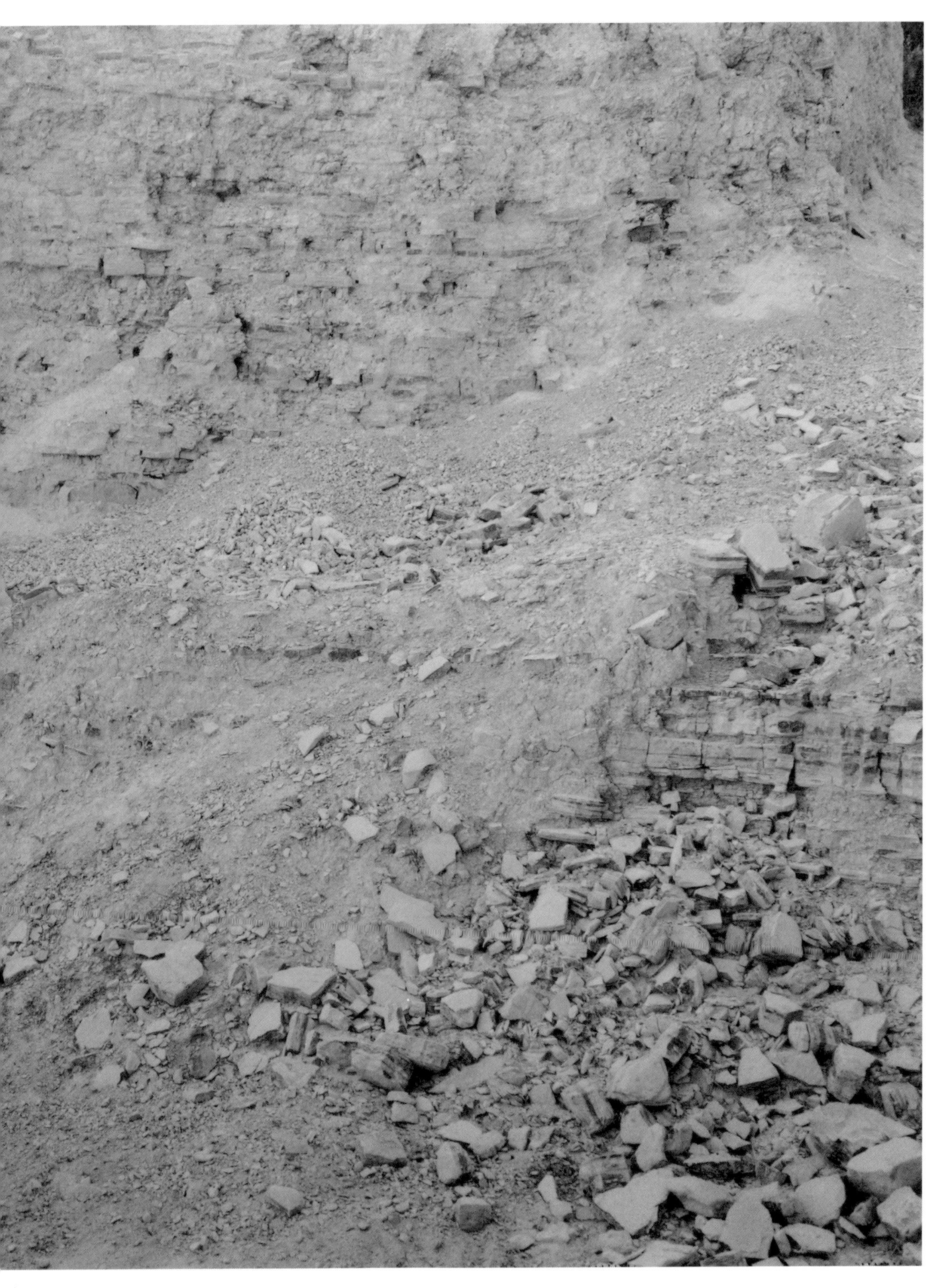

Ahlam Shibli
Aus | from: *The Valley,*
Arab al-Shibli, Palestine,
2007/08

Untitled (The Valley no. 5),
Arab al-Shibli, Palestine,
2007/08

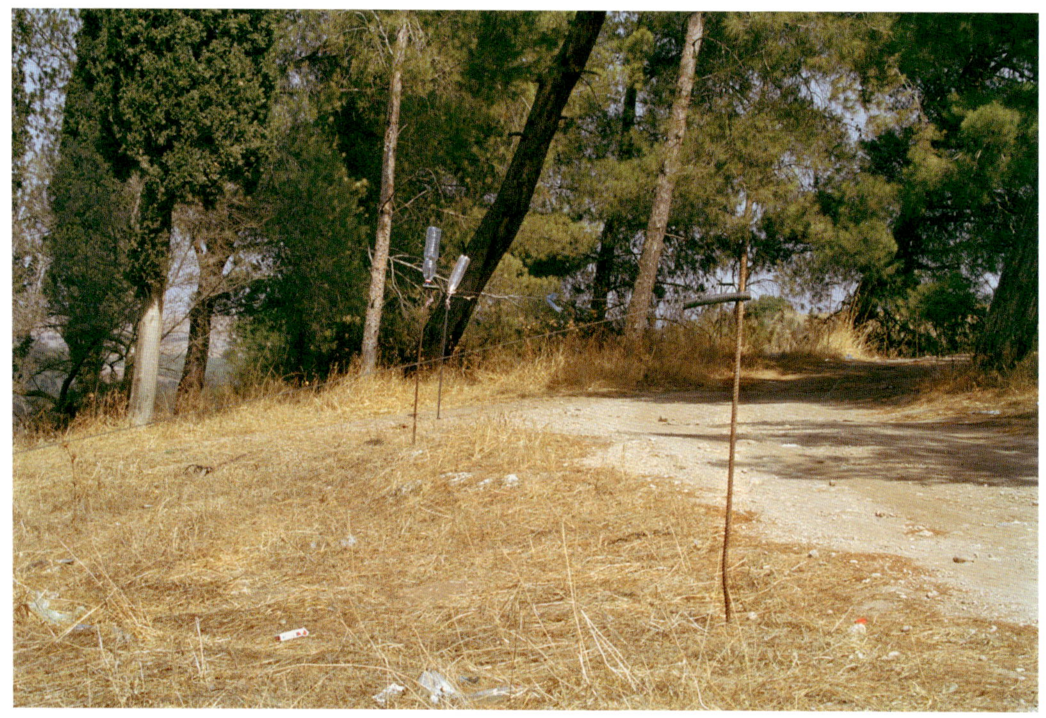

Ahlam Shibli
Aus | from: *The Valley,
Arab al-Shibli, Palestine,
2007/08*

*Untitled (The Valley no. 9),
Arab al-Shibli, Palestine,
2007/08*

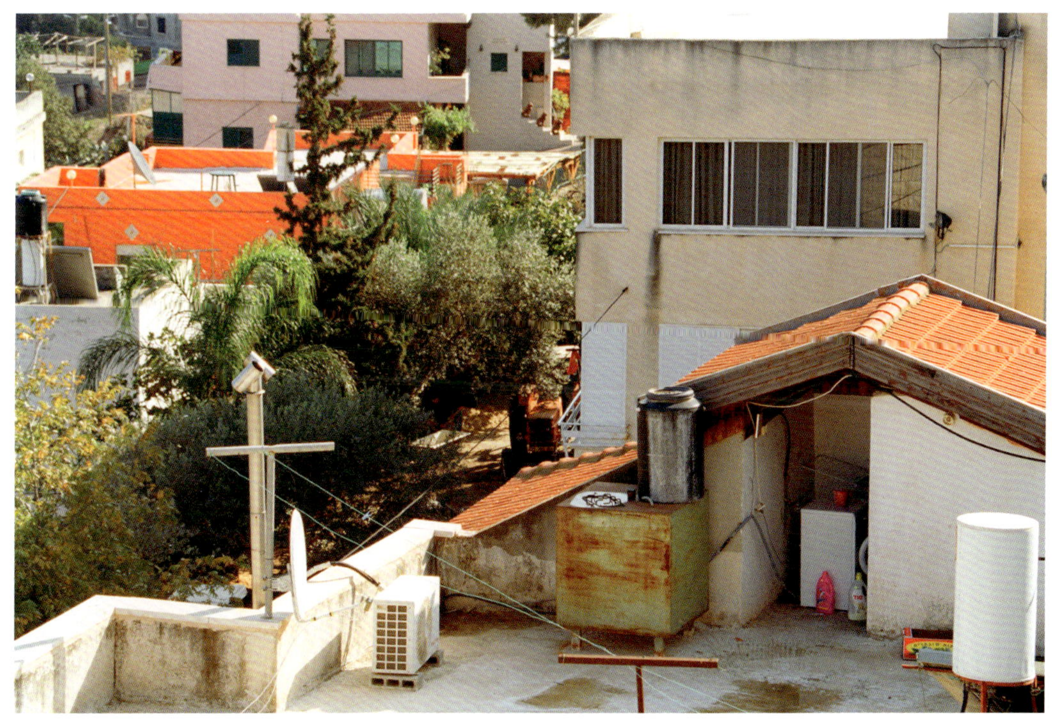

Efrat Shvili
Aus / from: *100 Years*, 2007

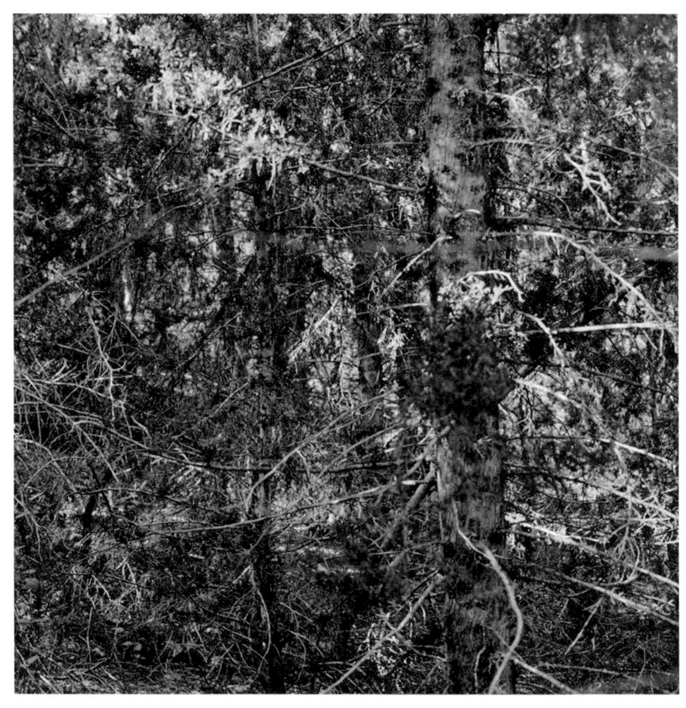

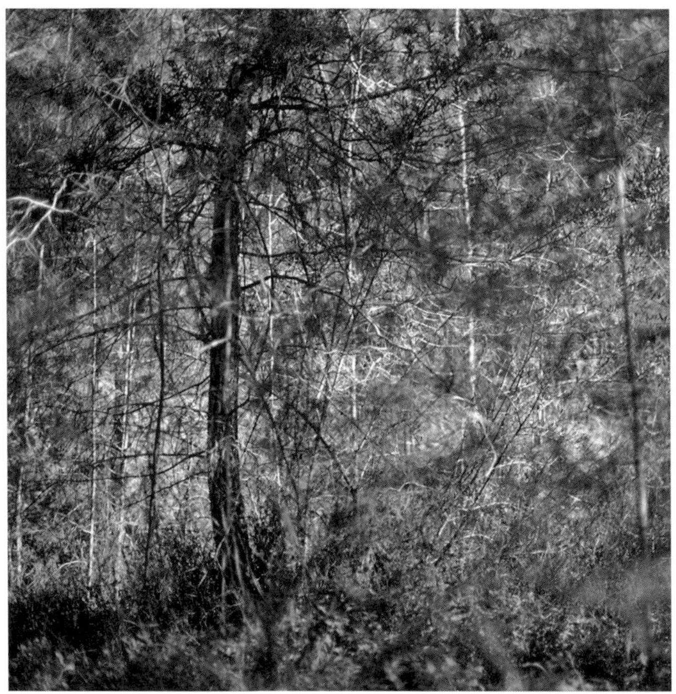

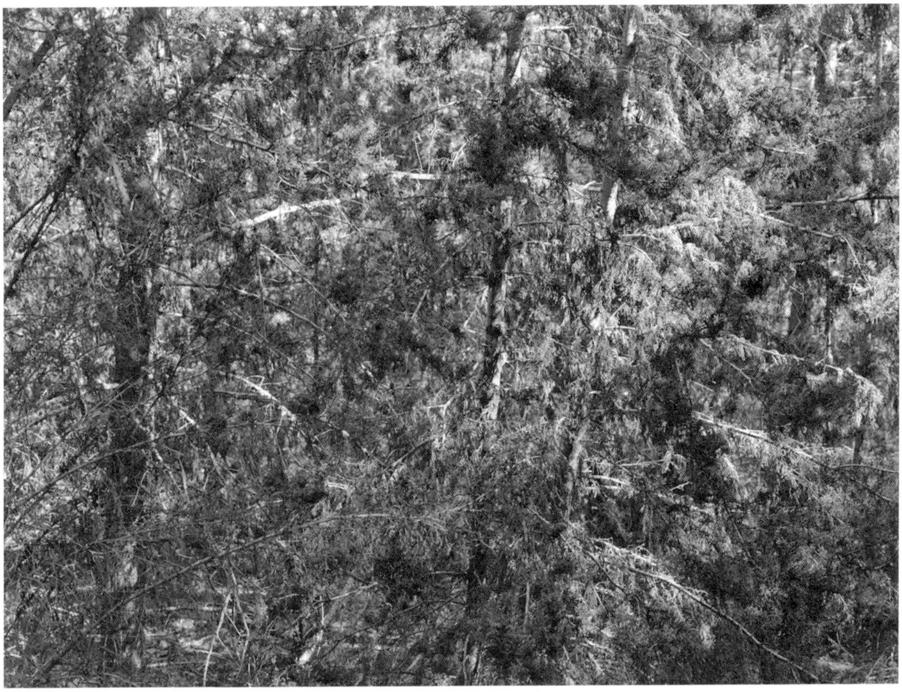

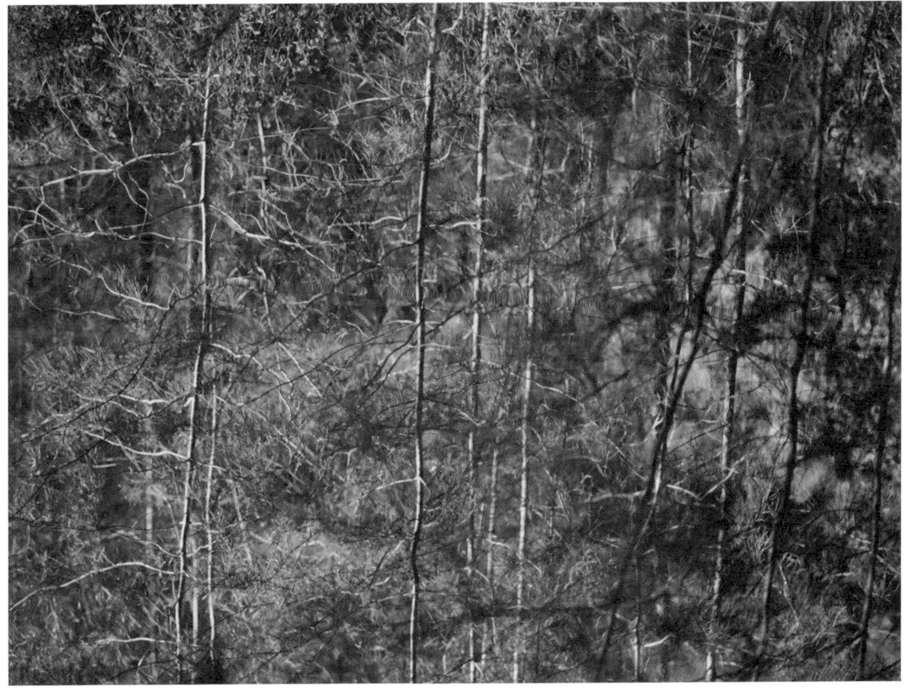

Nicole Six & Paul Petritsch
Aus der Serie / from the series:
Die Innere Grenze / Notranja
meja, Abb. 02 + 03 / Slika
02 + 03, 2008

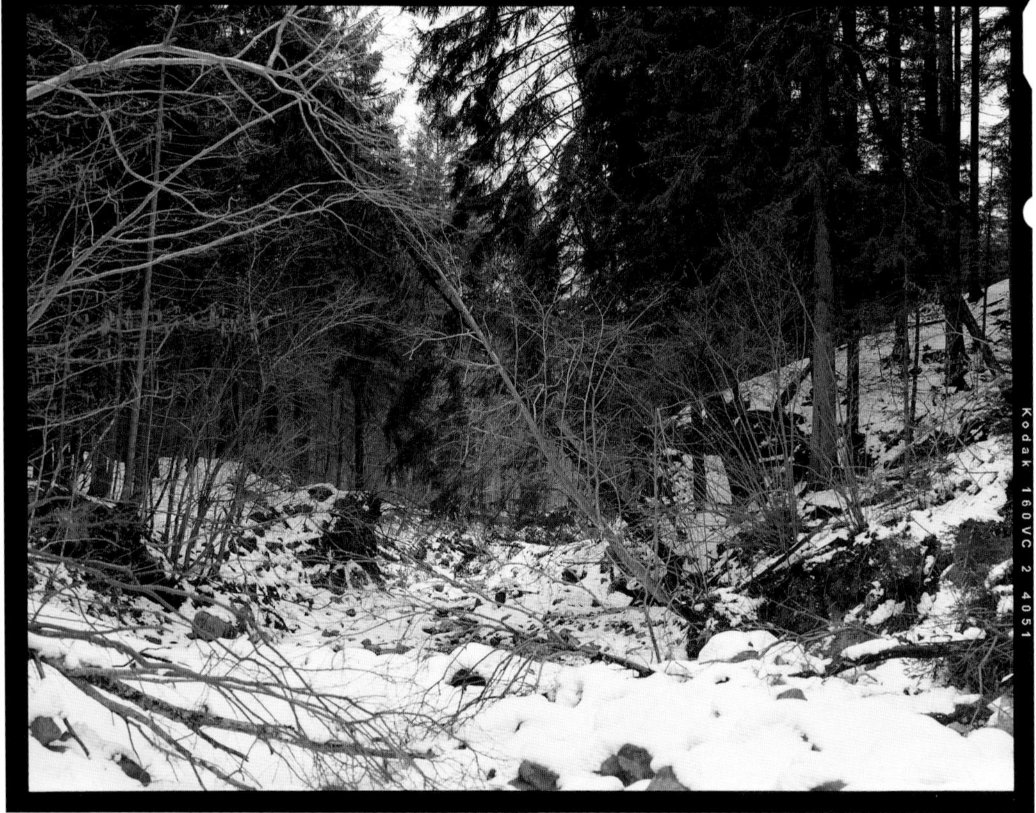

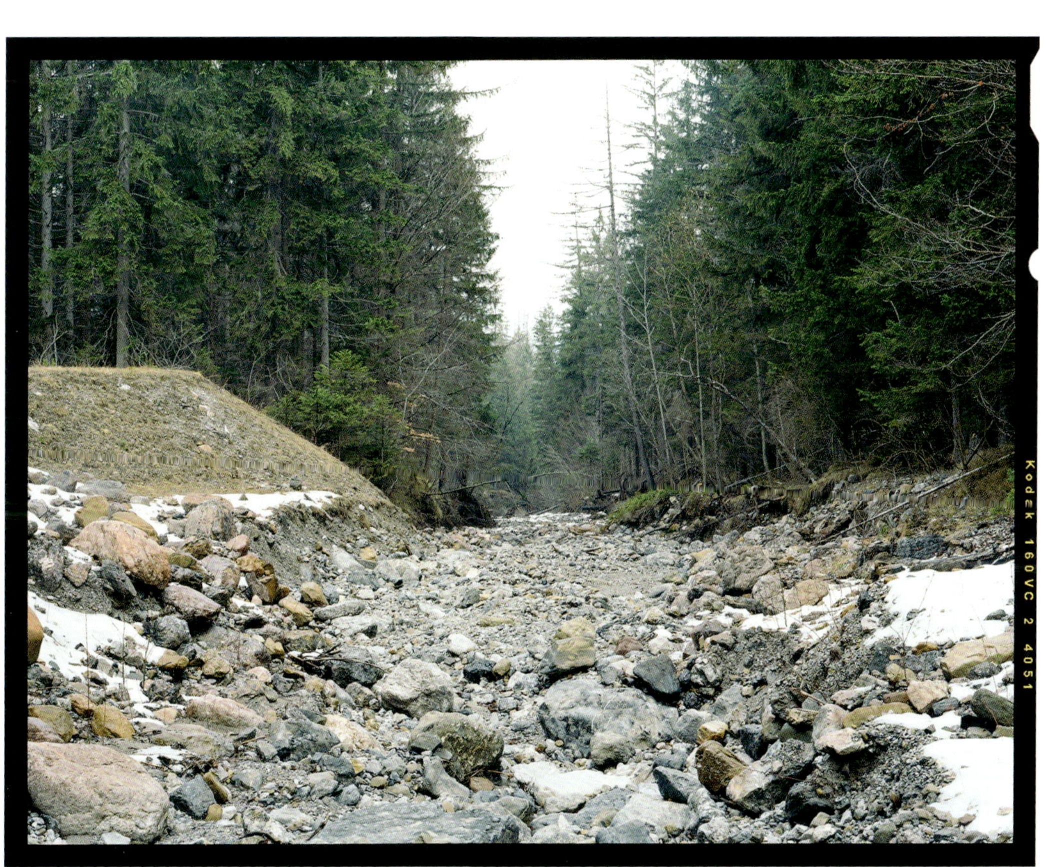

Sharon Ya'ari
*Tel Yavne Archaeological
Mound, Summer, 2012*

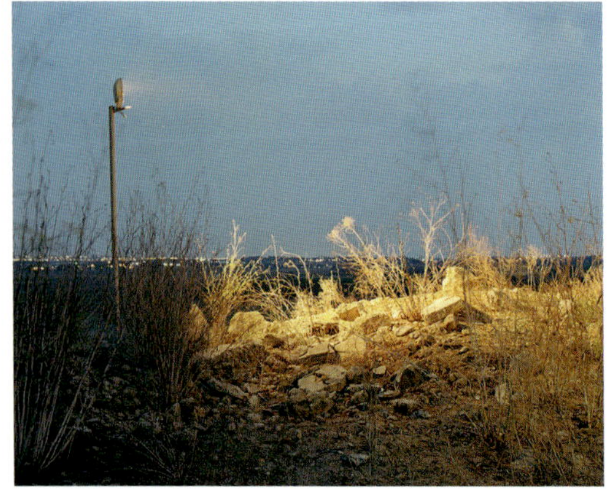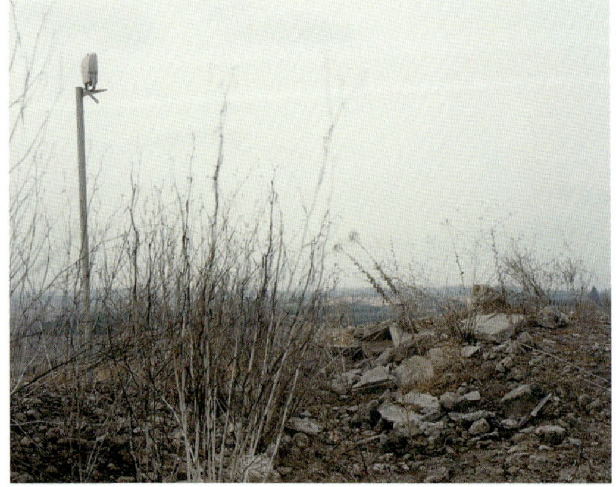

Sharon Ya'ari
*Safe Room, Beersheba Zoo,
Spring, 2013*

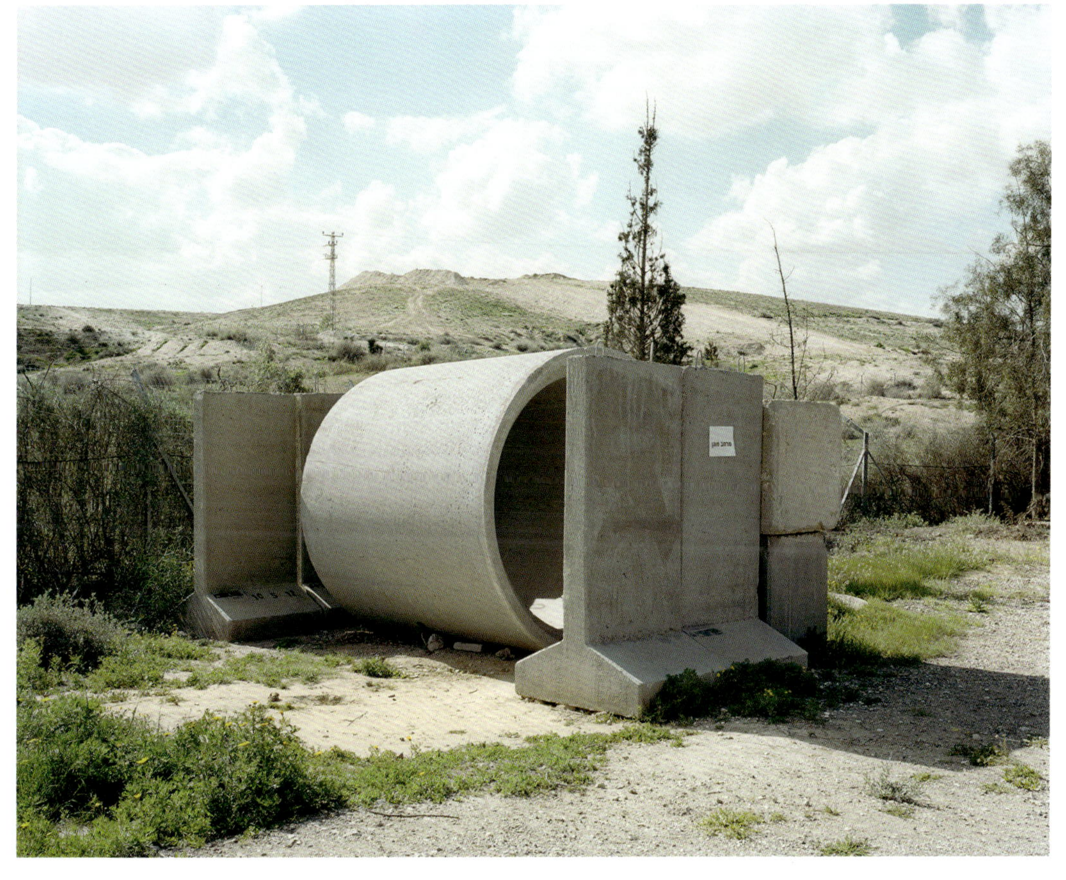

Politische Landschaft
Kunst – Widerstand – Salzkammergut
Political Landscape
Art – Resistance – Salzkammergut

Kunst im öffentlichen Raum Steiermark
Art in Public Space Styria

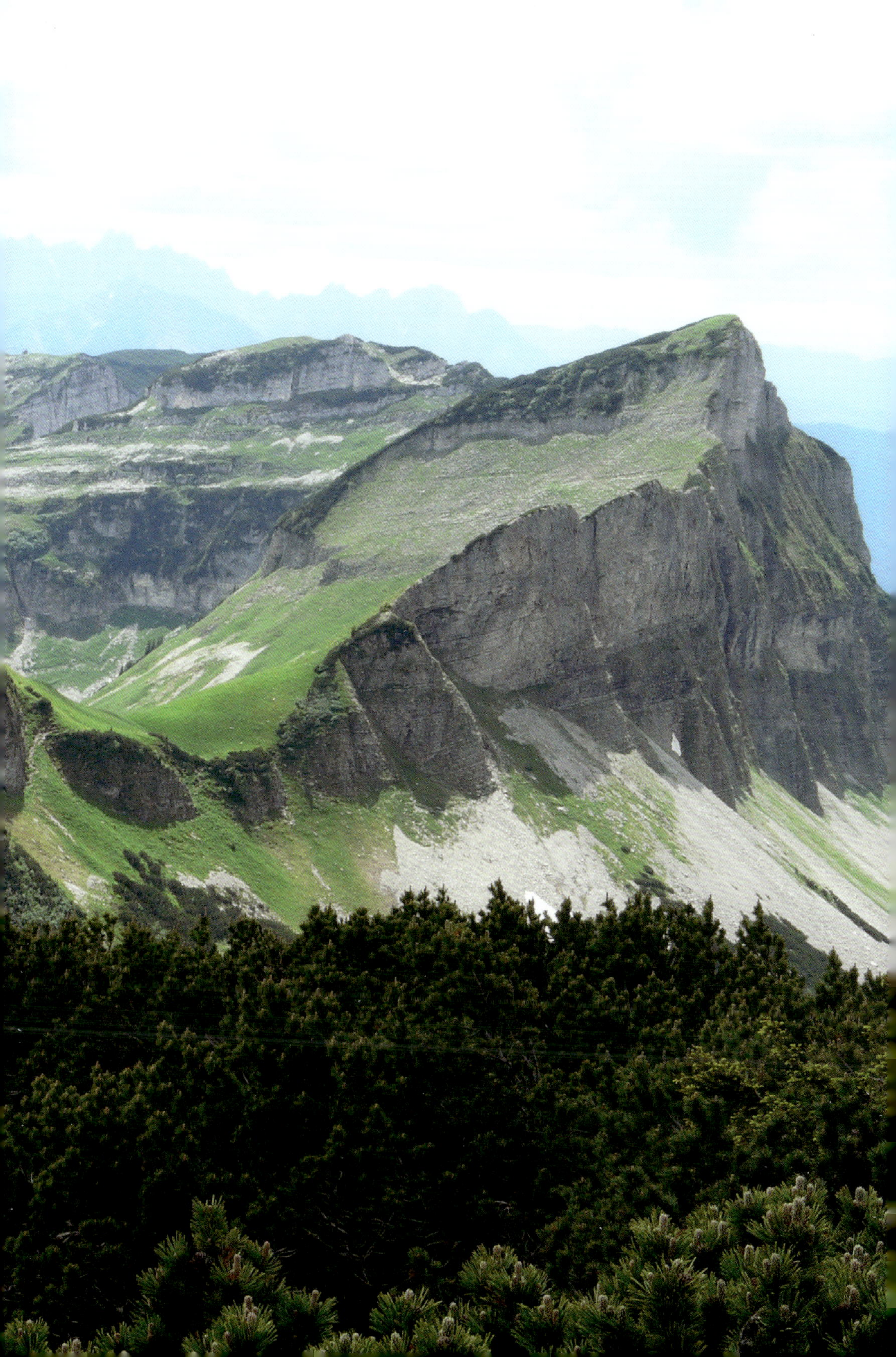

Clegg & Guttmann
Die Offene Bibliothek, Graz |
The Open Public Library, Graz,
1991

Die Offene Bibliothek,
Hamburg | The Open Public
Library, Hamburg, 1993

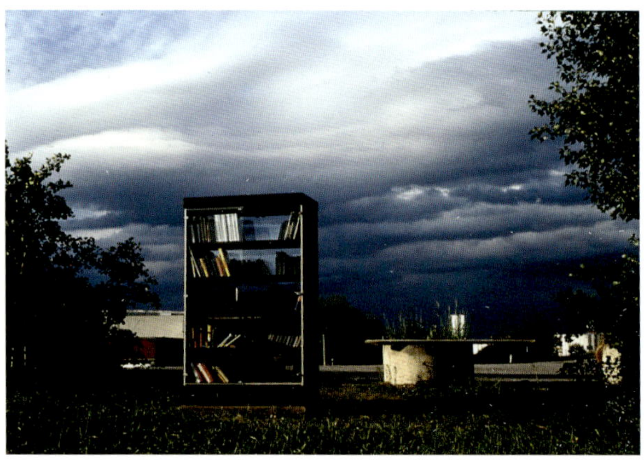

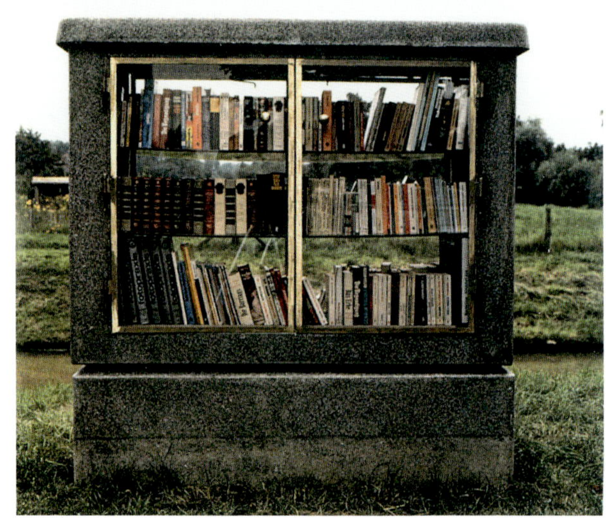

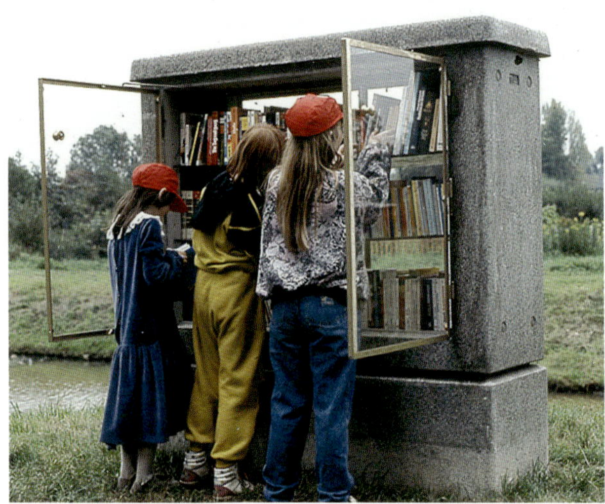

Clegg & Guttmann
Die Offene Bibliothek, Mainz |
The Open Public Library,
Mainz, 1994

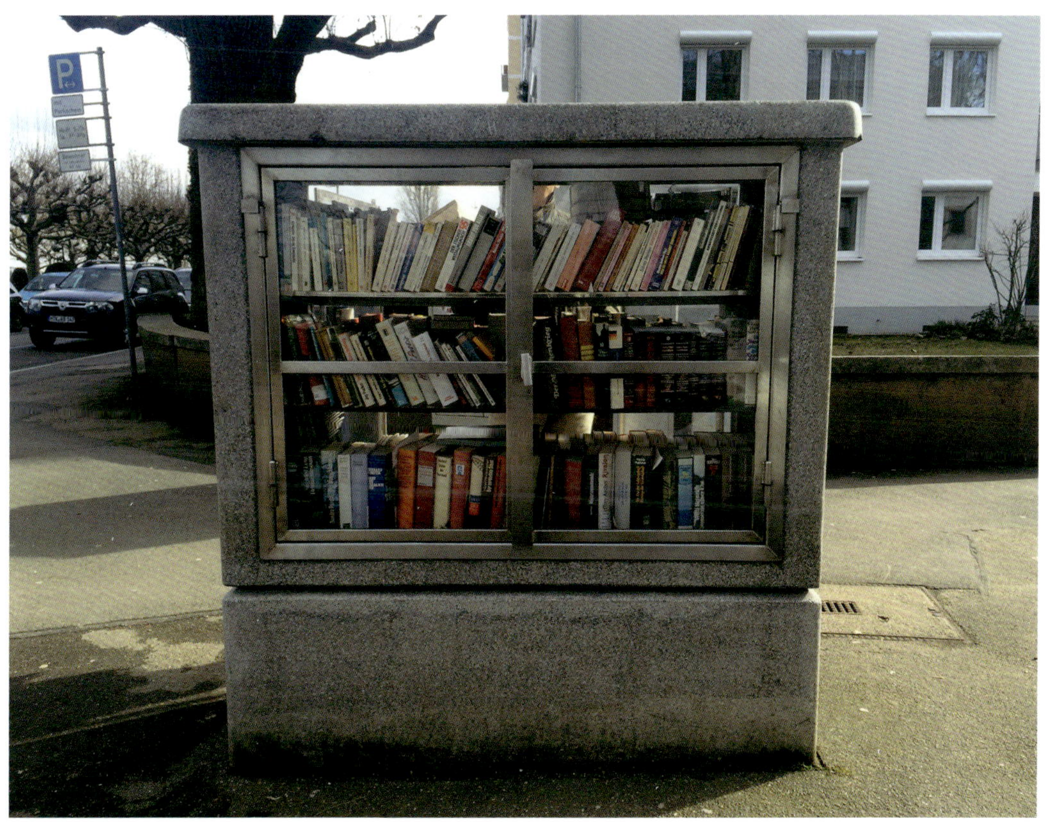

Eva Grubinger
Material für *Igel* / Material for
Hedgehog, Ausseerland, 2015

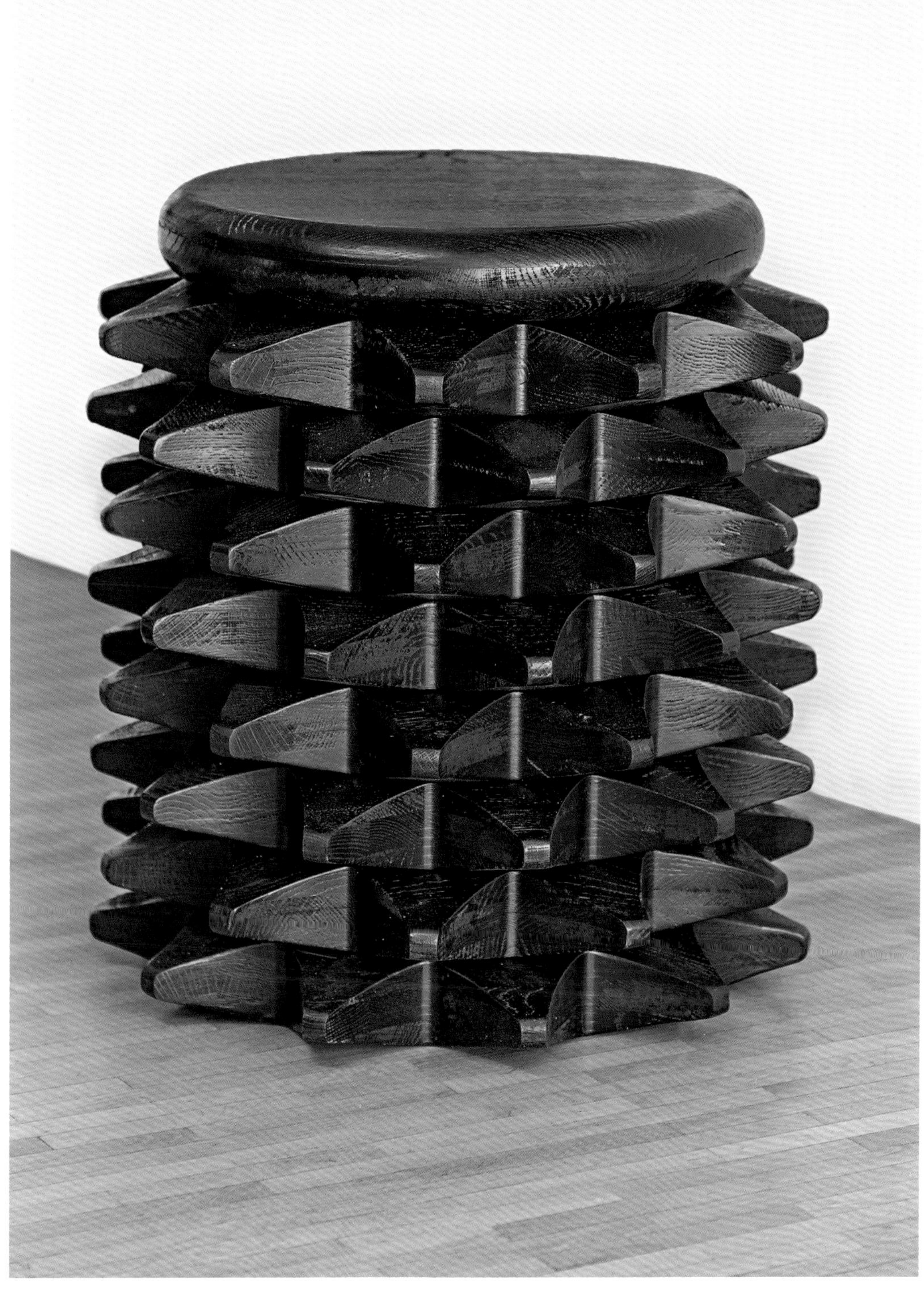

Florian Hüttner
*Freie Flusszone
Süderelbe*, 2014
(Plakat / poster)

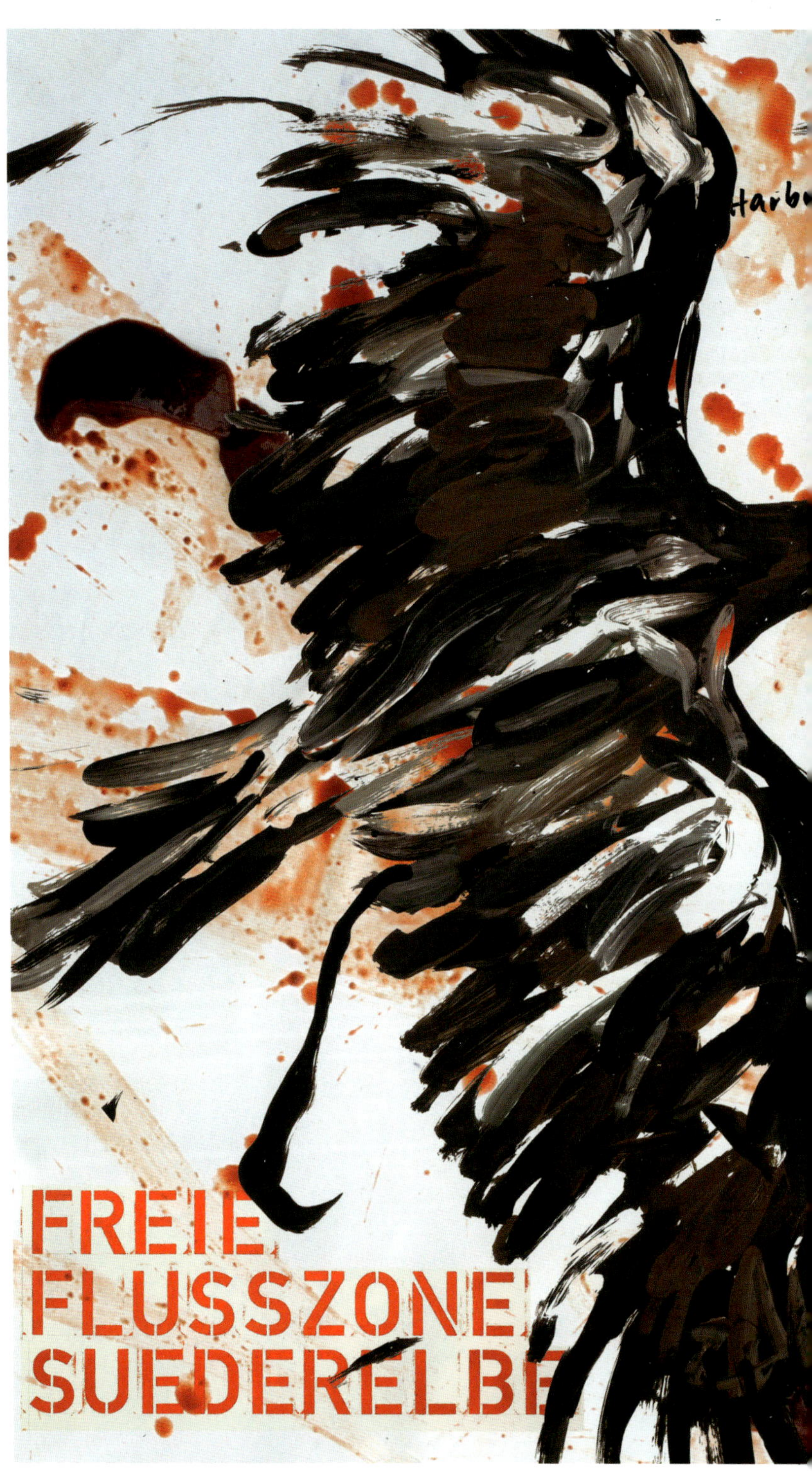

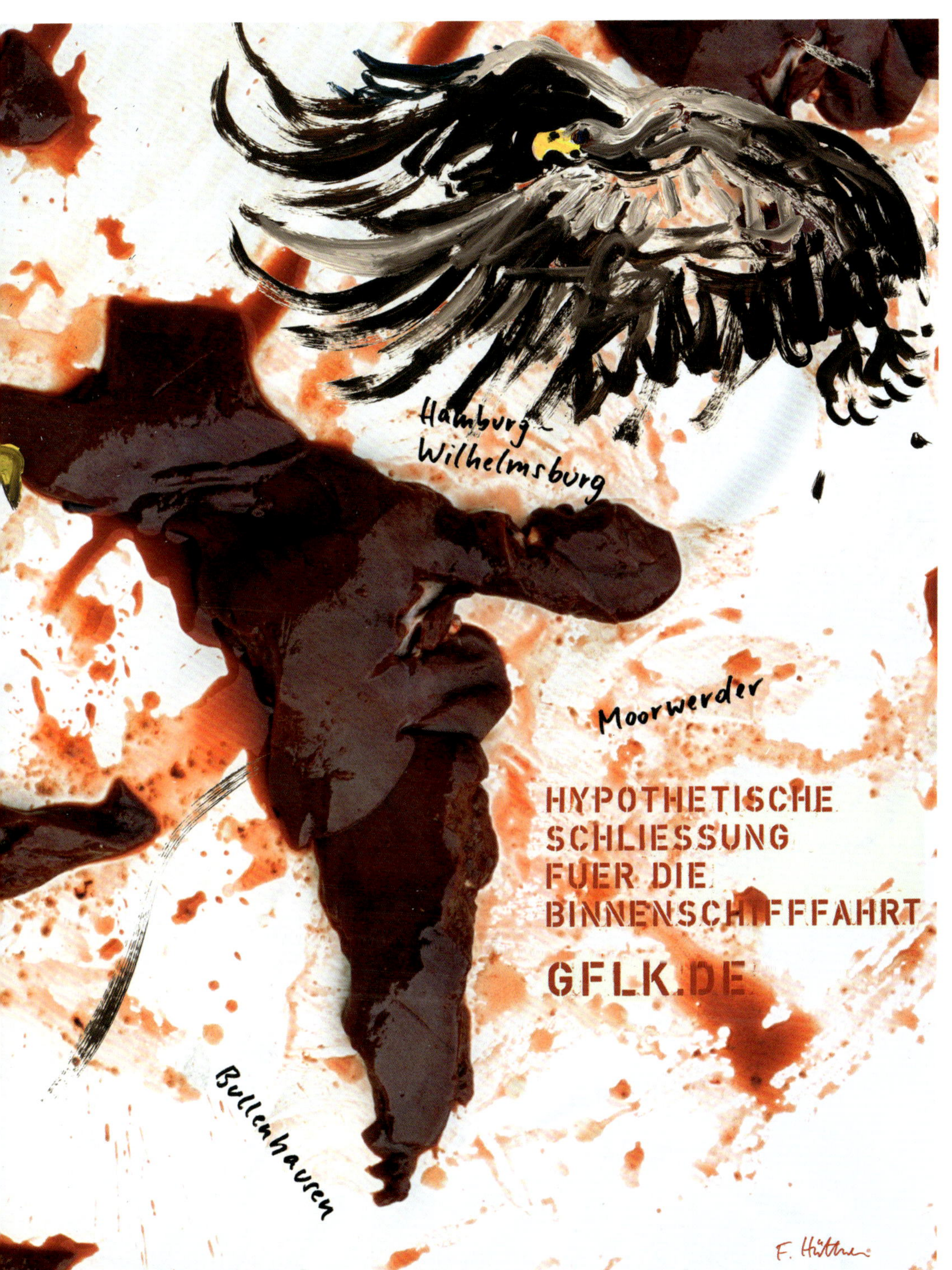

Hamburg-Wilhelmsburg
Moorwerder
Bullenhausen
HYPOTHETISCHE SCHLIESSUNG FUER DIE BINNENSCHIFFFAHRT
GFLK.DE
F. Hütter

Angelika Loderer
Schüttlöcher | Casted Holes,
2012

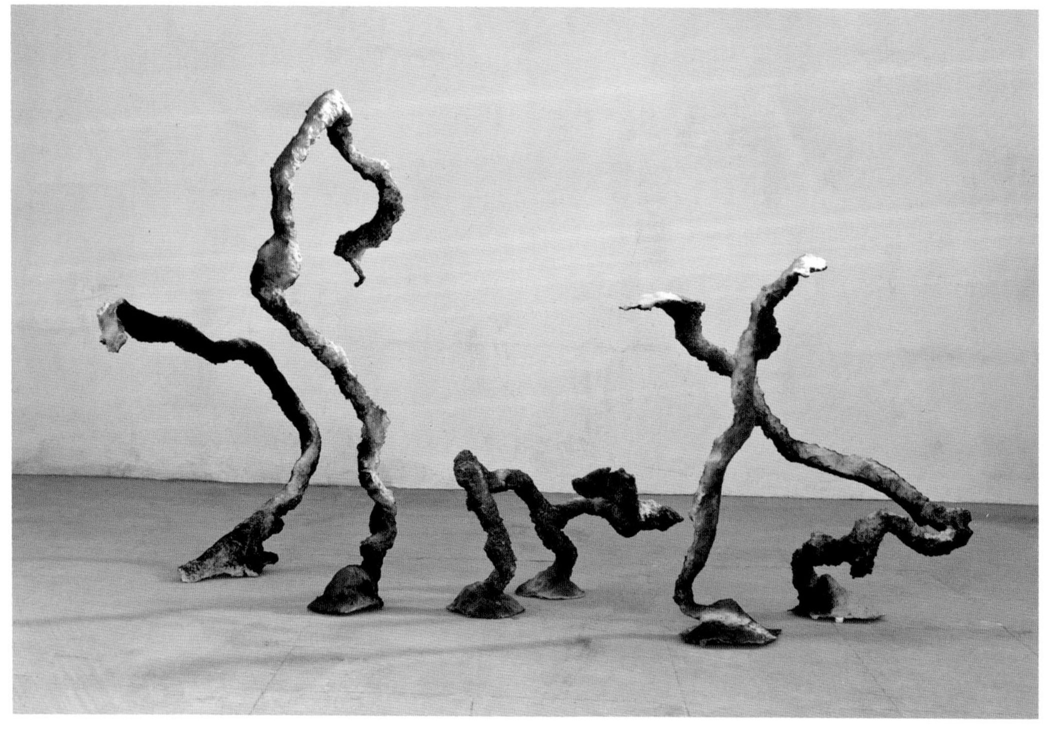

Angelika Loderer
Bäume, Entwurfsskizze für
Lärchen und Steine | Trees,
draft for *Larches and Stones*,
2015

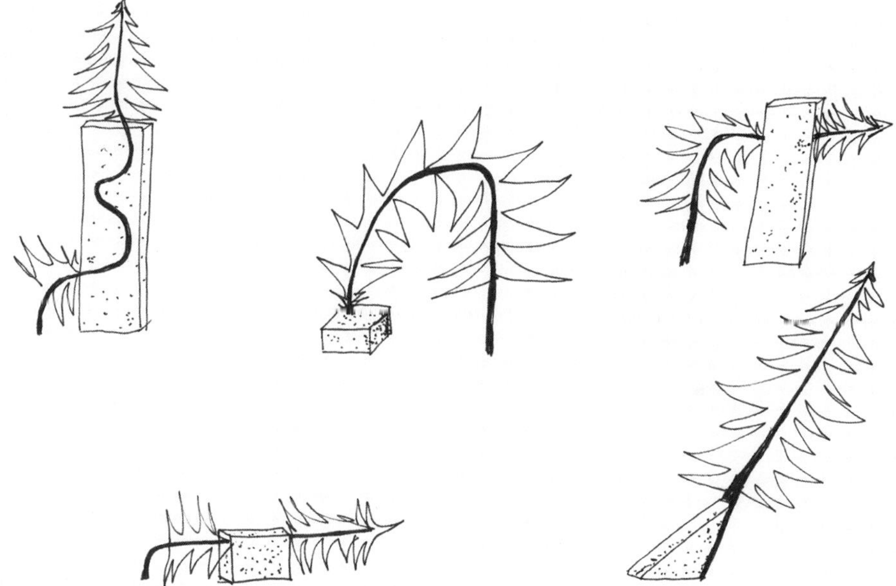

Susan Philipsz
Material für / material for *Slow
Fresh Fount*, Ausseerland,
2015

*Genter Altar, im Zustand
1945, Salzmine
Altaussee* / *Ghent altarpiece in
1945 condition, salt mine of
Altaussee*

Deckblatt zu *Slow Fresh
Fount*, Projektvorschlag für die
Salzmine Altaussee / cover for
Slow Fresh Fount, project
proposal for the salt mine of
Altaussee, 2015

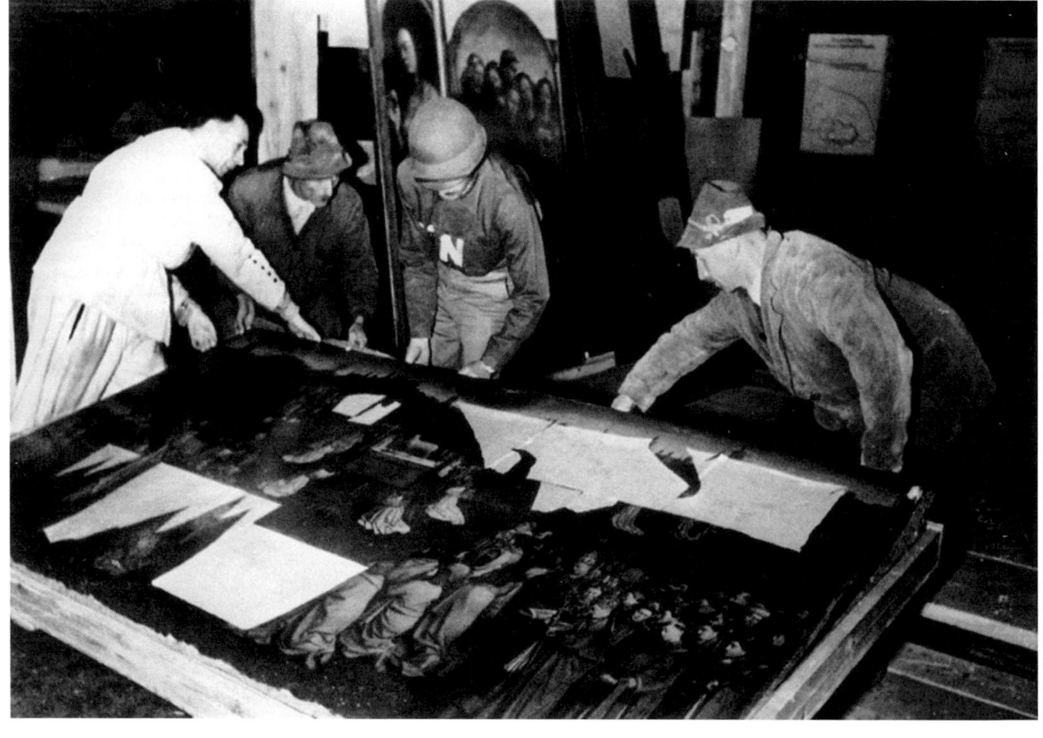

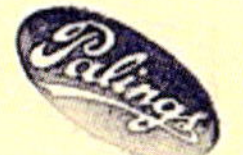

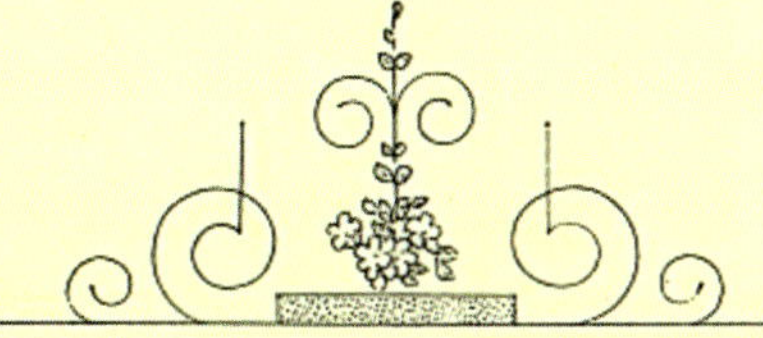

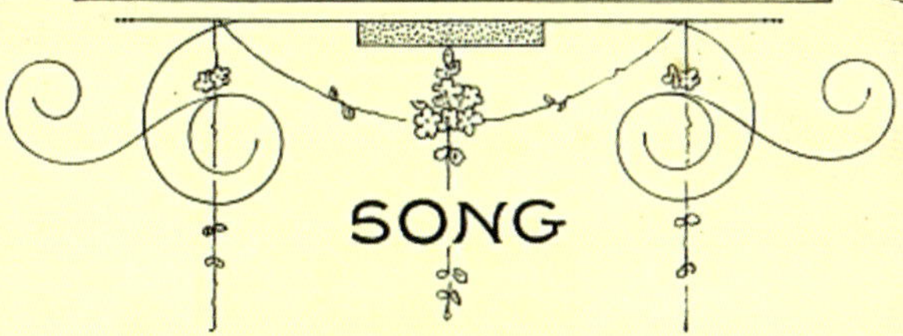

SLOW, SLOW, FRESH FOUNT

SONG

WORDS BY

BEN JONSON
[Elizabethan]

MUSIC BY

EDGAR L. BAINTON.

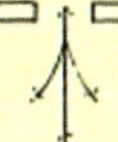

PRICE 2|- NET

JOSEPH WILLIAMS, LIMITED.
PUBLISHERS OF MUSIC, BOOKS AND DRAMATIC WORKS,
29, ENFORD STREET, MARYLEBONE
LONDON, W.1.

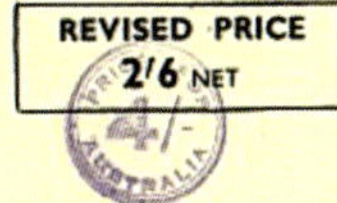

Bojan Šarčević
Material für / material for
The Partisan, Ausseerland,
2015

*Riesenmuschel Tridacna
gigas (Übernahme vom
österreichischen Zoll,
gemäß CITES Konvention /
Giant Clam Tridacna gigas
(Acquisition from Austrian
customs according to CITES
Convention)*

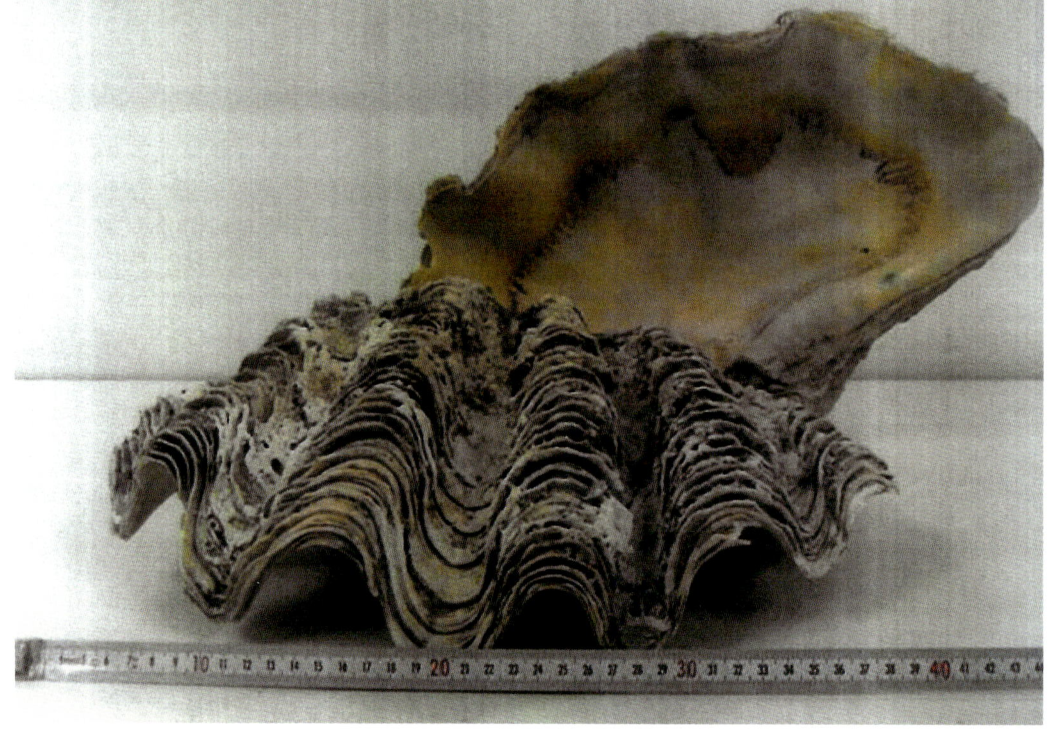

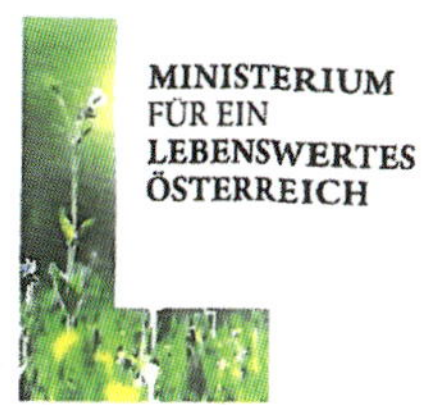

ÜBERNAHMEBESTÄTIGUNG
(zu Zl. BMLFUW-LE.1.5.5/0188-I/8/2014)

Das Institut für Kunst im öffentlichen Raum Steiermark des Joanneum Graz bestätigt die Übernahme von

2 Stück Riesenmuschelschalenhälften (wiss. Bez.: *Tridacna spp.*)

welche beschlagnahmt und als verfallen erklärt wurden und welche hiermit für Anschauungs-/Kunstzwecke in die Sammlung des Museums übertragen werden.

Datum: Unterschrift:

Stampiglie:
Universalmuseum
Joanneum GmbH

Mar… … 2-4, 8020 Graz, Austria

Concepts of Landscape
A Conversation
Sabine Flach, Peter Pakesch

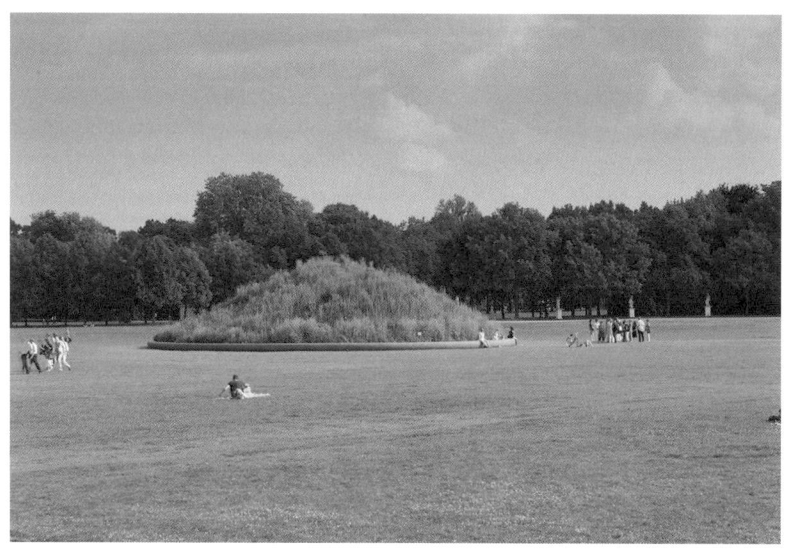

Song Dong
*Doing Nothing
Garden*, 2010-12,
documenta 13,
Kassel

Sabine Flach: Before we talk about the exhibitions on landscape,
the artistic positions and the Hyperrealism that dominated art of the
1970s, it seems to make sense first of all to outline the notion and
the concepts of landscape itself. Not only are landscape and nature
wrongly equated with one another, nature is likewise always thought
of in opposition to culture, which is simply incorrect. The artistic positions presented at documenta 13 showed clearly that not only can
this distinction no longer be maintained, but that it is in fact based on
fundamental misunderstandings. Take, for instance, the artistic positions of Claire Pentecost, Pierre Huyghe or of Song Dong, whose *Doing
Nothing Garden* seemed to invite us to idleness and contemplation.
There was a reason why the *Doing Nothing Garden* was located in the
pleasure garden, the Karlsaue. The apparent harmony of this work of

art, which addresses the classic *locus amoenus*, is subverted, however, when we realise that the hill on which grasses and flowers grew was artificially raised, and raised with rubbish, what's more—that is, largely with the remnants of consumer goods. We have to accept that when we consider modern art, say, a landscape with a rubbish dump is still a landscape. But what notion of landscape, of space, do we have in so doing?

Generally speaking, it is important to consider that a homogenous or homogenising notion of landscape does not exist any more than one of nature exists; and of course the same holds true for culture. In concrete terms, this means there is no uniform definition of landscape. Not only must we keep in mind that landscape can be utilised distinctly in geographical terms just as much as in philosophical-cultural terms, and thus implies other concepts, such as subjectivity, perception, space; landscape is also defined differently depending on the reference point concerned, be it aesthetic, economic, territorial, political or philosophical. And just as these reference points have to be kept separate from one another, so too do they all relate to one another. Overall, it is important to emphasise that notions and judgements about landscape are shaped by a history of culture and ideas, an essential role in which is played by art, art theory and aesthetics. In the arts, the aesthetic understanding of concepts of space and location are of course of vital importance, likewise the categories of perception and experience which are always linked to physical experience and thus sensory experiences. Clearly of significance here is also our historic understanding of landscape, which is quite different for Europe than for America. And it is precisely at this point that these concepts begin to take hold in art and show us which notions of landscape we must deal with. For America this is explicit, while we in Europe have quite a different image of landscape due to history, also because we originate from a continent of small states …

Peter Pakesch: Yes, our landscape was to some extent already distributed, while the American landscape was purportedly first settled, producing a different dynamic.

SF: And the romanticising image—a genre of art not to be underestimated, especially in the United States—also shapes ideas of landscape, of course: it comes from art and then works back into culture and our cultural interaction with landscape.

PP: I was greatly fascinated by the approach of the German environmentalist Hansjörg Küster, who also sees himself as a landscape scientist and would like to establish this as an interdisciplinary form of research. For example, he has demolished myths about nature and has pointedly told nature conservationists that there has been no pure natural space in Europe since time immemorial, that mankind has in fact always shaped it and that landscape without culture is inconceivable. Küster explicitly demands that we always reflect communally on the various aspects—whether scientific, political or historical in nature, or relating to the history of culture or art.[1] Thus entirely new concepts arise on the scientific, the environmentally-technological side—and what happens artistically plays an enormous part in that. Of course, the image of the Romantic landscape was also formed in this way, not only our understanding of landscape, but also specifically the way in which landscape functions and is used, and how it is then perverted once more by tourism, for example.

SF: Yes, indeed. I think that precisely the Romantic image of landscape shows that landscape is both subject and object at the same time, because I cannot have a landscape without a structure of mood as prescribed by a viewer who then conceives it. In this sense, landscape is always a projection, too. That would be the landscape painting, which also explicitly played a significant role in Sensibility, and then following that in Romanticism, with which the landscape as such was not depicted in a mimetic sense. What was depicted was a certain emotional structure, a mood. To this day, this still plays a significant role if it concerns the value placed on landscapes up to now. It is also interesting, however, when we look at Land Artists to see that a notion of landscape is used here that once again was formed quite differently. And so it is, I think, one of the most intriguing terms that one can use for contemporary art at the moment: what is the reality of landscape? And how does it work in the arts? For if we ascertain in this conversation that landscape is always first constructed, then one must consider: where has the reality of landscape gone to?

PP: I was interested by Smithson's text on one of the designers of Central Park, Frederick Law Olmsted.[2] It is fascinating to see how the artist draws on a romantic design of landscape, yet also interprets it as Land Art. He presents photos that look like Land Art and are part of a late Romantic design of landscape. Also, in his text *The Monuments of Passaic*,[3] he describes situations of an industrial nature as landscape and historical monument, and indeed at a time when that had not actually been thought of. I find it fascinating how explicitly he relocates these interventions into the description. Historically, that was an important step.

SF: I think in this context Land Art is—it shows in the name already—certainly one of the most important forms of art because it has so many variations. Though what I find interesting about Smithson is how intensely his works enter the realm of sculpture. He forms a sculpture from landscape itself, which is *materialiter* after all, while others work with the ephemeral things of landscape such as atmosphere.

PP: It is also exciting what has happened with *Spiral Jetty.* In the exhibition *Landscape in Motion* we see a film by James Benning, who filmed *Spiral Jetty* over a period of years, reflecting its passing and then its re-establishment in the restoration, bringing in a quite different dimension of time. We shall also show the reactions of other artists to it. Moreover, Benning is represented with his *California Trilogy,* an epochal work on the measuring of the present-day Californian landscape. The role of the sculptural, but also the filmic and the temporal dimension are quite fascinating.

→ p. 215

→ p. 214

SF: Would you say that when reflecting on America's landscapes, the factor of time plays a part? Due to the size of the country alone? If I take James Benning, to whom you also devoted an exhibition last year,[4] and the rolling trains he observed—these are fantastic investigations into landscape.

PP: In Benning's case time plays an important role for sure, and of course the dimension of magnitude as well. In the Benning solo show, *Decoding Fear,* located more historically, it concerned the importance of personalities such as Thoreau and his Romantic image of the landscape. What occurs concerning the specifically American: Karl Schlögel writes in his book *Im Raume lesen wir die Zeit* [Reading Time in Space] very impressively on the first map with the new federal states drawn by Jefferson, on which borders were first made using a ruler.[5] While the European landscape, the European geography was still determined by the topography, and history and topography have linked up here so to say, Jefferson broke with that in radical fashion. The original federal states still have topographical bearings, but then suddenly the new federal states are divided into orthogonal forms with the ruler. That immediately gives the structure for the land register—the division of America becomes an orthogonal one, the modular property thus becomes loanable and is introduced into the capitalist order, which is also useful for the financing of this conquest of land. So it is also interesting how cartographic processes provide the impetus for much else and what dynamics arise as a result. A great deal in America still belongs to this tradition. And precisely the railroad in Benning's works is significant in this regard. It was an important element in the conquest of the country.

SF: Yes, and it is relevant to see how different landscape constellations can be: because we don't have to deal so intensely with this

[4]
*James Benning.
Decoding Fear,*
Kunsthaus Graz, 2014.

[5]
Cf. Karl Schlögel: *Im
Raume lesen wir die
Zeit*, Munich 2003,
pp. 177ff.

relationship of the economy, in which the economy of space always has to be attached to the economy of the person. For us, everything was scattered in small states from the outset, and much more the case in earlier days than now. In America of course things are different. And so too the economisation of space with regard to one person who has to manipulate it is much more pronounced.

PP: In America the railroad was indeed replaced by the freeways, the highways. And so, as the railroad plays a part in Benning, so in Hyper-realism painting the automobile is important—as a representative of this exploitation of landscape and the interaction with it. Such elements of appropriation had an enormous significance from the 1950s on, greatly determining the definition of landscape.

SF: Absolutely. Also, in America landscape has to be connected more closely with the concept of nature than here. In Europe it had been a space of scattered settlements for centuries. As a result we deal with apparent spaces of nature quite differently. But if we think of Land Art works, for instance, then that is an 'experience'. The American-influenced artists exhibited here work very intensely with a notion of experience. It's not something one simply looks at. Many of the artists who work with landscape want to be experienced.

PP: Yes, and that is also often linked to interventions. That is a very active and dynamic concept.

SF: And in the intervention in turn, the political resonates. When we think of works by Hans Haacke or Gordon Matta-Clark, for example, where landscape is also lived-in urban space, then it becomes quite explicit.

PP: The Camera Austria exhibitions are very intensively involved with the political dimension, too—they negotiate other notions of landscape once again. This is also a highly charged topic in view of the continuing globalisation and the condensing of events: how can landscape be negotiated in future in a world that becomes ever more dense?

SF: And above all things: how has landscape changed? In the text on the exhibition *Landscape in Motion* you use a wonderful quotation from Max Frisch, *Man in the Holocene*. And if we now follow the latest discussions, then we have left the Holocene behind us, in which great interventions of 'nature' impact on us, and live now in the Anthropo-cene, which means that humankind determines geological and climatic changes, as Bruno Latour described it not only recently, but also in *We Have Never Been Modern*.[6] What is interesting for me, given that the

6
Bruno Latour: *We Have Never Been Modern.* Cambridge, MA 1993.

counter-movement to this exists in the arts, is: one shouldn't think anthropocentrically. These tendencies are among the most fascinating moments in contemporary art for me. For at the same time artists have to come to terms with the fact that the Anthropocene exists. We have placed ourselves at the centre of aesthetic, ecological, economic and political debates, and much depends on how we reflect upon landscape, upon nature, and especially the arts have a significant voice here.

PP: We are concerned here with a reconciliation between nature and culture among other things. Mankind sees himself as in between and has to come to terms with the possibilities of design.

SF: The Anthropocene presupposes that man is on the one side, doing something with things. If we see that the other way round, as it was seen in the arts throughout the whole of the 20th century, namely that man is a part of everything, then the whole picture shifts. Then one would have a setting in which man plays a part. And perhaps one could make progress if one—starting with the Smithson works, which show that wonderfully—no longer perpetuated this dichotomy between nature and culture. This is indeed the strength of the landscape picture in the arts. That landscape is precisely not nature, but rather always implies the *polis*. We make progress when we look closely at what the arts actually do. They show us in fact that what we assume to be landscape need not be in contradiction to us, nor to the concept of culture, but rather has always implied everything.

PP: Something decisive has happened in art in just the last 30 years. Here these definitions have been shifted correspondingly and man has been depicted more clearly as the actor—as someone who does act anyhow, but depicts it subsequently in a way that glosses it over.

SF: And the arts prove in a quite wonderful way that some things lie outside of a spectrum of experience. Works with animals, for instance, show, and we know this, that there is a world of perception that lies outside of our comprehension and which must yet be processed for us. Only then can we notice that all this belongs to it. If we think of works that deal with these gigantic dimensions of the US-American natural landscape, that also lies outside of our range of experience because it is simply too large. We can neither see it, nor include it, nor run it. It has a duration and an expanse that we cannot simply lay claim to.

PP: It is also interesting how, for example, legislators are considering to what extent the forest can become a legal entity—in one of Ursula Biemann's more recent works this is a theme.[7] Today people are

7
Forest Law, 2014, by Ursula Biemann and Paulo Tavares, was produced in the jungles of Ecuador where a few years ago nature was included in the constitution as a legal subject.

beginning to view plants differently, as it were to see the essence of plants in another way. Our understanding of this environment is becoming more complex, and for this quite different images are needed. Space is being redefined in a way that is new and quite emphatic.

SF: I really believe it is very important to pay heed to the artists who are showing that landscape is not something that is fixed, that tells us about nature or culture, but rather that it depends essentially on spatial experiences. This turn towards space which exists after all in theory already has its rationale, as we simply ascertain, as Michel Foucault formulated it, that we are living in a complexity of relations that are organised spatially and that must be understood. There is no one space, one landscape and one nature.

PP: Yes, these are quite different areas of meaning that merge into one another. And of course there is this date—which could be established as the 1970s and which is also interesting for our exhibitions—up to which point one had dealt with this resource, as we now call it so nicely these days, in a much more wasteful and unthinking way. And then suddenly this finiteness defines itself. It has a great deal to do with the quantities that we are confronted with, yet ultimately it is also a different comprehension of Earth, which is represented today in a quite different way to even 50 years ago. And I believe that it also requires a vision or the imagination of artists to define these things. Art delivers us with pictures for this, and in this context also other instructions on how to interact with them.

SF: Yes, if we think, for example, of the pictures of the universe by Thomas Ruff. They come after all from a quite different context; he didn't make them himself, he used them. So what do I see when I see that? But if one really engages with this kind of work, then actually one doesn't see anything anymore. It's rather like a challenge to question one's own range of experience: what do I see actually? It's no longer a question of recognising, rather of a question being put to me: what do you see now? And so I as viewer am dealt with in quite a different way. With photography, if you will. Is that still photography? I think that began in the 1970s, which is a decade in urgent need of research, as I find it one of the most important, because categories such as 'sculpture' or 'photography' began to totter.

PP: What was an important aspect for me within the landscape theme: there is a two complex of works by Thomas Struth, with pictures of all these large scientific machines and calculators—I found it interesting to interpret that as landscape, and briefly toyed with the idea of bringing it into the exhibition. Struth also photographs the settings of important events, including very many landscapes, because many important events have often occurred while walking takes place: take Lucius Burckhardt's *Strollology*.[8] The forms of movement that people make in space powerfully describe the notion of landscape, of course.

SF: With this we come to the beginning of modernism, Charles Baudelaire's *The Painter of Modern Life*.[9] Attached to modernity and in the experiential space of modernity, there belongs a certain form of behaviour in the sense of movement. With regard to walking through 'a spatiality', one of the great figures of the 20th century is surely the flâneur. And that is indeed quite typical for all of modernism: that a quite different habit was established of appropriating something in oneself. It is indeed interesting that everything near to us—in modernism and the present—also expects a quite special habit of appropriation. Practices of appropriation also play a part in landscape. But I wanted to come back to something else: what is actually our view of the Earth, you asked. I find that to be a great question! For where am I actually looking from when I sit at my computer and look at Google Earth and rush around the world with the camera and then zoom in. And then I am suddenly in the street where I live. What is then done actually? Where am I looking from then?

PP: Quite a lot coincides. Up to a certain point in time there may not have been eternity, but instead infinity and that stopped when the Americans conquered the territory in California. A great mythology resonates here too, which the Americans, primarily in their imagination, projected into outer space. These models came out of that, thus one speaks also of 'Space Ship Earth'. Here a perspective, which was absolutely binding for the image we see now, shifted drastically. I think that this question can also be understood from the zeitgeist of European philosophy at the time. Schlögel shows very beautifully how Jefferson introduces this very radical penetration of space and thus makes possible a quite different treatment of space from that which had been possible in the much more historically shaped Europe. And this space very much arises from an idealistic standpoint

SF: It also makes sense to have rationalistic, economic dealings with landscape. It depends on which country in Europe one is speaking of, as the British and Spaniards, for instance, with their policy of colonialisation, naturally had completely different ideas of landscape and occupation. To make something one's own is a gesture of usurpation that is incredible.

PP: Let us recall: in the 1970s and 1980s, when the woods dying was the all-dominating theme in Germany, the countries from Southern

8
Cf. Hannah Stippl: *What is Camouflage, What is Landscape?*, p. 334 in this catalogue.

9
Charles Baudelaire's essay *Le Peintre de la vie moderne* was published in 1863 in three parts in *Figaro*.

Europe shook their collective heads. The Spaniards, who on account of their colonial policies had long since chopped down the forests of the Iberian Peninsula, dealt with landscape in a completely different way. This heterogeneity still exists in Europe, I believe. At the same time, however, the European went to America with a certain idealistic concept, which in the spirit of a better world he wanted to do in a new and different way, and thus he determined this image of landscape, too. It is interesting how an entire mythology has arisen from this, which is still present in the most distant branches of Hollywood film; how one handles movement in this country.

SF: I think that also has to do with something that is very much embedded in European thought. This form of land grab, of immigration, but then also of expedition, if we think of Humboldt, for example, this setting off into unknown territory is of course determined in a completely different way, too. The reasons vary. And to migrate to America is not the same as exploring the Amazon. The gesture behind it, however, to set off into unknown territory, is a very European one, generally speaking.

PP: Of course, that has to do with the early periods of European science. The American land grab contained a mercantile, organisational aspect, yet derived from a similar attitude. It can only be understood from this culture.

SF: Absolutely, and I think we may not underestimate—I am very grateful for the prompt—the close connection to the sciences that the concept of landscape always has, too—if we think of Humboldt's cosmos, those are also publications that one may not forget. If we reflect on the notion of landscape today, scientific and aesthetic thinking mesh into one another very much.

PP: It will be interesting in a following phase to see how other cultural attitudes deal with the notion—keyword here East Asia—but also: what does that mean in Africa, what does that mean in other places. We touch upon these questions with single positions, but in this connection major themes are still to emerge.

SF: For sure major themes will arise which will have to be handled with the necessary caution. For as near as the Asian area seems to us, it is at the same time distant. I also find it right not to mix that in an exhibition. As globalisation shows, not all concepts are similar.

The Monuments of Passaic
Robert Smithson

Has Passaic replaced Rome as the eternal city?

He laughed softly. 'I know. There's no way out. Not through the Barrier. Maybe that isn't what I want, after all. But this … this …' He stared at the Monument. 'It seems all wrong sometimes. I just can't explain it. It's the whole city. It makes me feel haywire. Then I get these flashes …'
Henry Kuttner, *Jesting Pilot*

… today our unsophisticated cameras record in their own way our hastily assembled and painted world.
Vladimir Nabokov, *Invitation to a Beheading*

On Saturday, September 30, 1967, I went to the Port Authority Building on 41st Street and 8th Avenue. I bought a copy of the *New York Times* and a Signet paperback called *Earthworks* by Brain W. Aldiss. Next I went to ticket booth 21 and purchased a one-way ticket to Passaic. After that I went up to the upper bus level (platform 173) and boarded the number 30 bus of the Inter-City Transportation Co.
I sat down and opened the *Times*. I glanced over the art section: a 'Collectors', Critics', Curators' Choice' at A.M. Sachs Gallery (a letter I got in the mail that morning invited me 'to play the game before the show closes October 4th'), Walter Schatzki was selling 'Prints, Drawings, Watercolors' at '33⅓ % off,' Elinor Jenkins, the 'Romantic Realist,' was showing at Barzansky Galleries, XVIII—XIX Century English Furniture on sale at Parke-Bernet, 'New Directions in German Graphics' at Goethe House, and on page 29 was John Canaday's column. He was writing on *Themes and the Usual Variations*. I looked at a blurry reproduction of Samuel F. B. Morse's *Allegorical Landscape* at the top of Canaday's column; the sky was a subtle newsprint grey, and the clouds resembled sensitive stains of sweat reminiscent of a famous Yugoslav watercolorist whose name I have forgotten. A little statue with right arm held high faced a pond (or was it the sea?). 'Gothic' buildings in the allegory

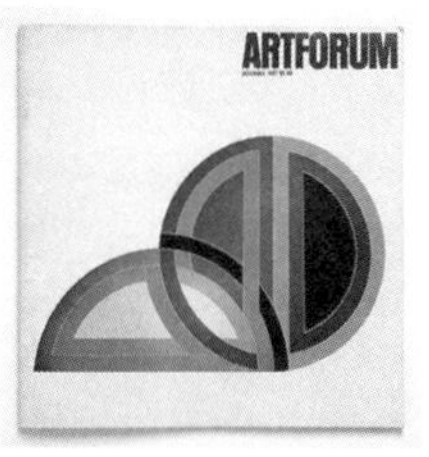

Artforum, December 1967

THE MONUMENTS OF PASSAIC

Has Passaic replaced Rome as the eternal city?

ROBERT SMITHSON

He laughed softly. 'I know. There's no way out. Not through the Barrier. Maybe that isn't what I want, after all. But this — this —' He stared at the Monument. 'It seems all wrong sometimes. I just can't explain it. It's the whole city. It makes me feel haywire. Then I get these flashes —'

—Henry Kuttner, *Jesting Pilot*

. . . today our unsophisticated cameras record in their own way our hastily assembled and painted world.

—Vladimir Nabokov, *Invitation to a Beheading*

On Saturday, September 30, 1967, I went to the Port Authority Building on 41st Street and 8th Avenue. I bought a copy of the *New York Times* and a Signet paperback called *Earthworks* by Brian W. Aldiss. Next I went to ticket booth 21 and purchased a one-way ticket to Passaic. After that I went up to the upper bus level (platform 173) and boarded the number 30 bus of the Inter-City Transportation Co.

I sat down and opened the *Times*. I glanced over the art section: a "Collectors', Critics', Curators' Choice" at A.M. Sachs Gallery (a letter I got in the mail that morning invited me "to play the game before the show closes October 4th"), Walter Schatzki was selling "Prints, Drawings, Watercolors" at "33⅓% off," Elinor Jenkins, the "Romantic Realist," was showing at Barzansky Galleries, XVIII — XIX Century English Furniture on sale at Parke-Bernet, "New Directions in German Graphics" at Goethe House, and on page 29 was John Canaday's column. He was writing on *Themes and the Usual Variations.* I looked at a blurry reproduction of Samuel F. B. Morse's *Allegorical Landscape* at the top of Canaday's column; the sky was a subtle newsprint grey, and the clouds resembled sensitive stains of sweat reminiscent of a famous Yugoslav watercolorist whose name I have forgotten. A little statue with right arm held high faced a pond (or was it the sea?). "Gothic" buildings in the allegory had a faded look, while an unnecessary tree (or was it a cloud of smoke?) seemed to puff up on the left side of the landscape. Canaday referred to the picture as "standing confidently along with other allegorical representatives of the arts, sciences, and high ideals that universities foster." My eyes stumbled over the newsprint, over such headlines as "Seasonal Upswing," "A Shuffle Service," and "Moving a 1,000 Pound Sculpture Can Be a Fine Work of Art, Too." Other gems of Canaday's dazzled my mind as I passed through Secaucus. "Realistic waxworks of raw meat beset by vermin," (Paul Thek) "Mr. Bush and his colleagues are wasting their time," (Jack Bush) "a book, an apple on a saucer, a rumpled cloth," (Thyra Davidson). Outside the bus window a Howard Johnson's Motor Lodge flew by — a symphony in orange and blue. On page 31 in Big Letters: THE EMERGING POLICE STATE IN AMERICA SPY GOVERNMENT. "In this book you will learn . . . what an Infinity Transmitter is."

The bus turned off Highway 3, down Orient Way in Rutherford.

I read the blurbs and skimmed through *Earthworks.* The first sentence read, "The dead man drifted along in the breeze." It seemed the book was about a soil shortage, and the Earthworks referred to the manufacture of artificial soil. The sky over Rutherford was a clear cobalt blue, a perfect Indian summer day, but the sky in *Earthworks* was a "great black and brown shield on which moisture gleamed."

The bus passed over the first monument. I pulled the buzzer-cord and got off at the corner of Union Avenue and River Drive. The monument was a bridge over the Passaic River that con-

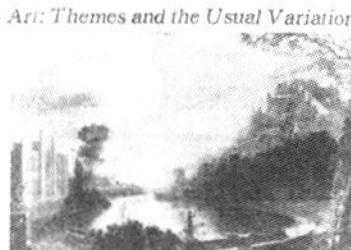

nected Bergen County with Passaic County. Noonday sunshine cinema-ized the site, turning the bridge and the river into an over-exposed picture. Photographing it with my Instamatic 400 was like photographing a photograph. The sun became a monstrous light-bulb that projected a detached series of "stills" through my Instamatic into my eye. When I walked on the bridge, it was as though I was walking on an enormous photograph that was made of wood and steel, and underneath the river existed as an enormous movie film that showed nothing but a continuous blank.

The steel road that passed over the water was in part an open grating flanked by wooden sidewalks, held up by a heavy set of beams, while above, a ramshackle network hung in the air. A rusty sign glinted in the sharp atmosphere, making it hard to read. A date flashed in the sunshine . . . 1899 . . . No . . . 1896 . . . maybe (at the bottom of the rust and glare was the name Dean & Westbrook Contractors, N.Y.). I was completely controlled by the Instamatic (or what the rationalists call a camera). The glare or of New Jersey defined the structural parts of the monument as I took snapshot after snapshot. A barge seemed fixed to the surface of the water as it came toward the bridge, and caused the bridgekeeper to close the gates. From the banks of Passaic I watched the bridge rotate on a central axis in order to allow an inert rectangular shape to pass with its unknown cargo. The Passaic (West) end of the bridge rotated south, while the Rutherford (East) end of the bridge rotated north; such rotations suggested the limited movements of an outmoded world. "North" and "South" hung over the static river in a bi-polar manner. One could refer to this bridge as the "Monument of Dislocated Directions."

Along the Passaic River banks were many minor monuments such as concrete abutments that supported the shoulders of a new highway in the process of being built. River Drive was in part bulldozed and in part intact. It was hard to tell the new highway from the old road; they were both confounded into a unitary chaos. Since it was Saturday, many machines were not working, and this caused them to resemble prehistoric creatures trapped in the mud, or better, extinct machines — mechanical dinosaurs stripped of their skin. On the edge of this prehistoric Machine Age were pre- and post-World War II suburban houses. The houses mirrored themselves into colorlessness. A group of children were throwing rocks at each other near a ditch. "From now on you're not going to come to our hide-out. And I mean it!" said a little blonde girl who had been hit with a rock.

As I walked north along what was left of River Drive, I saw a monument in the middle of the river — it was a pumping derrick with a long pipe attached to it. The pipe was supported in part by a set of pontoons, while the rest of it extended about three blocks along the river bank till it disappeared into the earth. One could hear

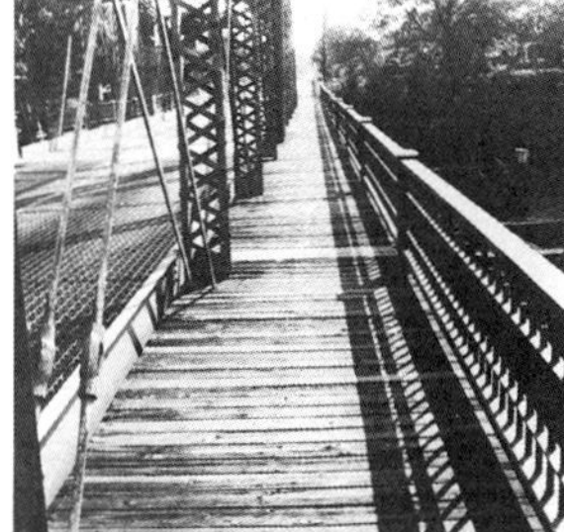
The Bridge Monument Showing Wooden Sidewalks. (Photo: Robert Smithson)

---

debris rattling in the water that passed through the great pipe.

Nearby, on the river bank, was an artificial crater that contained a pale limpid pond of water, and from the side of the crater protruded six large pipes that gushed the water of the pond into the river. This constituted a monumental fountain that suggested six horizontal smokestacks that seemed to be flooding the river with liquid smoke. The great pipe was in some enigmatic way connected with the infernal fountain. It was as though the pipe was secretly sodomizing some hidden technological orifice, and causing a monstrous sexual organ (the fountain) to have an orgasm. A psychoanalyst might say that the landscape displayed "homosexual tendencies," but I will not draw such a crass anthropomorphic conclusion. I will merely say, "It was there."

Across the river in Rutherford one could hear the faint voice of a P.A. system and the weak cheers of a crowd at a football game. Actually, the landscape was no landscape, but "a particular kind of heliotypy" (Nabokov), a kind of self-destroying postcard world of failed immortality and oppressive grandeur. I had been wandering in a moving picture that I couldn't quite picture, but just as I became perplexed I saw a green sign that explained everything.

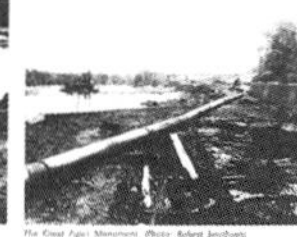
Monument with Pontoons: The Pumping Derrick. (Photo: Robert Smithson)

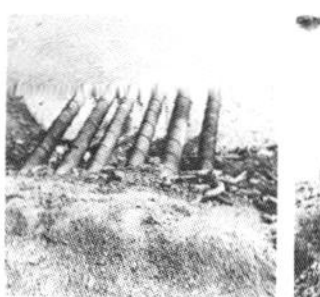
The Fountain Monument — Bird's Eye View. (Photo: Robert Smithson)

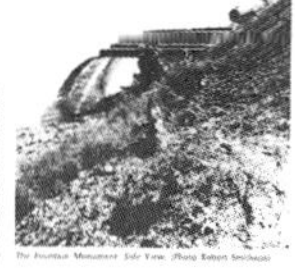
The Fountain Monument Side View. (Photo: Robert Smithson)

That zero panorama seemed to contain ruins in reverse, that is — all the new construction that would eventually be built. This is the opposite of the "romantic ruin" because the buildings don't fall into ruin after they are built but rather rise into ruin before they are built. This anti-romantic mise-en-scene suggests the discredited idea of time and many other "out of date" things. But the suburbs exist without a rational past and without the "big events" of history. Oh, maybe there are a few statues, a legend, and a couple of curios, but no past — just what passes for a future. A Utopia minus a bottom, a place where the machines are idle, and the sun has turned to glass, and a place where the Passaic Concrete Plant (253 River Drive) does a good business in STONE, BITUMINOUS, SAND and CEMENT. Passaic seems full of "holes" compared to New York City, which seems tightly packed and solid, and those holes in a sense are the monumental vacancies that define, without trying, the memory-traces of an abandoned set of futures. Such futures are found in grade B Utopian films, and then imitated by the suburbanite. The windows of City Motors auto sales proclaim the existence of Utopia through 1968 OVER TRACK PONTIACS — Executive, Bonneville, Tempest, Grand Prix, Firebird, GTO, Catalina, and LeMans — that visual

incantation marked the end of the highway construction.

Next I descended into a set of used car lots. I must say the situation seemed like a change. Was I in a new territory? (An English artist, Michael Baldwin, says: "It could be asked if the country does in fact change — it does not in the sense a traffic light does.") Perhaps I had slipped into a lower stage of futurity — did I leave the real future behind in order to advance into a false future? Yes, I did. Reality was behind me at that point in my suburban Odyssey.

Passaic center loomed like a dull adjective. Each "store" in it was an adjective unto the next, a chain of adjectives disguised as stores. I began to run out of film, and I was getting hungry. Actually, Passaic center was no center — it was instead a typical abyss or an ordinary void. What a great place for a gallery! Or maybe an "outdoor sculpture show" would pep that place up. At the Golden Coach Diner (11 Central Avenue) I had my lunch, and loaded my Instamatic. I looked at the orange-yellow box of Kodak Verichrome Pan, and read a notice that said:

After that I returned to Passaic, or was it the hereafter — for all I know that unimaginative suburb could have been a clumsy eternity, a cheap copy of The City of the Immortals. But who am I to entertain such a thought? I walked down a parking lot that covered the old railroad tracks which at one time ran through the middle of Passaic. That monumental parking lot divided the city in half, turning it into a mirror and a reflection — but the mirror kept changing places with the reflection. One never knew what side of the mirror one was on. There was nothing interesting or even strange about that flat monument, yet it echoed a kind of cliche idea of infinity; perhaps the "secrets of the universe" are just as pedestrian — not to say dreary. Everything about the site remained wrapped in blandness and littered with shiny cars — one after another they extended into a sunny nebulosity. The indifferent backs of the cars flashed and reflected the stale afternoon sun. I took a few listless, entropic snapshots of that lustrous monument. If the future is "out of date" and "old fashioned," then I had been in the future. I had been on a planet that had a map of Passaic drawn over it, and a rather imperfect map at that. A sidereal map marked up with "lines" the size of streets, and "squares" and "blocks" the size of buildings. At any moment my feet were apt to

fall through the cardboard ground. I am convinced that the future is lost somewhere in the dumps of the non-historical past; it is in yesterday's newspapers, in the jejune advertisements of science-fiction movies, in the false mirror of our rejected dreams. Time turns metaphors into things, and stacks them up in cold rooms, or places them in the celestial playgrounds of the suburbs.

Has Passaic replaced Rome as The Eternal City? If certain cities of the world were placed end to end in a straight line according to size, starting with Rome, where would Passaic be in that impossible progression? Each city would be a three-dimensional mirror that would reflect the next city into existence. The limits of eternity seem to contain such nefarious ideas.

The last monument was a sand box or a model desert. Under the dead light of the Passaic afternoon the desert became a map of infinite disintegration and forgetfulness. This monument of minute particles blazed under a bleakly glowing sun, and suggested the sullen dissolution of entire continents, the drying up of oceans — no longer were there green forests and high mountains — all that existed were millions of grains of sand, a vast deposit of bones and stones pulverized into dust. Every grain of sand was a dead metaphor that equaled timelessness, and to decipher such metaphors would take one through the false mirror of eternity. This sand box somehow doubled as an open grave — a grave that children cheerfully play in.

. . . all sense of reality was gone. In its place had come deep-seated illusions, absence of pupillary reaction to light, absence of knee reaction — symptoms all of progressive cerebral meningitis: the blanketing of the brain . . .

—Louis Sullivan, "one of the greatest of all architects," quoted in Michel Butor's *Mobile.*

I should now like to prove the irreversibility of eternity by using a jejune experiment for proving entropy. Picture in your mind's eye the sand box divided in half with black sand on one side and white sand on the other. We take a child and have him run hundreds of times clockwise in the box until the sand gets mixed and begins to turn grey; after that we have him run anti-clockwise, but the result will not be a restoration of the original division but a greater degree of greyness and an increase of entropy.

Of course, if we filmed such an experiment we could prove the reversibility of eternity by showing the film backwards, but then sooner or later the film itself would crumble or get lost and enter the state of irreversibility. Somehow this suggests that the cinema offers an illusive or temporary escape from physical dissolution. The false immortality of the film gives the viewer an illusion of control over eternity — but "the superstars" are fading. ∎

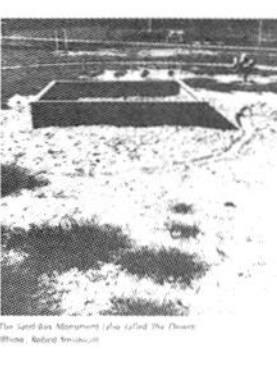
The Sand-Box Monument (also called The Desert). (Photo: Robert Smithson)

Negative Map Showing Region of the Monuments along the Passaic River.

had a faded look, while an unnecessary tree (or was it a cloud of smoke?) seemed to puff up on the left side of the landscape. Canaday referred to the picture as 'standing confidently along with other allegorical representatives of the arts, sciences, and high ideals that universities foster.' My eyes stumbled over the newsprint, over such headlines as 'Seasonal Upswing,' 'A Shuffle Service,' and 'Moving a 1,000 Pound Sculpture Can Be a Fine Work of Art, Too.' Other gems of Canaday's dazzled my mind as I passed through Secaucus. 'Realistic waxworks of raw meat beset by vermin,' (Paul Thek), 'Mr. Bush and his colleagues are wasting their time,' (Jack Bush), 'a book, an apple on a saucer, a rumpled cloth,' (Thyra Davidson). Outside the bus window a Howard Johnson's Motor Lodge flew by—a symphony in orange and blue. On page 31 in Big Letters: THE EMERGING POLICE STATE IN AMERICA SPY GOVERNMENT. 'In this book you will learn … what an Infinity Transmitter is.'
The bus turned off Highway 3, down Orient Way in Rutherford.
I read the blurbs and skimmed through *Earthworks*. The first sentence read, 'The dead man drifted along in the breeze.' It seemed the book was about a soil shortage, and the *Earthworks* referred to the manufacture of artificial soil. The sky over Rutherford was a clear cobalt blue, a perfect Indian summer day, but the sky in *Earthworks* was a 'great black and brown shield on which moisture gleamed.'
The bus passed over the first monument. I pulled the buzzer-cord and got off at the corner of Union Avenue and River Drive. The monument was a bridge over the Passaic River that connected Bergen County with Passaic County. Noonday sunshine cinema-ized the site, turning the bridge and the river into an over-exposed picture. Photographing it with my Instamatic 400 was like photographing a photograph. The sun became a monstrous light-bulb that projected a detached series of 'stills' through my Instamatic into my eye. When I walked on the bridge, it was as though I was walking on an enormous photograph that was made of wood and steel, and underneath the river existed as an enormous movie film that showed nothing but a continuous blank.
The steel road that passed over the water was in part an open grating flanked by wooden sidewalks, held up by a heavy set of beams, while above, a ramshackle network hung in the air. A rusty sign glared in the sharp atmosphere, making it hard to read. A date flashed in the sunshine … 1899 … No … 1896 … maybe (at the bottom of the rust and glare was the name Dean & Westbrook Contractors, N. Y.). I was completely controlled by the Instamatic (or what the rationalists call a camera). The glassy air of New Jersey defined the structural parts of the monument as I took snapshot after snapshot. A barge seemed fixed to the surface of the water as it came toward the bridge, and caused the bridgekeeper to close the gates. From the banks of Passaic I watched the bridge, and caused the bridgekeeper to close the gates. From the banks of Passaic I watched the bridge rotate on a central axis

in order to allow an inert rectangular shape to pass with its unknown
cargo. The Passaic (West) end of the bridge rotated south, while the
Rutherford (East) end of the bridge rotated north; such rotations
suggested the limited movements of an outmoded world. 'North' and
'South' hung over the static river in a bi-polar manner. One could refer
to this bridge as the 'Monument of Dislocated Directions.'
Along the Passaic River banks were many minor monuments such as
concrete abutments that supported the shoulders of a new highway
in the process of being built. River Drive was in part bulldozed and
in part intact. It was hard to tell the new highway from the old road;
they were both confounded into a unitary chaos. Since it was Saturday,
many machines were not working, and this caused them to resemble
prehistoric creatures trapped in the mud, or, better, extinct machines—
mechanical dinosaurs stripped of their skin. On the edge of this prehistoric Machine Age were pre- and post-World War II suburban houses.
The houses mirrored themselves into colorlessness. A group of children
were throwing rocks at each other near a ditch. 'From now on you're not
going to come to our hide-out. And I mean it!' said a little blonde girl
who had been hit with a rock.
As I walked north along what was left of River Drive, I saw a monument
in the middle of the river—it was a pumping derrick with a long pipe
attached to it. The pipe was supported in part by a set of pontoons,
while the rest of it extended about three blocks along the river bank
till it disappeared into the earth. One could hear debris rattling in the
water that passed through the great pipe.
Nearby, on the river bank, was an artificial crater that contained a pale
limpid pond of water, and from the side of the crater protruded six large
pipes that gushed the water of the pond into the river. This constituted
a monumental fountain that suggested six horizontal smokestacks that
seemed to be flooding the river with liquid smoke. The great pipe was
in some enigmatic way connected with the infernal fountain. It was as
though the pipe was secretly sodomizing some hidden technological
orifice, and causing a monstrous sexual organ (the fountain) to have
an orgasm. A psychoanalyst might say that the landscape displayed
'homosexual tendencies,' but I will not draw such a crass anthropomorphic conclusion. I will merely say, 'It was there.'
Across the river in Rutherford one could hear the faint voice of a P. A.
system and the weak cheers of a crowd at a football game. Actually,
the landscape was no landscape, but 'a particular kind of heliotypy'
(Nabokov), a kind of selfdestroying postcard world of failed immortality
and oppressive grandeur. I had been wandering in a moving picture that
I couldn't quite picture, but just as I became perplexed, I saw a green
sign that explained everything:

YOUR HIGHWAY TAXES   21
AT WORK

Federal Highway Trust Funds
2,867,000

U.S. Dept. Of Commerce
Bureau of Public Roads
State Highway Funds
2,867,000
New Jersey State Highway Dept.

That zero panorama seemed to contain ruins in reverse, that is—all the new construction that would eventually be built. This is the opposite of the 'romantic ruin' because the buildings don't fall into ruin after they are built but rather rise into ruin before they are built. This anti-romantic *mise-en-scene* suggests the discredited idea of *time* and many other 'out of date' things. But the suburbs exist without a rational past and without the 'big events' of history. Oh, maybe there are a few statues, a legend, and a couple of curios, but no past—just what passes for a future. A Utopia minus a bottom, a place where the machines are idle, and the sun has turned to glass, and a place where the Passaic Concrete Plant (253 River Drive) does a good business in STONE, BITU-MINOUS, SAND, and CEMENT. Passaic seems full of 'holes' compared to New York City, which seems tightly packed and solid, and those holes in a sense are the monumental vacancies that define, without trying, the memory-traces of an abandoned set of futures. Such futures are found in grade B Utopian films, and then imitated by the suburbanite. The windows of City Motors auto sales proclaim the existence of Utopia through 1968 WIDE TRACK PONTIACS—Executive, Bonneville, Tempest, Grand Prix, Firebirds, GTO, Catalina, and LeMans—that visual incantation marked the end of the highway construction.
Next I descended into a set of used car lots. I must say the situation seemed like a change. Was I in a new territory? (An English artist, Michael Baldwin, says, 'It could be asked if the country does in fact change—it does not in the sense a traffic light does.') Perhaps I had slipped into a lower stage of futurity—did I leave the real future behind in order to advance into a false future? Yes, I did. Reality was behind me at that point in my suburban Odyssey.

Passaic center loomed like a dull adjective. Each 'store' in it was an adjective unto the next, a chain of adjectives disguised as stores. I began to run out of film, and I was getting hungry. Actually, Passaic center was no center—it was instead a typical abyss or an ordinary void. What a great place for a gallery! Or maybe an 'outdoor sculpture show' would pep that place up.
At the Golden Coach Diner (11 Central Avenue) I had my lunch, and loaded my Instamatic. I looked at the orange-yellow box of Kodak Verichrome Pan, and read a notice that said:

After that I returned to Passaic, or was it the *hereafter*—for all I know that unimaginative suburb could have been a clumsy eternity, a cheap copy of The City of the Immortals. But who am I to entertain such a thought? I walked down a parking lot that covered the old railroad tracks which at one time ran through the middle of Passaic. That monumental parking lot divided the city in half, turning it into a mirror and a reflection—but the mirror kept changing places with the reflection. One never knew what side of the mirror one was on. There was nothing interesting or even strange about that flat monument, yet it echoed a kind of cliché idea of infinity; perhaps the 'secrets of the universe' are just as pedestrian—not to say dreary. Everything about the site remained wrapped in blandness and littered with shiny cars—one after another they extended into a sunny nebulosity. The indifferent backs of the cars flashed and reflected the stale afternoon sun. I took a few listless, entropic snapshots of that lustrous monument. If the future is 'out of date' and 'old fashioned,' then I had been in the future. I had been on a planet that had a map of Passaic drawn over it, and a rather imperfect map at that. A sidereal map marked up with 'lines' the size of streets, and 'squares' and 'blocks' the size of buildings. At any moment my feet were apt to fall through the cardboard ground. I am convinced that the future is lost somewhere in the dumps of the non-historical past; it is in yesterday's newspapers, in the *jejune* advertisements of science-fiction movies, in the false mirror of our rejected dreams. Time turns metaphors into *things*, and stacks them up in cold rooms, or places them in the celestial playgrounds of the suburbs. Has Passaic replaced Rome as The Eternal City? If certain cities of the world were placed end to end in a straight line according to size, starting with Rome, where would Passaic be in that impossible progression? Each city would be a three-dimensional mirror that would reflect the next city into existence. The limits of eternity seem to contain such nefarious ideas.

The last monument was a sand box or a model desert. Under the dead light of the Passaic afternoon the desert became a map of infinite disintegration and forgetfulness. This monument of minute particles blazed under a bleakly glowing sun, and suggested the sullen dissolution of entire continents, the drying up of oceans—no longer were there green forests and high mountains—all that existed were millions of grains of sand, a vast deposit of bones and stones pulverized into dust. Every grain of sand was a dead metaphor that equaled timelessness, and to decipher such metaphors would take one through the false mirror of eternity. This sand box somehow doubled as an open grave—a grave that children cheerfully play in.

… all sense of reality was gone. In its place had come deep-seated illusions, absence of pupillary reaction to light, absence of knee reaction—symptoms all of progressive cerebral meningitis: the blanketing of the brain …
—Louis Sullivan, 'one of the greatest of all architects,' quoted in Michel Butor's *Mobile*.

I should now like to prove the irreversibility of eternity by using a *jejune* experiment for proving entropy. Picture in your mind's eye the sand box divided in half with black sand on one side and white sand on the other. We take a child and have him run hundreds of times clockwise in the box until the sand gets mixed and begins to turn grey; after that we have him run anti-clockwise, but the result will not be a restoration of the original division but a greater degree of greyness and an increase of entropy.
Of course, if we filmed such an experiment we could prove the reversibility of eternity by showing the film backwards, but then sooner or later the film itself would crumble or get lost and enter the state of irreversibility. Somehow this suggests that the cinema offers an illusive or temporary escape from physical dissolution. The false immortality of the film gives the viewer an illusion of control over eternity—but 'the superstars' are fading.

American Space: The Poetics of the Highway

Karl Schlögel

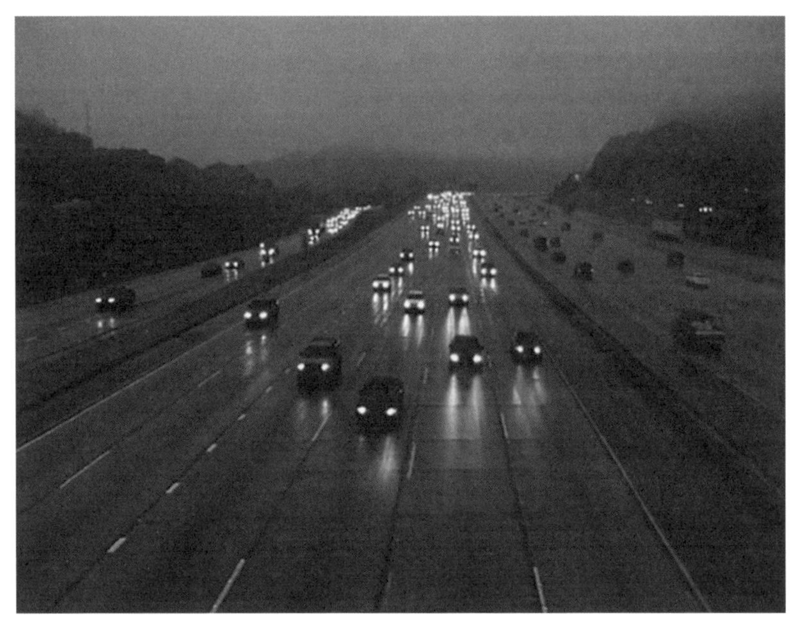

James Benning
Los, 2000, from:
California Trilogy,
1999–2001, film still

Excerpt from: *Im Raume
lesen wir die Zeit. Über
Zivilisationsgeschichte
und Geopolitik*. Fischer
Taschenbuchverlag /
Hanser: Munich 2003,
pp. 379–392.

The highway is the most conspicuous emblem of the American 20th
century. It stretches for well over a hundred thousand miles from
one end of the continent to the other. Perhaps the highway—or more
precisely, the entire web of freeways, expressways, turnpikes and park-
ways—is the preeminent hieroglyph engraved upon the planet by man.
It was the highway that turned the continent into America, that truly
made it the United States of America.[1] [...]
The highway network transforms mere space into a territory. It is the
way that leads into America and into a world that has become like
America. It is not just a form of movement but what Marx called a 'form
of intercourse.' It represents a social relation or, to use the American

term, a *way of life*; hardly surprising in a society in which more than 90 percent of adults have a car and daily life in many places would be impossible without one. The highway is where America is a 'nation on wheels', where the human being shows himself to be the 'territorial animal' par excellence, as John Brinckerhoff Jackson put it. The Interstate Highway System is a system of superlatives, of superhighways: although its roughly 50,000 miles are no more than 1 percent of the total road U.S. system, about one quarter of the country's passenger traffic and almost half of all freight traffic circulate on the interstates. The system is ten times the size of pre-reunification West Germany's autobahn and thirty times that of Great Britain's network of motorways. The traffic streaming on the highway is at the basis of the nation's markets and the relation between downtown and suburbia. The highway network produces the American space no less than the gridiron plan that structures the nation's territory.

The production of American space. Any visitor knows: you have not fully arrived in America when you have landed at JFK and taken the train into Manhattan. America starts somewhere else; perhaps with the rites of passage you have to go through at the agency—Budget, Hertz, Dollar—where you pick up the keys for your rental car. Then the final barrier has fallen, the last restriction is undone, there is no stopping you: the entire continent lies open before you, and you enter the 'America of the empty, absolute freedom of the freeways'.[2] You find yourself adopting a specific mode of movement. You are free to go or drive wherever you want. No one will detain you as long as you follow a basic set of rules and have enough money to pay your way when you need to stop or stray from the main route on a whim. The highway functions in accordance with uniform laws set down in the Federal Aid Highway Act of 1956. They apply where you enter the system no less than where you leave it, along the country's densely populated eastern seaboard no less than in the desert you must traverse. It overlies the country's relief without regard for its diversity. Wherever you go, it consists of at least two lanes per direction, each of which is exactly twelve feet wide, and a 10-foot shoulder. The median between the roadways for each direction is so wide that you would have to be insane to cause a head-on crash. The highway is designed for travel at 50 to 70 miles per hour and uninterrupted movement; there are no intersections where you might have to yield to other vehicles or so much as slow down. The only red lights you will encounter are at the toll plazas. The two roadways are parallel white ribbons of concrete drawn by man across the earth's surface, clinging to its relief, extending straight ahead toward the horizon, plunging into tunnels, feeding into the grid from which the towers of a downtown rise, bridging valleys and flying over plains, edging up hillsides or cutting through the steepest ridges in artificial canyons.[3] They are America's handwriting in the Garden of Eden—magnificent and

1
See Bruce E. Seely:
Building the American Highway System. Engineers as Policy Makers. Philadelphia 1987; James J. Flink: *The Automobile Age*. Cambridge, MA 1988. For a general history of traffic routes, see Maxwell G. Lay. *Ways of the World. A History of the World's Roads and of the Vehicles That Used Them*. New Brunswick 1992.

2
Jean Baudrillard: *America* (trans. Chris Turner). London/New York 1988, p. 5; see also James Howard Kunstler's excellent *The Geography of Nowhere. The Rise and Decline of America's Man-Made Landscape*. New York 1993. I have touched on the production of the American space in 'Glückliches Amerika, armes Rußland', in: Karl Schlögel: *Die Mitte liegt ostwärts. Europa im Übergang*. Munich 2002, pp. 168–85.

3
See also Laurence Ilsley Hewes: *American Highway Practice*, vol. 1. New York/London 1942.

powerful, grand flourishes of the planner's pen. Without ever leaving the highway, you can cover thousands of miles, crossing tens of thousands of bridges and, especially in urban areas, travelling high above the ground on viaducts, raised highways, overpasses. That is the monumental hieroglyph we espy from the airplane, the steady and unceasing stream of traffic as seen from police helicopters and in innumerable movies: endless in all directions, an even flow, always in keeping with the defined norms and standards set decades ago. The immense movements of the great multitude engenders its own form, uniformity, a mild monotony. John Brinckerhoff Jackson writes:

The highway never seems to end. There is an occasional brightly lit truck stop and the lights of a bypassed town. Rows of trucks are parked for the night at rest areas, and with the hours of solitary travel there comes a mood of introspection. A favorite episode in novels and movies and television shows laid in the American heartland is that lonesome ride through the night landscape: an occasion for remembering other times. You think back over your past, think about your work, think about your destination and about those you have left. The dashboard display shows how fast you are driving, tells you the hour and how many more miles you still have to go. The sameness of the American landscape overwhelms and liberates you from any sense of place. Familiarity makes you feel everywhere at home. A sense of time passing makes you gradually increase your speed. This all-pervading sameness is by and large the product of the grid—not simply the grid of streets in every town and city west of the Mississippi, but that enormous grid which covers two-thirds of the nation, stretching from the Mississippi and Ohio to the Pacific, from the Rio Grande to the Canadian border, beyond which it extends in a slightly modified form well into the northern subarctic forest. It is this grid, not the eagle or the stars and stripes, which is our true national emblem. I think it must be imprinted at the moment of conception on every American child, to remain throughout his or her life a way of calculating not only space but movement.[4] There are no bottlenecks, no unforeseen obstacles or bends. The road accommodates itself to nature, but it does not defer to it. Everything is foreseeable, everything can be adjusted to without stopping. Directions are provided en route, and so their language and symbolism must be easily legible, pared down to the gist: numbers and letters. The system is simple: the primary routes are assigned one- and two-digit numbers, odd for north-south highways and even for east-west highways. Numbering begins in the west for north-south routes and in the south for west-east routes. This scheme lets the driver navigate the North American continent with the greatest convenience imaginable.

Everything must be unambiguous and recognisable at first glance. Anyone and anything meant to be seen must be discernible and

4
John Brinckerhoff Jackson: *A Sense of Place, a Sense of Time.* New Haven 1994, pp. 152–53; see also John Brinckerhoff Jackson: *Discovering the Vernacular Landscape.* New Haven 1984.

recognisable from the moving car: visibility is the first principle of the roadside aesthetic. Whole landscapes come into being that are designed with a view to the automobile flâneur, that address the traveller and seek to attract his attention with their proportions, distances, colours, illuminations. Entire cities are built whose layout and life centres on the strip. Las Vegas was the prototype—now cities all over the world have 'learned from Las Vegas.'[5] The highway engendered the American landscape, the conjunction of city and wide country, the ebb and flow between the centers of civilisation and the national parks where visitors marvel at the volcanic labour of the geysers, the eagles circling above the canyons, and the primeval remnants of the flora and fauna of the Jurassic. A universe unto itself unfolds along the highway. Its emblems are impossible to miss. In passing we read the writing that spells out America: ESSO, Shell, Aramco, Texaco, Goodyear, Firestone, Kentucky Fried Chicken, Burger King, McDonald's, Lucky Strike, Holiday Inn, Howard Johnson's Motor Lodge, Wal-Mart, Coca-Cola, Marlboro. It is the lexicon of advertisement and persuasion. The range of services offered to the traveller is impressive: motels, garages, used cars, gas stations, truck stops, heated pools, breakfast, coffee shops, family accommodations, flags—especially in times of swelling patriotic sentiment—parking lots, rest areas, restaurants, cafés, amusement parks, fast-food drive-ins, open-air movie theaters, casinos, souvenir stalls. You might conduct what Venturi has called a 'comparative analysis of billboards'.

Entrusting yourself to the highway, you are in good hands. You move with undreamt ease. The highway puts the country within reach: every point in its territory is accessible without much difficulty and at any time. It teaches you the humility America's vastness inspires, but also the confidence that anything is feasible. Any destination, even one in the remotest wilderness, can be reached on time. The country's expanses are overwhelming, and yet you traverse them at your leisure. The highway is also a school of loneliness. Jean Baudrillard writes of the 'miracle of total availability, of the transparency of all functions in space, though this latter nonetheless remains unfathomable in its vastness and can only be exorcised by speed'; the highway, he argues, blends 'a marvel of easy living [...] with the fatality of the desert'.[6] All distances can be measured; all movements, calculated. America's highways are trajectories of transportation, not of bravado, tailgating, and latent civil war. The flow on the highway has its own rhythm, with a thousand nuances between unhindered passage and bumper-to-bumper traffic. The ceaseless tide of vehicles on the concrete ribbons has become part of America's second nature, an emblem of its sublimity no less compelling than Manhattan's urban canyons. The repertoire of forms as it evolved over the decades, the spectrum of colours that come in and out of style, the rhythm of taillights flashing up and dying

5
Robert Venturi, Denise Scott Brown, Steven Izenour: *Learning from Las Vegas*. Rev. ed. Cambridge, MA 2001.

6
Baudrillard, op. cit., p. 8.

down, the shimmering air above the macadam, the sequences of billboards pointing the way toward the horizon, the rhetoric of the direction signs—all these were an integral part of our vision of America even before we first travelled it. The highway has its tempers—the strained discipline early in the morning when everyone drives to work, the weariness when they go back the way they came in the evening—the arc of the day's moods between sunrise and sunset, between downtown and suburbia. The highway figures prominently in the works of poets from John Steinbeck to Jack Kerouac, it is the place of American melancholy and perhaps the American genius loci. Movement is everything; the different paths you might take to your destination matter as much as getting there. Americans perhaps no longer have any place in common, but they share the journey: the highway is their commons. Increasingly, Brinckerhoff Jackson has argued, roads 'are the scene of work and leisure and social intercourse and excitement. Indeed, they have often become for many the last resort for privacy and solitude and contact with nature. Roads no longer merely lead to places; they are places. And as always they serve two important roles: as promoters of growth and dispersion, and as magnets around which new kinds of development can cluster. In the modern landscape, no other space has been so versatile.'[7] But the highway is also the place of shared routines, of habituation to human interaction and intercourse, with all that entails: discipline, consideration, respect for boundaries and the appropriate distance. 'The question which insists on an answer is, What kind of small or local community can we hope to have? What we can be sure of is that it will not be based on territoriality. What seems to bring us together in the new landscape is not the sharing of space in the traditional sense but a kind of sodality based on shared uses of the street or road, and on shared routines.'[8] The highway trains the motorist's virtues: he does not mind driving for hours closely behind another car, at high speed or at a crawl, always alert so as to avoid a collision. It is a system of the conquest of space and contraction of distances. And the American highway would not be what it is without the sky above it. 'Clouds,' Baudrillard writes, 'spoil our European skies. Compared with the immense skies of America and their thick clouds, our little fleecy skies and little fleecy clouds resemble our fleecy thoughts, which are never thoughts of wide open spaces […] Europe has never been a continent. You can see that by its skies. As soon as you set foot in America, you feel the presence of an entire continent—space there is the very form of thought.'[9] To experience the highway as it should be experienced, you ought to drive a sedan. But traveling on the highway you do not strictly speaking drive: you coast. Baudrillard again: 'Nostalgia born of the immensity of the Texan hills and the sierras of New Mexico: gliding down the freeway, smash hits on the Chrysler stereo, heat wave. Snapshots aren't enough. We'd need the whole film of the trip in real

7
Brinckerhoff Jackson,
op. cit., *A Sense of
Place*, pp. 190-191.

8
Ibid, p. 10.

9
Baudrillard, op. cit.,
p. 16.

time, including the unbearable heat and the music. We'd have to replay it all from end to end at home in a darkened room, rediscover the magic of the freeways and the distance and the ice-cold alcohol in the desert and the speed and live it all again on the video at home in real time, not simply for the pleasure of remembering but because the fascination of senseless repetition is already present in the abstraction of the journey. The unfolding of the desert is infinitely close to the timelessness of film.'[10] The highway also has its distinctive soundtrack: in the 1960s, no road trip would have been complete without Jimi Hendrix, Frank Zappa, the Beach Boys, the Rolling Stones. [...]

Archaeology of America. The highway is not just the timeless medium of transcontinental communication, not just the transmission that keeps Leo Marx's 'machine in the garden' humming.[11] It has its own history and genealogy. In many places, the blacktop on which we zoom along is already the second, third, or fourth iteration. Buried beneath it in their several layers lie the footpaths of Native Americans and trappers, the rutted roads out toward the frontier and the Promised Land where milk and honey flowed, and the 1811 National Road from Cumberland, Md., to Vandalia, Ill. Buried, too, is U. S. Route 66, which ran from Chicago across the Southwest to the Pacific Coast near Los Angeles. Construction started in 1926: a thoroughfare from the storm-and-stress period of the automobile age and Fordism, but also the road on which hundreds of thousands migrated west during the Dust Bowl. To drive along it today is to make pilgrimage to an America that no longer exists, captured in pictures of the 'Mother Road' from John Steinbeck's Grapes of Wrath, with its lodges, inns, and motels, with gas stations in Amarillo and Albuquerque, a road lined by Great Depression-era museum pieces. The golden age of highway construction began several decades later, after the conclusion of World War II, which had delayed major projects of the New Deal, and at the height of the Cold War. It is not a coincidence that military men like Dwight D. Eisenhower and Lucius D. Clay, who orchestrated the Berlin Airlift, threw their weight behind the implementation of the 1956 interstate program. Like all large-scale road construction projects in history, the highway combined civilian with strategic military purposes, functioning as an engine of rapid dislocation. A system designed to mobilize society, it was also an instrument of military mobilization: the highway as a supply route toward the naval ports on the Atlantic and Pacific Coasts and the airbases. The highway moreover facilitated the migration of American industry from the Northeast to the West and Southwest that began during the war and picked up speed amid the frozen conflict that followed. It became for the twentieth century what Union Pacific had been for the nineteenth. Like Pan American World Airways and the guaranteed comforts of a Hilton Hotel, it was a symbol of the rising superpower's new global stature. When it was first conceived,

10
Ibid, p. 1.

11
Leo Marx's inspiring *The Machine in the Garden. Technology and the Pastoral Ideal in America.* New York 2000 remains the classic study of technology and the relation to nature in the United States.

the highway network was not only meant to combat unemployment, a primary objective of the New Deal, it also stood for a utopian vision. Models of six-lane highways were presented at the 1939 New York World's Fair, and in the Futurama pavilion, the designer Norman Bel Geddes envisioned a web of 14-lane superhighways, to be operational by 1960, on which vehicles would traverse the continent at speeds of up to 100 miles per hour. Traffic would pass through cities on multi-level roads. Reality soon caught up with his vision. By the time the oil crisis hit in 1973, the development of the highway system had perhaps already passed its peak. As the concrete tracks, crowded with traffic only yesterday, lay deserted, the country gave an adumbration of what the world might look like after the end of the automobile age, although we cannot truly imagine an America without the steady flow of traffic on the highway, an America in whose truck stops the last lights have been turned off. It would be an utterly changed country. Yet we need not speculate. If we want to check in on the state of America's health, we have to go where its pulse is felt most keenly: on the highway, America's Main Street. Stop-and-go traffic is a symptom of prosperity; so is a steady even flow of vehicles. The hieroglyph will let us know what shape America is in. When the highway will be abandoned, when the concrete will buckle and grass will sprout from the cracks, the American era will have come to an end.

The Documentary Style
Thomas Weski

Understanding photography as an art form equal to all others is a matter of course today. But when did this emancipation process begin and what were its reference points? Sixty years ago, art photography in the United States was dominated by a style known for its perfect technique and aesthetic roots in the sublime. Prominent representatives such as Ansel Adams and Edward Weston exposed negatives and prepared prints using an elaborate system that showed the finest greyscale values between the purest white and the deepest black. Their large-format plate cameras created extremely sharp, detailed shots that seemed artificial in their hyperreal feel. In their photographs, they articulated a myth of America as the promised, majestic land of unlimited resources. As a reaction to this worldview, but also to the static appearance of these crafted, masterpiece-style photographs, a younger generation of photographers gravitated toward the lively imagery of photojournalism and everyday subject matter. With daily news broadcasts bringing scenes from the Vietnam War to every living room, television began to replace the photography as the exclusive medium of news and reporting. Photojournalism experienced one last heyday due to the increased use of full colour photographs in the print media. Unlike the distancing effect of black and white photographs, the bright hues of colour photography brought current events closer to the readers. At a time when photography was reduced to its aesthetic or reporting qualities, younger photographers began to include radically personal points of view in their work, and to explore the limits of the medium. Rebelling against the established positions of art photography, they photographed spontaneously with hand-held cameras, reacted to scenes randomly encountered and welcomed coincidence as an enriching element in their imagery. Their subjects of choice could be found in ordinary, everyday life—a tendency found in art, literature, film and theatre as well. Many viewed their approach, which understand

1
'I don't have anything to say. (…) I photograph to find out what something will look like when photographed.' Garry Winogrand, quoted in: Gene Thornton: 'The New Photography. Turning Traditional Standards Upside Down', in: *ARTnews* 4 (1978), p. 76.

photography primarily as an aesthetic object with its own laws, as a provocative refusal.[1]

John Szarkowski, director of the photography department at the Museum of Modern Art starting 1962, played an important role in bringing this new photography to the public. The museum was the first in the world to begin showing regular photography exhibitions as early as 1938, and in 1940 the museum founded its own photography collection and department. Szarkowski's predecessor, Edward Steichen, had largely favoured representatives of the traditional canon. With his 1955 exhibition *Family of Man*, which toured both nationally and internationally to record crowds, Steichen created a visual argument advocating basic, humanitarian values in the age of the nuclear arms race and the Cold War. His successor focused primarily on young, unknown positions who worked from a different understanding of media. In the 1967 exhibition *New Documents*, Szarkowski presented three young photographers—Diane Arbus, Garry Winogrand and Lee Friedlander—distinguished by their radically personal way of seeing social outsiders, the everyday and street life.[2]

In Walker Evans, born 1903, Szarkowski found an artist who could serve as a model for his favoured documentary concept of photography. Evans' images are part of 20th-century American cultural heritage; his photographs, particularly those showing the country's impoverished Southern states in the mid-1930s (a population particularly devastated by the Great Depression and a drought) are part of the United States' collective memory.[3] It is a visual status report that, despite his high artistic quality, is primarily classified as documentary and considered a valid picture of society at that time.

Documentary photography refers to a visual approach that shows the subject in a seemingly direct way, without obvious interpretation. Because of its attributed neutrality, it stands for credibility, accountability, and thus for practicality. Walker Evans referred to these qualities in an interview in 1971, but when asked whether his own photography was documentary, he defined his work differently. Documentary photographs, he says, are what police take at a crime scene. They serve a purpose. But art never serves a purpose, so he himself is not creating documents, though he does have a documentary style.[4] With this distinction between a form of photography that is useful and serves a purpose and one that develops out of artistic criteria, the two poles and different characters of documentary photography are defined: if the traditional form aims to reproduce the visible world as close to reality as possible, the documentary style stands for a worldview in the form of the document. This is a crucial difference that puts one kind of photography in the service of a client, while the other approach relies on a highly personal point of view, and thus on a photographic author. In other words, while one type of documentary photography involves

2
'In the past decade this new generation of photographers has redirected the technique and aesthetic of documentary photography to more personal ends. Their aim has not been to reform life but to know it, not to persuade but to understand. The world, despite of its terrors, is approached as the ultimate source of wonder and fascination, no less precious for being irrational and incoherent.' John Szarkowski, quoted in: *New Documents*, Press Release No. 21, The Museum of Modern Art, Department of Photography, February 28, 1967, www.moma.org/ momaorg/pdfs/docs/ press_archives/3860/ MOMA_1967_Jan-Jun_0034_21.pdf?2010.

3
See Jeff Rosenheim: 'The Cruel Radiance of What Is: Walker Evans and the South'. Exh. cat. The Metropolitan Museum of Art, NY, in: *Walker Evans*. New York 1995, p. 69.

4
'Documentary? That's a very sophisticated and misleading word. And not really clear. (…) The term should be documentary style. An example of a literal document could be a police photograph of a murder scene. You see, a document has use, whereas art is really useless. Therefore art is never a document, though it can certainly adopt that style.' Walker Evans in a conversation with Leslie George Katz, *Art in America*, March/ April 1971, reprinted in: *Walker Evans: Incognito*. New York 1995, p. 18.

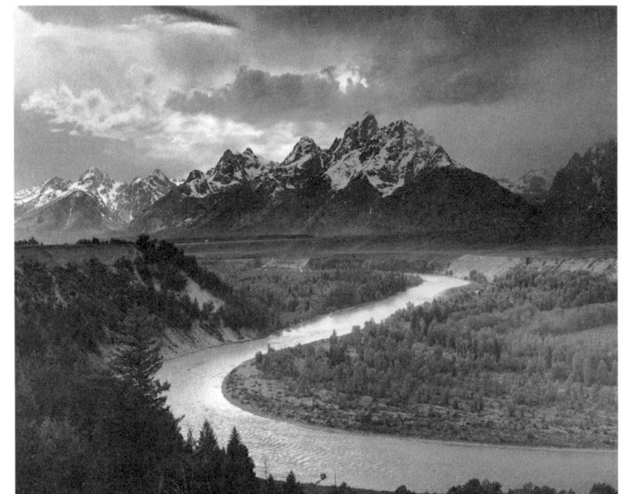

Ansel Adams
*The Tetons and the
Snake River, Grand
Teton National Park,
Wyoming, 1942*

5
*New Topographics:
Photographs of a Man-
altered Landscape,*
George Eastman House,
Rochester, January
1975. Participating
artists included: Robert
Adams, Lewis Baltz,
Bernd and Hilla Becher,
Joe Deal, Frank Gohlke,
Nicholas Nixon, John
Schott, Stephen Shore
and Henry Wessel Jr.

using photographic means to achieve the most accurate possible representation of the world, the other tries to formulate an idea of the world
that is rooted in subjectivity.

In the early 1970s, photographers such as Joel Meyerowitz, Stephen
Shore, Joel Sternfeld and William Eggleston discovered colour photography as a tool for exploring ordinary life in America. They did not
make direct reference to photorealism (which was emerging around the
same time) but instead drew inspiration from the imagery of Edward
Hopper paintings, Alfred Hitchcock's colour films for cinema or the
films of Andy Warhol and their attention to the ordinary. With William
Eggleston's solo exhibition at the Museum of Modern Art in 1976,
Szarkowski established colour photography as an artistic medium
that until then had been used mainly in advertising, photojournalism
and increasingly for private snapshots. Eggleston photographed his
personal surroundings—life in the suburbs in the southern United
States—in cryptic, atmospherically charged images. He used a technique from advertising for his colour-saturated prints, controlling the
individual tones for psychological effect. His photography quoted
amateur photography both formally and thematically, thereby attract-
ing strong criticism. In retrospect, however, the exhibition counts as a
milestone for the art world's recognition of colour photography within
the art context.

The 1975 exhibition *New Topographics*,[5] which was held at the George
Eastman House in Rochester and restaged at various locations in 2009,
experienced a similarly delayed reaction. Curator William Jenkins' vision
of contemporary photography went against the predominant type of
subjective photography, which emphasised the individual signature
as seen in the nascent auteur film. Instead, he focused on positions

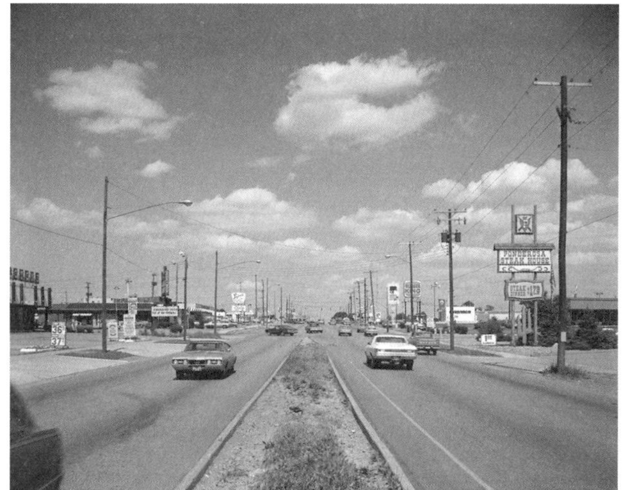

more formally akin to the documents of mid-19th century photo-graphers, who accompanied geological expeditions to little-studied areas of North America. Walker Evans had already assumed their formal restraint; his work paradoxically combined passionate interest with distant, seemingly signatureless photography, and young photogra-phers were influenced by him.[6] Jenkins' title probed the site-descriptive nature of photographs taken by participants who focused on the trans-formation of a natural landscape into a cultural one. Even the subtitle of the exhibition *(Photographs of a Man-altered Landscape)* points to a change in the concept of landscape. The 1970s were a period shaped by political events such as the Vietnam War and the Watergate scandal. Photographs of the earth from space raised awareness of the fragility of the planet, giving fuel to an ecological movement that would lead to the founding of Greenpeace in 1971. The organisation experienced a surge in popularity after the 1979 nuclear meltdown at Three Mile Island. What's more, growing prosperity meant that Americans could afford to take long car trips across the continent, heightening their understanding of sustained changes to the landscape. Robert Adams, Lewis Baltz and Stephen Shore depicted rapidly expanding cities with their suburbs, urban sprawl and new infrastructures such as industrial parks or recreational facilities. In *Learning from Las Vegas,* a project conducted at Yale University in 1968 and published in 1972, Robert Venturi and Denise Scott Brown referenced this new kind of primarily commercial, car-oriented cultural landscape.

Jenkins' exhibition title and term 'New Topographics' encompassed a number of different photographic approaches. Bernd and Hilla Becher were also represented, with several typologies of utilitarian buildings they had photographed in North America. Their work, which was first

6
'In regard to tone or inflection, or the appar-ent depersonalization of style (...) Walker Evans is most important. The attempt to make a pho-tograph from which the photographer seems to be absent is a strategy whose value and power all of us I think primarily have learned from him.' Frank Gohlke, quoted in: Britt Salvesen: *New Topographics.* Göttingen 2009, p. 17.

→ p. 242

perceived in Germany as heritage or monument protection, was now understood as conceptual art.[7] The artists' large-format tableaux of multiple, unique images invite comparative reflection and combine inherently different times and places, simultaneously constructing an artistic ideal of an architectural form. At the same time, artists for whom photography was just one technique among many began to investigate everyday life with other means. In the mid-1960s, Dan Graham made *Homes for America*, an artistic investigation of the phenomenon of standardised architecture and urbanism. As early as 1962, Ed Ruscha had been using the technical development of offset printing to publish inexpensive, unsigned artists' books in relatively large quantities. The books were devoted to the phenomena of everyday architecture such as gas stations, parking lots and all the buildings on the Sunset Strip in Los Angeles, which he portrayed in simple photographs. Land Artists had often filmed or photographed their ephemeral interventions in the landscape as a way of documenting and communicating their activities, as did the artists who worked performatively. Consequently, their photographs are distinguished by a more direct, documentary character than the individually developed aesthetic seen in photographs by 'New Topographics' artists. At that time, the exhibition in Rochester had few visitors and was barely noticed by the media. Yet the exhibition title[8] is still synonymous with a specific, artistic-documentary approach to photographing sites and landscapes. Although the artists and the photographers often dealt with the same subject matter, their works were only considered in their respective contexts. The 1977 exhibition documenta 6 directed by Manfred Schneckenburger in Kassel was no exception. A group of curators showed various stylistic positions in 20th-century photography, and though the medium was acknowledged as an equally relevant art form for the first time in the history of this event, it had to be presented in separate rooms. Shortly afterwards, European and American art institutions began to establish their own photography departments and collections. Still, most of the institutions categorised the artworks by technique and only rarely was there a dialogue between photography and the other arts. Only now—decades after the building of this infrastructure and the unpredictable success of photography in the art market—are these boundaries beginning to dissolve, establishing a better understanding of photography's diversity and validity as an art form.

7
The transatlantic network also included conceptual artist Robert Smithson, who presented his exhibition *Non-site Slag (Oberhausen, Germany)* in 1968 at Galerie Konrad Fischer in Düsseldorf—the same gallery that represented Bernd and Hilla Becher. Bernd Becher had accompanied Smithson during his work in Oberhausen. That same year, Bernd and Hilla Becher began to photograph in the United States. In 1973, they met Stephen Shore. Cf. Britt Salvesen: *New Topographics*, pp. 34-35.

8
'New Topographics Pool' is a group on the social network flickr, https://www.flickr.com/groups/newtopographics/pool.

Space Explorations
Land Art and Landscape
Philipp Kaiser

1
For more on the origins of Land Art, see Philipp Kaiser and Miwon Kwon: *Ends of the Earth: Land Art to 1974.* Exh. cat. Museum of Contemporary Art, Los Angeles / Haus der Kunst, Munich 2012.

2
Rosalind E. Krauss: *Passages in Modern Sculpture.* New York 1977, p. 282.

3
According to Michael Heizer, Walter De Maria used the term 'Land Art' as early as 1967. However, since this cannot be verified, Schum's artists' film with contributions from Heizer, De Maria, but also Richard Long, Dennis Oppenheim, Jan Dibbets, Robert Smithson, Barry Flanagan and Marius Boezem, must be considered eponymous.

In the late 1960s, when Land Art first clearly appeared on the horizon as a discursive formation and the overwhelming, monumental sculptures of Michael Heizer and Robert Smithson caught the attention of even the tabloids, it was less the starting-point than the end of a complex story of development. In the early 1960s, artists in various parts of the world had already begun to investigate space outside of the museum: the Fluxus artists, for example, imagined landscape-relevant works in proto-conceptual way or else landscape became the site of performative interventions. The latter can to some extent be understood as an expansion of 1950s gestural painting—one need only think of the Gutai group in Japan, for instance. And yet it was the emancipation and redefinition of sculpture that proved especially crucial for the formation of Land Art.[1] What is interesting in this context is not so much sculpture's outward mode of appearance—which, as we know, was heavily influenced by minimalism in the 1960s, and then radically broke away from it by developing a processual, ephemeral and post-minimal language; rather more important here is that within sculpture there was a negotiation of the ontological categories of sculpture *in itself*, but also of space. Genuinely engaged with three-dimensional space, the sculptural innovations of the 1960s show a clear paradigm shift that Rosalind Krauss described as 'phenomenological evidence', or 'passage'.[2] The concept of sculpture as passage was particularly popular among American artists and crucial for numerous works of Land Art, which attempted to articulate a new relationship with external space in general and its specific site in particular. It is hardly surprising that this paradigm shift led at first to transcontinental misunderstandings. Nevertheless, Western European reception played a very important role in establishing Land Art—a term[3] that, interestingly, was first used by German filmmaker Gerry Schum for his eponymous television programme.[4] Lutz Schirmer first reported on the new American

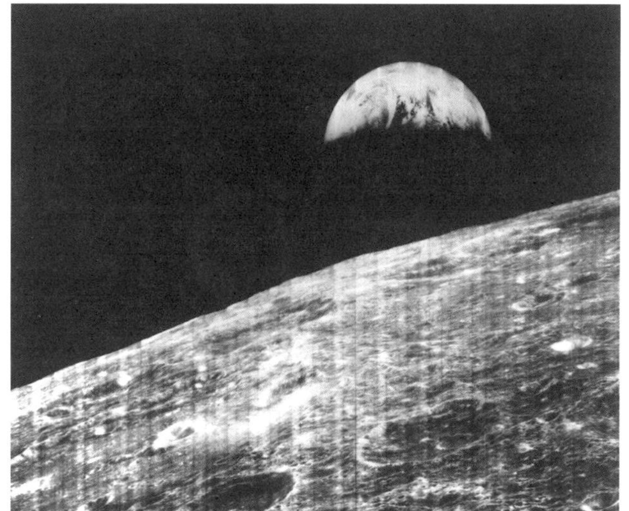

First view from space
of the Earth and the
Moon released by
NASA, photographed
by Lunar Orbiter I on
23.08.1966

4
The crucial events for
the establishment of
the Land Art discourse
in the United States
were the two exhibi-
tions *Earthworks*, which
was jointly conceived
by Robert Smithson and
gallerist Virginia Dwan
in 1968, and Willoughby
Sharp's *Earth Art*
exhibition at Cornell
University in Ithaca in
February 1969. After
it was aired on public
television in the spring
of 1969 (broadcaster
Freies Berlin), Gerry
Schum's film was shown
in Harald Szeeman's
legendary exhibition
*Live In Your Head: When
Attitudes Become
Form, Works-Concepts-
Processes-Situations-
Information* 1969 at the
ICA London.

5
Lutz Schirmer: 'Zur Land
Art', in: *Interfunktionen*
3, 1969, pp. 1–35.

6
Ibid., p. 6. NASA pub-
lished the first image
of Earth seen from the
Moon on August 23,
1966, almost three
years before the moon
landing.

phenomenon in 1969. In an article for the magazine *Interfunktionen*[5]
he observes that his text is being written at a point in time when
'departure to the Moon, the first look back at the entire planet from
beyond the atmosphere' has made 'the Earth the object of new visual
experiences'.[6] Schirmer finds it paradoxical that in the US of all
places—the most developed nation in the world, both technologically
and industrially—artists had turned to the Earth as their material, evidently rejecting a blind belief in progress. Schirmer's pertinent analysis
becomes puzzling in its radically Eurocentric worldview, however, when
he argues that proponents of Land Art are revisiting a Romantic tradition, reviving the idea of land as a landscape of the soul and spirit.[7]
Endeavouring a comparison with Caspar David Friedrich, Carl Gustav
Carus and Philipp Otto Runge, Schirmer understands the 'choice of
landscape as a subject and material of art as the symptom of a Romantic, internalised view of the world.'[8] Perhaps significantly, Gerry Schum
originally wanted to call his Land Art film *Landscape Art*, but decided
against it after conversations with the artists.[9] For American artists in
particular, the category of landscape was problematic if not irrelevant.
It was primarily associated with painting and thus with compositional,
idealised landscapes that, in the best-case (Romantic) scenario, would
unfold to sublime effect. Because of this, landscape as a category
played almost no role in considerations during the heyday of American
Land Art.[10] Instead, going back to Rosalind Krauss' phenomenological paradigm shift, landscape was reflected in a fundamental way or
stylised as mediated substitute reality. The following attempts to trace
a new treatment of space and its representation on the basis of a few
works of Land Art.

Michael Heizer
Double Negative,
1969/70, Mormon
Mesa, Overton,
Nevada

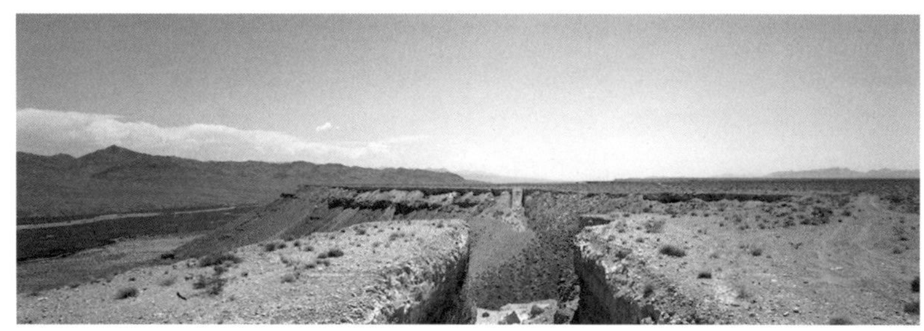

→ p. 250

7
Ibid., p. 7.

8
Ibid., p. 7.

9
Cf. Ursula Wevers:
'Liebe Arbeit Fernseh-
galerie', in: *Ready to
Shoot: Fernsehgalerie
Gerry Schum, Videoga-
lerie Schum*. Exh. cat.
Kunsthalle Düsseldorf.
Cologne 2004, p. 29.

10
Undoubtedly, the Ame-
rican protagonists differ
from the European and
especially British artists
in this regard.

11
Interview, Julia Brown
and Michael Heizer,
in: *Michael Heizer:
Sculpture in Reverse.*
Exh. cat. The Museum of
Contemporary Art, Los
Angeles. Los Angeles
1984, p. 12 and p. 36.

12
Rosalind E. Krauss:
op. cit. pp. 279ff.

In 1969/70, Michael Heizer created a 500-metre long cut in a Nevada desert mesa near Las Vegas, making it passable from both sides. This work, entitled *Double Negative*, became the first-ever monumental sculpture. Using dynamite and excavators, the then 25-year-old artist created a negative space with architectural qualities. For Heizer, it was first and foremost about the absence of sculptural mass; at the same time, he compared the size of the negative sculpture with the Empire State Building, thereby creating an explicit reference to Manhattan.[11] The specific experience of *Double Negative* can be likened to passing through urban space between stone skyscrapers—a substitution that makes Heizer's sculpture readable as a critique of urbanism, perhaps against his will. It hardly seems a coincidence that Smithson realised *Spiral Jetty* (1970) in Utah just a short time afterwards, creating the second monumental Land Art sculpture. The length of his spiral (after it was extended in a second attempt) is also 500 metres. The explicit reference to *Double Negative* stems not only from the artists' personal friendship, but from the fact that, as much as they differ in intent, the two monumental sculptures would have to be interpreted as relational: both works are strikingly simplistic in form and—to quote Merleau-Ponty, whose writings greatly influenced Smithson's generation—both must be walked in order to be physically experienced. The only subject of these monumental sculptures, Rosalind Krauss argues, is our bodies and their self-perception. We find ourselves *in* the sculpture, though it constantly decentres us; at the same time, it creates a presence com-parable to Proust's famous madeleine.[12] Robert Smithson discovered this as early as 1966, in his annotated and published documentation of excursions to upstate New York: first with Donald Judd and their wives, and a year later to visit his birthplace in Passaic, New Jersey. In both excursions, *The Crystal Land* (1966) and *The Monuments of Passaic* (1967) [13], Smithson takes up the old-fashioned genre of travelogue (or its contemporary counterpart, the sci-fi story), acting as a cicerone to the art world with evocative descriptions.[14] Smithson's sometimes enigmatic, abstruse travel reports are associative and highly idiosyn-cratic evidence of his landscape explorations. They arguably represent, to some extent, the counterpart to the physically phenomenological, experiential dimension of the sculptural works. Landscape does not appear as a counterpart or a tableau, as Lutz Schirmer suggested in his reference to the Romantics, but as a space of possibility that has to be physically walked or explored.[14] When it does appear as a tableau, then it does so only in an extremely clichéd way as a postcard—as a cliché of itself. Smithson writes in his account of Passaic that the mid-day sun 'cinema-ized' the site, and that photographing the bridge was akin to photographing a photograph. He follows this observation with the words: 'Actually, the landscape was no landscape, but "a particular kind of heliotypy" (Nabokov), a kind of self-destroying postcard world of failed immortality and oppressive grandeur. I had been wandering in a moving picture (…).'[15]

Though at first glance very different, both Smithson's descriptions and Rosalind Krauss' phenomenological 'turn' are very much based on the premise of bodies moving through the landscape, be it authentic landscape (in the sense of a location), as the setting of a specific, distinctive experience, or as a mediated substitute reality. One thing is certain: American Land Art left the contemplative, Romantic 'land-scapes of the soul' far behind.

13
See p. 308 in this catalogue.

14
Philip Ursprung: *Grenzen der Kunst. Allan Kaprow und das Happening, Robert Smithson und die Land Art*. Munich 2003, p. 222.

15
The film *Swamp* (1971), which Robert Smithson realised together with Nancy Holt, could serve as a good example of this. In *Swamp*, Holt manoeuvres the pastures of New Jersey with a handheld camera, while Smithson gives verbal instructions as to how to access the space through physical activity.

16
Robert Smithson: 'A Tour of the Monuments of Passaic, New Jersey', in: *Robert Smithson: The Collected Writings*. Berkeley 1996, pp. 68–75.

What is Camouflage, What is Landscape?
The Aesthetic and Anaesthetic of Landscape

Hannah Stippl

'The image of landscape par excellence is camouflage, both as its appearance and its abstraction.' (Lucius Burckhardt)

Landscape is invisible, Lucius Burckhardt claims. Initially that seems paradoxical, for the multiplicity of material things that landscape is made up of lie before us in full view. Yet the evident components of landscape are entangled in vast, immaterial currents of a historical, economic and cultural nature. To analyse these components, the sociologist Burckhardt founded the 'science of walking', also called 'promenadology' or 'strollology', in the 1980s. The subject of research of the new planning and design science is the investigation of complex conditions of perception of landscape and urban space. In this, Lucius Burckhardt is no fan of great plans or conceptual constructs, rather the opposite: guided by the idea of the smallest possible intervention, he assumes that design need not impinge upon the existing environment by means of brute force. Yet the multiple intertwining of aesthetics, theory, morality and habits of perception are shown to be knots that cannot be untangled by theoretical positing alone. On the contrary, most effective of all are those interventions that change the image of landscape in our heads, producing a new aesthetic understanding of the environment.

The walks undertaken in the context of the science of walking—also called 'scientific walks' or 'promenadological walks' to distinguish them from usual walks—are a changeable method that Burckhardt uses in different contexts and shapes, enabling what had hitherto remained unseen, unthought of and unrecognised, to be rendered visible. His attitude to this is always critical, political and self-confident—thus deliberate in terms of one's own standing and fallibility. The principle of the smallest possible intervention runs through his entire multi-layered work, in which he conveys connections, not only by means of scientific

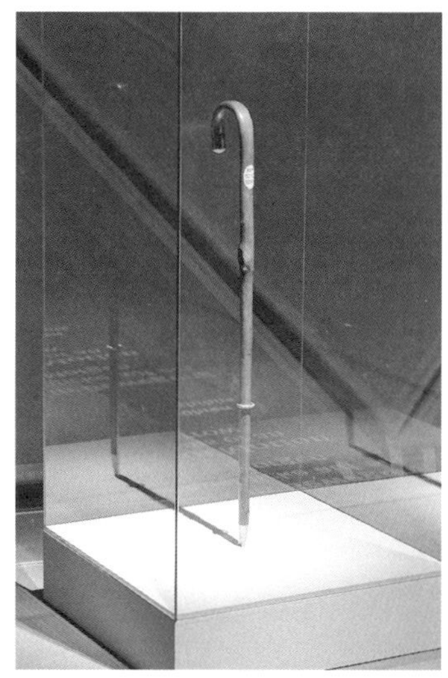

Andreas Gram
Walking stick with metal leaf *Hier ist es schön* [Here it is beautiful], 1993, exhibition view, Kunsthaus Graz, 2015

The canes emerged as a multiple for the action 'Das Zebra streifen' [To stripe the zebra]—a subversive appropriation of public space with Lucius Burckhardt.

texts, but also with artistic methods such as drawings, caricatures or watercolours that relate to the theory of landscape. These works, an important and certainly rich source of Burckhardt's reflections on the aesthetics of landscape, should not be mistaken for real or invented views of landscapes; rather they are diagrams of the multifarious conditions under which a society can perceive nature as landscape.

→ p. 218 Likewise the two early landscape-theoretical watercolours *Kriegerische Landschaft* [War-like Landscape] and *Evakuierte Landschaft* [Evacuated Landscape], which can be seen as counterparts that complement and determine one another. Italy is invisible, Lucius Burckhardt claims, for the charming landscape of Italy is a construct. The artists of the 17th and 18th century discover Italy: Goethe's *Land, wo die Zitronen blühn* [land where the lemons bloom], the pictures of Claude le Lorrain, those thirsting for knowledge and hungry for adventure combine the most beautiful places into an overall image. A young man in classicist folk costume carries the scenery of a Lorraine landscape under his arm, well known with its cypress trees and little round temples. The landscape is being evacuated, transported elsewhere and passed on. How the travellers would like to take the delightful landscape home with them. Save it from further destruction! Without intervention, meaning untouched, the landscape is not so delightful at all, rather full of unsightly realities that disrupt the pleasure: the former world empire of Rome has lain in ruins for centuries, the poor local population graze their cattle amidst the ruins, dirt and unwelcome odours distract from the aesthetic perception. An entire arsenal of tricks is deployed to produce the desired mode of perception: beggars and ragged children are simply turned into accessory figures, matching the painterly decay all around them.

Perceiving is also suppressing, not-perceiving, reversing, projecting. By inventing certain topoi of conceiving, artists steer the viewer's gaze, numbing perception. 'The aesthetic is executed as an anaesthetic', as Wolfgang Welsch notes. The sepia-coloured landscape prospect is not a portrait of an existing landscape, rather the idea of the aesthetic, now become transportable, as a term of conception. Welsch has provided this aesthetic with the notion of the 'anaesthetic'. 'Anaesthetic means that state whereby the elementary conditions of the aesthetic—the ability to feel—is lifted. While the aesthetic of feeling is forceful, the anaesthetic makes the lack of feeling its theme—in the sense of a loss, a prevention or the impossibility of sensibility, and this on all levels, too: from physical apathy to mental blindness.'[1]

The travellers who in the 18th century journeyed to Italy from England, Germany, France and the rest of Europe in order to acquire there the so-keenly desired education, helped to constitute the tourist's gaze. Prefabricated by these historical, social and cultural patterns of perception, the tourist's gaze offers a kind of mission statement by which itineraries and behavioural rituals find their bearings. First and foremost it is visual consumption that turns landscapes into commercially exploitable tourist destinations. The tourist's gaze is fundamentally reliant upon the production and reproduction of images. How one anticipates a particular destination, a key element in its touristic exploitation, is already structured by images. Likewise, the indispensable tourist guide, enabling one to explore a region or a place more efficiently, i.e. with less time expended, place in the foreground what is typical, worth seeing about a particular destination, while film and TV images as well as the internet also make their contribution. For the construction of these memories, the production of one's own images is of central importance. At an early stage the growing market for landscape prints, panorama images and picture postcards emerge, enabling the landscape, consumed visually to be captured too, without having to be drawn or painted in watercolours—artistic techniques whose mass distribution goes hand-in-hand with tourism. Today the tourist without a camera or mobile phone is almost unthinkable, while social media platforms or photo-sharing portals ensure the comprehensive, synchronous dissemination of rationalised touristic perception, prior to the journey as much as after.

One of the central insights of Marshall McLuhan is that media are extensions of the human body, of its organs or senses. The wheel extends the foot, the clothes expand the skin, the telescope enhances the eye. Media extend man's possibilities, his ability to perceive, his power, his speed. Conversely, these extensions that have thus been materialised now in turn have an effect on the body, continually

1
Wolfgang Welsch:
Ästhetisches Denken.
Stuttgart 2010, p. 10.

forming it. The relocation of the functions of certain parts of the body on to instruments or technologies is a process that initially distracts perception to such an extent that man is displaced into a state of shock and pain. In order to unburden the overtaxed psyche and to re-establish the balance in our senses, the central nervous system switches off the functions of the extended body part, so that this is amputated and the source of distraction removed. Man feels indigenous again in his surroundings, yet he finds himself, as in a real operation, in a state of anaesthesia, of narcosis.

At the same time as McLuhan describes the effects of the medial surroundings on perception as fundamental and irrevocable, Joachim Ritter works on his theories of landscape. Ritter's main theory is as follows: landscape could only emerge after modern man had succeeded in emancipating himself increasingly from nature and perceiving this consciously as something opposite him. The development of scientifically analytical methods eradicates the anaesthetic, unified experience of metaphysics, the cosmic connection between man-nature-God that held sway up to the Middle Ages. Read together with McLuhan, Ritter's theories on the development of the aesthetic perception of nature as landscape can be seen as an anaesthetic, narcotic shock reaction to the crumbling of the metaphysical experience of the wholeness of nature through scientific observation and exploitation. For Ritter, however, the splitting of nature that followed the technical domination of the same is also the prerequisite for aesthetic reconciliation with her. The aesthetic perception of nature constructs the individual wholeness of the landscape by means of an integrating perspective. But that which is whole in a landscape is not a connection that is substantive or material, not the complex structure between its components; rather it is a subject unity that is individually given. Thus a multi-layered fabric of reaction made up of the aesthetic and the anaesthetic (Welsch) or of narcosis (McLuhan) opens up. The aesthetic perception of nature is an anaesthetic shock reaction to the technological expansion of man. Already at this point, the viewing of landscape with regard to its aesthetic is shown to be based on a narcotic state.

The flood of images renders landscape invisible. Burckhardt reflects this relationship between visibility and invisibility in the watercolour *Kriegerische Landschaft* as well as the problem of making something invisible, as it is found primarily in the domain of the military as the art of camouflage. Camouflage covers the entire surroundings, it frames the scenery with well-known props from the landscape. If the small temple with the cypress trees symbolises the category of the lovely, charming landscape, then in the case of the Matterhorn it concerns a visual reference to an elevated landscape. The landscape that is vanishing due to the fleck of colour of camouflage directs our attention to the difference between being and the appearance of things. This difference is not present in daily consciousness. What the viewer sees in objects in everyday perception is not the real design, but rather what is inferred from what is seen, for consciousness is always focused on something, meaning it is a consciousness of something. The true appearance of the landscape disappears under the cloak of camouflage; the viewer is content with recognising it. Yet the *Kriegerische Landschaft* is a picture puzzle that can flip between two meanings. In the contour of the punched surface we can recognise the silhouette of a tank turret with a gun and access hatch, on which two helmeted soldiers are sitting. What is camouflage, what is landscape? The small temple and the Matterhorn function as a camouflage for the tank; the camouflage pattern actually constitutes the landscape.

Burckhardt believes that 'the landscape is comparable with a camouflage net, its reality rendered by the overlapping of heterogeneous forms and patches. The interaction of their disparities allows a system of lifelike moods to arise, whose existence extends beyond the simple addition of the fragments that make it up.'[2] The process of perception, seemingly so self-evident, is always based on a selection of environmental stimuli—filtered not through the physiological possibilities of the sensory organs, but rather through attention, through mental activity and social boundaries of perception. At this point it is shown that reality overall, that 'reality as such', like nature, is not accessible to perception. There is no innocent eye and likewise no immediate perception, for every perception has already been focused in a subjective way. Thus perception is an action guided by interests, an active achievement of construction, precisely oriented towards that which is worth seeing. Perception itself is already an achievement of cognition, and it is, as pointed out by Hoffmann-Axthelm, 'functionally seen, the exception, outside of work it only exists as tourism, art and love.'[3] Prefabricated pictures and constructions, and also projections of the self on to the other, thus determine perception to a large degree. In this way, cultivated, education-minded travellers are subject to that which has been seen before just as much as mass tourists, although they move in a different segment of the predictable. Tourist guides thus prove thoroughly ambivalent, for although they restrict the tourist's perspective, they frequently enable perception in the first place. The typical, the original, the authentic in a place, in the surrounding landscape and the people living it, has to a large extent been predicted and communicated by the perspective of others.

Landscape only becomes a homogeneous unity, a unity that is a construct, in the viewing and in the viewer. Yet landscape is just a

[2]
Lucius Burckhardt: *Die Kinder fressen ihre Revolution.* Cologne 1985, p. 3.

[3]
Dieter Hoffmann-Axthelm: *Wie kommt die Geschichte ins Entwerfen?* Braunschweig 1987, p. 201.

construct, in which the aesthetic and anaesthetic participate in equal measure. This process is certainly not a peaceful one, quite the contrary: landscape—an entirely synthetic construction—is war-like. With his science of walking, Lucius Burckhardt pursues the goal of creating awareness for this game of seeing and not-seeing, of the aesthetic and anaesthetic, which the unifying of heterogeneous elements brings to the landscape. The concern here is not with the exchanging or extending of old impressions, rather with acquiring an approach to thinking and perceiving that is non-affirmative, open and critically reflexive.

Anthropocene
On the Substance of a New Idea
Christian Schwägerl

In February 2000 Paul J. Crutzen erupted in anger at a scientific conference in Mexico. Five years previously the Dutch-born atmospheric chemist had been awarded the Nobel Prize for being one of the first to recognise and investigate the dangers nitrous oxides and CFC cooling gases posed to the protective shield around Earth. Crutzen's findings were a vital contribution to the international prohibition of the most harmful of these gases in 1988 and to enabling the ozone layer to slowly regenerate in the period of time since.
Throughout his career Crutzen had gathered materials showing how humans have changed, influenced and damaged Earth—often, as is the case with the ozone layer, not even with malicious intention, but rather from pure ignorance. And now, attending a symposium of the International Geosphere-Biosphere Programme, he was listening to one lecture after another in which the present period was being described as the 'Holocene', as geologists call the period in Earth's history since the end of the last ice age nearly 12,000 years ago. The Nobel Prize winner's dissatisfaction with this word grew steadily until finally he stood up to interrupt the speaker. 'We no longer live in the Holocene,' Crutzen bluntly declared. 'We live in the, in the, in the ... Anthropocene.'

In Greek 'Anthropos' means 'human being' as such, and the final syllable '-cene' is derived from the word for 'new': 'The new brought about by humans' could be a translation for Anthropocene. In geology 'cene' describes the Earth's epochs, i.e. important sub-chapters in the 4.6 billion year long history of the mineral planet and its inhabitants. 'The geological epoch of mankind' is thus another possible translation: the period in which humans have become the dominant force of change on Earth. Crutzen's small outburst created a stir in the specialised world of geology, but for quite a few years the new word was barely noticed outside of that scene. Recently, however, that has changed. The idea

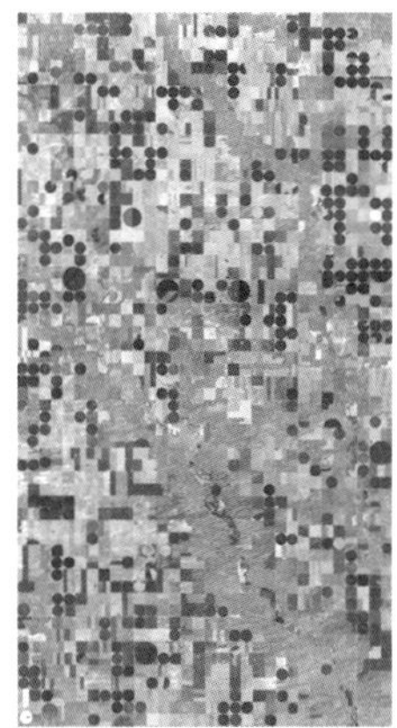

Agricultural landscape in the US

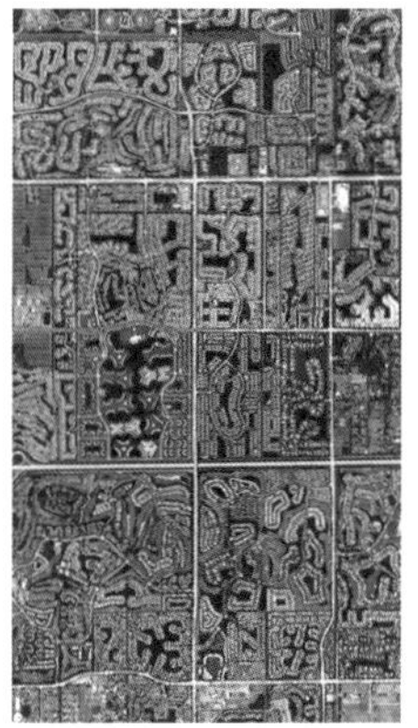

Housing estate in Florida

of the Anthropocene now engages politicians, artists, ecologists, as it does humanities scholars and ethicists.

Ban Ki-Moon, General Secretary of the United Nations, opened the last Rio environmental summit with the words: 'Welcome to the Anthropocene'. The Berlin 'House of World Cultures' (Haus der Kulturen der Welt) has received funding from the German Federal Parliament for a three-year international project to explore the idea jointly with the Max Planck Society and the Deutsche Museum. The Smithsonian in Washington is likewise occupied with the Anthropocene, as is Britain's Royal Society. Most important of all is probably the work of the 'Anthropocene Working Group'. This informal gathering of scientists has the task of casting a vote in 2016 on whether a new chapter in Earth history should officially be opened and called 'Anthropocene'. Astonishingly, Crutzen's spontaneous intervention has developed into a universal idea that has found attention worldwide and could even become the generic scientific term for all of mankind's activities.

Primarily the idea is no more than a geological hypothesis: mankind is changing the planet not only on a global scale, but also with an amazing speed and with long-term consequences, to the point that this will remain recognisable even in the far-off future. So it is not merely scratches in the Earth's systems that we leave behind, but our actions change the way Earth functions. Even if mankind disappeared from Earth tomorrow, interested visitors in 100,000 or even several million years could still see that we have been here. Just as geologists today investigate the shells of extinct ammonites or new kinds of rock strata as 'markers' of earlier stages in Earth's history, so in this imagined future there would be indications of the 'epoch of mankind' in persistent techno-fossils, new types of substances, globally altered distribution patterns of animals and plants, and in the bones and pollen grains of bred life-forms as well as in such artefacts as cities.

The hard pieces of evidence are numerous: CO_2 emissions, which have constantly grown since the onset of industrialisation, are sufficient to change the world's climate for tens of thousands of years, turning the seas so acidic that many algae and corals can no longer live in them. The Haber-Bosch process means that mankind, in the production of fertilisers, has already extracted more nitrogen from the air and introduced it into eco-systems than was there naturally—with massively negative consequences for biodiversity. Globally, forests and savannas are ploughed up in order to produce food for man. Between 2000 and 2012 alone, a surface area of forest measuring 1,100 by 1,100 kilometres was cut down, mainly to make room for soya and oil palm plantations. Taken together, global agricultural areas are as large as South America. While man and his livestock made up only a few percent of the biomass of larger animals at the end of the last ice age, today they comprise 97 percent. Wild animals make up just three percent when put on the scales. Accelerated consumerism has resulted in metals and minerals disappearing in certain places due to mining, and reappearing in other places in new material combinations, for example as heaps of electronic scrap.

There are numerous other long-term 'markers', measurable or visible, of the Anthropocene: for example, the artificial radioactive elements that have entered the world since 1945 as a result of atomic bomb explosions and the use of nuclear power; the vast amount of dumped plastic that could wrap the whole world once over in plastic film; and the millions of various synthetic chemicals that have spread and accumulated around the planet. Radionuclides and plastic are at present considered the clearest measurable signals to mark the official beginning of the Anthropocene around 1945.

Measured by this hard evidence, the Anthropocene sounds like something that should in fact be combatted. As a summation of all our environmental problems it summons up a terrifying vision. Or does it—even worse—legitimise yet more destruction of the environment? Critics assert that the word 'Anthropocene' sounds like 'Anthropocentrism'. Is this perhaps supposed to be the idea of the Anthoropocene: that Earth is owned by mankind, that humans have the right to finish their conquest with the help of technology and capitalistic logic, to exploit and rebuild the planet's surface according to their needs, and to make subjects of animals, plants and living spaces, not only in a metaphorical but a real sense, right down to the very last corner? And if something goes wrong, humans are entiteld to employ large-scale technology such as genetic engineering and artificial cooling gases as 'solutions'? Another critical approach to the Anthropocene idea is that it blurs who exactly is responsible for the many planetary problems. If all 'anthropos' are to blame, then are a family farmer in India and the CEO of an oil conglomerate equally responsible for climate change?

Such negative readings crop up repeatedly in the current debate—and I too consider it very important to examine the concept of the Anthropocene idea critically, to sound out a word that in the future could be given worldwide validity. Yet there are many other ways of reading it, some with very much a positive message to them.

– To speak of the Anthropocene means to integrate human history into that of the Earth and of nature. We no longer see ourselves as a power coming from outside, supernatural as it were, but rather we recognise our origins from the Earth's crust and our interconnectedness with all other forms in which nature manifests itself.

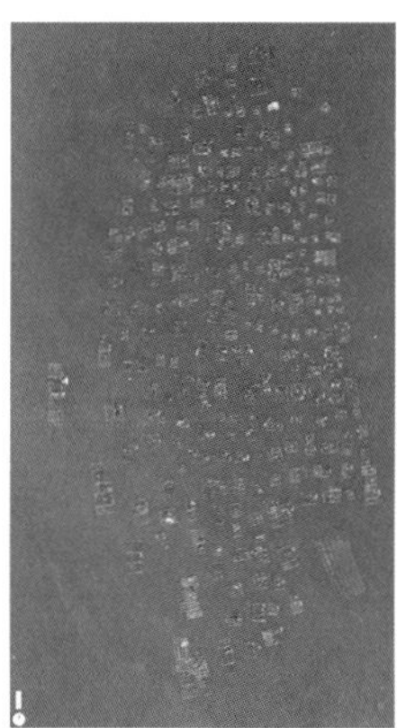

Fish farming in Taiwan

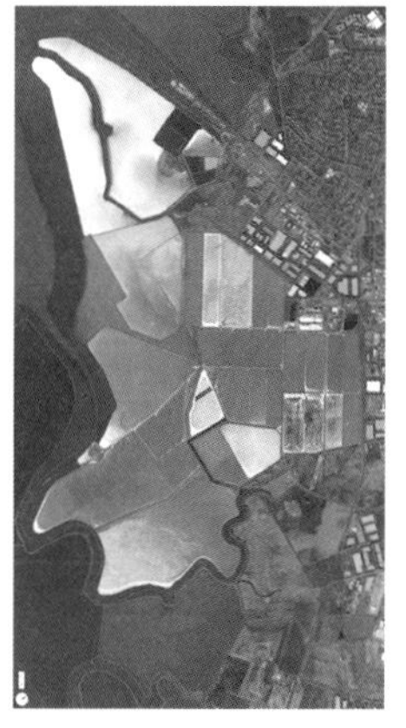

Salt production

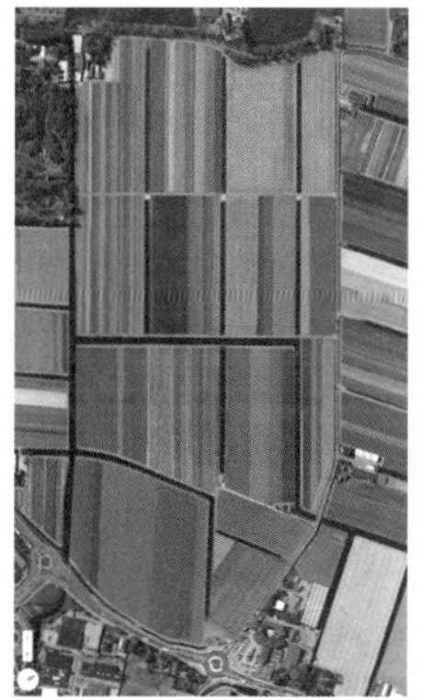

Tulip fields in the
Netherlands

– In an era in which billions of Euros are shifted around the world in nano-seconds, and companies, like governments, make decisions looking no more than a few months ahead, the Anthropocene idea creates the sense of a long past, and above all of a long future.

– By shifting the focus on to the far-off future, our sensors for the long-term consequences of our actions become heightened. Globalisation has broken down borders in spatial terms, and the internet has created a worldwide network. This creates the positive potential that global movements against destructive business activity can coordinate their activities, and can act on behalf of future inhabitants of Earth.

– The ideological basis of ruthless business—namely that there is a clear border between ecology and economy, between culture and nature, and that what we call 'environment' is an external, economically worthless factor—are refuted by the Anthropocene concept. Ecosystems appear as the primary economy of earth to which civilisation has to adapt.

– The powerful dimension hidden in a new Earth epoch expresses how momentous the decisions we make today are—from individual purchasing decisions, which in their accumulated form either help or damage rain forests and coral reefs, to far-reaching decisions reached by companies and governments. That could heighten a general sense of responsibility.

– While power and wealth today are concentrated in the hands of an ever smaller group—one percent of the world's population owns as much as the rest, with just 80 billionaires disposing of as much money as 3.5 billion of the world's poorest—every person, by virtue of the word 'anthropos', is called upon to be part of decisions about the future as equals, including small farmers and indigenous people.

– The Anthropocene concept does not grant humans any additional rights, but rather can open our eyes to our multifarious interconnectedness with all abiotic and biotic powers on earth, with stones and living creatures. Instead of promoting anthropocentric thinking, it could accelerate our embeddedness.

– By removing the illusion of a 'great out there' which we can use to extract 'resources' and dump our rubbish, the Anthropocene idea creates a new imperative: to design cities, agriculture, fishing, technology and production in such a way that they enrich rather than impoverish the biospheres, that they become 'sources' of biological wealth.

These are some of the possibilities that are uniquely expressed by this new word. Exactly how the Anthropocene will proceed is not laid down in any canon; there is no master plan nor an ideology. It is an open-source concept that everyone familiar with the geophysical basics can get involved in. Ultimately the Anthropocene is the sum and multiplication of everything humans think, feel, decide, do, individually or in large

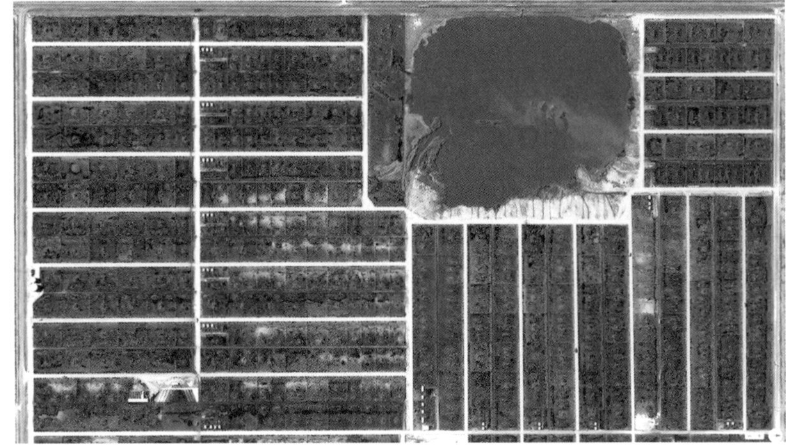

Pig breeding in the
US

groups. It reflects how humans live together with the diversity of Earth's
non-human inhabitants—and above all, too, how what we have called
the 'environment' reacts, responds, acts towards what humans do.
Once I accompanied Paul J. Crutzen to a conference. On the way there
he said to me in that characteristic mix of humility and brilliance: 'What
the Anthropocene is precisely? I don't know.' How the 'human epoch'
will proceed depends on collective actions, on social movements and
economic decisions. The fact that the consciousness of one species can
have such profound impact on Earth is something new in the history of
the planet. Jürgen Renn from the Max Planck Institute for the History
of Science describes it as follows: 'The Anthropocene is a process that
reflects upon itself.'

Landscape and the Politics of the Visual

Reinhard Braun

'Landscapes are neither simple realities meant to be captured by objectivising methods, nor codified texts meant to be read interpretively, but rather socially relevant processes of collective and subjective identity production. Inherent to landscape is thus something dynamic, performative. The word "landscape", as W. J. T. Mitchell programmatically notes in his introduction to the first edition of the anthology *Landscape and Power* published in 1994, should be understood as a verb rather than as a noun …: *to landscape*, engendering, spawning landscapes.'[1]

So when we speak of landscape, we must consider that it does not really involve something real (along the boundary between nature and culture?) or something given. Instead, we use the term to denote the one indissoluble 'combination of aesthetic, social, economic, symbolic, and spatial components'.[2] Landscape is thus also envisioned, negotiated and—even more importantly—produced in the medium of aesthetics and of the production of visibility. Here—as in general, by the way—representation is not to be understood as a passive mechanism of picturisation, but rather as an active process that evokes something, and not just something that would not exist in this form otherwise, but also something that in this way fosters new kinds of connections to other cultural practices. Representation may be perceived as an intrusion, as an intervention that engages with certain respective assumptions, mechanisms, and interests while also being partially defined by them. But it is also something that changes and reshapes these assumptions, thus opening up new related opportunities for *articulation*.[3] Like all photographic images, pictures of landscapes do not simply concern that which we see. They also deal with how we are even able to determine what we are seeing, how we translate this determination into images, and which meanings can be associated with this translation process. 'Therefore I will say my gaze is directed at "to look at what is there, to read it and its conditions and to make an image of that reading",' writes Ahlam Shibli about her work. Her photographic projects indeed deal with an interpretation, already inscribed in her gaze, of what can be seen.

1
Rainer Guldin: *Politische Landschaften. Zum Verhältnis von Raum und nationaler Identität.* Bielefeld 2014, p. 9.

2
Erik Meinharter: 'Landschaft ist Verhandlungssache: Ein Kommentar zum Diskurs der Landschaft', in: Barbara Pichler and Andrea Pollach (eds.), *moving landscape: Landschaft und Film*. Vienna 2006, pp. 71–80, esp. p. 73.

3
'Articulation is the production of identity on top of differences, of unities out of fragments, of structures across practices. Articulation links this practice to that effect, this text to that meaning, this meaning to that reality, this experience to those politics.' Lawrence Grossberg: 'Articulation and Culture', in: *We Gotta Get Out of This Place: Popular Conservatism and Postmodern Culture.* New York 1992, p. 54.

Landscape is produced, in any case. On the one hand, it is created through interventions, divisions among different forms of usage, agreements, boundaries, exploitation, destruction, and also by preventing destruction and repatriation or even through conservation. This list alone illustrates that landscape, rather than merely correlating with a real manifestation, actually oscillates between history and nature and is essentially the product of an ascription and projection. On the other hand, these interventions and ascriptions first become readable and renderable, or let us say framed, through specific forms of representation—through a framework that facilitates landscape's form, its context, and its coherency. This is a frame that also decides which narratives may be linked to landscape (and such framings are not even to be considered predominantly aesthetically or artistically connoted, but also geographically or scientifically). Indeed, *to landscape* is not another way of saying *farming*. Instead, it denotes processes that produce landscape through systems of representation, bringing it into circulation and allowing it to be integrated into discourses related to science, aesthetics, but also to subjectivisation and identification—processes that associate landscape with identities, with regional or national idioms and stereotypes, with cultural terms and concepts of collectivity, of social and societal facets, ultimately allowing it to become a political project.

In 1949, a National Geographic Society expedition explored the area that is now Kodachrome Basin State Park in Utah. That same year, Jack Breed called this terrain 'Kodachrome Flat' in an article published in National Geographic Magazine, named such after Kodak's Kodachrome diapositive film: 'It was a beautiful and fantastic country. A mile to the left near the base of the cliff I could see red pinnacles thrust up from the valley floor. The few natives who had been here called this area "Thorny Pasture", but we renamed it "Kodachrome Flat" because of the astonishing variety of contrasting colours in the formations.' Towards the end of 2010, Kodak stopped developing this film—but the landscape itself continues to bear its name.

This anecdote from the history of photography illustrates how the perception of landscape during modernism—meaning long before 1949—had become a question of the cultural techniques governing its recording, representation, dissemination and also archivisation. The expansion of the regime of visibility to include previously inaccessible or unknown regions gives rise to something that has found its way, by way of these images in particular, into the collective imagination and into social discourse. The success of the panorama in the late 18th century as a first visual mass medium, in the wake of the first stirrings of industrialisation and the spread of colonialism, elucidates

4
See Joel Snyder:
'Picturing Vision', in:
Critical Inquiry, vol. 6,
no. 3 (Spring 1980), pp.
499-526, esp. p. 503.
'Realistic depiction
is conceptually and
historically based upon
the adoption of a model
that permits both pic-
ture maker and viewer
to demand and, indeed,
to find systematic rela-
tions between picture
and object of depiction.
But this "object" is not
simply "the way the
world is", "the way the
world looks", nor even
"the ways we use our
vision"; it is rather a
standardized, or cha-
racterized, or defined
notion of vision itself.'

5
See Roland Barthes:
'Rhetoric of the Image',
in: *Image, Music, Text*.
London 1977, pp. 32-51,
esp. pp. 42-43. '(...) the
photograph (...) seems
to constitute a message
without a code.'

6
See Joel Snyder: op.
cit., p. 509: 'Only in the
most equivocal sense is
information "out there".
We find, or fail to find,
what we are trained to
look for.'

this dispositive quite exemplarily. European metropolises or foreign countries, Jerusalem, battles on other continents, exotic people and landscapes—all of this laid before the eyes of the 'Western' audience that fancied itself at the centre of the globe. In the process, this world became a visual spectacle and also a spectacle of the visual, not revolving around reality but rather primarily around power relations in which this reality was assigned a role. Visual appropriation in the panorama—and ultimately also, later, in photography—redoubled and validated the seizure of foreign lands by Western colonial powers, while simultaneously validating the superiority of their civilisation. But giving a new name to a landscape in Utah likewise implies becoming inscribed in this landscape, rewriting the history of this landscape, and thus also overwriting and extinguishing another history. From this point on, the new history became a part of the mythos of the American nation and it retrospectively anchored and legitimised the claim to this land.

This anecdote also substantiates the idea that a picturisation of vision occurs before the production of pictures themselves—a picturisation of vision that rests on the conviction that *vision* is precisely able to be captured because it is itself *pictorial*.[4] In this sense, photography may be spoken of as a cultural technique because it regulates the relation between vision, perception, and image according to certain premises for the technologisation and visualisation of culture and society. In con-trast to painting, the technique of photography appears to mask the moment of subjective interpretation and to be bound solely to reality itself. This, at least, did remain a topos of photography theory far into the 20th century.[5] Let us recall how Charles Baudelaire, around the time of photography's origin, denounced it for picturing everything in front of the camera—invariably and indiscriminately—and for selecting, determining, and interrelating the pictorial elements, which contrasted with the art of painting.
However, this selection in/of photography plays out on a different plane: we find (see) what we have learned to seek (recognise), or we do not find (see) it.[6] What photography produces is the excerpted and limited field of a representation that, outside of the picture itself, does not possess or embody any kind of referents. It is for this reason that Shibli insists on creating the image in such a way that it reads and interprets reality, that of the Palestinian village where she was born. Yet what emerges here is not a picture of the village (not in a literal sense, nor in a figurative one), but rather the—regulative, selective—visual access thereto, which is significantly impacted by the unsettled history of this village. It is also influenced by the way this history codetermines the visibility of the village, and by what the artist knows about this history and which role this knowledge plays when it comes to her gaze.

This moment of recognition—of decisions about what scattered traces even can or should be found within the 'real', which is completely inaccessible in its entirety—is more closely akin to a reconstruction than to vision. It inevitably leads to a further assumption: that, in turn, the (photographic) images themselves are not solely accorded to the realm of the visual.

The dispositive of (photographic) images is not actually visual. As Stuart Hall noted in 1984: '[T]here is no such thing as "photography"; only a diversity of practices and historical situations in which the photographic text is produced, circulated and deployed.'[7] Even if we reject the concept of 'image as text' as inadequate and reductionistic, a concept that was influenced by the 'linguistic turn' in the humanities of the 1970s, images must still be understood as something that is to be fundamentally classified between the *visible* and the *sayable*. That which can be found does not appear to be exclusively assigned to the visible but rather simultaneously linked to knowledge. 'There are no visual media. All media are mixed media, with varying ratios of senses and sign types.'[8]

Ultimately, through knowledge (and history), landscape is linked to—cultural, ethical, and national—identity, and images of landscape become enmeshed in processes of identification. Étienne Balibar writes: 'The imaginary dimension in which identities are shaped, and senses of belonging formed and unformed, is, then, the condition of conditions; it is, as it were, the "other scene" on which the effects of the autonomy and heteronomy of politics are engineered.'[9] Photography, too, counts among those 'other scenes' for which the image 'serves as a kind of relay connecting theories of art, language, and the mind with conceptions of social, cultural, and political value'.[10] In this sense, photographic images represent an *articulation:* they link *that* history with *this* view, *that* text with *this* identity, *that* memory with *this* object, *that* place with *this* history.

Countless geographic regions are associated with national-historical origin myths and the attendant political and military conflicts, or they constitute contested zones of national, ethical, cultural and economic conflict. Landscape as and in the image is a scene for these conflicts; it spatialises them, maps them within realities, verifies their claim and their validity there, and first and foremost allows them even to appear to begin with. These landscapes, which are also pictorial landscapes, thus embody a space for producing difference, and they are associated with identity, memory and experience, becoming the scene for the related inscriptions. Their manifestations are distinguished by designs for belonging and describe strategic processes for negotiating various living spaces and life concepts.

7
Stuart Hall: 'Reconstruction Work. Images of Post-War Black Settlement', in: *Critical Decade. Black British Photography in the 80s*, Birmingham 1992, pp. 2–9, esp. p. 2.

8
W. J. T. Mitchell: 'Showing Seeing: A Critique of Visual Culture', in: *What Do Pictures Want? The Lives and Loves of Images*. Chicago 2005, p. 343.

9
Étienne Balibar: 'Three Concepts of Politics: Emancipation, Transformation, Civility', in: *Politics and the Other Scene*. London/New York 2002, pp. 1–2.

10
W. J. T. Mitchell: *Iconology: Image, Text, Ideology*. Chicago 1986, p. 2.

Landscapes thus become a kind of historical formation and represent complex superimpositions, as Gilles Deleuze writes, 'from things and words, from seeing and speaking, from the *visible* and the *sayable*, from bands of visibility and fields of readability, from contents and expressions'.[11] Each historical formation, in turn, forms a specific distribution of the visible and the sayable, 'a way of saying and seeing' and "images falling into the midst of words, verbal flashes crisscrossing drawings, … discourse cutting into the form of things," and vice versa'.[12] So if no purely visual media exist, then photography can be said to be flashed by the verbal and traversed by knowledge and thought. Yet this does not make photography a 'message without a code' or even a 'universal language',[13] but rather a field of agency in which bodies, things, language, thought and experience become inscribed. It would be a mistake, however, to assume that in the photographic image these coinciding elements become 'reconciled' to us. On the contrary, in taking reference to Michel Foucault, Deleuze is concerned with the fundamental issue of the relation between images and texts, and with the understanding that they do not share a common space but are rather interreferential along the margin of difference.[14] This difference, this curious region between the word and the image, a 'distribution in space',[15] cannot be identified, described, named, classified, or coerced into a relationship where the one represents the other, becomes reduced to the other, or is expressed by the other. It is in this unclassified space that the politics of images could ultimately settle, including its specific modality that we communicate by way of pictures about identities, knowledge, history, affiliations, or cultural differences. Photography does not represent landscape as politics, knowledge as aesthetics, or vision as imagery. Instead, it articulates, through the *dispositifs* of its representations, the intertwining affinities among vision, image, expression, knowledge, body, and also landscape. Herein lies the politics of the photographic image.

Against this background, the exhibition series *Disputed Landscape* probes current photographic conditions as to how they can stage or make these photographic articulations visible in pictures. Some of the invited artists work in regions that are experiencing, or have been marked by, military or national struggles, from Tibet to the Middle East, from Africa to Ireland. The artists have set out to expose the forensic and symbolic traces of these areas ('Uncovering History'); others explore the fiction of landscape, historical photographic *dispositifs*, or the documentary conflict with a view to representation ('Visual Paradigm'); and still others focus on the temporal, spatial, corporeal and pictorial constructions of landscape ('Enacting Landscape'). Common to all projects appears to be the fact that the photographs produced in the process are themselves permeated by conflicts and ruptures,

11
Gilles Deleuze: *Foucault* (trans. Séan Hand). London/New York 1999, p. 41.

12
Ibid, pp. 42 and 56.

13
Cf. note 5 and see Allan Sekula: 'The Traffic in Photographs', in: *Art Journal*, vol. 41, no. 1 (Spring 1981), p. 16.

14
Gilles Deleuze, op. cit. (note 11), pp. 41ff.

15
Ibid, p. 60.

that they challenge existing articulations of *those* ideologies by way of *these* representations. Is it even possible to reconstruct (conflicting) histories like those inscribed in landscapes? How are these histories staged in image form, themselves being characterised by a suppression of visibilities, a suppression that is so often compounded and ingrained by a suppression of (other) histories? Which facets of historical forma-tions can be exposed, which aspects of things and words, vision and speech, content and expression? Against this backdrop, the exhibition project opens up an arena for coming to terms with articulations, a pursuit that ultimately infuses all of the pictures themselves.

Body and Landscape in the Colonial Matrix of Power

Alanna Lockward

'Modern life begins with slavery.'
Toni Morrison

Body and landscape, the mediated experience of our surroundings, are quintessential elements of what the Situationists articulated as psychogeography, considering it 'the study of the precise laws and specific effects of the geographical environment, whether consciously organised or not, on the emotions and behaviour of individuals.'[1] A decolonised reading of this indeed useful concept involves the necessary excoriation of the masquerade known as modernity and its inseparable shadow, coloniality.[2] Given that European modernity has been prolific in the politics of confusion, namely the interchangeable usage of terms such as modernism, modernisation and modernity to designate similar but different phenomena, I will start by clarifying how decoloniality sees the relationship between body and landscape within the colonial matrix of power.

Colonial matrix of power is a term coined by Aníbal Quijano in the early 1990s. Later, Walter D. Mignolo and Madina Tlostanova (2009) analysed how it has operated since the 16th century within its four interconnected spheres. In all of these spheres, for example, the notion of *individual* illustrates the first disambiguation from the Situationists' symptomatic reproduction of a so-called universal human condition, so treasured by the rhetoric of modernity. According to this narrative, the category human is self-explanatorily white, patriarchal hetero-normative, Christian and European. It is in the struggle to dominate entire populations outside of this notion of an 'authentic' human that the economic enterprise known as European colonialism came into being with brutal and continuous consequences. One of the four spheres of this modus operandi of coloniality is related to the control of knowledge and subjectivity. For the purpose of the ideas discussed below, I

1
Guy Debord: 'Introduction to a Critique of Urban Geography' [1955]. Trans. Ken Knabb, in: *situationist international online*, www.cddc.vt.edu/sionline/presitu/geography.html (accessed January 23, 2015).

2
The modernity/coloniality research programme was inspired by the groundbreaking contribution of Peruvian sociologist Aníbal Quijano. It offers a tool to dismantle the continuities of colonialism after formal decolonisation. Decolonial thinkers consider postcolonial studies to be limited in scope since, in addition to omitting this inextricability, their genealogy is anchored in rather provincial theories of (post)modernity based largely on Eurocentric historical and intellectual genealogies.

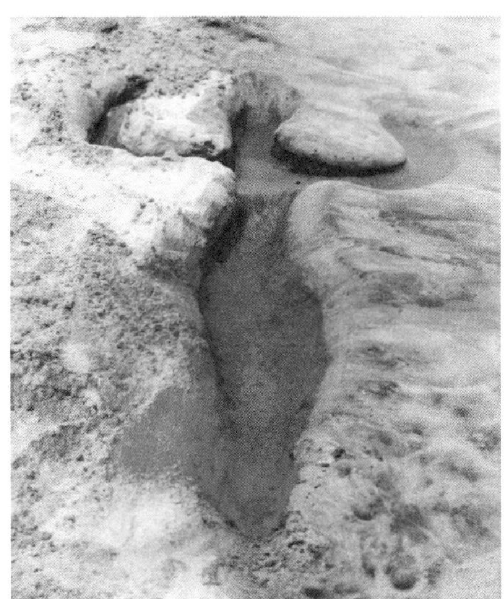

Ana Mendieta
Untitled (Silueta Series, Mexico), 1976

will focus on this particular one as the core of the ethical conundrums of aesthetic analysis in these times where, according to Kobena Mercer, 'the world maps of modern art inherited from the age of Eurocentrism have been thrown off-centre by the post-colonial breakthrough.'[3]

Before building further arguments questioning the ideal scenario proposed by Mercer, I will briefly name the other three spheres which offer an equally transcendental understanding of how an entire system known as modernity/coloniality has until today ruled human relations within the context of the nation-state. The first is the violent appropriation of land and its resources, which ensured that control of the economy rested in the hands of a few. The second sphere is the control of political, financial, military and governmental organisations which give authority to either the same few or others associated with them. Thirdly, we find the control of the public sphere organised around the inevitability of the nuclear family and its hetero-patriarchal capitalist gender relations. This set of spheres has mutated in different periods and moments, changing its rhetoric 'according to the needs and the leading forces shaping [them],' as Mignolo and Tlostanova observe: 'In the period from 1970 to 2000 neo-liberalism was consolidated in the wake of the collapse of the Soviet Union. The neo-liberal agenda translated the previous mission of development and modernisation, into the Washington Consensus of granting the market economy priority over social regulation.'[4]

If we listen to the songlines of Aboriginal Australians, we experience how these four spheres are articulated dramatically in the relationship between landscape and body. In these spiritual landscapes, coloniality—which is the preservation of the modus operandi of colonialism

3
Kobena Mercer, 'Introduction', in: Idem (ed.), *Exiles, Diasporas and Strangers*. London/ Cambridge, MA 2008, p. 13. I beg to differ with this rather optimistic perspective by Mercer. Recent statistical data developed as an art project in New York City reached the factual conclusion that the art scene is 200 per cent *whiter* than the current demographic ethnic imperatives of this city: Jillian Steinhauer: 'Report Finds NYC's Art World 200% Whiter Than Its Population', in: *Hyperallergic* (posted 30 June 2014) hyperallergic.com/135474/report-finds-nycs-art-world-200-whiter-than-its-population/ (accessed 30 July 2014).

4
Walter D. Mignolo and Madina Tlostanova; 'Global Coloniality and the Decolonial Option', in: *Kult* 6–Special Issue (Fall 2009), pp. 134–136.

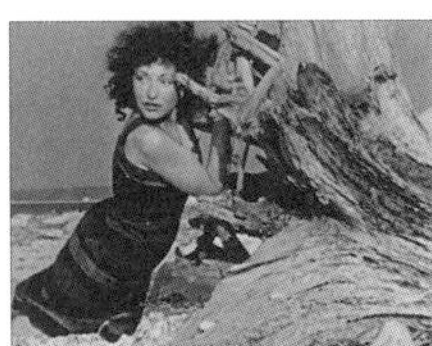

Maya Deren
At Land, 1943

5
Frontex is an external and internal borders programme, founded in 2005, with the fastest growing budget in the European Union; a European Union that was first known and conceptualised as inseparable from (the exploitation of) Africa and therefore named Eurafrica by its founders (cf. Peo Hansen and Stefan Jonsson, 'Bringing Africa as a "Dowry to Europe"', in: *Interventions: International Journal of Postcolonial Studies* 13,3 [2011], pp. 443-463). Indeed, there are irrefutable historical continuities between the Berlin Africa Conference (1884-1885), the original Eurafrica (European Union) project, and current 'mappings' of migration routes in the African Continent. This border externalisation 'initiative' could be defined as a de facto 'cartographic war' against Africa. For more information on Frontex see www.frontex. europa.eu.

after formal decolonisation—challenges the so-called crisis of testimony inherent to modernity/coloniality. Australian Aborigines experience a reality inseparable from their spiritual world, which they call dreaming, in the same way that Dominican and Haitian Vodoun practitioners understand the human condition as being one with the ancestors. Those landmarks that have been considered unworthy of legitimisation by canonical historiography, in the name of the so-called 'secular' imperative of modernity, have been carefully preserved orally and their physical locations—their psychogeographies—are poetically embedded in its accounts. There is a freedom of movement among these narratives that is completely lacking in Ferguson, Melilla, Gaza, the Mexican-US border, Guantánamo, the 'highlights' of coloniality today. In other words, in all these places the romantic endeavours of the Situationists' flâneur or flâneuse become irrelevant and even aggravating when mirrored with the criminalisation of movement institutionalised in Europe by Frontex[5] as well as the anti-Black racial profiling on the rise both in England as well as on the continent.

Legendary decolonial flâneuses such as Maya Deren, Ana Mendieta and Mona Hatoum have imprinted their own bodies in both natural and urban landscapes, challenging coloniality and becoming an obligatory reference on the subject. In *At Land* (1943), for example, Maya Deren immerses herself in a time-space capsule using her own body as the leitmotif that links dream-like scenes taking place in different contexts. This notion of inseparability between the visible and the invisible is a direct output of her scholarly and personal involvement with Haitian Vodoun cosmologies. As the mother of (North) American experimental cinema, Deren was, like Jean-Luc Godard and Sergei Eisenstein, also a film theorist, but unlike them her writings and films are almost exclusively discussed in feminist courses. According to Shelley Rice, 'Her years in Haiti and her intense involvement with [Vodoun] can be seen as her quest to experience a living culture that gave "credibility to the unreal", and thereby embody the vision she sought in her experimental films. Maya Deren's most significant contribution to postmodern discourse might be her profound understanding of the ties that link the avant-garde and the "primitive" [sic], the Western and the Other'.[6]

The inseparability of art and life, of nature and its invisible dwellers, is what kept Ana Mendieta eternally imprinted in the shadows and traces of her own earthy body silhouettes. This conscious interaction with landscape and the elements that are equally removed and still tabooed in the name of the so-called 'secularity' of the arts, one of the biggest and most successful delusions of the Enlightenment, is movingly expressed in her interview with legendary art-life performance artist Linda Montano: 'Now I believe in water, air and earth. They are

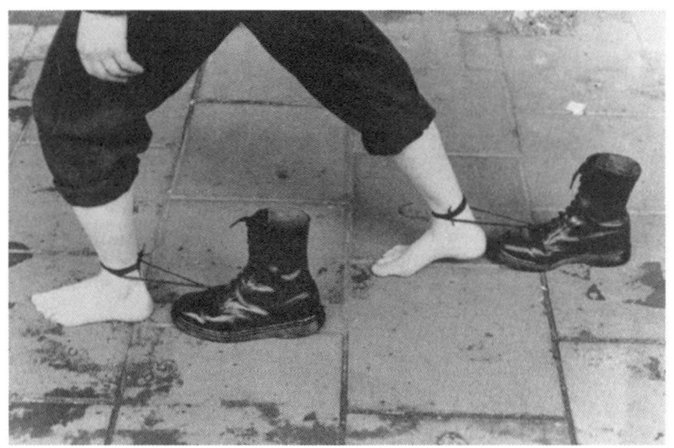

6
'Like Claude Cahun, she was a friend of André Breton. Deren, however, denied any connection with the movement's aesthetic aims. The Surrealist obsession with duality—with the lines separating the real and the imaginary, the rational and the irrational, the waking life and the dream—was, in fact, diametrically opposed to Deren's fascination with the continuity of life and death, the physical and the spiritual, and "I" and the "non-I". Her films were intended as imaginary arenas where this point of contact could be visualised—where boundaries normally fixed could dissolve, or become wildly flexible; where protagonists could move freely between dreams and waking life without ever resolving the differences between the two; where nature and culture, urban and rural environments could be separated (and linked) by a single step; where past and future selves could meet along the road, fracturing into clones moving along parallel paths of time and space.' Shelley Rice: *Inverted Odysseys: Claude Cahun, Maya Deren, Cindy Sherman.* New York 1999, p. 70.

all deities. They also speak. I am connected with the goddess of sweet water—this has been her year, and it is raining a lot. Those are the things that are powerful and important. I don't know why people have gotten away from these ideas.'[7]

In her iconic performance *Roadworks* (1985), British-Palestinian artist Mona Hatoum's bare feet were laced to a pair of Dr. Martens boots usally worn by the police or skinheads. Her pilgrimage through the urban landscape of Brixton had, according to the artist, an epistemically revealing moment: 'One comment I really liked was when a group of builders, standing having their lunch break, said: "What the hell is happening there? What is she up to?" And this Black woman, passing by with her shopping, said to them: "Well it is obvious. She's being followed by the police." Very cool, and just went off'.[8] The immediacy of the translation of the diasporic experience is strikingly self-evident in this anecdote. What I find even more fascinating is precisely the inability of the *white* workers to understand the action by Hatoum, since in coloniality the Black body in the landscape is either rendered invisible or imagined as a possible threat.

The romantic figure of the flâneur is hardly applicable in the same sense in Haiti, where Miami-based artist Adler Guerrier was born. His *Untitled (Nine to Five)* (2001), a three-channel video, features a man in a suit carrying a briefcase. He waits at the bus stop; walks down the street; walks into a building; enters a cafeteria. However, his activities begin at nine p.m., when it is dark and downtown is completely deserted. This is definitively the view of an immigrant that sees himself as part of the scene, not as an accessory; there is a strong sense of dignity and self-respect in this perspective. According to Guerrier[9] this film was based on three jazz compositions: Charles Mingus's *Haitian Fight Song* (1955), Duke Ellington's *Fleurette Africaine (African Flower,* 1963), and the Modern Jazz Quartet's *Valeria* (1972). *Haitian Fight Song* is the piece more strongly connected to the above-mentioned sequences of the

Adler Guerrier
Untitled (Nine to Five), 2001, video still

7
Ana Mendieta interviewed by Linda Montano, in: Idem: *Performance Artists Talking in the Eighties*. Berkeley 2004, p. 180.

8
Amna Malik: 'Conceptualising "Black" British Art Through the Lens of Exile', in: Kobena Mercer (ed.): *Exiles, Diasporas and Strangers*. Op. cit., p. 176.

9
Rebecca Zorach: 'Place Becomes Sweet and Great. A Conversation with Adler Guerrier', in: *Adler Guerrier: Formulating a Plot*. Exh. cat. Miami 2014, pp. 77-96, here p. 80.

film, where the idea of the flâneur[10] is linked to the maroon[11] leaders who conceived and ultimately achieved the first successful enslaved people uprising, the Haitian Revolution, which created the first Black Republic. This particular type of awareness implied by the presence of the Black body in the urban landscape represents both a transgression and an affirmation of being. In Guerrier's native Haiti, young people also transgress the unmarked boundaries of class and racialisation by becoming contemporary *pa gen pwogram* defying pervasive notions of belonging attached to public spaces such as those beaches that until very recently were only accessible to the elite, as well as the streets of Pétion-Ville which today are as promiscuous socially as the traditionally crowded areas of downtown Port-au-Prince. This displacement of landscapes' 'legitimacy' dooms any attempt at social engineering to be an exercise in futility. The illegality of the Black body is a de facto impossibility in Haiti and the absurdity of its criminalisation is what keeps the legacy of the Haitian Revolution a glorious reminder in the face of Ferguson et al. At least here the Black body in the landscape has a decolonial history that is as real as it gets, a living memory that has been consistently and painfully erased by colonial archives on the African continent and elsewhere.

In a video interview for the exhibition 'Contested Terrains' at the Tate Modern (2011), Sammy Baloji explains the genealogy of *Mémoire* by concluding that his aim was to create 'a new *dispositive*, a new narrative'. The translation, however, uses the term *slides* instead of the Foucauldian *dispositif*. And it is precisely in resonance with this misunderstanding—with this colonial misunderstanding, to paraphrase a film with the same title by French-Cameroonian documentary filmmaker,

10
'Literally translatable
as "stroll; strolling;
sauntering", flânerie is
most often associated
with a rich tradition
of unencumbered,
non-confrontational
movement through
physically and socially
shifting Francophone
geographies. In late
19th-century Parisian
visual and poetic
discourse, the aimless
looking of the 'gentle-
man of leisure' was key
to understandings of
the city's spatial trans-
formation into a center
of modern capital. For
Haitian writers in the
1920s living under
American occupation,
the wanderings of bour-
geois *pa gen pwogram*,
meaning those with no
programme or schedule,
were seen as central
to the gathering of
native knowledges that
might be amassed and
mobilised in the making
of a national culture.
And amid the upheavals
of mid-20th-century
France, the related
concept of the *dérive*,
or drift—an uncharted,
meandering journey
through an urban land-
scape—would become
central to the radical
practice of the Situ-
ationist International,
particularly group
members' exploration of
"the effects of the geo-
graphical environment
on the emotions and
behaviours of individu-
als".' Huey Copeland:
'Sinous Coordination:
On the Photography of
Adler Guerrier', in: *Adler
Guerrier: Formulating a
Plot*. Op. cit., pp. 42–52,
here p. 45.

Jean-Marie Teno—that I want to conclude these thoughts on body and landscape in the colonial matrix of power.

Mémoire, realised between 2006–2009, has been exhibited in iconic venues such as the above-mentioned Tate Modern, the Museum of African Art in New York and also received the prestigious Prince Claus Award in 2009. Some of the texts accompanying the series in its travels tend to preclude two pertinent aspects that I would like to outline. These two vacuums are linked to form and content respectively. On the formal vacuum, it is surprising to find the lack of interest in reading *Mémoire* as inscribed within the long-standing tradition of photomontage as a political tool that started in Germany with the Dadaists, and more specifically in Berlin with John Heartfield. Considering that Baloji describes himself as self-taught, any reference to his inspiration from European and African sources in his formal education could be easily dismissed. Nevertheless, it is crucial to remember that art critique must consistently relate to canonical genealogies in order to validate itself. Even decolonial readings such as this one must follow this unavoidable path.

The second vacuum is defined by the content and I will focus my last brief comments on this particular aspect. This gap is indeed very illustrative of the way in which European modernity has systematically fictionalised itself as completely independent from colonialism. Dismantling this narrative is the core of decolonial thinking and it is the reasoning behind my interpretation of *Mémoire* as a virtual 'manual on decoloniality'. According to Bogumil Jewsiewicki: 'The landscapes [that Baloji] portrays are of a kind seen throughout the world, as factories and production, resources and profits, are moved from one continent to another due to the vicissitudes of globalisation'.[12] In this judgment, globalisation is presented as a 'new' phenomenon, something that 'inevitably' carries with it the impoverishment of entire populations using a rather benevolent expression: 'the vicissitudes of globalisation'.
In *Mémoire*, Sammy Baloji creates a series of *tableaux vivants* where neo-liberalism is simultaneously re-enacted, dismembered and rigorously portrayed as the macabre fiction that it is. We feel that we are looking at different films where the actors only change costumes and the themes are repeated in a litany where the interconnectedness between enslavement and wealth is presented over and over again. This work is a result of his own personal confrontation with the hidden side of modernity. In 2005, while researching Lumumbashi's colonial architecture and industrial sites—which he has photographed extensively— the artist found the photographic archives of the Gécamines mining company, which was the main industry in the province of Katanga for many years. These photographs were completely unknown in Katanga until then, and he never learned about the stories portrayed in them

Sammy Baloji
From: *Mémoire,*
2006

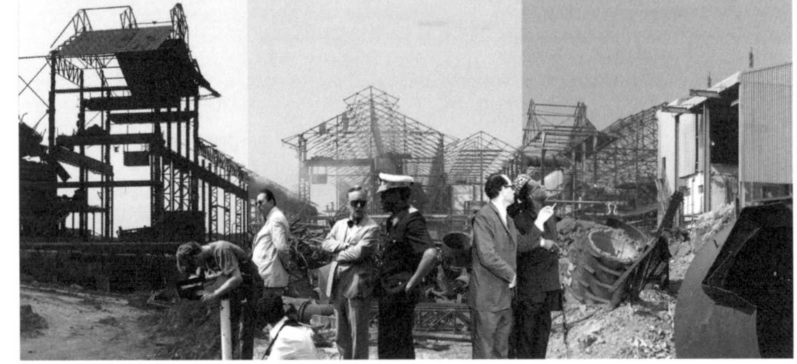

at school. These images reveal the genesis of the forced labour that created the by now long-gone 'economic success' of Lumumbashi. The ruins of the industrial backdrop operate as a signifier of an unbroken continuity. The landscapes are static but, contrasted with the dynamism evoked by the subjects superimposed on them, challenge any attempts to understand the different historical moments as ruptures. These are splendid illustrations of how the rhetoric of modernity and the logic of coloniality are inseparable, or rather mutually inclusive. It is impossible to understand the one without fully acknowledging 'the Other'.

Since the orchestrating quality of these images reminds me of the different movements of a symphony, and in order to avoid a misreading of his intentions (even decolonial misunderstandings should be avoided), I asked the artist how he would describe his work in musical terms. He answered by quoting Sun Ra's *Concert For Comet Kohoutek*. According to Jesse Jarnow, this album recorded in late 1973 and released in the early 1990s 'captures a typically inspired night by Sun Ra & the Intergalactic Space Research Arkestra, since it is guided by a musical theme composed around the idea of the Comet Kohoutek, which was passing close to Earth at the time.'

Sun Ra, a queer Black performer who has dismantled many music industry clichés, seems the perfect embodiment of the challenging of the coloniality of gender, economic control, knowledge and authority. By quoting this particular album by Sun Ra, Sammy Baloji is certainly outlining the liberating and decolonising potential of his images, because it is only by acknowledging the truth of inequality, of our differences, as the Black Feminist Audre Lorde commands us to do, that we will be able to materialise a true creative force for change. Only by decolonising our understanding of history in the colonial matrix of power it is possible to forge what Baloji calls a 'new *dispositive*, a new narrative' and Sun Ra defines as 'The fiery truth of Enlightenment'.

11
Marronage—the lifestyle, ethics and sociopolitical organisation of runaway enslaved communities outside the plantation system during colonialism—has been an intrinsic component of the radical imagination of countless liberation struggles in the Americas.

12
Bogumil Jewsiewicki,
*The Beautiful Time.
Photography by Sammy
Baloji.* New York 2010.

Authors

Reinhard Braun, born 1964 in Linz, studied art history at the University of Graz and currently lives in Graz. From 2007 to 2010 he was curator for visual arts at the steirischer herbst festival, Graz. Since 2011 he has been director and publisher of Camera Austria, Graz. His most recent curatorial projects include: *Art Is Concrete* (2012), *Sven Johne. Where the sky is darkest, the stars are brightest* (2013), *Joachim Koester. The Ghost Shop* (2014), *once documentary. Sven Augustijnen, Eric Baudelaire, Peggy Buth, Maryam Jafri* (2014), Camera Austria, Graz.

Sabine Flach is Professor for Modern and Contemporary Art at the Institute for Art History at the Karl-Franzens University, Graz, as well as a permanent member of the Faculty for Contemporary Art and Art Theory at the School of Visual Arts, NYC. Among other places, she has taught at the Universities of Kassel and Hamburg, at the Technical University Berlin, at Humboldt Universität Berlin as well as at the Mills College, Oakland, CA. From 2000 to 2010 she was Head of the Research Department 'Knowledge Arts. The Art of Knowing, and the Knowledge of Art' at the Centre for Literature and Culture Research, Berlin.

Philipp Kaiser studied Art History and German Literature at the Universities of Basel and Hamburg. After a period as curator at the Museum for Contemporary Art Basel, he worked as Senior Curator at the Museum of Contemporary Art, Los Angeles (MOCA) from early 2007, and headed up the Museum Ludwig in Cologne from 2012 to 2014. At present he is working as a freelance curator and critic in Los Angeles. He has curated numerous solo exhibitions, including those of Louise Lawler, Christian Philipp Müller, Simon Starling, Johanna Billing, Oscar Tuazon, Bruce Nauman, and Jack Goldstein, as well as *Flashback. Revisiting the Art of the Eighties* (2005), *Index. Conceptualism in California* (2008), and *Ends of the Earth. Land Art to 1974* (2012) at the MOCA, Los Angeles and the Haus der Kunst, Munich in collaboration with co-curator Miwon Kwon. Besides his work as a curator, he has published numerous texts on contemporary art and taught at the State Academy of Fine Arts in Karlsruhe as well as at the University of California, Los Angeles (UCLA).

Alanna Lockward, born in the Caribbean, is an author and independent curator based in Berlin. She is the founding director of Art Labour Archives, an exceptional platform centred on theory, political activism, and aesthetics. She is an academic advisor for Transart Institute (US), associate scholar of the Young Scholars Network Black Diaspora and Germany, and the general manager of the Transnational Decolonial Institute. As a curator she has received awards from the Allianz Cultural Foundation, Berlin, the Danish Arts Council, Copenhagen, and the Nordic Council of Ministers. She conceptualised and curated *BE.BOP. BLACK EUROPE BODY POLITICS* (2012–14) at Ballhaus Naunynstraße, Berlin. www.alannalockward.com

Peter Pakesch, born in Graz, began studying architecture, but also was active early on as an artist. His first experiences as an exhibition curator were gathered in the Forum Stadtpark in Graz from 1976 to 1979 and at the steirischer herbst. A period of study in New York followed in 1980. After his return to Austria, Pakesch opened his own gallery in Vienna in 1981, in which he presented exhibitions of artists such as John Baldessari, Herbert Brandl, Albert Oehlen, Mike Kelley, Martin Kippenberger, and Sol LeWitt. In 1986 he founded the Grazer Kunstverein together with the Graz-based cultural policy maker Helmut Strobl, which he led as artistic director until 1988. After a few years as a freelance curator for the National Gallery in Prague, he assumed the post of Director of the Kunsthalle Basel in 1996. Since 2003 Pakesch has been the Intendant and Artistic Director of the Universalmuseum Joanneum. At the Kunsthaus Graz, which opened in 2003 and which he also led until 2011, Pakesch has been responsible for various exhibitions of nationally and internationally prominent artists: *Warhol Wool Newman. Painting Real* and *Screening Real. Conner Lockhart Warhol* (2009), *Franz West. Auto-Theatre, Cologne – Naples – Graz* (2010), *Heimo Zobernig* (2013), *James Benning. Decoding Fear* (2014). Since 2015 Peter Pakesch has been Head of the Management Board of the Maria Lassnig Private Foundation.

Karl Schlögel, born in 1948, studied philosophy, sociology, East European history and Slavic studies at the Free University Berlin, in Moscow and Leningrad. He was Professor for East European History at the Europa University Viadrina in Frankfurt/Oder until his retirement with emeritus status. He received the European Essay Prize Charles Villon in 1990, the Anna-Krüger Prize of the College of Sciences, Berlin in 1999, the Hamburg Lessing Prize in 2005, as well as the Leipzig Book Prize for European Understanding in 2009. Publications: *Promenade in Jalta und andere Städtebilder, Die Mitte liegt ostwärts. Europa im Übergang, Terror und Traum. Moskau 1937, Archäologie des Kommunismus*, et al.

Christian Schwägerl, born in 1968, works as a journalist, author and biologist in Berlin. His book *Menschenzeit* (Riemann, 2010) inspired the Anthropocene Project at the House of World Cultures in Berlin and the special exhibition *Welcome to the Anthropocene* running at the Deutsches Museum in Munich until mid-2016. Recently *Menschenzeit* was published by the Synergetic Press with the title *The Anthropocene. The Human Era and How It Shapes Our Planet*. Other books by Christian Schwägerl are *11 drohende Kriege* (2012) and *Die analoge Revolution* (2014). The author works on a freelance basis for GEO, FAZ, Cicero and other media. In addition, he runs the 'Future of Science Journalism' masterclass at the Bosch Foundation.

Hannah Stippl, born in 1968, works with the theme of landscape as a fine artist, curator and theoretician. Important curatorial projects in recent years were *Die Lesbarkeit der Brache* and *(Landscape) with Flowers* in collaboration with the Botanical Garden of the University of Vienna and the IG Bildende Kunst Wien. Her dissertation *Nur wo der Mensch die Natur gestört hat wird die Landschaft wirklich schön* offers the first treatment of Lucius Burckhardt's landscape-theory related watercolours, and will be published by Martin Schmitz Verlag in 2017. Involvement with plants and painting lie at the root of her joint artistic work with Anita Duller under the label Duller/Stippl. At present she teaches landscape art at the University for Applied Arts, Vienna.

Thomas Weski, born in Hanover in 1953, was Curator for Photography and Media at the Sprengel Museum Hanover, Chief Curator at the Museum Ludwig, and initially Chief Curator and later Vice-Director at the Haus der Kunst, Munich. He has been Professor for 'Cultures of the Curated' at the Academy of Visual Arts, Leipzig since 2009. Co-curated exhibitions include: *How you look at it*, Sprengel Museum Hanover (2000), *Cruel & Tender*, Tate Modern, London and Museum Ludwig, Cologne (2003), *William Eggleston. Democratic Camera*, Whitney Museum of American Art, New York (2008), *Photography Calling*, Sprengel Museum Hanover (2011). Curated exhibitions include: *Robert Adams. What We Bought. The New World*, Sprengel Museum Hanover (1995), *Thomas Struth. Portraits*, Sprengel Museum Hanover (1997), *Click Doubleclick. The Documentary Factor*, Haus der Kunst, Munich (2006), *Andreas Gursky*, Haus der Kunst, Munich (2007), and *Michael Schmidt. Grey as Colour*, Haus der Kunst, Munich (2010).

Imprint

This catalogue is published on the occasion of the exhibitions

Disputed Landscape
Camera Austria
13.03.–06.09.2015

The Visual Paradigm
13.03.–10.05.2015

Uncovering History
16.05.–05.07.2015

Enacting Landscape
11.07.–06.09.2015

Camera Austria
Lendkai 1
8020 Graz, Austria
T: +43-316/81 55 50-16
office@camera-austria.at
www.camera-austria.at

Artistic Director, Curator
Reinhard Braun

Exhibition Management
Angelika Maierhofer

Archive, Exhibition
Installation
Christine Winkler

Team Exhibition Installation
Henrik Klug, Martin
Pelzmann, Eva
Schmartschan

Exhibition Guards and
Education
Barbara Augustinović,
Joana Theuer, Daniela
Zehetner

Exhibition Graphics
Satz & Sätze, Graz

Exhibition Documentation
Lupi Spuma

Office Management
Katrin Müller

Landscape in Motion
Cinematic Visions of an
Uncertain Tomorrow
Kunsthaus Graz,
Universalmuseum
Joanneum
13.03.–26.10.2015

HyperAmerica
Landscape – Image –
Reality
Kunsthaus Graz,
Universalmuseum
Joanneum
10.04.–30.08.2015

Kunsthaus Graz
Universalmuseum
Joanneum
Lendkai 1
8020 Graz, Austria
T: +43-316/8017-9200
kunsthausgraz@
museum-joanneum.at
www.kunsthausgraz.at

The Kunsthaus Graz is a
joint venture between the
Province of Styria and the
City of Graz within the
context of the Universal-
museum Joanneum.

Board
Wolfgang Muchitsch, Peter
Pakesch

Department Head Modern
and Contemporary Art
Peter Peer

Curators
Katrin Bucher Trantow,
Peter Pakesch (Landscape
in Motion)
Katia Huemer, Peter
Pakesch (HyperAmerica)

Assistant Curator
Elisabeth Schlögl
(Landscape in Motion)

Registrars
Elisabeth Ganser, Clemens
Mair (Landscape in Motion)
Magdalena Reininger,
Astrid Mönnich
(HyperAmerica)

Restoration
Paul-Bernhard Eipper,
Barbara Molnár-Lang

Exhibition Installation
Robert Bodlos, Ivan
Drlje, Fabian Egger,
Markus Ettinger, Daniel
Freudenberg, Helmut
Fuchs, Ivan Gorickic, Bernd
Klinger, Irmgard Knechtl,
Andreas Lindbichler, Josef
Lurger, Stefan Reichmann,
Klaus Riegler, Michael
Saupper, Stefan Savič,
Peter Semlitsch

Technical Team
Klaus Berghold, Lukas
Ditzer, Andreas Graf, Georg
Pachler, Stefan Reichmann,
Mit Loidl oder Co
(Christoph Loidl, Wolfgang
Petschnegg), zuvy.net,
Wien (Christian Zagler)
(Landscape in Motion)

Scientific Consultant
Thomas Weski
(HyperAmerica)

Architectonic Consultant
Niels Jonkhans
(HyperAmerica)

Educational Team
Monika Holzer-Kernbichler
and team

Graphics
Michael Posch

Office Management
Teresa Ruff

Staff Coordination
Anke Leitner, Eva Ofner,
Sigrid Rachoinig

Info Desk
Sarah Bundschuh,
Elisabeth Kampfhofer,
Thomas Kirchmair, Sabine
Messner

Press/Marketing and Public
Relations
Christoph Pelzl, Jörg
Eipper-Kaiser, Barbara
Ertl-Leitgeb, Anna Fras/
Elisabeth Weixler, Bärbel
Hradecky, Eva Pessenhofer-
Krebs, Astrid Rosmann

Event Management
Gabriele Filzwieser, Michael
Sladek, Franz Adlassnig

**Landscape: Transformation
of an Idea**
Art from 1800 to the
Present Day from the
Collection of the Neue
Galerie Graz
Neue Galerie Graz,
Universalmuseum
Joanneum
19.06.–06.09.2015

Neue Galerie Graz
Universalmuseum
Joanneum
Joanneumsviertel 2
8010 Graz, Austria
T: +43-316/8017-9100
neuegalerie@
museum-joanneum.at
www.neuegaleriegraz.at

Curators
Gudrun Danzer, Günther
Holler-Schuster

Registrars of the Collection
Monika Binder-Krieglstein,
Brigitte Lampl

Registrars
Astrid Mönnich, Magdalena
Reininger

Restoration
Paul Bernhard Eipper, Julia
Hüttmann, Barbara Molnár-
Lang, Melitta Schmiedel

Exhibition Installation
Robert Bodlos and Team

Educational Team
Monika Holzer-Kernbichler
and team

Graphics
Karin Buol-Wischenau,
Andrea Weishaupt

Office Management
Gertrude Leber

Staff Coordination
Anke Leitner, Eva Ofner,
Sigrid Rachoinig

Info Desk
Sarah Bundschuh, Thomas
Kirchmair, Gabriele Lind,
Petra Melinz-Schille,
Sabine Messner

Press/Marketing and Public Relations
Christoph Pelzl/Elisabeth Weixler and teams

Event Management
Gabriela Filzwieser and team

Political Landscape
Art – Resistance – Salzkammergut
Art in Public Space
from 11.07.2015,
Ausseerland
11.07.–06.09.2015,
Kunsthaus Graz

Institute for Art in Public Space Styria
Universalmuseum Joanneum
Marienplatz 1/1
8020 Graz, Austria
T: +43-316/8017-9265
kioer@museum-joanneum.at
www.kioer.at
www.politische-landschaft.org

Department Head
Elisabeth Fiedler

Curators
Dirck Möllmann, Elisabeth Fiedler

Assistant Curator
Johannes Leitich

Catalogue

Editors
Katrin Bucher Trantow, Katia Huemer, Peter Pakesch

Assistant Editors
Katia Huemer, Angelika Maierhofer, Elisabeth Schlögl

Translations
Dawn Michelle d'Atri, Andrew Horsfield, Amy Patton

Proofreading
Kate Howlett-Jones

Graphic Concept
Lichtwitz – Büro für visuelle Kommunikation

Graphic Design
Karin Buol-Wischenau

Image Editing
Leo Kreisel-Strauss, Michael Posch, Karin Buol-Wischenau

Print
Medienfabrik Graz

Paper
Invercote 300g,
Hello Silk 150g,
Biotop 3 100g

Fonts
Tram Joanneum,
ITC Charter Com

Printed in Austria

Source Materials and Translations

Peter Pakesch
Foreword
translated from the German by Andrew Horsfield

Gudrun Danzer, Günther Holler-Schuster
Landscape: Transformation of an Idea
translated from the German by Y'Plus: Susannah Chadwick and Maria Nievoll

Katia Huemer
HyperAmerica
Index
Katia Huemer (KH)
translated from the German by Amy Patton (AP)

Katrin Bucher Trantow, Monika Holzer-Kernbichler
Landscape in Motion
Index
Katrin Bucher Trantow (KBT), Monika Holzer-Kernbichler (MHK), Christian Höller (CH), Katia Huemer (KH), Claudia Slanar (CS), Elisabeth Schlögl (ES)
translated from the German by Andrew Horsfield (AH), Amy Patton (AP)

Estelle Blaschke (EB), Reinhard Braun (RB)
Disputed Landscape
translated from the German by Dawn Michelle d'Atri
Index
Jens Asthoff (JA), Reinhard Braun (RB)
translated from the German by Andrew Horsfield (AH)

Dirck Möllmann
Political Landscape
Index
Dirck Möllmann (DM)
translated from the German by Y'Plus: Susannah Chadwick and Maria Nievoll (SC/MN)

Sabine Flach, Peter Pakesch
Concepts of Landscape
translated from the German by Andrew Horsfield
The conversation took place on 27.01.2015.

Robert Smithson
The Monuments of Passaic
© Holt Smithson Foundation/Licensed by VAGA, New York, NY, © Artforum, December 1967

Karl Schlögel
American Space: The Poetics of the Highway
'American Space: Die Poesie des Highways', in: *Im Raume lesen wir die Zeit. Über Zivilisationsgeschichte und Geopolitik.*
Fischer Taschenbuch Verlag / Hanser: Munich 2003, pp. 379-392.
translated from the German by Gerrit Jackson

Thomas Weski
The Documentary Style
translated from the German by Amy Patton

Philipp Kaiser
Space Explorations
translated from the German by Amy Patton

Hannah Stippl
What is Camouflage, What is Landscape?
translated from the German by Andrew Horsfield

Christian Schwägerl
Anthropocene
translated from the German by Andrew Horsfield

Reinhard Braun
Landscape and the Politics of the Visual
translated from the German by Dawn Michelle d'Atri

Alanna Lockward
Body and Landscape in the Colonial Matrix of Power

Cover
James Benning, *El Valley Centro*, 1999, from: *California Trilogy* (film study) Courtesy of the Collection of the Austrian Film Museum

Published by
Verlag der Buchhandlung Walther König, Cologne
Ehrenstraße 4, 50672 Cologne, Germany
T: +49 (0) 221/20 59 6-53
F: +49 (0) 221/20 59 6-60
verlag@buchhandlung-walther-koenig.de

ISBN 978-3-86335-731-3

The Deutsche Nationalbibliothek lists this publication in the Deutsche Nationalbibliografie; detailed bibliographic data is available on the Internet at http://dnb.ddb.de

Distribution

Germany & Europe
Buchhandlung Walther König, Köln
Ehrenstr. 4, 50672 Köln
T: +49 (0) 221/20 59 6-53
F: +49 (0) 221/20 59 6-60
verlag@buchhandlung-walther-koenig.de

UK & Ireland
Cornerhouse Publications
70 Oxford Street
GB-Manchester M1 5NH
T: +44 (0) 161 200 15 03
F: +44 (0) 161 200 15 04
publications@cornerhouse.org

Outside Europe
D.A.P. / Distributed Art Publishers, Inc.
155 6th Avenue, 2nd Floor
New York, NY 10013
T: +1 (0) 212 627 1999
F: +1 (0) 212 627 9484
eleshowitz@dapinc.com

Kunsthaus Graz (HyperAmerica) thanks

Klaus Albrecht Schröder, Walter Moser, Sonja Eiböck, Barbara Kühnen: ALBERTINA, Vienna

André Buchmann, Erik Herkrath: Buchmann Galerie Berlin

Gabriele Conrath-Scholl, Rajka Knipper: Die Photographische Sammlung / SK Stiftung

Duncan Forbes, Thomas Seelig, Theresa Seeholzer, Andrea Hadem: Fotomuseum Winterthur

Julia Fabényi, Anna Bálványos, Zoltan Dragon: Ludwig Múzeum Budapest – Museum of Contemporary Art

Thomas Zander, Dagmar Kürschner: Galerie Thomas Zander, Cologne

Karl Schlögel

Sabine Schormann, Ulrike Schneider: Niedersächsische Sparkassenstiftung, Hanover

Yilmaz Dziewior, Miriam Halwani, Christin Wähner: Museum Ludwig, Cologne

Elizabeth K. Harris, Louis Meisel, Kat Kiernan: Louis K. Meisel Gallery, New York

Kevin Grogan, Jana Kende, Mindy Gales: Morris Museum of Art, Augusta

Heike Munder, Anna-Lena Gugger: Migros Museum für Gegenwartskunst

Karola Kraus, Susanne Neuburger, Marie-Therese Hochwartner, Sophie Haaser, Katharina Schendl, Eva Stimm: mumok, Vienna

Thierry Raspail, Milène Jallais, Hervé Percebois, Gaëlle Philippe: Musée d'art contemporain de Lyon

Inka Graeve Ingelmann, Simone Kober: Pinakothek der Moderne, Munich

F. C. Gundlach, Sebastian Lux, Franziska Mecklenburg: Stiftung F. C. Gundlach

Philomene Magers, Monika Sprüth, Erika Neufeld, Andrew Silewicz: Sprüth Magers Berlin London

Rock Hushka, Jessica Wilks: Tacoma Art Museum

Thomas Weski

Kunsthaus Graz (Landscape in Motion) thanks

Béatrice Josse, Valerie Audren-Guelton, Emeline Coulon: 49 NORD 6 EST – Frac Lorraine

Reinhard Braun, Angelika Maierhofer: Camera Austria

Nick Lesley: Electronic Arts Intermix

Sabine Flach

Krist Gruijthuijsen, Victoria Dejaco, Tanja Gurke: Grazer Kunstverein

Elisabeth Sann, Meriwether McClorey, Jess Pillar, Daniel Tsai: Jack Shainman Gallery, New York

Elyse Goldberg: James Cohan Gallery, THE ESTATE OF ROBERT SMITHSON

Merten Houfek: Kinoprojektion, Hamburg

Anna Bálványos, Soma Bradák, Krisztina Szipocs: Ludwig Múzeum Budapest – Museum of Contemporary Art

Veronica Castillo: M+, West Kowloon Cultural District Authority

Eva Scherr, Anna Himmelsbach: Meyer Riegger

Philipp Kaiser

Rose Lord, Catherine Belloy, Brian Loftus: Marian Goodman Gallery, New York / Paris

Igor Španjol, Sabina Povšič: Moderna galerija Ljubljana

Simone Moser: mumok, library

Martin Schmitz: Estate Lucius and Annemarie Burckhardt-Wackernagel

Lorenz Heiligensetzer, Francesco Carmenati, Noah Regenass: Public Library of the University of Basel

Alexander Horvath, Oliver Hanley: Austrian Film Museum, Vienna

Paul Petritsch and the Institute of Landscape Art at the University of Applied Arts, Vienna

Christian Schwägerl

Marianne Heller, Christiane Ostertag: Sigg Collection

Hannah Stippl

Bridget Chew, Connor Linskey: Studio 110

Caroline Fuchs: Studio Rosa Barba

Sarah Poppel: Studio Armin Linke

Yewen: Studio Qiu Anxiong

Mani Mazinani: Studio Michael Snow

Wim van der Meer: Studio Guido van der Werve

Marinko Sudac

Gabriele Schor, Theresa Dann: VERBUND AG SAMMLUNG VERBUND, Vienna

Art in Public Space thanks

Mayors Herbert Pichler (Altaussee), Franz Frosch (Bad Aussee) and Franz Steinegger (Grundlsee)

Günther Marchner, Karin Hochegger, Thomas Kranabitl and Bernhard Pliem

Herwig Loidl, Kurt Thomanek

Natalie Trautmannsdorff-Weinsberg, Albrecht Syen and Gudrun Suchanek

Christian Dirninger, Karin Hochegger, Fritz Idam, Helmut Kalss, Alexander Prenninger, Wolfgang Quatember, Erika Selzer, Anton Strobl, Markus Plasencia

transclaudia: Max Höfler, Johannes Schrettle

Olaf Pascheit

Kammerhofmuseum Bad Aussee

Camera Austria thanks

Jens Asthoff

Estelle Blaschke

Culture Ireland

Wilhelm Deuer: Landesarchiv Kärnten

ifa–Institut für Auslandsbeziehungen

Martin Janda, Susanne Rick: Galerie Martin Janda, Vienna

Raphaëlle Jehan: Galerie Stevenson, Cape Town / Johannesburg

Astrid Hamm: Galerie EIGEN + ART Leipzig / Berlin

Alanna Lockward

Museum Moderner Kunst Klagenfurt

Inbal Sommer: Sommer Contemporary Art, Tel Aviv

Neue Galerie Graz thanks

GrazMuseum, Graz

Galerie Auktionshaus Hassfurther, Vienna

Steiermärkische Landesbibliothek, Graz

Bernd Moser, Graz

Muzej Suvremene Umjetnosti, Zagreb

Schloss Trautenfels, UMJ

We also thank

Sammy Baloji

Sarah Bildstein

Patrizia Brumen: Library of
Neue Galerie Graz

Andreas Flach, Jugend am
Werk

Adler Guerrier

Mona Hatoum

Gerrit Jackson

Maximilian Marek,
Steirisches Imkerzentrum

Dieter Plankl

Thomas Rottleuthner und
Parkorchester Graz

Christina Töpfer

Sabine Tschürtz, Wegener
Center for Climate and
Global Change University
of Graz

Bernhard Wolf

**We owe special thanks
to the artists of the
exhibitions.**

Kindly supported by

Stadt Graz,
Land Steiermark

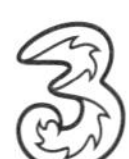 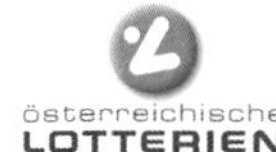 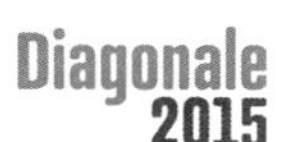 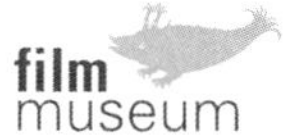 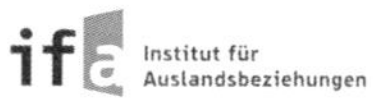 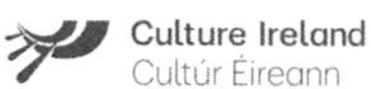

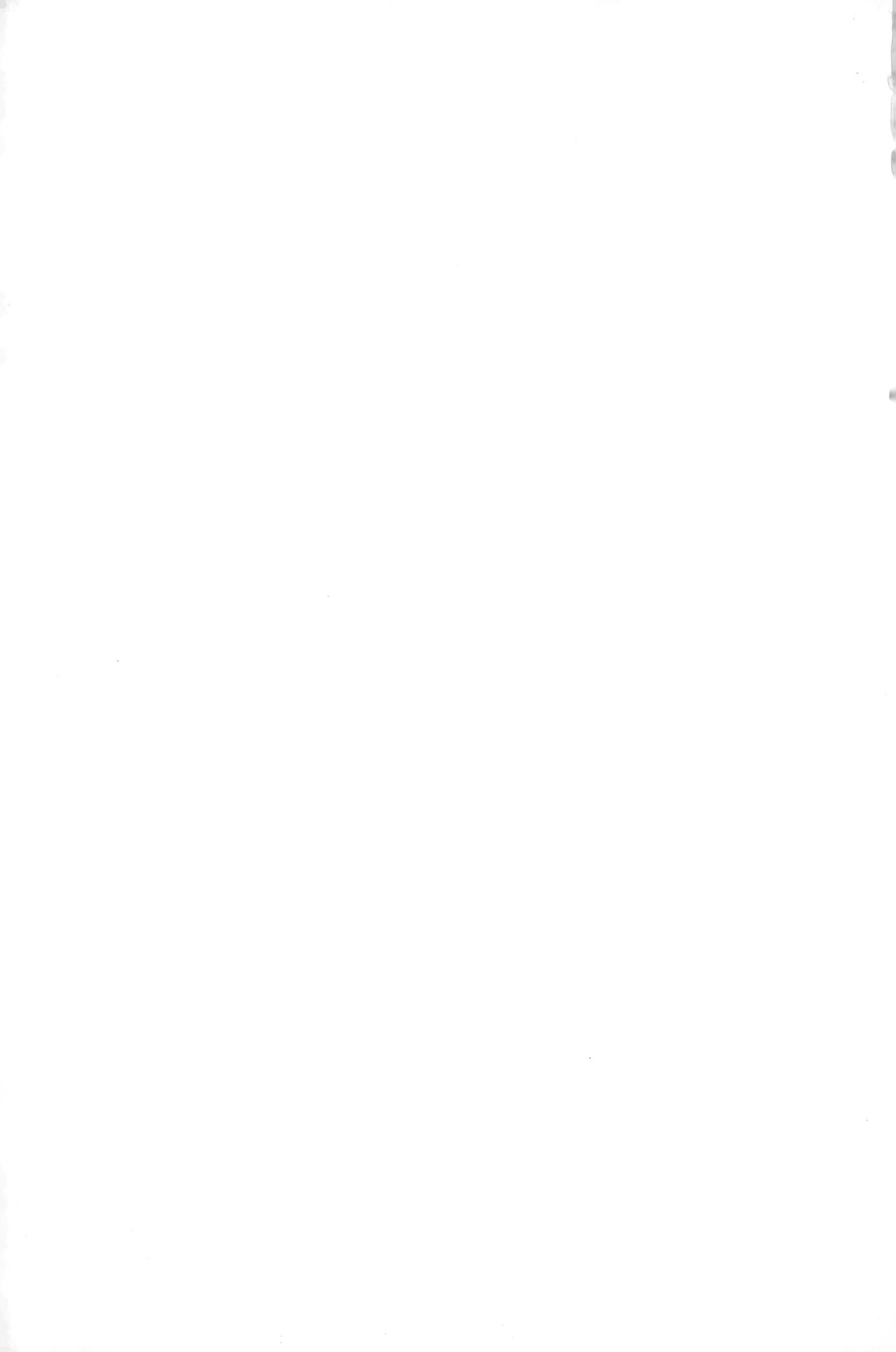